the Unofficial Guide® to

Hawaii

3rd Edition

Also available from John Wiley & Sons, Inc.:

Beyond Disney: The Unofficial Guide to Universal, Sea World, and the Best of Central Florida

Inside Disney: The Incredible Story of Walt Disney World and the Man Behind the Mouse

Mini Las Vegas: The Pocket-Sized Unofficial Guide to Las Vegas

Mini-Mickey: The Pocket-Sized Unofficial Guide to Walt Disney World

The Unofficial Guide to Bed & Breakfasts and Country Inns:
California Great Lakes States Mid-Atlantic
New England Northwest Rockies
Southeast Southwest

The Unofficial Guide to Best RV and Tent Campgrounds:
California and the West Florida and the Southeast
Great Lakes Mid-Atlantic Northeast Northwest
Southwest U.S.A.

The Unofficial Guide to Central Italy: Florence, Rome, Tuscany, and Umbria

The Unofficial Guide to Chicago

The Unofficial Guide to Cruises

The Unofficial Guide to Disneyland

The Unofficial Guide to Disneyland Paris

The Unofficial Guide to Golf Vacations in the Eastern U.S.

The Unofficial Guide to Florida

The Unofficial Guide to the Great Smoky and Blue Ridge Region

The Unofficial Guide to Las Vegas

The Unofficial Guide to London

The Unofficial Guide to Maui

The Unofficial Guide to Mexico's Best Beach Resorts

The Unofficial Guide to New Orleans

The Unofficial Guide to New York City

The Unofficial Guide to Paris

The Unofficial Guide to San Francisco

The Unofficial Guide to Skiing and Snowboarding in the West

The Unofficial Guide to South Florida

The Unofficial Guide to Traveling with Kids:
California Florida Mid-Atlantic
New England Southeast

The Unofficial Guide to Walt Disney World

The Unofficial Guide to Walt Disney World for Grown-Ups

The Unofficial Guide to Walt Disney World with Kids

The Unofficial Guide to Washington, D.C.

The Unofficial Guide to the World's Best Diving Vacations

the Unofficial Guide® to Hawaii

3rd Edition

Rick and Marcie Carroll

Please note that prices fluctuate in the course of time, and travel information changes under the impact of many factors that influence the travel industry. We therefore suggest that you write or call ahead for confirmation when making your travel plans. Every effort has been made to ensure the accuracy of information throughout this book, and the contents of this publication are believed correct at the time of printing. Nevertheless, the publishers cannot accept responsibility for errors or omissions or for changes in details given in this guide or for the consequences of any reliance on the information provided by the same. Assessments of attractions and so forth are based upon the author's own experience, and therefore, descriptions given in this guide necessarily contain an element of subjective opinion, which may not reflect the publisher's opinion or dictate a reader's own experience on another occasion. Readers are invited to write the publisher with ideas, comments, and suggestions for future editions.

Published by:
John Wiley & Sons, Inc.
111 River Street
Hoboken, NJ 07030

Produced by Menasha Ridge Press
Cover design by Michael J. Freeland
Interior design by Michele Laseau

For information on our other products and services or to obtain technical support, please contact our Customer Care Department within the U.S. at (800) 762-2974, outside the U.S. at (317) 572-3993 or fax (317) 572-4002.

John Wiley & Sons, Inc. also publishes its books in a variety of electronic formats. Some content that appears in print may not be available in electronic formats.

ISBN 0-7645-4192-7

Manufactured in the United States of America
5 4 3 2 1

Contents

List of Maps

About the Authors and Contributors

Rick Carroll, author of many Hawaii books, is the creator of the best-selling *Hawaii's Best Spooky Tales Series.* A former daily journalist at the *San Francisco Chronicle,* Carroll wrote award-winning travel and feature stories about Hawaii and the Pacific for the *Honolulu Advertiser* and United Press International. He is contributing editor to *Hawaii Magazine.* His stories appear on the Internet at www.hawaii.rr.com. His new book, *Madame Pele True Encounters with Hawaii's Fire Goddess,* celebrates Pele's 20-year tantrum at Kilauea Volcano, the world's longest continuous eruption, still underway.

Marcie Rasmussen Carroll, freelance travel writer and former communications director for the Hawaii Convention and Visitors Bureau, wrote political, environmental, and other news for the *San Francisco Chronicle, San Jose Mercury-News,* and UPI in Atlanta. She was a Journalism Fellow in Asian studies at University of Hawaii and in energy studies at Stanford University.

Together, the Carrolls, who moved to Windward Oahu in 1983, collected and edited the anthology *Travelers Tales Hawaii: True Stories of the Island Spirit,* which one reviewer praised as "the best collection of contemporary Hawaii travel stories." They are the authors of this extensively revised and rewritten third edition of the *Unofficial Guide to Hawaii.*

Betty ShimaBukuro, who updated the dining chapter for this edition, is the food editor at the *Honolulu Star-Bulletin,* a job that encompasses everything from good home cooking, to mom-and-pop ethnic restaurants, to the finest in Hawaii Regional Cuisine. After a long journalism career that has included a dozen different news beats, she considers this to be the best gig in town.

Introduction

Making the Most of Your Hawaiian Dream

Hawaii. Hear the word, and you're swept away by dreams of a tropical Eden, sensual swaying hula dancers, and visions of an endless, empty beach.

Can this place *really* be as magical as it seems? Or is it just an illusion? The right answers to those questions are yes and no respectively. The tropical Eden is for real, hula is the heartbeat of the Hawaiian culture, and empty beaches stretch for miles on all the smaller islands. And volcanoes are still making Big Island beaches even more magical. This is, in all ways, a very special destination, unlike any other.

But it's more than a pretty place; it's an experience that can change your life, and that has to do with the people and their way of living. The lighthearted island attitudes, the warmth of people who go out of their way for you, and the sense of extended family soon begin to melt even the most resolute holdouts. Your stakes are huge in making the most of your visit to the Islands. If you get Hawaii right, the place will grab you by the heart and make you feel good. The best way to enjoy it is to loosen up and let Hawaii happen to you.

Approach Hawaii like you would another country, which it was not so long ago. Be prepared for exotic customs, serendipity, and unexpected disruptions of your plans. Be a good sport. Brief yourself by reading this book, prowling the Internet, and talking to friends. For those who come to the Islands with advance knowledge and plenty of patience, delightful encounters are bound to happen. Bring your children and elders. They'll have a good time, and the people of Hawaii cherish *keiki* (kids) and *kupuna* (wise older folks).

In Waikiki, don't expect idyllic huts by the sea (although you can find them elsewhere on the Islands). Expect high-rise hotels in an urban cityscape. Expect hustling on the sidewalks, although quite tame by big-city standards (most Waikiki hustlers want to hand you an ad). Don't expect to be met with a lei of flowers at the airport unless you have already paid for the greeting service or are being met by a friend who lives in the Islands. Brace yourself for hugs and kisses on the cheek when you meet effusive strangers, if you're lucky. Hawaii is one of the world's safer destinations, but don't be surprised if your wallet and camera are pilfered when you leave them on the seat of a rental car while you run to look at a mesmerizing view.

Strip away the veil of Hawaii's natural beauty and you'll find many of the same problems that burden other American communities: economic struggles, drugs, increasing crime, and traffic congestion. But you'll also find people who still smile at strangers and largely rely on kindness, respect, and humor when dealing with one another. You'll discover skies that are blue rather than gray, seawater that is clear and warm, air that is soft and fresh, and scenery that soothes the soul.

A visit to Hawaii is too precious to waste. So we're here to help you pursue your dream and along the way find some unexpected memorable experiences. Our purpose is to present a realistic view of contemporary Hawaii that helps you make the most of your Island holiday. We'll provide some of the details in advance, so that you'll be free to have fun.

In this guide you'll discover how to find the best deals on lodging, whether you want hotels, condominiums, or bed-and-breakfasts. You'll get an up-to-date review of the best adventures, attractions, beaches, hotels, clubs, and restaurants. And you'll gain insights into local customs and learn a few Hawaiian words and phrases to make you feel more like a *kamaaina* ("child of the land"—longtime or native-born Hawaii resident).

Along the way, we'll answer frequently asked questions like these:

- When is the best time to go?
- Which islands should we visit?
- Where are the best beaches?
- What hiking trails are recommended for families?
- Who are Hawaii's must-see entertainers?

You want to make the most of your time in the Islands. You want to be at the right place at the right time, enjoying the very best Hawaii has to offer, especially if it is your first trip. This book will help you. For those of you who have been to the Aloha State many times before and are ready to dig deeper, this book will suggest new possibilities. You may find a new discovery. So mix up a mai tai, put on your favorite Hawaiian music, and start your Hawaiian adventure with *The Unofficial Guide to Hawaii.*

E komo mai! Welcome.

About This Guide

Why "Unofficial"?

Just as Hawaii inspires unconventional ideals and promotes individuality, so does the "Unofficial" series. Most "official" guides to Hawaii tout the well-known sights, promote the local restaurants and hotels indiscriminately, and leave out the nitty-gritty. This one is different. We'll be upfront with you. Instead of nabbing you by the ankles in a tourist trap, we'll tell you if it's not worth the wait for the mediocre food served at a well-known restaurant. We'll complain loudly about overpriced hotel rooms that aren't convenient, and we'll guide you away from the crowds and congestion for a break now and then. If a museum is boring or a major attraction is overrated, we say so—and, in the process, make your visit exactly that: *your* visit. We got into the guidebook business because we were unhappy with the way travel guides make the reader work to get any usable information. Wouldn't it be nice, we thought, if we made guides that were easy to use?

Other Guidebooks

Most guidebooks are compilations of lists. This is true regardless of whether the information is presented in list form or artfully distributed through pages of prose. There is insufficient detail in a list, and with prose the presentation can be tedious and contain large helpings of nonessential or marginally useful information. Not enough wheat, so to speak, for nourishment in one instance, and too much chaff in the other. Either way, other guides provide little more than departure points from which readers initiate their own quests.

Sure, many guides are readable and well researched, but they tend to be difficult to use. To select a hotel, for example, a reader must study several pages of descriptions with only the names of the hotels in bold type breaking up the text. Because each description essentially deals with the same variables, it is difficult to recall what was said concerning a particular hotel. Readers generally have no alternative but to work through all the write-ups before beginning to narrow their choices. The presentation of restaurants, clubs, and attractions is similar except that even more reading is usually required. To use such a guide is to undertake an exhaustive research process that requires examining nearly as many options and possibilities as starting from scratch. Recommendations, if any, lack depth and conviction. By failing to narrow travelers' choices down to a thoughtfully considered, well-distilled, and manageable few, these guides compound rather than solve problems.

How Unofficial Guides Are Different

Some Hawaii guidebooks are full of pretty pictures. Others present a tedious stream of words with little practical advice. Many Hawaii guidebooks lead you only to a sugarcoated version of the Islands, but this book strives to be different.

Our goal at *Unofficial Guides* is to help you make informed decisions about topics like this: Anyone can find the Bishop Museum, but when is the best time to go? How much walking is involved? Is the museum really worth the price of admission?

Hawaii offers more things to do and see than you could pack into a lifetime of vacations. If you have only a week or two and you really just want to relax on a palm-fringed gold sand beach, no problem. We'll suggest that perfect beach and provide the information you need to enjoy it in a concise, easy-to-read format.

The Unofficial Guide to Hawaii, written for repeat and first-time visitors alike, addresses typical planning concerns: "Can I leave my coat and tie at home?" or "Should I visit the Polynesian Cultural Center?" You'll find the answers to those questions and more in these pages.

Our philosophy: If it matters to you, then it matters to us. From the beginning, the people behind *Unofficial Guides* have worked diligently to deliver honest, straight-up reviews of major destinations and U.S. cities. For this book, the authors are former San Francisco daily newspaper journalists who have lived in Hawaii and written about the Islands for two decades. They combine island knowledge with the ability to evaluate experiences from the visitor's point of view.

Special Features

This *Unofficial Guide* includes these special features:

- Insightful introductions to Hawaii's six main islands, highlighting the special appeal and character of each.
- A brief look at Hawaii's fascinating history, from its discovery by the first Polynesians, through the missionaries, to today's multicultural, mid-Pacific reality.
- Explanations of local customs and island styles.
- Candid opinions on the best and worst of Hawaii, including accommodations, beaches, restaurants, attractions, shows, clubs, and shops.
- Practical information on driving distances and how to avoid crowds, dodge traffic jams, and park cheaply. Or, on Oahu, how to get around without a car.
- Suggested itineraries for families, honeymooners, seniors, and disabled travelers.
- A guide to the state's best golf courses.

Comments and Suggestions from Readers

We welcome your suggestions and comments about all our *Unofficial Guides,* including this book. Should you find any errors or omissions, we would appreciate hearing from you. Some of the best suggestions come from our readers.

How to Write the Authors

Rick and Marcie Carroll
The Unofficial Guide to Hawaii
P.O. Box 43673
Birmingham, AL 35243
unofficialguides@menasharidge.com

When you contact us by mail, be sure to put your return address on your letter as well as on the envelope. And remember, our work takes us on the road for long periods of time, so please forgive any delayed response.

How Information Is Organized: By Subject and By Geographic Zones

To give you quick access to information about the best Hawaii has to offer, we've organized material in several formats.

Hotels So many Islands hotels, condos, and bed-and-breakfasts seek your business that choosing the right one can be daunting. We offer easy-to-read charts, maps, and rating systems as well as pertinent information on room size, cleanliness, service, amenities, cost, and accessibility to the beach.

Restaurants A highlight of every Hawaiian vacation is sampling Islands cuisine. The menu is vast and tasty, ranging from simple local favorites like plate lunches to extravagant gourmet repasts and Hawaii's own regional cuisine. We take you to Hawaii's best restaurants.

Entertainment and Nightlife Most visitors to the Islands take in a couple of shows or nightspots during their stay. This is especially true of visitors to Oahu, where Waikiki is home to ongoing live theatrical productions and plenty of hot spots. We've reviewed a few of the best live productions, where the standards are reliably high. We also check out the best nightclubs and lounges.

Golf Golf is a major draw for many visitors. We detail vital stats of the state's top courses to help you choose the right one.

Geographic Zones For added convenience, we've divided Hawaii into geographic zones. Perhaps you're interested in staying somewhere in Kapalua Resort on the Island of Maui but aren't sure where it is. We'll note for you that Kapalua is in Zone 9, which covers West Maui, and all other Zone 9 resorts, hotels, attractions, and restaurants will be in that vicinity. Maps of each zone follow.

Zone 1	Waikiki
Zone 2	Greater Honolulu
Zone 3	Windward Oahu
Zone 4	The North Shore
Zone 5	Leeward Oahu
Zone 6	Central Oahu
Zone 7	Central Maui
Zone 8	South Maui
Zone 9	West Maui
Zone 10	Upcountry Maui and Beyond
Zone 11	Kona
Zone 12	Hilo and Volcano
Zone 13	Kauai
Zone 14	Molokai
Zone 15	Lanai

Please note that the islands of Niihau and Kahoolawe, while technically among the main southernmost islands in the Hawaiian Island chain, are not designated as zones, nor are the older Northwest Hawaiian Islands that stretch hundreds of miles into the North Pacific. Niihau is a private, family-owned island and is, with few exceptions, inaccessible to visitors. For decades, Kahoolawe, the red-dirt island that seems to be bleeding across the ocean from South Maui, was a target for United States Navy bombing practice. Now it is being transformed into a Hawaiian cultural preserve. The uninhabited island is off-limits, except by special invitation. Only one of the Northwest Islands is a limited visitor destination—Midway Islands, the famed World War II battle site and naval base that is now a wildlife refuge.

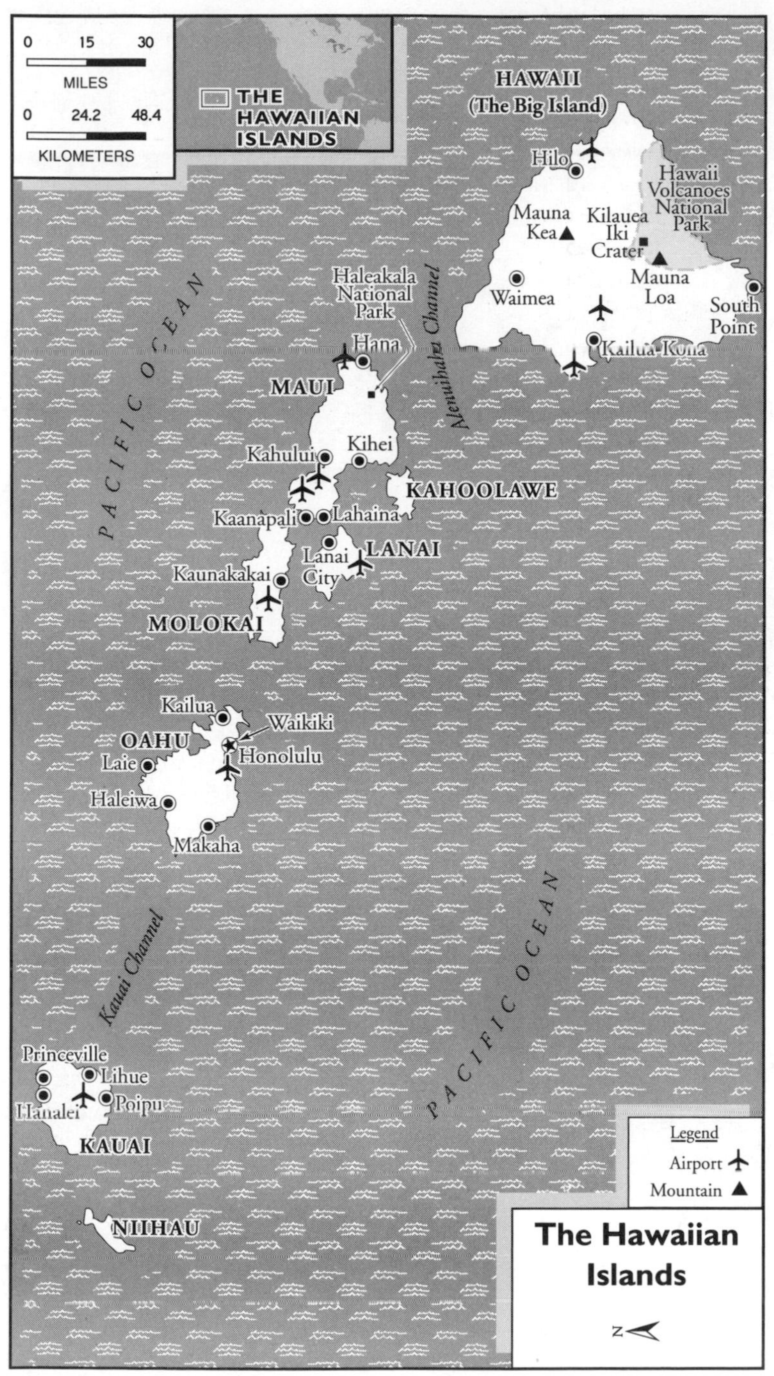
0 15 30
MILES
0 24.2 48.4
KILOMETERS
THE HAWAIIAN ISLANDS
HAWAII
(The Big Island)
Hilo
Hawaii Volcanoes National Park
Mauna Kea
Kilauea Iki Crater
Mauna Loa
Waimea
South Point
Kailua-Kona
Haleakala National Park
Hana
Alenuihaha Channel
MAUI
Kahului
Kihei
KAHOOLAWE
Kaanapali
Lahaina
Lanai City
LANAI
Kaunakakai
MOLOKAI
PACIFIC OCEAN
Kailua
Waikiki
OAHU
Honolulu
Laie
Haleiwa
Makaha
Kauai Channel
PACIFIC OCEAN
Princeville
Lihue
Hanalei
Poipu
KAUAI
NIIHAU
Legend
Airport
Mountain
The Hawaiian Islands
N

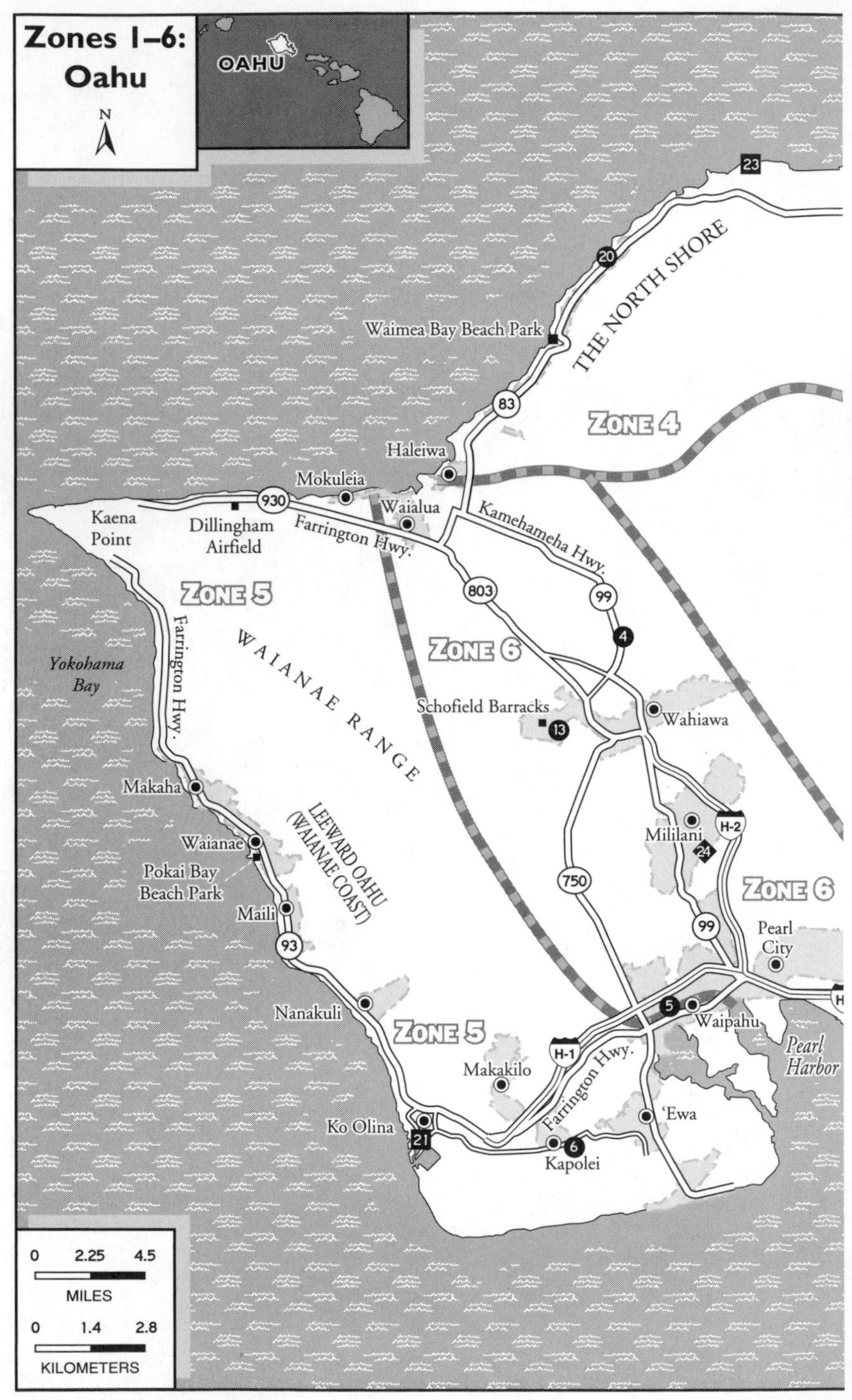
Zones 1–6: Oahu
N
OAHU
23
20
THE NORTH SHORE
Waimea Bay Beach Park
83
ZONE 4
Haleiwa
Mokuleia
930
Waialua
Kamehameha Hwy.
Kaena Point
Dillingham Airfield
Farrington Hwy.
803
99
4
ZONE 5
Farrington Hwy.
WAIANAE RANGE
ZONE 6
Yokohama Bay
Schofield Barracks
13
Wahiawa
Makaha
LEEWARD OAHU (WAIANAE COAST)
H-2
Mililani
24
Waianae
Pokai Bay Beach Park
750
ZONE 6
Maili
99
Pearl City
93
Nanakuli
5
Waipahu
ZONE 5
H-1
Farrington Hwy.
Pearl Harbor
Makakilo
'Ewa
Ko Olina
21
6
Kapolei
0 2.25 4.5
MILES
0 1.4 2.8
KILOMETERS

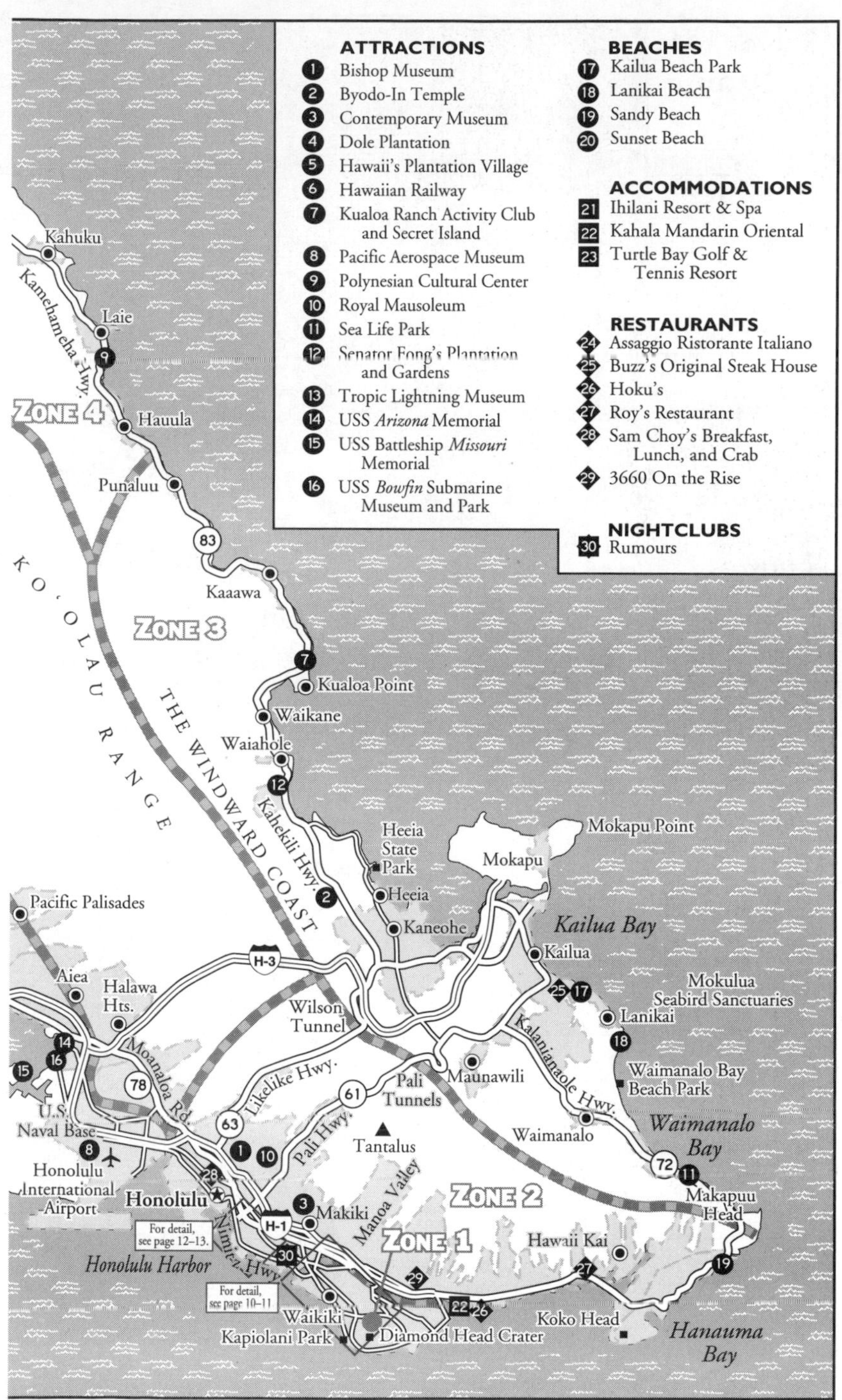
ATTRACTIONS
1 Bishop Museum
2 Byodo-In Temple
3 Contemporary Museum
4 Dole Plantation
5 Hawaii's Plantation Village
6 Hawaiian Railway
7 Kualoa Ranch Activity Club and Secret Island
8 Pacific Aerospace Museum
9 Polynesian Cultural Center
10 Royal Mausoleum
11 Sea Life Park
12 Senator Fong's Plantation and Gardens
13 Tropic Lightning Museum
14 USS Arizona Memorial
15 USS Battleship Missouri Memorial
16 USS Bowfin Submarine Museum and Park
BEACHES
17 Kailua Beach Park
18 Lanikai Beach
19 Sandy Beach
20 Sunset Beach
ACCOMMODATIONS
21 Ihilani Resort & Spa
22 Kahala Mandarin Oriental
23 Turtle Bay Golf & Tennis Resort
RESTAURANTS
24 Assaggio Ristorante Italiano
25 Buzz's Original Steak House
26 Hoku's
27 Roy's Restaurant
28 Sam Choy's Breakfast, Lunch, and Crab
29 3660 On the Rise
NIGHTCLUBS
30 Rumours
Kahuku
Kamehameha Hwy.
Laie
ZONE 4
Hauula
Punaluu
83
KO'OLAU RANGE
Kaaawa
ZONE 3
THE WINDWARD COAST
Kualoa Point
Waikane
Waiahole
Kahekili Hwy.
Heeia State Park
Heeia
Mokapu
Mokapu Point
Kaneohe
Kailua Bay
Kailua
Pacific Palisades
H-3
Aiea
Halawa Hts.
Wilson Tunnel
Mokulua Seabird Sanctuaries
Lanikai
Kalanianaole Hwy.
Moanalua Rd.
Likelike Hwy.
Pali Tunnels
61
Maunawili
Waimanalo Bay Beach Park
78
U.S. Naval Base
63
Pali Hwy.
Tantalus
Waimanalo
Waimanalo Bay
72
Honolulu International Airport
Honolulu
Manoa Valley
ZONE 2
Makapuu Head
Makiki
H-1
For detail, see page 12–13.
Honolulu Harbor
Nimitz Hwy.
ZONE 1
Hawaii Kai
For detail, see page 10–11.
Waikiki
Kapiolani Park
Diamond Head Crater
Koko Head
Hanauma Bay

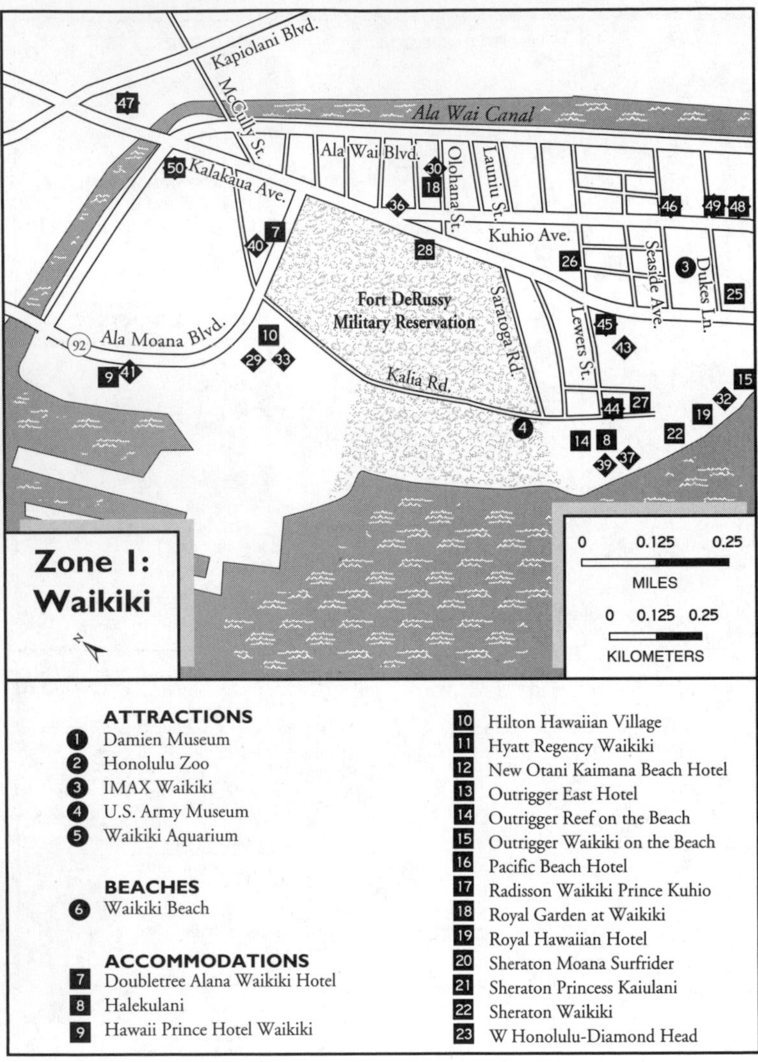
Zone 1:
Waikiki
Kapiolani Blvd.
McCully St.
Ala Wai Canal
Ala Wai Blvd.
Kalakaua Ave.
Olohana St.
Launiu St.
Kuhio Ave.
Seaside Ave.
Dukes Ln.
Fort DeRussy
Military Reservation
Saratoga Rd.
Lewers St.
Kalia Rd.
Ala Moana Blvd.
92
0 0.125 0.25
MILES
0 0.125 0.25
KILOMETERS
ATTRACTIONS
1 Damien Museum
2 Honolulu Zoo
3 IMAX Waikiki
4 U.S. Army Museum
5 Waikiki Aquarium
BEACHES
6 Waikiki Beach
ACCOMMODATIONS
7 Doubletree Alana Waikiki Hotel
8 Halekulani
9 Hawaii Prince Hotel Waikiki
10 Hilton Hawaiian Village
11 Hyatt Regency Waikiki
12 New Otani Kaimana Beach Hotel
13 Outrigger East Hotel
14 Outrigger Reef on the Beach
15 Outrigger Waikiki on the Beach
16 Pacific Beach Hotel
17 Radisson Waikiki Prince Kuhio
18 Royal Garden at Waikiki
19 Royal Hawaiian Hotel
20 Sheraton Moana Surfrider
21 Sheraton Princess Kaiulani
22 Sheraton Waikiki
23 W Honolulu-Diamond Head

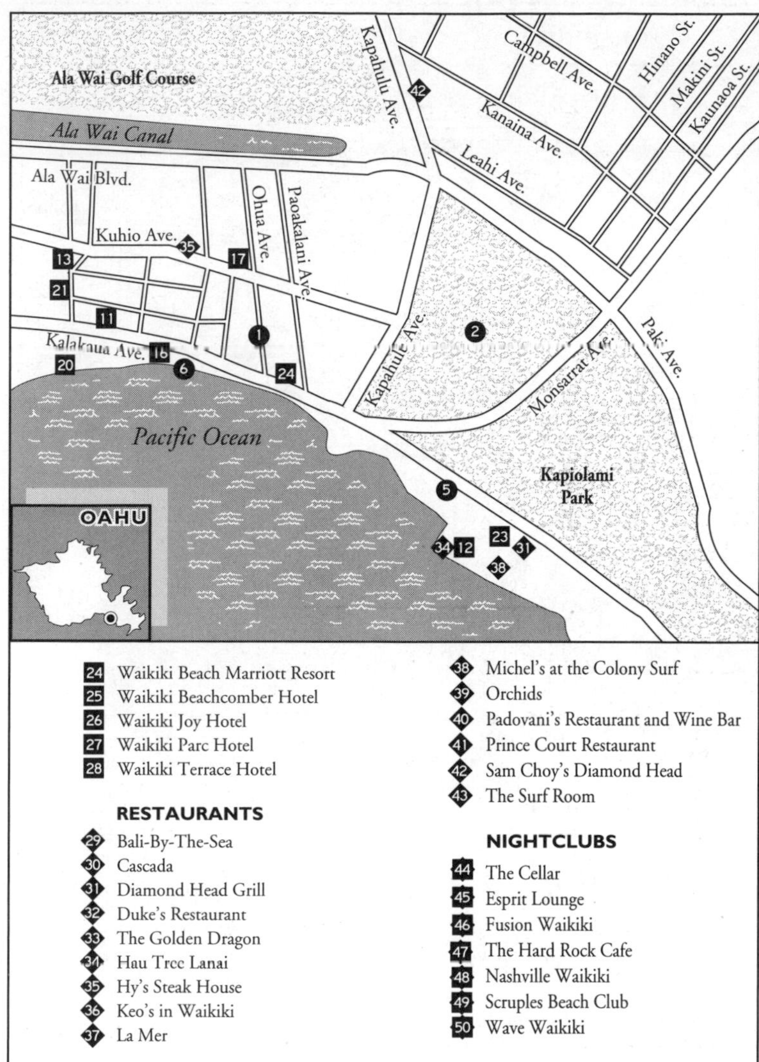

24 Waikiki Beach Marriott Resort
25 Waikiki Beachcomber Hotel
26 Waikiki Joy Hotel
27 Waikiki Parc Hotel
28 Waikiki Terrace Hotel

RESTAURANTS

29 Bali-By-The-Sea
30 Cascada
31 Diamond Head Grill
32 Duke's Restaurant
33 The Golden Dragon
34 Hau Tree Lanai
35 Hy's Steak House
36 Keo's in Waikiki
37 La Mer
38 Michel's at the Colony Surf
39 Orchids
40 Padovani's Restaurant and Wine Bar
41 Prince Court Restaurant
42 Sam Choy's Diamond Head
43 The Surf Room

NIGHTCLUBS

44 The Cellar
45 Esprit Lounge
46 Fusion Waikiki
47 The Hard Rock Cafe
48 Nashville Waikiki
49 Scruples Beach Club
50 Wave Waikiki

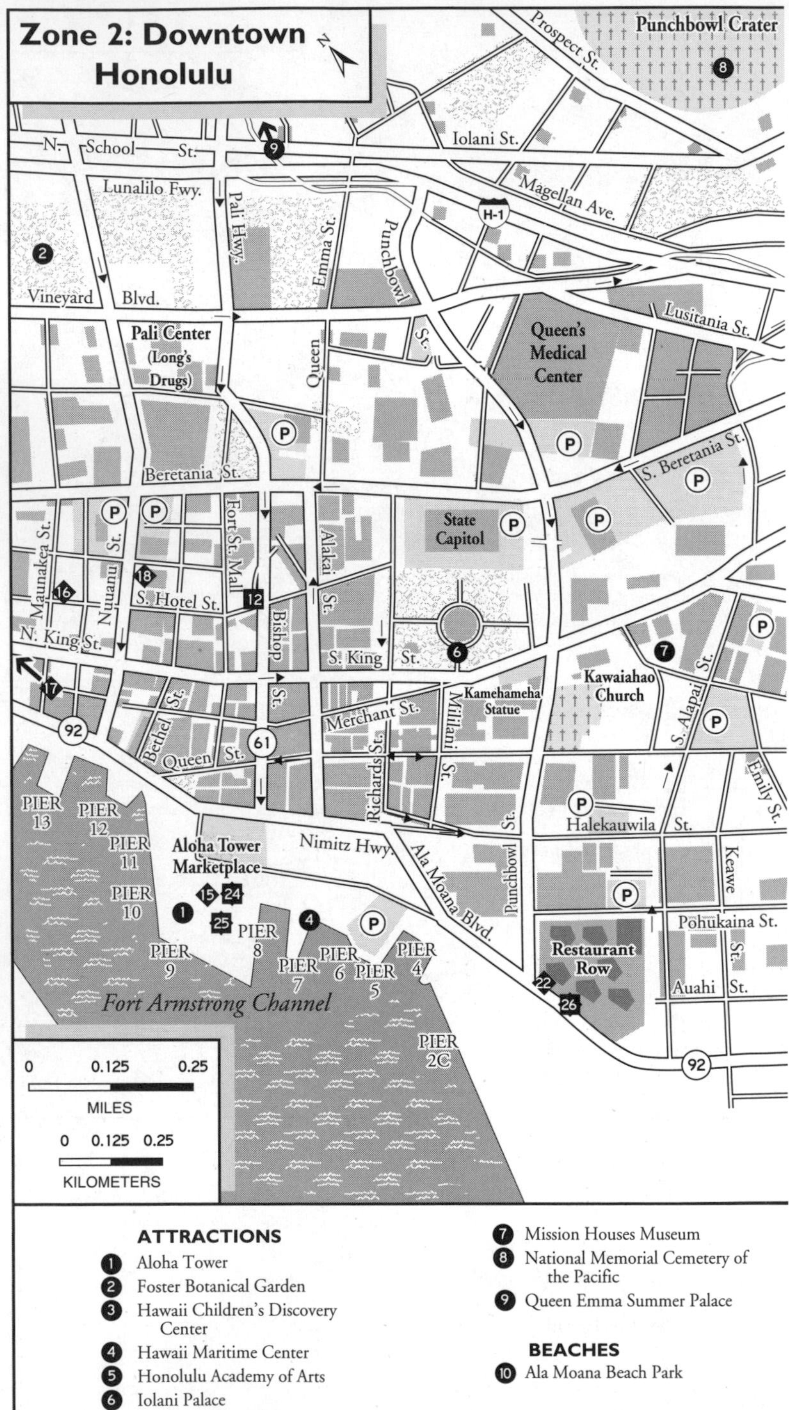
Zone 2: Downtown Honolulu
N
Punchbowl Crater
Prospect St.
Iolani St.
N. School St.
Lunalilo Fwy.
Magellan Ave.
H-1
Pali Hwy.
Emma St.
Punchbowl St.
Vineyard Blvd.
Lusitania St.
Pali Center (Long's Drugs)
Queen's Medical Center
Queen
Beretania St.
S. Beretania St.
State Capitol
Maunakea St.
Nuuanu St.
Fort St. Mall
Alakai St.
S. Hotel St.
Bishop St.
N. King St.
S. King St.
Kawaiahao Church
Kamehameha Statue
Mililani St.
Merchant St.
Bethel St.
Queen St.
Richards St.
S. Alapai St.
Emily St.
Halekauwila St.
Nimitz Hwy.
Ala Moana Blvd.
Punchbowl St.
Keawe St.
Pohukaina St.
Aloha Tower Marketplace
Restaurant Row
Auahi St.
PIER 13
PIER 12
PIER 11
PIER 10
PIER 9
PIER 8
PIER 7
PIER 6
PIER 5
PIER 4
PIER 2C
Fort Armstrong Channel
92
61
0 0.125 0.25
MILES
0 0.125 0.25
KILOMETERS
ATTRACTIONS
1 Aloha Tower
2 Foster Botanical Garden
3 Hawaii Children's Discovery Center
4 Hawaii Maritime Center
5 Honolulu Academy of Arts
6 Iolani Palace
7 Mission Houses Museum
8 National Memorial Cemetery of the Pacific
9 Queen Emma Summer Palace
BEACHES
10 Ala Moana Beach Park

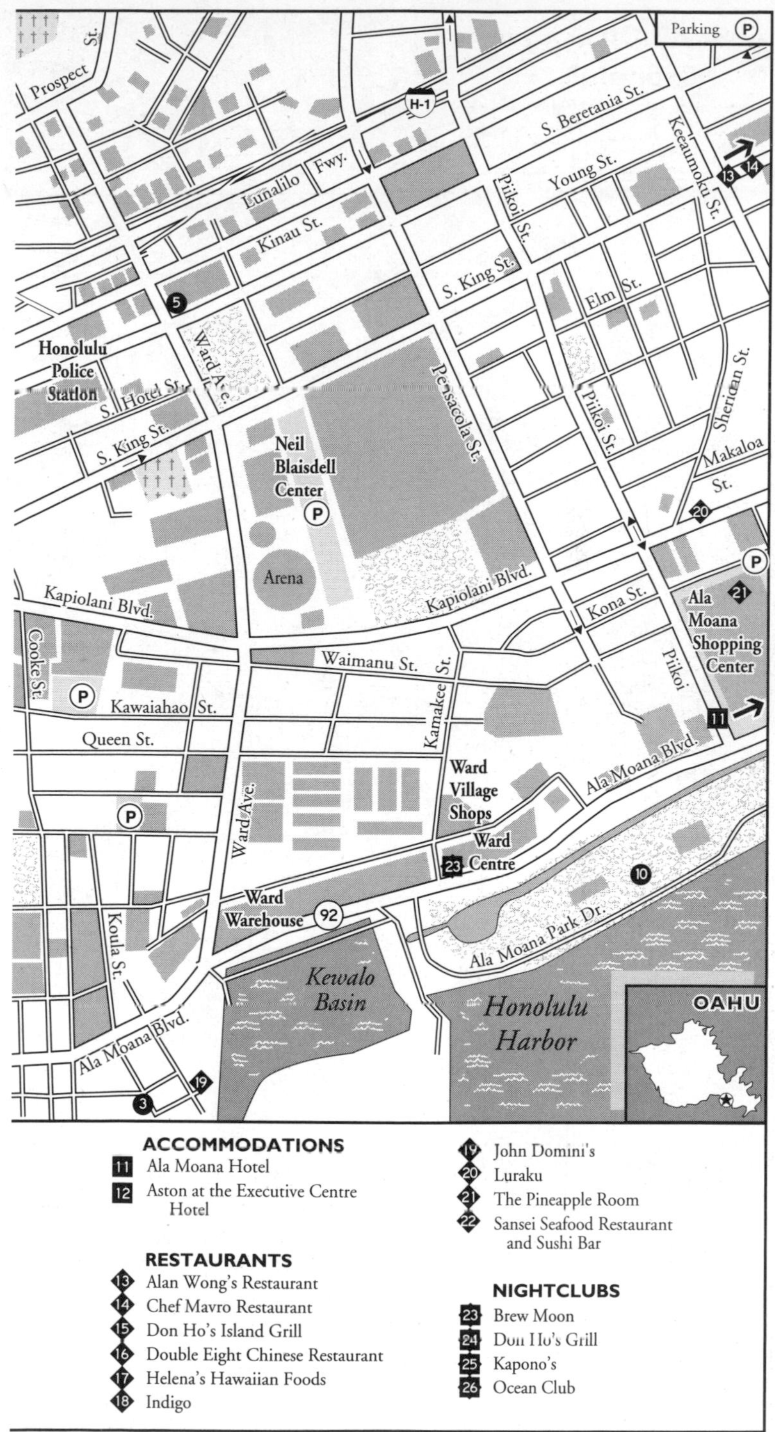
Parking
Prospect St.
H-1
S. Beretania St.
Lunalilo Fwy.
Young St.
Keeaumoku St.
Pikoi St.
Kinau St.
S. King St.
Elm St.
Honolulu Police Station
Ward Ave.
S. Hotel St.
S. King St.
Pensacola St.
Sheridan St.
Pikoi St.
Makaloa St.
Neil Blaisdell Center
Arena
Kapiolani Blvd.
Kapiolani Blvd.
Kona St.
Ala Moana Shopping Center
Cooke St.
Waimanu St.
Kamakee St.
Pikoi
Kawaiahao St.
Queen St.
Ala Moana Blvd.
Ward Village Shops
Ward Ave.
Ward Centre
Ward Warehouse
Ala Moana Park Dr.
Koula St.
Kewalo Basin
Honolulu Harbor
Ala Moana Blvd.
OAHU
ACCOMMODATIONS
11 Ala Moana Hotel
12 Aston at the Executive Centre Hotel
RESTAURANTS
13 Alan Wong's Restaurant
14 Chef Mavro Restaurant
15 Don Ho's Island Grill
16 Double Eight Chinese Restaurant
17 Helena's Hawaiian Foods
18 Indigo
19 John Domini's
20 Luraku
21 The Pineapple Room
22 Sansei Seafood Restaurant and Sushi Bar
NIGHTCLUBS
23 Brew Moon
24 Don Ho's Grill
25 Kapono's
26 Ocean Club

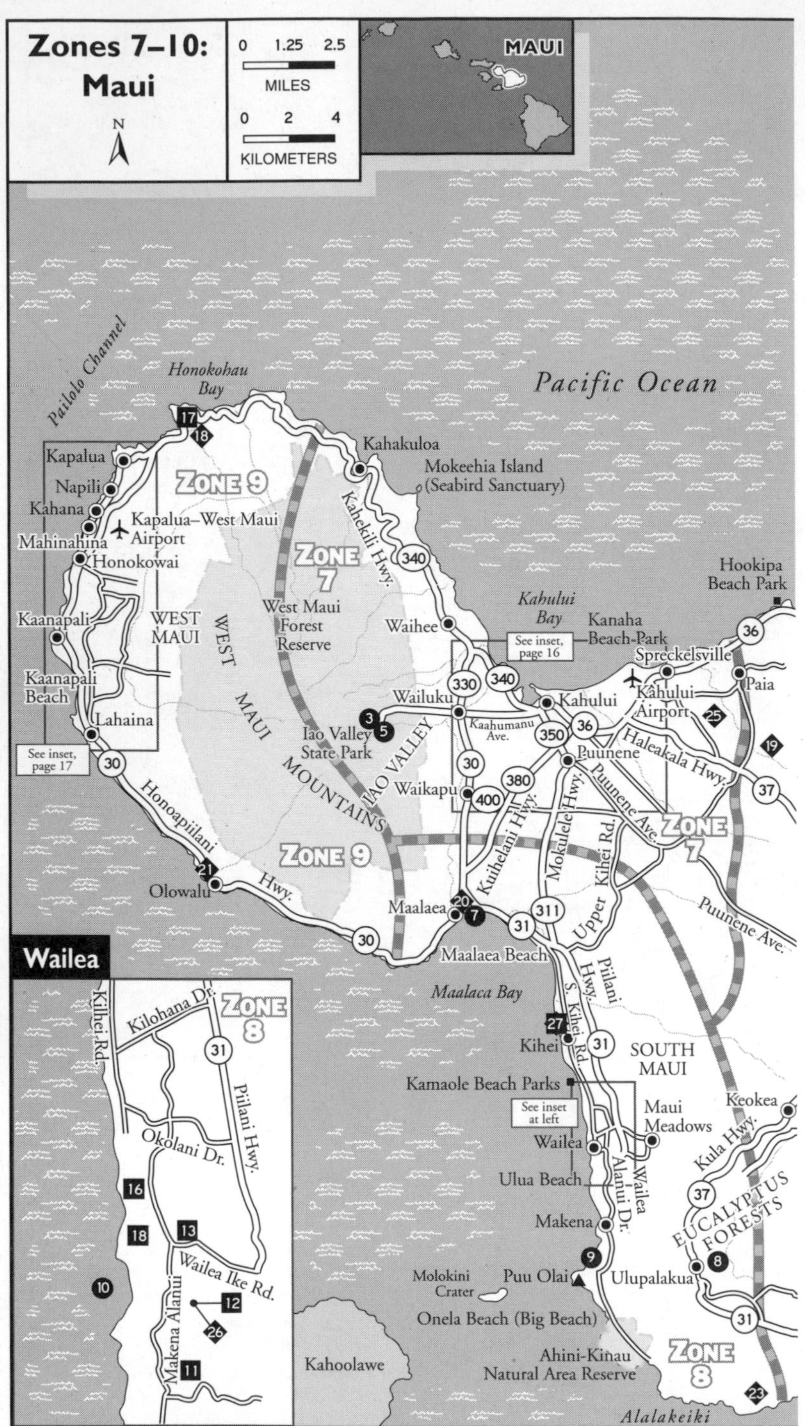
Zones 7–10: Maui
N
0 1.25 2.5
MILES
0 2 4
KILOMETERS
MAUI
Pacific Ocean
Pailolo Channel
Honokohau Bay
Kapalua
Napili
Kahana
Mahinahina
Honokowai
Kapalua–West Maui Airport
ZONE 9
ZONE 7
Kahakuloa
Mokeehia Island (Seabird Sanctuary)
Kahekili Hwy.
340
WEST MAUI
WEST MAUI MOUNTAINS
West Maui Forest Reserve
Waihee
Kahului Bay
Kanaha Beach Park
See inset, page 16
Hookipa Beach Park
36
Spreckelsville
Paia
Kaanapali
Kaanapali Beach
Lahaina
See inset, page 17
30
330
Wailuku
Kahului
Kahului Airport
Iao Valley State Park
IAO VALLEY
Kaahumanu Ave.
350
Puunene
Haleakala Hwy.
37
Honoapiilani Hwy.
Waikapu
380
400
Kuihelani Hwy.
Mokulele Hwy.
Puunene Ave.
Kihei Rd.
ZONE 7
ZONE 9
Olowalu
Maalaea
311
31
Upper Kihei Rd.
Puunene Ave.
Maalaea Beach
Maalaea Bay
Piilani Hwy.
S. Kihei Rd.
Kihei
SOUTH MAUI
Kamaole Beach Parks
See inset at left
Maui Meadows
Keokea
Kula Hwy.
Wailea
Ulua Beach
Wailea Alanui Dr.
Makena
EUCALYPTUS FORESTS
Molokini Crater
Puu Olai
Ulupalakua
Onela Beach (Big Beach)
Kahoolawe
Ahini-Kinau Natural Area Reserve
ZONE 8
Alalakeiki
Wailea
Kilohana Dr.
Kihei Rd.
ZONE 8
Piilani Hwy.
Okolani Dr.
Wailea Ike Rd.
Makena Alanui
3 5 7 8 9 10 11 12 13 16 17 18 19 20 21 23 25 26 27

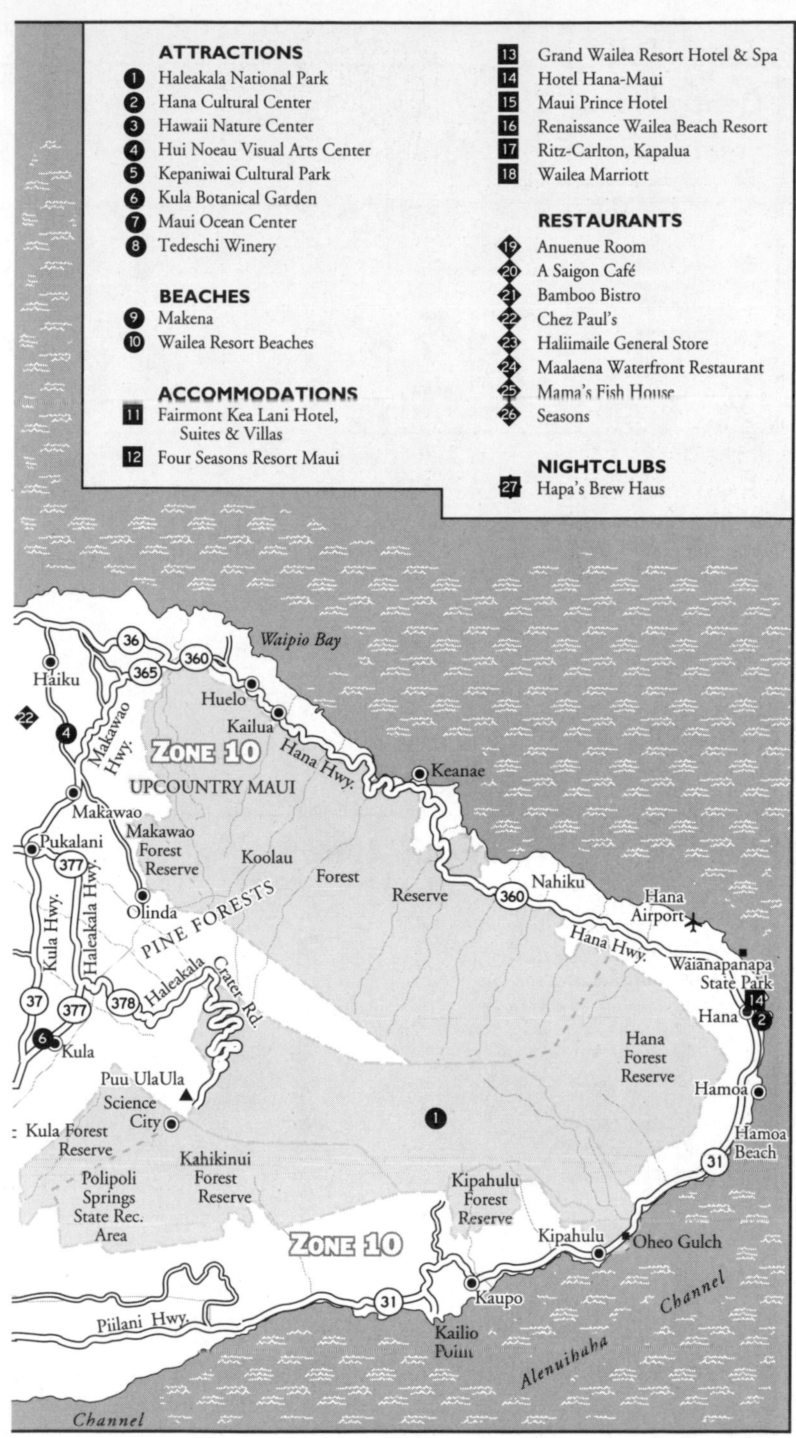
ATTRACTIONS
1 Haleakala National Park
2 Hana Cultural Center
3 Hawaii Nature Center
4 Hui Noeau Visual Arts Center
5 Kepaniwai Cultural Park
6 Kula Botanical Garden
7 Maui Ocean Center
8 Tedeschi Winery
BEACHES
9 Makena
10 Wailea Resort Beaches
ACCOMMODATIONS
11 Fairmont Kea Lani Hotel, Suites & Villas
12 Four Seasons Resort Maui
13 Grand Wailea Resort Hotel & Spa
14 Hotel Hana-Maui
15 Maui Prince Hotel
16 Renaissance Wailea Beach Resort
17 Ritz-Carlton, Kapalua
18 Wailea Marriott
RESTAURANTS
19 Anuenue Room
20 A Saigon Café
21 Bamboo Bistro
22 Chez Paul's
23 Haliimaile General Store
24 Maalaena Waterfront Restaurant
25 Mama's Fish House
26 Seasons
NIGHTCLUBS
27 Hapa's Brew Haus
Waipio Bay
Haiku
Huelo
Kailua
Hana Hwy.
Keanae
Makawao Hwy.
ZONE 10
UPCOUNTRY MAUI
Makawao
Pukalani
Makawao Forest Reserve
Koolau Forest Reserve
Nahiku
Hana Airport
Olinda
PINE FORESTS
Kula Hwy.
Haleakala Hwy.
Haleakala Crater Rd.
Hana Hwy.
Waianapanapa State Park
Hana
Kula
Puu UlaUla
Science City
Kula Forest Reserve
Hana Forest Reserve
Hamoa
Hamoa Beach
Polipoli Springs State Rec. Area
Kahikinui Forest Reserve
Kipahulu Forest Reserve
Kipahulu
Oheo Gulch
ZONE 10
Kaupo
Piilani Hwy.
Kailio Point
Alenuihaha Channel
Channel

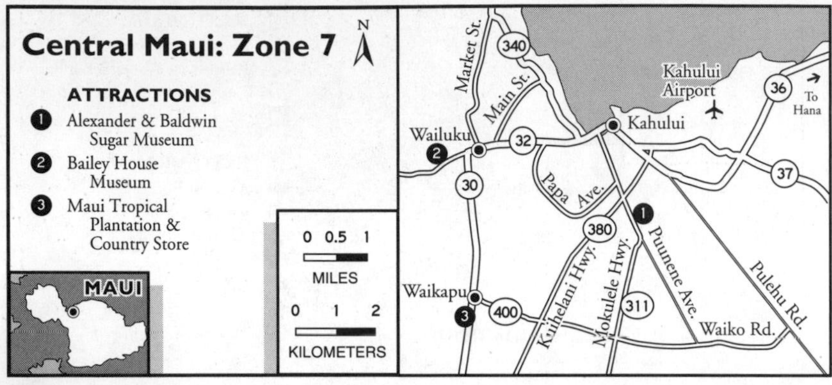

West Maui: Zone 9

ATTRACTIONS

1. Baldwin Home Museum
2. Brig Carthaginian
3. Hawaii Experience Theater
4. Lahaina-Kaanapali and Pacific Railroad
5. Whalers Village Museum
6. Wo Hing Temple Museum

BEACHES

7. Kaanapali Beach
8. Kapalua Beach

ACCOMMODATIONS

9. Embassy Vacation Resort
10. Hyatt Regency Maui
11. Kaanapali Beach Hotel
12. Kapalua Bay Hotel
13. Lahaina Inn
14. Maui Marriott Resort
15. Sheraton Maui
16. Westin Maui

RESTAURANTS

17. The Bay Club Restaurant
18. David Paul's Lahaina Grill
19. Gerard's
20. Hula Grill
21. Kimo's
22. Longhi's
23. Pacific O
24. Plantation House Restaurant
25. Roy's Kahana Bar & Grill and Roy's Nicolina
26. Sansei Seafood Restaurant and Sushi Bar

NIGHTCLUBS

27. Maui Brews

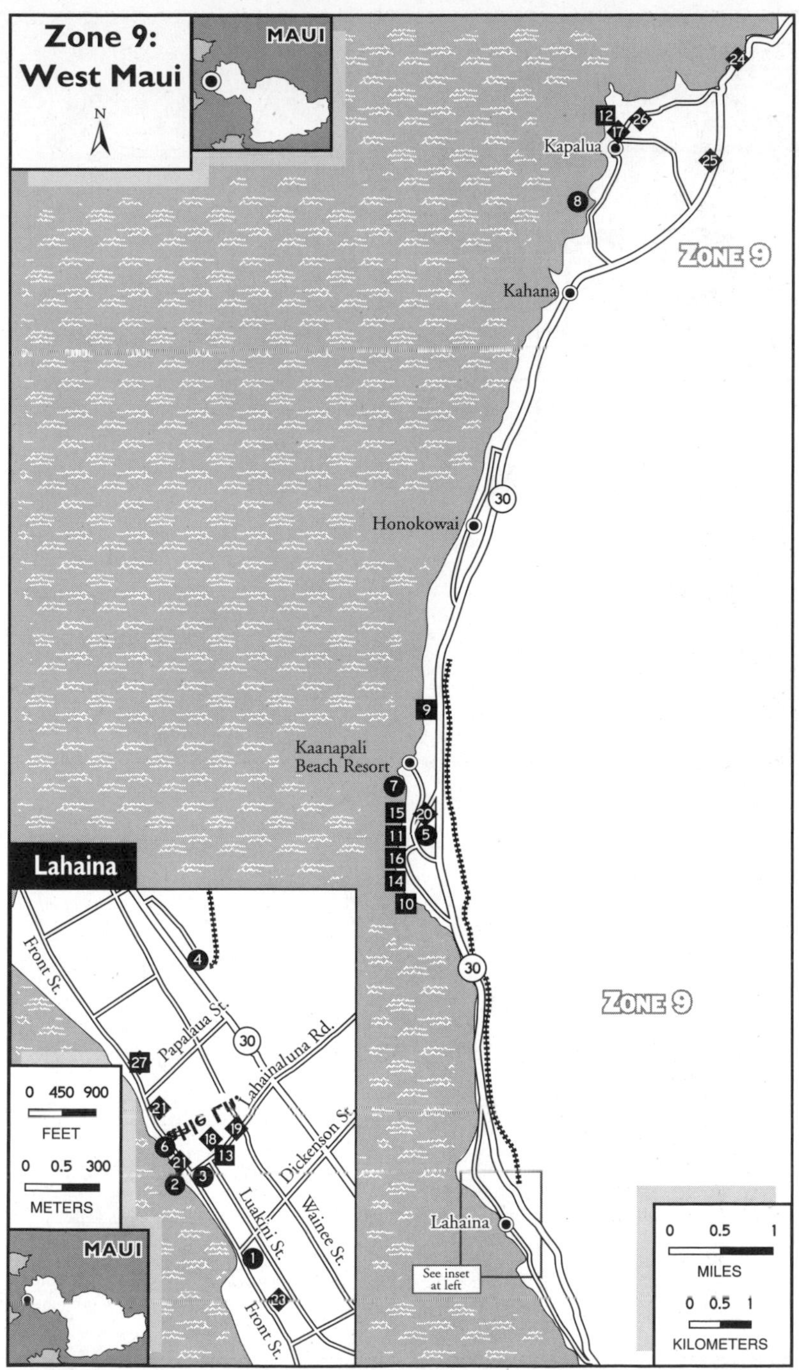

Zone 9: West Maui
N
MAUI
Kapalua
Kahana
ZONE 9
Honokowai
30
Kaanapali Beach Resort
Lahaina
See inset at left
0 0.5 1
MILES
0 0.5 1
KILOMETERS
Lahaina
Front St.
Papalaua St.
Lahainaluna Rd.
Dickenson St.
Luakini St.
Wainee St.
0 450 900
FEET
0 0.5 300
METERS

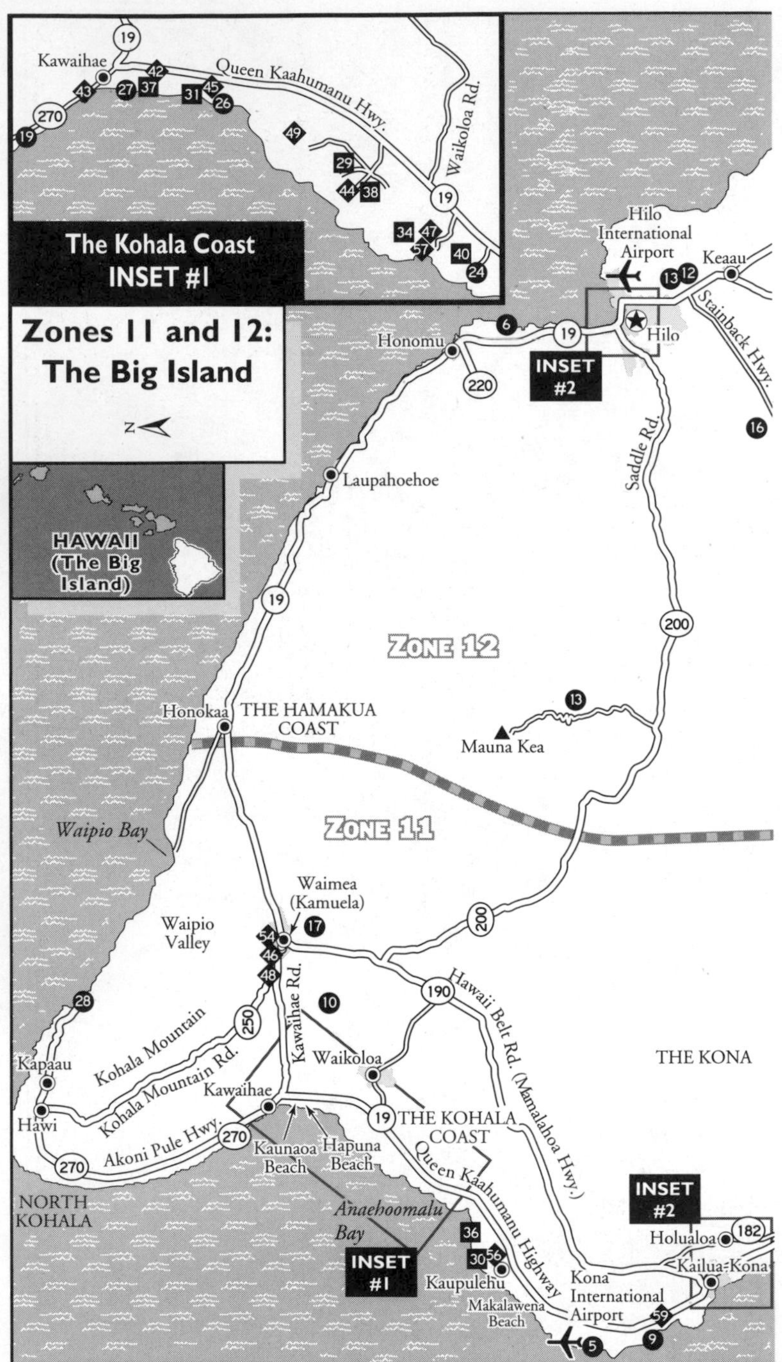
The Kohala Coast
INSET #1
Zones 11 and 12:
The Big Island
HAWAII
(The Big
Island)
Kawaihae
Queen Kaahumanu Hwy.
Waikoloa Rd.
Hilo
International
Airport
Keaau
Stainback Hwy.
Hilo
Honomu
INSET
#2
Saddle Rd.
Laupahoehoe
ZONE 12
Honokaa
THE HAMAKUA
COAST
Mauna Kea
ZONE 11
Waipio Bay
Waimea
(Kamuela)
Waipio
Valley
Hawaii Belt Rd. (Mamalahoa Hwy.)
Kawaihae Rd.
Kohala Mountain
Kohala Mountain Rd.
Waikoloa
THE KONA
Kapaau
Hawi
Kawaihae
THE KOHALA
COAST
Akoni Pule Hwy.
Kaunaoa
Beach
Hapuna
Beach
Queen Kaahumanu Highway
NORTH
KOHALA
Anaehoomalu
Bay
INSET
#1
INSET
#2
Holualoa
Kailua-Kona
Kaupulehu
Kona
International
Airport
Makalawena
Beach

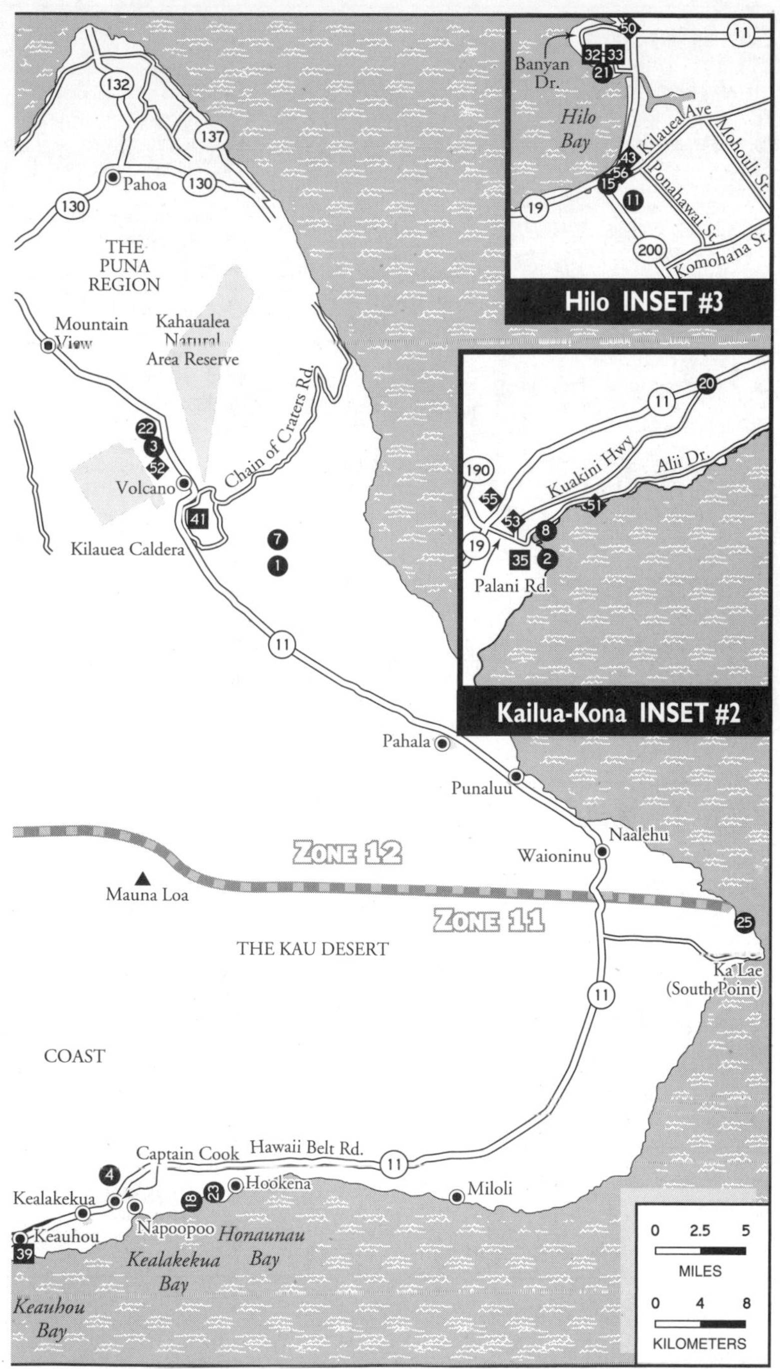

Hilo INSET #3
Banyan Dr.
Hilo Bay
Kilauea Ave
Mohouli St.
Ponahawai St.
Komohana St.
Kailua-Kona INSET #2
Kuakini Hwy
Alii Dr.
Palani Rd.
Pahoa
THE PUNA REGION
Mountain View
Kahaualea Natural Area Reserve
Chain of Craters Rd.
Volcano
Kilauea Caldera
Pahala
Punaluu
Naalehu
Waioninu
ZONE 12
ZONE 11
Mauna Loa
THE KAU DESERT
Ka Lae (South Point)
COAST
Captain Cook
Hawaii Belt Rd.
Hookena
Miloli
Kealakekua
Keauhou
Napoopoo
Honaunau Bay
Kealakekua Bay
Keauhou Bay
MILES
KILOMETERS

Zones 11 and 12: The Big Island

ATTRACTIONS

1. After Dark in the Park
2. Ahuena Heiau
3. Akatsuka Orchid Gardens
4. Amy B. H. Greenwell Ethnobotanical Garden
5. Astronaut Ellison S. Onizuka Space Center
6. Hawaii Tropical Botanical Garden
7. Hawaii Volcanoes National Park
8. Hulihee Palace
9. Kaloko-Honokohau National Historical Park
10. Kamuela Museum
11. Lyman Mission House and Museum
12. Mauna Loa Macadamia Nut Visitor Center
13. Nani Mau Gardens
14. Onizuka Center for International Astronomy and Mauna Kea Observatory
15. Pacific Tsunami Museum
16. Panaewa Rainforest Zoo
17. Parker Ranch Visitor Center and Historic Homes
18. Puuhonua O Honaunau National Historical Park
19. Puukohola Heiau
20. Sadie Seymour Botanical Gardens
21. Suisan Fish Market and Auction
22. Volcano Winery
23. Wakefield Botanical Gardens

BEACHES

24. Anaehoomalu Beach
25. Green Sand Beach
26. Hapuna Beach State Recreation Area
27. Kaunaoa Beach
28. Pololu Beach

ACCOMMODATIONS

29. Fairmont Orchid
30. Four Seasons Resort Hualalai
31. Hapuna Beach Prince Hotel
32. Hawaii Naniloa Resort
33. Hilo Hawaiian Hotel
34. Hilton Waikoloa Village
35. King Kamehameha's Kona Beach Hotel
36. Kona Village Resort
37. Mauna Kea Beach Hotel
38. Mauna Lani Bay Hotel & Bungalows
39. Ohana Keauhou Beach Resort
40. Volcano House
41. Waikoloa Beach Marriott

RESTAURANTS

42. Batik Restaurant
43. Café Pesto
44. CanoeHouse
45. Coast Grille
46. Daniel Thiebaut Restaurant
47. Donatoni's
48. Edelweiss
49. The Grill and Lounge at the Orchid
50. Harrington's
51. Huggo's
52. Kilauea Lodge
53. Kona Ranch House
54. Merriman's
55. Oodles of Noodles
56. Pahuia at Four Seasons
57. Royal Siam Thai
58. Roy's at the King's Shops
59. Sam Choy's Restaurant

Zone 13: Kauai

ATTRACTIONS

1. Grove Farm Homestead
2. Guava Kai Plantation
3. Kauai Museum
4. Kilauea Point National Wildlife Refuge
5. Kilohana Plantation
6. Kokee National History Museum
7. Limahuli Garden
8. Moir Gardens
9. National Tropical Botanical Garden Lawai and Allerton Gardens
10. Waioli Mission House Museum

BEACHES

11. Hanalei Bay
12. Kalapaki Beach
13. Kee Beach
14. Lumahai Beach
15. Poipu Beach Park
16. Polihale State Park (Barking Sands)
17. Secret Beach
18. Shipwreck Beach
19. Tunnels Beach

ACCOMMODATIONS

20. Hanalei Bay Resort & Suites
21. Hyatt Regency Kauai Resort & Spa
22. Kauai Marriott Resort & Beach Club
23. Princeville Resort
24. Radisson Kauai Beach Resort
25. Sheraton Kauai Resort

RESTAURANTS

26. The Beach House
27. Brennecke's Beach Broiler
28. Café Hanalei and Terrace
29. Casa di Amici
30. Duke's Canoe Club
31. Hamura Saimin
32. Keoki's Paradise
33. Mema Thai Chinese Cuisine
34. A Pacific Café
35. Plantation Gardens
36. Postcards
37. Roy's Poipu Bar & Grill
38. Shells, at the Sheraton Kauai Hotel
39. Tidepools

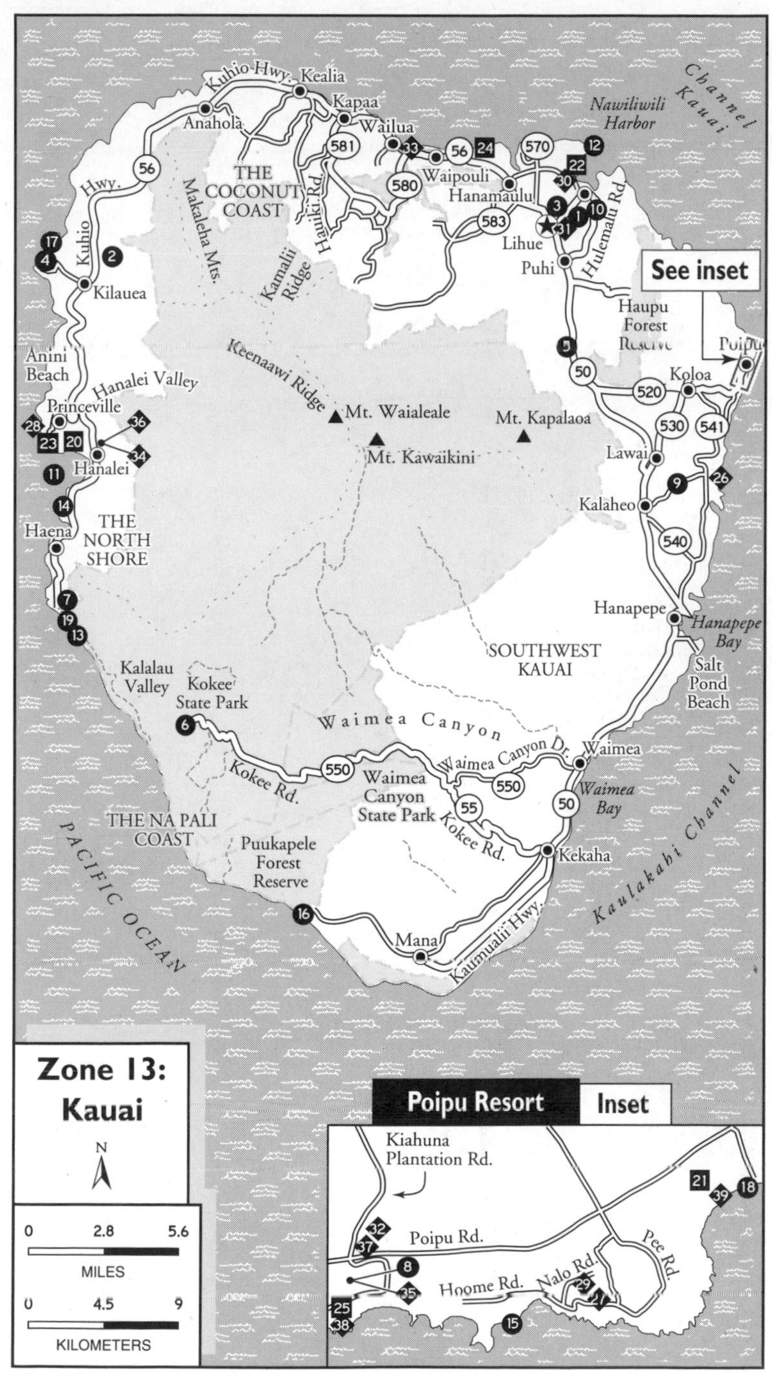
Zone 13: Kauai
Poipu Resort
Inset
See inset
Kuhio Hwy.
Kealia
Kapaa
Wailua
Anahola
Nawiliwili Harbor
Kauai Channel
THE COCONUT COAST
Waipouli
Hanamaulu
Lihue
Puhi
Hulemalu Rd.
Makaleha Mts.
Kamalii Ridge
Hauiki Rd.
Kilauea
Kuhio Hwy.
Anini Beach
Hanalei Valley
Princeville
Hanalei
Keenaawi Ridge
Mt. Waialeale
Mt. Kawaikini
Mt. Kapalaoa
Haupu Forest Reserve
Poipu
Koloa
Lawai
Kalaheo
Hanapepe
Hanapepe Bay
Salt Pond Beach
Haena
THE NORTH SHORE
SOUTHWEST KAUAI
Kalalau Valley
Kokee State Park
Waimea Canyon
Waimea Canyon Dr.
Waimea
Waimea Bay
Kokee Rd.
Waimea Canyon State Park
THE NA PALI COAST
Puukapele Forest Reserve
Kekaha
Kaulakahi Channel
PACIFIC OCEAN
Mana
Kaumualii Hwy.
N
0 2.8 5.6
MILES
0 4.5 9
KILOMETERS
Kiahuna Plantation Rd.
Poipu Rd.
Pee Rd.
Hoome Rd.
Nalo Rd.

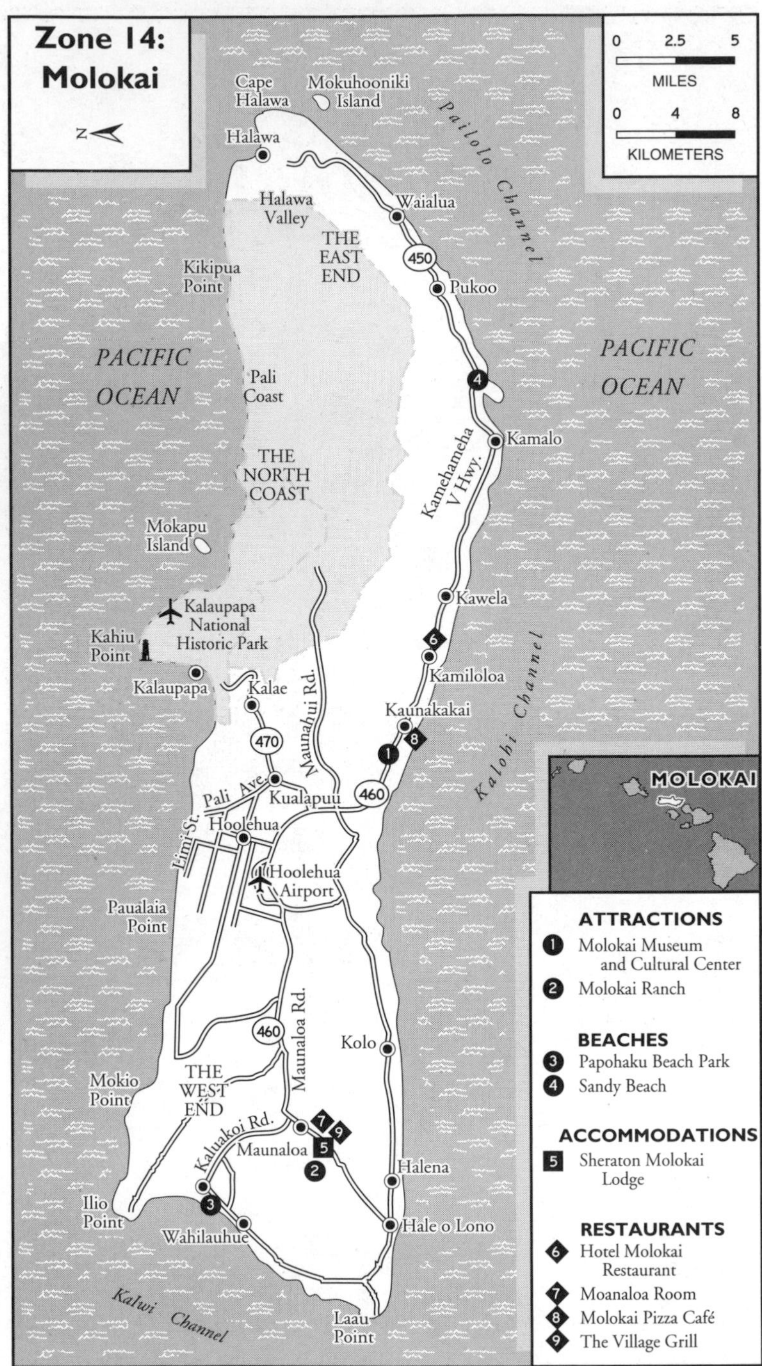
Zone 14:
Molokai
Z
0 2.5 5
MILES
0 4 8
KILOMETERS
Cape Halawa
Mokuhooniki Island
Pailolo Channel
Halawa
Halawa Valley
THE EAST END
Waialua
450
Pukoo
Kikipua Point
PACIFIC OCEAN
Pali Coast
PACIFIC OCEAN
Kamalo
THE NORTH COAST
Kamehameha V Hwy.
Mokapu Island
Kalaupapa National Historic Park
Kawela
Kahiu Point
Kamiloloa
Kalaupapa
Kalae
Kaunakakai
Kalohi Channel
470
Maunahui Rd.
MOLOKAI
Pali Ave.
Kualapuu
460
Hoolehua
Lihi St.
Hoolehua Airport
Paualaia Point
460
Maunaloa Rd.
Kolo
Mokio Point
THE WEST END
Kaluakoi Rd.
Maunaloa
Halena
Ilio Point
Wahilauhue
Hale o Lono
Kalwi Channel
Laau Point
ATTRACTIONS
1 Molokai Museum and Cultural Center
2 Molokai Ranch
BEACHES
3 Papohaku Beach Park
4 Sandy Beach
ACCOMMODATIONS
5 Sheraton Molokai Lodge
RESTAURANTS
6 Hotel Molokai Restaurant
7 Moanaloa Room
8 Molokai Pizza Café
9 The Village Grill

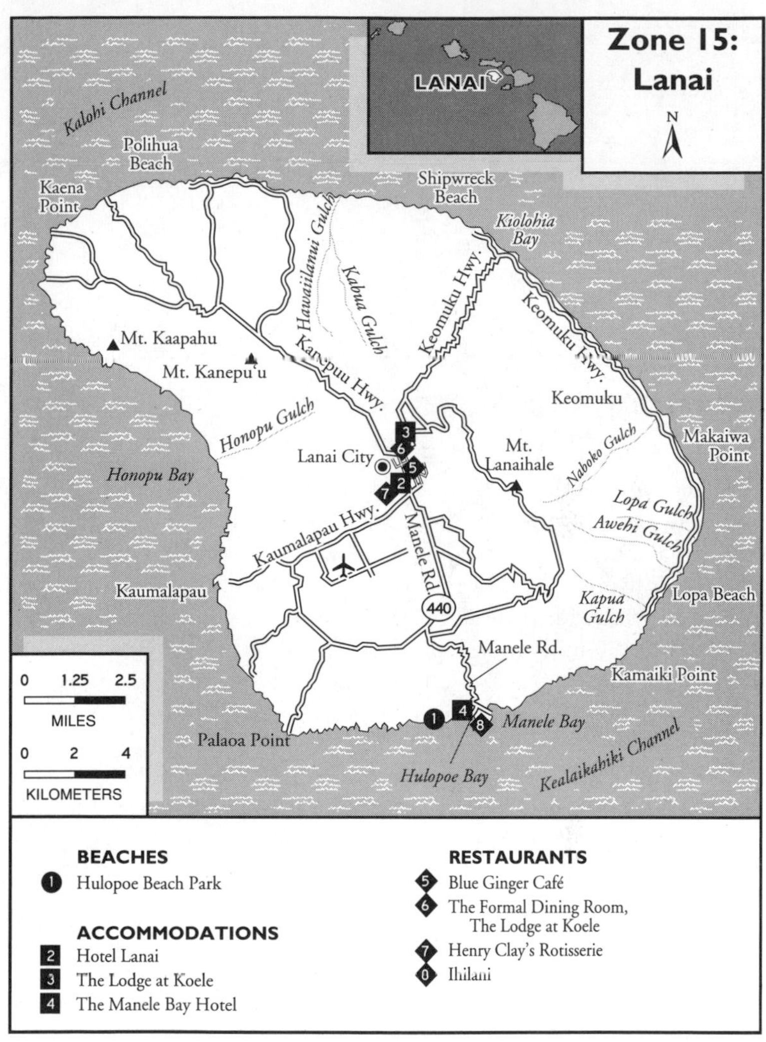

Zone 15:
Lanai
N
LANAI
Kalohi Channel
Polihua Beach
Kaena Point
Shipwreck Beach
Kiolohia Bay
Hawaiilanui Gulch
Kahua Gulch
Keomuku Hwy.
Keomuku Hwy.
Mt. Kaapahu
Mt. Kanepu'u
Kanepuu Hwy.
Keomuku
Honopu Gulch
Lanai City
Mt. Lanaihale
Naboko Gulch
Makaiwa Point
Honopu Bay
Lopa Gulch
Awehi Gulch
Kaumalapau Hwy.
Manele Rd.
440
Kaumalapau
Kapua Gulch
Lopa Beach
Manele Rd.
Kamaiki Point
0 1.25 2.5
MILES
0 2 4
KILOMETERS
Manele Bay
Palaoa Point
Hulopoe Bay
Kealaikahiki Channel
BEACHES
1 Hulopoe Beach Park
ACCOMMODATIONS
2 Hotel Lanai
3 The Lodge at Koele
4 The Manele Bay Hotel
RESTAURANTS
5 Blue Ginger Café
6 The Formal Dining Room, The Lodge at Koele
7 Henry Clay's Rotisserie
8 Ihilani

Part One

Getting Acquainted with Hawaii

About the Aloha State

The Hawaiian Islands, in the middle of the sea and far removed from any continent, are nonetheless an irresistible lure to anyone who's ever heard the word aloha. People from all over the world pay handsomely for the privilege of flying at least five hours to this jack's toss of islands in the tropical North Pacific. Hawaii is the most isolated population center in the world, 2,390 miles from California, 3,850 miles from Japan, 4,900 miles from China, and 5,280 miles from the Philippines. Only seven of the 132 blips in the Hawaiian Islands archipelago are even inhabited, and one of those, Niihau, is a private ranch.

Despite the remoteness of the destination, nearly seven million people find their way annually to Hawaii to roam the sandy shores and volcanic peaks, enjoy the nearly perfect weather and easygoing lifestyle, gaze at the spectacular natural beauty, and dream of ways to drop out of sight and stay here forever.

Plenty of people have done just that. Since the Islands were discovered in about A.D. 650 by Polynesian seafarers, probably from the Marquesas, a wide range of folks have washed ashore—British and European explorers, field workers from Asia and some from Europe and the Caribbean, German planters, Scottish merchants, American missionaries and whalers, South Pacific and other Polynesian Islanders, Southeast Asian refugees, and rogues of all nations who jumped ship and were unwilling, or unable, to leave. Some early-twentieth-century wayfarers ran out of fuel, crash-landed their planes in the sea, and swam ashore. It's a colorful history that led to the racial rainbow of people and cultures that comprise modern Hawaii. These Islands, America's only former royal kingdom complete with a fairy-tale palace, have been a state since 1959. In their remarkable population, people of mixed blood outnumber other groups, no one is a majority, and the rarest soul of all is a pure Hawaiian.

In the beginning the Islands were empty slates, volcanic slopes in a beneficent climate rich with potential to sustain the good life. Creatures and plants blew in or were carried by the settlers, along with their heritage, customs, and languages. Imports mingled and thrived in the fecund tropical atmosphere, often at the expense of earlier arrivals. The riotous birds that wake the day and the fragrant flowers, lush plants, and towering trees that dress the landscape hail from India, the Americas, Asia, and still farther regions. Subtle native plants and shy native birds were crowded into small corners or vanished altogether. As a result, Hawaii has the dubious reputation of being the endangered species capital of the world, with more than 75% of native birds extinct or threatened and more than 250 species on the endangered list.

Without the enemies of their homelands, exotic species have a very good life in the Islands. You don't often see the only native mammals, the hoary bat and the endangered monk seal, but men introduced hooved cattle, pigs, donkeys, deer, and sheep that went wild and flourished, to the detriment of the fragile landscape. Houseplants got loose to climb tree trunks, where they sprouted leaves as big as your face. The ficus trees pampered in pots in many a mainland living room are two-story giants with massive canopies in Hawaii. The bright lantana blooming in the wild is said to have sprung from a single garden plant tossed into a garbage heap. Anything grows, larger than life, including the cityscape of Honolulu and the elaborate, world-famous beach resorts where each building component, investment dollar, computer, bedsheet, fork, vehicle, and tourist was shipped thousands of miles from another shore. Hawaii is not only a special place; for better or worse, it's a marvel.

You can look forward to an unforgettable experience in Hawaii, which is likely to call you back again. Hawaii enjoys one of the highest repeat visitor rates of any destination.

Open your window shade on the plane and look out when the final descent begins, after miles of open sea, to see Mauna Kea and Mauna Loa looming through the clouds. Maui's Haleakala appears next, then the low red-dirt plains of Lanai across from moody Molokai. As the plane approaches Honolulu, the water seems to get bluer. Then Oahu appears, and the world's most remote and most unlikely city, sprawling along its southern shore. Excitement builds as you touch down and glide into Honolulu International Airport. You emerge in the open air, which smells of flowers, and feel the warm breeze on your skin. Welcome to Hawaii.

Choosing Your Island

Which island should you see first? It depends on what you want to do and who you're bringing along on this trip. Here's a thumbnail visitor's guide: The Big Island has active volcanoes, accessible cultural history, landscape diversity, and luxury golf resorts in the lava. Maui has wintering humpback whales, its own complement of big-time golf courses, and plenty of visitors to its sunny beach resorts, ranging from affordable condos to plush hotels. Molokai is the quietest and least oriented to tourism. Lanai is a virtually private former pineapple plantation with two classy hotels and golf courses. Oahu is the vibrant heart of the Islands—the cosmopolitan cities of Honolulu and Waikiki on one side and unspoiled country all around it. Kauai is the lush green movie set where nature pulls out all the beauty stops.

Want to simply kick back at a beach resort and get spritzed with Evian by the pool or have a butler fix your mai tais? Hawaii offers at least two dozen upscale luxury choices, most of them clustered on South and West Maui and the Big Island's Kona-Kohala Coast, where you can be pampered in butlered bungalows for $5,000 a night.

Want to hike spectacular sea cliffs or green rain forests? You can't miss on Kauai, with pure wilderness on its Na Pali (The Cliffs) Coast, or the Big Island with its *kipuka,* oases of green forest amid black lava, and Hamakua Coast waterfall valleys. Equally spectacular are Maui's Upcountry cloud forests, Oahu's sheer Koolau ridges, and Molokai's haunting fern-forested northeast coast.

Traveling with your family? Your kids, especially the teenagers, will love Waikiki. Maui's Kaanapali Resort is a top family destination, but kids love Poipu Beach on Kauai too. And what could be more educational than watching a Big Island volcano in action? You'll find kids are welcome, even cherished, all over the Islands.

Golf doesn't get much better than the spectacular courses of Maui, Lanai, Kauai, and the Big Island. Oahu adds its share, including the busiest and the most difficult courses in the nation.

You'd need more than a week to do justice to Oahu, but the trick is to hit the road. Rent a car, ride the bus, but do get out of town and see the beauty of the Koolau Mountains, the Windward Coast, the North Shore, central plains filled with pineapple, and other destinations. Wear your swimsuit if you want to stop every now and then to go for a swim at a roadside beach. Spend a morning snorkeling at crowded Hanauma Bay, break for plate-lunch surfer chow, then go find your own choice of an empty near-shore reef to snorkel in the afternoon. Save another day for learning how to surf at Waikiki; a day for hiking or riding in the Windward hills or watching big waves on the North Shore; a day at the USS *Arizona* and USS *Missouri,* the Bishop Museum and Honolulu Academy of Art; a day browsing the designer boutiques; a day exploring Honolulu's natural history; a day kayaking or windsurfing at Kailua Beach; and a day to rest after attending a Hawaiian music concert at Waikiki Shell and then boogying all night. Pretty soon it adds up to a real good time.

If you're island-hopping, it's important to realize that many of Hawaii's attractions and adventures—including a visit to the Polynesian Cultural Center on Oahu, a Zodiac boat ride along Kauai's Na Pali Coast, coasting on a special bike from Maui's lofty summit of Haleakala down to the sea, a snorkel cruise to Lanai, and a mule ride down Molokai's cliffs—take up most of a day or more. You need more than a day to fully explore the natural wonders of Hawaii Volcanoes National Park, home of fire goddess Madame Pele and her ever-erupting Kilauea Volcano.

To get the most out of your Hawaii visit, mix and match experiences: Combine the sparkle of Honolulu on Oahu with the meditative beauty of Hanalei, Kauai or Hana, Maui. Supplement your big-game fishing adventure on the Big Island with a rugged trail ride on Molokai. Soak up the sun in Wailea's luxury resorts on Maui, then sail across the channel to Lanai to cool off under the Upcountry pines at the affordable Hotel Lanai or luxurious Lodge at Koele.

The Weather Report

Blue skies, trade winds, and sunshine with almost 12 hours of daylight every day of the year: There's no better climate than Hawaii. The reason is geographic. The Hawaiian Islands are located in the North Pacific, 1,700 miles north of the Equator, inside the Tropic of Cancer (stretching from 154 degrees 40 minutes to 179 degrees 25 minutes west latitude and 18 degrees 54 minutes to 28 degrees 15 minutes north latitude, to be precise).

While the Islands share latitudes with Havana, Hong Kong, Calcutta, and the Sahara Desert, they enjoy a key advantage over these hot spots. Hawaii has natural air-conditioning. The islands are 2,781 miles south of Anchorage, Alaska, across open sea. The cold northeast winds, which historically propelled merchants' ships to Honolulu from the West Coast to earn the name "trade winds," still sweep down the Pacific, softening as the water warms. The tamed breezes arrive in Hawaii as cooling trade winds, welcome whether gentle or blustery. Now and then, they die off in what is called Kona (meaning leeward) weather, hot and still and fretful.

The coldest spot in Hawaii is atop Mauna Kea, where the February average is 31.1°; however, a minimum temperature of 11° was once recorded. The warmest spot is nearly 14,000 feet below at Puako, near Mauna Lani Resort on the Kohala Coast of the Big Island, with an August average of 80.7°. Pahala, at the island's southern tip, once reached 100°.

Hawaii's year-round average temperature of 77° is judged the best in the United States. The difference between winter and summer, and between night and day, is about five to ten degrees on the shorelines, where most people live. Daytime highs are usually somewhere in the 80s, although they can be lower in winter, when storms hide the sun, or rise to the low 90s in steamy August and September. Nights are in the 70s in summer and 60s in winter, with rare dips into the 50s. Winter nights at the coldest record in decades got down to 55° in Honolulu, where summer highs are unlikely to be higher than 94°. The rest of the thermometer seems superfluous.

But it's not that easy. The Aloha State encompasses 21 of the 22 world climatic zones and features no fewer than 88 ecosystems, ranging from snowy mountaintops, rain forests, wetlands, and deserts to sea cliffs, beaches, and volcanoes.

Temperature zones vary with altitude, rather than with latitude. Around the coastlines all the islands are warm (highs in the 80s) and mostly sunny. As you gain altitude in the Upcountry, with 2,000–3,000-foot elevations, the weather cools off on all islands and is often wetter too. On the mountaintops, the chill can be downright alpine, and the moisture turns to snow from time to time. Meteorologists estimate the temperature drops 3.5° for every 1,000-foot rise above sea level. If the heat gets you down, go up and cool off. You may need a jacket or sweater and a blanket at Kula, Maui; Waimea on the Big Island; Nuuanu on Oahu; Kokee State Park on Kauai; and Lanai City, Lanai.

All islands share another climatic trait: The weather is drier and hotter on the leeward sides; cooler, wetter, and windier on the windward sides. The line between is a northeast-southwest diagonal echoing the trade wind flow. Resorts tend to be located on the leeward coasts for the reliable sunshine: Waikiki and Ko Olina on Oahu; Makena, Wailea, Kihei, Lahaina, and Kaanapali on Maui; Kailua-Kona and the Kona-Kohala coast on the Big Island; and the South Shore of Kauai around Poipu Beach.

Vacationers may not always agree, but rain is a good thing on islands too remote to import water. Hawaiians wrote chants about rain. And they created onomatopoetic words for water—*wai huihui* (cool water), *wai kapipi* (sprinkling water), *wai konikoni* (tingling water), *wai noenoe* (misty water), and *wai kai* (brackish water). And more familiar, Waikiki (spouting water) was named not for the ocean but the fresh springs that gushed there. Oahu's municipal water is adjudged some of the best in the world, and it tastes better than bottled designer water because it is filtered through lava for a half-century to reach the water table.

The average humidity level in the state ranges from 56% to 72%, but annual precipitation varies widely. Waikiki gets 25 inches of rain a year, but Manoa Valley, five miles inland, receives 158 inches.

Two of the wettest spots on Earth are found in Hawaii:

- Mount Waialeale on Kauai gets more than 400 inches of rainfall a year. Waialeale means "rippling or overflowing water," an apt title for the Kauai peak that one year received 950 inches of rain, nearly 80 feet.
- Puu Kukui, the 5,871-foot-high summit of the West Maui Mountains, gets 350 inches a year. In 1982, it had a record rainfall of 654.83 inches, or 54.5 feet.

Hilo on the Big Island, meanwhile, has the soggy sobriquet of being the wettest city in the United States, averaging 128 inches of rain per year. A word about rain showers: Don't get too excited about getting wet. It feels good. No one wears raincoats. Umbrellas are more often used to keep off the sun than the rain, and showers often come on winds that turn umbrellas inside out. If it rains while you're on the beach, get in the water or under a tree. If it rains during your al fresco brunch, put up the table umbrella and don't sit under the drip. The shower will probably be gone in a minute or two. With the ubiquitous Hawaiian "pineapple juice" showers that drift over while the sun shines brightly, everyone just gets wet one moment and dries off the next. Showers are considered blessings.

Weather can get extreme on these mid-Pacific pinpricks of land, but it's uncommon (see below).

A Word about Directions

The familiar directions of north, east, south, and west won't be terribly helpful in Hawaii. Local usage has little to do with the compass. The words you want to know are *mauka* (uphill, inland, toward the mountains) and *makai* (toward the sea). The other directions are known by a bewildering variety of local landmarks. In Honolulu, these are generally *Ewa* (west, or where Ewa plantation used to be) and *Diamond Head* (that one's easy).

Perils of "Paradise"

No place is perfect, even this one that seems heavenly enough that many call it "paradise." While nobody in Hawaii likes to "talk stink" (say anything bad), each island has certain drawbacks.

Oahu suffers hellish chronic traffic congestion—too many cars and not enough roads—which is worst at rush hour and lunchtime. Traffic is much lighter in summer when school is out. If you drive, be patient and polite. Let cars merge in front of you, as you'll see others do. Remember that it's bad manners to honk in Hawaii unless you are signaling a friend, and rude gestures can get you in trouble. Don't worry unduly about mileage on your rental car. The longest distance you can drive in Hawaii on paved road, a two-lane blacktop, is from Hilo to Kailua-Kona around the southern end of the Big Island, a distance of 125.2 miles. On Oahu, you run out of island paved road after 46.2 miles, the distance between Honolulu and Kahuku via Wahiawa. Parking is inexpensive in downtown Honolulu compared to other big cities, but it can mount up unless you get validations from restaurants and offices you visit or park in municipal lots. Hotels in Waikiki and Kaanapali Beach Resort on Maui charge for guest parking. Metered parking on the streets is inexpensive, so long as you pay attention to the hours and tow-away zones.

Maui gets really windy most afternoons, when the breezes kick up whitecaps in the ocean, sling stinging sand in your face at the beach in Kihei, and make for bumpy landings at Kahului Airport. It's a natural phenomenon. Near-constant trade winds accelerate when they pass through Maui's funnel-like isthmus.

Maui and Kauai both have traffic jams when big jets unload passengers around quitting time for the sugar mills or other businesses. On Maui, the jam is worst from Lahaina to Kaanapali. On Kauai, it's worst between Lihue and Kapaa. You'll also encounter crowds at rental car stands when DC 10s and 747s arrive. The best policy is to slow down and cool off. Allow more time. Strike up a conversation. Island pace just isn't as *wiki-wiki* (speedy) as the stressful life you're vacationing from, so you might as well get used to it. It's called "Hawaiian time."

Kauai is nicknamed the "Garden Island" because it is so green and lush and tropical. It thrives because it gets watered a lot, especially on the North Shore where short torrential downpours are common. The rickety wooden bridge over Hanalei River gets flooded out at least once a year, briefly cutting off the North Shore from the rest of the world (there's no more celebrated excuse for being late for work). Residents put up with it because the old bridge guards their beautiful home ground from major bus and truck traffic and full-scale development. Lots of Hawaiian songs celebrate Kauai's beauty, but it takes rain to make those triple rainbows and waterfalls, sometimes lots of it. That's even more true of Hilo and the Hamakua Coast on the Big Island, where the verdant waterfall valleys and profusion of orchids, anthuriums, fruit, nuts, and other crops are a live giveaway to the moist climate.

The Big Island of Hawaii can thank its two active volcanoes, primarily Kilauea, for the hazy condition it often suffers, known as vog. That's short for "volcanic fog," which cloaks Kailua-Kona on many afternoons with a gray overcast that looks like doomsday. Sometimes a shift in the winds will carry the vog north to other islands. Vog can pose a discomfort to asthma victims and makes people drowsy or headachy. Something more acute, called laze, occurs close to active lava flows when volcano-produced sulfuric acid mixes with cool seawater and becomes hydrochloric acid, sometimes in a burst of steam. This is harmful to your health.

Molokai's only resort is the Sheraton Molokai Lodge. The island receives milk and staples by once-a-week barge from Honolulu. If you shop the markets for food, you plan dinner around what there is to buy.

Clouds that delay takeoffs and landings often shroud the island of Lanai. You may spend more time on Lanai than you planned. Since the island is remote and there are only two resorts, everything is more costly, a fact of little concern to most of its high-budget visitors.

Besides the drawbacks above, real perils are few, but be forewarned:

Insects love tropical Hawaii—huge centipedes (and they bite, painfully); delicate, small scorpions (a bite like a bee sting); several species of scary-looking cockroaches that don't bite; huge, fast, hairy but harmless cane spiders; several sizes of ants; your average fly and superfly; and mosquitoes that seem to prefer tender flesh fresh from the mainland. You might even see a bold fruit rat traveling on a power line.

Sunburn is a much bigger danger than bugs. Don't underestimate the power of tropical sun. It's strongest from 9 a.m. to 3 p.m. Do what you want when you want, but slather everyone with high-SPF waterproof sunscreen and use sunglasses and hats as well. If you get scorched, slather on even more aloe vera gel.

Shark attacks are rare in Hawaii, but sharks are not. Those clear blue waters harbor a variety of the creatures, which, by Hawaiian legend, are more revered than feared as *aumakua,* or family guardian spirits.

The islands are subject to earthquakes, mostly small Big Island rumbles from Kilauea Volcano. Rogue waves can sweep you out to sea, and rip tides can carry you off toward Tahiti. You can slip off a cliff trail or fall into the volcano. All of these awful things have happened to people on a holiday in normally benign Hawaii.

Hawaii's most threatening perils are the occasional tsunami, high surf, and the temporary flash flooding that occurs when tropical cloud bursts, usually brief and intense, run off steep slopes. Sudden, heavy rains pose flash-flood danger, particularly in a downhill waterfall valley or on a road that briefly becomes a raging waterfall course. If you get caught by a squall while hiking by a stream, go immediately to high ground. If driving, park before you get to the deep water on a roadway and wait an hour or two. It will all be gone soon as the water flows out to sea.

The Islands by Zone

Oahu: The Gathering Place

OAHU FACTS

Flower Ilima	**Color** Yellow
State Capital, County Seat Honolulu	**Area** 608 square miles
Length 44 miles	**Width** 30 miles
Population 876,156	**Coastline** 112 miles
Highest Point Kla Peak (4,003 feet)	

Oahu has a lot to brag about: two mountain ranges, great natural beauty, world-class shopping, lots of sandy beaches, accommodations ranging from surf shacks to five-star hotels, sleepy country villages, international sophistication, a modern city and urban resort with clean air and water, open space, high-rise towers, a multicultural population, nightlife, a major university, and considerable wealth, drawn by the quality of life.

Small wonder everyone sooner or later ends up on Oahu, America's gateway to the Pacific and most-visited island in the chain. Ironically, an island famous for so much gets a bad rap from critics who complain of too many buildings and people. Perhaps they never left Honolulu. The truth is that the entire cityscape, the urban resort of Waikiki, and the lion's share of suburban housing are squeezed into a narrow 26-mile-long corridor between the Koolau Mountains and the Pacific. Leave that corridor and you have another Oahu.

You need only cross over the mountains to the cool and scenic Windward Coast or head up the central valley between the Koolau and Waianae ranges to the North Shore to discover Oahu's more natural side, or go west past the airport to be surrounded by old sugar lands.

Zone 1: Waikiki

After a costly facelift, Waikiki sports new gardens, walkways, pools, and street lighting, as well as an emphasis on projecting Hawaiian culture to guests in the un-Hawaiian environment of tall buildings and busy streets.

If you think of Waikiki as a lively urban resort where an incredible variety of people enjoy the most famous beach in the world, you'll love it, as public theater if nothing else. If you seek the good old days when cruise ship passengers were met by men and maidens who jumped in the sea and swam to the boats, then escorted passengers to a handful of hotels where they resided royally for months, having shipped their Rolls Royces over, then you will surely be disappointed. You won't find grass shacks to sleep in—sadly, the Uniform Building Code outlaws even thatched roofs in most instances. You can see hula, Hawaiian arts and crafts, and nostalgia; hear Hawaiian music; and watch surfers as long as you want.

Waikiki packs into a square mile of space about 33,000 visitor rooms in 175 hotel and condo properties, plus apartments that house some 50,000 residents, restaurants, boutiques, theaters, nightspots, fast-food joints, museums, beaches, boats, churches, and just across the Ala Wai Canal, a major convention center. The district is a narrow peninsula between **Waikiki Beach** and the canal paralleled by Kalakaua Avenue, the main one-way inbound boulevard; secondary thoroughfare Kuhio Avenue, a block back from the beach; the one-way outbound Ala Wai Boulevard; and the canal, which defines the district on two sides. Kapahulu Avenue more or less defines the Diamond Head end. One big chunk of Waikiki at the beginning of the man-made peninsula is **Fort DeRussy,** the only open spot along this end of the beach. This fortunately situated Army installation has a couple of high-rises for military visitors, plus low-rise buildings and lots of green. With even fewer buildings and more green, 170-acre **Queen Kapiolani Park** at the other end, the foot of Diamond Head, is a similar beachfront respite from congestion. King Kalakaua created the park in 1877 and named it for his queen. It is the home of the **Waikiki Shell,** an outdoor entertainment venue, and **Honolulu Zoo.** It's a wonderful place for running, flying kites, having picnics, holding cultural festivals, and playing softball and tennis.

You could say Waikiki, in which an estimated 100,000 people sleep on any given night, is the antithesis of urban sprawl. The compaction puts everything within walking distance or a short bus ride. Waikiki is a city within a city, and while they might have done it better (no planners were used in the making of Waikiki), the resort accommodates, amazingly well, millions who seek sun and sand and a good time in a tropical urban setting.

Our suggestion is to visit Waikiki for at least two or three days, time enough to get your bearings, shake off jet lag, and press on, either elsewhere on Oahu or to a neighbor island. While you're in Waikiki, go out early one morning, walk the beach when it's deserted and the sand is cool, and stop for an al fresco breakfast at one of the hotels you pass.

At night, the sidewalks of Kalakaua and Kuhio are constant parades of passersby, including visitors from every corner of the globe. Prostitution thrives in Waikiki after dark, despite periodic attempts to control it. Prostitution is not legal here, but goes on just the same.

Waikiki is a safe area. The Honolulu Police Department maintains a strong and reassuring presence there. In addition, a citizens group calling themselves the "Aloha Patrol" prowls the streets at night, assisting visitors and keeping an eye out for trouble.

After years of traffic congestion during Waikiki's facelift, residents from outside the tourist district rarely go there. Venture outside Waikiki to experience the local lifestyle of Oahu.

Zone 2: Greater Honolulu

Honolulu has been the capital of Hawaii since 1850, when it was the heart of the kingdom. Today, its realms are financial, political, commercial, and cultural—during the daytime at least. The lively downtown shuts down at night. Except for Chinatown and parts of the waterfront, the downtown restaurants and bars are open in daytime only, and so are the stores. But retail continues unabated into the evenings in the out-of-downtown shopping centers.

The main street of town is Bishop Street, a continuation of the Pali Highway that goes one-way makai all the way down to Honolulu Harbor. The companion mauka-bound thoroughfare is Alakea Street. The downtown area extends several blocks around them. Other boundaries are Ala Moana Boulevard, paralleling the harbor front, and Vineyard Boulevard on the uphill side, named for onetime wine vineyards planted long ago by a Spaniard, Don Marin. Through the middle, King and

Beretania Streets, a pair of key one-way (through downtown) connectors, link neighborhoods for miles on either side of town. The downtown architecture is an interesting mix of historic buildings and new high-rises that speak of continued prosperity. Street trees and park areas, not to mention the mountain and ocean views at either end of the streets, make for a very attractive district. The government buildings and **Capitol District,** which includes **Iolani Palace** and other historic structures, are just Diamond Head of downtown, within easy walking distance.

Just Ewa of downtown is the historic **Chinatown** district, now populated more by Vietnamese than Chinese. Twice in the past, Chinatown burned to the ground and was rebuilt. The latest assault was a matter of rising crime and drug use, but citizens have banded together to take Chinatown back. One key advance was the $30 million renovation of the 1,400-seat **Hawaii Theatre,** a masterpiece in gilt and 1920s style.

Zone 3: Windward Oahu

For peace and scenic splendor without high-rise canyons, go over the mountains to the Windward beach town of **Kailua,** where hotels are banned but vacation rentals and bed-and-breakfasts offer affordable access to the excellent beaches; or **Haleiwa,** former plantation town and home of big-wave surfers on the North Shore; or **Ko Olina Resort,** the neighbor island-style luxury spread in west Oahu.

No signs point the way to Kailua, but it's over the Pali Highway from downtown. There's no tourist booth and not many tourists. Kailua's great beaches were largely unknown to visitors until recently, but **Kailua Beach** and **Lanikai Beach** have been named two of America's best, and now the secret's out. A quaint beach town at the foot of the Koolau, Kailua is a bedroom community of about 50,000 and the bed-and-breakfast capital of Oahu.

Bed-and-breakfasts in Hawaii are most often rooms or suites in people's houses with breakfast or light kitchen facilities provided, rather than the quaint inns of the East Coast. Scores of B&Bs and other low-key places to stay, including vacation rentals on or near the beaches, can be found on the Internet. Many operate underground since the City and County of Honolulu, in a poor display of civic aloha, banned new bed-and-breakfasts years ago.

Windsurfing, kayaking, swimming, and snorkeling are the main water attractions here in the home of Robbie Naish, former world champion windsurfer who is now pioneering kitesurfing (see details, page 269). The scenic **Mokulua,** two photo-op islets off Lanikai, are the most popular kayak destinations. Rent all the gear you need right in Kailua Beach Park or at one of the shops in town.

Hikers scale 603-foot-high **Kaiwa Ridge** for a panoramic view of the Windward side or hike other trails through the Koolau rain forests along the Windward Coast. Fearless hikers with sheer-cliff experience test their mettle on the spiky pinnacle of Olomana.

Kailua is the recommended choice on Oahu for families with small kids, who can safely play in gentle waves. Opting for a vacation rental is one way to control expenses while maximizing exposure to local life—discovering unfamiliar foods in the supermarkets, for instance (or at the hour-long Thursday morning "People's Market" at 9 a.m. beside Kailua Middle School). Kailua is a favorite of many visitors seeking to live Hawaiian style. A rental car is necessary to make the most of it and to enjoy the surrounding Windward Coast. Farther up the reef-protected Windward shores, more than 50 miles of empty beaches (busier on weekends) are suitable for snoozing, swimming, shorefishing, spearfishing in the lagoon-like waters, or snorkeling.

Natural attractions include **Kaneohe Bay,** one of the most beautiful in the Pacific, with snorkel and dive trips departing from Heeia Pier; **Kualoa Ranch,** a 4,000-acre cattle ranch with 75 horses for trail rides and myriad other outdoor activities; and **Hoomaluhia Botanical Park,** a 400-acre municipal garden with Hawaiian ethnic plants at the foot of the cathedral-like Koolau.

Zone 4: North Shore

Year-round, the sleepy North Shore sugar town of **Haleiwa** offers another alternative in Oahu, with its modest plantation-style buildings that house surf shops, clothing stores, art galleries, and restaurants.

The pace quickens considerably when the surf rises in winter, drawing the world's best wave riders and people who simply have never seen a 25-foot wave, much less someone surfing on it.

The North Shore has relatively few places to stay—a youth hostel; a few beach cottages, campgrounds, and private vacation rentals; plus the condo units and hotel rooms of Turtle Bay Resort Golf and Country Club. It is a great day-trip destination that shows Oahu's country face.

To the west from Haleiwa is **Mokuleia,** relatively undeveloped stretches of wild beach fronting old sugar lands. The road ends shortly after **Dillingham Airfield,** where gliders, skydiving, biplanes, and other aerial thrill rides are based. Oahu may have nearly a million residents, but it doesn't have a paved road that goes around the entire island. Kaena Point (see below) is a wilderness area for hiking and other pursuits. You can walk or bike around to the Waianae Coast, but you can't drive there.

Agricultural landscapes still dominate the middle and upper central valley areas that culminate in the North Shore.

Zone 5: Leeward Coast

The hot, dry **Waianae Coast** is sheltered from view and separated from the rest of the island by the Waianae Range. The beach area of **Makaha,** long a popular surf break, remains relatively unexplored and nearly unknown to visitors since the lone resort hotel closed several years ago. Some condos and timeshares exist—you can find affordable lodging in condos like the Hawaiian Princess and Makaha Beach Cabanas and in vacation rentals on the Internet.

Makaha means "gate" in Hawaiian, and it serves as the entry to Oahu's last true shoreline wilderness area, **Kaena Point Natural Area Reserve,** a world removed from Waikiki. On this remote shore at Oahu's westernmost point, albatross nest in sand dunes, Hawaiian monk seals loll on empty beaches, and humpback whales cruise by in winter. Winter and spring bring the huge swells that draw surfers like magnets to this shore as well as to the North Shore communities around the point. But the paved road doesn't go through. You can drive to the end at **Yokohama Bay** (an old train used to stop here and drop off Japanese fishermen to fish the bay). Then it's a 90-minute walk down a dirt road to Kaena Point.

On the city end of the coast, the welcome mat will be out at the nearest resort hotel, **Ihilani Resort and Spa,** a luxurious retreat and elaborate spa with a man-made beach lagoon, beachfront suites, two fine-dining restaurants, and nearby, 18-hole **Ko Olina Golf Course.**

Zone 6: Central Oahu

The valley formed by Waianae Mountains on the west and Koolau Mountains on the east is a broad, scenic plain that from the sky resembles an avenue leading to **Pearl Harbor** and its war memorials. That's one path the Japanese warplanes took in 1941. On the way they bombed **Schofield Barracks Army** installation, halfway along the plain.

Aloha Stadium, the 50,000-seat facility that is home to annual NFL Pro Bowl games and other sports and entertainment events, neighbors **Pearl Harbor Naval Base.**

Today the Central Valley is still bucolic in the northern reaches, carpeted with gray-green rows of pineapple in the rich red dirt and wild cane where sugar plantations used to hold sway. You can stop at **Dole Pineapple Plantation** to learn about and taste the golden fruit, once a major Hawaii crop. Toward the southern end are the newer suburbs of housing and shopping centers, including **Waikele Outlets.**

Maui: The Valley Isle

MAUI FACTS

Flower Lokelani (rose)
County Seat Wailuku
Length 48 miles
Population 128,094
Highest Point Haleakala (10,023 feet)
Color Pink
Area 729 square miles
Width 26 miles
Coastline 120 miles

Maui's sunny resorts on its south and west coasts are mainly the reasons why just about everybody knows the name of this island, Hawaii's second largest. Maui is composed of two volcanic masses joined by a valley with golden beaches and blue sea on either end. Then there's 10,000-foot Haleakala, the dormant volcano whose sheer bulk forms more than half the island. But Maui seems to have more appeal than the sum of its parts. It combines a hint of the flash of Oahu with the genuine country attitudes of a rural plantation island and the sophisticated influence of its luxury spreads and the people who frequent them.

Zone 7: Central Maui

Departing Kahului Airport, you may wonder why you came so far to see such familiar big-box landmarks (Costco, Wal-Mart, Barnes & Noble). Wander farther to find more shopping centers, neighborhoods of this amorphous waterfront town, the port, and, on either side, beaches. Beyond the retail center, you discover why everyone raves about Maui.

The famous windsurfing areas, **Kanaha** and **Hookipa Beaches,** are just beyond the airport on the way to Hana. In the opposite direction, a small road wanders off toward Waihee and eventually around the whole northwest shoulder of Maui to the western resort coast. This is one of Maui's most scenic and unspoiled drives along sea cliffs and through large ranches, although housing developments are threatening to overtake parts of it. The pavement narrows to one lane often as it winds around the base of the **West Maui Mountains,** so watch the road.

Beyond Kahului is the county seat of **Wailuku,** historic and quaint, and the countryside gets greener as you approach **Iao Valley State Park.**

The isthmus valley is a sea of waving green sugarcane fields, a vanishing sight in the Islands. Above it pokes the smokestack of still functional **Puunene Sugar Mill.**

From Kahului Airport the main roads lead to resort areas: Follow the signs to Kihei/Wailea/Makena in South Maui, Maalaea in the middle, and Lahaina, Kaanapali Beach Resort, and Kapalua Resort in West Maui. The Haleakala Highway leads up the flank of the mountain, and the Hana Highway along the North Shore leads around the back of Haleakala to the ranch village of Hana, hiding near the end of this windy road with its plentiful waterfalls.

Zone 8: South Maui

A 20-minute ride through the cane brings you to the resort coast. **Wailea, Makena,** and **Kihei** are the resorts of choice to the south. Straight ahead is **Maalaea,** home of condos; the **Maui Ocean Center Aquarium;** and the harbor where the boats for many snorkel, whale watching, and other cruise tours are sheltered.

If you're on a budget, go to Kihei. When money's no object or you're pining for spectacular golf, go to Kapalua or Wailea. Got your sociable kids along? Go to **Kaanapali,** where they can enjoy the action. Or head to serene Makena at Maui's southern end for more solitude. When time is no object, go to **Hana** and stay awhile in the quaint seaside village.

Thrifty travelers find affordable condos in Kihei, a beachside strip lined with shops and malls. Kihei is also the home of many people who work in the neighboring resorts, as well as the Air Force Super Computer complex nearby. The town fronts a ten-mile coast indented by black lava reefs that frame some excellent gold sand pocket beaches and broad strand beach parks. Most popular is **Kamaole Beach III,** in the heart of Kihei with a tree-shaded grass picnic area and park, views of Lanai and Kahoolawe, and free parking.

Hollywood celebrities, conference-goers, and honeymooners love **Wailea Resort,** a lush, groomed beauty spot where luxury and deluxe hotels share great beaches with green space in between. The lower slope of Haleakala helps the mid-rise hotels hide from view. **Grand Wailea Resort Hotel & Spa, Four Seasons Maui, Outrigger Wailea Beach, Renaissance Wailea Beach,** and Arabian fantasy-style **Fairmont Kea Lani** are interspersed with plush waterfront condo homes and resorts. These temples of pleasure feature Grand Wailea spa and lesser spas; an elaborate water complex with mini-river canyons, dives, waterfall caves, and a water-powered elevator so swimmers don't have to walk back up at Grand Wailea; gourmet restaurants; and suites costing $10,000 a night.

Find seclusion beyond Wailea at **Makena Resort,** where the **Maui Prince Hotel** stands alone amid 1,800 acres of dryland keawe forest and several splendid beaches. South Maui is punctuated by Polai, a cindercone peninsula that juts into the sea. Makena is an old village where cattle from the upland Ulupalakua Ranch were once herded into the water to swim for the ships that would take them to market. The tiny community has a picturesque Hawaiian-language church by the water. Haleakala's last eruption spilled down to the sea south of Makena about 1790. It's now traversed by rough hiking trails. There the road ends.

Wailea Resort has three scenic golf courses, and Makena adds two more. Horseback riding, a sporting clay shooting range, hiking, a coastal trail, a competition tennis complex, **Shops at Wailea** shopping village, and a shuttle bus to connect them are all part of the South Maui appeal.

Zone 9: West Maui

Head to the right from Maalaea around the foot of the West Maui Mountains and you'll approach historic **Lahaina** town and **Kaanapali Beach Resort,** prize-winning progenitor of the planned resort complex popular in Hawaii and other destinations.

Lahaina, the old whaling capital, retains charm because of its quaint and preserved historic buildings. It's a happy, honky-tonk jumble of art galleries, coral jewelry and T-shirt boutiques, bars, restaurants ranging from David Paul's Lahaina Grill to waterfront Pacific O to Cheeseburger in Paradise, and **Ulalena,** the best theatrical show in all Hawaii (see page 442 for details). You can stay at the century-old **Pioneer Inn** for a real taste of history. It was once the hangout of lusty whalers on R&R, until the disapproving missionaries prevailed. Lahaina also has a variety of condo resorts, inns, vacation rentals, and B&Bs. In Lahaina many people stop what they're doing and gather to watch when the sun starts dropping like a fireball behind Lanai and the boats in Lahaina harbor.

Kaanapali is a three-mile hop north of Lahaina, but when the traffic is heavy, it can take more than half an hour to get there. After nearly 40 years, park-like Kaanapali continues to reinvent itself and remains a popular destination. The 600-acre resort has two golf courses, mid-rise blocks of deluxe and luxury hotels and condos that line the four-mile beach and dot the hillside behind it, restaurants with a full range of open-air, ocean-view dining, and **Whalers Village Shopping Center.** The shops now include upscale European boutiques in an effort to attract Japanese shoppers. Kaanapali also includes beachfront tennis, public accessways and beach parks, and a shuttle that connects to Kapalua/West Maui Airport (small aircraft).

Farther north, the luxury coast culminates in **Kapalua Resort,** part of a 23,000-acre pineapple plantation with rows of spiky plants that stretch for miles in hilly fields below Puu Kukui, second tallest peak on Maui. This is the most beautiful part of West Maui, its wide-open vistas framed by Molokai offshore and wild lands to the north. Two hotels, several luxury condo resorts, three notable golf courses, and, for contrast, the tidy, prim red plantation buildings share this setting. The roads are lined with signature Islands pines. Kapalua-bound guests can fly from Honolulu to West Maui Airport and avoid the congestion of Kahului.

If Kapalua is outside your budget, investigate the resorts and condos of **Napili Beach** right next door on the southern side of the resort. You can enjoy many of the same benefits.

Zone 10: Upcountry Maui and Beyond

From central Kahului, a country road runs up Haleakala's lower slope and winds through the cool, pastoral community of **Kula,** where, at 3,000 feet, exotic protea, roses, carnations, and blue jacaranda trees bloom. Visitors can stay at **Kula Lodge** or in a variety of bed-and-breakfast bungalows. Kula is on the way to **Haleakala National Park.** It's an escape from tropical heat, featuring botanical gardens, flower farms, and the winery at Ulupalakua, **Tedeschi Vineyards.** They sell a lot of pineapple wine, but you can also taste other vintages and sparkling wine at the tasting room. A cool grassy setting under wild avocado trees is fine for picnics.

Maui's most famous road—the **Hana Highway**—winds by magnificent sea views, waterfalls, and botanical gardens on a skinny road for 53 miles to the ultimate tropical retreat. Count on three hours each way for the drive to Hana, more if you stop to swim in waterfall pools. The small coastal village is populated by Hawaiians (and a few celebrities) who wisely resist change. The rich and famous fly to Hana in small planes, and you can too. There is a small airport served by planes from Kahului.

A stay on Maui promises sunny beaches, great golf on championship courses, winter whale watching, snorkeling and sailing, hikes, sunrise at Haleakala Crater, and a quiet nightlife outside of Kihei and Lahaina.

While the island caters to the wealthy and free-spending corporate incentive winners at many elegant hotels and resort condos, it also offers some affordable bargains for budget travelers. Hikers and campers like Maui for its natural attractions and parks.

Folks who live on Maui have the motto, "Maui No Ka Oi," which means Maui is the best. Satisfied readers of *Condé Nast Traveler* agree. For five years in a row, they've named Maui the "best island in the world."

Hawaii: The Big Island

HAWAII FACTS

Flower Red lehua
Color Red
County Seat Hilo
Area 4,028 square miles
Length 93 miles
Width 76 miles
Population 148,677
Coastline 266 miles
Highest Point Mauna Kea (13,796 feet)

Long before tourism became Hawaii's livelihood, the pluckiest visitors were those who journeyed high above Hilo more than a century ago to see a live, erupting volcano. The volcano shows no sign of stopping. In its current phase, **Kilauea Volcano** has been erupting since January 1, 1983, adding ever more real estate to the already big Big Island of Hawaii. **Mauna Loa,** the most voluminous structure on Earth, is quiet but still active. It last erupted in 1984.

If you have but one day to spend on the Big Island, see Kilauea at **Hawaii Volcanoes National Park.**

The Big Island not only has five volcanoes (Kilauea, **Mauna Kea,** Mauna Loa, **Hualalai,** and **Kohala**) but also a sixth one, a work in progress named **Loihi,** now a seamount emerging from the ocean floor off the southeast coast. You can stargaze at the 9,000-foot-level Visitor Center of the 13,796-foot Mauna Kea, tallest mountain in the tropical Pacific, where the air is so clear and dark that scientists have set up a forest of high-tech telescopes to peer into deep space. If you are hardy, you can hike to the sub-Arctic summit of slightly shorter 13,680-foot-high

Mauna Loa. Both mountains rise more than 30,000 feet from the ocean floor, making them technically the tallest mountains on the planet.

Some visitors head for **Ka Lae** or **South Point,** the windswept southernmost point in the United States, where carbon dating on fish hooks shows early Polynesians arrived around 650 A.D. Others go to **Holualoa,** an artists' village amid backyard coffee farms on the hillside over Kailua. And lucky ones enjoy a sunny day in **Hilo,** gateway to the volcano park.

The Big Island is the only Hawaiian island big enough to take a road trip of more than an hour or two. Plan on three days to see natural attractions like **Akaka Falls, Waipio Valley,** Hawaii Volcanoes National Park, the catch of the day at **Honokohau Harbor,** the coffee plantations of **Kona,** and **Puu Honua O Honaunau,** the ancient refuge where hapless victims and law breakers could find sanctuary. Adventurers, vulcanologists, astronomers, hunters of marlin, and lovers of the outdoors now are joined by golfers, international conferees, and the rich and famous.

Zone 11: Kona

Kona is the word for "leeward" in Hawaiian, and it usually means warm and still. The Big Island's Kona Coast is the area where several hulking volcanoes act to block the ever-blowing northeast winds and calm the sea. **Kailua-Kona** is the fishing village–turned–junior Waikiki that serves as headquarters for the Kona district. It's filled with affordable condos, hotel rooms, and suites (none of them terribly appealing) as well as shopping plazas, restaurants, and bars. Beaches are noticeably in short supply, although the **King Kamehameha Kona Beach Hotel** has one. Instead, this is primarily a rocky shoreline where the waters are so dependably docile that walkways, restaurants, and rooms hang right over the floodlit waves in several places.

To the south of Kailua-Kona is the somewhat tonier **Keauhou Resort,** with many deluxe condo resorts like the **Kanaloa** and a renovated hotel worth a try, the **Aston Keauhou Beach Resort,** which has historic features (King Kalakaua's summer cottage and small fishpond) on the handsome grounds, a spa, a tide pool, and **Disappearing Sands Beach** next door.

To the north of the airport and Honokokau Harbor, where the world-famous Kona Coast marlin fishing fleet is moored, the lava spilled by Hualalai Volcano about 200 years ago lines the highway in endless, desolate reaches of black. The first time we saw it, we had decided to hold green Kauai for another visit and opted instead for the raw island of big hot volcanoes. Somewhere north of Kailua-Kona, our hearts sank. Then we cut across the lava to find palm-edged oases by the sea and discovered some of the world's great beach resorts.

The first is the area of **Kaupulehu,** an ancient fishing village before it was overrun by lava and later metamorphosed into low-rise bungalow resorts. Honeymooners, CEOs, and families (except in September, when it is a kid-free zone) seek the **Kona Village Resort,** a low-key but expensive enclave of traditional private bungalows on the ancient village site between the beach and surrounding protective lava. Kona Village has petroglyph fields, a famous luau, tennis, and many other pluses, but it is the only resort along this stretch of coast without a world-famous championship golf course. Next door is its opulent, and equally romantic modern neighbor, **Four Seasons Resort Hualalai,** which borders a golf course, exclusive condos and homes, and has several swimming pools, including one made to look like a lava tide pool complete with tropical fish.

Up the highway at **Waikoloa Beach Resort,** the **Hilton Waikoloa Village** is a fantasy resort where you can swim with captive dolphins, ride a sleek silver tram to your tower, or take an Italian launch on a rail through a second-story waterway. The pools, falls, and water slide are so elaborate that you can forget there's no natural beach. But a postcard-perfect beach is next door at **Anaehoomalu Bay,** fronting the completely revamped deluxe **Outrigger Waikoloa Beach Resort.** Both hotels have spas, and the resort features two golf courses, the **Kings Village** shops, restaurants, and well-maintained historic features.

Next up the highway to the north is **Mauna Lani Resort,** with golf, tennis, walking trails, historic features, and the luxurious **Mauna Lani Bay Hotel & Bungalows,** where you'll find butlered hideouts beside the beach and **Orchid at Mauna Lani,** where you can bliss out with a massage in a tent by the sea at a "spa without walls."

Just north of Mauna Lani is **Mauna Kea Beach Resort,** home of the venerable **Mauna Kea Beach Hotel** and newer **Hapuna Beach Prince,** two golf courses, access to the two best beaches on the island, and all the amenities wealth can summon. Hotels and golf courses on sites carved from beachfront lava can be traced to 1965, when Laurance Rockefeller opened the Mauna Kea Beach Hotel on a primo beach that belonged to **Parker Ranch,** then the largest privately held cattle spread in the nation. The simple, elegant resort became a top choice of executives in search of a comfortable retreat, and their heirs kept up the tradition. ("Now I know where old Republicans go to die," once quipped Merv Griffin.) The art-filled hotel set the tone for luxury Hawaii beach resorts to come.

History is right on the surface throughout this coast—Kona Village, Waikoloa, and Mauna Lani Resorts all serve as stewards of petroglyph fields, lava beds covered with thousands of ancient primitive drawings. Mauna Lani and Waikoloa also boast well-kept ancient fishpond complexes with signage to tell you how they work. Federal and state parks preserve cultural monuments throughout this area.

Vacation rentals and bed-and-breakfasts are plentiful in **Upcountry Holualoa,** in the coffee country above Kailua-Kona, and in **Waimea,** Parker Ranch headquarters and a charming ranch town. Parker Ranch has a historic compound and rodeo grounds.

Zone 12: Hilo and Volcano

Hilo tourism facilities were set up decades ago with great expectations for a tourism boom that didn't quite materialize. Some of the large hotels on Banyan Drive on **Hilo Bay** were transformed into residential dwellings. Reasonable rates predominate at the remaining ones, and some have been upgraded in recent years.

Hilo has a historic downtown district and a quiet charm. It gets plenty of rain and has the attributes of a wet, warm place—abundant flowers and tropical fruit (bananas hang in the lobbies of some hotels), huge shady trees, waterfalls and streams, and triple rainbows. Our recommendation is to stay a night or two at **Shipman House,** a restored Victorian bed-and-breakfast in a beautiful Hilo neighborhood, and to spend your days exploring Hawaii Volcanoes National Park and the nearby lava-watch area at **Kalapana,** where hot lava may still be rolling into the sea when you are there. Both are less than an hour's drive away. Stroll through one of Hilo's famous gardens, such as the **Onomea Tropical Botanical Garden,** go for a swim in Hilo Bay, and enjoy the uncrowded pace. The **Lyman Mission House Museum** in downtown Hilo is an excellent small facility whose exhibits will give you a feel for life of early immigrants to the area.

Vacation rentals and bed-and-breakfasts make up the accommodations in upcountry Volcano, where you'll find charming lodging like Tom and Brenda Carson's 1925 tin-roofed **Volcano Cottage** and tasty dinners along with quaint rooms at **Kilauea Lodge** in the misty fern forests.

If your goal is to get back to nature, the Big Island is your choice; there is too much to see and do in the great outdoors in just a week, including skiing on the occasionally snowcapped cinders. But if you only have a week, spend two days at Hawaii Volcanoes National Park, staying in Hilo or a nearby cottage, two days sightseeing or pursuing other activities, then splurge for three days at Kona Village, Four Seasons Hualalai, or Outrigger's Waikoloa Beach Resort, some personal favorites.

Kauai: The Garden Isle

KAUAI FACTS	
Flower Mokihana	**Color** Purple
County Seat Lihue	**Area** 549 square miles
Length 33 miles	**Width** 25 miles
Population 58,463	**Coastline** 90 miles
Highest Point Kawaikiki Peak (5,243 feet)	

Zone 13: Kauai

The island's a beauty all right, where roadside forests are a riot of flowering vines and mangoes fall ripe to the ground. But it's not just a pretty place. It's tough and gritty and made for adventure. In modern times, it survived two monster hurricanes in a decade. In olden times, it was the only island to resist Kamehameha the Great's military attempt to unite the kingdom in the late 1700s, although its independent-minded chiefs gave up without a fight later. While the young Big Island is still black with lava in many spots and raw with new life, Kauai is the oldest major island, and its jagged peaks, mantle of green over steep cliffs, and shoreline of beaches are all testimony to the scenic inevitability of erosion.

When you go you can hang out at a fancy hotel in **Princeville** on the North Shore or **Poipu Beach** on the South Shore, or choose the so-called **Coconut Coast** in between, sipping Blue Hawaiis by the pool, or you can get out and discover the island's true nature. Or both. The combination of rough nature and indulgent luxury is all the rage in Hawaii.

Some hike into the 3,000-foot-deep **Waimea Canyon,** a multicolored chasm, or brave the cliff-side 11-mile **Kalalau Trail** that winds along the remote **Na Pali Coast.** Some go up to **Kokee State Park** and venture into the cloud forests on the boardwalk trail into **Alakai Swamp,** last haunt of the Kauai oo, a black bird with bright yellow thigh feathers. This 20-square-mile highland bog is home to rare plants, native birds, Hawaii's only native land mammal, the hoary bat, and a mosquito-eating plant.

Others angle for big-game fish off nearby **Niihau,** snorkel **Kee Beach's** fishy lagoon, and helicopter up to the 5,243-foot-high summit of **Mount Waialeale,** a crater ribboned with waterfalls as befitting the wettest spot in the world. Twenty inches of rain in a single day is common.

All that water refreshes Kauai's seven rivers (you can kayak on the **Huleia, Hanalei,** and **Wailua**) and keeps the Garden Island the great green place it is.

Where to stay depends on the weather. Any place on Kauai can be sunny and hot, but showers are most likely to cool the moody green Hanalei (heavenly garland) area on the North Shore, a real-life version of movie land's Bali Hai (*South Pacific* was shot up here, a movie anyone over 50 might remember). **Princeville Resort,** a California-like development on a sea-cliff plateau with a spectacular view, has homes, condos, the Princeville Hotel with its over-the-top marble lobby, shopping, restaurants, a spa, and world-famous golf at Princeville Golf Course. Part of it overlooks **Hanalei Bay,** the taro patches of the **Hanalei River Valley,** a mile-long beach, and the bowl of 4,000-foot cliffs creased by waterfalls that surrounds the valley. Seven miles beyond friendly, picturesque Hanalei town, the road ends at **Kee Beach** and an ancient footpath leads into Na Pali wilderness. No roads cross the northwest section of the island, a series of dramatic deep valleys carved by ancient streams.

Midway between Hanalei and Poipu is the Coconut Coast, including a number of small communities from **Kapaa** past the Wailua River to **Lihue,** the county seat and site of the airport. Affordable to deluxe beachfront condos and hotels share a golden beach. Water conditions can be rugged for all but surfers and body surfers. There is a sheltered swimming area at **Lydgate Park** by the river mouth. **Coconut Marketplace** offers most of the shopping and restaurants.

Lihue, mostly devoted to commerce and county government, has a museum worth a stop—the small coral-block **Kauai Museum** on Rice Street. Kauai Lagoons by the airport was once a pinnacle of the fantasy resort movement. What's there now is the **Kauai Marriott,** part hotel and part time-shares, with an opulent lobby and ballroom/conference complex, seven-acre pool, extensive art collection, two well-regarded golf courses, and other amenities. Heading south, the highway passes a historic manor on the right known as **Kilohana,** which houses boutiques with fine examples of Nhau shell jewelry artistry, crafts and galleries, and a restaurant. It will give just a taste of how sweet life on Kauai was for the onetime owners, the Wilcox family, when sugar was king.

Sunseekers and families like **Poipu Beach Resort,** a coastal complex with a good swimming beach, golf courses, a tennis complex, several notable restaurants, a wide range of plentiful condo resorts, and a hotel row redefined by the 1992 hurricane. Hotels never get too old on Kauai. Presently Poipu features the **Hyatt Regency Kauai Hotel,** a fine example of Hawaii-style Art Deco architecture, on the southern end and **Sheraton Kauai Resort** on the northern end.

Children and adults enjoy **Spouting Horn,** a lava tube where surf sometimes shoots sea water 50 feet into the air. Inland is **Koloa Town** where the Hawaiian sugar industry was born more than 150 years ago. Now it's a collection of restaurants, bars, and surf-n-sun shops that you pass through to get from the highway to the beach.

Looking for flowers on the Garden Isle? Serious green thumbs go to **Lawai** to visit **National Tropical Botanical Garden,** a Congressionally chartered research facility that's 186 acres include an important collection of rare tropical plants, tropical experimental gardens, and, for contrast, the finely trimmed formal gardens of a former royal estate. Honeymooners and couples seeking a romantic getaway will enjoy Kauai, as will those who come back with tiny shells in their pockets and red dirt on their hiking shoes.

Molokai: The Friendly Isle

MOLOKAI FACTS

Flower White kukui blossom	**Color** Green
County Seat Kaunakakai	**Area** 260 square miles
Length 38 miles	**Width** 10 miles
Population 6,717	**Coastline** 88 miles
Highest Point Kamakou Peak (4,961 feet)	

Zone 14: Molokai

If you crave bright lights and busy nights; avoid Molokai. One of Hawaii's main islands, Molokai can be described by what it doesn't have: traffic lights, shopping malls, nightclubs. The lifestyle is slow and unpretentious, and people pride themselves on being a traditional Hawaiian community.

For better or worse, Molokai has spurned, or been spared, "progress." Actually the island has sustained a number of economic hits over recent years—sugar and pineapple production ceased, residents decided against new hotels and tourism, and federal officials ordered all the cows killed to stamp out an obscure ailment that had been around for decades.

Islanders grow prized produce: watermelons, sweet potatoes, boutique veggies, honey, coffee, and macadamia nuts. Molokai folks are uncommonly friendly and down-home. And honest. Once we left an airplane coupon ticket at the rental car counter in Molokai's tiny airport. Three days later, it was still there—not far from the sign reminding passengers that airline rules prohibit carrying watermelons in the overhead racks.

The island is not a destination for everyone, especially those who like creature comforts. The beaches are wild and lengthy but not usually safe or desirable for swimming. The greatest natural feature, the world's tallest sea cliffs on the jungled North Shore, is virtually inaccessible. The most famous, and poignant, attraction is an isolated but still inhabited former leprosy colony and the mule ride down a steep switchback trail to get there. **Kalaupapa National Park,** where Hansen's Disease victims were banished by royal edict in the 1860s, was the last home of famed Belgian priest Father Damien, who gave his own life treating the sick.

Why go to Molokai? There's plenty to do: mountain biking, horseback riding, snorkeling, diving, kayaking, fishing. The Nature Conservancy runs preserves and hike programs at **Moomomi Dunes,** where bones of flightless birds surface and at **Kamakou** in the high country, a cloud forest filled with rare native plants. Hikers have been known to trek through scenic **Halawa Valley** wilderness on the East End, although the ancient Hawaiian settlement was declared off-limits to visitors by the private owner. Check the status when you are on-island.

Sightseers find an odd assortment of natural and historic sites like ancient fishponds, the **Smith-Bronte Landing** (where the first airplane to Hawaii crash-landed in 1927), **Mapalehu Mango Grove,** and **Iliiliopae,** temple ruins of an ancient school of sacrificial rites.

The frontier-like town of **Kaunakakai** is a sleepy crossroads with a handful of stores and a beloved bakery. At Hoolehua Post Office, you can address, stamp, and send a Molokai coconut home like a postcard.

Turn left out of town onto Kamehameha V Highway and you'll soon find the East End—lush, green, and tropical with ancient fishponds lining the coco-palm coast. Go right and you'll encounter the West End, arid and spiked with cactus. Condo resorts, bed-and-breakfasts, and vacation beach houses are available in either direction.

Go west to find **Sheraton Molokai Lodge and Beach Village,** with distinctive and recently built tourism facilities, including a stylish 22-room lodge, done in what might be called upscale *paniolo* (cowboy) decor recalling ranch history. The lodge has a fine-dining restaurant, capacious bar, and comfortable great room. You can sign up there for adventures, including mountain biking, kayaking, beach toys, and cultural hikes.

The rebuilt plantation town of **Maunaloa** encompasses the lodge and its Outfitters Center. The small community now offers movies, shops, eateries (including the island's first genuine fast-food joint, a KFC outlet), and new, "affordable" plantation-style homes that start at $250,000. Some locals don't take well to change and are still seething.

However, the island has generally retained its pastoral character. The **Molokai Ranch,** with 6,000 head of cattle, covers one-third of Molokai, mostly with wide-open spaces. You're sure to get a good night's sleep overlooking quiet pastures and the sea. Just don't expect nightlife. After dark it's so quiet you can hear the cows dream.

Lanai: The Pineapple Island

LANAI FACTS

Flower Kaunaoa
County Seat Lanai City
Length 18 miles
Population 2,800
Highest Point Lanaihale (3,366 feet)
Color Orange
Area 141 square miles
Width 13 miles
Coastline 47 miles

Zone 15: Lanai

A short flight from Honolulu, Lanai is a world removed. On this smallest of Hawaii's six accessible islands, you can still see most of the island from its loftier spots.

Buildings are dwarfed by the rolling terrain of what was the world's biggest pineapple plantation until they surrendered in the 1980s and planted seeds for resorts and upscale tourism instead. The quaint plantation cottages of **Lanai City** are still there, in remarkable contrast to the elegant **Lodge at Koele,** which resembles a British hill station, and the Mediterranean-style **Manele Bay Hotel,** nestled on a coastal hillside.

When your plane lands in Palawai Basin, where pineapple grew as far as the eye could see, you discover an island of anomalies. It is rural yet sophisticated, with only three paved roads but a 100-mile network of red-dirt plantation lanes and a fleet of small SUVs to go four-wheeling on them. In former times, the days started with a plantation whistle at 5 a.m. Now, days in the sun begin with more discreet wake-up calls.

Lanai is owned mostly by an American tycoon, who acquired it incidentally in a corporate purchase, and inhabited largely by Filipinos, who immigrated to work the pineapple fields and stayed to retrain as luxury hotel workers. Most plantation families still live there, sharing the streets of town with well-heeled world travelers and, increasingly, neighbors.

Golfers play either of the island's magnificent 18-hole courses—the ocean-side **The Challenge at Manele** or the upland **The Experience at Koele,** possibly the most beautiful course anywhere. Yet while visitors are signing up for substantial fees, locals choose the little nine-hole upland course where fees are paid on the honor system, a few bucks in a tin can.

When it was a plantation, nobody went to Lanai unless invited or fortunate enough to get one of the ten rooms in the 1920s-era Hotel Lanai. Now the island appeals to those with means enough to enjoy peace and solitude. Pricey spreads are going up on the hillside so wealthy vacationers can stay longer under their own roofs.

Honeymooners, this is your island. Bill and Melissa Gates took over the island to get married here. Outdoors lovers like it too. You can shoot clay pigeons at Lanai Pine Shooting Clays or hunt game like turkey, Mouflon sheep, and Axis deer. Lodge facilities include a riding stable and croquet on the lawns. Hiking trails lead off through the woods. Nightlife, however, is limited to whatever amusements the hotels have lined up.

Anyone who seeks peaceful surroundings with luxurious accommodations will want to visit Lanai if only to explore a most atypical Pacific island. The island is a combination of hot, dry coastal cliffs and cool uplands with pine groves planted by a farsighted plantation manager long ago to trap clouds and bring water to the dry island. This is no tropical wonderland; its deep gorges and eroded plains speak of a hard agricultural life. But there's beauty to its hinterlands, headlands, and wide-open red-dirt valley touched only by blue sky and puffy white clouds. While prowling the four-wheel roads, explorers can find historic sites like a crumbled sugar town and an ancient king's summer fishing residence.

On a clear day, from **Lanaihale,** the 3,379-foot island summit, you can see five of the seven main Hawaiian islands in a single glance. Only distant Kauai and Niihau remain over the horizon.

Overall, Lanai will appeal to anyone looking to get away from it all whatever the price. In addition to a half-dozen bed-and-breakfasts, you have two resort choices and the little lodge, all under the same ownership—you can go back and forth by shuttle van. The lodge sits on a 1,700-foot-high hill at the head of a lane lined with tall pines and looks so ostentatious that you think a king might greet you instead of a uniformed hostess with a flower lei. It is cooler here, especially at night, which is why the lodge is a favorite with weekending Honolulu residents who love to dress up in sweaters and sit by a roaring fire. Downhill, beside the only safe swimming beach at **Hulopoe Bay,** Manele Bay Hotel simmers around its pool, a lobby full of Asian art, and tropical gardens lining a man-made stream teeming with koi carp.

A drive into Lanai City is like entering a time warp. Most of the island's residents live in tidy little tin-roofed plantation houses with a riot of flowers, fruits, and vegetables growing in their front yards.

You can stop and "talk story" with the locals about the not-so-good old days when pineapple farming dominated life. And by all means, frequent the shops, restaurants, and art galleries in the tree-lined town square.

A Brief History

Scientists believe the Hawaiian Islands were formed millions of years ago, each rising from a single "hot spot" on the floor of the Pacific Ocean and then moving north with shifting tectonic plates. The islands were barren until seeds carried by the wind or ocean currents took root and began to grow. Slowly but surely, birds and insects found their way to these islands, and humans too.

Historians believe seafaring Polynesian voyagers first discovered Hawaii in the fourth century A.D. and took residence along the coasts and valleys where freshwater was plentiful. They introduced dogs, pigs, chickens, and plants, including taro, coconut, breadfruit, banana, sweet potato, and sugarcane. A second wave of Polynesian seafarers, this time from Tahiti, arrived some 500 years later.

The early Hawaiians embraced a simple lifestyle. Taro was a chief food source: Its root was pounded and mixed with water to make poi, the paste-like starch that remains a staple of Hawaiian diets and appears at every luau. Ahead of their time in understanding nature's ecosystem, early Hawaiians built and maintained large fishponds to ensure their chiefs an abundant supply of fish. Back then, a typical *hale* (house) was a wooden frame covered with pili grass; it looked like a haystack.

Hawaiians lived under a strict caste system, and high-ranking *al* (chiefs or rulers) wielded power by imposing many *kapu* (laws or prohibitions). In some cases, even to cross the shadow of a powerful *al* meant sure death. This system brought much bickering among the people, adding to the hostilities among chiefs eager to gain more territory under their rule.

Still, the Hawaiians thrived. When Captain Cook arrived in the Islands in 1778, an estimated 400,000 Hawaiians were living on Oahu, the Big Island of Hawaii, Maui, Kauai, Molokai, Lanai, Niihau, and Kahoolawe.

Captain Cook's Arrival

On January 21, 1778, Captain James Cook, commander of Britain's HMS *Resolution* and HMS *Discovery,* became the first European to set foot on Hawaiian soil, landing at Waimea on the west coast of Kauai. Cook and his crew spent five days on Kauai before a short visit to Niihau, where they traded salt and yams for goats, pigs, and water.

Cook's second contact with the Hawaiians occurred a year later, this time at Kealakekua on the Big Island. As fate would have it, his arrival coincided with the Hawaiians' annual *makahiki* celebration, a four-month festival honoring Lono, the god of peace, agriculture, and fertility. (Today, this event is echoed in the statewide Aloha Festivals.) Historians believe the Hawaiians, seeing these strange vessels heading for shore, thought it was Lono himself returning to the island. Cook and his men were treated to the greatest welcome in Hawaii's history: Hawaiians greeted the ships by the thousands. Cook wrote: "I have nowhere in this sea seen such a number of people assembled in one place; besides those in the canoes, all the shore of the bay was covered with people, and hundreds were swimming about the ship like shoals of fish."

After the *makahiki* ended and Lono-like Cook began to act more human, however, the Hawaiians were no longer quite so hospitable. A scuffle broke out and more than 200 warriors attacked Cook's landing party. Five British marines were killed, including Cook himself. His remains were buried in the deep blue water of Kealakekua Bay.

The Kamehameha Dynasty

One Big Island warrior who took great interest in the foreigners was Kamehameha I. He had been wounded by a gun during the fight, and he realized that any chief who possessed such powerful weapons would have a decided advantage during battles.

Kamehameha set out to conquer all the Hawaiian Islands and bring them under his rule. He secured Maui and Lanai in 1790, then conquered Maui again after losing it for a short time. He had his chief rival on the Big Island killed to claim sole leadership over the island. Then he conquered Molokai and Oahu, but two attempts to invade Kauai failed. In 1810 Kauai's chief peacefully surrendered his island (and the neighboring island of Niihau) to his persistent rival. The entire Hawaiian kingdom was finally unified under one ruler: King Kamehameha I.

Under Kamehameha's reign, trade with Europeans increased. Foreigners particularly valued Hawaii's sandalwood, and the king allowed the exportation of the precious wood to China until the forests were cut to the ground and the supply exhausted.

Kamehameha succumbed to a lengthy illness in 1819 in the area now known as Kailua-Kona on the Big Island. His bones were hidden at a secret location "known only to the moon and the stars," believed to be somewhere on the Kona Coast. Historians estimate he was in his early 60s when he died.

His son and successor, Liholiho (Kamehameha II), had a short but eventful reign. Kaahumanu, the favorite of Kamehameha's numerous wives, made herself the joint ruler, or queen regent, of the Hawaiian kingdom and almost immediately abolished the despised *kapu* system of religious prohibitions. She did so by persuading Liholiho to sit down with her at a feast (it was *kapu,* or forbidden, for men and women to eat together). Seeing that the gods did not punish the guilty parties, Hawaiians' faith in their system crumbled. Kaahumanu and Liholiho declared that all idols and temples be destroyed.

Without their places of worship, the Hawaiians experienced a gaping spiritual vacuum. They were ripe for conversion when fate intervened. In 1820, 14 American missionaries from New England arrived aboard the brig *Thaddeus.* They preached in Honolulu and in Kona for what was supposed to be a one-year trial period. They never left, marrying Hawaiian royals and gaining land and power.

Liholiho and his queen, Kamamalu, died of the measles in 1924 in London, where they had journeyed in hopes of meeting King George IV. Liholiho's successor was his younger brother, Kauikeaouli (Kamehameha III). Kaahumanu, meanwhile, embraced Christianity and announced a new system of laws based on the missionaries' teachings.

The missionaries' impact on Hawaii overwhelmed the old culture. They built churches and schools throughout the Islands and condemned the people for their manner of dress. Hula, regarded by the missionaries as lewd, was banned. Christianity became the new religion in Hawaii. The chiefs were converted first, and the commoners followed suit.

Kamehameha III took control of the kingdom in 1825. By then the whaling industry had replaced the exhausted sandalwood trade. From the mid-1820s through the 1850s, when whale blubber was replaced by oil as a source for light, the whaling industry was the kingdom's economic savior, and Lahaina became one of the most vital ports in the Pacific.

The king's 29-year reign was marked by several landmark events. The first came in 1843, when the Hawaiian kingdom fell to British control for a brief time. More significantly, in 1848 Kauikeaouli issued The Great Mahele, which divided Hawaii's lands among the monarchy, government, and common people. For the first time, the working class could own land. Just two years later, foreigners were also allowed to own land, and 40 years after the Great Mahele was decreed, two-thirds of all government lands belonged to foreigners.

By this time, the introduction of foreign diseases, including syphilis and smallpox, to the Hawaiians who had no immunity was taking a terrible toll. By the end of Kamehameha III's reign, the Hawaiian population dropped to 70,000.

Sugar was fast emerging as the new lifeblood of the Islands' economy, and Kauikeaouli knew he had to find more laborers to work in the plantations. He turned to contract workers from other countries—the Chinese first, in 1852, when 293 laborers began working on the plantations for $3 a month. Then came the Japanese, Portuguese, Filipinos, Koreans, Puerto Ricans, Okinawans, Germans, Russians, and Spaniards. By the turn of the century, Polynesians were no longer the majority of Hawaii's population.

Kauikeaouli died in 1854, and his nephew Alexander Liholiho ascended the throne as Kamehameha IV. He reigned for eight years before dying of an asthmatic attack at 29. His brother, Lot (Kamehameha V), served as king from 1863 to 1872, and upon his death, William Lunalilo was elected his successor. Lot's cousin, the Princess Bernice Pauahi, had been next in line to take the throne but adamantly refused. Lunalilo's reign was short-lived, however—he died after only a year as king.

The Merrie Monarch

David Kalakaua was elected to succeed Lunalilo, and his tenure as Hawaii's king proved to be as colorful as the man himself. Known as the "Merrie Monarch" for his passion for Hawaiian music and dance, Kalakaua began to restore traditional Hawaiian culture. He commissioned construction of Iolani Palace, an extravagant masterpiece. With a fondness for the good life, he took a trip around the world, hosted gala balls, and bet on local horse races.

Kalakaua was the first reigning king to visit Washington to meet with the president, Ulysses S. Grant, and Congress. The *New York Herald* reported, "[Kalakaua] is no common king, but one to whom we can give our allegiance with a clean conscience for we believe him to be a good man who has the happiness of his nation at heart." Kalakaua returned home with a desirable reciprocity treaty giving Hawaii "favored nation" status and eliminating tariffs on sugar. While recognizing the benefits of a strong relationship with America, Kalakaua fought to maintain Hawaii's independence. The stronger the sugar industry grew, however, the more power shifted from the king to influential American businessmen. In 1887, an armed insurrection by this foreign political group forced Kalakaua to accept a new constitution that severely diminished his authority. The king's remaining years weren't happy ones, as he was relegated to a figurehead role in government. His health failing, he sought treatment in California in 1891. He died that year in San Francisco's Palace Hotel.

End of the Monarchy

Kalakaua's successor, his sister Liliuokalani, was determined to restore the Hawaiian monarchy to power. But the queen was severely outmatched.

In January 1893, pro-annexation forces struck. John B. Stevens, the United States Minister in Hawaii, ordered American Marines from the visiting USS *Boston* to occupy Honolulu. It was a daring move that was not authorized by Washington, but it worked: The next day, a new government led by Sanford B. Dole was in place. Liliuokalani was forced to abdicate her throne.

President Grover Cleveland was dismayed by the action, calling it "an act of war against a peaceful nation." His attempts at reinstating Liliuokalani as Hawaii's ruler, however, were resisted by Congress. In 1894, the new government, the Republic of Hawaii, named Dole as its first president.

In January 1895, a group of royalists led by Robert Wilcox attempted a coup. The battle lasted for two weeks, with skirmishes erupting at Diamond Head Crater and in Manoa Valley, Punchbowl, and other sites on Oahu. Ultimately, the revolt failed, and the government arrested the royalists and the queen, charging them with treason. She was imprisoned at Iolani Palace—her own home—for nearly a year.

In 1898, members of the republic got what they had wanted all along: Hawaii was annexed to the United States. Two years later, it became a United States territory.

World War II and Statehood

The next four decades brought the birth of Hawaii's tourist industry, as well as the sweet days of pineapple and sugar, backbone of the islands' economic system. Then came December 7, 1941, when Japanese war planes bombed Pearl Harbor. The bombs sunk the USS *Arizona* and sent 1,200 sailors aboard the 608-foot battleship to a watery grave. The air raid on Hawaii brought America to war with the battle cry: "Remember Pearl Harbor!"

Islands residents, devastated by the attack, enlisted and did what they could at home to support the American effort. In Waikiki, hotels were closed to visitors, then reopened to accommodate servicemen. The famed "Pink Palace," the Royal Hawaiian Hotel, was turned into an R&R center for military officers on leave. Barbed wire was strung all along the beach.

In the years following the war, Hawaii pursued statehood and finally won it on August 21, 1959. The *Honolulu Advertiser* reported, "A phone call from Governor Quinn in Washington today is expected to set off the biggest wingding in Island history to celebrate Statehood Day . . . the 52 air raid sirens on Oahu will start screaming out the news . . . . Every church bell in town will begin pealing. Every ship in harbor will blow her whistle. Most folks will do a little shouting on their own, and, of course, there's nothing to stop you from hula-ing in the streets if you want to." And they did. President Dwight D. Eisenhower made it official, signing the proclamation welcoming Hawaii as the 50th state in the union.

Not all Hawaiians favored statehood, but they were too few to stand in the way of history, and a once-proud Polynesian nation became an American state.

Hawaii's Diverse Population

One of the outstanding features of Hawaii is the diversity of its people. In the 50th state, no ethnic group comprises a majority of the state's population. The breakdown is as follows:

Caucasian	23.3%	Korean	1.4%
Japanese	20%	Hawaiian	0.8%
Filipino	10.4%	Samoan	0.5%
Chinese	4.6%	Puerto Rican	0.4%
Black	1.8%	Mixed race	37% *(about half are part-Hawaiian)*

Each ethnic group has made its mark on Hawaiian culture, contributing its foods, arts, music, and customs to Hawaii's melting pot community. Many cultural groups hold annual festivals in Honolulu to celebrate their heritage—a great chance to sample the food, music, dance, national dress, and pride of the culture at hand. Several cultures share a passionate affinity for fireworks, which are more abundant in Hawaii than anywhere else in the country. Fireworks are big for western New Year, Chinese New Year, Japanese New Year, Fourth of July, and, for good measure, every Friday night at the Hilton Hawaiian Village in Waikiki.

The Chinese were the Islands' first immigrants. Nearly 300 workers from southeastern China came to the Islands in 1852 after signing five-year contracts to work the sugar plantations for food, clothing, shelter, and a salary of $3 per month. Most of the Chinese lived near Honolulu Harbor on Oahu and Lahaina on Maui. It was in Honolulu where Dr. Sun Yat-sen, regarded as the father of modern China, founded the Hsing Chung Hui, a revolutionary group instrumental in China's movement against foreign powers. The Chinese influence on the local community is visible today in the distinctively Hawaiian-style Chinese New Year celebrations, Chinese cuisine and arts, Chinese heritage of many prominent citizens, and a little Chinese blood in many local residents.

The first Japanese immigrants arrived in 1868 to work on the plantations. Although the conditions were often miserable, more Japanese made their way to what they referred to as Tenjiku, or "Heavenly Place." By the beginning of the twentieth century, more than 60,000 Japanese laborers and their families lived in Hawaii. Like all immigrants, Japanese faced racial prejudices, but far more so after Japan's attack on Pearl Harbor. Many Japanese-Americans were taken away to internment camps on the mainland, and many more lost their family businesses, even though not a single case of Japanese-American treason or sabotage was ever documented. But they rebounded strongly in Hawaii after the war, gained prominence in politics and education, and integrated Japanese customs and design into everyday life. Today, Japanese-Americans are a major presence in Hawaii, and most residents embrace at least some degree of Japanese custom, including removing shoes before entering a home. Sushi, sashimi, mochi, and miso soup are part of the Hawaiian table.

In 1903, the first Koreans arrived to work on the plantations. Ambitious and hardworking, Koreans today have the highest education and income level per capita of any ethnic group on the islands. Korean cuisine is extremely popular among Hawaiian residents, and you'll find Korean restaurants in every town. Try beef kal-bi (marinated beef) with rice and spicy kimchee (pickled vegetables).

A group of 15 Filipino laborers began working on Islands plantations in 1906; by midcentury, that number had swelled to 125,000. Every summer, the Filipina Fiesta festivals, held throughout the state, celebrate the colorful traditions and customs of the Filipino culture. Dishes such as chicken adobo and lumpia are favorites on any local menu.

Samoans are among the newer ethnic groups in Hawaii, arriving from American Samoa shortly after the end of World War I. Most settled in the Mormon community in Laie on Oahu. Their many contributions to the Islands include the celebrated fire-knife dance that highlights most Polynesian luau. Local Samoans have also made their mark in the world of football: In the 1990s, Jesse Sapolu (San Francisco 49ers), Mark Tuinei (Dallas Cowboys), and Maa Tanuvasa (Denver Broncos) all played significant roles in helping their teams win Super Bowl championships.

In multicultural Hawaii, intermarriage is the norm rather than the exception, and a dizzying number of ethnic groups coexist at both the top and bottom of the economic scale. This tends to even things out. The ability to get along, born of necessity in plantation villages and perfected in the modern mix, may be Hawaii's most valuable contribution, far more lasting than a suntan and an aloha shirt.

In order to get along, plantation people from around the world had to communicate, so they developed Hawaiian pidgin—a true creole language according to many scholars, one that borrows words and grammar from several languages. Pidgin endures today, despite efforts of many inside and outside the education system to stamp it out, at least in school. Unofficially, it is lovingly cultivated as a kind of jive talk among kids, families, friends, and lovers. You'll see graffiti in pidgin. It's also still useful, since myriad ethnic immigrants continue to arrive. (See page 155 for a quick lesson in pidgin basics.)

Most people are proud of their diversity, but ethnic prejudices and stereotypes still occur. Caucasians can be the targets of slurs and jokes, along with everybody else. The word *haole* (foreigner) is widely used to refer to Caucasians, usually in a descriptive way. When using words to describe islanders, beware of a linguistic minefield. Don't call us "Hawaiians" unless you mean Hawaiians, not just residents of the islands. Don't call anyone a "native" unless you're wearing your pith helmet, although "native Hawaiian" is still acceptable to distinguish the cultural group. "Local" is a somewhat more loaded word in Hawaii than elsewhere, applying to the multicultural people with broader antecedents who were born here. It's more neutral when it means the opposite of "just visiting." *Kamina* (child of the land, as described earlier) and *malahini* (newcomer) refer to length of stay rather than race or culture. Now you see why the most popular pidgin phrase is *da kine* (as in "the kind"), a handy catch-all to refer to anything you can't or don't want to name specifically.

Local Customs and Protocol

- When going to the *lua* (rest room) make sure you know the difference between *kane* (man) and *wahine* (woman), since many rest rooms are only identified in Hawaiian.
- Close your middle three fingers of either hand while keeping your thumb and pinkie finger fully extended. Shake your hand a few times in the air. That's the *shaka* sign, a hand gesture expressing acknowledgment, goodwill, or appreciation. It's like *mahalo* (thank you).
- Every Friday is aloha Friday, when residents wear aloha shirts and *muumuu* in celebration of Islands culture and lifestyle. Aloha wear is so in these days that it is worn any day. The first aloha shirt was sold in the mid-1930s in Honolulu. Boys during the time had been wearing similar shirts made from Japanese prints, and the idea caught on. The origin of the first muumuu traces to missionary days when the missionary wives sewed "Mother Hubbard" nightgowns to clothe the half-dressed Hawaiian women.
- If you get lucky and are invited to a *kamina* home, remember that most follow the custom of removing shoes before entering the house. The forest of shoes in front of the door is your reminder.
- Local people of all kinds profess a deep reverence for the *aina* (land), although all that litter along Hawaii's roads can't be from visitors alone. This is a beautiful place that deserves respect. Please don't trash it.

Part Two

Planning Your Visit to Hawaii

Best Time to Go

It's hard to think of a bad time to go to Hawaii, but some times are better than others for you to visit, depending less on the weather than on your own plans. Seasonal changes are subtle, and the tourism industry is largely a year-round operation.

Hawaii has winter, of a sort, when the daily highs lurk down around 80°, sometimes even lower. It's the season of higher hotel and condo rates, when the weather where you live is more likely to be awful and more snowbirds flock to the tropics to escape. It's also the time to see migrating humpback whales, big surf, major golf events, squalls rolling across the horizon, and (perhaps) snow at nearly 14,000 feet atop Mauna Kea and occasionally down at 10,000 feet atop Haleakala. It's the rainier, slightly cooler, often less breezy time between late November and late March when bright amaryllis lilies spring up wild by the roadsides, the hills are particularly green, and at dusk you might need a windbreaker. Room rates peak from mid-December through March. In our first year on Oahu, we were anxious to see what winter would bring. One late afternoon everyone got cold, rummaged around for a sweatshirt, and checked the thermometer: 74°. Everything's relative.

The land of perpetual good weather has a summer too. It starts in June, the time of ripe mangoes, calmer seas on north shores, bigger surf on south shores, hurricanes and tropical storms marching west across the Pacific, somewhat warmer and drier weather, and an explosion of flowers (not that there weren't plenty in winter too). The Southern Cross and Perseid meteor showers appear in the skies in late summer. Summer is a busy time in Hawaii since school is out and families head for fun in the sun.

Spring in Hawaii has the added advantage, like autumn, of lower rates and lesser crowds. If you're budget-conscious, time your trip between September and the December holidays or from mid-March to mid-June (excluding Easter), when hotel room rates dip. To see the world's finest hula dancers, come the week after Easter for the annual Merrie Monarch Festival, to Hilo if you are lucky enough to get tickets. Elsewhere, local television carries the colorful contest live.

If you just want to kick back under the tropical sun, watch the ads and the Net and catch the next plane that suits your purse and schedule. The weather's not much of a deterrent any time of year.

Gathering Information Before You Leave

Know where you're going before you get there: Get a map. The best Hawaiian Islands maps are created by cartographer James A. Bier and published by the University of Hawaii Press. Each topographic map includes island highways, roads, and trails as well as large-scale inset maps of population centers. The maps include points of natural, cultural, and historic interest; parks and beaches; sea channels; peaks and ridges (with altitudes); and Hawaiian words spelled with all their accent marks. These maps are $3.95; printed on heavy paper, they fold and fit easily into a carry-on bag or backpack.

If your bookstore doesn't carry these maps, order them directly from Marketing Department, University of Hawaii Press, 2840 Kolowalu Street, Honolulu, HI 96822. Specify the island map you want. You can also request a free catalog of books about Hawaii and the Pacific. Call the University of Hawaii Press at (808) 956-8255 or visit www.uhpress.edu.

If you plan to camp at national parks and other popular spots, you may have to compete long before you arrive for reservations for rustic cabins and tent grounds. (See "Camping in the Wilds," page 284.)

Surf the Internet

Hawaiian Spoken Here, Again For centuries, Hawaiians were master chanters, orators, songwriters, and storytellers. In the 1800s, when missionaries put the sounds into letters and words and taught Hawaiians to read them, the literacy rate in Hawaii was higher than in any other part of the world. The overthrow of the Hawaiian monarchy in 1893 brought a ban on the Hawaiian language in public schools. Over the next century, the language was nearly extinguished.

Now mellifluous Hawaiian is making a comeback, with attention to proper pronunciation, spelling, and marking of its words. It is being resurrected in language courses, special language immersion schools designed to teach young children in Hawaiian, on street signs, in the media, and on the Internet. *Oiwi: A Native Hawaiian Journal,* a contemporary online anthology, features the work of Hawaiian writers and artists. The website (www.hawaii.edu/oiwi) presents stories in both Hawaiian and English. Surf over to www.olelo.hawaii.edu to find the University of Hawaii Hilo's Kualono page, which contains links to

Hawaiian-language dictionaries, books, computer fonts, and a radio program, "Alana I kai Hikini," that broadcasts in Hawaiian online.

Chinatown, Honolulu-Style It's easy to solve the mysteries of Chinatown by visiting its home page at www.chinatownhi.com. Tour the historic 17-block district, visit open markets, pick up Alan Lau's herbal remedy for the common cold at Tak Wah Tong in the Chinese Cultural Center, and even read about the adventures of Charlie Chan.

Visit Maui The Maui Visitors Bureau home page (www.visitmaui.com) makes you want to go there now. It offers lots of solid information and useful links, including seven remote cameras with scenes of the island (one focuses on Hookipa windsurfers). Check out the surf report and daily temperatures, order a free vacation planner, book a B&B, and tour resorts.

Mighty Mo, WW II Dreadnought The battleship USS *Missouri,* upon whose deck Japan surrendered in Tokyo Bay to end World War II, is now anchored in Pearl Harbor next to the USS *Arizona* Memorial and also in cyberspace at www.ussmissouri.com (where you can take a virtual tour).

"Mighty Mo" was saved from mothballs and towed across the Pacific to Hawaii to commemorate peace. The relics are bookends to World War II—the attack on the *Arizona* during the surprise air raid on Pearl Harbor launched the American entry in the war; the surrender aboard the *Missouri* came 3 years, 9 months, and 25 days later.

Surf Molokai For such an atavistic island, Molokai has a big Internet presence: at least 54 home pages, from Molokai Ranch (www.molokairanch.com) to Monkey Pod Records (www.monkeypod.com), which promotes local musicians. One notable site details the somber history of the Kalaupapa Peninsula, where victims of leprosy were once banished. Now it's a national historic park reached by way of the Island's most famous attraction, the Molokai Mule Ride (www.muleride.com).

Visitors and Convention Bureaus

In the early 1900s, several hoteliers in Hawaii formed a tourist information bureau to attract those who had previously only dreamed of visiting the islands. Their earliest marketer went to San Francisco to foster those dreams and drew crowds with a stereo opticon lecture. The boosters later hired Mark Twain to extol the virtues of a Hawaiian vacation, mailed out enticing photos and postcards, and sent Hawaiian entertainers on the road to deliver aloha in person, a practice that continues today as the next best thing to being here. Today, the Hawaii Visitors and Convention Bureau spends millions of dollars globally to promote Hawaii as a top travel destination. Part of that job is to disperse information on islands, activities, accommodations, restaurants, and a calendar of festivals, cultural celebrations, sports events, and activities.

HAWAII'S VISITORS BUREAUS

Hawaii Visitors and Convention Bureau
2270 Kalakaua Avenue, 8th Floor
Suite 801
Honolulu, HI 96815
(808) 923-1811 or (800) GO-HAWAII
www.gohawaii.com

Request a free copy of *The Islands of Aloha,* the bureau's vacation planner.

Oahu Visitors Bureau
733 Bishop Street, Suite 1872
Honolulu, HI 96813
(808) 524-0722 or (877) 525-OAHU
www.visit-oahu.com, or link from www.gohawaii.com

Big Island Visitors Bureau (Hilo)
250 Keawe Street
Hilo, HI 96720-2823
(808) 961-5797 or (800) 648-2441
www.bigisland.org, or link from www.gohawaii.com

Big Island Visitors Bureau (Kona)
250 Waikoloa Beach, Suite B15
Waikoloa, HI 96738
(808) 886-1655 or (800) 648-2441
www.bigisland.org, or link from www.gohawaii.com

Maui Visitors Bureau
1727 Wili Pa Loop
Wailuku, HI 96793-1250
(808) 244-3530 or (800) 525-MAUI
www.visitmaui.com, or link from www.gohawaii.com

Call or write for a free copy of *Maui, The Magic Isles,* a travel planner featuring the Maui County destinations of Maui, Molokai, and Lanai.

Kauai Visitors Bureau
4334 Rice Street, Suite 101
Lihue, HI 96766-1801
(808) 245-3971 or (800) 262-1400
www.kauaivisitorsbureau.org, or link from www.gohawaii.com

Molokai Visitors Association
P.O. Box 960, 10 Kamehameha Hwy
Kaunakakai, HI 96748
(808) 553-3876 or (800) 800-6367
www.molokai-hawaii.com, or link from www.gohawaii.com

Destination Lanai
P.O. Box 700, 730 Lanai Avenue, Suite 102
Lanai City, HI 96763
(808) 565-7600 or (800) 947-4774
www.visitlanai.net, or link from www.gohawaii.com

International Contacts

United Kingdom
Hawaii Visitors and Convention Bureau
P.O. Box 208, Sunbury on Thames
Middlesex TW165RJ, England
44 (208) 941-4009
xcd16@dial.pipex.com

Australia
Hawaii Visitors and Convention Bureau
c/o The Sales Team
Suite 2, Level 234 Burton Street
Milsons Point, NSW 206, Australia
61 (2) 9955-2619
rlane@thesalesteam.com.au

New Zealand
Hawaii Visitors and Convention Bureau
c/o Walshes World
18 Shortland Street, Level 6
Auckland, New Zealand
64 (9) 379-3708
darragh@walwor.co.nz

Canada
Comprehensive Travel Industry Services
1260 Hornby Street, Suite 104
Vancouver, BC V6Z1W2, Canada
(604) 669-6691
compre@intergate.bc.ca

Recommended Magazines

Hawaii is featured often in magazines like *Condé Nast Traveler, National Geographic Traveler,* and *Travel and Leisure,* as well as airline in-flight magazines. Only a few feature magazines devote full coverage to the islands:

- *Hawaii Magazine,* (800) 365-4421
- *Honolulu Magazine,* (808) 524-7400
- *Maui No Ka Oi Magazine,* (808) 871-7765 or www.mauinokaoi.net

Packing Wisely

Everyone brings too many of the wrong kinds of clothes to Hawaii. Californians, most of your wardrobe is too warm. East Coasters, think summer year-round. For packing purposes, it's always summer here.

If you're planning to ride horses, bring covered footwear and jeans and hang onto your hat. If you're going camping, you can bring or rent gear, according to your preference and the percentage of your trip you plan to camp. A night or two? Rent. A month? You might prefer your own stuff.

What men need: shorts, T-shirts and informal tops, favorite Hawaiian shirts, swim trunks, lightweight slacks, a light jacket or sweatshirt for going Upcountry, and sandals, sports shoes, or loafers. Don't even bring a tie. If you're hanging out at stuffy fancy restaurants, bring a jacket or be forced to wear one of theirs for dinner.

What women need: sundresses, swimsuits, cover-ups, shorts, tops, light sweater or jacket, sandals, and maybe a muumuu for the luau (it's best to buy one here). Lose the heels, and other banes of your wardrobe. Unless you're staying in butlered digs, minimize the high-maintenance wear of wrinkling silk and linen. Many hotel rooms come equipped with an iron and a board, if you insist. Tennis shoes and athletic socks turn into hot, sweaty foot sponges in the tropics and are heavy to pack. Bring them if you plan to hike the Upcountry. Local folks prefer to wear sandals or cool, airy rubber flip-flops, known as "slippers."

Unless you're heading for Mauna Kea's 13,976-foot summit, you won't need any apparel heavier than a sweatshirt.

If you pack wisely for Hawaii's climate, you can put all your lightweight clothes in one case and bring an empty one for all you'll probably buy.

Getting to Hawaii

The flight to Honolulu International Airport is about 5 hours from the West Coast, 8 from Dallas, 9 from Atlanta, and 11 from New York. Most major U.S. and several international airlines serve Hawaii, along with charters from other countries. Hawaii-based Aloha Air Lines and Hawaiian Airlines connect the islands with various West Coast cities and Las Vegas (Hawaii residents' favorite destination).

Honolulu International Airport (HNL) on Oahu is one of the nation's busiest airports, with 1,400 daily operations, many of them to and from Asian and Pacific destinations, and more than 24 million passenger arrivals and departures annually.

Although the majority of flights from the U.S. mainland to Hawaii touch down in Honolulu, some land on the Neighbor Islands. United has daily flights from Los Angeles and San Francisco to Keahole-Kona on the Big Island and Kahului on Maui, and from Los Angeles to Lihue on Kauai. Delta and American fly to Kahului from Los Angeles. Hawaiian Airlines offers flights between Seattle and Kahului.

Call the toll-free numbers below for updated information.

AIRLINES

Air Canada	(800) 776-3000	Continental Airlines	(800) 523-3273
Air New Zealand	(800) 262-1234	Delta Airlines	(800) 221-1212
Aloha Airlines	(800) 367-5350	Hawaiian Airlines	(800) 367-5320
American Airlines	(800) 433-7300	Northwest Airlines	(800) 225-2525
British Airways	(800) 247-9297	United Airlines	(800) 241-6522

Traveler Advisory

Honolulu's International Airport is currently undergoing a $200 million improvement project to add an efficient security checkpoint, new people movers, and an information center. While renovations are under way, travelers may experience disruption, confusion, and construction noise. The project is scheduled to be completed by 2006.

Airports on the Neighbor Islands include Keahole Airport in Kona and Hilo Airport in Hilo on the Big Island; Kahului Airport, Hana Airport, and Kapalua Airport on Maui; Lihue Airport on Kauai; Molokai Airport on Molokai; and Lanai Airport on Lanai. You can't fly directly to all of these (see above), but all are used by island-hoppers (see "Interisland Flights," page 64).

Booking your vacation through a travel agent may save you time and money, as the agent can plow through myriad fares and rates to find you the best airfares, lodgings, and car rentals and take advantage of specials offered only to agents.

If you make the arrangements on your own, here are some tips and advisories on finding a good deal on airfares.

- To get the lowest possible fare, be flexible in your travel plans. The best deals are usually limited to travel on certain days of the week or hours of the day. Ask the reservations agent how you might save money by leaving a day earlier or later or by taking a different flight. Check carefully into fare restrictions and penalties if you change plans after purchase. Check various travel-related sites on the Internet. You can hold your telephone reservation on most airlines for a day or so before you commit to the ticket. In some cases you may have to call to cancel. In others you have to call to activate the reservation.

- If your travel itinerary falls into a busy flight period, book early. Flights during holidays may sell out months ahead of time.
- Many discount fares are nonrefundable and, in most cases, nontransferable (one exception is the coupon books offered at times by Hawaii's airlines). If you want to change your discounted booking, you will pay more if that fare is not available on the new flight.

How to Avoid Jet Lag

Start to combat jet lag before you depart. Jet lag, known in scientific terms as circadian desynchronization, occurs after flying across several time zones. It is not a state of mind; it is a condition with physical and mental ramifications, lasting anywhere from a few hours to a few days. You feel sleepy, disoriented, and a little out of sync.

Several books offer remedies to ease jet lag. One of the best is *Jet Smart* by Diana Fairechild, a veteran flight attendant whose 21 years of experience took her often to and from the Hawaiian Islands.

Here are some practical tips.

- Avoid coffee for a day or two before and after your flight and drink water, rather than coffee, sodas, or alcohol on the plane. Alcohol can sharply intensify jet lag. Drink lots of water to prevent dehydration—an eight-ounce glass for each hour of flight, according to our doctor.
- During flight, remove your shoes to improve circulation. Flex your feet, ankles, and legs often. If possible, stroll through the cabin and stand for a while.
- Adjust your watch to Hawaii Standard Time (see the following section) as soon as you board the plane. This mentally prepares you as you adjust to Hawaiian time. Think of the time it is where you're going, not where you've been. On the ground, get acclimated to local time as soon as possible. Stay up until bedtime in the islands if you can, even though you may feel extremely tired.
- Take a long soak in a bathtub or a warm pool or ocean. Not only will it replenish moisture lost during your flight; it also relaxes your nervous system. Don't attempt too much activity on the day or night of your arrival.
- Try to spend some time outside while it's sunny, as bright daylight helps the body adjust its internal clock. Take care, however, to avoid overexposure; a sunburn is a miserable way to start your vacation.

What Time Is It in Hawaii?

On standard time, when it's noon in San Francisco, it's 10 a.m. in Honolulu. Hawaii is two hours behind the West Coast and five hours behind the East Coast. Hawaii doesn't change to daylight saving time, so when it's daylight saving time on the mainland, April to October, then Hawaii is three hours behind the West Coast and six hours behind the East Coast.

With an average of 12 hours of sunshine daily, year-round, Hawaii doesn't need to save daylight. Hawaii's longest day, June 21, is 13 hours and 26 minutes long. Its shortest day, December 21, is 10 hours and 50 minutes. Hawaii's time zone is known as Hawaii Standard Time or HST.

What Not to Bring

- Forget drugs, especially marijuana. Dogs are on duty at baggage claim and check-in areas to sniff out illegal drugs, and the carriers are taken into custody on the spot.
- The Department of Agriculture bans most animals and plants from Hawaii. Dogs and cats bound for Hawaii end up in month-long, expensive quarantine. Snakes end up in the zoo or dead.
- Importation of unchecked flora and fauna can have a negative impact on Hawaii's fragile ecosystem. The Department of Agriculture restricts shipping of fruit, plants, and other items from Hawaii to the mainland to prevent the spread of fruit flies and other insects.

For inquiries, call the USDA Plant Quarantine Branch at (808) 586-0844 or the Animal Quarantine Branch at (808) 483-7171.

HAWAII'S AIRLINES

Aloha Airlines
Toll-free: (800) 367-5250
Oahu: (808) 484-1111
Maui: (808) 244-9071
Big Island: (808) 935-5771
Kauai: (808) 245-3691
www.alohaairlines.com

Hawaiian Airlines
Toll-free: (800) 367-5320
Oahu: (808) 838-1555
Maui: (808) 871-6132
Big Island: (808) 326-5615
Kauai: (808) 245-1813
Molokai: (808) 553-3644
Lanai: (808) 565-7281
www.hawaiianair.com

Island Air
Toll-free: (800) 652-6541
Molokai: (808) 567-6115
Lanai: (808) 565-6744
www.islandair.com

Molokai Air Shuttle
Oahu: (808) 567-6847

Pacific Wings
Toll-free: (800) 575-4546
Maui: (808) 873-0877
www.pacificwings.com

Paragon Air
Toll-free: (800) 428-1231
Maui: (808) 244-3356
www.maui.net/wing/index.htm

Interisland Flights

The islands are linked by frequent, efficient jet service all day from sunrise to late evening by two Honolulu-based airlines, Aloha Airlines and Hawaiian Airlines, which share the interisland terminal at Honolulu Airport. Other airports served are Kona and Hilo on the Big Island; Kahului, Maui; Lihue, Kauai; and Molokai and Lanai.

Island Air flies smaller twin-engine planes to smaller airports, including Kapalua and Hana on Maui and Kalaupapa on Molokai. Hawaiian has smaller craft as well.

Both Aloha and Hawaiian have small first-class seating areas, but the flights only take 25 to 45 minutes, so the chief advantage, besides bigger seats and personal service, is that you can board and deplane first. Check with the airlines for their carry-on baggage rules. Boogie boards, surfboards, full coolers, skateboards, and strollers are not allowed in the cabin.

When booking your interisland flight, ask about special promotions that may lower fares, such as coupon books. Or check Aloha's and Hawaiian's websites.

Car Rentals

Once you've landed on an island, renting a car provides the greatest flexibility and mobility in Hawaii. On Oahu, a car can also put you right in the middle of the biggest traffic jam in the Pacific.

It's fun to cruise Hawaii in a shiny convertible, but it's no fun to sit sweating in gridlock while heading back from the beach. So watch your timing to avoid rush-hour traffic, which runs early in the islands, a legacy from plantation days. Plan to leave later than 8:30 a.m. on weekday mornings and avoid the highways in the late afternoons, roughly 4–6 p.m. Listen to the radio for updates on particular problems. Summer driving is much easier because school's out.

Carry as little as possible in your rental car that might appeal to thieves. We usually leave ours empty and open; there's no sense in paying for a broken window. Whatever you do, don't leave your valuables in the car while you dash out to view the Windward Side from the Pali Lookout or the Blow Hole on the South Shore. These are favorite rip-off sites.

You can get by without a car on Oahu, which has a highly praised municipal bus system, one of the best in the United States, as well as taxis, private transit, and (often) free shuttle vans. But it is a lot easier to explore the Windward Coast and North Shore and enjoy museums, botanical gardens, adventure areas, and vacant beaches with a car. One solution is to rent a car just for a day or two.

On Maui, Hawaii, Kauai, and Molokai, where beaches and natural attractions are all over the islands, renting a car is a must unless you plan to hole up at your resort and commute on foot or by resort shuttle between your room and the beach or golf course.

On Lanai, a resort shuttle will take you to most sites. But one of Lanai's more popular activities is exploring the back roads in a rented four-wheel-drive vehicle, allowing you to discover backcountry and island history on your own.

Car rentals are available on all islands, and the cost is around $30 a day for an economy car. Rental car rates are lower in Hawaii than in the rest of the nation as a whole. Shop for rates by telephone or the Internet, if making your own arrangements. Most major car rental firms offer special rates frequently and include car rentals in money-saving travel packages with airfare and accommodations. Check with your travel agent or call the car rental agencies for details before you go.

When making interisland flight reservations, ask the airlines for any special deals on rental cars. They often partner with car agencies in promotional fly/drive packages. You may get a break of 5–15% for association memberships, credit cards, frequent-flier clubs, and coupons. Agency Internet sites (listed later) can offer up to 20% off regular rates.

All the major car rental agencies are located at or near the airports, and many have reservations desks at various resorts or stores. On Maui, besides Kahului Airport and the hotels, many car rental agencies operate at the Kaanapali Transportation Center (30-1 Halawai Drive), a five-minute ride from the Kapalua Airport in West Maui (linked by free shuttle service).

As with car rentals in any destination, you can rent a car after you arrive, presuming one is available. Courtesy phones and free shuttles in airport terminals connect you to their nearby offices. However, you'd do better to reserve a car with the national agency before you go, usually a week or more ahead for the best rate. Rental rates are based on the number of cars available, so they constantly fluctuate. Because you don't have to pay up front, you can always recheck rates.

Expect to see that rental fee jump by the time you do pay. Car rentals on all islands are subject to a $3 per day state road tax and a nominal vehicle license tax (24–45 cents a day on Oahu and 17–45 cents a day on the Neighbor Islands). In addition, transactions that take place at an airport are subject to an airport concession fee of 10% of the rental fee per day on Oahu and 7.5% on the Neighbor Islands.

Optional insurance rates vary by car rental agency. It's a hard-sell situation when you're picking up the car, but remember that your own car insurance and often your major credit card provide insurance coverage when you're driving rental cars. Check before you leave.

Gas prices will look astronomical in Hawaii compared to almost any mainland location, particular the East Coast. The islands are small enough, though, that you seldom rack up major mileage.

About island driving: Hawaiian Islands (even Oahu) don't have a lot of roads. Most roads are two lanes, and speed limits are lower than in other states. Oahu has three short "interstate" highways that absorb much of the traffic. Mainland drivers will find the entry and exit setups otherworldly. But island driving manners are such that people will let you in if you landed in the wrong lane. Just take it slow, signal, look, smile a lot, and wave your thanks. Leave your aggressive driving habits at home. Hawaii is a no-fault insurance state.

People talk of driving "around the island," but you can't really do that around the entire coastline of any of the islands. You can circle most but not all of the Big Island without backtracking, at least until the volcano rewrites the Chain of Craters Road map again.

CAR RENTAL AGENCIES

Alamo Rent-A-Car

Toll-free: (800) 327-9633
www.goalamo.com

Oahu
Honolulu Int'l. Airport: (808) 833-4585
Ilikai Hotel Nikko Waikiki: (808) 947-6112

Maui
Kahului Airport: (808) 871-6235
Kaanapali Transportation Center: (808) 661-7181

Big Island
Keahole-Kona Int'l. Airport: (808) 329-8896
Hilo Int'l. Airport: (808) 961-3343

Kauai
Lihue Airport: (808) 246-0646

Avis Rent-A-Car

Toll-free: (800) 331-1212
www.avis.com

Oahu
Honolulu Int'l. Airport: (808) 834-5536
Outrigger East Hotel: (808) 971-3700

Maui
Kahului Airport: (808) 871-7575
Kaanapali: (808) 661-4588
Kihei: (808) 874-4077
Renaissance Wailea Beach Resort: (808) 879-7601

Big Island
Keahole-Kona Int'l. Airport: (808) 327-3000
Hilo Int'l. Airport: (808) 935-1290

Kauai
Lihue Airport: (808) 245-3512
Princeville Airport: (808) 826-9773
Hyatt Poipu Kauai: (808) 742-1627

Budget Rent-A-Car

Toll-free: (800) 777-0169
www.budgetrentacar.com

Oahu
Honolulu Int'l. Airport: (808) 836-1700
Hyatt Regency Waikiki: (808) 921-5808

Maui
Kahului Airport: (808) 871-8811
Kaanapali: (808) 661-8721

Big Island
Keahole-Kona Int'l. Airport: (808) 329-8511
Hilo Int'l. Airport: (808) 935-6878

Kauai
Lihue Airport: (808) 245-1901

Molokai
Molokai Airport: (808) 567-6877

Dollar Rent-A-Car

Toll-free: (800) 367-7006
www.dollarcar.com

Oahu
Honolulu Int'l. Airport: (808) 831-2330
Hawaiian Regent Hotel: (808) 952-4264
Hale Koa Hotel: (808) 952-4264
Waikiki: (808) 952-4242

Maui
Kahului Airport: (808) 877-2731
Hana: (808) 248-8237
Kaanapali Transportation Center: (808) 667-2651

Big Island
Keahole-Kona Int'l. Airport: (808) 329-2744
Hilo Int'l. Airport: (808) 961-6059

Kauai
Lihue Airport: (808) 245-3651

Molokai
Molokai Airport: (808) 567-6156

Lanai
Lanai Airport: (808) 565-7227

Harper Car and Truck Rentals

Toll-free: (800) 852-9993
www.harpershawaii.com

Big Island
Kauai: (808) 969-1478
Kona Int'l. Airport: (808) 969-1478
Hilo: (808) 969-1478

CAR RENTAL AGENCIES *(continued)*

Hertz Rent-A-Car
Toll-free: (800) 654-3011
www.hertz.com

Oahu
Honolulu Int'l. Airport: (808) 831-3500
Hyatt Regency Waikiki: (808) 971-3535

Maui
Kahului Airport: (808) 877-5167
Westin Maui: (808) 667-5381
Maui Marriott: (808) 667-1966

Big Island
Keahole-Kona Int'l. Airport: (808) 329-3566
Hilo Int'l. Airport: (808) 935-2896

Kauai
Lihue Airport: (808) 245-3356
Kauai Marriott Resort: (808) 246-0027

National Car Rental
Toll-free: (800) CAR-RENT
www.nationalcar.com

Oahu
Honolulu Int'l. Airport: (808) 831-3800
Kahala Mandarin Oriental: (808) 733-2309

Maui
Kahului Airport: (808) 871-8851
Kaanapali Transportation Center: (808) 667-9737

Big Island
Keahole-Kona Int'l. Airport: (808) 329-1674
Hilo Int'l. Airport: (808) 935-0891

Kauai
Lihue Airport: (808) 245-5636

So Many Islands, So Little Time

Because Hawaii has six major islands to see, two weeks still wouldn't be enough time to do and see it all. This is one factor that keeps visitors coming back again and again, to see their favorite sites and sample new ones.

We suggest that newcomers spend the first two or three days in Waikiki or elsewhere on Oahu, slowing down enough to enjoy the pace of the islands. But that's just a suggestion. We have a friend who comes to Waikiki at least once a year and never goes anywhere else. Other visitors shun Waikiki completely.

All the ingredients of a grand tropical holiday can be found on Oahu—sunny days, warm water, great beaches, stunning scenery, a wide range of accommodations (mostly hotels, from budget to upscale), museums and cultural events, stimulating atmosphere, cuisines of many cultures, excellent shopping, and great nightlife. If you want quiet, check into a B&B or vacation rental elsewhere on Oahu, or pick another island and spend the rest of your time there.

Maui is the next most popular choice after Oahu, followed by the Big Island of Hawaii, Kauai, Molokai, and Lanai.

To Hop or Not to Hop?

First-time visitors may have ambitious visions of island-hopping from one end of the Hawaiian chain to the other. One word of advice: don't. You may think you can see all the Hawaiian Islands in a single week. You can *see* most of them in 20 minutes at 20,000 feet on the way in. But clearly, that's not enough. This is too fine a place to gloss over, so count on spending some time on one or two islands and coming back someday. If you do move between islands, the flights are only half an hour or so, but the airport transfers are time-consuming and plane tickets are expensive. Below are some factors to consider before island-hopping.

- A round-trip interisland airline ticket is about $190 per person. Most island flights are to and from Honolulu. You may have to go to Honolulu just to connect to flights to other islands. *Tip:* Ask the airlines about discount coupons, where you can buy multiple flights' worth in advance for a cheaper rate.
- Expect to spend several hours commuting from place to place—to pack, check out, get to the airport, return your rental car if you have one or go early in a transit vehicle, check in for your flight and go through security, wait for the plane, board the plane, fly, deplane, get your luggage, get another rental car, drive to another hotel, register your room, and unpack.
- You can save money by staying longer on each island. Some major hotels offer a free night's stay when you book four to six consecutive nights.

We think a two-island stay is plenty for one vacation. But keeping the costs (in money and time) in mind, you can easily add a day trip for a specific activity, such as a round of golf or a look at the volcano.

The quickest way to see the islands is a scenic flight on a twin-engine airplane. Several companies offer low-altitude, half-day, and full-day scenic air tours over the main islands. One is Pacific Wings: Call (808) 873-0877 or e-mail info@pacificwings.com.

Cruise lines offer voyages with port calls in Honolulu and on Maui, Kauai, and the Big Island of Hawaii. (See "Cruising Hawaii," page 175.)

Hawaii from Above

Volcanic islands defy road-building, and Hawaii is filled with remote wilderness which remains rugged and untrammeled. How to see it? Perhaps a helicopter flight that reveals glorious scenery and then lands for a brief visit in a beautiful spot.

- **Alexair** lifts off from busy Kahului Airport, Maui, to travel back in time along the Hana Coast to old Hawaii, flight-seeing the Hana rain forest and waterfalls before landing at a black-sand beach for a snack and respite. Then it's up, up and over Haleakala crater, descending back to earth amid the rays of sunset. With a four-passenger minimum, you might prefer to buy out the flight.
- **Sunshine Helicopters** will show you the sights, then land at Kaupo Gap on the wilderness side of Maui, relating the history of this ancient place and its *heiau*, a national monument. Or Sunshine will fly you to an ocean cliff on the remote Mendes Ranch, where the West Maui Mountains seem to fall like rumpled sheets of green velvet into the sea. If the agenda includes a proposal or other special toast, they'll pack iced flutes for your champagne.
- Check out the bright Honolulu city lights at night with a flight on **Makani Kai Helicopters** that takes off from Waikiki and includes a snack of sushi. If you

want, the flight can be yours alone. Makani Kai will also charter a daytime flight with a landing in a secret scenic spot in the hinterlands.

- Float over all in Hawaii's only seaplane tour. **Island Seaplane Service, Inc.** takes off from Keehi Lagoon near the Honolulu Airport for flight-seeing over Waikiki, the cityscape and scenic rural Windward Coast before returning over Pearl Harbor—an airy way to get a sense of this complex city/country island.
- Haven't been the same since *The English Patient*? Grab your silk scarf and head for the Kona Coast of the Big Island, where **Classic Aviation Biplanes** will take two of you up together for a tour of the area in an open-cockpit reproduction of a 1935 biplane.

Suggestions for Special Travelers

Singles

Best Island to Visit Oahu

Other Recommended Islands Maui, Big Island

Things to See and Do On Oahu, join the crowd on Waikiki Beach, catch a ride on an outrigger canoe, and have a beer and listen to live Hawaiian music at Duke's Canoeclub at the Outrigger Waikiki. Check out the *pau hana* (after-work) action at Aloha Tower Market Place, shop at Ala Moana Center. Discover local food—an instant picnic of inexpensive plate lunches or *mana pua* (stuffed Chinese steamed buns, otherwise known as *char siu bao*) from downtown lunch wagons. Explore Hawaii's history at the Bishop Museum or Hawaii Maritime Center. Climb Diamond Head Crater. Boogie in Waikiki nightclubs and indulge yourself the next day with a spa extravaganza at Hilton Hawaiian Village, the newest addition to the spa lineup.

On the Big Island, don't miss the volcano, and have a drink at the Volcano House, which overlooks a steaming live crater. Explore Waimea and Parker Ranch country. Share a fishing charter at Honokohau Harbor. Join a pickup golf group and play a round on a course you'll never forget.

If you choose Maui, ride with a bike tour down Haleakala or take a snorkel tour to Molokini or Lanai. Drive to Makawao and Paia and poke around the villages. Head further upcountry to Kula and taste Tedeschi wines at the winery at Ulupalakua Ranch. The places to party are Lahaina and Kihei.

Comments Oahu has the most things to do and places to see and will keep your itinerary filled. If you're hoping to meet new friends during your trip, Oahu is the island with the most dance clubs and best nightlife.

Couples

Best Island to Visit Kauai

Other Recommended Islands Lanai, Maui, Big Island

Things to See and Do Hang out in Hanalei, a naturally romantic setting you'll never want to leave; swim or body surf in Hanalei Bay; get to know some of the local citizenry at Tahiti Nui or neighboring spots. Go for a waterfall trail ride at Princeville Stables. Kayak down the Hanalei River to the bay and try to catch a wave on the way back. If the moon is full, go down to the beach to see if anyone is dancing hula in the moonlight, and join them. See for yourself what inspired Bob Nelson to write "Hanalei Moon," a well-known song describing a tropical moonrise.

Stay at Princeville, which provides gorgeous views of Hanalei Bay and the surrounding mountains. Pick a new North Shore beach to discover every day, and don't forget your snorkel gear. Take the boat ride up Wailua River to Fern Grotto. Walk up the Kalalau Trail the first two miles to the unforgettable Hanakapiai Valley, and return. Go south to Poipu Beach for at least a day, ride horses by the beach near Hyatt Regency Kauai (a honeymoon hotel), and don't miss dinner at Tidepools.

On Lanai, divide your time between the seaside Manele Bay, where you can wake up to spinner dolphins in the waters, and Lodge at Koele, where evenings in the romantic environs are chilly enough for cuddling. Hike or drive out to the hinterlands, or ride a horse through the woods. Witness a green flash together, that magical prism phenomenon that sometimes happens when the sun meets the sea at the horizon. On Maui, get up early to see the spectacular sunrise over Haleakala, then relax with massages for two in tents by the sea at Four Seasons Wailea and take a stroll on Wailea Beach. Then go to Hana to discover Maui's true cultural heart. On the Big Island, stay at Four Seasons Hualalai, but make time to drive over one afternoon and watch the lava flowing at sunset or hike the trails in Hawaii Volcanoes National Park.

Comments Kauai is *the* choice for Hawaii's most romantic island, offering a combination of postcard scenery and uncrowded settings.

Hikers

Best Island to Visit Kauai

Other Recommended Islands Big Island, Maui

Things to See and Do Hike Kalalau Trail on Na Pali Coast (a difficult trek)—this is a round-trip with a stopover of at least a night in the valley.

Or hike one way and arrange to catch a ride up the awesome coast on a Zodiac raft the other way.

Take the boardwalk on a sunny day through Alakai Swamp up at Kokee State Park. Explore the trails of 4,000-acre Kokee Wilderness Forest, or see how the goats hang onto the precipitous ledges in Waimea Canyon. Hike the ridgeline above Kapaa to the Sleeping Giant.

On the Big Island, hike across simmering Kilauea Iki Crater and cool off by walking through Thurston Lava Tube. Hike the summit of Mauna Loa, but only if you're in shape for the high-altitude walking and are very experienced. On Maui: Hike the falls and forest at Kipahulu, beyond Hana.

Comments Hikes on Kauai are the most dramatic because of the natural landscape, from thin ledges along the seacoast to miles of trails in a cloud forest.

Bikers

Best Island to Visit Big Island

Other Recommended Islands Maui, Kauai

Things to See and Do Maui invented the sport of coasting down a volcano, but you can bike down a lower slope of Mauna Kea as well. Touring the Big Island in three or four days on a bike remains a challenge. This is the only island where roads allow you to circumnavigate without retracing your route. Pedal around Hawaii, proceeding counterclockwise from Kona on the Upper Highway. Head south past the backyard coffee plantations, down across the lava wasteland of Kau Desert, then up through Hawaii Volcanoes National Park to the village of Volcano. From there, you can coast downhill nearly 40 miles to Hilo. If you still have steam, pedal on to Waimea along the lush, green Hamakua Coast and cut across the wide, open lava fields of the Kohala Coast before reaching your starting point at Kona.

On Maui, you will always remember the thrill of coasting down 10,000-foot-high Haleakala 38 miles to the sea on a specially built bicycle on a guided cruise, the only sensible way to descend the mountain on two wheels. Mountain bikers should head for Kauai, Molokai, and Oahu.

Comments Bike enthusiasts test their stamina against the Big Island, the best all-around cycling island in the Pacific, because of its many challenging features: terrain that varies from lava desert to rain forest, steep inclines, and radically different temperatures from one area to the next.

Nature Lovers

Best Island to Visit Kauai

Other Recommended Islands Big Island, Maui

Things to See and Do Snoop on boobies and goonies (Pacific seabirds) at Kilauea Point. See 600 species of palm trees and other tropicals at 300-acre National Tropical Botanical Garden. Wander in Waimea Canyon, the "grand canyon" of the Pacific. Spend the day in Limahuli Gardens, a botanical refuge for endangered native plants.

On the Big Island, explore Hawaii Volcanoes National Park, hike Chain of Craters Road to witness red-hot lava flow into the Pacific, cool your heels in lush Onomea Botanical Garden near Hilo. Watch for rarely seen native Hawaiian forest birds. On Maui, look for rare silversword plants and the endangered Hawaiian nene geese at Haleakala National Park.

Comments Hawaii's natural beauty is legendary; its wildlife (monk seals, nene geese, and native Hawaiian birds) may be endangered, but you will not be disappointed by the great outdoors, especially on Kauai, a botanical wonder all its own. The diverse nature of the Big Island with its lava rock coasts and highland rain forests is like nowhere else on Earth. Maui's fabled town of Hana is a prime destination for people who like to feel overwhelmed by the majesty of nature. If you're lucky you may win admission to the Puu Kukui nature preserve in the West Maui Mountains.

Beachcombers

Best Island to Visit Oahu

Other Recommended Islands Kauai, Maui

Things to See and Do With 50 miles of sandy shore, Oahu has the most beaches in Hawaii. People-watch at Waikiki Beaches. Windsurf Kailua Beach. Snorkel Hanauma Beach. Search for shells at Malaekahana Beach in spring and summer and at Pupukea Beach on the North Shore. Watch big winter waves at Waimea Beach. Explore empty Yokohama Beach. Hide out at Lanikai Beach. Have a picnic at Kualoa or Kaaawa or Hauula Beach Parks. Take a break from shopping at Ala Moana Beach, just across the street from the mall.

On Kauai, go body boarding at Poipu Beach, summer swimming at Hanalei Beach, snorkeling at Kee Beach and Tunnels Beach, or camping on 17-mile Polihale Beach, longest in Hawaii. Maui's best beaches include golden Wailea Beach and scenic Kapalua Beach, as well as remote black-sand Hamoa Beach in Hana.

Comments The best, safest, and most dramatic beaches of Hawaii are found on Oahu, where the abundance of choice suits almost everyone's style. Some beautiful beaches are found on Kauai and Maui, but Oahu is the beach capital of Hawaii.

Families

Best Island to Visit Oahu

Other Recommended Island Maui

Things to See and Do If you enjoy paid attractions, take the family to Sea Life Park, the Honolulu Zoo, Waikiki Aquarium, and Bishop Museum. See beneath the sea without getting wet with Atlantis Submarines. Enjoy some sun, surf, and sand at Waikiki Beach and Ala Moana Beach Park, two of the most swimmable beaches in Hawaii.

Let the kids learn about the islands and make new friends at supervised children's programs at the many hotels (the one at the Hilton Hawaiian Village is outstanding), while Mom and Dad get to enjoy some time on their own. Or, see if Hawaii Nature Center programs coincide with your visit so the kids can discover what's in the forested hills behind Honolulu. A visit to the USS *Arizona* Memorial and the USS *Missouri* will help your family understand what World War II was about.

On Maui, don't miss the Maui Ocean Center, Hawaii Nature Center, and Whalers Village Museum, all family-oriented attractions designed to educate as well as entertain.

Comments Maui's Kaanapali Beach is the most popular family destination after Waikiki, but Oahu offers more family-oriented attractions and activities than all other islands combined.

Active Seniors

Best Island to Visit Oahu

Other Recommended Islands Big Island, Kauai, Maui

Things to See and Do Visit Oahu's historical attractions, including the Bishop Museum, Iolani Palace, Aloha Tower, Hawaii Maritime Center, and the Mission Houses Museum. Hike up Diamond Head crater. Ride the open-air Waikiki Trolley. See Don Ho, still performing "Tiny Bubbles" and still a consummate entertainer who gives young singers and dancers a start. Learn Hawaiian crafts, like stringing lei, dancing a hula, or playing the ukulele. Swim in the comfort of the warm and salty Pacific, even if you're not comfortable in a bikini. Many couples renew their wedding vows on the beach at sunset.

Seniors will find excellent tours by Elder Hostel that probe the Islands' interesting and educational facets at affordable rates. Contact Elder Hostel at www.elderhostel.org or (877) 426-8056.

On the Big Island, a functioning volcano is a prime draw for the awestruck of all ages. Don't miss this sight. If you love gardens, you will be intrigued by Honolulu's five municipal botanical gardens, including Foster Gardens downtown with its array of towering exotic trees. On Maui, the Maui Tropical Plantation gives a glimpse of sample fields of island crops, plus a great produce market. The only federally chartered research gardens, the National Tropical Botanical Garden, are definitely worth a visit on Kauai, at Lawai near Poipu Beach and Limahuli on the North Shore. On Maui, the 125-acre Kahanu garden of Pacific Island plants includes the state's largest archaeological site, Piilanihale Heiau. Plenty of privately operated botanical gardens are sprinkled throughout the islands.

Comments Anyone with gray in their hair is viewed with respect in Hawaii. You are considered a wise *kupuna* (elder), and doors are not closed to you. The healthy seniors who live in the islands surf, dance, play golf, swim daily, and do anything else they want. So can you. Many visitor attractions and some stores offer discounts for seniors.

Visitors with Disabilities

Best Island to Visit Oahu

Other Recommended Islands Maui, Big Island

Things to See and Do Take in a concert, film, or dance performance at the historic Hawaii Theatre in Honolulu, which provides special seating areas for the disabled.

Visit Iolani Palace, Sea Life Park, Polynesian Cultural Center, Honolulu Zoo, Hawaii's Plantation Village, and Mission Houses Museum on Oahu; Haleakala National Park, Maui Tropical Plantation, and Maui Ocean Center on Maui; Hawaii Volcanoes National Park, Panaewa Rainforest Zoo, Nani Mau Gardens, and Puuhonua O Honaunau on the Big Island; and the Kauai Museum, Fern Grotto, and Kilauea Point National Wildlife Refuge on Kauai—all of which accommodate disabled visitors.

On Oahu, curb-to-curb transportation service is provided by the City and County of Honolulu via the Handi-Van (call (808) 456-5555 for reservations, (808) 454-5050 for customer service). A sister company to TheBus, the Handi-Van transports some 2,000 passengers daily, operating from 5:30 a.m. to 11 p.m. Fares are $2 each way. City buses have elevator lifts for wheelchairs.

Comments *The Aloha Guide to Accessibility,* published by the State Disability and Communication Access Board, provides detailed information on accessibility features of island hotels, attractions, beaches, parks, theaters, shopping centers, transportation services, and medical and support services. Special transportation services are limited on the Neighbor Islands, but this free brochure covers that information as well. Write to the commission at 919 Ala Moana Boulevard, Room 101, Honolulu, HI 96814, or call (808) 586-8121; you can also visit them online at www.hawaii.gov/health/dcab.

Hawaii Centers for Independent Living has a website that provides useful information for the disabled at www.assistguide.com.

Art Aficionados

Best Island to Visit Oahu

Other Recommended Islands Maui, Big Island

Things to See and Do The Honolulu Academy of Arts and the Contemporary Museum, both in Honolulu, are the state's two best art museums. Maui has a thriving arts community, with galleries in Lahaina, the Maui Arts and Cultural Center, and Hui Noeau Visual Arts Center. When you visit the Big Island, don't miss Volcano Art Center, housed in a historic building by the entrance of Hawaii Volcanoes National Park. Doris Duke's Shangri-La, a $100 million oceanfront mansion east of Honolulu, is now open to tours by small groups. A work of art itself, the house on five acres is filled with America's most extensive collection of Islamic art, collected globally over six decades by one of the world's richest women, the late tobacco heiress.

Comments You can see and buy some local handicrafts by Hawaiian artisans at various crafts fairs held throughout the islands almost year-round, especially in November and December.

Hawaiian Culture Seekers

Best Island to Visit Oahu

Other Recommended Islands Maui, Kauai, Big Island

Things to See and Do Hawaiian culture is on display year-round but is especially in the spotlight during the Aloha Festivals, the biggest annual cultural celebration in the state. Colorful parades and pageantry, demonstrations of arts and crafts, and performances of music and dance are among the features. Aloha Festivals take place September through October, and each island has its own nine- or ten-day program. The Aloha Festivals committee sets festival dates years in advance; call (808) 545-1771 for a schedule.

The multiplicity of ethnic groups that contributed to the Hawaii of today have heritage events throughout the year, on all islands but particularly on Oahu. The University of Hawaii often features its own cultural series of indoor and outdoor performances—showcasing contemporary Hawaiian music and dance, Chinese opera, and Japanese noh theater, among others. The Bishop Museum, repository of more than 20 million Pacific Islands cultural artifacts, is the best place to explore Hawaii's rich past. The museum's new Waikiki annex at Hilton Hawaii Village offers a preview. A must-visit spot for art lovers is the new $3.5 million Luce Pavilion at Honolulu Academy of Arts, where guests can see ink sketches by John Webber (who sailed with Captain Cook), Maui landscapes by Georgia O'Keeffe, and fiery canvases of Volcano School artists Jules Tavernier, Charles Furneaux, and D. Howard Hitchcock, who painted Madame Pele's volcanoes.

Comments Look for *hula halau* (school) fundraisers, slack key festivals, talk story events, and quilt shows; all offer a glimpse into the Hawaiian culture. You can also turn on the radio to an all-Hawaiian music station and get in the groove.

Gourmands

Best Island to Visit Oahu

Other Recommended Islands Maui, Big Island, Lanai

Things to See and Do Superb fine-dining establishments can be found on every island. The best concentration of great restaurants, however, is in Honolulu on Oahu. Many of Hawaii's top regional cuisine chefs—including Roy Yamaguchi, Alan Wong, Sam Choy, Phillipe Padovani, and George Mavrothalassitis—have restaurants on Oahu. In addition, Honolulu enjoys fine fusion versions of Japanese, Chinese, Thai, Vietnamese, Swiss, Korean, French, Italian, American, and other favorite cuisines.

The enthusiasm for creative chefs spreads to other islands too, fed by the notable kitchens of luxury hotels that gather talented staffs and excellent fresh local foods.

Comments Be sure to treat your palate to a dinner of Hawaii regional cuisine at Roy's, Alan Wong's, or Chef Mavro's, featuring fresh ingredients produced or grown in the islands. Not surprisingly, these restaurants are run by Hawaii's trio of James Beard Award–winning chefs—Roy Yamaguchi, Alan Wong, and George Mavrothalassitis.

History Buffs

Best Island to Visit Oahu

Other Recommended Islands Big Island, Maui, Lanai

Things to See and Do The greatest concentration of historical attractions is in a two-block area of downtown Honolulu, where the Iolani

Palace, the State Capitol, the Governor's Mansion, Mission Houses Museum, Kawaiahao Church, and the Hawaii State Library are within easy walking distance of each other. Waikiki has a long history, but you have to look very closely to find it, or go with a knowing guide—such as the intrepid *kupuna* (elders) of the Native Hawaiian Hospitality Association who lead free "talk story" walks that reveal the resort through native eyes. The Waikiki History Trail's surfboard-shaped trail markers lead a path through Waikiki's high-rise hotels. The two three-hour history walks encompass 23 historic sites that help explain how the area's original mosquito-choked fishponds, gold sand beach, and famous surf attracted ancient Hawaiian kings and queens in old Hawaii and evolved into a world-class beach resort. Tours are held twice daily except Sunday. The Queen's Tour starts at the information kiosk at Kalakaua and Kapahulu Avenues. The Kalia Tour starts on the second floor of Kalia Tower, Hilton Hawaiian Village. Contact the Native Hawaii Hospitality Association, (808) 841-6442, or www.waikikihistorictrail.com.

But in the tropics, where history vanishes quickly in the hot sun, salt air, and bug-laden environment, heritage sites are not always buildings. Rock platforms are all that's left of most *heiau,* or temple ruins, all over the islands. They are still sacred to many, however.

On the Big Island, clues to the somewhat mysterious past are everywhere if you care enough to search. The Kona-Kohala Coast resorts feature fields of ancient carvings and examples of early Hawaiian aquaculture techniques still in use today in fishponds. Out in the nearby lava, the C-shaped rock shelters built by early soldiers are still visible. In many places, including Waikoloa, you can make out the pathway through the lava made by bare human feet of royal messengers centuries ago. Ambitious plans are proceeding to raise some $30 million to unearth a particularly prized cultural treasure—Mokuula, the royal palace of King Kamehameha III—which lies buried beneath a county ball park but will one day be revealed by the restoration project.

The Piilanihale Heiau dig near Hana will appeal to archaeology buffs.

On Lanai, you can drive and hike up to petroglyph rocks on a hill over Palawai Basin, or pilot a vehicle over rough roads to Kaunolu, King Kamehameha I's summer fishing camp.

Comments Spend a day in the Bishop Museum, the best place to get a handle on Hawaii's history; it's in Kalihi at the Likelike Highway exit from H-1, a 20-minute drive from Waikiki.

Sports Fans

Best Island to Visit Maui

Other Recommended Islands Oahu, Big Island

Things to See and Do Football fans have something to cheer about on Oahu, scene of the NFL Pro Bowl every year and a Christmas Day doubleheader featuring two NCAA postseason bowl games. In December, the University of Hawaii hosts the prestigious Rainbow Classic, an eight-team collegiate basketball tournament. Other major Oahu sporting events include the Honolulu Marathon and Sony Open Golf Tournament, the Triple Crown of Surfing, the Kenwood Cup, the Trans-Pacific and other sailing races, annual lifeguard competitions, and a full schedule of outrigger canoe paddling contests.

Maui hosts the annual Hula Bowl (the college football all-star game), Maui Invitational (a nationally televised college basketball tournament), Kapalua's annual Mercedes Open (a golf tournament), windsurfing competitions, and the Maui Marathon.

The Big Island is home to the world's most famous triathlon, the annual Ironman Triathlon—which includes a 2.4-mile ocean swim, a rugged 112-mile bike ride, and a hot 26.2-mile run—and its one-up cousin, the Ultraman, which raises the bar to a 6.2-mile swim, 251.4-mile bike ride, and 52.3-mile run.

Comments Sports teams may not be able to swing a regular Hawaii playing schedule, but pros and collegiate all-star champions alike wouldn't miss their reward trip to Hawaii to end a stellar season with the Hula Bowl and Pro Bowl games. For Hula Bowl tickets, see www.idatasports.com/hulabowl/tickets.html or call (808) 871-4141. For Pro Bowl tickets and special packages, you can find lots of options on the Internet, including official National Football League offerings at www.nfl.com/tickets. Or contact the Aloha Stadium box office, (808) 486-9300.

Business Travelers

The Aloha State is the only place in the world where you can conduct business live with major financial centers in New York, Japan, China, and Hawaii all on the same day. The Islands are a good place to do business, especially when transactions involve linking U.S. concerns with Asia and the Pacific Rim. There's a convention facility in Honolulu as well.

The Islands are a great place for corporate groups to meet for fun and profit, rewarding top performers, top customers, and top prospects. The extensive choice of luxury resorts, outdoor sports and team-building events, al fresco parties, and other only-in-Hawaii features draw groups back year after year. Hawaii's remote setting, high degree of international air service, controlled access, and relatively safe and secure environment make it a favored choice for diplomats, scientists, political and economic leaders, and other international group gatherings. Hotels increasingly cater to business needs with office and fitness centers, in-room dataports, competent staff, and a hip-to-technology attitude. The fiber-optic system linking the islands to the West Coast is one of the best in the world, thanks to the presence of an Air Force supercomputer on Maui.

The Hawaii Convention Center

Located on the edge of Waikiki, the Hawaii Convention Center combines high-tech wizardry with a Hawaiian sense of place. Designed by Hawaii's own architectural firm of Wimberly Allison Tong and Goo, the airy four-story center opened to wide acclaim in the summer of 1998. The center has 100,000 square feet of meeting space, 200,000 square feet of exhibit space, a 36,000-square-foot ballroom, a 35,000-square-foot registration/lobby area, and an 800-space parking garage.

The ground floor houses the lobby area and exhibit hall, which is large enough to accommodate a reception for some 28,000 attendees. The second floor is reserved for parking; the third level features meeting rooms; and the fourth (top) floor houses the grand ballroom and rooftop garden terrace. A two-story glass wall enhances the lobby, where palms and tropical plants grow inside and out.

High-tech features include fiber-optic cables providing speedy, state-of-the-art communication; a press room with global links to any nation in the world; a built-in, six-station simultaneous translation room, allowing translators to view the speakers through a video monitor; a meeting room capable of hosting 400 computers working simultaneously; and an auditorium with built-in projection room and concert-quality sound system.

More than 30,000 hotel rooms and condominium units are within a one-mile radius of the center. The nearest, Ala Moana Hotel, is directly across the street. Plenty of restaurants are an easy walk away. Nearby Ala Moana Center offers dozens of restaurants and a food court. The older area around the convention center is still something of a mother lode of girlie bars, strip clubs, Korean bars, and just plain bars, despite some efforts to banish them.

For more information, call the Hawaii Visitors and Convention Bureau at (808) 923-1811 or surf over to www.visit.hawaii.org.

Tying the Knot

Hawaii is one of America's favorite places to get married and go on a honeymoon. Lovers can get married on the beach (check out www.beachweddingshawaii.com for information), by waterfalls, underwater amid tropical fish, in churches old and new, on sailboats, on offshore islets, and up in the air while skydiving.

In old Hawaii marriage ceremonies were reserved only for high-ranking citizens, *alii.* The first Christian marriage took place in 1822, two years after the arrival of American missionaries. For a time, it was illegal for non-Christian marriages to be held in the islands. Today, more than 10,000 out-of-state couples are wed here every year. For a time, legal same-sex marriages drew couples to Hawaii. However, voters amended the state constitution in 1998 to classify marriage as pertaining to male-female relationships, and the state's supreme court upheld that in 1999. The long tradition in Polynesian culture of tolerance to the "third sex," or *mahu,* still means gay-oriented travel companies and commitment ceremonies are commonly accepted on the islands.

How to Get Married

To get married in Hawaii, you'll need a valid marriage license. You can obtain one at the State Department of Health, Marriage License Office, 1250 Punchbowl Street, Honolulu, HI 96813, (808) 586-4545. The office is open from Monday to Friday, 8 a.m. to 4 p.m. (closed on holidays). Both bride and groom must be present when the license is issued. The license is valid statewide for 30 days. The fee is $60 in cash.

On the Neighbor Islands, you can get a license from a marriage license agent (ask your hotel concierge or wedding coordinator to direct you to the nearest agent).

Both the bride and the groom must be at least 18 years of age to be married without parental consent. If either partner has been married before, he or she is required to provide the date, county, and state (or country) in which the divorce was finalized for each previous marriage. The names of each person's parents and place of birth must also be provided.

A free "Getting Married" pamphlet is available from Hawaii's Marriage License Office. Write to the address above or call them at (808) 586-4544. In addition, the Hawaii Visitors and Convention Bureau has a list of wedding planners on all islands at www.gohawaii.com.

Eight Romantic Places to Get Married in Hawaii

Oahu

Kawaiahao Church, downtown Honolulu. This landmark coral block church, designed by New England missionary Hiram Bingham and dedicated in 1842, is one of Oahu's most popular and stately venues for couples seeking a formal church wedding. Contact Kawaiahao Church at (808) 522-1333, 957 Punchbowl Street.

Waikiki Beach

Just walk out on the gold sand at sunset, adorned in flowers with your intended mate and your officiator, and say "I do" before lots of witnesses, who may join you in singing the "Hawaiian Wedding Song" as you dance across the *lanai* (patio) at the House Without a Key. Don't forget to hire a photographer to capture the moment. Meanwhile, the Moët Chandon is chilling up in your Halekulani honeymoon suite. Contact Halekulani at (808) 923-2311 or www.halekulani.com.

Maui

Waterfall Garden, Westin Maui Prince. At the waterfall pool in the open-air atrium where golden Japanese carp splash in black lava tide pools, many couples get married every weekend on Maui. It's been a popular wedding site in South Maui since the hotel opened more than a decade ago. Contact Westin Maui Prince Hotel at Makena, (808) 874-1111.

Big Island of Hawaii

On a beach framed by palms and serene ancient fishponds, one of Hawaii's most romantic locations appeals to many wedding couples as the place to recite vows. Contact Waikoloa Beach Marriott, (808) 886-6789.

Kauai

On Kauai's North Shore, the Princeville Hotel overlooks the Bali Hai image you dream about: Hanalei Bay with jagged, waterfall-creased volcanic peaks in the background. *Akamai* (with-it) couples wait for the golden hour around sunset when the blue sky is streaked with red and gold rays. Contact Princeville Resort, (808) 826-9644.

Molokai

High noon or sundown, a wedding way out west on the Molokai Ranch is the way to go if the two of you love horses. You can choose a hilltop, a cliffside, or a beach for the main event before moseying back to the 22-room Sheraton Molokai for a reception overlooking the pastures and the sea. Call (808) 552-2791.

Lanai

At the Conservatory on Lanai, exchange vows amid thousands of exotic orchids in the misty, glass-paned conservatory, then dance your wedding waltz in The Lodge at Koele, a very romantic setting for weddings and honeymoons. Contact The Lodge at Koele, (808) 565-7300.

On the Ocean Blue

If your shipboard romance becomes the love of your life and you can't wait to tie the knot, have a wedding at sea. There's a little chapel aboard the *Norwegian Star* where you can get hitched and be on your tropical honeymoon in the time it takes to say, "I do." The 24-seat Starlight Chapel on Deck 12 hosts weddings, vow renewals, and special celebrations.

Part Three

Accommodations

Where to Stay

On the six main islands in Hawaii, you can choose the hotel that's just right for you from among more than 70,000 rooms, suites, condo units, apartments, and bungalows—from budget surfer digs to first-rate palaces, with prices to match. Most are on or near a beach.

You'll find the familiar names of international hotel management firms—such as Westin, Hilton, Hyatt, Marriott, Prince, Sheraton, Ritz-Carlton, Four Seasons, Mandarin, and Fairmont—as well as locally owned Aston and Outrigger hotels and family-operated independents.

With the same spectacular settings as their hotel neighbors, other lodging choices—condos, executive vacation homes, and increasingly, time-share units—offer families and small groups private, relaxed alternatives to multiple hotel rooms and high-cost hotel meals. Particularly on Maui and Kauai, portions of large luxury hotels have been remade into "vacation club" time-share operations run by well-known firms like Westin, Embassy Suites, and Marriott. Rooms were combined into larger efficiency units which devoted returnee guests can buy for a week or more each year. Kauai is home to 37% of Hawaii's growing time-share market.

Time-shares helped Kauai properties recover from lingering physical and legal ravages of Hurricane Iniki more than a decade ago. The latest example is the Marriott Waiohai Beach Club at Poipu Beach, converted from a favorite old hotel in a prime setting on the South Shore. With their upfront financing, time-shares help cushion the island economy from the swings of financial fortune. Time-share owners have already paid for their lodging and tend to be less likely to cancel for wars, SARS, and other travel threats. What difference does it make to visitors' experience whether their rooms are hotel or time-share? Probably not much. The larger units may be a better rate deal, minus some hotel services and plus a hard-sell pitch if guests agree to "free" time-share marketing offers.

Views range from outstanding to average. In Waikiki, "ocean" views can be a peek of blue between high-rises or a mesmerizing wall-to-wall panorama of the beach framed by Diamond Head or the city and sunset behind the Waianae Mountains in the distance. If you're off the beach, you may have a mountain view that reveals the haunting beauty of the Koolau Range, the twinkling neighborhood lights halfway up the slopes at night, and the busy paddlers on the Ala Wai Canal below. Garden rooms usually deliver tropical garden views. Most rooms have sliding glass doors that open to outdoor lanai for balmy breezes.

The chief factors we used to rate hotels are: location (on the beach or nearby), views, service, amenities, character, price, and value. When you choose your lodging—whether through a travel agent or on your own—ask about nearby construction, recent room renovations, balcony or patio availability, any extras included in the rate (such as daily paper, movies, dataports, minibar, beach gear, Continental breakfast), and whether airport transfers are available. Most deluxe and luxury rooms come equipped with in-room coffeemakers, hair dryers, irons and boards, and safes; some also come with CD players. Ask about them too.

If you're going upscale, inquire about the club floors. Rooms on these floors have keyed elevator access, a lounge with free drinks, Continental breakfast, light buffet lunch, evening *pupu* (appetizers), and sinful fresh-baked cookies, plus a concierge to call their own. The rates are higher, of course, but the buffets take care of breakfast, lunch, snacks, and cocktails, which are costly at resorts.

You don't have to go first class to get great service. Usually service at Hawaii hotels is friendly and courteous at every level from maids to general managers. Staff members exhibit lots of "aloha spirit" and wear flowers and tropical uniforms. They may not all speak your language, but they will find someone who does, and they are anxious to please you.

Waikiki gets the lion's share of visitors from around the world, but it's not for everyone. When you seek a quieter getaway on Oahu, plan to stay at J W Marriott Ihilani Resort and Spa on the Leeward side, Kahala Mandarin Oriental Hotel in suburban Kahala southeast of Waikiki, Turtle Bay Golf & Country Club on the North Shore, or a B&B or vacation rental on the Windward side.

On Maui, Kaanapali Beach Resort, like Waikiki, handles the greatest number of people very well, but the quieter resorts of Wailea, Kapalua, and Makena top our recommended list. Our favorite Big Island hotels are on the Kona-Kohala Coast. On Kauai, Poipu, and Princeville Resorts are our favorites. Lanai has two fine hotels and a small lodge; Molokai has an excellent 22-room lodge.

All accommodations are subject to an 11% state tax (7% room tax plus 4% excise tax, charged at 4.17%).

Great Places to Stay

Some of the world's greatest beach resort hotels and resorts are found in Hawaii. They range from traditional favorites, like the century-old Sheraton Moana Surfrider Hotel on Waikiki Beach, to newer stars, like the Four Seasons Hualalai Resort on the Big Island, that seem to define the Hawaiian experience for visitors of different eras. Some, like the Four Seasons Wailea Resort and Kapalua Bay Hotel, are elegant retreats; others are fantasies come true, like Grand Wailea Resort, Hyatt Regency Maui, Hilton Waikoloa Village on the Big Island, and Kauai Marriott. A precious few evoke the memory of old Polynesia, such as Kona Village Resort. Here's our list of favorites by category.

Hopelessly Romantic

Halekulani, Oahu No finer hotel exists in Waikiki for lovers or for anybody who can handle the five-star tab. You can watch the sunset from the House Without a Key as a hula dancer sways gracefully to old songs, or, if you prefer, watch the sunset reflect on Diamond Head from your in-room tub. Then settle into a private booth at La Mer for French champagne and haute cuisine. Phone (800) 367-2343 or visit www.halekulani.com.

Ritz-Carlton Kapalua, Maui Hawaii's only Ritz commands the last outpost of resort life in West Maui. Its caring management and celebrations of Hawaiian culture and art add to this romantic oasis on an old pineapple plantation at the foot of the West Maui Mountains. You can get married in the historic little church on the grounds. Phone (800) 262-8448 or visit www.ritzcarlton.com.

Kona Village Resort, Big Island Sleep under thatch in a private island *hale* at Kona Village, created in the mid-1960s before there was road access. Guests flew or sailed into this retreat. Now you can drive from the airport in a few minutes across the lava field, but the sense of seclusion continues. The ultimate escape, this exclusive beach retreat is a collection of coastal huts in various Pacific Islands styles of architecture. It's ideal for kids and families (September, couples only). When you seek genuine peace and quiet, stay here. When you want privacy, put your coconut by the door. This is one of the few island resorts that's rates include three meals a day. Phone (800) 367-5290 or visit www.konavillage.com.

Hotel Hana-Maui, Maui This inn by the sea offers private Sea Ranch cottages for two with a bubbly hot tub and thick Turkish towels. Explore the neighborhood on foot or horseback—this sleepy area is all part of a large ranch. Phone (800) 321-HANA or visit www.hotelhanamaui.com.

Hyatt Regency Kauai Resort & Spa On one of Kauai's wild beaches, this hotel echoes island architecture of the 1920s to create a romantic setting with gardens, pools, and intimate restaurants often frequented by hand-holding couples, not all of them honeymooners. Phone (800) 55-HYATT or visit www.kauai-hyatt.com.

Island Retreat, Kilauea, Kauai A private lakeside estate for lovers seeking escape, Steve Hunt's Island Retreat has been featured by bridal magazines. With its own 20-acre lake, beach, tropical gardens, boats, kayaks, boat dock, and putting green, the $750-a-night estate is a honeymoon hideaway. Phone (310) 379-7842 or visit www.kauai.honeymoon.com.

Great for Families

Hilton Hawaiian Village Flamingos, peacocks, penguins, a lagoon, 3 pools, and 3,000 rooms on 20 acres on Waikiki Beach: What more could a kid want? A busy children's program full of daily surprises keeps everyone happy. Plenty of grown-up entertainment is available as well, plus restaurants and a whole village full of shops. Kalia Tower opened in 2001, offering Waikiki's newest guest rooms, a spa, and a wellness center. Contact at (800) 949-4321 or www.hawaiianvillage.hilton.com.

Westin Maui at Kaanapali Beach Resort This open, airy beachfront hotel looks like a Disney fantasy jungle—tropical foliage, waterfalls, and parrots everywhere inside the open atrium and Kaanapali outside. Kids love the aquatic playground with a 128-foot slide, the easy-breezy feeling, and year-round summer camp–like fun. It's a big hit with big kids too. Phone (866) 500-8313 or visit www.westinmaui.com.

Fairmont Kea Lani, Wailea, Maui Like something out of *Arabian Nights,* the luxurious Fairmont Kea Lani hotel delivers more than just fantasy. All the rooms are well-equipped suites with high-tech stereos and kitchens, except for the special villas with private plunge pools. Scenic beach, great restaurants. There's a separate family pool and one for adults only. The south end of Wailea Resort is walking distance on the coastal trail to neighboring shops and restaurants. Phone (800) 659-4100, (866) 540-4457, or visit www.kealani.com.

Great Historic Traditions

Sheraton Moana Surfrider Hotel Enter this century-old hotel, and ghosts of old Waikiki past surround you. That could be Queen Liliuokalani's carriage at the porte cochere. You can almost hear Webley Edwards broadcasting "Hawaii Calls" from the Banyan Court. The graceful grande dame of the beach has been revived with a painstaking historic renovation. Now entering its second century, Waikiki's first hotel is on the National Register of Historic Places. If only the walls could talk. Phone (866) 325-3535 or visit www.moana-surfrider.com.

Royal Hawaiian Hotel They call it the "pink palace," from pink carpet to pink beach umbrellas. A hot flamingo pink landmark by the blue sea, the Royal Hawaiian is the bright spot in Waikiki's bland concrete jungle. It was nspired by a Rudolph Valentino movie and built by Matson Steamship Lines in 1927 during Waikiki's golden age. Phone (866) 500-8313 or visit www.royal-hawaiian.com.

Pioneer Inn, Lahaina, Maui Overlooking Lahaina Harbor, the Pioneer Inn turned 100 years old in 2001, holding on after a $5 million face-lift. This once-rowdy sailors' haunt is now a charming relic fit for all who "collect" old hotels and prefer tradition over trend. Phone (800) 457-5457 or visit www.pioneerinn-maui.com.

Mauna Kea Beach Hotel, Big Island Nelson Rockefeller started a trend in 1965 when he arranged for this classic, gracious hotel and its world-famous golf course to stand beside a beautiful beach and invited the captains of industry to come take their rest. Now their grandchildren carry on the tradition. He filled it full of Asian and Pacific art and triggered a renaissance in Hawaiian quilting arts by commissioning handmade quilts for wall hangings. A path was blasted through the lava to reach the hotel. The soaring indoor/outdoor architecture befits the climate. Phone (800) 882-6060 or visit www.maunakeabeachhotel.com.

Waimea Plantation Cottages, Waimea, Kauai This is a resort composed of restored tin-roof sugar shacks situated in a palm grove by the sea. History buffs will be delighted. Cottages are named for families who lived in them. Dating from the 1880s to 1930s, the cottages are updated with modern kitchens and baths and furnished with period wicker and rattan. Some are on the beach. The setting, near the Waimea River in West Kauai, is off the beaten track, but Captain Cook stepped ashore nearby more than 200 years ago and "discovered" Hawaii in the process. Phone (800) 92-ASTON or visit www.astonhotels.com.

Great for High Rollers

The Lodge at Koele, Lanai Live like a grand poobah, if only for a few days, in this highland inn on a nearly private, red-dirt island of abandoned pineapple fields. It's deliciously decadent, outrageously expensive, and captivating. You won't ever want to leave. It begins to feel like a friend's country estate. Phone (800) 321-4666 or visit www.lanai-resorts.com.

Four Seasons Resort Hualalai, Big Island Under dormant Hualalai volcano, this is Hawaii's only new resort that didn't come out a high-rise—instead, it is a series of clusters of handsome private bungalows arranged around pools by the beach, with outdoor shower gardens, tasteful decor, and oceanfront restaurants a step off the sand. From the thatched roofs over its outdoor whirlpool tubs to the natural amphitheater in a lava formation, Four Seasons Hualalai is wonderfully different and expensive, with rates up to $6,000 a night for bungalows by the sea. The resort is surrounded by golf greens, ranks of swanky condos, and private home lots. If you want a second home here, a lot with ocean view sans house goes for $1 million. Phone (888) 340-KONA or visit www.fourseasons.com.

Mauna Lani Beach Hotel and Bungalows, Big Island Fishponds, lava caves, petroglyphs—the physical evidence of early habitation is abundant on this shore. But it's doubtful they lived as well as current guests do, even though this was once a retreat for Hawaiian royalty. The Mauna Lani is the namesake hotel of Mauna Lani Resort, a 3,200-acre Kohala Coast retreat favored by Hollywood royalty who like the $4,900-per-night butlered bungalows by the shore. The Fairmont Orchid, two spectacular golf courses, plush condos, and private homes also share the enclave, which is protected by a lava wasteland. Phone (800) 327-8585 or visit www.maunalani.com.

Hapuna Beach Prince Hotel, Big Island Built by a Tokyo tycoon, the Hapuna Beach Prince is a paean to the ocean view from a cliff beside Hapuna Beach. The beauty is in the materials—burnished wood and slate with minimal interior decor. Critics call it stark, but think of the Hapuna Beach public and private rooms as mere frames for the marine-scene painting beyond. The huge pool awaits those reluctant to take on the golden sands and nearly secret cove below. A $7,000-per-night, three-bedroom villa awaits VIPs. The golf course is a spare intrusion on the natural setting, a links-style natural course with native plants and par-busting views. Phone (800) 882-6060 or visit www.hapunabeachprincehotel.com.

Great Bargains

New Otani Kaimana Beach, Oahu Under Diamond Head, this small hotel with a big attitude has a slightly removed view of Waikiki. Its beachfront location, gentle hospitality, famed Hau Tree Lanai (where Robert Louis Stevenson read poems to Princess Kaiulani), and decent rates make New Otani an old and valued favorite of repeat guests. Choose a corner suite and ask for the corner you want—ocean or Kapiolani Park view with Diamond Head or city/sunset exposure. On a budget, get a regular room (they're small) and enjoy your peaceful perch surrounded by the park instead of the traffic and crowds of central Waikiki. Phone (800) 356-8265 or visit www.kaimana.com.

Waikoloa Beach Marriott, an Outrigger Resort, Big Island In this ritzy neighborhood of high-end beach hotels, the newly remodeled, deluxe Waikoloa Marriott, with the same great location, is the best value on the Kohala Coast. New features include a beach-view restaurant, a spa, and many upgrades. The hotel commands a site by a huge fishpond complex and palm-fringed Anaehoomalu Beach, one of the Big Island's best. Phone (800) 922-5533 or visit www.outrigger.com.

Garden Island Inn, Kauai Kalapaki Beach and Nawiliwili Harbor (where freight ships and cruise ships call) plus shops and restaurants are all across the street from your spacious, $125-per-night suite with kitchen, wet bar, and private lanai, with free tree-ripe papayas daily. Phone (800) 648-0154 or visit www.gardenislandinn.com.

The Mauian on Napili Beach Centered on an ideal golden beach where swimming is good and views even better, the 44 studio condos come with breakfast buffet, kitchen, lanai, comfortable furnishings, and warm Hawaiian atmosphere as only a local family can provide. Check Internet special rates. Phone (800) 367-5034 or go to www.mauian.com.

Malihini Hotel, Oahu This small, no-frills, two-story, 28-unit hotel is a half block from Waikiki Beach, across from Fort DeRussy and costs just $50 a night. That's no typo, just the best deal for a clean, well-lighted place near the beach. Phone (808) 923-9644.

Good for Your Health

Like to stay where you can breathe easy? Outrigger has designated all of its Ohana Reef Lanai hotel near Waikiki Beach as a no-smoking zone. After a renovation with special attention to changing or cleaning fabrics and filters, rugs, and wall coverings, the moderately priced Ohana Reef Lanai is totally smoke-free, from its popular steak house restaurant in the lobby throughout its 110 rooms, some with kitchenettes, on 12 floors above. Phone (808) 923-3881 or e-mail orl@outrigger.com.

Getting a Good Deal on a Room

Now that you've had a preview of some of Hawaii's great places to stay, here's how to get the best deal.

- Book early.
- Go in fall and spring months (September–November, April, May, and early June).
- Educate yourself on what you want and where and when you want it before you talk to a travel agent. They may have suggestions that alter your plan, but they'll surely do a better job for you if you narrow the search for them. More agents are charging customers a fee for their services these days, as well as collecting a percentage of the booking as their commission. In Hawaii, hotel and condo commissions are usually 10%. Ask about your agent's fee policies in advance.
- Ask a travel agent to research package rates and other specials that combine your room with sports, spa, rental car, and other features. They have access to information you won't find as a consumer.
- Call the hotel to see what rate you can negotiate. Ask for the best rate they offer, not the published rack rate. Sometimes rates and fares are cheaper if you book via Internet.
- Pursue discounts for corporate travel, seniors, kids staying free in your room, military personnel, travel clubs, and other special status travel. See what frequent flier mileage you may gain from your hotel stay.

Several factors determine a hotel's room rate: demand, location, season, availability, view, grade of room, proximity to the beach, shopping centers, and entertainment.

Hawaii room rates are highest from late December through late March, when everyone wants to escape winter. Rates rise again in summer, when school's out and families flock to the Islands from the West Coast. The average hotel room rate then is $146–$151. In the spring and fall, average room rates fall to $130–$144.

Hawaii's visitor industry provides a quarter of the gross state product, a quarter of the state's tax revenue, and a third of the jobs. Hawaii's dependency on tourism means competitive rates and good deals for you.

Where the Deals Are

Check travel sections of major newspapers for good room deals and combinations with airfare, hotel or condo rental, and car rental. Surf the Internet to preview islands, beaches, golf courses, hotels, condos, and vacation rentals. Try your luck with Internet brokers, such as priceline.com, hotel discount.com, travelocity.com, and others dedicated to travel bargains.

Other Money-Saving Suggestions

Many hotels offer their own periodic package deals with value-added amenities like a free rental car, food and beverage credits, rounds of golf, spa treatments, extra-special treatment for honeymooners (chocolates and champagne) and for families, and free or cheaper second rooms when you book the first room. Some hotels offer a free extra night if you book a room for a certain number of nights (usually four to seven). Hotels off the beach are cheaper; so are mountain- or garden-view rooms. Ask if kids can stay in your room free.

Travel Packages

Those travel packages featured in the newspaper are the choice of many Hawaii vacationers. The plans, assembled by tour wholesalers for sale to travel agents or directly to the public, offer plenty of flexibility in price and places to stay and often include extras like lei greetings, luau, scuba dives, or golf rounds. Hotels, condos, and B&Bs offer packages too, featuring lodging combined with activities. Package travelers may be part of a large flock on the same schedule, but it's by chance, and their arrangements are independent. Packages differ from traditional group tours, which are conducted en masse and shepherded by guides who take care of all the details and charge accordingly. More than 100 tour wholesalers offer Hawaii travel packages, including these:

- Classic Custom Vacations, (800) 221-3949
- Creative Leisure International, (800) 426-6367
- Globetrotter/MTI Vacations, (800) 635-1333
- Pleasant Holidays, (800) 2-HAWAII

If You Make Your Own Reservation

If you hunt your own bargains, call the hotel directly instead of the chain's toll-free number. The clerk at a central site may not know about special local rates. The quoted, or rack, room rates—the ones printed once a year for brochures to be placed in a rack—are flexible. Virtually no one pays the full rack rate, except perhaps at peak travel times or for last-minute bookings. Don't be shy about inquiring about lower rates, especially during the low season, when your bargaining position is improved. Inquire about any other special deals. Hotels would rather fill rooms at discounted prices than leave them empty. Do your bargaining, however, when you reserve a room, not after your arrival.

Corporate Rates

Many hotels provide corporate rates (up to 20% off regular rack rates). Ask your hotel about them. Generally, you do not need to work for a large company or have a special relationship with a hotel to obtain corporate rates. Some hotels require a written request on company letterhead or some other verification of your employment status, but others will guarantee the rate over the phone.

Travel Clubs

Travel clubs offer discounts of up to half off participating hotels' rack rates, but with restrictions. They generally apply on a space-available basis and are not available in blackout periods (usually during peak travel times). Some may apply only on certain days of the week. Not all hotels offer a true 50% discount. Some base their discount on an exaggerated rack rate. Before joining a discount program, compare the rates offered to members with those available elsewhere.

Most travel clubs or half-price programs charge an annual fee, up to $125 or more. When you join, you receive a membership card and directory of participating hotels, including about 100 in Hawaii. Evaluate your long-term travel plans when considering membership in a travel club, as you may not recoup the membership fee in a single trip. Clubs work best for frequent travelers and travelers with flexible schedules.

The following travel club programs offer lodging in Hawaii:

- Encore, (800) 638-0930; www.preferredtraveller.com
- Entertainment Publications, (800) 285-5525; www.entertainment.com
- International Travel Card, (800) 342-0558
- Quest, (800) 638-9819

Travel Advisory

The following advice applies to each of the money-saving methods of booking a room described above.

- Be wary of deals that seem too good to be true.

- Don't be pressured into accepting a deal on the spot. A good offer today should be a good offer tomorrow. Do not send money by messenger or overnight mail. Question any requests for you to send money immediately. Do not provide your credit card number or bank information over the phone unless you know the company.
- Ask questions. Find out what's covered in the total cost. Ask if there are additional charges. Ask about cancellation policies and refunds.
- Get all the information in writing before you agree to purchase a tour or travel package, and read it.

Other Ways to Stay

Condominiums

Condos can be the perfect solution for family trips, two couples traveling together, or one couple seeking more space, privacy, convenience, and value than a hotel room might offer.

Hawaii condo resorts are not your bare-bones ski units. They range from standard to first-rate with all the comforts home may not have. They come in small clusters or large buildings, by the beach or not, often with lobbies, front desks, maid service, and other hotel services. Frequently, they are located in major resort areas with the full menu of extras available to hotel guests, including golf, tennis, pools, restaurants, and shuttle service. The difference between some resort condos and hotels is hard to discern as a guest, other than the larger units and homelike facilities of condos. The units are individually owned, but the rentals are managed in a group. Units in one complex may be managed by several different companies, some of them hotel firms—just to confuse it further—and individual owners may rent out their own units too.

Units range from 700–800 square feet for a one-bedroom unit to 2,000 square feet or more for a two-bedroom unit. Three-bedroom units and villas are larger still. With kitchens, you have the option of cooking meals or just putting together breakfast or lunch home-style, then having dinner in restaurants. This gives you the chance to indulge in fresh tropical fruit, Kona coffee, and other Hawaii specialties. Condo unit prices can range from as low as $45 per night to more than $300 per night, depending on the type of accommodation, location, and dates of stay.

One choice is to book your condo through one of the dozens of central condo reservations agencies around the islands and the nation (some are listed below) to find Hawaii units that suit your needs. State your preferences on location, unit size, price range, amenities, ambience, and the number in your party, and you'll receive a list of properties from which to choose. Some condo representatives offer extra services, like car rentals and lei greetings, and some handle private resort home rentals as well.

Kapalua Resort on Maui is one of several luxury resorts that has an on-site management operation handling some 200 luxury units and homes in several areas of the resort. Destination Resorts Hawaii at Wailea Resort is another, handling a wide variety of condo units at Wailea.

If you shop for travel deals on your own, you'll find plenty of condo travel packages are available in the same way that hotel packages are offered. Watch the ads, use the Internet, ask your friends, and keep on top of special offers.

Terms and policies differ. A deposit is usually required, payable by a major credit card. It's wise to book at least three months in advance, although late reservations are entirely possible. Again, holidays and other high-demand periods will mean more competition for the unit you want.

RECOMMENDED CONDO RESERVATIONS AGENTS

Statewide

Hawaiian Condo Resorts
(800) 487-4505, (808) 949-4505
www.hawaiicondo.com

Aston Hotels and Resorts
(800) 92-ASTON
www.aston-hotels.com

Outrigger Hotels and Resorts
(800) 688-7444
www.outrigger.com

Big Island

Keauhou Property Management (deluxe, Keauhou Resort)
(800) 745-KONA, (808) 326-9075

South Kohala Management (luxury units and homes, Kohala Coast)
(800) 822-4252, (808) 883-8500

Kona Hawaii Vacation Rentals (affordable, Kailua-Kona)
(800) 553-5035, (808) 329-9393
www.konahawaii.com

Maui

Destination Resorts Hawaii (Wailea Resort)
(800) 367-5246, (808) 879-1595

Kihei Maui Vacations (affordable; homes too)
(800) 541-6284, (808) 879-7581
www.maui.net/~kmv

Kauai

Kauai Vacation Rentals (homes too)
(800) 367-5025, (808) 245-8841

Oahu

Aloha Waikiki Vacation Condos (Waikiki)
(800) 655-6055, (808) 923-4402
www.waikiki-condos.com

Here are our favorite condos, selected for their location, value, facilities, and the good time we had there.

Oahu: Waikiki Shore The only beachfront condo on Waikiki Beach, this is a true find beside the open Fort DeRussy beachfront. Beach, ocean, city, and mountain views in studios, one-bedroom, and two-bedroom units priced from $154 per night for two people. For a fee, guests can use services of neighboring Outrigger Reef on the Beach Hotel—offering pool, club floor, fitness center, lounge, massage facility, and signing privileges.

Write 2161 Kalia Road, Honolulu, HI 96815; call (800) 655-6055, (808) 923-4402; or visit www.waikiki-condos.com/shore.html.

Maui: The Kapalua Villas Luxurious, spacious villas in low-rise clusters with views and proximity to beach and golf course. One bedroom to three bedrooms are available. Write 500 Office Road, Kapalua, HI 96761; call (800) 545-0018, (808) 669-8088; or visit www.kapaluavillas.com.

Kauai: Hanalei Colony Resort These condos boast an incredibly beautiful and remote location. Take seven one-lane bridges past Princeville on the North Shore to find this low-rise hideaway of 48 two-bedroom units. Get groceries at Hanalei on the way, because commerce comes to a halt when you arrive, leaving only the breathtaking beachfront setting. Step off your lanai onto sand. There's a restaurant next door, movie stars' homes just beyond that, and then the road ends at Na Pali Coast. Write P.O. Box 206, Hanalei, HI 96714; call (800) 628-3004, (808) 826-6235; or visit www.hcr.com.

Big Island of Hawaii: Kanaloa at Keauhou Palatial bathrooms are a key feature of these one-, two-, and three-bedroom units that are comfortable, and well furnished. The low-rise units sprawl over a rocky headland at Keauhou, south of Kailua-Kona, with a restaurant, tennis, three pools, and lots of lanai ambience. Some are on the waterfront. They're great for families. Write 78-261 Manukai Street, Kailua-Kona, HI 96740; call (800) 688-7444, (808) 322-9625; or visit www.kanaloakona.com.

Molokai: Paniolo Hale Wrapped in greens of the Kaluakoi Golf Course beside golden Kepuhi Beach, this is an architecturally appealing ranch-style retreat and the most interesting of several small low-rise condo complexes next to Kaluakoi Resort at Molokai's west end. The resort and golf course are currently closed, but not Paniolo Hale, which operates independently. Normally, one bonus of this complex is to be golf cart driving or walking distance from the tees. But it's also close to the beach, moderately priced, and probably the best way to stay on Molokai. You can shop for food and find movies up the hill at Maunaloa. Write P.O. Box 190, Maunaloa, HI 96770; call (800) 367-2984, (808) 552-2731; or visit www.paniolohaleresort.com.

Bed-and-Breakfasts and Vacation Rentals

A Hawaii-style bed-and-breakfast or vacation rental can offer a satisfying personal island experience much like staying in a friend's home. Some B&B guests stay year after year in the same spot and indeed become friends of the family. They find that staying at B&Bs gets them out of the artificial resort atmosphere and into real Hawaii life.

On the mainland, a "bed-and-breakfast" usually means a refurbished mansion or historic house. In Hawaii, it's usually a cottage, studio, or guest room in a private home. Most prevalent are studios with kitchenettes or full kitchens. There are exceptions, such as Shipman House Bed & Breakfast, a traditional inn in Hilo (131 Kaiulani Street, Hilo, HI 96720; (808) 934-8002 or (800) 627-8447; www.hilo-hawaii.com).

You probably won't get home-cooked breakfast at most of the in-house B&Bs, thanks to restrictive laws. But you can expect a basket of tropical fruit, breads, and Kona coffee. Most operators require a minimum three-night stay. Ask whether units have private baths and entries.

Search the Internet to preview and reserve a B&B. There are 700 B&B operations in Hawaii. Beach properties rent quickly and are usually booked year-round, often by returning guests. Plan to make reservations two or three months in advance, longer for holiday periods.

Prices range from $65 to $300 a night. A room in a private home averages between $55 and $75 a night for two people with Continental breakfast. A studio with private entrance, bath, and kitchenette ranges from $75 to $95 a night. A cottage averages $80 to $150 per night for two people. Call the hosts directly or use a reservation service, such as the following.

All Islands Bed & Breakfast
(800) 542-0344, (808) 263-2342
www.hawaii.rr.com/allislands

Bed & Breakfast Hawaii
(800) 733-1632, (808) 822-7771
www.bandb-hawaii.com

Bed & Breakfast Honolulu
(800) 288-4666, (808) 595-7533
www.aloha-bnb.com

Hawaii's Best Bed & Breakfasts
(800) 262-9912, (808) 885-4550
www.bestbnb.com

At most bed-and-breakfast agencies, a 20% deposit, plus 4.17% excise tax on the deposit, is required to hold a reservation. A portion of the deposit is retained by the agency as a fee. Otherwise, deposits are generally refundable if you cancel your reservation at least two weeks in advance, but ask what the policy is before you commit yourself. Personal checks and credit cards are accepted for deposits. The balance is usually paid in cash to the host family, though some agencies require full payment before you arrive. You will receive a confirmation letter shortly after your deposit is received, followed by a welcome letter, map, and brochure.

The following are a few of our favorite B&Bs, cottages, and other rentals.

RECOMMENDED HAWAII B&BS

Oahu

Hawaiian Islands Bed & Breakfast/
Lanikai Bed & Breakfast
1277 Mokulua Drive
Kailua, HI 96734
(808) 261-1059, (800) 258-7895
www.lanikaibb.com

Ke Iki Hale
59-579 Ke Iki Road
Haleiwa, HI 96712
(808) 638-8229

Pat's Kailua Beach Properties
204 S. Kalaheo Street
Kailua, HI 96734
(808) 261-1653
www.10kvacationrentals.com/pats

RECOMMENDED HAWAII B&BS *(continued)*

Maui

Blue Horizons B&B
3894 Mahinahina Street
Lahaina, HI 96761
(808) 669-1965, (800) 669-1948
www.bluehorizonsmaui.com

Silver Cloud Ranch
RR II, Box 201
Kula, HI 96790
(808) 878-6101, (800) 532-1111
www.maui.net/~slvrcld

Kauai

Aloha Country Inn
505 Kamalu Road
Kapaa, HI 96746
(808) 947-6019, (800) 634-5115
www.aloha.net/~wery

Poipu Bed & Breakfast Inn
2720 Hoonani Road
Poipu, HI 96756
(808) 742-1146, (800) 227-6478
www.poipu.net

Big Island *(Hilo/Volcano)*

Carson's Volcano Cottage
P.O. Box 503
Volcano, HI 96785
(808) 967-7683, (800) 845-5282
www.carsonscottage.com

Wild Ginger Inn
100 Puueo Street
Hilo, HI 96720
(808) 935-5556, (800) 882-1887
www.wildgingerinn.com

Volcano Bed & Breakfast
P.O. Box 998
Volcano, HI 96785
(808) 967-7779, (800) 937-7786
www.volcano-hawaii.com

Big Island *(South Kona Coast)*

Dragonfly Ranch Tropical Fantasy Lodging
P.O. Box 675
Honaunau-Kona, HI 96726
(808) 328-9570, (800) 487-2159
www.dragonflyranch.com

Lanai

Dreams Come True
547 12th Street
Lanai City, HI 96763
(808) 565-6961, (800) 566-6961
www.go-native.com/Inns

Molokai

Kamalo Plantation B&B
HC01, Box 300
Kaunakakai, HI 96748
(808) 558-8236
www.molokai.com/kamalo

Hotels Rated and Ranked

We've ranked more than 60 hotels in Hawaii, based on room quality (cleanliness, spaciousness, views, amenities, visual appeal), value, service, and location. These factors are combined into an overall rating, which is expressed on a five-star scale. These are our ratings, independent of any travel organization or club. The evaluations are relative to properties on the islands. See the hotel profiles later in this section for more details. These descriptions will help you understand the reasoning behind a hotel's rank.

The overall rating takes into consideration all facets of a hotel. A property with a prime location, excellent restaurants, or a gorgeous lobby might rank highly despite mediocre rooms. Conversely, a property with elaborate rooms and little else may rank lower overall. Hence the one- to five-star room quality ratings. Obviously, a room's size, the quality of its furnishings, and its level of cleanliness are prime factors in room quality. However, *Unofficial Guide* researchers also take careful note of the things most guests only notice when something is awry: noise levels, lighting, temperature control, ventilation, and security.

WHAT THE RATINGS MEAN

★★★★★	Best of the best
★★★★½	Excellent
★★★★	Very good
★★★½	Good
★★★	Average
★★½	Below average
★★	Poor

The value ratings, also given on a five-star scale, are a combination of the overall and room quality ratings, divided by the cost of an average guest room. They indicate a general idea of value for money. If getting a good deal means the most to you, choose a property by looking at the value rating. Otherwise, room and overall ratings are better indicators of a satisfying experience. If a wonderful property is fairly priced, it may only get an average or ★★★ value rating, but you still might prefer the experience to an average property with a ★★★★★ value rating.

COST INDICATORS

$$$$$	Above $350
$$$$	$250–$350
$$$	$150–$250
$$	$100–$150
$	Below $100

The chart above indicates the symbols used in the subsequent table and profiles to correlate with various hotel prices. The rates used here are based on the rack rate for a standard ocean-view room (or suitable equivalent) during the tourism high season, which runs from December through March. Don't be intimidated by the cost indicators. Lower and higher prices (depending on the room category) are available at each hotel.

HOW THE HOTELS COMPARE IN HAWAII

Hotel	Overall Rating	Room Rating	Value Rating	Cost	Zone
Oahu					
Halekulani	★★★★★	★★★★★	★★★	$$$$$	1
J W Marriott Ihilani Resort & Spa	★★★★★	★★★★★	★★★	$$$$$	5
Hyatt Regency Waikiki	★★★★½	★★★★½	★★★	$$$$$	1
Hawaii Prince Hotel Waikiki	★★★★½	★★★★	★★½	$$$$$	1
Hilton Hawaiian Village	★★★★½	★★★★	★★★	$$$$	1
Kahala Mandarin Oriental	★★★★½	★★★★	★★	$$$$$	2
Royal Hawaiian Hotel	★★★★½	★★★★	★★½	$$$$$	1
Sheraton Moana Surfrider	★★★★½	★★★★	★★½	$$$$$	1
Sheraton Princess Kaiulani	★★★★	★★★★	★★	$$$$	1
Sheraton Waikiki	★★★★	★★★★	★★	$$$$$	1
W Honolulu-Diamond Head	★★★★	★★★★	★★	$$$$	1
Waikiki Beach Marriott Resort	★★★★	★★★★	★★	$$$$	1
Waikiki Parc Hotel	★★★★	★★★★	★★★½	$$$	1
Ala Moana Hotel	★★★★	★★★½	★★★½	$$$	2
Royal Garden at Waikiki	★★★★	★★★½	★★★	$$$	1
Turtle Bay Golf & Tennis Resort	★★★★	★★★½	★★★	$$$	4
Waikiki Joy Hotel	★★★★	★★★½	★★★	$$$	1
New Otani Kaimana Beach Hotel	★★★★	★★★½	★★½	$$$	1
Aston at the Executive Centre Hotel	★★★★	★★★½	★★	$$$$	2
Waikiki Beachcomber Hotel	★★★★	★★★	★★½	$$$	1
Outrigger Waikiki on the Beach	★★★½	★★★½	★★★	$$$$	1
Doubletree Alana Waikiki Hotel	★★★½	★★★½	★★	$$$$	1
Outrigger East Hotel	★★★½	★★★½	★★	$$$	1
Outrigger Reef on the Beach	★★★½	★★★½	★★	$$$$	1
Radisson Waikiki Prince Kuhio	★★★½	★★★½	★★	$$$	1
Waikiki Terrace Hotel	★★★½	★★★½	★★	$$$	1
Pacific Beach Hotel	★★★½	★★★	★★	$$$	1
Maui					
Ritz-Carlton, Kapalua	★★★★★	★★★★★	★★★½	$$$$$	9
Four Seasons Resort Maui	★★★★★	★★★★★	★★★	$$$$$	8
Grand Wailea Resort Hotel & Spa	★★★★½	★★★★½	★★½	$$$$$	8
Fairmont Kea Lani Hotel, Suites & Villas	★★★★½	★★★★	★★★	$$$$$	8
Embassy Vacation Resort	★★★★½	★★★★	★★½	$$$$$	9
Wailea Marriott	★★★★	★★★★	★★★	$$$$$	8
Hyatt Regency Maui	★★★★	★★★★	★★½	$$$$$	9

HOW THE HOTELS COMPARE IN HAWAII *(continued)*

Hotel	Overall Rating	Room Rating	Value Rating	Cost	Zone
Maui (continued)					
Westin Maui	★★★★	★★★★	★★½	$$$$$	9
Hotel Hana-Maui	★★★★	★★★★	★★	$$$$$	10
Kapalua Bay Hotel	★★★★	★★★★	★★	$$$$$	9
Maui Marriott Resort	★★★★	★★★★	★★	$$$$	9
Renaissance Wailea Beach Resort	★★★★	★★★★	★★	$$$$	8
Sheraton Maui	★★★★	★★★★	★★	$$$$$	9
Kaanapali Beach Hotel	★★★★	★★★½	★★★	$$$$	9
Maui Prince Hotel	★★★★	★★★½	★★	$$$$	8
Lahaina Inn	★★★★	★★★	★★★½	$$	9
The Big Island					
Four Seasons Resort Hualalai	★★★★★	★★★★★	★★½	$$$$$	11
Mauna Lani Bay Hotel & Bungalows	★★★★½	★★★★½	★★½	$$$$$	11
Fairmont Orchid	★★★★½	★★★★	★★	$$$$$	11
Hapuna Beach Prince Hotel	★★★★½	★★★★	★★	$$$$$	11
Hilton Waikoloa Village	★★★★½	★★★★	★★	$$$$$	11
Kona Village Resort	★★★★½	★★★★	★★	$$$$$	11
Mauna Kea Beach Hotel	★★★★½	★★★★	★★	$$$$$	11
Hawaii Naniloa Resort	★★★★	★★★½	★★★	$$	12
Ohana Keauhou Beach Resort	★★★★	★★★½	★★½	$$$	11
Waikoloa Beach Marriott	★★★★	★★★½	★★★	$$$$	11
Hilo Hawaiian Hotel	★★★½	★★★½	★★½	$$	12
King Kamehameha's Kona Beach Hotel	★★★½	★★★	★★★½	$$$	11
Volcano House	★★★½	★★★	★★	$$	12
Kauai					
Hyatt Regency Kauai Resort & Spa	★★★★½	★★★★½	★★½	$$$$$	13
Princeville Hotel	★★★★½	★★★★	★★	$$$$$	13
Hanalei Bay Resort & Suites	★★★★	★★★★	★★½	$$$$	13
Kauai Marriott Resort & Beach Club	★★★★	★★★★	★★	$$$$$	13
Sheraton Kauai Resort	★★★★	★★★★	★★	$$$$$	13
Radisson Kauai Beach Resort	★★★★	★★★½	★★	$$$	13
Molokai					
Sheraton Molokai Lodge & Beach Village	★★★★½	★★★★	★★★	$$$$$	14

HOW THE HOTELS COMPARE IN HAWAII *(continued)*

Hotel	Overall Rating	Room Rating	Value Rating	Cost	Zone
Lanai					
The Lodge at Koele	★★★★½	★★★★	★★½	$$$$$	15
The Manele Bay Hotel	★★★★½	★★★	★★½	$$$$$	15
Hotel Lanai	★★★½	★★★	★★★	$	15

HAWAII HOTELS BY ZONE

Zone 1: Waikiki

Doubletree Alana Waikiki Hotel
Halekulani
Hawaii Prince Hotel Waikiki
Hilton Hawaiian Village
Hyatt Regency Waikiki
New Otani Kaimana Beach Hotel
Outrigger East Hotel
Outrigger Reef on the Beach
Outrigger Waikiki on the Beach
Pacific Beach Hotel
Radisson Waikiki Prince Kuhio
Royal Garden at Waikiki
Royal Hawaiian Hotel
Sheraton Moana Surfrider
Sheraton Princess Kaiulani
Sheraton Waikiki
W Honolulu-Diamond Head
Waikiki Beach Marriott Resort
Waikiki Beachcomber Hotel
Waikiki Joy Hotel
Waikiki Parc Hotel
Waikiki Terrace Hotel

Zone 2: Greater Honolulu

Ala Moana Hotel
Aston at the Executive Centre Hotel
Kahala Mandarin Oriental

Zone 4: The North Shore

Turtle Bay Golf & Tennis Resort

Zone 5: Leeward Oahu

J W Marriott Ihilani Resort & Spa

Zone 8: South Maui

Fairmont Kea Lani Hotel, Suites & Villas
Four Seasons Resort Maui
Grand Wailea Resort Hotel & Spa
Maui Prince Hotel
Renaissance Wailea Beach Resort
Wailea Marriott

Zone 9: West Maui

Embassy Vacation Resort
Hyatt Regency Maui
Kaanapali Beach Hotel
Kapalua Bay Hotel
Lahaina Inn
Maui Marriott Resort
Ritz-Carlton, Kapalua
Sheraton Maui
Westin Maui

Zone 10: Upcountry Maui and Beyond

Hotel Hana-Maui

Zone 11: Kona

Fairmont Orchid
Four Seasons Resort Hualalai
Hapuna Beach Prince Hotel
Hilton Waikoloa Village
King Kamehameha's Kona Beach Hotel
Kona Village Resort
Mauna Kea Beach Hotel
Mauna Lani Bay Hotel & Bungalows
Ohana Keauhou Beach Resort
Waikoloa Beach Marriott

HAWAII HOTELS BY ZONE *(continued)*

Zone 12: Hilo and Volcano

Hawaii Naniloa Resort

Hilo Hawaiian Hotel

Volcano House

Zone 13: Kauai

Hanalei Bay Resort & Suites

Hyatt Regency Kauai Resort & Spa

Kauai Marriott Resort & Beach Club

Princeville Hotel

Radisson Kauai Beach Resort

Sheraton Kauai Resort

Zone 14: Molokai

Sheraton Molokai Lodge & Beach Village

Zone 15: Lanai

Hotel Lanai

The Lodge at Koele

The Manele Bay Hotel

Hotel Profiles

Details on hotels and resorts in alphabetical order by island follow.

Oahu

Ala Moana Hotel *$$$*

OVERALL ★★★★ | QUALITY ★★★½ | VALUE ★★★½ | ZONE 2

410 Atkinson Drive, Honolulu, HI 96814; (888) 367-4811 or (808) 955-4811; fax: (808) 944-6839; amhiresv@get.net; www.alamoanahotel.com

It doesn't front Waikiki Beach, but it does have a great central location, close to everything. A sky bridge leads you to Ala Moana Center; the Hawaii Convention Center is across the street; and it's a five-minute walk to Ala Moana Beach Park. Traffic in this area is always busy and views are disappointing, but everything is handy.

SETTING & FACILITIES

Location On the fringe of Waikiki. **Dining** Aaron's is the signature restaurant here, offering fine Continental cuisine. Other dining options include Royal Garden (Chinese) and Tsukasa (Japanese). The Plantation Café serves a variety of international cuisine for breakfast, lunch, and dinner. **Amenities & Services** Room service, laundry facilities (coin-operated), ice and soda machines, ATM machine, business center, sundry shop, shopping arcade, concierge, self-parking ($9/day), valet parking ($12), swimming pool.

ACCOMMODATIONS

Rooms 1,152. Includes 67 suites; 28 rooms equipped for the disabled; 800 nonsmoking rooms. **All Rooms** A/C, color TV, pay movies, clock radio, mini-fridge, in-room safe, two double beds, direct-dial phone system, dataport, in-room coffee, hair dryer, voice mail. **Some Rooms** King and two doubles, concierge services, in-room steam and Jacuzzi unit, iron and board, yukata robes. IBM PC–compatible systems available for additional $15/night. **Comfort & Decor** Very clean and well maintained. Rooms small to medium, decorated with light colors and Hawaiian-accented artwork, airy and bright ambience.

PAYMENT, RESERVATIONS, & RESTRICTIONS

Family Plan Children age 18 and under stay free in room with parents if using existing bedding. Each additional adult, $25/night. Maximum of 4 people/room (maximum of

2/room in Kona Tower). Rollaway bed, $25/night; cribs free. **Deposit** To guarantee reservation, a deposit of one night's room rate is required within 10 days of confirmation. Cancellation notice must be given at least 72 hours prior to scheduled arrival for refund. **Credit Cards** All major credit cards accepted. **Check-In/Out** 3 p.m./noon. Early check-in possible if the room is available.

Aston at the Executive Centre Hotel $$$$

OVERALL ★★★★ | QUALITY ★★★½ | VALUE ★★ | ZONE 2

1088 Bishop Street, Honolulu, HI 96813; (800) 321-2558 or (808) 539-3000; fax: (808) 523-1088; res.exc@aston-hotels.com; www.aston-hotels.com

Stylish, all-suite hotel for the business traveler who must be on Honolulu's Bishop Street. The service staff is friendly and professional, and the swimming pool and fitness center are welcome amenities. Don't expect a resort atmosphere. Though downtown Honolulu is populated by an intriguing mix of people by day, the streets are nearly deserted at night. If you're here on business, this downtown hotel is the best choice.

SETTING & FACILITIES

Location In the heart of the downtown business district. **Dining** Bronson Restaurant serves a full menu of local-style favorites, but is closed on weekends. **Amenities & Services** Swimming pool, fitness center, parking facilities ($9/day), laundry and dry cleaning service.

ACCOMMODATIONS

Rooms 116. All suites. **All Rooms** A/C, color TV, partial kitchen. **Some Rooms** Full kitchen, washer and dryer, fax machines. **Comfort & Decor** Well-appointed, spacious suites. Some rooms have fax machines (be sure to request a room with one if you need it). The decor is elegant but subdued. Floor-to-ceiling windows provide superb views of downtown Honolulu.

PAYMENT, RESERVATIONS, & RESTRICTIONS

Family Plan Children age 18 and under stay free with parents. **Deposit** $400 (cash or credit card) refundable damage deposit. Cancellation notice must be given at least 72 hours prior to scheduled arrival for refund. **Credit Cards** All major credit cards accepted. **Check-In/Out** 3 p.m./noon. Early check-in and late checkout available on request (no guarantees).

Doubletree Alana Waikiki Hotel $$$

OVERALL ★★★½ | QUALITY ★★★½ | VALUE ★★ | ZONE 1

1956 Ala Moana Boulevard, Honolulu, HI 96815; (800) 367-6070 or (808) 941-7275; fax: (808) 949-0996; www.alana-doubletree.com

The hotel's website claims that the property is just "steps" away from the beach and Ala Moana Shopping Center, but it doesn't tell you how many. The truth is, it's about a 15-minute walk either way. What this boutique hotel lacks in location, it makes up for in hospitality. Service is friendly and efficient, and there's a level of charm and comfort here that you won't find in larger hotels. Padovani's, one of Hawaii's favorite restaurants, offers fine dining. Room views are so-so, because most of Diamond Head is obscured by other hotel properties. Decorator suites are exceptional, especially one with an outdoor lanai that wraps much of the building.

SETTING & FACILITIES

Location On the fringe of Waikiki, 15-minute walk to beach. **Dining** Breakfast, lunch, and dinner at Padovani's Bistro & Wine Bar, one of Oahu's top fine-dining establishments, which serves superb classic southern French cuisine. **Amenities & Services** Room service, valet parking ($10), dry cleaning and laundry service, 24-hour business center, fitness center, swimming pool.

ACCOMMODATIONS

Rooms 313. Includes 25 suites and a penthouse suite. Nonsmoking rooms available. **All Rooms** A/C, private lanai, TV, mini-cooler, in-room safe, coffeemaker, hair dryer, iron and board. **Some Rooms** Living room with sofa-bed. **Comfort & Decor** Very spacious, tastefully appointed with plush sofas and chairs. Hawaiian-themed artwork adorns the walls.

PAYMENT, RESERVATIONS, & RESTRICTIONS

Deposit Credit card guarantee with 1-night deposit. **Credit Cards** All major credit cards accepted. **Check-In/Out** 3 p.m./noon. Early check-in and late checkout available by request.

Halekulani $$$$$

OVERALL ★★★★★ | QUALITY ★★★★★ | VALUE ★★★ | ZONE 1

2199 Kalia Road, Honolulu, HI 96815; (800) 367-2343 or (808) 923-2311; fax: (808) 926-8004; www.halekulani.com

The Halekulani is the best hotel in Waikiki, the best on Oahu, and the only hotel in Hawaii to win the prestigious AAA Five Diamond Award for both hotel and restaurant categories. It lives up to its reputation.

Amid the hustle and bustle of Kalakaua Avenue, the Halekulani remains a peaceful, elegant oasis with a postcard view of Waikiki Beach and Diamond Head.

No experience exemplifies this more than sunset cocktails at the House Without a Key, where a former Miss Hawaii dances the hula to soothing Hawaiian music as the sun sinks in the Pacific.

Service is impeccable, and the rooms are spacious and well appointed—all with an ocean view. The two restaurants, La Mer and Orchids, are open-air and face the sea, the cuisine is outstanding, and the service almost fawning. A weekly manager's reception serves complimentary heavy hors d'oeuvres.

Geared more toward well-to-do couples than large families, the hotel has gained a loyal following; many come back every year.

SETTING & FACILITIES

Location On Waikiki Beach. **Dining** The Halekulani has several notable fine dining establishments, including the AAA Five Diamond Award–winning La Mer, which serves neoclassic French cuisine. Orchids serves breakfast, lunch, and dinner. **Amenities & Services** Fresh fruit bowl and chocolates on arrival, complimentary morning newspaper, valet parking, self-parking ($10/day), fitness center, business center, heated swimming pool.

ACCOMMODATIONS

Rooms 456. Includes 44 suites, 16 rooms for the disabled. Nonsmoking rooms available. **All Rooms** A/C, lanai, 3 phones, cable TV, mini-fridge, clock radio. **Some Rooms** 2 bedrooms. **Comfort & Decor** Spacious, stylishly appointed decor with light colors and tasteful furnishings, high ceilings, plenty of drawer space. Large balconies include table, two chairs, and an adjustable folding chair.

PAYMENT, RESERVATIONS, & RESTRICTIONS

Family Plan Children age 17 and under stay free in room with parents if using existing bedding; extra bed, $40/night. **Deposit** Credit card guarantees reservation with 1-night deposit within 14 days of confirmation. Cancellation notice must be given at least 72 hours prior to scheduled arrival for refund. **Credit Cards** All major credit cards accepted. **Check-In/Out** 3 p.m./noon. Hospitality room available for early arrivals and late departures. Early check-ins and late checkouts based on availability.

Hawaii Prince Hotel Waikiki $$$$$

OVERALL ★★★★½ | QUALITY ★★★★ | VALUE ★★½ | ZONE 1

100 Holomoana Street, Honolulu, HI 96815; (800) 321-6248 or (808) 956-1111; fax: (808) 946-0811; reservationsHPHW@hiprince.com; www.hawaiiprincehotel.com

An upscale pink marble monument overlooking Ala Wai Yacht Harbor, the Hawaii Prince offers exceptional service and proximity to Ala Moana Center, Ala Moana Beach Park, and the Hawaii Convention Center, all within easy walking distance. The hotel's business facilities and services are excellent. All 521 hotel rooms provide yacht harbor and ocean views. The expansive Italian marble lobby features a tuxedo-clad piano player. The fifth floor is often windy, but is still a favorite hangout, with a swimming pool, sun deck, and terraces for sunset cocktails. If you're looking for a tee time, the Hawaii Prince Golf Club isn't anywhere near the hotel (it's a 40-minute drive away on the Ewa side of Oahu), but this is the only Waikiki hotel with a golf course to call its own. Guests of this hotel receive preferred tee times and shuttle service.

SETTING & FACILITIES

Location On the outskirts of Waikiki at Ala Wai Yacht Harbor, 15-minute walk to Ala Moana Beach. **Dining** Two restaurants of note are the Prince Court, which features Hawaiian regional cuisine, and Hakone, specializing in exquisite Japanese fare. **Amenities & Services** Hot towels on check-in, valet parking, business facilities, fitness center, in-room safes, babysitting services, daily newspaper.

ACCOMMODATIONS

Rooms 521. Includes 57 suites; 10 rooms for the disabled. Nonsmoking rooms available. **All Rooms** A/C, cable TV with pay movies, mini-fridge, in-room safe, hair dryer, robes. **Some Rooms** Extra bedroom and bath. **Comfort & Decor** Very spacious, with lavish decor and floor-to-ceiling windows that partially open, but no lanai. Floral-themed artworks adorn walls in well-lit room with bright, warm colors.

PAYMENT, RESERVATIONS, & RESTRICTIONS

Family Plan Children age 17 and under stay free in room with parents if using existing bedding. Maximum occupancy is 3 adults or 2 adults and 2 children/room; extra adult, $40/night. **Deposit** 1-night deposit due 14 days within booking. Cancellation notice must be given 72 hours prior to scheduled arrival for refund. **Credit Cards** Visa, MC, AmEx, DC. **Check-In/Out** 2 p.m./noon. Early check-in and late checkout available on request.

Hilton Hawaiian Village $$$$

OVERALL ★★★★½ | QUALITY ★★★★ | VALUE ★★★ | ZONE 1

2005 Kalia Road, Honolulu, HI 96815; (800) 445-8667 or (808) 949-4321; fax: (808) 947-7898; www.hawaiianvillage.hilton.com

Hawaii's largest hotel, this beachfront village epitomizes the term *self-contained* resort. You really don't have to leave. Expect crowds here, because the Hilton is top choice for tour groups. The hotel rooms are currently housed in five separate towers: Tapa, Rainbow, Diamond Head, upscale Alii, and the 453-room, 25-story Kalia Tower that opened May 2001 at the hotel entry, where Buckminster Fuller's geodesic dome once stood. The tower includes a health and wellness spa, Hawaiian cultural center, and four floors of retail shops. Yet another new tower is planned.

The HHV also has five bars (with nightly entertainment provided), more than 100 shops and services, and activities ranging from undersea submarine rides to wildlife tours. This hotel is terrific for young families, as it offers one of Hawaii's best year-round children's programs (including excursions to nearby attractions such as the Honolulu Zoo and Waikiki Aquarium). Lei making, hula, and ukulele lessons are daily activities. Every Friday, the King's Jubilee and Fireworks show features a precision rifle drill team, Hawaiian music, and fireworks.

SETTING & FACILITIES

Location Fronting Duke Kahanamoku Beach (part of Waikiki Beach) near gateway to Waikiki. **Dining** Of the 7 restaurants located here, 2 stand out as among the finest on Oahu: Bali-by-the-Sea, an oceanfront restaurant serving innovative cuisine with an island accent, and Golden Dragon, serving Cantonese and Szechuan specialties. **Amenities & Services** 3 outdoor swimming pools, valet parking, parking garage, travel services, laundry and dry cleaning, wedding chapel, physicians on call, beauty and barber shops, post office and express mail pickup and delivery, meeting and banquet space, business services, children's program, florist.

ACCOMMODATIONS

Rooms 2,998. Includes 363 suites; 526 nonsmoking rooms; 75 rooms for the disabled. **All Rooms** A/C, cable TV with pay movies, in-room safe, refreshment center. **Some Rooms** Evening *pupu*, concierge service, robes, sparkling water, in-room fax, upgraded bathroom amenities, valet laundry service. **Comfort & Decor** Moderate space, well-lit with airy, attractive Hawaiian decor that includes wicker furnishings and floral-themed bedspreads.

PAYMENT, RESERVATIONS, & RESTRICTIONS

Family Plan Children age 17 and under stay free in room with parents if using existing bedding. **Deposit** 1-night deposit due within 10 days after confirmation. Cancellation notice must be given at least 72 hours prior to scheduled arrival for refund. **Credit Cards** All major credit cards accepted. **Check-In/Out** 2 p.m./11 a.m. Early check-in and late checkout available (confirmed on arrival).

Hyatt Regency Waikiki $$$$$

OVERALL ★★★★½ | QUALITY ★★★★½ | VALUE ★★★ | ZONE 1

2424 Kalakaua Avenue, Honolulu, HI 96815; (800) 233-1234 or (808) 923-1234; fax: (808) 923-7839; info@hyattwaikiki.com; www.hyattwaikiki.com

Everything, including the beach, is just a short walk away. The Hyatt is composed of twin 40-story towers connected by the open-air Great Hall and has three floors of shops. The lobby features free entertainment next to Harry's Bar and a ten-story atrium with a man-made waterfall. Free entertainment is provided in the lobby next to Harry's Bar. The Hyatt also has a new full-service spa and a children's program, Camp Hyatt, that provides kids ages 3–12 with fun and educational activities with an emphasis on Hawaii's history and culture. The neighborhood is noisy at night.

SETTING & FACILITIES

Location Across the street from Waikiki Beach. **Dining** Several restaurants here, including the Texas Rock 'n' Roll Sushi Bar (country-style food with a wide range of sushi creations) and Ciao Mein (Italian and Chinese food). **Amenities & Services** Room service, valet parking ($12) and self-parking ($10/day), children's program.

ACCOMMODATIONS

Rooms 1,230. Includes 18 suites; 193 nonsmoking rooms; 24 rooms for the disabled. **All Rooms** A/C, TV, lanai, refrigerator, minibar, hair dryer, iron and board, in-room safe, coffeemaker. **Some Rooms** Connecting parlor. **Comfort & Decor** Spacious, well maintained. Decor is sparse but gracious, with rattan furnishings and subdued colors.

PAYMENT, RESERVATIONS, & RESTRICTIONS

Family Plan Children age 17 and under stay free in room with parents if using existing bedding. **Deposit** 1-night deposit required within 10 days of confirmation. Cancellation notice must be given at least 72 hours prior to scheduled arrival for refund. **Credit Cards** All major credit cards accepted. **Check-In/Out** 3 p.m./noon. Early check-in and late checkout available on request.

JW Marriott Ihilani Resort & Spa $$$$$

OVERALL ★★★★★ | QUALITY ★★★★★ | VALUE ★★★ | ZONE 5

92-1001 Olani Street, Kapolei, HI 96707; (800) 626-4446 or (808) 679-0079; fax: (808) 679-0080; reservations@ihilani.com; www.ihilani.com

The Ihilani, which translates to "heavenly splendor," was built by the Japanese for Tokyo moguls on holiday, and today it's a favorite of Oahu visitors seeking an alternative to Waikiki, which is only an hour but seemingly a world away.

Situated on the first of four man-made lagoons, Ihilani overlooks a gold-sand beach. The resort's full-service spa is regarded as one of the finest in the world.

Six state-of-the-art tennis courts, an acclaimed spa using seawater therapies, and nearby Ko Olina Golf Club make this a favorite for sports-minded visitors. Sports celebrity alert: During NFL Pro Bowl week (usually the first week in February), Ihilani hosts players and their families. Practices are often held on a nearby field.

SETTING & FACILITIES

Location At the Ko Olina Resort in Kapolei, on the Leeward side of the island. **Dining** Azul is Ihilani's signature restaurant, serving an extensive menu blending the flavors of the Mediterranean and Hawaii. **Amenities & Services** Twice-daily maid service, turndown service, daily ice delivery, 24-hour room service, full-service health spa, tennis club, beauty salon, year-round children's program. Self and valet parking ($10/day).

ACCOMMODATIONS

Rooms 387. Includes 36 luxury suites; 120 nonsmoking rooms; 14 rooms equipped for the disabled. **All Rooms** A/C, ceiling fan, color TV, in-house movie library, in-room safe, AM/FM radio with CD player, minibar, 3 phones, private lanai, hair dryer, robes. **Some Rooms** Whirlpool spas, walk-in closets, large-screen TVs, 2 bathrooms. **Comfort & Decor** Very spacious (the smallest room is 640 square feet) and clean, rooms are decorated with local art and teak furnishings. One amenity here is that you can turn lights on and off, adjust the room temperature (in 1° increments), and even find out the current time anywhere in the world—right from your phone, which has instructions in six languages.

PAYMENT, RESERVATIONS, & RESTRICTIONS

Family Plan Children age 17 and under stay free in room with parents if using existing bedding. Rollaway bed, $35. **Deposit** To guarantee reservation, a 1-night deposit is required within 14 days of booking. Cancellation notice must be received at least 72 hours prior to scheduled arrival for refund. **Credit Cards** All major credit cards accepted except Discover. **Check-In/Out** 3 p.m./noon. Early check-in available by request.

Kahala Mandarin Oriental $$$$$

OVERALL ★★★★½ | QUALITY ★★★★ | VALUE ★★ | ZONE 2

5000 Kahala Avenue, Honolulu, HI 96816; (800) 526-6566 or (808) 739-8888; fax: (808) 739-8800; sales@mohg.com; www.mandarin-oriental.com

Old-timers recall this grand old beach hotel as the Kahala Hilton. The Mandarin is a good choice if you are a security-conscious golfer. This hotel sits between a private golf course and the ocean, so presidents and kings, who do stay and tee off here, sleep well.

Complimentary shuttle service transports you to and from major shopping destinations: Kahala Mall, Ala Moana Shopping Center, and Royal Hawaiian Shopping Center. The Mandarin has its own reef-protected beach, exotic gardens, waterfall, turtle ponds, dolphin lagoon, and beachfront lawn.

SETTING & FACILITIES

Location In the upscale Kahala neighborhood, about 15 minutes from Waikiki. **Dining** The oceanfront Hoku's is one of Oahu's best restaurants, serving fine international cuisine with fresh local ingredients. **Amenities & Services** Room service, laundry service, valet parking, business facilities, fitness center, children's program, 24-hour medical services.

ACCOMMODATIONS

Rooms 371. Includes 33 suites. Nonsmoking and ADA-approved rooms available. **All Rooms** A/C, cable TV, CD player, clock radio, video games, 3 phones, minibar, computer outlets, dataport, hair dryer, in-room safe, bathrobes. **Some Rooms** Upgraded amenities. **Comfort & Decor** Spacious, luxurious, and clean, rooms have a stylish turn-of-the-twentieth-century motif, mahogany furnishings, and teak parquet floors, rendering them warm, relaxing, and comfortable.

PAYMENT, RESERVATIONS, & RESTRICTIONS

Family Plan Children age 17 and under stay free in room with parents if using existing bedding. Rollaway bed, $40. **Deposit** All reservations guaranteed by credit card. Cancellation notice must be given at least 72 hours prior to scheduled arrival for refund. **Credit Cards** All major credit cards accepted. **Check-In/Out** 3 p.m./noon. Early check-in and late checkout available on request.

New Otani Kaimana Beach Hotel $$$

OVERALL ★★★★ | QUALITY ★★★½ | VALUE ★★½ | ZONE 1

2863 Kalakaua Avenue, Honolulu, HI 96815; (800) 421-8795 or (808) 923-1555; fax: (808) 922-9404; rooms@kaimana.com; www.kaimana.com

What we like best about the Kaimana is its location. It's in Waikiki, yet somehow removed from traffic and noise of the main drag. A low-key hotel with stylish touches from the Orient, the Kaimana fronts Sans Souci Beach with Kapiolani Park in its backyard. The small, well-situated hotel is popular with residents who often lunch on the Hau Tree Lanai overlooking Sans Souci Beach. Robert Louis Stevenson noted over a century ago, "If anyone desires lovely scenery, pure air, clear sea water, good food, and heavenly sunsets, I recommend him cordially to Sans Souci." We second the motion. This is Oahu's best small hotel.

SETTING & FACILITIES

Location On Sans Souci Beach, near Diamond Head, across from Kapiolani Park. **Dining** The oceanfront Hau Tree Lanai has one of Hawaii's most romantic settings and offers Continental cuisine. Miyako serves traditional Japanese fare. **Amenities & Services** Room service, laundry and dry cleaning service, valet parking ($11), fitness center, business facilities.

ACCOMMODATIONS

Rooms 124. Includes 5 suites and 3 ADA-approved rooms. All rooms permit smoking. **All Rooms** A/C, TV, VCR, lanai, refrigerator, in-room safe, hair dryer; coffeemaker available on request. **Some Rooms** Minibar. **Comfort & Decor** Rooms are smallish, but clean and well maintained, with light, soft pastels and contemporary island-themed decor.

PAYMENT, RESERVATIONS, & RESTRICTIONS

Family Plan Children age 12 and under stay free. Rollaway bed, $30; crib, $10. **Deposit** Credit card guarantee or 1-night deposit required. Cancellation notice must be given at least 72 hours prior to scheduled arrival for refund. **Credit Cards** All major credit cards accepted. **Check-In/Out** 2 p.m./noon. Hospitality room available for early arrivals and late departures.

Outrigger East Hotel *$$$*

OVERALL ★★★½ | QUALITY ★★★½ | VALUE ★★ | ZONE 1

150 Kaiulani Avenue, Honolulu, HI 96815; (800) 688-7444 or (808) 922-5353; fax: (808) 926-4334; www.outrigger.com

One of Outrigger's more popular properties, the Outrigger East is a good choice if you don't require unobstructed ocean views, because it's in the center of Waikiki and the beach is just a few minutes away on foot. It's situated near the International Market Place and next to Kaiulani Park. It has suites with kitchenettes for visitors on extended stays. Nothing exceptional, but nothing subpar, either.

SETTING & FACILITIES

Location At Kuhio and Kaiulani Avenues, 2 blocks from beach. **Dining** A trio of restaurants, including Pepper's Waikiki Grill & Bar (American, Southwest, and Mexican cuisine) and Chuck's Cellar (prime rib and seafood specialties). **Amenities & Services** Room service (7 a.m.–9:30 p.m.), activities desk, parking ($9/day), coin-operated washer and dryer.

ACCOMMODATIONS

Rooms 445. Includes 25 suites; 5 rooms for the disabled. Half the rooms are designated nonsmoking. **All Rooms** A/C, cable TV, refrigerator, in-room safe, coffeemaker. **Some Rooms** Lanai, kitchenette. **Comfort & Decor** Rooms are small to medium sized, with island-accented art and furnishings. Rooms were recently renovated.

PAYMENT, RESERVATIONS, & RESTRICTIONS

Family Plan Children age 17 and under stay free in room with parents if using existing bedding. **Deposit** Credit card guarantee or 1-night deposit required. Cancellation notice must be given at least 72 hours prior to scheduled arrival for refund. **Credit Cards** All major credit cards accepted. **Check-In/Out** 3 p.m./noon. Early check-in and late checkout available on request.

Outrigger Reef on the Beach $$$$

OVERALL ★★★½ | QUALITY ★★★½ | VALUE ★★ | ZONE 1

2169 Kalia Road, Honolulu, HI 96815; (800) 688-7444 or (808) 923-3111; fax: (808) 924-4957; www.outrigger.com

The Outrigger Reef provides all the island hospitality this kamaaina chain is known for, plus the added convenience of being right on Waikiki Beach. The atmosphere here is very informal and is great for young families (the hotel offers a children's activity program). The lobby area includes 15 specialty shops. The Outrigger Reef is the home of the Honolulu Marathon, which takes place each December, and during the week of the event you can expect to see a lot of international runners here.

SETTING & FACILITIES

Location On Waikiki Beach near Ft. DeRussy. **Dining** A quartet of eateries, including Shorebird Beach Broiler, a lively nightspot serving burgers and sandwiches. **Amenities & Services** Room service, activities desk, parking, valet parking ($11), coin-operated washer and dryer.

ACCOMMODATIONS

Rooms 883. Includes 25 suites; 450 nonsmoking rooms; 10 rooms for the disabled. **All Rooms** A/C, cable TV, refrigerator, in-room safe, coffeemaker. **Some Rooms** Kitchenette. **Comfort & Decor** Medium-sized, well-lit rooms are clean and comfortable with cool colors, simple furnishings.

PAYMENT, RESERVATIONS, & RESTRICTIONS

Family Plan Children age 17 and under stay free in room with parents if using existing bedding. **Deposit** 1-night deposit or credit card guarantee. Cancellation notice must be given 72 hours prior to scheduled arrival for refund. **Credit Cards** All major credit cards accepted. **Check-In/Out** 3 p.m./noon. Early check-in and late checkout available on request.

Outrigger Waikiki on the Beach $$$$

OVERALL ★★★½ | QUALITY ★★★½ | VALUE ★★★ | ZONE 1

2335 Kalakaua Avenue, Honolulu, HI 96815; (800) 688-7444 or (808) 923-0711; fax: (808) 921-9749; beachfront@outrigger.com; www.outrigger.com

This is considered Outrigger's flagship property, and we know why. A short stroll around the second-floor lobby tells you right away you're in Hawaii, with soft Hawaiian music, floral-motif carpeting, island artworks, a seashell-shaped chandelier, and, most telling, the soothing sounds of the beach. The location is fabulous too. Not only is the Outrigger Waikiki right on the beach; it is also next door to Waikiki's largest shopping complex, the Royal Hawaiian Shopping Center. Duke's Canoe Club, the hotel's best-known restaurant, is worth a visit just to peruse the memorabilia paying tribute to Duke Kahanamoku,

Hawaii's surfing legend. The Outrigger Waikiki is also the home of the popular *Society of Seven* show, one of Waikiki's longest-running dinner shows (see page 442 for a description). The atmosphere is informal, colorful, and friendly.

SETTING & FACILITIES

Location On Waikiki Beach, next to the Royal Hawaiian Shopping Center. **Dining** Duke's Canoe Club is a Waikiki favorite, serving breakfast, lunch, and dinner. **Amenities & Services** Room service, parking, valet parking ($11), activities desk, coin-operated washer and dryer.

ACCOMMODATIONS

Rooms 530. Includes 30 suites. Half of the rooms are designated nonsmoking. Rooms for the disabled are available. **All Rooms** A/C, cable TV, refrigerator, in-room safe, coffeemaker. **Some Rooms** Kitchenettes. **Comfort & Decor** Medium-sized rooms with subdued colors and few adornments are clean and well maintained.

PAYMENT, RESERVATIONS, & RESTRICTIONS

Family Plan Children age 17 and under stay free in room with parents if using existing bedding. **Deposit** 1-night deposit or credit card guarantee. Cancellation notice must be given at least 72 hours prior to scheduled arrival for refund. **Credit Cards** All major credit cards accepted. **Check-In/Out** 3 p.m./noon. Early check-in and late checkout available on request.

Pacific Beach Hotel $$$

OVERALL ★★★½ | QUALITY ★★★ | VALUE ★★ | ZONE 1

2490 Kalakaua Avenue, Honolulu, HI 96815; (800) 367-6060 or (808) 922-1233; fax: (808) 923-2566; reservation@hthcorp.com; www.pacificbeachhotel.com

Every Waikiki hotel tries to distinguish itself from the others in some form or fashion, and the Pacific Beach Hotel makes a big splash with its three-story, 280,000-gallon oceanarium, featuring hundreds of marine plants and animals. The oceanarium is the centerpiece of the hotel's dining establishments. A busy hotel with friendly service and a prime location, it's next to the beach.

SETTING & FACILITIES

Location Across the street from Waikiki Beach. **Dining** Oceanarium, whose star attraction is not the food but the fish in 280,000-gallon saltwater tank. Shogun is a popular Japanese restaurant, and Neptune's Garden serves seafood, steaks, and Continental fare. **Amenities & Services** Swimming pool and whirlpool, full spa, tennis, parking, laundry service, travel desk, 24-hour fitness center, business facilities, meeting rooms.

ACCOMMODATIONS

Rooms 837. Includes 10 suites; 5 floors of nonsmoking rooms; 13 rooms for the disabled. **All Rooms** A/C, cable TV, balcony, lanai, coffeemaker, in-room safe, mini-fridge, bath slippers. **Some Rooms** Bathrobes, iron and board, vanity kit. **Comfort & Decor** Rooms are small to medium in size. Soft, pastel colors help brighten them. Lanai are open to scenic mountain or ocean views.

PAYMENT, RESERVATIONS, & RESTRICTIONS

Family Plan Children age 18 and under stay free in room with parents if using existing bedding. Maximum of 4 people/room. **Deposit** 1-night deposit required within 14 days of confirmation. Cancellation notice must be given at least 72 hours prior to scheduled arrival for refund. **Credit Cards** All major credit cards accepted. **Check-In/Out** 3 p.m./noon. Early check-in and late checkout based on availability.

Radisson Waikiki Prince Kuhio $$$

OVERALL ★★★½ | QUALITY ★★★½ | VALUE ★★ | ZONE 1

2500 Kuhio Avenue, Honolulu, HI 96815; (800) 688-7444 or (808) 922-0811; fax: (808) 923-0330

Centrally located Prince Kuhio is a short hike to Waikiki Beach. The Ala Wai Canal, Honolulu Zoo, and Kapiolani Park are also nearby. Kuhio Avenue can be just as busy as Kalakaua Avenue, and the area tends to get noisy at night. The lobby area is attractive but rather dimly lit. The hotel recently added a new fitness room and renovated its swimming pool.

SETTING & FACILITIES

Location On Kuhio Avenue in Waikiki, 2 blocks from beach. **Dining** Trellises serves nightly theme buffets and Sunday brunch. Shanghai Garden serves Chinese cuisine and seafood specialties. **Amenities & Services** Room service, activities desk, parking (self, $9/day, valet $12), coin-operated washer and dryer, swimming pool.

ACCOMMODATIONS

Rooms 623. Nonsmoking rooms and rooms for the disabled available. **All Rooms** A/C, cable TV, refrigerator, in-room safe, coffeemaker. **Some Rooms** Balcony, kitchenette. **Comfort & Decor** Rooms are small to medium, tastefully appointed, and very clean, with floor-to-ceiling windows, Hawaiian artwork, and comfortable furnishings. Rooms were recently renovated.

PAYMENT, RESERVATIONS, & RESTRICTIONS

Family Plan Children age 17 and under stay free in room with parents if using existing bedding. **Deposit** 1-night deposit or credit card guarantee required. Cancellation notice must be given 72 hours prior to scheduled arrival for refund. **Credit Cards** All major credit cards accepted. **Check-In/Out** 3 p.m./noon. Early check-in and late checkout available on request.

Royal Garden at Waikiki $$$

OVERALL ★★★★ | QUALITY ★★★½ | VALUE ★★★ | ZONE 1

440 Olohana Street, Honolulu, HI 96815; (800) 367-5666 or (808) 943-0202; fax: (808) 945-7407; hotel-info@royalgardens.com; www.royalgardens.com

It's a decent walk to the beach from this property—about 20 minutes—but the boutique Royal Garden is still a great recommendation. Everything is first-class here, from the service to the amenities. The setting is one of quiet refinement, with interiors inspired by Hawaii's natural beauty. Lush gardens surround two swimming pools. The new King Kalakaua Plaza nearby—with Niketown, All Star Café, and Banana Republic—makes shopping simple. Jogging along nearby Ala Wai Canal is pleasant.

SETTING & FACILITIES

Location In Waikiki, near Ala Wai Canal, 20-minute walk to beach. **Dining** Cascada serves Mediterranean and Pacific Rim cuisine; Shizu offers Ginza-style teppanyaki and traditional Japanese delicacies. **Amenities & Services** Laundry facilities, business center, fitness center, sauna, Jacuzzi, swimming pool, soda machines, shuttle service. Hair dryer, iron and board, and crib available on request.

ACCOMMODATIONS

Rooms 220. Includes 19 suites. Nonsmoking rooms and rooms for the disabled available. Inquire when placing reservation. **All Rooms** A/C, cable TV, private lanai, refrigerator, coffeemaker, voice mail, wet bar, in-room safe. **Some Rooms** Separate shower and Jacuzzi. **Comfort & Decor** Luxurious, with marble bathrooms, extra closet space, and tropical plants.

PAYMENT, RESERVATIONS, & RESTRICTIONS

Family Plan Children age 12 and under stay free in room with parents if using existing bedding. **Deposit** 1-night deposit required within 10 days of confirmation. Cancellation notice must be given at least 72 hours prior to scheduled arrival for refund. **Credit Cards** All major credit cards accepted. **Check-In/Out** 3 p.m./noon. Early check-in and late checkout available on request (no guarantees).

Royal Hawaiian Hotel $$$$$

OVERALL ★★★★½ | QUALITY ★★★★ | VALUE ★★½ | ZONE 1

2259 Kalakaua Avenue, Honolulu, HI 96815; (800) 500-8313 or (808) 923-7311; fax: (808) 924-7098; www.royal-hawaiian.com

This is the famed "Pink Palace." Few hotels in Hawaii have a history like that of this property, which opened in 1927, inspired by a Rudolph Valentino movie. The Royal Hawaiian has aged well and still offers a great old-Waikiki experience. Reminiscent of Waikiki's golden years, the hotel's design reflects a Moorish influence. The lobby area is cool and elegant, decorated in various outrageous shades of pink. The initial views are of lush gardens and shady lawns, but the back end opens up to a dreamlike beach setting with imported gold sand and azure waters. Take a short walk to the Royal Hawaiian Shopping Center. The hotel holds a lavish luau every Monday evening ($60 for hotel guests, free for their children ages 12 and under; $81 for non-hotel guests, $48 for children ages 5–12). Over the years, the Royal has hosted numerous dignitaries and celebrities, from Franklin Roosevelt to the Beatles.

SETTING & FACILITIES

Location On Waikiki Beach, behind Royal Hawaiian Shopping Center. **Dining** The Surf Room serves breakfast, lunch, and dinner, including Friday seafood buffet and Sunday brunch. **Amenities & Services** Fresh flower lei greeting, fresh-baked Hawaiian banana bread on arrival, nightly turndown service, concierge, 24-hour fax service, morning newspaper, laundry and dry cleaning service, parking (valet $15, self $10/day), nurse and physician service.

ACCOMMODATIONS

Rooms 527. Includes 33 suites; 58 nonsmoking rooms; 6 rooms with roll-in showers for wheelchair users. **All Rooms** A/C, color TV, refrigerator, in-room safe, robes. **Some Rooms** Wet bar, Continental breakfast. **Comfort & Decor** Very spacious bedrooms have high ceilings, chandeliers, and classic decor with Old World charm. The bathrooms are a little cramped, however.

PAYMENT, RESERVATIONS, & RESTRICTIONS

Family Plan Children age 17 and under stay free in room with parents if using existing bedding. Rollaway bed, $25/night. **Deposit** Credit card guarantee or 1-night deposit required within 10 days of booking to guarantee reservation. Cancellation notice must be given 72 hours prior to scheduled arrival for refund. **Credit Cards** All major credit cards accepted. **Check-In/Out** 3 p.m./noon. Hospitality suite available for early arrivals and late departures.

Sheraton Moana Surfrider $$$$$

OVERALL ★★★★½ | QUALITY ★★★★ | VALUE ★★½ | ZONE I

2365 Kalakaua Avenue, Honolulu, HI 96815; (800) 782-9488 or (808) 922-3111; fax: (808) 923-0308; www.moana-surfrider.com

Opened in 1901, this is Waikiki's oldest hotel. Nicknamed the "First Lady of Waikiki," the Moana has lost none of her charm. We like the second-floor balcony overlooking Kalakaua Avenue where you can kick back in a rocking chair and watch the world go by. Ocean and beach views are excellent. The staff is efficient, courteous, and smartly dressed. Visit the mini-museum for a look at the golden age of the Moana and Waikiki. Memorabilia include historic photos, postcards, room keys, stock shares, sheet music, menus, and old brochures. You'll also see a sofa that once belonged to King Kalakaua, Hawaii's "Merrie Monarch." A historic centerpiece is the hotel's 75-foot-high, 150-foot-wide banyan tree, near where "Hawaii Calls" was broadcast for 40 years. The central portion of the Moana is listed on the National Register of Historic Places.

SETTING & FACILITIES

Location On Waikiki Beach. **Dining** The Ship's Tavern serves contemporary cuisine; the Beachside Café offers breakfast, lunch, and dinner in a casual setting; Banyan Veranda serves breakfast, afternoon tea, cocktails, and an evening buffet. **Amenities & Services** 24-hour room service, maid service, valet service, self-parking ($9/day), fitness center, concierge, children's program.

ACCOMMODATIONS

Rooms 793. Includes 46 suites; 18 ADA-approved rooms. Nonsmoking rooms available. **All Rooms** A/C, cable TV, in-room safe, hair dryer, slippers, bathrobe, coffeemaker. **Some Rooms** Oceanfront lanai, wet bar, refrigerator, pullout sofa. **Comfort & Decor** Rooms are small to medium in size, with high ceilings, oversized windows, and great views. The design is an interesting mix of old and new, with Old World furnishings and modern amenities, including a video message and checkout system.

PAYMENT, RESERVATIONS, & RESTRICTIONS

Family Plan Children age 17 and under stay free in room with parents if using existing bedding. Maximum of 4 people/room. **Deposit** 1-night deposit or credit card guarantee within 10 days of placing reservation. Cancellation notice must be given 72 hours prior to scheduled arrival for refund. **Credit Cards** All major credit cards accepted. **Check-In/Out** 3 p.m./noon. Early check-in and late checkout available on request.

Sheraton Princess Kaiulani $$$$

OVERALL ★★★★ | QUALITY ★★★★ | VALUE ★★ | ZONE I

120 Kaiulani Avenue, Honolulu, HI 96815; (800) 782-9488 or (808) 922-5811; fax: (808) 931-4577; www.princess-kaiulani.com

Named after Hawaii's beloved Princess Victoria Kaiulani, last heir to the Hawaiian throne, this hotel is situated on the site of her garden estate, Ainahau, where the princess spent her childhood.

The Princess Kaiulani has 1,150 rooms in three separate wings—Princess, Kaiulani, and Ainahau—surrounded by lobby areas, specialty shops, and gardens. The lobby area is airy, bright, and busy during the day. Original artwork and mementos from the era of Princess Kaiulani are displayed throughout the hotel. Arts and crafts demonstrations are done daily, and poolside entertainment is provided nightly. The hotel offers *Creation—A Polynesian Odyssey* dinner show in Ainahau Showroom (see page 441).

SETTING & FACILITIES

Location In Waikiki, next to the International Market Place, across the street from Waikiki Beach. **Dining** Momoyama serves Japanese specialties in a traditional setting, Lotus Moon features an extensive Chinese menu. **Amenities & Services** Room service, swimming pool, valet parking ($15), self-parking ($8/day), coin-operated laundry machines.

ACCOMMODATIONS

Rooms 1,150. Includes 12 suites; 13 ADA-approved rooms and 6 rooms with roll-in showers. Smoking-designated areas are available. **All Rooms** A/C, cable TV, mini-fridge, in-room safe ($4/day), hair dryer. **Some Rooms** Lanai. **Comfort & Decor** Spacious, very clean. Simple but pleasant decor reflects island accents.

PAYMENT, RESERVATIONS, & RESTRICTIONS

Family Plan Children age 17 and under stay free in room with parents if using existing bedding. Maximum of 4 people/room. **Deposit** 1-night deposit or credit card guarantee. Cancellation notice must be given by 6 p.m. on date of scheduled arrival for refund. **Credit Cards** All major credit cards accepted. **Check-In/Out** 3 p.m./noon. Early check-in and late checkout available on request (no guarantees).

Sheraton Waikiki $$$$$

OVERALL ★★★★ | QUALITY ★★★★ | VALUE ★★ | ZONE 1

2255 Kalakaua Avenue, Honolulu, HI 96815; (800) 782-9488 or (808) 922-4422; fax: (808) 923-8785; www.sheraton-waikiki.com

With its entire second floor dedicated to meetings and featuring Waikiki's largest indoor ballroom (26,000 square feet), this busy beach hotel is the second largest in the state—a 30-story wall of rooms full of conventioneers. The main lobby's centerpiece is a striking collection of colorful, ocean-themed glass sculptures, from fish and sharks to sea turtles. It personifies the hotel as a whole: pleasant but not stuffy. Hawaiian entertainment is provided nightly. For club-goers, the Sheraton offers Esprit nightclub.

SETTING & FACILITIES

Location On Waikiki Beach. **Dining** Up on the 30th floor, Hanohano is renowned for its incredible views (it has the highest vantage point on Waikiki Beach) and award-winning Continental menu. Other restaurants include Ciao, serving Italian cuisine, and Ocean Terrace, with buffets with various international themes. **Amenities & Services** Valet parking ($15), self-parking ($10/day), meeting facilities, secretarial business services, nightly poolside entertainment, fitness center, travel services, daily children's program.

ACCOMMODATIONS

Rooms 1,852. Includes 127 suites; 10 rooms for the disabled. Most rooms are nonsmoking. **All Rooms** A/C, private lanai, color TV with first-run movies, clock radio, minibar, refrigerator, in-room safe, safety deposit box, in-room video message and checkout facilities, room service, coffeemakers. **Some Rooms** Full kitchen. **Comfort & Decor**

Rooms feature high ceilings, spacious bathrooms, a complete line of amenities, and stylish furnishings with island-accented decor.

PAYMENT, RESERVATIONS, & RESTRICTIONS

Family Plan Children age 17 and under stay free in room with parents if using existing bedding. **Deposit** Credit card guarantee or 1-night deposit required. Cancellation notice must be given before 6 p.m. on scheduled day of arrival for refund. **Credit Cards** All major credit cards accepted. **Check-In/Out** 3 p.m./noon. Hospitality suite available for early arrivals and late departures.

Turtle Bay Golf & Tennis Resort $$$

OVERALL ★★★★ | QUALITY ★★★½ | VALUE ★★★ | ZONE 4

57-091 Kamehameha Highway, Kahuku, HI 96731; (800) 445-8667 or (808) 293-8811; fax: (808) 293-9147; www.turtlebayresort.com

Situated on Oahu's North Shore, the Turtle Bay rests on a scenic peninsula that juts into the Pacific. It's far removed from Waikiki but still has all the creature comforts.

A former Hilton, it was sold after a major face-lift and now the new owner may cinch up its laid-back service. Atmosphere is comfortable and relaxed. Hawaiian entertainment is provided at the Bay View Lounge, with dancing on weekends. A choice spot for golfers and tennis players, the resort also offers snorkeling and horseback riding.

SETTING & FACILITIES

Location On Oahu's North Shore, at the tip of Kuilima Point. The hotel is near the North Shore's best surfing spots and beaches, including the legendary Banzai Pipeline. **Dining** The Palm Terrace serves breakfast, lunch, and dinner daily, including theme buffets. **Amenities & Services** Room service, laundry service, valet and self-parking, swimming pool and Jacuzzi, exercise room, activity desk, tennis, golf, horseback riding.

ACCOMMODATIONS

Rooms 485. Includes 26 suites; 5 rooms for the disabled. Nonsmoking rooms available. **All Rooms** A/C, cable TV, refrigerator, in-room safe, coffeemaker, dataport. **Comfort & Decor** Very spacious and clean, and rooms feature well-maintained light tropic colors, Hawaiian artwork, and tropical plants.

PAYMENT, RESERVATIONS, & RESTRICTIONS

Family Plan Children age 17 and under stay free in room with parents if using existing bedding. **Deposit** 1-night deposit or credit card guarantee required. Cancellation notice must be given 48 hours prior to scheduled arrival for refund. **Credit Cards** All major credit cards accepted. **Check-In/Out** 3 p.m./11 a.m. Early check-in and late checkout available for fee ($25 for 2 p.m. check-in, $50 for 5 p.m. checkout).

W Honolulu–Diamond Head $$$$

OVERALL ★★★★ | QUALITY ★★★★ | VALUE ★★ | ZONE 1

2885 Kalakaua Avenue, Honolulu, HI 96815; (888) 924-7873 or (808) 924-3111; fax: (808) 923-2249; www.whotels.com

Formerly known as the Colony Surf Hotel, this small hotel is a hidden gem nestled at the foot of Diamond Head. The setting here is not beachfront, but it is peaceful and calm—a far cry from the nonstop action in the center of Waikiki. The service is very personal and friendly, about what you would expect of a hotel of this size. The views here are eye-catching no matter what room you're in, and if you decide to stay here, spend at least one evening at Diamond Head Grill, one of Oahu's best restaurants. Waikiki Aquarium and Honolulu Zoo are a block or two away.

SETTING & FACILITIES

Location Diamond Head end of Waikiki, short walk to beach. **Dining** Diamond Head Grill serves New American cuisine. **Amenities & Services** Room service, laundry service, valet parking ($15).

ACCOMMODATIONS

Rooms 48 **All Rooms** A/C, radio, TV, refrigerator, lanai, minibar, coffeemaker, hair dryer. **Some Rooms** 2 bedrooms. **Comfort & Decor** Spacious and clean, the rooms' understated Balinese-style decor reflects tropical ambience. Sunny colors add to the overall pleasant look of the interiors.

PAYMENT, RESERVATIONS, & RESTRICTIONS

Family Plan Rollaway bed, $45. **Deposit** Credit card guarantees reservation. Cancellation notice must be given 72 hours prior to scheduled arrival for refund. **Credit Cards** All major credit cards accepted. **Check-In/Out** 3 p.m./noon. Early check-in and late checkout okay if available.

Waikiki Beachcomber Hotel $$$

OVERALL ★★★★ | QUALITY ★★★ | VALUE ★★½ | ZONE 1

2300 Kalakaua Avenue, Honolulu, HI 96815; (800) 622-4646 or (808) 922-4646; fax: (808) 923-4889; www.waikikibeachcomber.com

Although not as well known as many of Waikiki's name-brand hotels, the Beachcomber has a lot going for it. One asset is its front-and-center location in the heart of Waikiki, next to the International Market Place, where you can find bargains on all kinds of souvenirs and gifts, and directly across Kalakaua Avenue from the upscale Royal Hawaiian Shopping Center. The beach is also across the street, about a block away. The small lobby area displays a large pair of saltwater aquariums as well as striking Hawaiian artworks, including paintings, portraits, and framed Hawaiian quilts. We like the second-floor pool deck overlooking Kalakaua Avenue. The Beachcomber is the home of the *Don Ho Show* and the *Magic of Polynesia* (see page 441).

SETTING & FACILITIES

Location In the heart of Waikiki, across street from beach. **Dining** Hibiscus Café serves everything from burgers and pizzas to a wide selection of international specialties. **Amenities & Services** Maid service, parking ($9/day), washer and dryer, swimming pool, ice machine.

ACCOMMODATIONS

Rooms 500. Includes 7 suites; 7 wheelchair-accessible rooms. Nonsmoking rooms available on request. **All Rooms** A/C, cable TV with in-room movies, lanai, refrigerator, in-room safe, voice mail, coffeemaker. **Some Rooms** 2 TV sets, 2 balconies, king-sized bed. **Comfort & Decor** Spacious and clean. Soft tropical colors lead to a soothing and relaxing atmosphere. Decor is simple but pleasant, with Hawaiian paintings adorning the walls.

PAYMENT, RESERVATIONS, & RESTRICTIONS

Family Plan Children age 17 and under stay free in room with parents if using existing bedding. Rollaway bed, $30/night. Maximum of 4 people/room. **Deposit** 1-night deposit due no later than 10 days after confirmation. Cancellation notice must be given 72 hours prior to scheduled arrival for refund. **Credit Cards** All major credit cards accepted. **Check-In/Out** 3 p.m./noon. Additional charge for early check-in of 50% the 1-day rack rate (guarantees check-in at 10 a.m.).

Waikiki Beach Marriott Resort $$$$

OVERALL ★★★★ | QUALITY ★★★★ | VALUE ★★ | ZONE I

2552 Kalakaua Avenue, Honolulu, HI 96815; (800) 367-5370 or (808) 922-6611; fax: (808) 921-5222; www.marriott.com

One of Hawaii's larger hotels, the former Hawaiian Regent is now the Waikiki Beach Marriott Resort, with a fresh new look. All public areas and rooms in the Kuhio Tower were redone in a tropical style with new art and furnishings. Hospitality here is warm and friendly. Another definite plus is the hotel's family-friendly location: Kuhio Beach Park (part of Waikiki Beach) is just a walk across the street (the ocean views from the hotel are dazzling), the Damien Museum is next door, and Kapiolani Park and the Honolulu Zoo are also nearby. One of Waikiki's more popular nightspots, Eurasia, is on the first floor of the hotel's Kalakaua Tower. You can enjoy Hawaiian entertainment nightly at the lobby bar.

SETTING & FACILITIES

Location Across the street from Waikiki Beach, 1 block from Honolulu Zoo. **Dining** Acqua serves cuisine which combines Mediterranean and Pacific Rim flavors. **Amenities & Services** Room service, laundry, parking, business center, fitness center.

ACCOMMODATIONS

Rooms 1,308. Includes 6 suites; 4 nonsmoking floors; 18 ADA-approved rooms. **All Rooms** A/C, TV, in-room safe, refrigerator, lanai; hair dryer and coffeemaker available on request. **Some Rooms** More space, upgraded amenities. **Comfort & Decor** Tastefully appointed, medium-sized rooms have island-accented furnishings and decor.

PAYMENT, RESERVATIONS, & RESTRICTIONS

Family Plan Children age 17 and under stay free in room with parents if using existing bedding. **Deposit** Credit card guarantee or 1-night deposit within 10 days of booking to guarantee reservation. **Credit Cards** All major credit cards accepted except Diner's Club. **Check-In/Out** 3 p.m./noon. Early check-in and late checkout available on request.

Waikiki Joy Hotel $$$

OVERALL ★★★★ | QUALITY ★★★½ | VALUE ★★★ | ZONE I

320 Lewers Street, Honolulu, HI 96815; (800) 922-7866 or (808) 923-2300; fax: (808) 924-4010; res.joy@aston-hotels.com; www.aston-hotels.com

This is one of Waikiki's best boutique hotels. Its location puts you near the action in Waikiki, but the beach is a couple of blocks away. The Italian marble open-air lobby sets the tone, but what makes it special are lavish touches in the rooms, half of which are suites with kitchenette facilities. Music lovers will appreciate the impressive stereo system in guest rooms, and each room features its own Jacuzzi tub. Every guest receives a free hour at the property's G. S. Studio, a karaoke center with 15 private rooms and more than 4,000 songs to select.

SETTING & FACILITIES

Location In the center of Waikiki, a block mauka of Kalakaua Avenue, 15-minute walk to beach. **Dining** Cappucinos Café serves lunch and dinner. **Amenities & Services** Laundry service, valet parking ($10).

ACCOMMODATIONS

Rooms 94. Includes 47 suites; 2 wheelchair-accessible rooms and 1 room with roll-in shower. Nonsmoking rooms available on request. **All Rooms** A/C, stereo entertainment center, cable TV, Jacuzzi, mini-fridge, hair dryer, dataport, voice mail, 1 hour free karaoke. **Some Rooms** Full kitchen. **Comfort & Decor** Spacious, ultra-luxurious, and clean. Rooms have their own marble entries, a state-of-the-art entertainment system with Bose speakers, and private Jacuzzis.

PAYMENT, RESERVATIONS, & RESTRICTIONS

Family Plan Children age 18 and under stay free in room with parents if using existing bedding. **Deposit** Credit card required, 1-night deposit will be charged. Cancellation notice must be given 72 hours prior to scheduled arrival for refund. **Credit Cards** All major credit cards accepted. **Check-In/Out** 3 p.m./noon. Early check-in and late checkout available on request (no guarantees).

Waikiki Parc Hotel $$$

OVERALL ★★★★ | QUALITY ★★★★ | VALUE ★★★½ | ZONE 1

2233 Helumoa Road, Honolulu, HI 96815; (800) 422-0450 or (808) 921-7272; fax: (808) 931-6638; www.waikikiparc.com

The Halekulani's little sister, this hotel isn't visually appealing—it's crammed in among its neighboring properties—but it has some practical advantages, like being near the Royal Hawaiian Shopping Center. It's also about 100 yards from the beach. If you want tastefulness without an ocean view, the Waikiki Parc might be for you.

SETTING & FACILITIES

Location In Waikiki, across from Halekulani, a short walk to beach. **Dining** The Parc Café's buffets are popular with visitors and residents alike. Kacho serves traditional Japanese fare. **Amenities & Services** Room service, laundry service, parking, concierge desk, business facilities.

ACCOMMODATIONS

Rooms 298. Includes 3 floors of nonsmoking rooms; 1 room equipped for the disabled. **All Rooms** A/C, cable TV, 2 phones, mini-fridge, in-room safe, hair dryer; hot pots available on request. **Some Rooms** Lanai. **Comfort & Decor** Spacious and well-maintained rooms have tile floors with plush carpeting, shutters, tinted glass lanai doors, and custom rattan furnishings. Color scheme is soft shades of white with accents of Pacific blue.

PAYMENT, RESERVATIONS, & RESTRICTIONS

Family Plan Children age 14 and under stay free in room with parents if using existing bedding. Maximum of 3 people/room. **Deposit** Credit card guarantee or 1-night deposit due within 14 days of booking. Cancellation notice must be given 72 hours prior to scheduled arrival for refund. **Credit Cards** All major credit cards accepted. **Check-In/Out** 3 p.m./noon. Early check-in and late checkout available on request (may be charged, depending on length).

Waikiki Terrace Hotel $$$$

OVERALL ★★★½ | QUALITY ★★★½ | VALUE ★★ | ZONE 1

2045 Kalakaua Avenue, Honolulu, HI 96815; (800) 367-5004 or (808) 955-6000; fax: (808) 943-8555; www.castle-resorts.com

Three blocks from the beach, this affordable hotel neighbors Fort DeRussy and the King Kalakaua Plaza shopping/restaurant complex. The Waikiki Terrace recently renovated all 242 of its guest rooms and suites. Service is friendly and enthusiastic, and the atmosphere is comfortable. Overall, a good value.

SETTING & FACILITIES

Location At the gateway to Waikiki, next to Ft. DeRussy, 10-minute walk to beach. **Dining** The Eastern Garden serves breakfast, lunch, and dinner. **Amenities & Services** Room service, laundry and dry cleaning, swimming pool, Jacuzzi, business center, fitness center, parking ($9/day).

ACCOMMODATIONS

Rooms 242. Includes 2 suites; 7 ADA-approved rooms. Nonsmoking rooms available. **All Rooms** A/C, cable TV, mini-fridge, lanai, in-room safe, hot pot, hair dryer. **Some Rooms** Separate sleeping quarters, extra bathroom. **Comfort & Decor** Medium-sized rooms are clean and comfortable with soft colors and subtle island accents and decor.

PAYMENT, RESERVATIONS, & RESTRICTIONS

Family Plan Children age 17 and under stay free with parents. **Deposit** Credit card guarantee or 1-night cash deposit due 14 days after booking. Prepay entire stay plus $50 deposit at registration. Cancellation notice must be given 72 hours prior to scheduled arrival for refund. **Credit Cards** All major credit cards accepted. **Check-In/Out** 3 p.m./noon. Early check-in and late checkout available on request.

Maui

Embassy Vacation Resort $$$$$

OVERALL ★★★★½ | QUALITY ★★★★ | VALUE ★★½ | ZONE 9

104 Kaanapali Shores Place, Lahaina, HI 96761; (800) 669-3155 or (808) 661-2000; fax: (808) 667-5821; www.mauiembassy.com

Opened in 1988, this was the first Hawaii property to offer all-suite accommodations. Ninety percent of the suites provide ocean views (you can also see the neighboring islands of Molokai and Lanai). A variety of island-flavored art adorns the resort's lobby. A popular feature here is the 42-foot water slide, which plops you straight into a one-acre swimming pool. The young ones can participate in Beach Buddies, the resort's year-round children's program (for ages 5–12), which includes lei making, beachcombing, coconut weaving, and other activities. A miniature golf course is also on the premises, although serious golfers may prefer taking on the championship courses located elsewhere at the Kaanapali Resort.

SETTING & FACILITIES

Location On Kaanapali Beach. **Dining** The North Beach Grille serves steaks, seafood, chicken, and other American favorites. **Amenities & Services** Room service, laundry and housekeeping service, workout room, parking, children's day care.

ACCOMMODATIONS

Rooms 413. All suites. 12 ADA-approved rooms. Most rooms are designated nonsmoking. **All Rooms** A/C, cable TV, VCR, microwave, mini-fridge, in-room safe, hair dryer. **Comfort & Decor** Extremely spacious suites (over 800 square feet) have separate living rooms. An oversized soaking tub, separate shower, walk-in closets, dual marble vanities, and 35-inch-screen TV are among the luxuries. Decor has cool tropical appeal; cheerful and airy.

PAYMENT, RESERVATIONS, & RESTRICTIONS

Family Plan Children age 17 and under stay free in room with parents if using existing bedding. **Deposit** 1-night deposit due within 10 days of booking. Cancellation notice must be given 72 hours prior to scheduled arrival for refund. **Credit Cards** All major credit cards accepted. **Check-In/Out** 4 p.m./11 a.m. Early check-in and late checkout available on request. Hospitality suite available for early arrivals and late departures.

Fairmont Kea Lani Hotel, Suites & Villas $$$$$

OVERALL ★★★★½ | QUALITY ★★★★ | VALUE ★★★ | ZONE 8

4100 Wailea Alanui Drive, Wailea, HI 96753; (866) 540-4457 or (808) 875-4100; fax: (808) 875-1200; info@kealani.com; www.kealani.com

This all-suite hotel features an extensive menu of in-room amenities, including a complete entertainment system. The hotel's open-air, stark white, Arabian-nights fantasy architecture is bold, but inside the resort evokes a quaint village feel. Children ages 5–12 can participate in Keiki Lani, the hotel's year-round children's program, which features hula and lei-making lessons and swimming. The hotel has two marvelous swimming lagoons that are connected by a 140-foot water slide and swim-up beverage bar. One tasty feature on the property is the Organic Garden, which features more than 150 varieties of produce, including 18 varieties of rare exotic fruits. (The produce is used in the hotel's restaurants; inquire about a guided garden tour.) Readers of *Condé Nast Traveler* voted the Kea Lani one of the top five resorts in the Pacific region.

SETTING & FACILITIES

Location On Polo Beach. **Dining** Nick's Fishmarket Maui is a popular seafood bistro, with fine dining under the stars on its terrace. Caffe Ciao serves Italian cuisine in a garden setting. **Amenities & Services** Spa and fitness center, 3 swimming pools, tennis, golf, children's program, indoor and outdoor meeting/conference space.

ACCOMMODATIONS

Rooms 413. All suites. Includes 37 oceanfront villas; 201 nonsmoking suites; 11 suites for the disabled. **All Rooms** A/C, cable TV, stereo entertainment center (with CD player, VCR, and laser disc player), private lanai. **Some Rooms** Private villas with pool, gourmet kitchen, sun deck, barbecue grill, extra bedrooms. **Comfort & Decor** Soft tropical colors provide cheerful ambience to very spacious suites, with separate living rooms. Exceptionally clean, suites feature luxurious furnishings with island-themed artworks and large European marble bathroom with soaking tub and twin pedestal sinks.

PAYMENT, RESERVATIONS, & RESTRICTIONS

Family Plan Children age 18 and under stay free in room with parents if using existing bedding. Rollaway bed, $30. **Deposit** 2-night deposit due within 14 days after booking. Cancellation notice must be given 72 hours prior to scheduled arrival for refund. **Credit Cards** All major credit cards accepted. **Check-In/Out** 4 p.m./noon. Early check-in and late checkout available on request.

Four Seasons Resort Maui $$$$$

OVERALL ★★★★★ | QUALITY ★★★★★ | VALUE ★★★ | ZONE 8

3900 Wailea Alanui Drive, Wailea, HI 96753; (800) 334-6284 or (808) 874-8000; fax: (808) 874-6449; resmaui@fourseasons.com; www.fourseasons.com

Condé Nast Traveler magazine named the Four Seasons the "Top Tropical Resort in the World" in 1993, and this luxurious resort continues to rate high among travel experts and patrons. (The resort garnered the AAA Five Diamond Award in 1999.) The breezy, open lobby is testament to the resort's island-accented architectural design, which includes commissioned reproductions of early Hawaiian furniture as well as Hawaii-inspired paintings, sculptures, and other artwork. On-site features include a children's program, health club, game room, and salon. The service is professional and courteous. To top it all off, the Four Seasons is located at Wailea Resort, which offers three championship golf courses and the 11-court Wailea Tennis Center (known as "Wimbledon West"). Overall, the Four Seasons has to rate as one of the best resorts (if not the very best) on Maui.

SETTING & FACILITIES

Location On Wailea Beach. **Dining** Spago, Ferraro's, and Pacific Grill. **Amenities & Services** 24-hour room service, full laundry service, workout facilities, salon, business center, children's program, game room.

ACCOMMODATIONS

Rooms 380. Includes 75 suites. ADA-approved and nonsmoking rooms available. **All Rooms** A/C, cable TV, VCR, lanai, in-room safe, minibar, hair dryer, dataport, robes. **Some Rooms** Fax machines, extra bedroom. **Comfort & Decor** Very spacious, exceptionally comfortable, and well maintained. Soft white and gentle sunset hues, deep-cushioned rattan and wicker furnishings, large bathrooms with marble counters and dual vanities, and island-themed artwork add to the warm atmosphere.

PAYMENT, RESERVATIONS, & RESTRICTIONS

Family Plan Children age 17 and under stay free in room with parents if using existing bedding. **Deposit** 1-night deposit due within 7 days of booking. Cancellation notice must be given 14 hours prior to scheduled arrival for refund during January 3–April 30; 7 days prior during May 1–December 18. **Credit Cards** All major credit cards accepted. **Check-In/Out** 3 p.m./noon. Early check-in and late checkout available on request.

Grand Wailea Resort Hotel & Spa $$$$$

OVERALL ★★★★½ | QUALITY ★★★★½ | VALUE ★★½ | ZONE 8

3850 Wailea Alanui Drive, Wailea, HI 96753; (800) 888-6100 or (808) 875-1234; fax: (808) 879-4077; info@gwrmail.com; www.grandwailea.com

Even if you don't stay here, this $600 million ultra-luxury resort is a worthy destination. Stroll through the 40-acre property to see six major design themes—flowers, water, trees, sound, light, and art. There's more than $30 million in artwork in public areas, including an exceptional collection of huge lounging Botero bronze sculptures in the lobby and an impressive collection of works by Hawaii artists commissioned for the resort. Among the features here are Camp Grande, a 20,000-square-foot children's facility; the 50,000-square-foot Spa Grande; a breathtaking wedding chapel (complete with stained glass windows); and a 2,000-foot-long river pool that includes valleys, water slides, waterfalls, caves, grottos, whitewater rapids, a Jacuzzi, a sauna, and the world's only "water elevator," which lifts guests from the lower-level pool to the higher-level pool. If you want opulence, this is it.

SETTING & FACILITIES

Location On Wailea Beach. **Dining** Kincha serves Japanese cuisine in a traditional setting that includes rocks imported from Mt. Fuji. Bistro Molokini offers fine Italian fare, and the Humuhumunukunukuapuaa specializes in fresh seafood in a romantic open-air atmosphere. It is situated in a tide pool–like pond, with tropical fish and its own set of bronze sculptures commissioned by Hawaiian artists. **Amenities & Services** Room service, full-service spa and fitness center, wedding chapel, extensive conference facilities with a separate entrance, 3 championship golf courses, complimentary scuba lessons, squash/racquetball court, valet parking ($10), excellent children's program, high-tech water complex and Hawaii's largest swimming pools (one with a man-made beach adjacent to the real beach). A $10/day resort fee is automatically charged to each room.

ACCOMMODATIONS

Rooms 761. Includes 52 suites; 10 rooms for disabled. Nonsmoking rooms available. **All Rooms** A/C, cable TV, lanai, in-room safe, honor bar, coffeemaker, hair dryer, robes, slippers. **Some Rooms** Larger accommodations, extra baths, 3-bedrooom suite. **Comfort & Decor** Very spacious, luxurious, with opulent furnishings and decor.

PAYMENT, RESERVATIONS, & RESTRICTIONS

Family Plan Children age 18 and under stay free in room with parents if using existing bedding. Rollaway bed, $30. Maximum 4 people/room. **Deposit** 2-night deposit required within 14 days of booking (or reservation will be automatically canceled). Cancellation notice must be given 72 hours prior to scheduled arrival for refund (14 days for suites). **Credit Cards** All major credit cards accepted. **Check-In/Out** 3 p.m./ noon. Early check-in and late checkout available on request.

Hotel Hana-Maui $$$$$

OVERALL ★★★★ | QUALITY ★★★★ | VALUE ★★ | ZONE 10

P.O. Box 9, Hana, HI 96713; (800) 321-4262 or (808) 248-8211; fax: (808) 248-7202; www.hotelhanamaui.com

What this cozy small hotel lacks (television and air-conditioning), it makes up for in charm, location, and friendly, attentive service. Hana sits on 66 acres of landscaped gardens, and the ocean and mountain views are, like Hana, heavenly. Remote, quiet, romantic, this is the epitome of a honeymoon hotel. A weekly luau is held on the beach. Available outdoor activities include horseback riding, hiking, snorkeling, bike riding, and historical tours. A wellness center offers everything from massages to yoga. A favorite celebrity haunt, the Hotel Hana-Maui can only get better since it's been purchased by the owner of the Post Ranch in California's Big Sur.

SETTING & FACILITIES

Location In Hana, east end of Maui, shuttle to Hamoa Beach. **Dining** The dining room serves Continental cuisine. **Amenities & Services** Room service (breakfast only), laundry service, parking, wellness center.

ACCOMMODATIONS

Rooms 65. Includes 7 suites. Nonsmoking suite available. **All Rooms** Wet bar, lanai, coffee- and tea-maker. **Some Rooms** Jacuzzis. **Comfort & Decor** Rooms are small to medium with comfortable atmosphere, bleached hardwood floors, wicker and bamboo furnishings, handmade quilts, and private patios.

PAYMENT, RESERVATIONS, & RESTRICTIONS

Family Plan Children age 12 and under stay free in room with parents if using existing bedding. **Deposit** 1-night deposit required. Cancellation notice must be given 72 hours prior to scheduled arrival for refund. **Credit Cards** All major credit cards accepted. **Check-In/Out** 3 p.m./noon. Early check-in and late checkout available on request.

Hyatt Regency Maui $$$$$

OVERALL ★★★★ | QUALITY ★★★★ | VALUE ★★½ | ZONE 9

200 Nohea Drive, Lahaina, HI 96761; (800) 233-1234 or (808) 661-1234; fax: (808) 667-4497; www.hyatt.com

At first glance, it's easy to stamp the Hyatt Maui as a typical Hyatt hotel, but dig a little deeper and you'll uncover some unusual features.

The hotel's nightly "Tour of the Stars" program gives guests a guided tour of the Hawaiian skies and allows them to peer through a state-of-the-art, computer-controlled 16-inch reflector telescope. A wildlife tour brings visitors face-to-face with the resort's menagerie of penguins, swans, parrots, macaws, flamingos, and koi. You can also tour the tropical gardens (it's about a two-mile walk) or browse the $2 million art collection. This hotel, one of the first fantasy-style hotels in the islands, offers something for travelers of all ages and interests, including a health spa. In 1996, the property underwent a $16 million renovation of all its guest rooms.

SETTING & FACILITIES

Location On Kaanapali Beach. **Dining** Romantic Swan Court features Continental cuisine with Pacific Rim flair by a pool with stately swans swimming up for a handout, Spats Trattoria serves Italian food, and Cascades Grille and Sushi Bar offers fresh seafood and steak. **Amenities & Services** Fitness center, tennis, golf, outdoor dinner theater, activities desk, children's program, shops, meeting and convention facilities, rooftop astronomy program.

ACCOMMODATIONS

Rooms 815. Includes 31 suites; 4 rooms for the disabled. Nonsmoking rooms available. **All Rooms** A/C, cable TV, honor bar, in-room safe, hair dryer, robes, coffeemaker. **Some Rooms** Living room, dining area, wet bar, refrigerator. **Comfort & Decor** Spacious and clean rooms have stylish earth and mauve Asian Pacific decor, comfortable furnishings, and attractive wall hangings.

PAYMENT, RESERVATIONS, & RESTRICTIONS

Family Plan Children age 17 and under stay free in room with parents if using existing bedding. Maximum 4 people/room. **Deposit** 2-night deposit due within 14 days after booking. Cancellation notice must be given 72 hours prior to scheduled arrival for refund. **Credit Cards** All major credit cards accepted. **Check-In/Out** 3 p.m./noon. Early check-in and late checkout based on availability.

Kaanapali Beach Hotel $$$$

OVERALL ★★★★ | QUALITY ★★★½ | VALUE ★★★ | ZONE 9

2525 Kaanapali Parkway, Lahaina, HI 96761; (800) 262-8450 or (808) 661-0011; fax: (808) 667-5978; info@kbhmaui.com; www.kaanapalibeachhotel.com

Located on one of the widest stretches of Kaanapali Beach, the Kaanapali Beach Hotel is called Maui's "most Hawaiian" hotel. The management and staff here, schooled in Hawaiian hospitality, pride themselves on their aloha spirit, and the smiles and friendliness are downright contagious. Modern amenities aside, everything here is reminiscent of the Islands' romantic plantation era. Four separate wings form a semicircle around a ten-acre courtyard. A variety of Hawaiian activities—including hula lessons, lei making, lau hala weaving, and ti leaf skirt making—are held daily, and employees provide Hawaiian entertainment three days a week. *Travel & Leisure* ranked this hotel tops for best value in Hawaii. For visitors seeking a hotel that places a strong emphasis on Hawaiian hospitality, look no further.

SETTING & FACILITIES

Location On Kaanapali Beach. **Dining** The Tiki Terrace Restaurant serves Continental and island cuisine. *Kupanaha Dinner Show,* 5:30 p.m. Sunday–Thursday, is a Polynesian show with magicians Jody and Kathleen Baran: $72–$83, adults, $52, children/students ages 13–20, $31, children ages 6–12. **Amenities & Services** Laundry service, valet parking ($9), self-parking ($6/day), children's program.

ACCOMMODATIONS

Rooms 430. Includes 14 suites. Nonsmoking rooms and rooms for the disabled available on request. **All Rooms** A/C, cable TV, in-room safe, refrigerator, coffeemaker. **Some Rooms** More space, upgraded amenities. **Comfort & Decor** Spacious, clean, and well maintained. Tropical green and golden sand hues accentuate the Hawaiian mood, along with Hawaiian quilt–style bedspreads, light tropical furniture, and local artwork.

PAYMENT, RESERVATIONS, & RESTRICTIONS

Family Plan Children age 17 and under stay free in room with parents if using existing bedding. Rollaway bed, $15. **Deposit** 1- or 2-night deposit due 10 days after booking. Cancellation notice must be given 3–7 days prior to scheduled arrival for refund. **Credit Cards** All major credit cards accepted. **Check-In/Out** 3 p.m./noon. Early check-in and late checkout available on request.

Kapalua Bay Hotel $$$$$

OVERALL ★★★★ | QUALITY ★★★★ | VALUE ★★ | ZONE 9

One Bay Drive, Kapalua, HI 96761; (800) 367-8000 or (808) 669-5656; fax: (808) 669-4694; www.kapaluabayhotel.com

The Kapalua Bay Hotel doesn't have the pedigree of its neighbor, the Ritz-Carlton Kapalua, but it is in the same worldly class and has the added advantage of fronting one of Maui's finest beaches. The hotel, a gracious veteran recently redone, blends into its natural surroundings and lush tropical gardens. Piano and Hawaiian music are provided nightly at the Lehua Lounge, located below the lobby area. The Kapalua Shops, a mini-mall of some 20 boutiques, shares the premises, and golf aficionados have a choice of three championship golf courses, one of which hosts the prestigious PGA Mercedes Open each January.

SETTING & FACILITIES

Location On Kapalua Bay, adjoining a perfect beach cove. **Dining** The Bay Club serves seafood specialties for lunch and dinner. Gardenia Court offers international fare, including Friday night seafood buffet and Sunday brunch. **Amenities & Services** Room service, laundry service, valet parking ($10), self-parking ($6/day), tennis courts, children's program, shops.

ACCOMMODATIONS

Rooms 194. Includes 12 suites; 1 floor designated for nonsmoking rooms; 6 rooms for the hearing impaired; 8 wheelchair-accessible rooms. **All Rooms** A/C, cable TV, in-room safe, minibar, lanai, 3 phones, hair dryer. **Some Rooms** Washer and dryer, Jacuzzi, second bedroom. **Comfort & Decor** Oversized rooms have natural colors and marble accents and large private lanai.

PAYMENT, RESERVATIONS, & RESTRICTIONS

Family Plan Children age 17 and under stay free in room with parents if using existing bedding. **Deposit** 1-night credit card guarantee (5-night deposit during the Christmas holidays). Cancellation notice must be given 72 hours prior to scheduled arrival for refund. **Credit Cards** All major credit cards accepted except Discover. **Check-In/Out** 3 p.m./noon. Early check-in and late checkout available on request.

Lahaina Inn $$

OVERALL ★★★★ | QUALITY ★★★ | VALUE ★★★½ | ZONE 9

127 Lahainaluna Road, Lahaina, HI 96761; (800) 669-3444 or (808) 661-0577; fax: (808) 667-9480; inntown@lahainainn.com; www.lahainainn.com

This hotel is proof that good things can come in small packages. Rick Ralston, founder and owner of the popular Crazy Shirts stores, is also a collector of fine antiques and other historic buildings. Ralston restored the dozen rooms of this historic inn; pieces from his personal collection furnish each individually decorated room. Because of the value of the furnishings, children under age 15 are not allowed at this inn. A complimentary Continental breakfast is served at the end of the hall every morning. The inn's close proximity to Front Street is a "good news, bad news" situation: It's good to be close to the action (Lahaina is the island's most bustling town), but it also tends to get noisy. Also, keep in mind that there are no TV sets at the inn.

SETTING & FACILITIES

Location In the heart of Lahaina, across from the waterfront, no beach. **Dining** David Paul's Lahaina Grill, one of Maui's best restaurants, serves New American cuisine. **Amenities & Services** Parking ($5/day), Continental breakfast.

ACCOMMODATIONS

Rooms 12. Includes 3 suites. All are nonsmoking rooms (smoking permitted on lanai). **All Rooms** A/C, ceiling fans. **Some Rooms** Lanai, full bath and shower, king-sized bed. **Comfort & Decor** Rooms are smallish and dimly lit, but well maintained and clean. Antique furnishings include restored brass and wood beds, period wall decorations, and wood armoires.

PAYMENT, RESERVATIONS, & RESTRICTIONS

Deposit 50% deposit required. Cancellation notice must be given 10 days prior to scheduled arrival for refund. **Credit Cards** All major credit cards accepted except Discover. **Check-In/Out** 3 p.m./11 a.m. Late checkout (until noon) on request.

Maui Marriott Resort $$$$

OVERALL ★★★★ | QUALITY ★★★★ | VALUE ★★ | ZONE 9

100 Nohea Kai Drive, Lahaina, HI 96761; (800) 763-1333 or (808) 667-1200; fax: (808) 667-8300; www.marriott.com

This is a full-service resort with a casual, family-oriented atmosphere and friendly service. Waterfalls, koi ponds, and tall coconut palms adorn the attractive grounds. A year-round children's program is available, as are Hawaiian crafts lessons and a full menu of recreational sports and activities. The Marriott also has one of the island's best luau, held almost nightly on the beach. A mini-mall with 20 shops is on the premises.

SETTING & FACILITIES

Location On Kaanapali Beach. **Dining** VaBene serves Italian cuisine, 3 meals daily. **Amenities & Services** Room service (until 10 p.m.), valet parking and self-parking ($8/day), nightly luau (except Monday), 2 swimming pools, 2 Jacuzzis, fitness center, coin-operated laundry service, meetings and convention facilities.

ACCOMMODATIONS

Rooms 606. Includes 16 suites; 14 rooms for the disabled. Nonsmoking rooms available. **All Rooms** A/C, cable TV, lanai, refrigerator, in-room safe, coffeemaker. **Some Rooms** Sofa sleeper, larger lanai, separate dressing area. **Comfort & Decor** Spacious rooms have tasteful furnishings and island artwork. Soft, pastel colors add to the overall pleasant ambience.

PAYMENT, RESERVATIONS, & RESTRICTIONS

Family Plan Children age 17 and under stay free in room with parents if using existing bedding. Maximum of 2 adults and 2 children/room. **Deposit** Credit card guarantee. Cancellation notice must be given 72 hours prior to scheduled arrival for refund. **Credit Cards** All major credit cards accepted. **Check-In/Out** 3 p.m./noon. Early check-in and late checkout available on request (no guarantees).

Maui Prince Hotel *$$$$*

OVERALL ★★★★ | QUALITY ★★★½ | VALUE ★★ | ZONE 8

5400 Makena Alanui, Kihei, HI 96753; (800) 321-6248 or (808) 874-1111; fax: (808) 879-8763; www.princehawaii.com

Situated on the shore below the cool slopes of Mount Haleakala and fronting lovely Maluaka Beach, this 1,800-acre resort is an isolated haven on the edge of wilderness. The picturesque grounds offer an interior courtyard with a koi pond and waterfall, which adds to the resort's tranquil, understated atmosphere. All rooms have views of the ocean as well as the neighboring islands of Molokai, Lanai, and Kahoolawe. The service here is impeccable. Snorkeling and scuba diving are among the outdoor activities available; there are six tennis courts nearby at the Makena Tennis Club, and two championship golf courses. A hula show is presented at the oceanfront Molokini Lounge. Resort shuttles run between the sports facilities, the hotel, and nearby Wailea Resort's shopping village.

SETTING & FACILITIES

Location In Makena in south Maui, short walk to Makena Beach. **Dining** The Prince Court features Continental and island cuisine; Hakone offers traditional Japanese fare and a sushi bar. **Amenities & Services** Room service, welcome baskets on arrival, laundry service, fitness center, parking, children's program.

ACCOMMODATIONS

Rooms 310. Includes 19 suites; 5–10 rooms for the disabled. Nonsmoking rooms available. **All Rooms** A/C, cable TV, lanai, in-room safe, hair dryer, iron and board, bottled water, coffeemaker. **Some Rooms** Second bedroom. **Comfort & Decor** Spacious rooms have clean, simple decor with creamy pastel tones and island-themed artworks in a modern, casual setting.

PAYMENT, RESERVATIONS, & RESTRICTIONS

Family Plan Children age 17 and under stay free in room with parents if using existing bedding. Extra adult, $40. **Deposit** 1-night deposit required. Cancellation notice must be given 72 hours prior to scheduled arrival for refund. **Credit Cards** All major credit cards accepted. **Check-In/Out** 3 p.m./noon. Early check-in and late checkout available on request.

Renaissance Wailea Beach Resort $$$$

OVERALL ★★★★ | QUALITY ★★★★ | VALUE ★★ | ZONE 8

3550 Wailea Alanui Drive, Wailea, HI 96753; (800) 992-4532 or (808) 879-4900; fax: (808) 874-5370; www.renaissancehotels.com

Another jewel property in Wailea. Opened in 1978 as the Stouffer Wailea Beach Resort, this 15-acre property received a dramatic face-lift in 1990. The main lobby is made of marble and limestone and features hand-blown Italian glass fixtures and a grand stairway. Outside, the landscape is dotted with waterfalls and tropical flora. Golfers choose from three championship courses in Wailea, and tennis action is available at the 11-court Wailea Tennis Center. The Renaissance also offers a recreational rarity among Hawaii resorts: half-court basketball. For ambience and scenery, enjoy late-afternoon cocktails at the Sunset Terrace.

SETTING & FACILITIES

Location At Wailea Resort, on the beach. **Dining** The Palm Court features Mediterranean cuisine and buffets for dinner. Hana Gion is an intimate Japanese eatery. Sunset luau held in oceanside garden setting. **Amenities & Services** Room service, laundry service, valet parking, self-parking ($5/day), fitness center.

ACCOMMODATIONS

Rooms 345. Includes 12 suites. Rooms for the disabled and nonsmoking rooms available. **All Rooms** A/C, cable TV, VCR, private balcony, mini-fridge, hair dryer, coffeemaker. **Comfort & Decor** Spacious and clean; light colors and subtle tropical touches add to the bright atmosphere. Island-themed furnishings and artworks.

PAYMENT, RESERVATIONS, & RESTRICTIONS

Family Plan Children age 17 and under stay free in room with parents if using existing bedding. **Deposit** 1-night deposit due within 10 days of booking. Cancellation notice must be given 72 hours prior to scheduled arrival for refund. **Credit Cards** All major credit cards accepted. **Check-In/Out** 3 p.m./noon. Early check-in and late checkout available on request.

Ritz-Carlton, Kapalua $$$$$

OVERALL ★★★★★ | QUALITY ★★★★★ | VALUE ★★★½ | ZONE 9

One Ritz-Carlton Drive, Kapalua, HI 96761; (800) 241-3333 or (808) 669-6200; fax: (808) 669-2028; www.ritzcarlton.com

The Ritz is a perennial AAA Five Diamond Award recipient, and it's not hard to understand why. Everything here, from the service to guest rooms to dining, is perfect, with the exception of the weather, which can be surprisingly windy and cool. The atmosphere here is one of blissful luxury that isn't stuffy. Set on 50 acres, the Ritz features two six-story wings that step down the seaside slope, sheltering pools that step down with waterfalls in between. Public areas are enhanced by eighteenth- and nineteenth-century artwork as well as large murals, paintings, and ceramics created by local artists. Recently added to the property was a 19,200-square-foot special-function pavilion located adjacent to the hotel's entrance. The Ritz Kids program allows children (ages 5–12) to learn about Maui's culture, nature, art, and ecology. Evening entertainment is provided at the Terrace Restaurant and Lobby Lounge. Kapalua Resort has a trio of championship golf courses and ten tennis courts. The Ritz hosts several notable annual events, including the PGA Mercedes Championships (January), Celebration of the Arts (April), Kapalua Wine and Food Symposium (usually July), and the Earth Maui Nature Summit (September). The Ritz-Carlton Kapalua is currently the world's only Audubon Heritage Cooperative Sanctuary Resort Hotel.

SETTING & FACILITIES

Location At Kapalua Resort in West Maui, a short, but steep, walk to the beach. **Dining** The Anuenue Room, one of Maui's finest restaurants, features Hawaiian/Provençal cuisine with fresh island flavors, and enjoys a superlative view. The Terrace Restaurant serves a popular buffet for breakfast and fresh local seafood for dinner. It also serves a Friday night seafood buffet and Sunday night Italian buffet. **Amenities & Services** 24-hour room service, twice-daily maid service, laundry service, fitness center, spa treatments, multilevel swimming pool, hydrotherapy pools, business facilities, children's program, golf, tennis, ocean activities.

ACCOMMODATIONS

Rooms 548. Includes 58 suites. ADA-approved rooms and nonsmoking rooms available. **All Rooms** A/C, cable TV with pay movies, 3 phones, lanai, in-room safe, honor bar, hair dryer, dataport, robes. **Some Rooms** Personal concierge service, complimentary food and beverages. **Comfort & Decor** Oversized rooms are well maintained with warm colors, opulent tropical-inspired furnishings, Hawaiian artworks, and large private lanai (80% of rooms have ocean views).

PAYMENT, RESERVATIONS, & RESTRICTIONS

Deposit Cancel reservations 7 days prior to scheduled arrival for refund. **Credit Cards** All major credit cards accepted. **Check-In/Out** 3 p.m./noon. Early check-in and late checkout available on request (no guarantees).

Sheraton Maui *$$$$$*

OVERALL ★★★★ | QUALITY ★★★★ | VALUE ★★ | ZONE 9

2605 Kaanapali Parkway, Lahaina, HI 96761; (800) 782-9488 or (808) 661-0031; fax: (808) 661-0458; www.sheraton-maui.com

After extensive renovation, the Sheraton Maui is again a luxurious full-service resort. Its 23 acres comprise the premier real estate at Kaanapali Beach Resort—front and center, incorporating the volcanic landmark Black Rock into its architectural design (some facilities were built atop the rock). Its elevated lobby opens to a wide panorama of the Pacific Ocean and a spectacular 147-foot-long oceanfront swimming lagoon. Children ages 5–12 can participate in the Keiki Aloha Club (available during the summer), beach activities, and field trips to historic sites. Legendary Black Rock, a place where Hawaiians believed spirits of the dead departed this world, is considered one of the best snorkeling areas on Maui, and cliff divers used it for decades for spectacular sunset rituals.

SETTING & FACILITIES

Location On Kaanapali Beach. **Dining** The Coral Reef serves seafood specialties. Teppan Yaki Dan offers a noteworthy blend of European and Pacific cuisines (chefs prepare meals while you watch). **Amenities & Services** Swimming pool, room service, laundry facilities, valet parking ($15), self-parking ($10/day), fitness center, spa, children's program (summer). A $12/day resort fee is added to the room charge.

ACCOMMODATIONS

Rooms 510. Includes 46 suites; 15 rooms for the disabled. Nonsmoking rooms available. **All Rooms** A/C, cable TV, in-room safe, mini-fridge, coffeemaker, iron and board, hair dryer. **Some Rooms** Microwave, second TV, parlor. **Comfort & Decor** Spacious and well-maintained rooms have custom bedspreads, tropical furnishings, and large lanai. Hawaiian artwork adorns the walls, and fine Hawaiian crafts are displayed throughout the public areas.

PAYMENT, RESERVATIONS, & RESTRICTIONS

Family Plan Children age 17 and under stay free in room with parents if using existing bedding. **Deposit** 1-night deposit due 10 days after booking. Cancellation notice must be given 72 hours prior to scheduled arrival for refund. **Credit Cards** All major credit cards accepted. **Check-In/Out** 3 p.m./noon. Early check-in and late checkout available on request.

Wailea Marriott $$$$$

OVERALL ★★★★ | QUALITY ★★★★ | VALUE ★★★ | ZONE 8

3700 Wailea Alanui Drive, Wailea, HI 96753; (800) 688-7444 or (808) 879-1922; fax: (808) 874-8331; www.outrigger.com

Although it was opened as the Maui Inter-Continental Resort and formerly known as the Aston Wailea Resort, this oceanfront resort came under Outrigger management in early 1999 and underwent an extensive renovation after that. The resort's low-rise building design is a comfortable fit on 22 oceanfront acres. Lei-making classes and crafts demonstrations are offered regularly, and Hawaiian entertainment is provided nightly. Luau is staged four nights a week on the lawn. Arcade games, billiards, darts, and air hockey are among the diversions offered at Paani, a game bar. A shuttle provides transportation to the Maui Ocean Center, half an hour away in Maalea. Overall, the Wailea Marriott is a pleasant gem suitable for families and couples alike.

SETTING & FACILITIES

Location At Wailea Resort, on the beach. **Dining** Kuma Bar & Grill specializes in steak and seafood; poolside Hula Moons features lighter fare and popular island favorites. **Amenities & Services** Laundry service, children's program, parking, business facilities, game room.

ACCOMMODATIONS

Rooms 524. Includes 46 suites; 446 nonsmoking rooms; 10 rooms for the disabled. **All Rooms** A/C, cable TV, in-room safe, refrigerator, coffeemaker, hair dryer, iron and board. **Some Rooms** Robes. **Comfort & Decor** Very spacious, clean, well-appointed rooms have sunny pastels, attractive tropical furnishings, artwork, and private lanai.

PAYMENT, RESERVATIONS, & RESTRICTIONS

Family Plan Children age 17 and under stay free in room with parents if using existing bedding. **Deposit** 1-night deposit required. Cancellation notice must be given 72 hours prior to scheduled arrival for refund. **Credit Cards** All major credit cards accepted. **Check-In/Out** 3 p.m./noon. Early check-in and late checkout available on request.

Westin Maui $$$$$

OVERALL ★★★★ | QUALITY ★★★★ | VALUE ★★½ | ZONE 9

2365 Kaanapali Parkway, Lahaina, HI 96761; (800) 937-8461 or (808) 667-2525; fax: (808) 661-5764; www.westin.com

A fantasy resort, the Westin has an elaborate water complex, sculpture and art displayed throughout, parrots and macaws stationed by the flagstone walkways, and a breezy casual atmosphere overall. The most notable physical feature here is the 87,000-square-foot aquatic playground. There are five pools, three joined together by a pair of water slides, and two divided by a swim-through grotto with twin waterfalls and a hidden Jacuzzi. One of the pools is designated for adults only and features a swim-up bar. The Westin Kids Club provides supervised fun and games for the keiki. Island-style entertainment is provided nightly. For night owls, a side benefit of staying in Kaanapali is that it's just a five-minute drive away from Lahaina, where most of West Maui's after-dark action takes place.

SETTING & FACILITIES

Location On Kaanapali Beach. **Dining** Sen Ju features traditional Japanese delicacies. **Amenities & Services** Room service, laundry/valet service, parking, business center, health club, children's program.

ACCOMMODATIONS

Rooms 741. Includes 28 suites; 14 rooms for the disabled. Nonsmoking rooms available. **All Rooms** A/C, cable TV, balcony, minibar, in-room safe, coffeemaker, iron and board, hair dryer. **Some Rooms** Sofa bed in living room, upgraded amenities. **Comfort & Decor** Spacious and clean rooms feature light colors and comfortable furnishings in a modern setting. The ambience is classy without being stuffy.

PAYMENT, RESERVATIONS, & RESTRICTIONS

Family Plan Children age 17 and under stay free in room with parents if using existing bedding. Maximum of 4 people/room. **Deposit** 2-night deposit due within 15 days after booking. Cancellation notice must be given 72 hours prior to scheduled arrival for refund. **Credit Cards** All major credit cards accepted. **Check-In/Out** 3 p.m./noon. Early check-in and late checkout if available.

The Big Island of Hawaii

Fairmont Orchid $$$$$

OVERALL ★★★★½ | QUALITY ★★★★ | VALUE ★★ | ZONE 11

One N. Kaniku Drive, Kohala Coast, HI 96743; (800) 441-1414 or (808) 885-2000; fax: (808) 885-8886; www.fairmont.com

When Ritz-Carlton originally opened this property, they built a beautiful European hotel but forgot the Hawaiian touches. When people come to Hawaii they want something that looks like Hawaii. Now the Orchid delivers a Hawaiian "sense of place" and a first-class experience. Exquisite Hawaiian quilts and original artworks adorn the walls. Hawaii's native koa wood is used prominently, from elevator walls to stairway banisters. Other physical features at this U-shaped hotel (divided into two six-story wings) include a 10,000-square-foot swimming pool, a gold-sand beach, and jogging and walking trail. Children ages 5–12 can make new friends at the Keiki Aloha Program—call (800) 845-9905 ($60 per child, full day, lunch included; $40 per child, no lunch)—while adults relax at the Centre for Well-Being. The Orchid shares with Mauna Lani Resort access to two famous golf courses, a competition tennis complex, and the Puako petroglyph field and other historic features.

SETTING & FACILITIES

Location On the Kohala Coast, a short walk to beach. **Dining** The Grill offers fresh seafood specialties. The Orchid Court serves California cuisine and American favorites.

Brown's Beach House serves island fare with a "California twist." **Amenities & Services** Room service, twice-daily maid service, spa and fitness center, business facilities, concierge desk, swimming pool, golf, tennis, child care, daily newspaper. A daily resort fee of $12 is added to room charge.

ACCOMMODATIONS

Rooms 540. Includes 100 suites. **All Rooms** A/C, cable TV, lanai, 3 phones, honor bar, robes. **Some Rooms** Living room, extra bath, pullout sofa. **Comfort & Decor** Spacious and clean rooms have large Italian marble bathrooms, Hawaiian-accented decor with neutral tones and hand-crafted quilts, and private lanai.

PAYMENT, RESERVATIONS, & RESTRICTIONS

Family Plan Children age 18 and under stay free in room with parents if using existing bedding. **Deposit** Credit card guarantee only. Cancellation notice must be given 7 days prior to scheduled arrival for refund. **Credit Cards** All major credit cards accepted. **Check-In/Out** 4 p.m./noon. Early check-in and late checkout (up to 2 p.m.) available on request.

Four Seasons Resort Hualalai $$$$$

OVERALL ★★★★★ | QUALITY ★★★★★ | VALUE ★★½ | ZONE 11

P.O. Box 1269, Kailua-Kona, HI 96745; (888) 340-5662 or (808) 325-8000; fax: (800) 325-8200; www.fourseasons.com

Hawaii's newest resort is less a hotel than an exclusive hideaway. Sitting on a dramatic landscape formed by eruptions from Hualalai volcano some 200 years ago, this AAA Five Diamond property features 36 low-rise, ocean-view bungalows strategically organized to ensure quiet and privacy. Hawaiian works of art—some dating back to the eighteenth century—are displayed throughout the resort. Located below the lobby is one of our favorite features at Hualalai: the Kaupulehu Cultural Center, which presents Hawaii's culture and history through artwork, exhibits, video and audio recordings, and hands-on educational programs. An additional special plus is the sports club/fitness center/spa facility, and yet another is the natural amphitheater formed by lava.

Enjoy swimming and snorkeling in the King's Pond, a large black lava pool inspired by the natural tide pools and brackish onshore lava ponds of this coast. You'll share it with some 3,500 colorful reef fish. The pond was sculpted from an ancient lava flow and is fed by natural artesian springs as well as water from the sea. It's one of several pools around which the bungalows are clustered. Ocean swimming here is limited by rough, shallow, rocky conditions.

SETTING & FACILITIES

Location At Kaupulehu on Kohala Coast, beachfront. **Dining** Pahuia serves international and local specialties from its spectacular setting on the beach. **Amenities & Services** Valet and laundry service, self-serve washer and dryer, valet and self-parking, concierge service, Hawaiian cultural center, golf, tennis, 3 swimming pools, children's program.

ACCOMMODATIONS

Rooms 243. Includes 31 suites; 14 rooms for the disabled. Most rooms are designated nonsmoking. **All Rooms** A/C, color TV, refrigerated private bar, lanai, in-room safe, walk-in closets, fax line. **Some Rooms** Private, walled shower gardens afford the option of bathing indoors or out. Bathroom windows look into the private garden. **Comfort & Decor** The suites are our favorite rooms of any luxury hotel, done up in beautiful woods, warm-colored slate, plantation shutters, and plenty of Indo-Pacific tropical chic. Large bathrooms have oversized tubs and separate showers.

PAYMENT, RESERVATIONS, & RESTRICTIONS

Family Plan Children age 18 and under stay free in room with parents if using existing bedding. **Deposit** 1-night deposit due 7 days after booking. Cancellation notice must be given 14 days prior to scheduled arrival for refund Jan. 3–April 30, and 7 days prior to scheduled arrival May 1–Dec. 18. Greater deposit required during the Christmas holidays. **Credit Cards** All major credit cards accepted. **Check-In/Out** 3 p.m./noon. Early check-in and late checkout available on request.

Hapuna Beach Prince Hotel *$$$$$*

OVERALL ★★★★½ | QUALITY ★★★★ | VALUE ★★ | ZONE 11

62-100 Kaunaoa Drive, Kamuela, HI 96743; (800) 882-6060 or (808) 880-1111; fax: (808) 880-3142; www.hapunabeachprincehotel.com

The Hapuna Beach Prince Hotel is located next to its sister property, the Mauna Kea Beach Hotel. The layout of the property includes a large number of suites intermixed with guest rooms in buildings that ensure that every room has ocean views, a signature of Prince Hotels in Hawaii. Built with a contemporary design, the hotel includes an open foyer and lobby that provide a stunning view of Hapuna Beach, regarded as one of the best beaches in Hawaii. The fourth level of the hotel includes an indoor recreation area equipped with pool tables, table tennis, shuffleboard, foosball, board games, and a fully stocked bar (guests must be at least 21 years of age). There's a competition-sized pool. Ocean activities include swimming, snorkeling, scuba diving, sailing, and whale watching.

SETTING & FACILITIES

Location On the Big Island's Kohala Coast, overlooking Hapuna Beach. **Dining** Coast Grille specializes in fresh island seafood. Hakone serves traditional Japanese fare. The Ocean Terrace offers a wide menu of breakfast selections, including an extensive buffet. **Amenities & Services** Freshwater pool spa, Jacuzzi, welcome amenities, golf, water sports, beauty salon, game room, business services.

ACCOMMODATIONS

Rooms 350. Includes 36 luxury suites; 2 floors designated for nonsmoking; 10 rooms for the disabled. One suite is a separate 3-bedroom house. **All Rooms** A/C, cable TV, lanai, refrigerators, in-room safes. **Some Rooms** Sitting rooms, upgraded amenities. **Comfort & Decor** Spacious and attractive, all rooms have ocean views, soft tropical colors, island-accented furnishings, and artwork.

PAYMENT, RESERVATIONS, & RESTRICTIONS

Family Plan Children age 17 and under stay free in room with parents if using existing bedding. Maximum 2 adults and 2 children or 3 adults/room. **Deposit** 1-night deposit due 15 days after booking. Cancellation notice must be given 14 days prior to scheduled arrival for refund. **Credit Cards** All major credit cards accepted except Discover. **Check-In/Out** 3 p.m./noon. Early check-in and late checkout available on request.

Hawaii Naniloa Resort *$$*

OVERALL ★★★★ | QUALITY ★★★½ | VALUE ★★★ | ZONE 12

93 Banyan Drive, Hilo, HI 96720; (800) 367-5360 or (808) 969-3333; fax: (808) 969-6622; hinon@aloha.net; www.naniloa.com

At first glance, this bayside hotel doesn't look like much. The exterior is rather drab and unattractive, although the bay is picturesque. The lobby, on the other hand, is airy and adorned in pleasant pastels. What we like best about the Naniloa is its attentive service and facilities, including the excellent fitness center and spa featuring exercise equipment, an oceanfront aerobics studio, whirlpool, sauna, and steam room (body massages are also available). The swimming pool is large and inviting. All in all, the Naniloa is a good-value hotel that rivals the neighboring Hilo Hawaiian Hotel as the premier Hilo resort. The hotel is also the headquarters of the Merrie Monarch Festival, the world's most prestigious hula competition.

SETTING & FACILITIES

Location Fronting Hilo Bay, no beach. **Dining** Continental fare is served at the Sandalwood Room, and Ting Hao Seafood Restaurant offers sumptuous Chinese cuisine. **Amenities & Services** Courtesy airport transfer service, laundry service, gift and sundry shop, ice machine, safety deposit box (at front desk).

ACCOMMODATIONS

Rooms 325. Includes 20 suites; 3 floors with nonsmoking rooms; 1 floor for the disabled. **All Rooms** A/C, cable TV with pay movies. **Some Rooms** Kitchen. **Comfort & Decor** Rooms are small to medium, with attractive island decor and tasteful furnishings.

PAYMENT, RESERVATIONS, & RESTRICTIONS

Family Plan Children age 17 and under stay free in room with parents if using existing bedding. **Deposit** 1-night deposit due within 10 days of confirmation. Cancellation notice must be given at least 72 hours prior to scheduled arrival for refund. **Credit Cards** All major credit cards accepted. **Check-In/Out** 3 p.m./noon. Early check-in and late checkout available on request.

Hilo Hawaiian Hotel $$

OVERALL ★★★½ | QUALITY ★★★½ | VALUE ★★½ | ZONE 12

71 Banyan Drive, Hilo, HI 96720; (800) 367-5004 or (808) 935-9361
fax: (808) 961-9642; www.castle-group.com

The Hilo Hawaiian doesn't qualify as a luxury resort, but it still rates as one of the best hotels in Hilo. Its sloping arc design blends well with its surroundings, including Hilo Bay. Built in 1974 and renovated in 1992, the hotel has attractive rooms, a friendly staff, and a popular seafood buffet (it's even a favorite among locals), but nothing stands out as extraordinary. This is a good choice for travelers who plan to spend most of their time exploring the island and want a comfortable, clean, and affordable place to stay.

SETTING & FACILITIES

Location At Hilo Bay, no beach. **Dining** Queen's Court serves nightly seafood buffets. **Amenities & Services** Free parking, coin-operated laundry.

ACCOMMODATIONS

Rooms 286. Includes 18 suites; 7 wheelchair-accessible rooms. Half the rooms are designated nonsmoking. **All Rooms** A/C, cable TV, refrigerator, hair dryers, and iron and board available on request. **Some Rooms** Lanai, coffee, tea, miso soup. **Comfort & Decor** Spacious, mostly clean, and well-maintained rooms have simple furnishings with a few island-inspired artworks but dim lighting.

PAYMENT, RESERVATIONS, & RESTRICTIONS

Family Plan Children age 18 and under stay free in room with parents if using existing bedding. **Deposit** 1-night deposit or credit card guarantee within 10 days after booking. Cancellation notice must be given 72 hours prior to scheduled arrival for refund. **Credit Cards** All major credit cards accepted. **Check-In/Out** 3 p.m./noon. Early check-in and late checkout available on request.

Hilton Waikoloa Village $$$$$

OVERALL ★★★★½ | QUALITY ★★★★ | VALUE ★★ | ZONE 11

425 Waikoloa Beach Drive, Waikoloa, HI 96738; (800) 445-8667 or (808) 886-1234; fax: (808) 886-2900; waikoloa_rooms@hilton.com; www.hilton.com

Think of this 62-acre resort as an island-style Disneyland dedicated to vacation fun, complete with boat rides, lush tropical gardens, and encounters with some exotic but friendly creatures (ranging from parrots and macaws to Atlantic bottlenose dolphins). The Hilton Waikoloa, the ultimate creation of Hawaii's fantasy resort era of the late 1980s, consists of three separate towers surrounding a beautiful five-acre lagoon where the dolphins live and play. You can explore the hotel via canal boats or Swiss trams or by hoofing it on the mile-long museum walkway, which is adorned with a multimillion-dollar collection of Asian and Pacific replicated art. A daily lottery determines which lucky guests can get into the water and pet the dolphins and learn about these ocean mammals from a marine specialist. Another property that epitomizes the phrase *self-contained resort*, the Hilton Waikoloa has something for everyone: restaurants, swimming and beach activities at neighboring Anaehoomalu Beach, shops, a health spa, children's programs, luau, entertainment, golf, and tennis. Families with children, in particular, will love this resort.

SETTING & FACILITIES

Location In Waikoloa Beach Resort, oceanfront (no beach). **Dining** The Palm Terrace offers a wide range of international specialties. Donatoni's serves fine Italian cuisine. Imari features traditional Japanese fare. Kamuela Provision Company serves steak and seafood. **Amenities & Services** Room service, laundry service, valet parking ($8), business center, health spa, children's program, Dolphin Encounter program.

ACCOMMODATIONS

Rooms 1,241. Includes 57 suites. Rooms for the disabled and nonsmoking rooms available. **All Rooms** A/C, cable TV, lanai, honor bar, refrigerator, coffeemaker, in-room safe, hair dryer, iron and board. **Some Rooms** Second bedroom, upgraded amenities. **Comfort & Decor** Spacious rooms (standard rooms are 530 square feet) have bright atmosphere, lavish furnishings, and tasteful Hawaiian artwork.

PAYMENT, RESERVATIONS, & RESTRICTIONS

Family Plan Children age 18 and under stay free in room with parents if using existing bedding. **Deposit** 1- or 2-night deposit due at least 10 days before arrival. Cancellation notice must be given 72 hours prior to scheduled arrival for refund. **Credit Cards** All major credit cards accepted. **Check-In/Out** 3 p.m./noon. Early check-in and late checkout available on request (no guarantees).

King Kamehameha's Kona Beach Hotel $$$

OVERALL ★★★½ | QUALITY ★★★ | VALUE ★★★½ | ZONE 11

75-5660 Palani Road, Kailua-Kona, HI 96740; (800) 367-6060 or (808) 329-2911; fax: (808) 923-2566; www.konabeachhotel.com

King Kamehameha's Kona Beach Hotel sits next to historic grounds once home to royalty. In old Hawaii, high-ranking alii used this site as a summer retreat. Kamehameha the

Great himself made this his royal residence nearly two centuries ago. The focal point of this historic area is the Ahuena heiau, which dates back to the fifteenth century and was used for human sacrifices. The hotel is centrally located, within easy walking distance to restaurants, shops, and a small gold-sand beach. The hotel is also popular among kamaaina visiting from other islands.

SETTING & FACILITIES

Location In the heart of Kailua-Kona, on the (only) beach. **Dining** The Kona Beach Restaurant serves breakfast and dinner buffets, plus Sunday champagne brunch. **Amenities & Services** Free parking, room service, laundry facilities, swimming pool, Jacuzzi, tennis.

ACCOMMODATIONS

Rooms 457. Includes 12 suites; 10 rooms for the disabled. Nonsmoking rooms available. **All Rooms** A/C, cable TV, mini-fridge, in-room safe, coffeemaker, hair dryer, iron and board available on request. **Some Rooms** Refrigerator, pay movies. **Comfort & Decor** Medium-sized rooms with subdued colors, simple furnishings, and Hawaiian artworks.

PAYMENT, RESERVATIONS, & RESTRICTIONS

Family Plan Children age 18 and under stay free in room with parents if using existing bedding. **Deposit** Credit card guarantee or 1-night deposit required. Cancellation notice must be given at least 72 hours prior to scheduled arrival for refund. **Credit Cards** All major credit cards accepted. **Check-In/Out** 3 p.m./noon. Early check-in and late checkout (up to 1 p.m.) available on request.

Kona Village Resort $$$$$

OVERALL ★★★★½ | QUALITY ★★★★ | VALUE ★★ | ZONE 11

P.O. Box 1299, Kailua-Kona, HI 96745; (800) 367-5290 or (808) 325-5555; fax: (808) 325-5124; kvr@aloha.net; www.konavillage.com

The ultimate retreat. Set between black lava fields and the blue Pacific, isolated, tranquil Kona Village offers the great tropical escape. No other place comes close, except maybe neighboring Four Seasons Hualalai, but there the ambience is obviously upscale. Here, you'll pay handsomely too, for well-appointed but less fancy digs. This venerable resort, built in the mid-1960s when access was by boat or plane only, more closely echoes the old village on the same site where ancient fishermen once dwelt. Kona Village boasts a petroglyph field depicting symbols of life by the sea, including sailing and fishing, unique in the area. It has an ancient fishpond and ruins of houses among its clusters of guest quarters and enough specimen trees and Hawaiian medicinal plants to warrant a botanical tour. Lava fields on the mauka side keep the twenty-first century at a safe distance, but you can cross them in minutes via a gated road. No one cares whether the guests are CEOs (many are), famous authors (some write novels there), movie producers, or just folks. Kona Village offers the kind of hang-loose peace and quiet that restores souls. Kids are cherished in this camp-like compound, except in September when it's adults only.

This collection of huts of different Pacific Island architectural styles strewn along the coast does without televisions, radios, phones, and air-conditioning in the guest bungalows. (Phones are available by the office.) Each *hale*, or house, is a thatched-roof bungalow with king-sized beds, mini-fridge, lanai, and other choice amenities. Some have a hot tub on the lanai.

Upon arrival, you're greeted with a fresh flower lei and a glass of rum punch. Then you're set for an extraordinary holiday of total relaxation. Beach activities, snorkel sailing, spa, tennis, and a renowned Friday night luau are recreational options. Less is more here; you will know what we mean on the day you leave, reluctantly.

SETTING & FACILITIES

Location In Kaupulehu, 14 miles north of Kailua-Kona, fronting a beach cove. **Dining** Hale Moana serves a wide variety of international and American favorites for breakfast, al fresco lunch buffet, and dinner; the more formal Hale Samoa specializes in Pacific Rim cuisine. **Amenities & Services** Fitness center, beach facilities, tennis, complimentary programs for children ages 6–12, transportation to and from airport.

ACCOMMODATIONS

Rooms 125 hale. 8 rooms for the disabled. Smoking permitted in all hale. **All Rooms** Ceiling fan, lanai, mini-fridge, hair dryer, in-room safe, coffeemaker. No A/C, TV, or phone. **Some Rooms** Private whirlpool spa. **Comfort & Decor** Spacious, with high ceilings; furnishings are comfortable and simple, with a tropical motif in rich earth tones and tasteful island-themed art.

PAYMENT, RESERVATIONS, & RESTRICTIONS

Family Plan Children age 3 and under stay free. However, note that during months of May and September, children pay the adult rates. **Deposit** 2-night deposit due within 14 days of booking. Cancellation notice must be given 14 days prior to scheduled arrival for refund (60 days for the Easter holiday, 90 days for the Christmas holiday). **Credit Cards** All major credit cards accepted except Discover. **Check-In/Out** 3 p.m./ noon. Hospitality room available for early arrivals and late departures.

Mauna Kea Beach Hotel $$$$$

OVERALL ★★★★½ | QUALITY ★★★★ | VALUE ★★ | ZONE 11

62-100 Mauna Kea Beach Drive, Kamuela, HI 96743; (800) 882-6060 or (808) 882-7222; fax: (808) 882-5700; mkrres@maunakeabeachhotel.com; www.maunakeabeachhotel.com

The oldest Big Island resort—it opened in 1965—remains a favorite. The Mauna Kea keeps its loyal, graying clientele and adds their junior replacements with babes in arms. Three generations of guests have checked in to this grand old lady of the Kohala Coast. The open-air architectural design, art-stuffed halls, perfect gold-sand crescent beach, and old-fashioned Hawaiian hospitality all contribute to the enduring success of this luxury inn. Longtime patrons were concerned when the hotel was renovated, but it reopened with all its old charm intact. Golfers have their choice of the Mauna Kea Golf Course or the Hapuna Golf Course; tennis players can serve and volley at the oceanside Tennis Park, which features 13 Plexi-pave courts. Mauna Kea Stables offers Parker Ranch trail rides. After dinner, it's customary to wander down to the floodlit platform by the water where manta rays come to have their evening meal, smaller fish attracted to the lights.

SETTING & FACILITIES

Location On the Big Island's Kohala Coast, fronting Kauna Oa Beach, down a short incline from most rooms. **Dining** The Batik features classical Provence-inspired cuisine. The Pavilion offers Italian and Pacific Rim cuisine. The Terrace/Copper Bar serves steaks and fresh seafood. **Amenities & Services** Swimming pool, Jacuzzi, fitness center, maid service, golf, tennis, horseback riding, meeting facilities, beauty salon, children's program.

ACCOMMODATIONS

Rooms 310. Includes 10 suites; 10 rooms for the disabled. No nonsmoking rooms designated. **All Rooms** A/C, private lanai, clock radio, coffeemaker, TV (upon request). **Some**

Rooms 2 full baths, sitting room, 2 TVs. **Comfort & Decor** Very spacious. Classy tropical adornments include rattan furnishings. Original watercolors are among the island-themed artworks.

PAYMENT, RESERVATIONS, & RESTRICTIONS

Family Plan Children age 17 and under stay free in room with parents if using existing bedding. **Deposit** 1-night deposit due within 15 days after booking. Cancellation notice must be given 14 days prior to scheduled arrival for refund. **Credit Cards** All major credit cards accepted except Discover. **Check-In/Out** 3 p.m./noon. Early check-in and late checkout available on request (no guarantees).

Mauna Lani Bay Hotel & Bungalows $$$$$

OVERALL ★★★★½ | QUALITY ★★★★½ | VALUE ★★½ | ZONE 11

68-1400 Mauna Lani Drive, Kohala Coast, HI 96743; (800) 367-2323 or (808) 885-6622; fax: (808) 885-1484; reservations@maunalani.com; www.maunalani.com

A perennial AAA Five Diamond Award winner, the Mauna Lani is one of our favorite resorts—especially the bungalows.

Service is friendly, island-style hospitality gracious, and the site ideal for a beach resort. And if you're fortunate, you can a stay at one of the resort's five world-class bungalows, only $4,900 a night. Each 4,000-square-foot bungalow has two bedrooms, a private swimming pool, and 24-hour butler service.

The hotel's main structure directly faces the ocean and has an atrium-style design with waterfalls, ponds, trees, and flora. Golf, tennis, and water sports are among the outdoor diversions available here, and kids ages 5–12 can participate in Camp Mauna Lani, which offers lei making, hula dancing, history tours, and other activities. The resort hosts the annual Cuisines of the Sun, a summer food festival spotlighting cuisines from around the world. Don't miss the Puako petroglyph field beside the resort or the self-guided history tour of the ancient dwelling caves and fishpond by the hotel. Mauna Lani Resort's coastal path makes a nice morning or late afternoon walk.

SETTING & FACILITIES

Location On Big Island's Kohala Coast, fronting beach. **Dining** The Canoe House serves Pacific Rim cuisine. The poolside Ocean Grill features salads, gourmet pizza, fresh seafood. **Amenities & Services** 24-hour room service, twice-daily maid service, laundry and dry cleaning service, concierge service, meeting and banquet facilities, secretarial assistance, golf, tennis, spa, children's program.

ACCOMMODATIONS

Rooms 350. Includes 5 exclusive bungalows, 10 suites, 28 villas; 12 rooms for the disabled. Nonsmoking rooms available. **All Rooms** A/C, cable TV, VCR, private lanai, honor bar, in-room safe, refrigerator, clock radio, hair dryer, ceiling fan, flashlight, umbrella, robes, slippers. **Some Rooms** Bungalows have private swimming pool, 24-hour butler service, whirlpool spa. **Comfort & Decor** Very spacious and well kept, rooms reflect a tropical theme, with tasteful island decor and furnishings. Cool tones of white and beige, large private lanai (more than 90% of the rooms have ocean views), atrium gardens, and pools lend a peaceful, tropical atmosphere.

PAYMENT, RESERVATIONS, & RESTRICTIONS

Family Plan Children age 12 and under stay free in room with parents if using existing bedding. Maximum of 2 adults and 2 children or 3 adults/room. **Deposit** 2-night deposit required to guarantee reservation. Cancellation notice must be given at least

72 hours prior to scheduled arrival for refund (14 days for villas). **Credit Cards** All major credit cards accepted. **Check-In/Out** 3 p.m./noon. Early check-in and late checkout available on request.

Ohana Keauhou Beach Resort $$$

OVERALL ★★★★ | QUALITY ★★★½ | VALUE ★★½ | ZONE 11

78-6740 Alii Drive, Kailua-Kona, HI 96740; (800) 922-7866 or (808) 322-3441; fax: (808) 322-3117; www.ohanahotels.com

This ten-acre oceanfront property reopened in March 1999 after an extensive $15 million renovation to its guest rooms and public areas. It remains a favorite for kamaaina visiting from other islands. The resort also features several prominent historic Hawaiian sites, including heiau and a replica of King Kalakaua's vacation hale. Children are welcome to explore several on-site tidal pools, and adults can enjoy snorkeling, scuba diving, or tennis on six courts.

SETTING & FACILITIES

Location Oceanfront near Kahaluu Bay in Kailua-Kona. **Dining** Kamaaina Terrace serves local favorites, pork, chicken, and fish. **Amenities & Services** Daily maid service, fitness center, activities and travel desks, parking, swimming pool, sundry shop.

ACCOMMODATIONS

Rooms 311. Includes 6 suites; 4 floors with nonsmoking rooms; 14 rooms for the disabled. **All Rooms** A/C, cable TV, private lanai, clock radio, crib, hair dryer, iron and board, refrigerator available on request. **Some Rooms** Ceiling fans, bathtub. **Comfort & Decor** Spacious, with earthy tones, Hawaiian-style decor, and attractive wicker furnishings.

PAYMENT, RESERVATIONS, & RESTRICTIONS

Family Plan Children age 18 and under stay free in room with parents if using existing bedding. **Deposit** 1-night deposit due 10 days after booking. Cancellation notice must be given at least 72 hours prior to scheduled arrival for refund. **Credit Cards** All major credit cards accepted. **Check-In/Out** 3 p.m./noon. Early check-in and late checkout based on availability.

Volcano House $$

OVERALL ★★★½ | QUALITY ★★★ | VALUE ★★ | ZONE 12

P.O. Box 53, Hawaii Volcanoes National Park, HI 96718; (808) 967-7321; fax: (808) 967-8429

On the edge of a volcano, inside Hawaii Volcanoes National Park, this funky old lodge is a good place to stay if you plan to spend time at the park. The lobby features a warm fireplace (sometimes visited by Madame Pele herself) for those chilly nights, and the walls are covered with nostalgic photographs and paintings of Hawaiian royalty. The hotel's lone restaurant fills quickly with a busload of tourists during lunch hour.

SETTING & FACILITIES

Location Inside Hawaii Volcanoes National Park. **Dining** The Ka Ohelo Dining Room specializes in prime rib, and also features breakfast and lunch buffets. **Amenities & Services** Parking, snack shop.

ACCOMMODATIONS

Rooms 42. Includes 1 wheelchair-accessible room. All rooms permit smoking. **All Rooms** Portable heater, telephone. No TV. **Comfort & Decor** Spacious, with koa furnishings, Hawaiian comforters, and tasteful decor.

PAYMENT, RESERVATIONS, & RESTRICTIONS

Family Plan Children age 12 and under stay free in room with parents if using existing bedding. **Deposit** 1-night deposit due within 15 days of booking. Cancellation notice must be given at least 72 hours prior to scheduled arrival for refund. **Credit Cards** All major credit cards accepted. **Check-In/Out** 3 p.m./noon. Early check-in and late checkout available on request.

Waikoloa Beach Marriott $$$$

OVERALL ★★★★ | QUALITY ★★★½ | VALUE ★★★ | ZONE 11

69-275 Waikoloa Beach Drive, Waikoloa, HI 96738; (800) 688-7444 or (808) 886-6789; fax: (808) 886-7852; www.outrigger.com

Always the best bargain in a neighborhood of upscale beach hotels, the Waikoloa Beach Marriott is, after a $25-million renovation, now one of the best looking too. It always had the best location, overlooking Anaehoomalu Bay's fishponds and a picturesque gold-sand crescent beach framed by palm trees.

The reconstructed 15-acre property has a new open-air lobby, porte cochere, restaurant, lounge, and meeting rooms. The lobby overlooks the resort's pool and gardens, and cultural sites, such as the extensive petroglyph field near the hotel front and large ancient Hawaiian fishpond, add a sense of relevance and history. The King's Shops, one of the better shopping spots in the area, is just across the road, and golfers can play one (or all) of three nearby courses in Waikoloa. In all, this is a good value hotel, and we expect even bigger and better things now that it's under Outrigger ownership.

SETTING & FACILITIES

Location Anaehoomalu Bay, on the Big Island's Kohala Coast. A short walk to the beach. **Dining** Hawaii Calls serves breakfast, lunch, and dinner, and island favorites. **Amenities & Services** Room service, laundry service, swimming pool, business center, spa and fitness center, tennis, golf, children's program.

ACCOMMODATIONS

Rooms 545. Includes 21 suites; 11 rooms for the disabled. Nonsmoking rooms available. **All Rooms** A/C, cable TV with pay movies, lanai, in-room safe, coffeemaker, hair dryer, refrigerator, iron and board, robes. **Some Rooms** Oversized rooms, concierge service. **Comfort & Decor** Well-appointed, spacious, and clean. Rattan furnishings and island artwork add to tropical flavor.

PAYMENT, RESERVATIONS, & RESTRICTIONS

Family Plan Children age 17 and under stay free in room with parents if using existing bedding. **Deposit** 2-night deposit required. Cancellation notice must be given at least 72 hours prior to scheduled arrival for refund. **Credit Cards** All major credit cards accepted. **Check-In/Out** 3 p.m./noon. Early check-in and late checkout available on request.

Kauai

Hanalei Bay Resort & Suites $$$$

OVERALL ★★★★ | QUALITY ★★★★ | VALUE ★★½ | ZONE 13

5380 Honoiki Road, Princeville, HI 96722; (800) 827-4427 or (808) 826-6522; fax: (808) 826-6680; www.hanaleibaykauai.com

This 22-acre resort, with some hotel rooms but mostly vacation condo units ranging up to three bedrooms in size, has ocean views and a gold-sand beach down a steep cliff. Carved into a hillside and featuring lush tropical landscaping, the resort offers privacy and solitude, ideal for honeymooners. There are eight tennis courts on the premises, and a pair of world-class golf courses nearby.

SETTING & FACILITIES

Location In the Princeville Resort area on North Shore. **Dining** The Bali Hai Restaurant serves Pacific Rim cuisine amid breathtaking views of Hanalei Bay below. **Amenities & Services** Free parking, coin-operated laundry facilities, dry cleaning service, 2 swimming pools, Jacuzzi, 8 tennis courts, children's programs (seasonally), babysitting.

ACCOMMODATIONS

Rooms 250. Includes 50 suites; 2 rooms for disabled. Smoking permitted on lanai. **All Rooms** A/C, cable TV, lanai, refrigerator, in-room safe, coffeemaker. **Some Rooms** Full kitchens, washer and dryer, separate bedroom and bathroom. **Comfort & Decor** Spacious and tastefully appointed with island-themed art and furnishings and cool, tropical colors.

PAYMENT, RESERVATIONS, & RESTRICTIONS

Deposit 1-night deposit or credit card guarantee due within 10 days after booking. Cancellation notice must be given at least 72 hours prior to scheduled arrival for refund. **Credit Cards** All major credit cards accepted. **Check-In/Out** 3 p.m./noon. No early check-ins granted. Hospitality room available.

Hyatt Regency Kauai Resort & Spa $$$$$

OVERALL ★★★★½ | QUALITY ★★★★½ | VALUE ★★½ | ZONE 13

1571 Poipu Road, Koloa, HI 96756; (800) 554-9288 or (808) 742-1234; fax: (808) 742-1557; www.hyatt.com

Kauai's best beach resort, the Hyatt Regency Kauai is an architectural treat, recalling the 1920s nostalgia of Hawaii's golden age. The open-air lobby is one of the most beautiful of a galaxy of luxurious ocean-view, gardened, waterfalled, opulent Hawaiian hotel offerings. View settings are dressed with Art Deco finishes, brilliant tropical flowers, koa wood furnishings, and handsome Italian marble. In terms of amenities and services, the Hyatt, last of the fantasy-oriented hotel boom, pulls out all the stops. One of the splashier centerpieces is a huge playground of saltwater lagoons and freshwater pools, complete with water slides. Among the highlights are a creative program of cultural and ecotourism activities, a children's program, a luxurious health spa, great dining, and nightly entertainment. Of course, it doesn't hurt that Poipu is a marvelous resort destination with a good-looking gold-sand beach, but stick to the pools for safe swimming.

SETTING & FACILITIES

Location Fronting Keoneloa Bay in Poipu, a short walk to beach. **Dining** Tidepools features Pacific Rim specialties; Dondero's serves northern Italian cuisine. **Amenities & Services** Room service, parking, laundry service, business center, spa, beauty salon, children's program.

ACCOMMODATIONS

Rooms 602. Includes 37 suites; 26 rooms for the disabled. Nonsmoking rooms available. **All Rooms** A/C, cable TV, lanai, coffeemaker, iron and board, hair dryer. **Some Rooms** Kitchen, daily Continental breakfast and snacks. **Comfort & Decor** Very spacious (standard rooms are 600 square feet) and well-maintained rooms have comfortable ambience with handsome wood furnishings and Hawaiian-themed art.

PAYMENT, RESERVATIONS, & RESTRICTIONS

Family Plan Children age 18 and under stay free in room with parents if using existing bedding. **Deposit** 2-night deposit due within 14 days after booking. Cancellation notice must be given at least 72 hours prior to scheduled arrival for refund. **Credit Cards** All major credit cards accepted. **Check-In/Out** 3 p.m./noon. Early check-in and late checkout available on request.

Kauai Marriott Resort & Beach Club $$$$$

OVERALL ★★★★ | QUALITY ★★★★ | VALUE ★★ | ZONE 13

Kalapaki Beach, Lihue, HI 96766; (800) MARRIOTT or (808) 245-5050;
fax: (808) 245-2993; www.marriott.com

This well-sited resort (a mile from the airport on a sheltered beach by the harbor) has toned down its glitzy former self—it was one of the last fantasy resorts—but remains a world-class destination offering excellent service. The hotel, half of it now a time-share operation, offers a seven-acre swimming pool for a focal point, lavish furnishings and artwork, and a major ballroom and conference facility. Tranquil lagoons and inland waterways are traversed via mahogany launches, and horse-drawn carriages provide a leisurely exploration of the resort grounds. Kalapaki Beach is an excellent locale for swimming and promenading, making the Kauai Marriott a good choice for families. Golfers are advised to play at least a round at one of the resort's two championship Jack Nicklaus courses.

SETTING & FACILITIES

Location On Kalapaki Beach. **Dining** Duke's Canoe Club serves steak, fish, and seafood specialties. The poolside Kukui's Restaurant & Bar features Pacific Rim cuisine. **Amenities & Services** Room service, coin-operated laundry facilities, free parking, maid service, valet service, business center, golf, tennis, free airport transportation, fitness spa.

ACCOMMODATIONS

Rooms 356. Includes 11 suites; 10 rooms for the disabled. Nonsmoking rooms available. **All Rooms** A/C, cable TV, minibar, in-room safe, coffeemaker, hair dryer, iron and board. **Some Rooms** Kitchenette, microwave. **Comfort & Decor** Rooms are small to medium and pleasant, with subtle tropical decor and artwork.

PAYMENT, RESERVATIONS, & RESTRICTIONS

Family Plan Children age 17 and under stay free in room with parents if using existing bedding. **Deposit** 1-night deposit due within 10 days of booking. Cancellation notice must be given at least 72 hours prior to scheduled arrival for refund. **Credit Cards** All major credit cards accepted. **Check-In/Out** 4 p.m./noon. Early check-in (from 2 p.m.) and late checkout (until 2 p.m.) available on request.

Princeville Hotel $$$$$

OVERALL ★★★★½ | QUALITY ★★★★ | VALUE ★★ | ZONE 13

5520 Ka Haku Road, Princeville, HI 96722; (800) 826-4400 or (808) 826-9644; fax: (808) 826-1166; www.princeville.com

With the best view in the Islands, Princeville is a Versailles by the sea, with a lobby full of black marble, glittering chandeliers, and Greek statues. The hotel overcomes its ostentation by setting a high standard of excellence, sufficient to win AAA's Five Diamond Award. Every effort is made to bring Hawaiian culture into the scene.

It's all here: shopping, fine dining, a swimming pool, nightly Hawaiian entertainment, a small gold-sand beach, and that incredible view of Hanalei Bay. Come here to be pampered in the world-class spa and play the Prince Course, considered the best golf experience in the islands.

SETTING & FACILITIES

Location At Princeville Hotel on North Shore, rooms step down a sea cliff; a short walk to beach, with elevators handling most of the grade. **Dining** La Cascata serves Italian cuisine. Café Hanalei serves three meals a day with a to-die-for view of Hanalei Bay. **Amenities & Services** 24-hour room service, laundry service, concierge desk, valet service, health and fitness center, swimming pool, business center.

ACCOMMODATIONS

Rooms 252. Includes 51 suites; 7 rooms for the disabled. 7 of the resort's 11 floors are designated for nonsmoking rooms. **All Rooms** A/C, cable TV, honor bar, safe, oversized bathroom, hair dryer, iron and board, robes, most with no lanai but with large windows that drink in the view. **Some Rooms** Lanai, second TV, fax machine. **Comfort & Decor** Very spacious, with custom-designed furnishings and original artwork. Shower window provides wonderful scenic views of the ocean and surfers below (for you, not them; the liquid crystal glass goes opaque at the flip of a switch).

PAYMENT, RESERVATIONS, & RESTRICTIONS

Family Plan Children age 17 and under stay free in room with parents if using existing bedding. Cots, $60. **Deposit** 1-night deposit required. Cancellation notice must be given at least 72 hours prior to scheduled arrival for refund. **Credit Cards** All major credit cards accepted. **Check-In/Out** 3 p.m./noon. Early check-in and late checkout available on request.

Radisson Kauai Beach Resort $$$

OVERALL ★★★★ | QUALITY ★★★½ | VALUE ★★ | ZONE 13

4331 Kauai Beach Drive, Lihue, HI 96766; (808) 245-1955; fax: (808) 246-9085; www.radisson.com

Just a few minutes away from Lihue Airport, this 25-acre former Outrigger property is now Radisson Kauai Beach Resort, providing everything you want in a great hotel including a great beach (but with unsafe ocean conditions). The open-air design promotes a relaxing and refreshing atmosphere, and its central location makes the property a good starting point for adventure. The hotel offers four tennis courts. Golfers tee off at adjacent Wailua Golf Course, Hawaii's best municipal course.

SETTING & FACILITIES

Location In Lihue, just minutes from the Lihue Airport. **Dining** The Naupaka Terrace steak house serves breakfast, lunch, and dinner, featuring American favorites. **Amenities & Services** Room service, free parking, business center, meeting facilities.

ACCOMMODATIONS

Rooms 341. Includes 3 suites; 12 rooms for the disabled. One-third of the rooms are designated nonsmoking. **All Rooms** A/C, cable TV, lanai, voice mail, mini-fridge, in-room safe, coffeemaker. **Some Rooms** Separate parlor, upgraded amenities. **Comfort & Decor** Small but attractive (recently renovated), with rattan furnishings, quilted bedspreads, and island artworks.

PAYMENT, RESERVATIONS, & RESTRICTIONS

Family Plan Children age 17 and under stay free in room with parents if using existing bedding. **Deposit** 1-night deposit or credit card guarantee due within 10 days after booking. Cancellation notice must be given at least 72 hours prior to scheduled arrival for refund. **Credit Cards** All major credit cards accepted. **Check-In/Out** 3 p.m./noon.

Sheraton Kauai Resort $$$$$

OVERALL ★★★★ | QUALITY ★★★★ | VALUE ★★ | ZONE 13

2440 Hoonani Road, Koloa, HI 96756; (800) 782-9488 or (808) 742-1661; fax: (808) 742-9777; www.sheraton-kauai.com

A $45 million renovation project created a Sheraton Kauai that blends with its beachfront surroundings. Half of the resort embraces Poipu Beach, and the other half seems to explode in a garden of ginger, anthurium, heliconia, and bamboo. No building is taller than a coconut tree, which adds to the sense of seclusion celebrated at this 20-acre resort. The 413 rooms are housed in a trio of four-story buildings, each identified by major views (ocean, beach, and garden). All amenities are here, including a children's program, swimming pools, a fitness center, and beach activities.

SETTING & FACILITIES

Location On Poipu Beach. **Dining** Shells Steak & Seafood serves a variety of international cuisine for breakfast, lunch, and dinner. Naniwa is a fine-dining Japanese restaurant. **Amenities & Services** Room service (breakfast and dinner only), parking, valet parking ($5), fitness center, laundry facilities, tennis, business facilities, children's program. An $11/day resort fee is added to the room charge.

ACCOMMODATIONS

Rooms 413. Includes 14 suites; 12 rooms for the disabled. Smoking is permitted on lanai only. **All Rooms** A/C, cable TV, radio, video games, refrigerator, in-room safe, hair dryer, iron and board, dataport, robes. **Some Rooms** Larger space, fresh flowers. **Comfort & Decor** Spacious and bright, rooms have warm earth tones and handsome wood furnishings.

PAYMENT, RESERVATIONS, & RESTRICTIONS

Family Plan Children age 18 and under stay free in room with parents if using existing bedding. Children age 12 and under eat free in dining rooms when accompanied by an adult. **Deposit** 1-night deposit due within 10 days of booking. Cancellation notice must be given at least 72 hours prior to scheduled arrival for refund. **Credit Cards** All major credit cards accepted. **Check-In/Out** 3 p.m./noon. Early check-in and late checkout available on request. Hospitality room available.

Molokai

Sheraton Molokai Lodge and Beach Village $$$$$

OVERALL ★★★★½ | QUALITY ★★★★ | VALUE ★★★ | ZONE 14

8 Maunaloa Highway, Maunaloa Island, HI 96770; (808) 552-2741; fax (808) 552-2773; www.sheraton-molokai.com

Molokai's only upscale lodge sits on a 53,000-acre working cattle ranch with a long-distance view of the Pacific. The 22-room inn is decorated on a paniolo heritage theme with low-key, friendly service that isn't particularly wikiwiki. This is, after all, Molokai, and where else would the waitstaff bring your dinners and then dance hula among the tables?

You can go to the beach, but it's a long, bumpy ride; you might prefer to splash in the infinity pool and hot tub.

Activities include horseback trail riding, mountain biking, kayaking, beachcombing, dude rodeo, archery, beach adventures, children's programs, clay shooting, cultural hikes, ocean expeditions (shoreline casting, throw netting, guided snorkeling/spearfishing), paniolo roundup, and spa treatments.

SETTING & FACILITIES

Location Rare old Hawaii ambience in a handsome new lodge, overlooking horse pastures and the blue Pacific. Located at the entrance to the historic (and rebuilt) plantation town of Maunaloa, it features wraparound verandas for the panoramic views. **Dining** Breakfast and dinner are served in the Maunaloa Dining Room. Lunch, cocktails, and lighter fare are served in the Paniolo Lounge. **Amenities & Services** Great room with fireplace, meeting room, heated swimming pool, day spa and fitness center, in-room Internet access, complimentary local and toll-free calls, room service, activities desk, on-ranch transportation. A $10/day resort fee is added to room charge. Activity rates range from $35 to $145.

ACCOMMODATIONS

Rooms 22. **All Rooms** Private lanai, cable TV, refrigerator, in-room safe, high-speed dataports. **Comfort & Decor** Each room, with a big ocean-facing view and outdoor lanai, is furnished differently in tasteful rustic ranch style. Claw-foot tubs, hikiee (large Hawaiian bedlike couch), and other spots offer space to curl up and read.

PAYMENT, RESERVATIONS, & RESTRICTIONS

Family Plan Children 12 and under stay free with a paying adult. **Deposit** 1-night deposit, refundable on cancellation within 72 hours of scheduled arrival. **Credit Cards** All major credit cards accepted. **Check-In/Out** 3 p.m./11 a.m.

Lanai

Hotel Lanai $

OVERALL ★★★½ | QUALITY ★★★ | VALUE ★★★ | ZONE 15

P.O. Box 630520, Lanai City, HI 96763; (800) 795-7211 or (808) 565-7211; fax: (808) 565-7377; hotellanai@aloha.net; www.hotellanai.com

Opened in 1923 for visiting Dole Pineapple execs, the 11-room upcountry lodge known as Hotel Lanai has always attracted a loyal following, even more so since Henry Clay Richardson opened his Creole-inspired bistro. If you can't afford to stay at the Lodge at Koele or Manele Bay Hotel, this is your alternative. Rooms are comfortable, service is friendly, and you'll probably meet some interesting local characters at pau hana time.

SETTING & FACILITIES

Location In village of Lanai City; beach is a 20-minute shuttle ride away. **Dining** Henry Clay's Rotisserie serves a hearty selection of spit-roasted meats, seafood, pasta, gourmet pizzas, and more. **Amenities & Services** Free parking. No room service or laundry service.

ACCOMMODATIONS

Rooms 11. All are nonsmoking. **All Rooms** Ceiling fans. **Some Rooms** TV, bathtub. **Comfort & Decor** Medium-sized rooms with pine floors, ceiling fans, custom quilts, and original photographs depicting the island's plantation days.

PAYMENT, RESERVATIONS, & RESTRICTIONS

Family Plan Children age 8 and under stay free in room with parents if using existing bedding. **Deposit** Pay deposit of half of total stay in advance on booking. Cancellation notice must be given 14 days prior to scheduled arrival for refund. Cancellations are charged a $12 processing fee. **Credit Cards** Visa, MC, AmEx. **Check-In/Out** 1 p.m./11 a.m. Early check-in and late checkout available on request.

The Lodge at Koele $$$$$

OVERALL ★★★★½ | QUALITY ★★★★ | VALUE ★★½ | ZONE 15

P.O. Box 630310, Lanai City, HI 96763; (800) 321-4666 or (808) 565-7300; fax: (808) 565-3868; reservations@lanai-resorts.com; www.lanai-resorts.com

Nestled on the island's central highlands, the Lodge at Koele is reminiscent of an English hill station, complete with manicured lawns, cozy fireplaces, and afternoon tea. Paintings, sculptures, and artifacts adorn the resort's interiors. Paths meander through flower gardens, past an English conservatory, to an inviting swimming pool. The atmosphere is calm and relaxed, providing a welcome escape, but there is plenty to do: work out at the new fitness center; explore the rugged countryside astride a horse or a mountain bike, or on foot, or by four-wheeler; play tennis; or enjoy a round at one of Lanai's two award-winning championship courses. Not much nightlife on this quiet island, but the lodge offers a weekly Visiting Artist Program, where guests meet and mingle with noted authors, chefs, and entertainers.

SETTING & FACILITIES

Location Upcountry, on the island's central highlands; beach is a 25-minute shuttle ride away. **Dining** The award-winning Formal Dining Room showcases Pacific Rim cuisine with local ingredients. **Amenities & Services** Room service, concierge, laundry service, fitness center, swimming pool, golf, valet parking, children's programs, free shuttle service.

ACCOMMODATIONS

Rooms 102. Includes 14 suites; 2 rooms for the disabled. The lodge is a nonsmoking facility. **All Rooms** Ceiling fans, cable TV, VCR, private lanai, mini-bar, in-room safe, robes, slippers. **Some Rooms** Fireplaces, larger space, upgraded amenities, butler service. **Comfort & Decor** Very spacious and comfy with country-chic, chintz interiors à la Laura Ashley, hand-carved poster beds, quiet ceiling fans, and oil paintings by local artists.

PAYMENT, RESERVATIONS, & RESTRICTIONS

Family Plan Children age 14 and under stay free in room with parents if using existing bedding. Maximum of 4 guests/room (2 adults and 2 children). Extra person, $75. **Deposit** 2-night deposit due within 14 days of booking. Cancellation notice must be given 14 days prior to scheduled arrival for refund. **Credit Cards** All major credit cards accepted except Discover. **Check-In/Out** 3 p.m./noon. Hospitality rooms available.

The Manele Bay Hotel $$$$$

OVERALL ★★★★½ | QUALITY ★★★ | VALUE ★★½ | ZONE 15

P.O. Box 310, Lanai City, HI 96763; (800) 321-4666 or (808) 565-7700; fax: (808) 565-2483; reservations@lanai-resorts.com; www.lanai-resorts.com

Perched atop windswept sea cliffs, the Manele overlooks Lanai's magnificent coastline and Hulopoe Bay, a favorite playground of spinner dolphins. A blend of Mediterranean and Hawaiian designs, the Manele Bay Hotel is full of exotic artifacts and grand murals, some hand-painted by local residents. Lush tropical gardens add color to the resort's otherwise arid landscape, but still fall short of the spectacular ocean views. It's just a short stroll downhill to Hulopoe Beach, one of the best beaches in Hawaii, with excellent water clarity for snorkeling and scuba diving. Great golf awaits you at the Challenge at Manele. Like the Lodge at Koele, Manele delivers a memorable experience.

SETTING & FACILITIES

Location At Hulopoe Bay, short walk to beach. **Dining** The Ihilani Restaurant serves fine Hawaii regional cuisine. **Amenities & Services** Room service, valet and self-parking, spa, golf, tennis, concierge service, children's program, babysitting.

ACCOMMODATIONS

Rooms 249. Includes 13 suites; 6 rooms for the disabled. Nonsmoking rooms available. **All Rooms** A/C, cable TV, VCR, radio, in-room safe, lanai, minibar, hair dryer, sitting area, tub and shower. **Some Rooms** Butler service. **Comfort & Decor** Spacious, comfortable rooms have refined furnishings, floral-themed decor, and accessories collected from around the world.

PAYMENT, RESERVATIONS, & RESTRICTIONS

Family Plan Children age 15 and under stay free in room with parents if using existing bedding. Maximum of 4 people/room (2 adults and 2 children). Extra person, $75. **Deposit** 2-night deposit due within 14 days of booking. Cancellation notice must be given 14 days prior to scheduled arrival for refund. **Credit Cards** All major credit cards accepted except Discover. **Check-In/Out** 3 p.m./noon. Early check-in and late checkout available on request (no guarantees).

Part Four

Aloha! Welcome to Hawaii

When You Arrive

Honolulu International Airport, one of the busiest in the United States, is simple to navigate. Gates have numbers; just follow the signs. Baggage claim areas are designated by letters of the alphabet in the primary mainland arrival terminals, and by numbers in the interisland terminal. Note that mainland flights by the local carriers, Hawaiian Airlines and Aloha Airlines, use the interisland terminal for ticketing and baggage. Latest arrival and departure times appear on the video monitors. Upon your arrival, follow the clearly marked signs to baggage claim on the street level. The wait only seems long because you're anxious to hit the beach.

Arriving in Hawaii is a sensual experience. You smell flowers, hear ukulele and people singing Hawaiian music, and feel the tropical warmth and tradewinds. If you elect to walk to baggage claim outdoors rather than taking the Wikiwiki transit, look beyond the airport to the moody mountains ahead of you and the city and Diamond Head off to your right for your first big-picture view.

In baggage claim, you will find car rental agencies and courtesy phones. Outside, you will find taxis, buses, Waikiki shuttles, car rental shuttles, and private or hotel limousines.

If you arrive on an international flight, the first to wish you "aloha" in their fashion are U.S. Customs and Immigration agents. Honolulu is today a far better staffed and more efficient port of entry than it was in the past.

Flying Interisland

We've noticed that interisland airlines and airports tend to be very efficient at handling the constant loads of passengers and bags—much more so than commuter connections on the mainland. For people who live on the Islands, this process replaces public transit. Neighbor Islands airports are smaller, less formal, and easier to navigate. An exception is Maui's main Kahului Airport, where the extra security measures of the post–September

11 era sometimes cause an exasperating jam-up that creates long slow lines and demands extra time to navigate. Plan accordingly.

Of Maui's three airports, Kahului Airport, at the island's center, is the main terminal for interisland and mainland flights. Car rental desks and taxi service are available outside baggage claim. Most people take a shuttle to the car compound a few minutes away. Kapalua/West Maui Airport serves only interisland flights on smaller aircraft but is handy to area resorts and towns. Car rentals are available nearby, and resort shuttles serve the airport. Tiny Hana Airport serves small plane traffic.

The Big Island of Hawaii has two major airports. Keahole-Kona International Airport is a full-service, open-air facility carved from the lava fields of the Kona Coast, eight miles from Kailua-Kona. Landing on this black landscape below a dormant volcano is a bit like landing in a barbecue pit. You get used to it, especially after you notice explosions of neon-colored bougainvillea and palm trees growing out of the cinders. Rental car desks are in an open building across the street from the terminal; you take a shuttle to get to most of the car compounds, located a few minutes away.

Hilo Airport at General Lyman Field serves the east side of the island. Hilo Airport is much larger than you might expect. It was designed and built a few decades ago when Hilo was expected to become a major port of entry into Hawaii because it was closest to the U.S. mainland. Car rental agencies are on site.

The Lihue Airport is Kauai's main airport and is an upgraded, enclosed, and air-conditioned facility. Princeville Airport on the North Shore serves primarily general aviation and helicopters.

Molokai's airport is an older, island-style, open-air facility located mid-island near Kaunakakai. Lanai's airport is a new, modern facility below Lanai City. Arriving guests are met by resort staff and transported by resort bus.

Ground Transportation

Oahu: Honolulu International Airport

Rental Cars Five car rental agencies—Avis, Budget, Dollar, Hertz, and National—have customer service desks in most baggage claim areas at street level. Other car rental agencies are located in the vicinity of the airport and have courtesy phones inside the baggage claim area. See the section on car rentals in Part 2 for more details.

Airport-Waikiki Express From the baggage claim area, head outside and look for any ticket agent wearing a blue aloha shirt; the agent will direct you to the nearest pickup point. The cost is $8 per person one-way and $13 per person round-trip (cash only). The 18-seat, air-conditioned red, white, and blue shuttle—clearly marked Airport-Waikiki Express—arrives every half-hour 6 a.m.–10 a.m., after 10 a.m. every 20–25 minutes. Call (808) 566-7340 for more information.

Taxis Cabs are available just outside the baggage claim area. Look for a dispatcher wearing a mustard-colored shirt. The fare from the airport to Waikiki ranges from $25 to $28, not including tip.

The Bus The bus is the cheapest airport transfer, if you are traveling light. The fare is $1 per adult and 50 cents per child, exact change required. Luggage is limited to one bag measuring no more than 24" × 18" × 12" that must fit under your seat or in your lap.

Look for the #19 and #20 buses marked Waikiki Beach & Hotels. Bus stops—two at the main terminal and one at the interisland terminal—are located on the second-floor (departures) level.

Buses arrive every 30 minutes depending on route number. In the evening, only the #19 bus serves the airport. Call (808) 848-5555 for more information. The bus takes about 30 minutes to reach Waikiki, depending on traffic.

Maui: Kahului Airport

Rental Cars Alamo, Avis, Budget, Dollar, Hertz, and National are just outside the main terminal (turn right as you leave the baggage area). Thrifty, Regency, and Word of Mouth have courtesy phones at the airport's information board inside the baggage claim area.

Taxis Maui Airport Taxi has a dispatcher inside baggage claim. Or you can just walk directly across the street and hail a cab at the curb.

Shuttles Use the courtesy phone mentioned above to contact the Airport Shuttle or Speedy Shuttle. The wait is usually less than 15 minutes; costs vary depending on the destination. The Airport Shuttle, for example, charges $22 for two passengers bound for Wailea and $32 to Kaanapali. To reserve a shuttle in advance, call the Airport Shuttle at (808) 661-6667 or Speedy Shuttle at (808) 875-8070.

Roberts Hawaii at (808) 539-9400 also provides transportation to the Kaanapali Beach Resort area from 9 a.m. to 4 p.m. daily, with an evening run between 6:30 and 7 p.m. Look for the customer service desk marked Airport Hotel Shuttle in the baggage claim area (directly across from carousel #4). Shuttles depart every half-hour. The cost is $15 per person.

Maui: Kapalua Airport

Rental Cars and Taxis Use the courtesy phone at the baggage claim area for a free shuttle van to car rental offices. Taxis are curbside outside baggage claim area.

The Big Island of Hawaii: Keahole-Kona International Airport

Rental Cars The car rental counters for Avis, Alamo, Budget, Dollar, Hertz, National, and Thrifty are all located across the street from the main terminal (directly across from the Onizuka Space Center).

Taxis Cabs are parked across the street from the baggage claim area.

Public Transportation No public transportation service is available at the airport.

Shuttles Various hotel shuttles will pick up arriving guests with advance notice. Be sure to let them know your arrival time. You can also call for a pickup at the information booth, just outside the baggage claim area.

The Big Island of Hawaii: Hilo International Airport

Rental Cars Car rental pickups for Alamo, Avis, Budget, Dollar, Hertz, and National are located directly across the street from the airport restaurant, near the main gates.

Taxis Taxis are available curbside near the baggage claim area.

Public Transportation No public transportation service is available at the airport.

Shuttle The only shuttle that serves the airport is for guests of the Hawaii Naniloa Resort in Hilo, and even this is based on availability. Visitors booked at the Naniloa should call (800) 442-5845 or check with a customer service agent at the visitors information desk near the baggage claim area.

Kauai: Lihue Airport

Rental Cars Car rental pickups for Alamo, Avis, Budget, Dollar, Hertz, and National are conveniently located directly across the street from the airport restaurant, near the main gates.

Taxis Taxis are lined up and available curbside near the baggage claim area, or use the dispatch phone by the visitors information desk to summon a cab.

Public Transportation No public transportation service is available at the airport.

Shuttle The neighboring Kauai Marriott has a free shuttle for guests. At the visitors information desk, phone the hotel and request a pickup.

Molokai: Molokai Airport

Rental Cars Budget and Dollar are the only car rental agencies at the Molokai Airport. Their customer service desks are located by the baggage claim area.

Taxis Two cab companies serve the airport: Kukui Tours (call (808) 336-0944 or (808) 553-4227 after 5 p.m.) and Molokai Off-Road (call (808) 553-3369). Neither has a courtesy phone. Look outside the baggage claim area to spot either taxi van. If none are around, call either for a pickup.

Lanai: Lanai Airport

Rental Cars Dollar Rent-A-Car is the only car rental agency on Lanai. Upon arrival, walk to the reception desk and use the red courtesy phone.

A van will pick you up and transport you to Dollar's pickup location, about three miles away.

Shuttle A convenient way to get around is Lanai Resort's shuttles. The $12 per person charge includes round-trip airport transportation and all shuttles between the island's two resorts, The Lodge at Koele and the Manele Bay Hotel. The shuttle vans are located right outside the airport's baggage claim area.

Things the Locals Already Know

The Lei Tradition

A Hawaiian flower lei is one of the most extravagant presents in the world. Some lei take more than a thousand flowers and quite a bit of time and artistry to make. They fade and perish within hours or days of their creation. Often they are worn only once.

Lei giving is one of the most colorful traditions in Hawaii. You'll see it first at the airport. But it isn't an embarrassing designation of a newly arrived tourist. Lei are a sign of honor, for a family member, friend, or special guest, of either gender.

Having a garland placed around your neck is a special welcome, farewell, or congratulations, usually followed by a hug or kiss on the cheek, especially if you know the donor. A lei greeting remains Hawaii's most tangible expression of aloha. Local tradition is to drape loved ones up to their noses with lei at graduations; they are also given for anniversaries, birthdays, and other special celebrations. They're great ice breakers with local strangers, who want to admire the lei and congratulate you on your special occasion. It's also customary to share the lei around after you wear it for a while (take it off and give it to someone else to wear).

Hawaiian language advisory: The word *lei* is singular and plural; there is no "s" in the Hawaiian language.

The tradition of lei giving may have originated with Hawaii's earliest settlers, who brought flowering plants to use for adornment. Early Hawaiians offered lei to their gods during religious ceremonies.

Today, long lei are also draped over the statues or images of important people in Hawaiian history, or over the bows of victorious racing canoes, or on anything worthy of commemoration. Each June, the King Kamehameha Day celebration kicks off with a colorful lei-draping ceremony at the King Kamehameha statue in downtown Honolulu.

Writer-poet Don Blanding initiated Lei Day, an annual May 1 celebration held since 1928. The biggest event is held at Kapiolani Park in Waikiki, where floral creations by the state's top lei makers are displayed.

Fresh flower lei can be purchased throughout Hawaii, at every major airport and many supermarkets, as well as florists. Home-style is to make your own, and many families still do. You'll find lei made of all kinds of flowers, including plumeria, gardenias, ginger, orchids, pakalana, roses, ilima, and carnations, as well as fragrant maile leaves, braids of ti leaves, kukui nuts, sea shells, flowers made of dollar bills, and, for the kids back home, even candy and gum.

Many high-quality, lower-priced lei stands are concentrated in Honolulu's Chinatown. Costs range from a few dollars for a simple crown flower or sweet-smelling tuberose lei to $40 for an intricately crafted rope lei. One of the most popular new lei is the cristina, an expertly sewn garland made of purple dendrobium orchids ($25–$30).

Often people try to keep a lei alive by refrigerating it. Here's another suggestion: Drape it over a doorknob or lampshade in your hotel room or some other place where it cheers you to see the flowers and smell the fragrance.

A Tip about Tipping

Many service workers in Hawaii depend on tips for their living. At the airport, tip a porter a dollar or two per bag. Taxi drivers receive a 15% tip of the total fare plus 25 cents per bag or parcel. At the hotel, tip the bellhop $5 for transporting your luggage to and from your room, and give the parking valet a couple of dollars. Tip your room housekeeper $1 for each day of your stay. For dining, tip 15% to 20% of the bill.

State Holidays

In addition to all major U.S. holidays, Hawaii celebrates three state holidays.

- Kuhio Day (March 26). This holiday honors Prince Jonah Kuhio Kalanianaole (1871–1922), a statesman and member of the royal family who served in the U.S. Congress in the early 1900s.
- King Kamehameha Day (June 11). Hawaii's great king, Kamehameha I, united the Islands into a kingdom under one rule. An imposing figure—some reported him as tall as eight feet—the Big Island–born monarch died in May 1819, when he was believed to be in his early sixties, and his bones were hidden at a secret location on the Kona Coast. Modern islanders celebrate the life of Kamehameha with colorful festivities, including lei-draping ceremonies, parades, and hoolaulea (public parties).
- Admission Day (third Friday in August). On August 21, 1959, U.S. President Dwight D. Eisenhower signed the proclamation welcoming Hawaii as the 50th state, following a long, often emotional campaign for statehood that originated more than a century earlier. Many expected Hawaii to be named the 49th state, but that distinction went to Alaska in 1958. Today, "Hawaii—49th State" memorabilia, ranging from record labels to buttons, is highly prized by collectors.

Saying It in Hawaiian

In Hawaii, English and Hawaiian are both official languages.

The Hawaiian alphabet has only 12 letters—the vowels a, e, i, o, and u and the consonants h, k, l, m, n, p, and w. A diacritical mark called the okina, pronounced as a glottal stop, is almost as vital as a letter, so that those vowels can do extra duty. The language takes practice and patience.

Here are some general rules of thumb for you to remember:

- Vowels are pronounced this way: *a* as "uh," as in the second a in "lava"; e as "ay," as in "hay"; *i* as "ee," as in "fee"; *o* as "oh," as in "low"; and *u* as "oo," as in "moon."
- All consonants are pronounced as in English except for *w*, which is usually pronounced as *v* when it follows an *i* or e. Example: Ewa Beach is pronounced as "Eva" Beach. When following a *u* or *o*, *w* is pronounced as *w*. When it is the first letter in the word or follows an *a*, there is no designated rule, so the pronunciation follows custom. Which means Hawaii and Havaii are both acceptable.
- Some vowels are slurred together in a diphthong, forming single sounds. Examples: ai as in "Waikiki," au as in "mauka," ei as in "lei," oi as in "poi," ou as in "kou," and ao as in "haole."
- Some are separated by a glottal stop, or okina, an upside-down and backward apostrophe that emphasizes a separate vowel sound, acting like another consonant, and keeps identically spelled words from being confused. For instance, pau means "finished," but pa'u is a skirt worn by women horseback riders. Pau is pronounced as "pow," and pa'u is pronounced as "pah-oo." We've kept the okina out of this guide for simplification.
- A macron, or *kahako,* designates a long vowel. A macron is marked as a line directly over the vowel. Logically enough, long vowels last longer than regular vowels. The macron isn't needed often to distinguish between words. This book, like most English publications from Hawaii, excludes macrons. However, don't be surprised if you see them over the i's in Waikiki. They indicate that the word is correctly sounded "why-kiki" rather than "why-kee-kee."
- Every Hawaiian syllable ends with a vowel. Thus, every Hawaiian word ends with a vowel. Which means the word "Hawaiian" isn't a Hawaiian word.
- If a word contains no macrons, the accent usually falls on the next-to-last syllable. Examples: a-LO-ha, ma-HA-lo, ma-li-HI-ni, and o-HA-na.

In our opinion, the most authoritative Hawaiian language book is the *Hawaiian Dictionary,* by Mary Kawena Pukui and Samuel H. Elbert.

COMMONLY USED HAWAIIAN WORDS AND PHRASES

Aina	Land, earth
Aloha	Love, kindness, or goodwill; can be used as a greeting or farewell
E komo mai	Welcome!
Hale	House
Hana hou	Do again, repeat, or encore
Haole	Formerly any foreigner, now primarily anyone of Caucasian ancestry
Holoholo	To go out for a walk, ride, or other activity
Hoolaulea	A big party or celebration

COMMONLY USED HAWAIIAN WORDS AND PHRASES *(continued)*

Hooponopono	To correct or rectify a situation
Ikaika	Strong, powerful
Ilima	A native shrub bearing bright yellow or orange flowers; used for lei
Kahuna	Priest, minister, expert
Kala	Money
Kamaaina	Native-born or longtime island resident
Kanaka	Person, individual
Kane	Male, husband, man
Kapu	Taboo
Keiki	Child
Kohola	Humpback whale
Kokua	Help, assistance, cooperation
Kolohe	Mischievous, naughty; a rascal
Kupuna	Grandparent
Kuuipo	My sweetheart
Lanai	Porch, verandah
Lua	Toilet, bathroom
Luna	Foreman, boss, leader
Mahalo	Thank you
Makahiki	Ancient Hawaiian harvest festival with sports and religious activities
Makai	Toward the ocean; used in directions
Malihini	Newcomer
Mana	Spiritual power
Mauka	Inland direction, toward the mountain
Me ke aloha pumehana	With warm regards
Mele	Song
Menehune	Legendary small people who worked at night, building fishponds, roads, and temples; according to legend, if the work was not completed in one night, it was left unfinished
Ohana	Family
Ono	Delicious
Pau	Finished, done
Pupu	Hors d'oeuvre, appetizer
Tutu	Grandmother
Wahine	Female, wife, woman

Pidgin

You may hear people talking in what sounds like abbreviated English, except that it's more colorful. Hawaii-style pidgin, the local patois, is the third language of the islands. It combines words and syntax of several languages and was developed so that multicultural plantation people could communicate. Although it is a true creole language and not simply slang, it's definitely not an official tongue.

The pros and cons of pidgin have long been debated by local educators and cultural experts. Some say that the practice is not an acceptable manner of speech, whereas others insist that pidgin is a treasured cultural asset that should not be looked down upon. In Hawaii, it's not uncommon for a kamaaina to speak perfect English in an office setting, then pick up the phone and speak pidgin to a friend. Here are some commonly used pidgin words and phrases you might hear during your stay.

COMMONLY USED PIDGIN WORDS AND PHRASES

An den?	So? And then?
Braddah	Brother or friend
Brah	Short for "braddah"
Bumbye	Do it later.
Bummahs!	That's unfortunate!
Da kine	The kind of, that thing
Fo' real?	Really?
Garans	Guaranteed
Geev um!	Go for it!
Go fo' broke	Give it your all (famous motto of the 442nd battalion in WW II).
How you figgah?	How do you think that happened?
Howzit?	How are you?
Laytahs	See you later.
Li'dat	Like that
Minahs	Minor; no problem; don't worry about it
Mo' bettah	Better
No shame	Don't be shy or embarrassed!
'Nuff already!	That's enough!
Shaka	Greetings; good job; thank you
Small keed time	Childhood
Soah?	Does it hurt?
Stink eye	Disapproving glance, a dirty look

COMMONLY USED PIDGIN WORDS AND PHRASES *(continued)*	
Talk story	Converse, talk, or gossip
T'anks, eh?	Thank you
Whatevahs	Whatever
Who dat?	Who is that?
Yeah, no?	That's right!

Twenty Words Every Hawaii Visitor Should Know

If you can pronounce Aiea, Kalanianaole, Keeaumoku, and Anaehoomalu correctly, know *hapa* from *hapai,* then you are *akamai, brah.* No need to read *da kine.* If you no can understand a word of this, *mo' bettah you read da kine.*

Da kine is one of 20 words or phrases every Hawaii visitor should know. So are *akamai* and *pau.* When you *go pau* reading *da kine,* you will be *akamai, li'dat.*

Welcome to Hawaii, the linguistically rich and confusing Islands with not one but two official languages—Hawaiian and English—and everybody speaks a little of the unofficial third language, pidgin.

You probably can get by with a now-and-then *aloha* and a mumbled *mahalo,* but to understand what's really going on in Hawaii, you need to know a few basic words like: *huhu, da kine, humbug,* and *mo' bettah.*

Everyone knows *wahine* from *kane* and *mauka* from *makai,* but what about *kokua* and *holoholo?* Most *haole* (that's you, *seestah* and *blahlah*) have trouble saying Hawaiian words because they are repetitive, have too many vowels, and look like the bottom line of an eye chart, e.g. , *Kaaawa, Kuliouou,* and *Napoopoo,* or *humhumunukunukapuaa,* the state fish.

To *haole* eyes honed on brittle consonants, Hawaiian looks impossible. Once spoken, the way Hawaiian was intended, the soft, round, soothing vowels are music to your ears. Banned after the Monarchy was toppled at the turn of the last century, the native tongue survived underground to carry a nation's culture down through generations in warrior chants, hula lyrics and "talk story," or storytelling.

And then there is pidgin, the local creole attributed to Chinese immigrants, said to have created it in order to do business without a common lingo. The root word of pidgin is, in fact, business.

A caveat: Before you go to Hawaii and put your foot in your mouth, it's probably a good idea to clip and save this lexicon for future review. Or, as any local might put it: *Good t'ing, brush up on da kine, brah, so no make A* (polite shorthand for making an ass of yourself).

Here are 20 Hawaii words in everyday usage which you should know. Fo' real.

1. **kokua** (ko-coo-ah) noun or verb; help, as in assist, (please *kokua*), or contribute *(kokua luau),* or a gentle reminder, ("Your *kokua* is appreciated.") A *kokua* barbecue, should you be invited to one, is a potluck. Bring something to grill and share.
2. **pau** (pow) adverb; finished, all gone, quitting time *(pau hana).* Politely as dishes are removed when you finish kaukau ("*All pau?*"), when your car or other mechanical object breaks down ("Eh, dis buggah *pau.*"). Not to be confused with *make* (mah kay) which means dead, a permanent form of *pau.*
3. **malihini** (mah lee hee nee) noun; non-derisive term for newcomer, opposite of *kamaaina.* If it's your first time to come to Hawaii, that's you, *brah,* a stranger, someone who wears socks and shoes instead of rubbah slippahs and eats rice with a fork instead of chopsticks.
4. **mo' bettah** (mow bedder) adjective; contemporary pidgin, for preferable or even outstanding, as in *"Dis beach mo' bettah."* Sometimes spelled "moah bettah."
5. **no ka oi** (no cuh oy) Hawaiian adjective phrase for superlative or the best, as in *"Maui no ka oi." Maui* is the best; a stage just beyond *mo' bettah.*
6. **hana hou** (huh nuh ho) verb phrase for do it again; Hawaiian equivalent of encore, most often heard at music concerts.
7. **to da max** (to dah macks) adverbial phrase for boundless enthusiasm, no limits, or another famous pidgin phrase, *go fo' broke,* the motto of the 442nd Battalion in WW II. Also title of popular book, *Pidgin To Da Max.*
8. **akamai** (ah kah my) noun for clever, common sense as opposed to intelligence. "Many are smart but few are *akamai.*" Name of high-tech Internet outfit.
9. **chance 'em** verb for give it a try. Often heard in Las Vegas at 21 tables in California Hotel and in Honolulu at Aloha Stadium late in fourth quarter when Warriors are behind. Fourth and inches on the five; coach says, "Chance 'em."
10. **chicken skin** adjective for goose bumps, frisson, shiver of excitement; title of best-selling local spooky book by favorite author (also of this book). *"Oh, da spooky kine gives me chicken skin."*
11. **laters** adverb for good-bye, sayonara, adios.
12. **howzit?** (houze it) phrase of greeting, always a question; contraction of "how is it?" or "how's by you?" Preferred response is, "'s good, brah!" Or, maybe not so good if feeling *junk* (poorly).

13. **shaka brah** (shah kah brah) pidgin gesture with phrase for hang loose. A *shaka* is a hand signal with thumb and pinkie extended; index, middle, and ring fingers closed; then a brisk flip of wrist or horizontal—a public sign that everything is cool, no problem. "Life is good, brah," followed by *shaka*. Made famous by entertainer Don Ho; seen daily on local TV news sign-off. *Brah* (braw), noun for brother, not to be confused with bra.
14. **holoholo** (hoe low hoe low) adverb with "go," old Hawaiian word for going around on pleasure trips. Not to be confused with similar sounding ***halohalo,*** (hah low hah low), the classic Filipino dessert made with ice cream and chopped fruit.
15. **wikiwiki** (wee key wee key) adverb meaning quickly; name of Honolulu International Airport shuttle bus. This is also a concept missing on the islands of Molokai and Lanai, as in to move rapidly or to hurry, not to be confused with *hele* (hell lay), which means to go or let's continue, as in "*Hele* on."
16. **mauka/makai** (mao cah/mah kigh) adjectives for two of four key directions, i.e., up and down. *Mauka* and *makai* are used on all Hawaiian Islands. *Mauka* means toward the mountain, or inland; *makai* means toward the ocean. Where it gets tricky is the other two directions on circular islands with little use for western compass points. In Honolulu or Waikiki, they are *'Ewa* (eh vah), generally toward the airport and the 'Ewa Plantation that used to be there and no longer is, and Diamond Head, for the Waikiki crater known in Hawaiian as *Leahi* (lay ah hee) or *tuna brow*. Other local landmarks define the side-to-side directions on other islands and other parts of Oahu. On Maui, the term in English *Upcountry* (uhp-kuhn-tree) means same t'ing, *mauka, brah.*
17. **kapu** (kuh poo) adverb corresponding to taboo or forbidden; means off-limits, or keep out. Often seen on signs in danger spots, or religious sites and geothermal plants.
18. **hapa haole** (hapa hawlee) adjective or noun describing many modern-day citizens of the Islands. *Haole* is what early Hawaiians called first European visitors who looked pale as death, or breathless. *Hapa* is Hawaiian for half, not to be confused with *hapai* (hah pie) which is one and a half, or pregnant. *Hapa-haole* is half white, or part dis and dat, li'dat, or not quite chop-suey (lots of antecedents). *Haole* may be considered derogatory if prefaced by "stupid" or "dumb."
19. **da kine** (dah kyne) literally "the kind of something"; perfectly understood but not defined, a one-size-fits-all generic expression used when two or more people know what they are talking about

but nobody can think of the right word. "Cannot explain, you know, *da kine.*"

20. **li'dat** (lye daht) adverbial existential pidgin phrase, that's the way it is, like that. Agreement or confirmation that an idea, concept, or statement is what it is. It is, *li'dat.* Similar to English "uh-huh," and Japanese "honto desu."

Note: All definitions of Hawaiian words based loosely on original interpretations by Mary Kawena Pukui and Samuel H. Elbert, authors of *Hawaiian Dictionary.*

Important Phone Numbers

Here's a list of phone numbers that may come in handy during your stay. For interisland calls, use the area code (808) before the number. Be aware these calls generally are charged long-distance rates.

All Islands

Police, fire, ambulance: 911

Directory assistance: 1411

Oahu

Weather forecast: 973-4380, 973-4381

Marine conditions: 973-4382

Time of day: 983-3211

Honolulu International Airport: 836-6413

Honolulu Physicians Exchange: 524-2575

Hawaii Dental Association Hotline: 593-7956

Information and complaints: 523-4385

Office of Consumer Protection: 586-2630

Better Business Bureau: 536-6956

Maui

(Note: Maui County also includes Molokai and Lanai)

Weather forecast: 877-5111

Marine conditions: 877-3477

Time of day: 242-0212 (Maui), 553-9211 (Molokai), 565-9211 (Lanai)

Kahului Airport: 872-3803, 872-3893

Kapalua Airport: 669-0623

Hana Airport: 248-8208

Molokai Airport: 567-6140

Kalaupapa Airport: 567-6331

Lanai Airport: 565-6757

Office of Consumer Protection: 984-8244

The Big Island of Hawaii

Weather forecast: 961-5582, 935-8555 (Hilo)

Marine conditions: 935-9883

The Big Island of Hawaii *(continued)*

Time of day: 961-0212

Volcano eruption information: 985-6000

Keahole-Kona International Airport: 329-3423

Hilo International Airport: 934-5801

Office of Consumer Protection: 974-6230

Kauai

Weather forecast: 245-6001

Marine conditions: 245-3564

Time of day: 245-0212

Lihue Airport: 246-1400

Newspapers

Local daily newspapers include the *Honolulu Advertiser* and *Honolulu Star-Bulletin* on Oahu; the *Hawaii Tribute-Herald* and *West Hawaii Today* on the Big Island of Hawaii; the *Maui News* on Maui; and the *Garden Island* on Kauai.

A key source for entertainment news and listings is the *Honolulu Advertiser's* "TGIF" section, published each Friday.

Safety Tips

You won't find state, city, or tourism spokespeople bragging about this, but *Money Magazine* calls Honolulu the safest large city in the United States, according to an analysis of FBI crime statistics. Hawaii is a peaceful state with few violent crimes. Much is invested in the safety of tourists, the state's biggest industry, but the state is not crime-free. We urge you to use the same common sense and self-protective measures you would at home.

- Carry only as much cash or traveler's checks as you need for the day.
- Never leave your luggage unattended until you arrive at your hotel.
- Never display large amounts of cash during transactions, such as at automated teller machines.
- Beware of pickpockets, especially in crowds.
- Carry your purse close to your body.
- Carry your wallet in a front pocket rather than a rear pocket.
- Avoid waiting alone at a bus stop after dark.
- Never leave valuables in your rental car.
- If your vehicle is bumped from behind at night, do not stop; instead, proceed to the nearest public area and call 911 for assistance.
- Leave your hotel room key with the front desk when going out.

Part Five

Getting Around Hawaii

Transportation Considerations

It's easy to get around Hawaii when you know how.

Only Oahu is large and busy enough to pose a problem, and that's only during Honolulu's morning and evening commute hours, when traffic chokes freeways and city streets. Traffic in and out of Waikiki can get congested on weeknights and weekends. Hawaiian street names are difficult to read and recall, and gas is expensive. Fortunately Oahu is also the island with an outstanding municipal bus system. It's called TheBus.

You can ride TheBus, take shuttle vans, or hail a taxi to get almost anywhere you want to go. An open-air, motorized Waikiki Trolley tour stops at visitor attractions and shopping.

What you won't find in the islands are trains or subway systems.

Before choosing your primary mode of transportation, weigh the factors of convenience, flexibility, time, and cost. For example, catching a taxi from Waikiki to the *Arizona* Memorial may be the fastest and most convenient option, but it will also set you back about $25–$28. Catching TheBus is the cheapest way to go, but it will take longer and you won't have as much flexibility.

The only new highway, the Interstate H-3, links Pearl Harbor with Kaneohe Bay Marine Air Station on the Windward side of the island. This highway broke the bank (the most expensive in the nation at the time, topping $1 billion a mile) and triggered controversy because its route violated a sacred area and an ancient temple site. But the roadway today is underused and very scenic. It's worth a spin just for the views.

Traffic Advisory

If you decide to explore Oahu by car, remember that Oahu reputedly has more cars per capita than any city in the United States. Avoid the freeways and major highways—H-1 in particular—during morning and evening weekday rush hours. It's worst on school days, particularly when classes start in August and September, and tends to jam up around downtown Honolulu at lunchtime. Road work is as big a cause of traffic backup as anything. The truth is that even Oahu's traffic looks tame next to many a big mainland city's problems. Drivers regularly exceed the posted speed limit here, but be aware that the Honolulu Police Department uses radar and cameras to nail offenders. Chief problem areas, says the HPD, are the H-1 Freeway, Pali Highway, and the Kalanianaole Highway, so be especially lawful on these roads.

Getting Around Neighbor Islands

You won't have to worry about major traffic jams on any of the Neighbor Islands, where the population is a small fraction of Oahu's. Barring accidents, traffic backups are nonexistent on Molokai and Lanai and the Big Island, the one island with well-designed roads, longer driving distances, and fewer cars. Maui and Kauai have developed their own commuter traffic, with the busiest times being 6:30–8:30 a.m. and 3:30–5:30 p.m. Road congestion intensifies on Maui and Kauai when jumbo jets and other planes land at once, and in Kapaa on Kauai during lunch hour.

Hawaii's road system is simple if somewhat arcane, with posted signs (white lettering against a dark green background) providing directions. Considering the number of vehicles, particularly on Oahu where the number of registered vehicles doubled in the past two decades, Hawaii's roadways and streets are in relatively good repair. You may hit rough spots along the H-1 (eastbound) near the Aiea exit and on Kamehameha Highway on Windward Oahu and the island's North Shore.

Drive Times

Here are some estimated drive times from popular resort areas to specific points of interest. The estimations are given for periods outside rush hour.

DRIVE TIMES

Oahu

From Central Waikiki to:	*Time to Travel*
Ala Moana Shopping Center	7 minutes
Aloha Tower Marketplace	15 minutes
Arizona Memorial	30 minutes
Bishop Museum	20 minutes
Chinatown Honolulu	15 minutes
Haleiwa	1 hour
Hanauma Bay	30 minutes
Honolulu International Airport	25 minutes

DRIVE TIMES *(continued)*

Oahu (continued)

From Central Waikiki to:	*Time to Travel*
Polynesian Cultural Center	1 hour, 15 minutes
Sea Life Park	40 minutes
University of Hawaii–Manoa	15 minutes

Maui

From Kahului Airport to:	*Time to Travel*
Haleakala National Park	1 hour, 45 minutes
Hana	2 hours, 30 minutes
Kaanapali	50 minutes
Kapalua	1 hour
Kihei	25 minutes
Lahaina	45 minutes
Makena	40 minutes
Wailea	35 minutes
Wailuku	10 minutes

Big Island

From Kona to:	*Time to Travel*
Hilo	2 hours, 15 minutes
Volcano	2 hours, 30 minutes
Waimea (Kamuela)	50 minutes

From Hilo to:	*Time to Travel*
Volcano	45 minutes
Waimea (Kamuela)	1 hour, 15 minutes

Kauai

From Lihue to:	*Time to Travel*
Kilauea	50 minutes
Kokee	1 hour, 30 minutes
Poipu	30 minutes
Princeville	1 hour
Waimea Canyon	1 hour, 15 minutes

Molokai

From Molokai Airport to:	*Time to Travel*
Halawa Valley	2 hours
Kaunakakai	15 minutes
Kepuhi Beach	25 minutes
Mapulehu	35 minutes

DRIVE TIMES *(continued)*

Molokai (continued)	
From Molokai Airport to:	***Time to Travel***
Maunaloa	15 minutes
Papohaku Beach	30 minutes
Lanai	
From Lanai Airport to:	***Time to Travel***
Garden of the Gods	45 minutes
Hulopoe and Manele Bays	25 minutes
Lanai City	5 minutes
Munro Trail	15 minutes
Shipwreck Beach	35 minutes

Parking

Finding a parking spot isn't a problem in most areas. Waikiki hotels and downtown Honolulu offices charge the highest parking rates in Hawaii. Your hotel will charge you a daily rate of at least $12 to park your car. Some Neighbor Islands resorts charge a daily fee if valets park your car long term, but they have free self-park lots as well.

Parking rates in private lots in Honolulu's main business district start at $3.25 per half hour, but banks, stores, restaurants, and most professional offices validate.

There are two city-operated affordable parking structures to keep in mind: the Alii Place lot at Alakea and Hotel Streets (enter off of Alakea) charges $1 per half hour for the first two hours and $2 per each following half hour. On weekends and evenings, the rate is only 50 cents per half hour, with a $3 maximum. The Chinatown Gateway Plaza lot at King and Bethel Streets (enter off of Bethel) also charges 50 cents per half hour for the first two hours and $1 per each additional half-hour.

In the downtown area near Iolani Palace, your best bet is finding a metered parking spot on the street, either Richards or Punchbowl Streets (the rate is $1 per hour, with a two-hour limit). There is no metered parking available on King Street.

You can also try to find a metered parking spot on Bethel, Merchant, and Nuuanu Streets in Chinatown. The best times to find an empty space are mid-morning and mid-afternoon.

If you're catching a show at the Hawaii Theatre downtown, we recommend parking at the Liberty House lot at King and Bethel (enter off Bethel Street). It's a flat rate of $4 any time after 4 p.m.

In Waikiki, the best option is to leave the car in your hotel parking garage and explore the area on foot. If you're driving into Waikiki, however, the best parking option is the multilevel IMAX garage located on Seaside Avenue (on the right immediately after turning left from Kalakaua Avenue). This parking garage is centrally located and has the most affordable rate (a flat fee of $6 for all-day parking). In the Honolulu Zoo and Kapiolani Park area, street parking becomes much easier to find. Metered stalls there cost only 50 cents per hour, with a four-hour limit at Kapiolani Park and a three-hour limit near the zoo.

On Neighbor Islands, finding an available parking space is most difficult in Maui's congested Lahaina. The best option is to park at the Lahaina Center (enter from either Papalaua or Wainee Street). If you purchase anything from a shop—even a single postcard—they'll validate your parking, up to four hours.

Currently, no parking meters exist on the Neighbor Islands except near a few public office buildings. Downtown Hilo had meters, but they recently discontinued them.

All parking lots are fairly well lit, almost always filled to near capacity with frequent turnover (particularly in Waikiki), and considered safe for your person if not your valuables. Do not leave valuables in your car, even in the trunk.

Public Transportation

Using the Bus

TheBus is the inexpensive way to get from here to there on Oahu. It is safe, friendly, and efficient and has twice been recognized by the American Public Transit Association as the best in the nation. Each day, the fleet of buses collectively transports 260,000 passengers and travels 60,000 miles, equal to two and a half trips around the world.

The advantages of riding TheBus go beyond cost. This is an excellent opportunity to mingle with local residents too (chances are you'll want to ask their help in figuring out which stop you want). Strike up a conversation and, hopefully, enjoy a sampling of Hawaii's aloha spirit. Outside rush-hour traffic, the buses are usually uncrowded and the ride is pleasant. Tell the driver where you want to go, and he'll help make sure you get off at the right place.

The exact-change, one-way fare on TheBus is $2 for adults and $1 for students (ages six through high school); exact change, please, dollar bills accepted; child sitting on adult lap, free (max age 6). You can request a free transfer, which entitles you to board up to two other buses where routes intersect, at the time you pay your fare. Stopovers or picking up a bus again in a continuous direction is not permitted, and there is a time limit to the transfer. You can pay $1–$2 per person and ride around the whole circle-island route, which takes about four hours.

If you plan on using TheBus frequently during your stay, we recommend purchasing a $20 visitor pass, which allows you unlimited rides for four days, or a $40 monthly pass ($20 for students). These passes are available at all ABC stores in Waikiki.

For bus route information, call (808) 848-5555 between 5:30 a.m. and 10 p.m. daily. Be sure you have a pencil and paper handy, and be ready to provide the following information: your current location, your desired destination, and the time of day you need to arrive at that destination. TheBus also has an informative website, www.thebus.org, with a complete schedule you can download.

Also, you can get recorded route information from Waikiki to some of the most popular visitor attractions by calling (808) 296-1818, entering code number 8287, and then following the directions. If you want to take TheBus to the Polynesian Cultural Center, for example, select option 13 and listen to the recording, which will instruct you to board any Ewa-bound bus numbered 8, 19, 20, 47, or 58; ride to Ala Moana Shopping Center; then transfer to the #55 bus, which will take you to the cultural center. It's that simple.

For customer service information, call (808) 848-4500.

Abbreviated List of Bus Numbers and Their Destinations

Note: Routes and numbers are subject to change.

3	Kaimuki/Pearl Harbor	47	Waipahu
4	Nuuanu/Punahou	52C	Wahiawa/Circle Island
6	Pauoa/Woodlawn (University of Hawaii)	55C	Kaneohe/Circle Island
8	Waikiki/Ala Moana	57	Kailua/Waimanalo/ Sea Life Park
19	Waikiki/Airport and Hickam	58	Hawaii Kai/Sea Life Park
20	Airport/Halawa Gate	88A	North Shore Express

Riding the Waikiki Trolley

Take the Waikiki Trolley for a fun and pleasant way to get around Waikiki and Honolulu. You can choose the **Red Line, Blue Line,** or **Yellow Line.** You'll get a good look at Oahu as you go.

The trolley's **Red Line** covers all of Waikiki and Honolulu, stopping at the Honolulu Zoo, Waikiki Aquarium, Bishop Museum, Chinatown, Aloha Tower, and Iolani Palace (26 stops in all).

The **Blue Line** traces Oahu's scenic southern coast, including stops at Hanauma Bay and Sea Life Park (11 stops in all).

The **Yellow Line** takes passengers on a shopping and dining excursion, with dropoff/pickup points at Ala Moana Center, Ward Warehouse, Ward Centre, Duty Free Shoppers, and other locales (20 stops in all).

Four-day passes are available at the following rates: $25 per adult ($12 per child ages 4–11) for unlimited rides on either the Red and Yellow or Blue and Yellow routes, and $45 per adult ($18 per child) for unlimited rides on all three routes. For a one-day pass, the cost is $25 per adult ($18 per child) for either the Red and Yellow or Blue and Yellow routes, and $30 ($12 per child) for all three routes. Passes may be purchased at all major hotel tour desks or from service representatives at selected stops.

The **Waikiki Trolley,** operated by E Noa Tours, runs daily from 8:30 a.m. to 11 p.m. Red Line trolleys arrive/depart at appointed stops every 20 minutes; Blue Line trolleys every 60 minutes; and Yellow Line trolleys every 10 to 30 minutes. All routes originate from the Royal Hawaiian Shopping Center depot in Waikiki on Royal Hawaiian Avenue.

E Noa Tours also operates several tours via trolleys and air-conditioned vans to popular visitor attractions, such as the *Arizona* Memorial. Call (800) 824-8804 for more information.

Taxis

A taxi is probably the best way to travel through Honolulu when you don't know your way around. Taxis are not cheap, but they will save you time and frustration. If you are staying in Waikiki for, say, only three days and have no plans to leave the beach resort, your best bet may be to take a taxi.

A fare from the Honolulu International Airport to Waikiki will be from $25 to $35, depending on which end of Waikiki your hotel is located. Typically, meters begin at $2, with 25 cents added for each eighth of a mile. A few taxi companies provide sight-seeing excursions at a fixed rate. At the airport, curbside attendants assign taxis to riders on a first-come, first-served basis outside baggage claim.

Of the 30 taxi cab companies on Oahu, you may choose those with a flat rate, metered rate, or hire a limo for sight-seeing trips around the island.

If you need to call a cab, we recommend **Charley's Taxi and Tours,** one of the oldest, locally owned companies, (808) 531-1333.

TAXI COMPANIES

Oahu	
Aloha State Taxi (808) 847-3566	City Taxi (808) 524-2121
Americabs (808) 591-8830	Royal Taxi and Tours (808) 944-5513
Charley's Taxi and Tours (808) 531-1333	TheCab (808) 422-2222

TAXI COMPANIES *(continued)*

Maui

AB Taxi (808) 667-7575	Kihei Taxi (808) 879-3000
Alii Cab (808) 661-3688	La Bella Taxi (808) 242-8011
Central Maui Taxi (808) 244-7278	Royal Sedan and Taxi Service (808) 874-6900
Classy Taxi (808) 661-3044	Wailea Taxi and Tours (808) 874-5000
Kahului Taxi Service (808) 877-5681	

Big Island

A-1 Bob's Taxi (808) 963-5470	Kona Airport Taxi (808) 329-7779
Ace One Taxi (808) 935-8303	Luana's Taxi (808) 326-5466
Aloha Taxi (808) 325-5448	Marina Taxi (808) 329-2481
Alpha Star Taxi (808) 885-4771	Paradise Taxi (808) 329-1234
C&C Taxi (808) 329-0008	Percy's Taxi (808) 969-7060
Hilo Harry's Taxi (808) 935-7091	

Kauai

Ace Kauai Taxi (808) 639-4310	City Cab (808) 245-3227
Akiko's Taxi (808) 822-7588	Poipu Taxi (808) 639-2044

Molokai

Molokai Off-Road Tours and Taxi (808) 553-3369

Kukui Tours and Limousines (808) 336-0944 or (808) 553-4227 after 5 p.m.

Lanai

No full-time taxi companies serve Lanai. **Dollar Rent-A-Car** provides taxi service on a driver-available basis. Call (808) 565-7227.

Resort and Shopping Shuttles

Take a shuttle van, which is often free or inexpensive. Shuttles are air-conditioned vans or buses that go to and from a specific destination. Many hotels and resorts operate shuttles of their own, while private operators, who pick up passengers by request or at multiple designated sites, tend to offer more elaborate routes. Ask your hotel concierge for any shuttles that serve your hotel. Some widely used shuttle services are the following.

Oahu

A trolley service between Waikiki and the Aloha Tower Marketplace is available daily from 9:15 a.m. (departing the Hilton Hawaiian Village) to 9 p.m. (departing the Marketplace). Pickup/dropoff points in Waikiki include the Hilton, Outrigger Islander Hotel, the Duke Kahanamoku Statue, Honolulu Zoo, Waikiki Aquarium, Outrigger Prince Kuhio, Outrigger West, Outrigger Waikiki Surf, and Waikiki Parkside. The one-way fare is $2 for adults and $1 for children. Call (808) 528-5700.

Maui

Free shuttles offer visitor transportation within the island's Wailea Resort, with stops at the Renaissance Wailea Beach Resort, Grand Wailea Resort, Four Seasons Resort Wailea, Outrigger Wailea Resort, and the area's golf courses and (on request) tennis facilities. The shuttle operates daily from 6:30 a.m., with the final dropoff at 8:30 p.m. Call (808) 879-2828.

In Kaanapali, a shuttle transports guests between the Whalers Village Shopping Center and hotels within the resort area. The service is provided daily from 9 a.m. to 11 p.m. and costs $2 per person. Call (808) 669-3177.

Guests staying at Kapalua Resort can take advantage of a free shuttle that stops at the major hotels, golf courses, tennis facilities, and shops in the area. The daily service runs from 6 a.m. to 11 p.m. Call (808) 669-3177.

Big Island of Hawaii

In the Hilo area, the Hele-On Bus can get you to where you want to go. Fares can range from 75 cents to $6, depending on the length of the route. Several bus pass options are available. Call (808) 961-8744.

The daily shuttles of Roberts Hawaii's Kona Coast Express System link resorts on the island's northeastern Kohala coast with shops along its southeastern Kona coast. All-day passes on one of three shuttles are $4, while a system-wide pass costs $13. Shuttles begin running between 6 and 8 a.m. and stop running between 10 and 11 p.m. A round-trip averages two hours and ten minutes. For more information, including route stops, visit www.robertshawaii.com or call (800) 767-7551.

Lanai

Guests staying at either The Lodge at Koele or Manele Bay Hotel on Lanai enjoy shuttle service between the hotels and the airport. Other shuttles transport guests to the island's two championship golf courses: the Experience at Koele and the Challenge at Manele. The charge of $10 per person covers rides during the entire length of your stay. Call (808) 565-7600.

The Lahaina-Lanai Ferry

Visitors to Maui and Lanai can take advantage of Expeditions' Lahaina-Lanai Passenger Shuttle, which makes five round trips daily between the two islands.

Departure times from Lahaina Harbor on Maui are 6:45 and 9:15 a.m. and 12:45, 3:15, and 5:45 p.m. Departure times from Lanai are 8 and 10:30 a.m. and 2, 4:30, and 6:45 p.m. The fare is $25 each way for adults, $20 for children age 11 and under. Each trip takes between 45 and 55 minutes. If you're prone to motion sickness, take your Dramamine ahead of time, as the ride can get bumpy. Call (808)

Part Six

Excursions

Adventures on Your Own

Exploring Downtown Honolulu

Downtown Honolulu is small enough to conquer on your own, mostly on foot, with an abundance of historic buildings linked by gracious green public areas. In between, busy streets abound, so try to choose your timing around rush-hour traffic for a more relaxed experience.

Mission Houses Museum hosts a three-hour walking tour of downtown Honolulu on Thursdays at 9:30 a.m. You'll see the museum, pass by Kawaiahao Church, the gilded statue of King Kamehameha, Iolani Palace, Washington Place (the Governor's Mansion), and the State Capitol. Admission is $20 for adults, $19 for senior citizens and military, $6 for students, and free for children ages 6 and under. Reservations are recommended. Call (808) 531-0481.

But you can do the two- or three-block route yourself. Bring the kids, provided they are older than age 5 and able to handle the walk. You are bound to gain insights about Hawaii (especially if you take a tour of Iolani Palace) like the sad tale of how it came to be that Hawaii's last queen, Liliuokalani, was imprisoned in her own palace while her kingdom was taken away. Call a day or two in advance to reserve space on palace tours, led by docents (see contact and schedule information following).

If you're in town on the third Wednesday in January, head for the State Capitol for the cultural and culinary extravaganza that traditionally marks opening day of the legislature. You'll never see the likes of it elsewhere. The nation's youngest legislature is in business through April in the volcano-shaped Capitol.

Take TheBus

In Waikiki, catch the #2 or #13 bus on Kuhio Avenue and get off at Punchbowl Street. The drivers are friendly; ask them to let you know where to get off for the Capitol District. You can drive into town and pay to park in lots under the Capitol or City Hall complexes or the inexpensive city lot in Alii Plaza on Alakea (on the right just before Hotel Street).

What to Wear and Bring

This downtown is tropical, so sundresses, shorts, and aloha shirts are acceptable. Wear comfortable walking shoes, and sun protection. Don't forget your camera.

What It Will Cost

Bus fare is $2 per adult and $1 per child ages 6–18. Admission for Grand Tour to Iolani Palace is $20 for adults and $5 for children ages 5–17 (children ages 4 and under not admitted to the palace); Gallery self-guided tour is $6 for adults and $3 for children ages 5-17 (children ages 4 and under free). Mission Houses Museum admission is $10 for adults; $8 for seniors and military; $6 for high school and college students; and free for children ages 5 and under.

If You Get Hungry

Snacks and restaurants (a bonanza of ethnic eateries) are a short walk away in the main business district along Bishop and Alakea Streets.

Sights to See

Iolani Palace (mauka (mountain) side of King Street) The most unusual downtown sight you'll see outside of Europe is Iolani Palace. The Italianate architectural gem is the only royal palace on American soil and a far cry from the grass shacks of early Hawaii residents. (The docent may tell you that the kings actually lived in a grass shack nearby and kept the palace for affairs of state.) Built in 1882, Iolani was the official residence of the kingdom's last two monarchs, King Kalakaua (who had it built for $360,000, which nearly bankrupted the kingdom) and Queen Liliuokalani. Liliuokalani surrendered the throne under hostile pressure from American businessmen in 1893 and later was imprisoned in her own rooms at the palace. Guided tours last about 45 minutes and are scheduled at 15-minute intervals. Pick up your tickets at Iolani Barracks, located on the palace grounds. The palace is open Tuesday–Saturday, 9 a.m.–2:15 p.m. Make advance reservations. Call (808) 522-0832.

State Capitol Building Behind the palace, linked by a walkway through shady grounds, is the State Capitol, designed to reflect the Islands' volcanic and oceanic origins. On the makai (seaward) side of the building is a bronze statue of Queen Liliuokalani. On the mauka side is a statue of Father Damien, the Belgian priest who dedicated his life to ministering to leprosy patients on Molokai.

Washington Place (Governor's Mansion) Across busy Beretania Street on the Richards Street or downtown end of the Capitol is the historic governor's residence, slated to become a museum when funds are raised. Banyan trees with giant roots shade the grounds.

The Mission Houses Museum From the corner of Punchbowl and South King Streets, walk in the Diamond Head direction to the Mission Houses Museum, a complex of missionary-era buildings located on the makai side of King Street. This is where the first American missionaries established their headquarters in 1820. The structures are the oldest surviving Western-style buildings in the state. The first printed works in the North Pacific were produced in the Coral House. Guided tours of the complex are scheduled 9:30 a.m.–3 p.m. The museum is open Tuesday–Saturday, 9 a.m.–4 p.m. Call (808) 531-0481.

Kawaiahao Church From the museum, head ewa (west) to nearby Kawaiahao Church. Dedicated in 1842, this historic church was a favorite place of worship for many Hawaiian monarchs. This handsome coral-block structure was the setting for Kamehameha IV's coronation and wedding. Listed on the State and National Registers of Historic Places, Kawaiahao is one of the few churches left in Hawaii that still offers services in the Hawaiian language.

The King Kamehameha Statue Cross Punchbowl Street and walk on King Street until you reach the King Kamehameha statue, one of Hawaii's most photographed. The king is shown holding a spear in his left hand, and his right arm is outstretched in a welcoming gesture.

Hawaii State Library Return to the palace and walk right, toward Diamond Head, passing by the State Archives building. The next big building is the Hawaii State Library. Its Hawaii and Pacific section houses the state's largest collection of Hawaii-related books, periodicals, and documents. Library hours vary, but it usually opens at 9 a.m. on weekdays. Call (808) 586-3500.

Honolulu Hale Across Punchbowl Street is Honolulu Hale, otherwise known as City Hall. This California-Spanish-style structure, built in 1927, is worth a visit with the kids at night during the Christmas season, when the grounds are a festive display of oversized cartoon characters and other holiday adornments.

From Honolulu Hale, cross South King Street and Punchbowl to the bus stop nearest the main intersection. Catch the #2 or #13 bus back to Waikiki.

Dinner Cruises

For those who want to enjoy views from the sea, Hawaii offers several nightly dinner cruises, daily sunset sails, and other short cruises. The scenery, especially at sunset, is mesmerizing, and most of the boats and crews provide state-of-the-art facilities and cheerful service. On Oahu, Royal Hawaiian Cruises (call (808) 848-6360) operates the 141-foot

Navatek I, a smooth-riding vessel that uses SWATH (Small Waterplane Area Twin Hull) technology to minimize motion sickness; the ship glides above the surface while twin submarine-like hulls ride below the waves. Rates are $120–$180 for adults and $72–$134 for children ages 2–11.

Also on Oahu is Paradise Cruises (call (808) 983-7827), which operates the *Star of Honolulu,* a 232-foot, four-deck ship that offers daily and nightly cruises. The dinner cruises are $30–$199 per adult and $15–$60 per child age 3–11.

Both these ships sail from Honolulu Harbor and cruise waters off Honolulu and Waikiki.

Neighbor Islands cruise providers include the *Navatek II* (call (808) 873-3475) and Windjammer Cruises (call (808) 661-8600) on Maui; Captain Beans Cruises (call (808) 329-2955) and Body Glove Cruises (call (808) 326-7122) on the Big Island; and Captain Andy's (call (808) 335-6833) and Holoholo Charters (call (808) 246-4656) on Kauai. Call for a schedule of available trips, which may range from morning excursions and whale-watching tours to sunset cruises. Lunch and sunset meals are usually served buffet-style; evening dinners are typically sit-down affairs with a set beef/seafood menu.

At Wailua State Park on Kauai, you can putter up the Wailua River on a leisurely boat ride to the famous tourist stop of Fern Grotto. Smith's Tropical Paradise (call (808) 821-6892) offers the 90-minute cruises daily.

Helicopter Tours

Helicopter flight-seeing rides aren't for everyone, and they are not without risk, particularly in the weather conditions sometimes encountered. Helicopters are a good way to see the big picture, especially in roadless wilderness areas like Na Pali Coast, the rainy summit of Waialeale, or the active lava pool of Kilauea Volcano.

We've seen several adventurers returning to terra firma needing a place to lie down. For those for whom motion sickness is not a problem, the best views of Hawaii are from the air aboard a chopper.

Schedule flight-seeing tours early in your vacation; if the weather doesn't cooperate on the day of your tour, you'll have an opportunity to reschedule. Try to book a few days in advance—tours are often filled if you wait until the last minute, especially during high-season holidays. You can secure reservations with a major credit card.

Prices generally are $99 per person for a 20-minute flight, $179 for a 45-minute flight, and about $210 for a full-hour adventure. There are no age restrictions, but passengers weighing over 250 pounds are assessed an additional charge (usually 50%) because an extra seat will be blocked off for added comfort. Only a few operators offer ground transportation to and from hotels.

Passengers are weighed before the tour, and seats are assigned based on body weight to balance the helicopter. Generally, every other passenger is assigned a window seat. Most tours, however, use the new A-Star aircraft, which provides better viewing conditions than previous helicopters from interior seats. Accommodating up to six passengers, the A-Star is comfortable, air-conditioned, and fully enclosed.

Helicopter tours provide dramatic panoramas of such locales as Pearl Harbor, Punchbowl National Cemetery of the Pacific, and Diamond Head on Oahu; Kilauea Volcano and the steep rain forest valleys of the Big Island; Haleakala and the West Maui Mountains on Maui; and the rugged Na Pali and Mt. Waialeale crater on Kauai. You'll get to see some spectacular hidden spots—waterfalls, black-sand beaches, lava fields, and cinder cones—that are otherwise inaccessible.

Each tour is fully narrated by the pilot, adding to the music humming in your specially equipped headset. Many pilots are certified tour guides, providing insights on history, geology, and nature and adding an educational facet to the tour.

The pilot also operates a multicamera system within the helicopter, capturing the scenery (and sometimes you!) on tape. You can buy the video at the end of your journey, usually for about $25.

About motion sickness: In addition to over-the-counter and prescription drugs that may help prevent motion sickness, you may want to try elastic wristbands that are designed to stimulate an acupuncture point on your wrist and counter air- or seasickness without drugs. Ginger is a favorite local remedy to prevent motion sickness; try drinking real ginger ale or snacking on ginger shortly before the flight.

A caveat: Choppers, like any aircraft, crash. It's a fact. Bad weather, mechanical failure, pilot errors all cause helicopters to go down. While the safety record in Hawaii is excellent, it's not faultless. Each year at least one helicopter crashes somewhere in the Islands. Keep an eye on weather conditions, especially on Kauai, and postpone your tour if the weather is unsettled. Go early in the day, when the air is still and calm. If you're flying over water, make sure your bird has pontoons, and you have a life vest.

HELICOPTER OPERATORS

Oahu

Magnum Helicopters (808) 833-1133
Makani Kai Helicopters (808) 834-5813

Maui

Alex Air Helicopters (808) 877-4354
Blue Hawaiian Helicopters (808) 871-8844
Hawaii Helicopters (808) 877-3900
Sunshine Helicopters (808) 871-0722

The Big Island

Blue Hawaiian Helicopters (808) 961-5600
Safari Helicopters (808) 969-1259

HELICOPTER OPERATORS *(continued)*

Kauai
Air-1 Inter-Island Helicopters (808) 335-5009
Bali Helicopter Tours (808) 335-3166
Jack Harter Helicopters (808) 245-3774
Safari Helicopters (808) 246-0136

Molokai Mule Ride

In today's era of high-tech attractions and showbiz wizardry, it's heart-warming to see that this rugged mule ride remains a favorite tourist activity. The Molokai Mule Ride to Kalaupapa stars surefooted mules that carry their riders down a hair-raising, 26-switchback trail. The 90-minute excursion includes breathtaking views of Molokai's northern coast. Kalaupapa is the historic settlement where Father Damien de Veuster ministered to leprosy patients from 1873 to 1889. Offered daily except Sunday, the per-person tour includes a picnic lunch. Call (800) 567-7550 or check out the website at www.molokai-muleride.com.

Submarine Rides

If you can't bring yourself to put your face in the water to snorkel, there is another way to admire the undersea beauty off Hawaiian shores. Atlantis Submarines offers narrated, air-conditioned tour rides on three islands in which you never get wet but can observe coral reefs teeming with yellow tangs, parrot fish, moray eels, and many other types of colorful sea life. On Oahu, catch the sub ride at Hilton Hawaiian Village, where you board a shuttle boat and transfer to large (48–64 passenger) vessels. On Maui, shuttle boats depart from Lahaina and take you to a 48-passenger sub that explores the ocean channel between Maui and Lanai. In Kailua-Kona on the Big Island, Atlantis's 48-passenger sub examines a large natural coral reef.

Rates are $79–$84 for adults and $39–$42 for children. For more information, call (800) 543-8359 or visit www.atlantissubmarines.org.

Cruising Hawaii

If you haven't sailed among the Hawaiian Islands, you've missed one of the best experiences in the Pacific. A seven-day cruise delivers the true nature of the islands. You can lounge on the sun deck with a good book, but there's much to see: sunsets, rainbows, whales, and, when Kilauea Volcano is pumping, the eerie night spectacle of red-hot lava running like jelly into the sea. Shore excursions offer the chance to sample the sights, nature, and culture of the islands, not to mention golf and other outdoor sports.

Norwegian Cruise Line operates luxury steamships in Hawaii for weeklong interisland voyages. *Norwegian Star,* a new, 2,200-passenger, $400 million "supership" reputed to be "the largest cruise ship ever to set sail in the Islands," launched weekly seven-day interisland cruises in late 2001. It shared duty with *Norwegian Wind* for the past two years while NCL was busy building and refitting two newly American-registered ships that are due to launch Hawaii cruising in mid-2004.

The new ships are the *Pride of America* and *Pride of Aloha. Pride of America* will be the first passenger ocean liner built to sail under the American flag in nearly half a century. *The Pride of Aloha* is an existing 2,000-passenger ship, formerly the *Norwegian Sky,* that will be reflagged and staffed with an American crew. Their addition to Hawaiian waters will allow the cruise line to expand its passenger capacity by nearly one-third to 200,000 a year on cruises varying from 3 to 11 days during 2004. Although the 2004 schedule includes all four ships, the *Star* and *Wind* will be returned to mainland service during the year and the new ships will run seven-day and three- or four-day itineraries with lots of in-port time for passengers to enjoy shore excursions in the Islands.

Miami-based Norwegian Cruise Line is offering some bargain fares to launch their new service. Check out the fare and cruise schedule on the Internet or with a travel agent.

Norwegian Cruise Line

(800) 327-7030; www.ncl.com

Type of Ship New and refurbished luxury ocean liners.

Type of Cruise Destination, family oriented, casual and flexible.

Comments New to Hawaii, the *Norwegian Star* and *Norwegian Wind* fill the void caused by the demise of American Classic Voyages, parent of American Hawaii Cruises, whose ships cruised the Islands for several decades, and United States Lines, whose new liner sailed only a year. The New Orleans–based cruise firm filed bankruptcy in the fall of 2001, and the ships were sold at auction.

The new Norwegian Cruise Line ships began service after our press deadline so we are unable to provide the usual rating and review comments. However, cruise line officials have gone to some lengths to assure their ships will reflect the culture through crew and decor, right down to the hull design on the *Pride of Aloha,* subject of a Hawaiian art competition. That local focus, plus new ships and attractive prices, makes these cruises appealing and worth a try.

Rather like a floating resort, the *Norwegian Star* has 15 decks, 10 restaurants, and 14 cocktail lounges with a crew of 1,100 to attend to as many as 2,200 passengers. The 91-ton, 971-foot-long vessel, powered by twin diesels, cruises at 25 knots under a Bahamas flag. It was built for

Hawaii service and is presently the only ship devoted exclusively to inter-island cruises.

The ship embarks Sundays from Honolulu's Aloha Tower and Fridays from Lahaina Harbor on voyages with ports of call including Nawiliwili, Kauai; Hilo or Kailua-Kona, Hawaii; and an exotic new destination way down in the Central Pacific: remote Fanning Island (Tabuaeran) in the Republic of Kiribati, part of the equatorial Line Islands.

One possible downside: The ship spends two full days at sea, cruising 2,000 miles south to Fanning Island and back. The side trip to remote Fanning, a tiny coral atoll, for a day-long foreign port of call, enables the cruise line to skirt the Jones Act which bans foreign-flagged vessels from sailing exclusively between U.S. ports. It also poses an interesting comparison for modern, American Hawaii. Fanning is the Pacific paradise some dreamers expect to find in the wealthy, worldly islands to the north. On the other hand, Fanning's 1,300 residents are experiencing weekly visits by up to 2,200 cruising guests, which is bound to change the local culture more than any event since World War II.

The 754-foot, 50-ton *Norwegian Wind,* formerly the *Windward,* cruises at a top speed of 18 knots. She was built in 1993, refurbished and stretched with a new 130-foot midsection in 1998, and now offers spacious surroundings and picture-window ocean views from most staterooms. With a capacity of 1,748 passengers and 689 crew, the *Norwegian Wind* is scheduled to make 10- and 11-day Hawaiian voyages, spending four days at sea en route to and from Fanning, with two days in Lahaina on the longer cruise and a sail-by view of Kilauea Volcano's fiery ribbons of lava, if they are flowing, on the shorter. The *Norwegian Wind* features ten passenger decks, five restaurants, a dozen bars and lounges, and a casino, which won't feature gambling on Hawaii cruises (Hawaii is one of the few states where offshore gambling is still against the law). This ship will cruise Australian and Alaskan waters before sailing to Hawaii, where cruises are scheduled September through April.

Cruising, Pro and Con

If you've never visited Hawaii and want to see two or more islands, a cruise is a good solution. A slow boat between the islands is relaxing. You'll avoid changing hotels and save time and money, but there's a trade-off. Because a sea cruise usually allows only a day in each port, you'll only get of a hint of each island. Think of a cruise as a scouting expedition.

You can sign up for shore excursions offered by the cruise line or strike out on your own on foot, by taxi, or by rental car. If you have a place you simply must see, hire a rental car and go. You can reserve and rent a car while still on board ship.

Otherwise, check out the full roster of shore excursions offered by the cruise line. All cruise ships that call on Hawaiian ports offer shore excursions—a helicopter tour of Kauai, hikes and kayak tours, Kona deep-sea fishing, snorkeling, and dive trips—all easily booked on board.

With the exception of the Big Island and Oahu, you can see a lot of an island in a day in a rental car. If you sail from Honolulu, arrive a day or two early to see the island, or stay two or three days after the cruise.

All meals are included in the price, which means you will miss the best of the Islands' regional cuisine. Food aboard is abundant, but it's not the same as dining at Alan Wong's Restaurant.

If you love the beach, you're out of luck except on Kauai, where Kalapaki Beach is a five-minute walk from Nawiliwili Harbor, the ship's anchorage.

Other Touring Suggestions

Around Oahu

Hawaii's most famous landmark, Leahi Crater, was renamed Diamond Head in the early 1800s by British sailors who claimed to see diamonds glittering on the crater. (The "diamonds" turned out to be merely sparkling calcite crystals.)

Waikiki Beach is actually a collection of small beaches, some with imported sand (from Molokai's empty beaches). The hotels block all ocean views from Kalakaua Avenue until Kuhio Beach, site of the Honolulu Police Department's Waikiki precinct house, surfboard racks, and the larger-than-life statue of Duke Kahanamoku, Hawaii's legendary sports hero. He stands cast in bronze, back to the sea he loved, arms outstretched in perpetual greeting.

Duke Kahanamoku was a record-setting swimmer (he captured gold medals in the 1912 and 1920 Summer Olympics) who set the 100-meter freestyle world record in 1911. In later years, Kahanamoku traveled the world, staging surf exhibitions to popularize the sport. He died in 1968 at the age of 77.

In 1850, **Honolulu** became the capital of the kingdom. Today it is a 26-mile-long urban strip, but the City and County of Honolulu not only encompasses all of Oahu but also extends 1,400 miles northwest up the island chain to Kure Atoll. In Hawaii, folks call Honolulu "town" and everything else that lacks a building over three stories tall "country." Waikiki is Waikiki.

Drive up Ala Moana Boulevard to **Honolulu Harbor**. Until Pearl Harbor was made navigable in the early 1900s, Honolulu Harbor was the only protected body of water of its size in Hawaii. In 1794, the English ship *Butterworth,* led by Captain William Brown, became the first foreign vessel to enter the harbor.

The centerpiece of the harbor remains the ten-story **Aloha Tower**, the tallest building in Honolulu when it opened in 1926. Its tenth-floor observation deck provides sweeping views of Oahu's southern coastline.

From the 1930s to the 1950s, steamships carrying dreamy-eyed visitors radioed their arrival schedule to harbormasters at the tower. And as luxury liners such as Matson's, SS *Lurline*, and SS *Monterey* pulled into port, a festive celebration—"Boat Day"—took place, as residents welcomed *malihini* (visitors) with Hawaiian music, hula, and sweet-smelling flower lei. A modern version of Boat Day occurs when interisland steamships depart the harbor from the area of **Aloha Tower Marketplace,** a retail-restaurant complex with open-air waterfront restaurants that offer a seat on the busy harbor plied by tugboats and in- and outbound ships.

From the harbor, take Alakea up to get on the Pali Highway and head to **Nuuanu Valley,** gateway to the Koolau Mountains and Oahu's Windward side.

At the top of the Pali in 1795, Kamehameha I and his army drove 300 Oahu defenders over the cliff to their deaths. You can still see the squared outline of a gun rampart on top of the mountain from the highway, a reminder of the battle.

Today, the **Pali Lookout** is one of the island's most visited spots, as evidenced by the parking lot full of tour buses. Stop to be blown by the wind and admire the striking views of haunting Windward Oahu.

Travelers Advisory: Pali Lookout is a prime area for *cockaroaches,* the pidgin term for car clout thieves who smash car windows and grab purses, cameras, or anything in sight. You can lock your car doors and trunk and still lose. It is best to take all items of value with you, or leave the car empty, open, and unlocked.

Up behind Waikiki is misty **Manoa Valley**, formed in part by the 2,013-foot **Mount Tantalus.** The rainbow-laced valley is home to **University of Hawaii–Manoa,** with an enrollment of 20,000 students. The sprawling campus, shaded by specimen tropical tress, is a mix of disparate architecture, with Korean temples beside World War II–like barracks. The most graceful building is the East West Center, a think tank begun by President Lyndon B. Johnson with congressional funds to foster alliances in Asia and the Pacific.

Back in Waikiki, drive east on the H-1 to find the tony eastern neighborhood of **Kahala** and the Kahala Mandarin Oriental Hotel, surrounded by grandiose estates from the Japanese property-buying heyday of the 1980s, now passed. Continuing on Kalanianaole Highway, you enter suburban **Hawaii Kai,** home to Roy's Restaurant, where foodies worship nightly at one of Hawaii's first regional cuisine restaurants. **Koko Head Crater** looms over the suburban homes and marks the spot where Oahu at last begins to reveal its raw, natural self along the Kaiwi Coast with its rocky shoreline, sandy beaches, famous spouting **Halona**

Blowhole (a geyser-like phenomenon caused when big waves hit a hole in the rocks), pocket beaches, and view of Molokai 26 miles across the sea. The 2,000-foot-deep Kaiwi Channel between Oahu and Molokai, considered one of the world's most dangerous because it funnels open ocean currents between the Islands, is the course for the celebrated Molokai Hoe outrigger canoe race each year, featuring daring paddlers from around the Pacific battling the seas and each other from Molokai to Waikiki Beach.

The main attraction here is not the crater (which you can climb on a steep trail) but **Hanauma Bay,** a coastal crater with a blown-out sea wall; the reef is a tropical fish preserve and the most popular snorkel spot in Hawaii, attracting 3,000 visitors a day. Believe it or not, fish still outnumber snorkelers.

Windward Oahu

Continuing east from Koko Head crater affords you a scenic drive along Oahu's southeastern coastline. To your right you will spot **Makapuu Beach Park** and the crashing waves beyond. Note also a pair of offshore islands; the larger one (67 acres) is **Manana,** or Rabbit Island. In the late 1800s, its owner, John Cummins, used the island to raise European hares, and a small population of rabbits still resides there, although the island is mainly a seabird sanctuary.

Ahead is **Sea Life Park,** an old-fashioned marine attraction where captive creatures like dolphins jump through hoops. The park also serves as a rehab center for injured sea life rescued from Hawaii waters.

Rising up 2,000 feet and more, the jagged spine of the majestic **Koolau Mountains** begins here, dramatic backdrop to the Windward towns of Waimanalo, Kailua, and Kaneohe. Geologists believe the sheer precipice of the Koolau may have been formed when a huge portion of the coast dropped off into the sea, leaving a vertical wall now cloaked in rain forest green.

In **Waimanalo,** a country settlement with a great bodysurfing beach, farmers grow abundant food and flower crops in the broad fertile plain below the cliffs. Nearby, the U.S. military has maintained a 1,500-acre seaside retreat beside an airfield known as Bellows. The first Japanese prisoner of war was captured on **Bellows Beach** shortly after the December 7, 1941, raid on Pearl Harbor, when his small submarine struck the reef in Waimanalo Bay and sank.

With nearly 60,000 residents, **Kailua** is the second largest town in the state. Kailua (it means "two seas") sits between the **Kawainui Marsh** and the Pacific Ocean. The marsh, the largest body of freshwater in Hawaii, is slowly becoming a meadow. But Kailua is blessed with splendid beaches, a picturesque bay, natural vistas, and a strong sense of community. **Kailua Beach** is one of the state's best beaches, famous as a windsurfing spot (onshore tradewinds blow nearly all the time). Nearby, **Lanikai Beach** is becoming a kind of Malibu West with celebrities like actress Michelle Pfeiffer and cookie magnate Wally "Famous" Amos in residence and others such as Robin Williams and Mel Gibson among the frequent visitors.

Neighboring Kaneohe, an undistinguished strip mall of a town, borders one of the world's most beautiful azure bays, **Kaneohe Bay,** dotted with islets and surrounded by steep cliffs.

Further up the Windward Shore, bound for the North Shore, you'll come to Kaaawa, home to **Kualoa Ranch,** a working cattle ranch that has turned to tourism to make ends meet and to share its magnificent setting. Activities offered here include horseback riding, helicopter tours, scuba diving, all-terrain-vehicle (ATV) riding, Jet Skiing, shooting range, hiking, an ancient fishpond, and a hidden beach.

About 600 yards off **Kualoa Beach Park** stands one of Hawaii's most photographed little islands: **Mokolii,** known as Chinaman's Hat. Ancient Hawaiians fancied the islet looked like a lizard's tail. Modern folks gave it the nickname Chinaman's Hat because its conical shape resembles the straw coolie hats once favored by immigrant workers.

The best and safest way to take its photo is to leave the highway, either to enter the park or to pull off along one of the beaches, and to shoot it with Kaneohe Bay in the background.

North Shore

Laie is where you'll find the **Polynesian Cultural Center,** one of the state's notable attractions.

Driving on around the northern point of the island, you approach the famous North Shore surfing beaches. Gone are the sweet-smelling scents of coconut oil and suntan lotion, replaced by the aroma of fresh salt air. Gone is the jungle of hotels and condominiums, replaced by surfer cottages and homes frequently threatened by massive winter surf. Gone are the friendly ocean waves of Waikiki, replaced by gigantic swells that have helped the North Shore gain worldwide notoriety as the undisputed capital of surfing.

Each winter, the world's top professional and amateur surfers make their annual pilgrimage to such renowned surf spots as **Sunset Beach, Alii Beach,** and **Ehukai Beach** (and its famous Banzai Pipeline).

The heart of Oahu's North Shore is **Haleiwa,** a funky village of surf shops, art galleries, mom-and-pop shops, shaved ice stands, and small main-street bistros like Kua Aina Sandwiches and Café Haleiwa, where surfers stoke up when waves are flat. Jameson's by the Sea is an irresistible but crowded steak and seafood restaurant with an always-popular lanai at sundown.

The best attraction is the **Haleiwa Surf Museum,** which traces the origins and history of the sport with photographs, artifacts, and memorabilia from Hollywood to Haleiwa.

Leeward Oahu

Here on the **Waianae Coast** in towns like Nanakuli and Makaha, pit bulls guard plantation houses with rusty pickups in the yard. This is one of the last enclaves of Hawaiians on Oahu. In general, the western side of Oahu turns its hot, dry back on tourists. Seldom (if ever) featured in travel magazines, this side of Oahu has, however, some spectacular unspoiled places.

Once you get comfortable with the local scene, you'll begin to enjoy the reef-fringed 20-mile-long stretch of coast that ends in exclamation at needle-nosed **Kaena Point,** Oahu's westernmost point and a popular fishing spot.

Though Kaena "points" toward Kauai, early Hawaiians believed the point was one place where human souls departed Earth—good souls to the right, less virtuous to the left.

Kaena means "heat" in Hawaiian. You'll understand why when you take the hike to the point that "throbs in the sun," according to a chant. Sunsets here are red hot. Bring plenty of water.

Heading back toward Honolulu, you'll arrive at **Makaha,** site of a popular longboard surf contest, emphasizing the surfing style favored in the 1950s and 1960s. The North Shore attracts worldwide attention, but true surfing insiders know Makaha as one of Hawaii's hottest surf spots. Here you'll find some of the finest surfers in the state, from young prodigies to legendary old-timers.

Beyond Makaha and Nanakuli is **Waianae,** a place often ignored by visitors. However, this may soon change. Recently, community leaders have talked about boosting Waianae's economic potential through cultural tourism, recognizing visitors' desires to learn about Hawaii's culture. One realization of these discussions is the **Na Hana Lima Store,** a cooperative of a dozen Waianae-area artisans, located at Waianae Mall Shopping Center. The store includes Hawaiian jewelry, sculptures, woodwork, kapa, prints, pottery, and other items.

Nearby is **Ko Olina,** a lavish resort area featuring Ihilani Resort and Spa, a 387-room luxury retreat. The resort's eye-catching man-made lagoons are now open to all for swimming.

Maui

On a map, Maui looks almost like a person. It's easy to make out a head, a neck, and a body. The **West Maui Mountains** form the head, the neck is the isthmus of the Valley Isle, and **Haleakala** is the body. Such diverse geographical anatomy makes it Hawaii's second most popular island, attracting more than two million visitors a year.

Most arrive at the airport in Kahalui, the trafficky center of commerce, and head straight to one of the main resorts in Wailea, Kihei, Kapalua, or

Kaanapali. A lucky few avoid the crowds and fly from Honolulu directly to Kapalua/West Maui Airport or to the lush tropical retreat of Hana. Wherever you choose to stay on Maui, go for a ride at least once to get a glimpse of the rest of the island, outside the resort zone. Here are some day trips to consider.

At Maui's "chin" is **Maalaea,** a small waterfront community with a boat harbor, condos, surfing area, and a stop worth your attention, the **Maui Ocean Center.** It features a 600,000-gallon aquarium with hundreds of ocean creatures, including rays, sea turtles, reef fish, and sharks.

South Maui

Driving south, you reach **Kihei,** a busy beach town with more than 100 small hotels and condos, shops, restaurants, and businesses. Kihei has nightlife, a rarity on the Neighbor Islands, in nightclubs, sports bars, and karaoke bars.

South of Kihei is the master-planned resort of **Wailea** ("water of Lea," goddess of canoes), a 1,500-acre oasis of luxury hotels and condos, set on five crescent beaches. After Wailea, the paved road ends at the isolated resort and old community of **Makena,** where the elegant Maui Prince Hotel sits amid 1,800 acres of mostly rugged, natural dryland slope and two championship golf courses. Beyond the Prince, the road continues past beachfront homes until it ends on an old lava flow.

Driving west from Maalaea, two-lane Highway 30 passes through a tunnel on the coastal route; there's a whale-watch lookout nearby at **McGregor Point,** as well as miles of open coastline and small tree-shaded beach parks, old graveyards, and views of Lanai and Molokai.

West Maui

Turn left into **Lahaina** (it means "the heat") to discover its historic buildings, harbor, and Front Street hangouts, popular day or night. The entire town is designated a National Historic Landmark, and Lahaina's storied past lives on in its restored relics that cluster around a mammoth banyan tree in the town square.

In the eighteenth century, Maui's ferocious high chief Kahekili, said to have built houses out of the skulls of defeated warriors to keep his enemies terrified, declared Lahaina his capital. He favored the area for its weather, lush thickets of banana and breadfruit trees, and defensible location between steep West Maui slopes and the sea, where it afforded a natural harbor. Kahekili, who gives his name to a nearby beach, survived all his foes and died in Waikiki in his 80s.

Lahaina was the focal point of the whaling industry in the mid-nineteenth century; at the height of the whaling era, more than 100 whaling ships dropped anchor at the town's harbor. Along with the ships came hundreds of pleasure-seeking sailors, the bane of the disapproving

Christian missionaries. In 1825, a mob of British sailors threatened to kill missionary settler William Richards and set his house on fire unless a law forbidding prostitution and alcohol was repealed. Two years later, a cannon struck Richards's home from a visiting whaler.

A short drive up from Lahaina is Kaanapali Beach Resort, where Alexander and Baldwin converted sugarcane fields into the island's first master planned resort—a parklike setting on a four-mile gold-sand beach with two championship golf courses, hotels, condos and homes, and an open-air mall with shops and restaurants.

Beyond Kaanapali other communities of condos and apartments dot the shoreline, but at the northwest end of the resort coast, **Kapalua Resort,** a picturesque resort with five exquisite bays, puts an end to human work and lets nature take over. For hiking enthusiasts, the Kapalua Nature Society offers guests hikes in the West Maui Mountains. The road continues on to Kahului, paved now but still tortuous, skinny, and slow going. It's a great drive through a relatively unspoiled area of the island.

North Shore

Heading toward Hana from Kahului on Highway 36 takes you to **Paia,** a breezy former sugar plantation town full of quaint brightly painted shops and bistros that look more Caribbean than Hawaiian. Paia is unofficial headquarters for nearby windsurfing favorite **Hookipa Beach.** Hookipa's strong year-round winds and ideal wave conditions draw the world's top windsurfers, dubbed the Maui Air Force for their aerial antics. It is a sight to see these daredevils hit waves head-on, to gain "hang time" up in the air, before splashing down in the sea. Nearby, **Haiku** has inexpensive lodging in B&Bs and vacation rentals.

Upcountry

From Paia, you can head inland up through the open fields to the cooler heights of Maui called Upcountry. The drive up the foothills of Haleakala, a dormant volcano, takes you to **Makawao.** This *paniolo* (cowboy) town has avoided becoming a ghost town by becoming a kind of arts center. It's the scene of an unforgettable July 4 parade and rodeo.

Farther upcountry is **Kula,** a scenic community that clings to Haleakala's side at 3,000 feet and is known for its cool climate, its thriving flower farms (growing the strange South African flowers known as protea), its sweet onions, and **Ulupalakua Ranch.** The 20,000-acre ranch, a nearly vertical spread where the volcano last erupted around 1790, raises cattle and elk and grows wine grapes.

Drop by the tasting room at **Tedeschi Vineyards** to sample the pineapple wine. Better yet, bring a picnic basket, pair it with a Maui vintage, and enjoy the afternoon in the cool uplands.

From Kula you can take the road up to the island's greatest natural spectacle, **Haleakala National Park.** According to Hawaiian legend, the demigod Maui captured the sun with his magic lasso on Haleakala. He convinced the sun to slow down its travels, lengthening the days and giving his mother, Hina, more time to dry her tapa cloths.

Haleakala is one of only two places in the world—the Big Island is the other—where you may see the exotic silversword, an odd-looking plant with silvery leaves and tall spikes of yellow and violet florets, from June through October.

Hana

Taking a different route from Paia starts you on the long drive to **Hana,** a three-hour trip, that crosses 56 one-lane bridges and takes 617 twists and turns (about 12 curves a mile). The rental car parade goes slowly so everyone can ogle Maui's natural beauty: crashing surf, steep green hills, waterfalls, and flowers.

Hana is a small community of about a thousand residents. The lifestyle here is slow and unpretentious. Highlights include the **Hana Cultural Center,** which retells area history, **Hana Coast Gallery, Hana Gardenland,** and **Hasegawa General Store.** In Hasegawa's General Store, "You'll find a baseball bat and a piano hat, sunburn creams and the latest magazines, muumuu and mangoes and ukuleles, too," according to the lyrics by Paul Weston who wrote the 1961 hit song "The Hasegawa General Store." Best of all, you can buy the sheet music and, if you're lucky, a cassette recording of the song "Hasegawa General Store" by Arthur Godfrey, Hilo Hattie, and local residents Jim Nabors and Carol Burnett. The other noted local musician, the late George Harrison of Beatles fame, frequently shopped Hasegawa's but somehow never got around to recording the song.

Hana also has a single resort hotel, Hotel Hana-Maui (now owned by the California folks who developed Big Sur's famed Post Ranch), a few condos, and B&Bs that provide limited lodging.

Ten miles south of the town of Hana is **Kipahulu,** where Charles Lindbergh is buried in the backyard of a cliffside church. The famed American aviator—in 1927, he became the first person to fly solo across the Atlantic Ocean—first visited Kipahulu in the 1950s. "I love Maui so much, I would rather live one day in Maui than one month in New York," a cancer-stricken Lindbergh told his doctor. The "Lone Eagle" died on August 26, 1974, at age 72. Lindbergh's grave lies near **Palapala Hoomau Congregational Church,** beneath *iliili* stones and a block of Vermont granite.

Big Island of Hawaii

Youngest of the Hawaiian Islands, the Big Island of Hawaii, which lends its name to the entire archipelago, is by far the largest—twice the size of all other Hawaiian Islands combined, with a grand total of 4,028 square miles. And of the 13 climatic regions on Earth, the Big Island has all but the two most extreme: Arctic and Saharan. Birthplace of Hawaii's greatest king, Kamehameha I, the island is full of history, legend, and spirits.

The easiest way to plan your vacation itinerary here is to take a Big Island map and draw a vertical line right down the middle of the island. Locals refer to the left half of the island as the "Kona" side, and the right half is the "Hilo" side. Both sides are well worth a visit, necessitating a rental car.

Kona Side

The hub of visitor activity is on the Kona side, particularly at the seaside village of **Kailua-Kona.** American humorist Mark Twain, who fell in love with the Hawaiian Islands during his visit in March 1866, once described Kailua-Kona as "the sleepiest, quietest, Sundayest-looking place you can imagine."

If Twain were alive today, perhaps he would put on his brightest aloha shirt and join the parade of people walking and driving along **Alii Drive.** His "Sundayest" place now is a Friday-night kind of place. Although a few landmarks from Twain's day remain, the town is now a busy jumble of hotels, condominiums, bars, restaurants, and shops.

Each August, Kailua-Kona hosts the **Hawaiian International Billfish Tournament,** a prestigious fishing event luring the world's top anglers. The largest fish caught during the event was a 1,166-pound marlin in 1993.

Five miles and 1,400 feet uphill from Kailua-Kona sits **Holualoa,** a village of coffee groves and artists' studios and galleries on the slopes of Hualalai.

South of Kailua-Kona and down the slope to the sea is mile-wide **Kealakekua Bay,** a state marine conservation district and favorite place to snorkel. A 27-foot white obelisk marks the spot of Captain Cook's death in 1779. The British sea captain and four of his men were killed in a skirmish with Hawaiians (4 Hawaiian chiefs and 13 commoners were also killed in the battle).

Farther south, 22 miles from Kailua-Kona, is **Puuhonua O Honaunau National Historical Park,** which in old Hawaii was a sanctuary or place of refuge where anyone who violated *kapu* (religious taboo) could escape a death sentence, if he ran fast enough. The hapless could seek absolution and do penance, then be forgiven and allowed to return home safely.

Hawaiians of old strongly enforced their laws, believing that sins left unpunished would incur the wrath of their gods in the form of earthquakes, tidal waves, famines, and volcanic eruptions. They pursued violators relentlessly and killed them. Puuhonua O Honaunau is the best preserved of all Hawaii's places of refuge. More than 400,000 visitors visit this 180-acre site each year. Each summer, the park hosts a cultural festival of Hawaiian arts and crafts, with *lau hala* weaving demonstrations, games, hula performances, and food.

Traveling all the way down the south coast is a full-day outing that ends at the southernmost part of the island, of any state in fact, **Ka Lae** (South Point).

Kohala Coast

Go north from Kailua-Kona to find the sunny Kohala Coast and its luxury resorts, hiking trails, and gold-sand beaches. Historical points of interest are also prevalent here. The area has several ancient fishponds, where fish were raised for royalty. The fish would be wrapped in *ti* leaves and delivered by servants to their *alii* in Kailua-Kona. Parts of this "King's Trail" are still visible from the coast.

Inland from the Kohala Coast, in the foothills of Mauna Kea, is **Waimea** (also called Kamuela), the peaceful village where the *paniolo* (cowboy) lifestyle still thrives on rolling emerald hills and lush pastures that disappear in the often misty distance. This cool uplands is the home of the 225,000-acre **Parker Ranch,** one of the largest cattle ranches in the United States, and the site of a major rodeo held every July 4. The nearby **Parker Ranch Visitor Center and Museum** recites the history of the ranch as well as six generations of the Parker family.

North Kohala, the peninsula that forms the northernmost tip of the Big Island and ends in the village of Hawi, is the birthplace of Kamehameha I. His birthplace is near the giant **Mookini Luakini Heiau,** Hawaii's first National Historic Landmark. The stones used for the construction of the *heiau* (temple) were supposedly passed hand to hand for nine miles from the coastline.

Hamakua Coast

Heading east from Waimea, toward Hilo, is **Waipio Valley,** a deep gorge of 2,000-foot cliffs laced with waterfalls and carpeted with taro patches that run down to a black-sand beach. Once a thriving community and favorite retreat of Hawaiian royalty, the valley is accessible via a steep cliff, by shuttle tour, by four-wheel-drive vehicle, or on foot. It's easy going down, but a tough pull back up, so most take the shuttle.

Hilo is the island's county seat and largest town, with a population of 47,639. Yet it never outgrew its small-town feel. Most years, Hilo ranks as the wettest city in the United States. It rains 128 inches a year there; that's more than ten feet, and the result is a profusion of tropical flowers, trees, and fruit. Orchids and anthuriums are everywhere.

Hilo was once the center of trade. The activity heightened with the arrival of Westerners, as Hilo Bay gave foreign vessels safe harbor. In August 1881, however, a lava flow from neighboring Mauna Loa cut a path straight toward Hilo, threatening to consume the growing town.

On August 9, Princess Ruth Keelikolani—an imposing figure at six feet tall and 400-plus pounds—arrived from Honolulu and, standing at the edge of the lava flow, prayed and presented offerings of *ohelo* berries, tobacco, flowers, red silk, and brandy to the goddess Pele.

Hilo was not as fortunate when it came to tidal waves. On April 1, 1946, the Hawaiian Islands were struck by devastating tidal waves, the result of an Alaskan earthquake. Hilo was the hardest hit, with nearly 100 deaths. In 1960, another tsunami struck Hilo, killing 61 residents.

When in Hilo, go downtown and walk around the restored historic buildings to find interesting shops and restaurants, and the twice-weekly Farmer's Market.

Other Hilo highlights include the 20-acre **Nani Mau Gardens, the Lyman Mission House and Museum,** and the new **Pacific Tsunami Museum,** which recalls the waves that almost wiped out Hilo.

It's nearly an hour's drive uphill from Hilo to **Volcano,** an upcountry art community in a fern forest just outside **Hawaii Volcanoes National Park,** the top visitor attraction in the state. Volcano viewing conditions depend on the weather and lava activity. Call (808) 985-6000 for recorded updates.

Kauai

The northernmost major island and the oldest is also the most beautiful. Many believe that it was the first to be populated, rather than the Big Island. It is certainly the most independent, located as it is off on the remote end of the cluster of main islands, about 70 miles across the water from Oahu. It's proven to be quite the movie star, serving as a setting for more than 50 films, including *South Pacific, Blue Hawaii, King Kong, Raiders of the Lost Ark,* and *Jurassic Park.*

The beauty runs deep. Kauai suffered and survived devastating damage from two major hurricanes in recent times, Iwa in 1982 and Iniki in 1992. But Kauai's 54,000 residents and abundant attributes have long since recovered.

South Shore

You land in **Lihue,** a one-time plantation town with an airport surrounded by cane fields and sea on the southeastern part of the island. A drive along Rice Street takes you to the **Kauai Museum,** where the island's history is retold with artifacts, artworks, photographs, and other exhibit items. Also in Lihue is the island's major seaport, **Nawiliwili Harbor** and the **Alekoko Fish Pond** (also known as the Menehune Fish Pond) further up the Huleia River. The Menehune, legendary elfin people, are credited with great feats of engineering overnight to create fishponds, roads, and temples. Just beyond Lihue are **Grove Farm Home-**

stead, a plantation-era home turned into a museum, and, a few miles further, **Kilohana,** another plantation manor.

West just after the 520 turnoff toward Koloa and Poipu Beach Resort is Lawai, home of the **National Tropical Botanical Garden,** a 186-acre Eden that maintains the largest collection of tropical flora in the world.

West Kauai

Farther leeward at the mouth of the Waimea River are the rocky remains of **Fort Elizabeth,** built in 1816 by Anton Schaeffer in an unsuccessful attempt to claim Kauai for the Russian crown.

In the town of **Waimea** stands a statue of Captain James Cook, who first set foot on Hawaiian soil at Waimea Bay on January 20, 1778.

Nearby is 3,567-foot **Waimea Canyon,** a 15-mile-long gorge with waterfalls, wild goats, and colorful striations that glow in fading light. Mark Twain dubbed it "the Grand Canyon of the Pacific." You can hike or ride horses in the canyon.

Just north of Waimea is the **Barking Sands Missile Range.** Check in at the gate and head to **Barking Sands Beach,** so named because of the "barking" sounds the sand makes as you hoof it on the beach. The beach is a safe distance from the still-active missile range.

Beyond lies 17-mile **Polihale Beach,** the longest beach in Hawaii, which ends on the island's northwest shore where Na Pali begins.

Driving uphill from Waimea, you'll come to **Kokee State Park,** a favorite spot for camping and hiking, with 45 miles of trails into the **Alakai Swamp,** last stand of Kauai's endangered native birds. In old Hawaii, Kokee was revered as a sanctuary for the gods.

Coconut Coast

The Wailua River and **Wailua State Park** mark an ancient historic area, with prominent heiau and birthing stones. High-ranking ancient women gave birth on such stones because they believed the children would grow up to be powerful chiefs. The baby's umbilical cord would be placed in a cloth and hidden in or under the navel stone (or *piko* stone), a practice continued very privately in some places today.

North Shore

When you pass the busy town of Kapaa, the crowds and buildings fall away and the road leads to the fabled North Shore. On the way, turn right at Kilauea and stop at the **Kilauea Point National Wildlife Refuge,** home to the largest seabird nesting areas and historic **Kilauea Lighthouse.** Spinner dolphins, humpback whales, sea turtles, monk seals, and albatross often can be seen here.

In another ten miles or so, you approach Princeville Resort on a high cliff marking one side of **Hanalei River Valley,** a green patchwork of taro ponds along the river surrounded by a bowl of mountains. It's worth stopping at the overlook. Then the road leads down to the valley floor, through Hanalei and on around the next mountain base, past seven one-lane bridges and several narrow valleys cut by streams. This is the scenery of your tropical dreams. Keep on until the road ends at the base of the magnificent **Na Pali Coast.** Na Pali ("the cliffs") is a dramatic 25-mile stretch of wind- and wave-worn precipices and hanging valleys cloaked in green. It is accessible only by foot on the ancient 11-mile Kalalau Trail, or by boat during summer months.

Molokai

Molokai, where less is more, is always described in negatives: Molokai has no Disneyesque fantasy resorts, no fancy restaurants, no stoplights, no malls or fast food, no freeways, and no buildings taller than a coconut tree. The beaches are too small or too dangerous for swimming; fish-ponds are muddy and mostly off-limits, one third of the island is a private ranch, and the main tourist attraction is a leper colony. So what's the big deal about Molokai? The simple life and absence of contemporary Americana landmarks is what attracts those in search of old Hawaii.

You arrive at Hoolehua Airport, the small, open-air lava rock terminal with rental cars and a lunch counter serving chili rice and Spam musubi. Which way you leave the airport depends on whether you like it hot and dry or lush and tropical. The 38-mile-long island divides at **Kaunakakai,** the funky main town, into two different climate zones, known locally as the West End and the East End. The West End looks like Mexico. The East End resembles Tahiti.

"The Cockeyed Mayor of Kaunakakai," a hapa-hauole song performed by Hilo Hattie, put Molokai's biggest town on the map in the 1940s. The song was written in 1934 by the late, great R. Alex Anderson. Others among his nearly 200 songs included "Lovely Hula Hands" and "I Will Remember You." FYI: There is no mayor of Kaunakakai.

A sun-faded, three-block town with harbor and pier, Kaunakakai looks more like an old western movie than a tropical village. Molokai's chief settlement includes a bank, post office, drug and grocery store, medical center, and family-run businesses: Molokai Drive-Inn, Oviedo's Filipino Restaurant, and Kanemitsu Bakery, where 19 different types of bread are baked fresh daily. The brightest lights in town shine on **Mitchell Pauole Center,** site of softball games, chicken roasts, and community events.

Above Kaunakakai, defunct **Kamakou Volcano,** the island's tallest mountain, is home to a virgin forest of native trees, including rare sandalwood. The Nature Conservancy runs the 2,774-acre **Kamakou Preserve,** home to native Hawaiian birds and 200 indigenous plants, which you can see on monthly tours given by the Nature Conservancy. Call (808) 553-5236 or fax (808) 553-9870. Or e-mail hike-molokai@pop mailnc.org to take part in tours of this or other preserves on the island.

Most visitors head to the West End, where the **Molokai Ranch** dominates the red-dirt rolling hills covered by kiawe brush and cactus, above and below the road. The 5,300-acre spread is headquartered at **Maunaloa,** the restored plantation town where the ranch has branched into tourism with its Outfitters Center and stables—starting points for outdoor adventure. You can even learn traditional rodeo events like barrel racing. The ranch features the island's only upscale retreat, the 22-room Sheraton Molokai Lodge and Beach Village, an expensive lodge with fine dining and lots of ranchy ambience, as well as the 40-unit seaside Kaupoa Camp, an ecotourism-oriented collection of tent cabins nestled by a beautiful, remote beach.

East of Kaunakakai, you'll find the top edge of the world's highest sea cliffs, which rise 3,250 feet from sea level and stretch 14 miles on the island's North Shore. On the way, you pass coffee plantations, the **Ironwood Hills Golf Course,** and **Molokai Museum and Cultural Center** in a restored sugar mill.

Nearby, on a plateau of Mauna Loa, is **Kaana,** a hill setting where tradition holds Laka, the goddess of the hula, created the native Hawaiian dance. Molokai celebrates the birth of the hula at the annual Molokai Ka Hula Piko, held each May at **Papohaku Beach Park,** a shady seaside grove on the island's West End. The daylong festival features hula performances, Hawaiian music, food, and local arts and crafts.

As you head to the East End, the island becomes lush, green, and tropical. Fishponds like 54-acre Keawanui Pond line the shore for 20 miles. Take a swim at **Waialua Beach at Mile Marker 19,** one of the island's best beaches, or **Mile Marker 20 Beach** for snorkeling.

At the **Mapulehu Mango Grove,** where 2,000 mango trees flourish by the sea, you can hitch a ride on the Molokai Horse and Wagon Ride to one of the spookiest places in Hawaii: **Iliiliopae Heiau,** a school of sacrifice where kahuna taught final rites in the massive temple of doom that's three stories high and bigger than a football field. More than 700 years old, the heiau, legend has it, was built of car-sized boulders passed hand to hand from Molokai's opposite side in exchange for shrimp. (*Iliili* means rock and *opae* means shrimp in Hawaiian.)

On Kamehameha V Highway you'll discover affordable seaside condos, like Wavecrest Resort, and perfectly sited vacation rentals like Dunbar Beachfront Cottages and the Country Cottage at Puu O Hoku Ranch. The highway turns to hairpins on the very eastern end. After scenic vistas of pocket beaches, offshore islets, and dense jungles, it deadends at **Halawa Valley.**

Inundated by a tsunami in 1946, Halawa Valley, an ancient settlement, was abandoned. Now privately owned, the valley is closed, and the trailhead to 250-foot Moaula Falls is posted with no trespassing signs. Observe the kapu but enjoy **Halawa Beach County Park** and its black-sand beach with the island's only decent surf break.

People stricken with leprosy in 1860 were banished to **Kalaupapa Peninsula,** a lava shelf down below the famous sea cliffs. The victims were literally pushed from a boat into the waters off the peninsula and had to swim to shore. Father Damien de Veuster, a Belgian priest, arrived in 1873 and embraced the outcasts, cared for them, and sought medicine, food, shelter, and clothing for them. It was an exhausting labor of love, and Father Damien was mostly alone in his efforts. Any contributions by visiting doctors were left on a fencepost to avoid physical contact with patients. By the end of the 1870s, approximately 1,000 people had been exiled to Kalaupapa. On April 15, 1889, Damien himself died of leprosy at age 49. Some 60 patients, their disease controlled by modern medicine, still live at the settlement and serve as tour guides.

Lanai

Long ago Hawaiians believed Lanai was haunted by spirits so wily and vicious that no human who went there could survive. Today, nearly everyone who goes there not only gets a good night's sleep but leaves reluctantly. Spirits still haunt the island, but they are thought to be benign.

In 1904, American businessman Charles Gay began purchasing various parcels on Lanai; four years later he owned the entire island. Gay sold it in 1922 to James Dole, who quickly turned his $1.1 million investment into the pineapple capital of the world. For the next six decades, pineapple was king on Lanai. Lanai survives now by cultivating a few privileged visitors seeking peaceful surroundings, luxurious hotels, outstanding golf, and one of the best dive spots in the Pacific. The sweet and juicy pineapple once covered more than 19,000 acres of the island's red-dirt Palawai Basin; all that remains is a relic field so visitors can see what pineapple looks like.

Most people will never know the taste of a fresh plucked Hawaiian pineapple, which 1930s poet laureate Don Blanding wrote "tastes like champagne and honey . . . the most delicious fruit grown in any Garden of Eden." Neither pine, nor apple, nor Hawaiian in origin, the South American import that became the symbol of the Islands is now grown and harvested in Third World tropical nations (Honduras, Costa Rica, Dominican Republic, Mexico, Thailand, and the Philippines) where labor is less costly. Sweet and juicy, the king of fruit ruled the island of Lanai for a half century; inspired its nickname ("The Pineapple Island"); provided wages, shelter, and jobs for plantation workers (also imported to Hawaii); and made global conglomerate Dole Foods a household name. Now an exhibition crop in most of Hawaii, pineapple on Lanai is represented in two thin rows of spiky gray-green specimen plants that line the lane to Lanai's little airport in Puuwai Basin, where rows upon rows once filled the old volcanic crater. Today, a lone golden painted pineapple looms larger than life on the pediment arch of The Lodge at Koele; the mural, too, is fading in the tropic sun.

In 1987, California tycoon David Murdock bought a controlling interest in Castle & Cooke, owners of Dole, and found that the deed to 98% of Lanai came with the deal, along with plans for hotel development. He envisioned an island resort like no other, and in the early 1990s, The Lodge at Koele and the Manele Bay Hotel opened. Visitors content with less palatial properties might enjoy the venerable 1920s-era Hotel Lanai, a ten-room highland lodge with a popular restaurant, Henry Clay's Rotisserie, a New Orleans–inspired Creole bistro many think is the island's best.

Golf is the sport of choice on Lanai, at two 18-hole championship courses: **The Experience at Koele,** designed by golf superstar Greg Norman and architect Ted Robinson, and **The Challenge at Manele,** designed by Jack Nicklaus.

The chief landmark is 3,366-foot **Lanaihale,** the highest point on the island.

A drive up **Munro Trail** to the summit on a clear day will afford a view of Maui, Molokai, Kahoolawe, and the Big Island. Historians believe Lanaihale served as a strategic vantage point so that chiefs could keep an eye on canoe traffic in the sea lanes.

Lanai is regarded as a five-star locale among divers. *Skin Diver Magazine* rated **Cathedrals,** two large underwater caves near Hulopoe Bay, as Hawaii's top diving spot. On the opposite end of the island is **Shipwreck Beach,** where the rusted remains of the *Helena Pt. Townsend,* a World War II liberty ship, are still stuck on the reef.

On the slopes of Lanaihale overlooking the broad Palawai Basin, you can find on 20 boulders stone-age art known as petroglyphs. The best time to search is mid-afternoon when the declining sun lights up the pecked and incised stick figures. It's a most amazing cast of characters unlike any others on Lanai or any other island for that matter. You can see a canoe sailing across a gigantic red boulder, a curly-tailed dog barking at a centipede, two turtles inching along, and a horseman with a hat riding a thin steed while two V-chested men walk down a trail.

The most significant historic site is **Kaunolu,** where once there was the summer retreat for King Kamehameha I, who tried his hand at fishing with the blessing of Kunihi, a three-foot stone fish god, filled with *mana* (power). The idol is believed to still exist somewhere on Lanai. If you spot it, think twice before touching it. The last person to touch the idol is said to have died as a result.

Niihau: The "Forbidden" Island

You cannot go easily to Niihau, Hawaii's other privately owned island, because ranch owners want to preserve the old ways in this last Hawaiian enclave where about 150–200 residents still speak Hawaiian and pay little heed to the world beyond.

Long off-limits to visitors without an invitation, the forbidden island can sometimes be seen by travelers like us whose curiosity gets the best of them. It takes written permission from the owners. You can go to beachcomb, fish, hunt wild pigs and goats, or just see a mostly raw island. You may not see any of the Hawaiians who live there. Interest in Niihau, for most of us, began when we first read about this strange island bought for $10,000 in gold from a king more than 100 years ago and inhabited only by a "lost" tribe of 200 Hawaiians who are said to choose a pure and simple life over twenty-first-century trappings.

It all sounds wonderfully arcane, the stuff of Swiss Family Robinson: a 6- by 18-mile late-eighteenth-century island, 17 miles northwest of Kauai. It's actually owned now by a man named Robinson. Cattle ranching is Niihau's primary business, along with helicopter tours, hunting safaris, and its precious shell jewelry.

To visit Niihau, fax a written request to the Robinson family at (808) 338-1463 or sign up for a helicopter tour of its beaches.

Kahoolawe: The Target Island

From Maui or Lanai, the island of Kahoolawe appears forbidding and bleak, forgotten in time. Its huge red scars show where U.S. Navy pilots, who for nearly a half century practiced air-raid skills here, dropped tons of bombs.

The bombing was halted in 1990 by President George Bush, who was shocked to learn the U.S. Navy was still bombing one of the Hawaiian islands. The 45-square-mile island, about the size of San Francisco, was returned to native Hawaiians to become a cultural retreat someday, after the unexploded ordnance is all cleaned up. A $400 million Navy cleanup sweep then commenced.

Kahoolawe variously served in the past as penal colony in the monarchy period, as a cattle ranch during territorial days, and as the staging zone for World War II U.S. forces preparing for the invasion of Okinawa. In 1965, the U.S. Navy dropped a 500-ton TNT bomb on Kahoolawe to simulate an atomic explosion; the impact irreparably cracked a submarine water lens and turned the island's freshwater brackish.

Tour Companies

Looking for more assistance in planning your Hawaii trip? One option is to set up a tour through a local tour company. Each offers an extensive menu of sight-seeing excursions. The destination descriptions in this chapter and the profiles of specific attractions which follow in Part Seven allow you to determine what you most want to do with your time in Hawaii. With that in mind, you can determine if a guided tour suits your agenda. Tours operate according to set itineraries, so flexibility is clearly limited; however, they can also provide a very efficient day of sight-seeing. Day tours range in price from $20 to $75, with extras such as luaus and meals ratcheting up the price further. Interisland day and overnight tours are pricier, but may well appeal to travelers bent on seeing another island despite time or budgetary constraints. Here are a few suggestions among the dozens of tour firms available in the Aloha State.

TOUR COMPANIES

Oahu
E Noa Tours
(808) 591-2561; (800) 824-8804
www.enoa.com

Kauai
Hawaii Movie Tours
(808) 822-1192; (800) 628-8432
www.hawaiimovietour.com

Oahu, Maui, Big Island, Kauai
Polynesian Adventure Tours
(808) 833-3000 (Oahu)
(808) 877-4242 (Maui)
(808) 329-8008 (Big Island)
(808) 246-0122 (Kauai)
(800) 622-3011 (toll-free)
www.polyad.com

Roberts Hawaii
(808) 523-7750 (Oahu)
(808) 871-6226 (Maui)
(808) 245-9101 (Kauai)
(800) 767-7751 (toll-free)
www.roberts-hawaii.com

Part Seven

Hawaii's Attractions

Choosing which attractions to visit during your Hawaii vacation is daunting. So much to see and do and so little time! Most of Hawaii's top visitor attractions, from museums and gardens to historic sites, have a nominal fee, but many are free. Reference the maps in the introduction to locate the attractions.

The following profiles provide basic information on the attractions, such as location, hours of operation, and cost. Each also features a rating for five age groups and a brief description. Given on a five-star scale, the ratings don't guarantee that a certain segment of visitors will love or hate the attraction, but they do provide a reliable evaluation of each group's typical reaction. For example, some teenagers want to visit historical sights, but more want to go to the beach. Together, the information, ratings, and descriptions will help you plan an itinerary pleasing to all members of your family or group.

HAWAII ATTRACTIONS BY ISLAND

Name	Type of Attraction	Rating	Zone
Oahu			
Aloha Tower	Shopping/Restaurants	★★★	2
Bishop Museum	Museum	★★★★½	2
Byodo-In Temple	Temple/Gardens	★★	3
Contemporary Museum	Museum	★★★	2
Damien Museum	Museum	★★½	1
Dole Plantation	Historic Home/Gardens	★★½	6
Doris Duke's Shangri-La	Palace/Art, History	★★★★★	2
Foster Botanical Garden	Gardens	★★★	2
Hawaii Children's Discovery Center	Museum	★★★★	2
Hawaii Maritime Center	Museum	★★★	2

HAWAII ATTRACTIONS BY ISLAND *(continued)*			
Name	**Type of Attraction**	**Rating**	**Zone**
Oahu *(continued)*			
Hawaii's Plantation Village	Historic Home/Museum	★★★	4
Hawaiian Railway	Train Ride	★★½	5
Honolulu Academy of Arts	Museum	★★★★	2
Honolulu Zoo	Zoo	★★★	1
Iolani Palace	Historic Home/Museum	★★★★½	2
Kualoa Ranch and Activity Club and Secret Island	Outdoor Activities Complex	★★★★	3
Mission Houses Museum	Museum	★★★	2
National Memorial Cemetery of the Pacific	Historic Memorial	★★★	2
Pacific Aerospace Museum	Museum	★★½	2
Polynesian Cultural Center	Museum/Theater	★★★★½	4
Queen Emma Summer Palace	Historic Home	★★★	2
Royal Mausoleum	Historic Memorial	★★½	2
Sea Life Park	Aquarium	★★★½	3
Senator Fong's Plantation and Gardens	Historic Home/Gardens	★★★	3
Tropic Lightning Museum	Museum	★★½	6
U.S. Army Museum	Museum	★★★½	1
USS *Arizona* Memorial	Historic Memorial	★★★★	6
USS Battleship *Missouri* Memorial	Historic Memorial	★★★★	6
USS *Bowfin* Submarine Museum and Park	Museum	★★★½	6
Waikiki Aquarium	Aquarium	★★★½	1
Maui			
Alexander & Baldwin Sugar Museum	Museum	★★★	7
Bailey House Museum	Museum	★★★	7
Baldwin Home Museum	Museum	★★★	9
Brig Carthaginian	Museum	★★★	9
Haleakala National Park	National Park	★★★★	10
Hana Cultural Center	Museum	★★★	10
Hawaii Experience Theater	Theater	★★★½	9
Hawaii Nature Center	Museum	★★★★	7
Hui Noeau Visual Arts Center	Gallery	★★★	10
Kepaniwai Cultural Park	Gardens	★★★	7
Kula Botanical Garden	Gardens	★★★	10
Lahaina-Kaanapali & Pacific Railroad	Hawaiian Railway	★★★	9
Maui Ocean Center	Aquarium	★★★★	8

HAWAII ATTRACTIONS BY ISLAND *(continued)*

Name	Type of Attraction	Rating	Zone
***Maui** (continued)*			
Maui Tropical Plantation & Country Store	Historic Home/Gardens	★★★	7
Tedeschi Winery	Winery	★★★	8
Whalers Village Museum	Museum	★★½	9
Wo Hing Temple Museum	Museum	★★½	9
The Big Island			
After Dark in the Park	National Park	★★★★★	12
Ahuena Heiau	Temple	★★½	11
Akatsuka Orchid Gardens	Gardens	★★★	12
Amy B. H. Greenwell Ethnobotanical Garden	Gardens	★★★	11
Astronaut Ellison S. Onizuka Space Center	Museum	★★★½	11
Hawaii Tropical Botanical Garden	Gardens	★★★½	12
Hawaii Volcanoes National Park	National Park	★★★★★	12
Hulihee Palace	Historic Home/Museum	★★★	11
Kaloko-Honokohau National Historical Park	National Park	★★★	11
Kamuela Museum	Museum	★★½	11
Lyman Mission House and Museum	Museum	★★★	12
Mauna Loa Macadamia Nut Visitor Center	Visitor Center/Gardens	★★★½	12
Nani Mau Gardens	Gardens	★★	12
Onizuka Center for Int'l. Astronomy and Mauna Kea Observatory	Observatory	★★★★½	12
Pacific Tsunami Museum	Museum	★★★	12
Panaewa Rainforest Zoo	Zoo	★★½	12
Parker Ranch Visitor Center and Historic Homes	Visitor Center/ Historic Home	★★★½	11
Puuhonua O Honaunau National Historical Park	National Park	★★★½	11
Puukohola Heiau	Temple	★★★	11
Sadie Seymour Botanical Gardens	Gardens	★★★	11
Suisan Fish Market and Auction	Market	★★½	12
Volcano Winery	Winery	★★½	12
Wakefield Botanical Gardens	Gardens	★★½	11
Kauai			
Grove Farm Homestead	Historic Home/Museum	★★½	13
Guava Kai Plantation	Historic Home/Gardens	★★½	13

HAWAII ATTRACTIONS BY ISLAND *(continued)*

Name	Type of Attraction	Rating	Zone
Kauai *(continued*			
Kauai Museum	Museum	★★★½	13
Kilauea Point National Wildlife Refuge	Wildlife Refuge	★★½	13
Kilohana Plantation	Historic Home/Gardens	★★★	13
Kokee National History Museum	Museum	★★★	13
Limahuli Garden	Gardens	★★★★	13
Moir Gardens	Gardens	★★★	13
National Tropical Botanical Garden Lawai and Allerton Gardens	Gardens	★★½	13
Waioli Mission House Museum	Museum	★★½	13
Molokai			
Molokai Museum and Cultural Center	Museum	★★½	14
Molokai Ranch	Outdoor Activities Complex	★★★★★	14

HAWAII ATTRACTIONS BY TYPE

Name	Rating	Zone
Aquarium		
Maui Ocean Center	★★★★	8
Sea Life Park	★★★½	3
Waikiki Aquarium	★★★½	1
Gallery		
Hui Noeau Visual Arts Center	★★★	10
Gardens		
Akatsuka Orchid Gardens	★★★	12
Amy B. H. Greenwell Ethnobotanical Garden	★★★	11
Foster Botanical Garden	★★★	2
Hawaii Tropical Botanical Garden	★★★½	12
Kepaniwai Cultural Park	★★★	7
Kula Botanical Garden	★★★	10
Limahuli Garden	★★★★	13
Moir Gardens	★★★	13
Nani Mau Gardens	★★	12
National Tropical Botanical Garden Lawai and Allerton Gardens	★★½	13

HAWAII ATTRACTIONS BY TYPE *(continued)*

Name	Rating	Zone
***Gardens** (continued)*		
Sadie Seymour Botanical Gardens	★★★	11
Wakefield Botanical Gardens	★★½	11
Historic Home		
Queen Emma Summer Palace	★★★	2
Historic Home/Gardens		
Dole Plantation	★★½	6
Grove Farm Homestead	★★½	13
Guava Kai Plantation	★★½	13
Hawaii's Plantation Village	★★★	4
Hulihee Palace	★★★	11
Iolani Palace	★★★★½	2
Kilohana Plantation	★★★	13
Maui Tropical Plantation & Country Store	★★★	7
Senator Fong's Plantation and Gardens	★★★	3
Historic Memorial		
National Memorial Cemetery of the Pacific	★★★	2
Royal Mausoleum	★★½	2
USS *Arizona* Memorial	★★★★	6
USS Battleship *Missouri* Memorial	★★★★	6
Market		
Suisan Fish Market and Auction	★★½	12
Museum		
Alexander & Baldwin Sugar Museum	★★★	7
Astronaut Ellison S. Onizuka Space Center	★★★½	11
Bailey House Museum	★★★	7
Baldwin Home Museum	★★★	9
Bishop Museum	★★★★½	2
Brig Carthaginian	★★★	9
Contemporary Museum	★★★	2
Damien Museum	★★½	1
Doris Duke's Shangri-La	★★★★★	2
Hana Cultural Center	★★★	10
Hawaii Children's Discovery Center	★★★★	2
Hawaii Maritime Center	★★★	2
Hawaii Nature Center	★★★★	7

HAWAII ATTRACTIONS BY TYPE *(continued)*		
Name	**Rating**	**Zone**
Museum *(continued)*		
Honolulu Academy of Arts	★★★★	2
Kamuela Museum	★★½	11
Kauai Museum	★★★½	13
Kokee National History Museum	★★★	13
Lyman Mission House and Museum	★★★	12
Mission Houses Museum	★★★	2
Molokai Museum and Cultural Center	★★½	14
Pacific Aerospace Museum	★★½	2
Pacific Tsunami Museum	★★★	12
Tropic Lightning Museum	★★½	6
U.S. Army Museum	★★★½	1
USS *Bowfin* Submarine Museum and Park	★★★½	6
Waioli Mission House Museum	★★½	13
Whalers Village Museum	★★½	9
Wo Hing Temple Museum	★★½	9
Museum/Theater		
Polynesian Cultural Center	★★★★½	4
National Park		
After Dark in the Park	★★★★★	12
Haleakala National Park	★★★★	10
Hawaii Volcanoes National Park	★★★★★	12
Kaloko-Honokohau National Historical Park	★★★	11
Puuhonua O Honaunau National Historical Park	★★★½	11
Observatory		
Onizuka Center for Int'l Astronomy and Mauna Kea Observatory	★★★★½	12
Outdoor Activities Complex		
Kualoa Ranch and Activity Club and Secret Island	★★★★	3
Molokai Ranch	★★★★★	14
Shopping/Restaurants		
Aloha Tower	★★★	2
Temple		
Ahuena Heiau	★★½	11
Puukohola Heiau	★★★	11

HAWAII ATTRACTIONS BY TYPE *(continued)*

Name	Rating	Zone
Temple/Gardens		
Byodo-In Temple	★★	3
Theater		
Hawaii Experience Theater	★★★½	9
Train Ride		
Hawaiian Railway	★★½	5
Lahaina-Kaanapali & Pacific Railroad	★★★	9
Visitor Center/Gardens		
Mauna Loa Macadamia Nut Visitor Center	★★★½	12
Visitor Center/Historic Home		
Parker Ranch Visitor Center and Historic Homes	★★★½	11
Wildlife Refuge		
Kilauea Point National Wildlife Refuge	★★½	13
Winery		
Tedeschi Winery	★★★	8
Volcano Winery	★★½	12
Zoo		
Honolulu Zoo	★★★	1
Panaewa Rainforest Zoo	★★½	12

Attraction Profiles

Oahu

Aloha Tower — *Zone 2 Greater Honolulu*

Location Aloha Tower Marketplace, Pier 9 at Honolulu Harbor

Phone (808) 528-5700

Website www.alohatower.com

Hours Daily, 9 a.m.–sunset

Admission Free

When to Go Anytime

How Much Time to Allow 20 minutes

Author's Rating ★★★; Go to the top, look around, come down.

Overall Appeal by Age Group

Pre-school ★	Teens ★★★	Over 30 ★★★½
Grade school ★½	Young Adults ★★★	Seniors ★★★½

Description and Comments Now dwarfed by high-rises in downtown Honolulu, Aloha Tower was once the tallest building in Hawaii. The slender, square-shaped ten-story tower was erected in 1926 as a landmark welcoming passenger ships arriving at Honolulu Harbor. Now the centerpiece of the Aloha Tower Marketplace shopping/restaurant complex, the historic tower is perhaps the most recognized man-made structure in the Islands, with its large clock with faces on each side, the huge letters A-L-O-H-A, and the 40-foot flagstaff. In 1997, the tower closed for two years, undergoing an extensive renovation (among the additions were handicapped-accessible rest rooms, security cameras, and emergency exits). It reopened to visitors in April 1999. Take the elevator to the tenth floor and take in 360° views of Honolulu. You'll have sweeping views of the downtown area, Honolulu Harbor, and the leeward mountains.

Touring Tips Be sure to bring your camera or video camera.

Other Things to Do Nearby Aloha Tower Marketplace features shops, live entertainment, and restaurants. The tower is a short walk away from the Hawaii Maritime Center.

Bishop Museum — *Zone 2 Greater Honolulu*

Location 1525 Bernice Street

Phone (808) 847-3511

Website www.bishopmuseum.org

Hours Daily (except Christmas), 9 a.m.–5 p.m.

Admission $14.95 for adults; $11.95 for children ages 4–12

When to Go Anytime

How Much Time to Allow 2½ hours

Author's Rating ★★★★½; Don't miss the best natural-history museum in Hawaii and the Pacific.

Overall Appeal by Age Group

Pre-school ★★	Teens ★★★½	Over 30 ★★★★★
Grade school ★★★	Young Adults ★★★★★	Seniors ★★★★★

Description and Comments The Bernice Pauahi Bishop Museum boasts the world's largest collection of Hawaiian and Pacific artifacts. Literally thousands of cultural treasures are housed here, including ancient weaponry, feather cloaks, clothing, jewelry, koa bowls, photographs, illustrations, and even a re-created Hawaiian grass hale (house). At the entrance to the museum, you'll see the gift shop to the left (be sure to pay a visit before you leave, as the shop carries an impressive line of Hawaiian books, artwork, crafts, and souvenirs) and a small exhibit on Hawaii's political and natural histories to your right. From the ticket office, proceed to Hawaiian Hall, the distinguished stone building that houses the bulk of the Hawaiian artifacts. Take your time and read the descriptions of each display—the galleries here provide probably the most powerful and effective way of discovering Hawaii's rich past. The adjacent Castle Building houses visiting interactive exhibits. The planetarium educates visitors on how ancient Polynesian voyagers used the stars to navigate their arduous journeys throughout the Pacific.

Also, sports fan should take note that one of the newer attractions at the museum is the Hawaii Sports Hall of Fame, located in the Paki Building. This insightful gallery pays tribute to Hawaii's most storied athletes, coaches, promoters, and other contributors to local sports. Among them are famed surfer/swimmer Duke Kahanamoku, Alexander J. Cartwright (the father of baseball lived in Hawaii for much of his life), sumo pioneer Jesse "Takamiyama" Kuhaulua, and legendary women's surfer Rell Sunn. Lei making and craft demonstrations at the museum are held regularly.

Touring Tips Guided tours of the museum's Hawaiian Hall are scheduled daily at 10 a.m. and noon. Also, a garden tour is held at 12:30 p.m. The Journey by Starlight program at the planetarium is conducted daily at 11:30 a.m.

Byodo-In Temple — *Zone 3 Windward Oahu*

Location Valley of the Temples Memorial Park, 47-200 Kahekili Highway

Phone (808) 239-8811

Hours Daily, 9 a.m.–4 p.m.

Admission $2 for adults; $1 for senior citizens and children ages 6–12

When to Go Anytime

How Much Time to Allow 45 minutes

Author's Rating ★★; A peaceful spot to visit.

Overall Appeal by Age Group

Pre-school ★★	Teens ★★	Over 30 ★★★
Grade school ★★	Young Adults ★★	Seniors ★★★½

Description and Comments Nestled at the foot of the scenic Koolau Mountains, the Byodo-In Temple is a replica of the famous 900-year-old temple in Japan. A stroll of the temple grounds leads you to an immaculate Oriental garden, a colorful carp pool, a nine-foot Buddha statue, and a stately teahouse. Peacocks, swans, ducks, and shimmering waterfalls add to the scenery.

Contemporary Museum — *Zone 2 Greater Honolulu*

Location 2411 Makiki Heights Drive

Phone (808) 526-0232

Website www.tcmhi.org

Hours Tuesday–Saturday, 10 a.m.–4 p.m.; Sunday, noon–4 p.m. Closed major holidays.

Admission $5 for adults; $3 for students with valid ID and senior citizens; free for children under age 12

When to Go The museum provides free admission to all comers on the third Thursday of each month.

How Much Time to Allow 75 minutes

Author's Rating ★★★; If you love modern art, you'll enjoy this.

Overall Appeal by Age Group

Pre-school ★★	Teens ★★★½	Over 30 ★★★½
Grade school ★★½	Young Adults ★★★½	Seniors ★★★½

Description and Comments Originally built in 1925 as a residence of a wealthy socialite, the Contemporary Museum opened its doors in 1988 as a modern art collection. The small museum features 1,300 works, dating from 1940 to the present, on rotating exhibits. A special highlight is a permanent walk-in multimedia exhibit by David Hockney, inspired by Maurice Ravel's opera *L'Enfant et les Sortiliges*. Works by local artists are also on display.

You'll probably spend as much time outside the museum as you will inside: The museum's 3.5-acre garden is dotted by a variety of bronze, ceramic, stainless steel, copper, and aluminum sculptures. The garden was originally created in the 1930s by a Honolulu reverend with a passion for landscape design, and it remains a blissful retreat. The Contemporary Café is a favorite spot for lunch, and shoppers will want to visit the museum's gift boutique.

Other Things to Do Nearby Continue your drive up Mount Tantalus to see sweeping views of Honolulu.

Damien Museum — *Zone 1 Waikiki*

Location 130 Ohua Avenue

Phone (808) 923-2690

Hours Monday–Friday, 9 a.m.–3 p.m.; Saturday, 9 a.m.–noon

Admission Free

When to Go Anytime

How Much Time to Allow 30 minutes

Author's Rating ★★½; Make a pilgrimage to this Damien shrine before you go to Molokai and Kalaupapa.

Overall Appeal by Age Group

Pre-school ★	Teens ★★½	Over 30 ★★★
Grade school ★	Young Adults ★★★	Seniors ★★★

Description and Comments This mini-museum houses several artifacts belonging to Father Damien deVeuster (1840–1889), the Belgian priest who dedicated his life to caring for patients stricken with Hansen's disease (leprosy) at Kalaupapa settlement on Molokai. Among the displays here are some of Father Damien's possessions, including books, work tools, candlesticks, and personal letters. A 20-minute video highlights the minister's life and reflects on this sad chapter in Hawaiian history.

Other Things to Do Nearby The Honolulu Zoo and Kapiolani Park are a block away, and Waikiki Beach beckons just across Kalakaua Avenue, Waikiki's main thoroughfare.

Dole Plantation — *Zone 6 Central Oahu*

Location 64-1550 Kamehameha Highway

Phone (808) 621-8408

Website www.dole-plantation.com

Hours Daily, 9 a.m.–5:30 p.m.

Admission Plantation free; Pineapple Express: $7.50 for adults, $5.50 for children; Pineapple Garden Maze: $5 for adults, $3 for children; Plantation Garden Tour: $3.50 for adults, $2.50 for children

When to Go Anytime

How Much Time to Allow 90 minutes

Author's Rating ★★½; The maze is more popular than the pineapple.

Overall Appeal by Age Group

Pre-school ★½	Teens ★★★★	Over 30 ★★★
Grade school ★★★★	Young Adults ★★★	Seniors ★★★

Description and Comments Situated just outside the town of Wahiawa, the Dole Plantation features outdoor displays of Hawaii's pineapple history as well as the life of the plantation founder, Jim Dole. Sample some pineapple juice and stroll through the Pineapple Garden, which features 21 different varieties of the prickly fruit. Since its debut in 1998, the biggest attraction here (and the one the children most want to see) is the Pineapple Garden Maze, which covers nearly 2 acres and has a path length of 1.7 miles. The maze was built from 11,400 Hawaiian plants, including varieties of the official state flower, the hibiscus. The maze was recognized in 1998 by the *Guinness Book of World Records* as the world's largest maze.

Doris Duke's Shangri-La — *Zone 2 Greater Honolulu*

Location Honolulu Academy of Arts, 900 South Beretania Street

Phone (808) 532-8701

Website www.honoluluacademy.org

Hours Tuesday–Saturday, 10 a.m.–4:30 p.m.

Admission $25

When to Go Wednesday through Saturday

How Much Time to Allow 2 to 3 hours for tour and round-trip from Honolulu to Black Point

Author's Rating ★★★★★; A unique palace of art, history, culture.

Overall Appeal by Age Group

Pre-school ★	Teens ★★★	Over 30 ★★★★
Grade school ★★	Young Adults ★★★★	Seniors ★★★★★

Description and Comments Inspired by the Taj Mahal, built by the richest little girl in the world, the late Doris Duke's "Shangri-La," a $100 million Islamic-style palace on five oceanfront acres of Honolulu's exclusive Black Point enclave, is now open to a few lucky art lovers and curiosity seekers. Inside the seldom seen or photographed 14,000-square-foot palace is one of the most extensive collections of Islamic art, paintings, ceramics, and textiles in the United States, more than 3,500 objects collected by Miss Duke over six decades.

The mansion itself is a work of art with painted ceilings, elaborately carved doorways, inlaid stone and mosaic tile panels set amid lush gardens and a saltwater swimming pool at the edge of the Pacific. A part-time Oahu resident, the tobacco heiress died in 1993 at age 80 at her Beverly Hills estate, Falcon's Lair. Born November 22, 1912, in New York City, Miss Duke was the daughter of James Buchanan "Buck" Duke, the tobacco tycoon who founded American Tobacco Company, maker of Lucky Strike cigarettes. When her father died in 1925, the 13-year-old Miss Duke personally inherited $30 million. Educated in Europe, married twice (once to Dominican Republic playboy Porfirio Rubirosa), she founded Duke University in North Carolina, funded the Doris Duke Foundation, and became an orchid grower and patron of the Metropolitan Museum of Art. In her will, she created the Doris Duke Foundation for Islamic Art to "promote the study and understanding of Middle Eastern art and culture" and to manage her Honolulu home as an art center open to the public.

Touring Tips The $25 tour, Wednesday through Saturday, originates at Honolulu Academy of Arts which serves as the orientation center for tours to Shangri-La and hosts educational programs on Islamic art and culture. Visitors are shuttled to and from Shangri-La. Only a few visitors are permitted on tours. Reservations required. Make reservations far in advance on the Academy's website at www.honoluluacademy.org.

Other Things to Do Nearby Black Point is one of Honolulu's most private, upscale neighborhoods; you will ooh and ahh at the houses and may even spot someone rich and famous out walking their dog or working on their tan. The ocean view from the Duke mansion is one in a $100 million.

Foster Botanical Garden — *Zone 2 Greater Honolulu*

Location 50 North Vineyard Boulevard

Phone (808) 522-7066

Hours Daily, 9 a.m.–4 p.m.

Admission $5 for adults; $1 for children ages 6–12

When to Go In the morning, when it's coolest

How Much Time to Allow 1 hour

Author's Rating ★★★; A thoroughly pleasant outing.

Overall Appeal by Age Group

Pre-school ★★	Teens ★★★	Over 30 ★★★½
Grade school ★★½	Young Adults ★★★	Seniors ★★★½

Description and Comments One of Oahu's most popular tropical gardens, right on the edge of downtown Honolulu, is a beautiful 14-acre oasis. Foster Botanical Garden boasts one of the nation's largest collections of tropical plants (about 10,000 species), including many rare and endangered species. Among the highlights are an exquisite orchid garden, several rare and endangered trees (some of which are extinct in the wild), an herb garden, and an "economic" garden, which displays plants that are used for food, fabrics, dyes, and medicine. Foster Botanical Garden was placed on the Hawaii Register of Historic Places in 1988 and was the setting for several Hollywood films and TV shows. It is the best known of Honolulu's five municipal botanical gardens.

Touring Tips Guided tours are available weekdays at 1 p.m. Call for reservations.

Hawaii Children's Discovery Center — *Zone 2 Greater Honolulu*

Location 111 Ohe Street

Phone (808) 524-5437

Hours Tuesday–Friday, 9 a.m.–1 p.m.; Saturday and Sunday, 10 a.m.–3 p.m.

Admission $8 for adults; $6.75 for children ages 2–17; $5 for seniors. No strollers permitted in the exhibit area.

When to Go Anytime

How Much Time to Allow 2 hours

Author's Rating ★★★★; Excellent children's museum; the kids will love it.

Overall Appeal by Age Group

Pre-school ★★★★	Teens ★★★★	Over 30 ★★★
Grade school ★★★★★	Young Adults ★★★½	Seniors ★★★

Description and Comments Originally opened in 1989 as the Hawaii Children's Museum at Dole Cannery, the $10 million Children's Discovery Center reopened in 1998 at a larger, 37,000-square-foot location. Four separate galleries—Fantastic You, Our Town, Hawaiian Rainbows, and Your Rainbow World—are featured on three floors, each with a variety of hands-on, interactive galleries designed for children. Our favorites were Fantastic You, which helps children understand their bodies and organs, and Our Town, which features a working television station that lets children take on roles as news anchors and camera technicians. A gift shop sells a variety of educational toys, games, and books. The center stresses fun as much as education. The president of the center once explained its mission this way: "The museum isn't really to educate children. Instead, it's to motivate them, stimulate them, to arouse their curiosity about things, and to give them an excitement and joy about learning."

Other Things to Do Nearby Kakaako Waterfront Park, directly across the street, provides a great picnic setting.

Hawaii Maritime Center — *Zone 2 Greater Honolulu*

Location Pier 7, Honolulu Harbor

Phone (808) 536-6373

Website www.holoholo.org/maritime

Hours Daily, 8:30 a.m.–5 p.m.

Admission $7.50 for adults; $4.50 for children ages 6–17

When to Go Anytime

How Much Time to Allow 75 minutes

Author's Rating ★★★; If you love ocean history and messing around with boats, see this shipshape museum.

Overall Appeal by Age Group

Pre-school ★★	Teens ★★★	Over 30 ★★★½
Grade school ★★★	Young Adults ★★★½	Seniors ★★★½

Description and Comments Hawaii's colorful ocean history is the story line, from ancient Polynesian voyagers and rowdy whalers to the legendary Waikiki beach boys and the luxury liners of the 1920s and 1930s. Take an audio tour and browse through 50 displays, including a skeleton of a humpback whale (one of only two such displays in the world). Two major attractions here are the *Falls of Clyde* (built in 1817) and the welltraveled Polynesian voyaging canoe *Hokulea*. You can board the *Falls of Clyde,* which is the last four-masted, full-rigged ship in the world and is a National Historic Landmark. The *Hokulea* is a double-hulled sailing canoe in which modern Hawaiians retraced the voyages of ancient Polynesians in the 1970s and 1980s using only the stars and ocean currents to guide them.

Other Things to Do Nearby The Aloha Tower Marketplace is next door.

Hawaii's Plantation Village — *Zone 4 The North Shore*

Location 94-695 Waipahu Street

Phone (808) 677-0110

Website www.hawaiiplantationvillage.org

Hours Monday–Friday, 9 a.m.–4:30 p.m.; Saturday, 10 a.m.–4:30 p.m. (guided tours begin at the top of every hour)

Admission $10 for adults; $7 for military personnel and seniors; $4 for children ages 5–17

When to Go Anytime

How Much Time to Allow 90 minutes

Author's Rating ★★★; Best place to learn about Hawaii's plantation history.

Overall Appeal by Age Group

Pre-school ★	Teens ★★½	Over 30 ★★★
Grade school ★★	Young Adults ★★★	Seniors ★★★

Description and Comments Located in the former plantation town of Waipahu, this outdoor museum pays tribute to Hawaii's plantation era. Included are artifacts, household items, photos, and documents representing the cultures and lifestyles of eight different ethnic groups that labored on the sugar plantations: Japanese, Chinese, Okinawans, Filipinos, Koreans, Puerto Ricans, Portuguese, and Hawaiians. Nearly 30 replicated dwellings dot the village's three acres, including a Chinese cookhouse, a plantation store, and a community bath. The different types of architecture illustrate the cultural differences of those workers and how they had to figure out how to get along while living together so closely. The park also features a display of medicinal plants.

Hawaiian Railway — *Zone 5 Leeward Oahu*

Location 91-1001 Renton Road

Phone (808) 681-5461

Hours Sundays only, 12:30 and 2:30 p.m. (charter groups may schedule weekday rides)

Admission $8 for adults; $5 for seniors and children ages 2–12

When to Go Anytime

How Much Time to Allow 2 hours

Author's Rating ★★½; For train buffs.

Overall Appeal by Age Group

Pre-school ★★	Teens ★★★	Over 30 ★★★
Grade school ★★★	Young Adults ★★★	Seniors ★★★

Description and Comments In the heyday of Hawaii's plantation era, more than 40 sugar plantations utilized private railway systems to transport their crops. (Trains ran on every populated island except Niihau.) Today, the Hawaiian Railway Society strives to preserve what's left of Hawaii's railroad history with this 6.5-mile stretch of track. A trio of vintage diesel locomotives has been restored as well. The 90-minute ride begins at the Ewa station and travels at a leisurely pace of 15 miles per hour. Trained narrators tell of Hawaii's railway history, explain how the trains were used by plantations, and point out sites along the way. The end of the line, literally, is scenic Kahe Point, and passengers can spend a few minutes enjoying views of the Pacific Ocean. Back at the Ewa station, you can browse the train yard, enjoy a picnic lunch, and visit the gift shop.

Honolulu Academy of Arts — *Zone 2 Greater Honolulu*

Location 900 South Beretania Street

Phone (808) 532-8701 or (808) 532-8700

Website www.honoluluacademy.org

Hours Tuesday–Saturday, 10 a.m.–4:30 p.m.; Sunday, 1–5 p.m.

Admission $7 for adults; $4 for students, seniors, and military personnel; free for children age 12 and under

When to Go Anytime

How Much Time to Allow 90 minutes

Author's Rating ★★★★; The biggest and best Hawaii art museum.

Overall Appeal by Age Group

Pre-school ★½	Teens ★★★	Over 30 ★★★★
Grade school ★★½	Young Adults ★★★½	Seniors ★★★★

Description and Comments Founded by Anna Rice Cooke, Hawaiian-born daughter of New England missionaries, the Honolulu Academy of Arts opened in 1927 with 4,500 donated works of art. That number has grown to more than 34,000 pieces, ranging from paintings and textiles to sculptures and prints. With 32 galleries and 34,000 works of art from cultures around the globe, Honolulu Academy of Arts long ago achieved its reputation as the premier East-West art center. Now, 75 years after it opened, the Academy presents the best at last: the art of Hawaii. Hawaii-themed artworks are a primary feature of the new two-story, $9 million Henry R. Luce Pavilion Complex. The Complex welcomes visitors with a skylight by contemporary American glass artist Dale Chihuly and four sculptures called Dangos (a Japanese word for dumpling) by Japanese artist Jan Kaneko. Once inside you discover two 4,000-square-foot galleries, one for traveling exhibits and the other dedicated to Hawaii. Unrivaled anywhere, the Hawaii gallery (named for John Dominis and Patches Damon Holt) chronicles the history of the Islands from pen-and-ink sketches of John Webber (1752–1793), who accompanied Capt. James Cook on his voyages to Hawaii and gave the Western world its first glimpses of exotic Hawaiians and island lifestyle, to erotic works by Georgia O'Keeffe (1887–1986), who came to Hawaii to paint pineapples in 1939 for the Hawaii Pineapple Co., later Dole Corp., but grew bored and began painting vaguely suggestive waterfalls and tropical flowers. On view are some of Hawaii's most vivid works of art—"Hawaiian Fisherman" by Dutch portrait artist Hubert Vos (1855–1935); Hilo-born Lloyd Sexton's (1912–1990) triptych "Egrets and Pandanus"; and "The Lei Maker" by San Francisco painter Theodore Wores (1859–1939). The fiery canvases of the Volcano School artists—a self-titled group of artists and friends who painted volcanoes and included Jules Tavernier (1844–1889), Charles Furneaux (1835–1913), and D. Howard Hitchcock (1862–1943)—are worth the price of admission. Funded by the late Claire Booth Luce, a Honolulu resident and former Secretary of the Treasury (her signature was on all U.S. currency), the Luce Pavilion is named for her husband, the late cofounder and editor-in-chief of *Time* magazine.

The Western art collection includes Roman, Greek, and Egyptian works that date as far back as the third millennium B.C. to American and European works of the 1990s. The Academy's collection of Asian works is among the most highly regarded in the country and includes paintings, sculptures, ceramics, lacquerware, and prints. Of special note is the sizable collection—more than 8,000 works in all—of Japanese woodblock prints, most of which were donated by the famous American novelist James Michener. The collection represents the wood block printmaking masters of Japan in the eighteenth and nineteenth centuries. Also, the Academy's collection of Chinese works includes more than 100 paintings, some of which date back to the Ming dynasty.

Touring Tips Guided tours are scheduled at 11 a.m. Tuesday–Saturday and 1:15 p.m. on Sunday. The museum is fairly large, and the tour will likely make your visit here more enjoyable.

Other Things to Do Nearby The Pavilion Café is Honolulu's newest (some say best) place for lunch. Across the street is Thomas Square Park, a leafy green space that often hosts local arts and craft fairs.

Honolulu Zoo — *Zone 1 Waikiki*

Location 151 Kapahulu Avenue, Kapiolani Park; the entrance is on the makai side of the zoo

Phone (808) 971-7171

Website www.honoluluzoo.org

Hours Daily, 9 a.m.–4:30 p.m. (Special "Moonlight Walks" are offered from 6:30 to 8:30 p.m. once a month, before the full moon.)

Admission $6 for visitors age 13 and over; $1 for children ages 6–12; free for children under age 6

When to Go Anytime

How Much Time to Allow 2 hours

Author's Rating ★★★; A zoo is a zoo, but why not if you've had enough sun?

Overall Appeal by Age Group

Pre-school ★★★	Teens ★★★½	Over 30 ★★★
Grade school ★★★★	Young Adults ★★★½	Seniors ★★★★

Description and Comments Set on 42 acres at Kapiolani Park, the Honolulu Zoo is the largest zoo in the state—and the largest within a 2,300-mile radius. It is also big on history: The land for the zoo was donated in 1876 by King Kalakaua, Hawaii's "Merrie Monarch." The zoo began exhibiting animals in 1914; a monkey, a bear, and a few lion cubs were among the first furry occupants. Today, the roster of wildlife has expanded to include more than 120 different species divided into four separate exhibits. The African savanna includes lions, hippos, gazelles, rhinoceros, giraffes, zebras, cheetahs, chimpanzees, crocodiles, warthogs, hyenas, flamingos, tortoises, pelicans, and more. The tropical rain forest features tigers, monkeys, sun bears, gibbons, alligators, black swans, Amazon parrots, king vultures, toucans, Burmese pythons, iguanas, and the zoo's biggest (literally) attractions: Mari and Vaigai, a pair of Indian elephants. A popular spot for the kids is the Children's Zoo, with a variety of donkeys, sheep, llamas, potbellied pigs, and common farm animals. The Islands of the Pacific exhibit spotlights a few indigenous bird and reptile species. The zoo has several spots for picnicking, and food stands and strollers are available. Also, the Zootique gift shop carries an impressive selection of wildlife-related merchandise that stresses education as well as fun.

Touring Tips The zoo holds moonlit tours each month from 6:30 to 8:30 p.m. These evening programs reveal some of the nocturnal habits of the zoo's residents and include some fascinating folk tales. Admission is $10 for adults and $7 for children under age 12 (not recommended for children under age 5). Purchase tickets in advance at the zoo's front desk.

Other Things to Do Nearby The zoo is located at Kapiolani Park, a great place for picnicking. The Waikiki Aquarium is within easy walking distance, as is Waikiki Beach.

Iolani Palace — *Zone 2 Greater Honolulu*

Location 364 South King Street

Phone (808) 522-0832

Website www.iolanipalace.org

Hours Tuesday–Saturday, 8 a.m.–3:30 p.m.

Admission $20 for adults; $5 for children ages 5–17 (Children under age 5 are not allowed into the palace. Reservations are required.)

When to Go Anytime

How Much Time to Allow 1 hour

Author's Rating ★★★★½; The only palace in America is the last vestige of the Monarchy Period and one of Hawaii's architectural treasures.

Overall Appeal by Age Group

Pre-school —	Teens ★★★½	Over 30 ★★★★½
Grade school ★★½	Young Adults ★★★★½	Seniors ★★★★½

Description and Comments Built in 1882, Iolani Palace—the only royal palace standing on American soil—served as the royal residence of Hawaii's last two monarchs, King Kalakaua and Queen Liliuokalani. In its heyday, the palace was the scene of spectacular galas and events, including the fun-loving Kalakaua's extravagant 50th birthday jubilee. Sadly, it was also the site of political chaos, which led to the downfall of the kingdom in the late 1890s at the hands of American sugar planters. From then until 1969, when the State Capitol building was completed, the palace served as the capitol of the republic, territory, and finally state of Hawaii. The palace was restored to museum-quality condition, and restoration efforts continue.

Now operated by the nonprofit Friends of Iolani Palace, this remarkable building is open five days a week for docent-guided public tours. The inside is striking, with a large koa wood staircase serving as a magnificent centerpiece. The Throne Room, adorned in maroon and gold, was the setting for royal audiences, receptions, and events of state. The Blue Room was the site of more informal gatherings and parties; the Dining Room is beautifully appointed with portraits of various world leaders of the past. The second floor includes the King's Suite, the Queen's Room, two guest rooms, and the Music Room.

A royal uproar of more recent vintage occurred in the summer of 1998, when the president of Friends of Iolani Palace actually sat on one of the palace's thrones for a photo session with a *Life* magazine photographer. Her faux pas caused some damage to the fabric. Bishop Museum officials later said that the throne's silk material was in such a deteriorated condition that any touch would have caused damage. The damage was repaired, but the president—a great-grandniece of King Kalakaua—was forced to resign.

Touring Tips Guided tours are scheduled at 15-minute intervals, each lasting about 45 minutes. Pick up your tickets at Iolani Barracks, located on the palace grounds. The palace is wheelchair-accessible; call ahead about other special requirements.

Other Things to Do Nearby The Mission Houses Museum, Kamehameha Statue, Hawaii State Archives, Hawaii State Library, and the State Capitol are all within easy walking distance from the palace.

Kualoa Ranch and Activity Club *Zone 3 Windward Oahu*

Location 49-560 Kamehameha Highway

Phone (808) 237-7321 or (800) 231-7321

Website www.kualoa.com

Hours Daily, 9 a.m.–5 p.m.

Admission Rates for individual activities range $15–$79

When to Go Anytime

How Much Time to Allow 2–6 hours

Author's Rating ★★★★; Offers myriad activities, with something for every age group, outdoors in one of the Islands' most beautiful settings.

Overall Appeal by Age Group

Pre-school ★★½	Teens ★★★★	Over 30 ★★★★
Grade school ★★★	Young Adults ★★★★★	Seniors ★★★

Description and Comments One of Oahu's best attractions, this 4,000-acre working cattle ranch offers more than 15 active outdoor activities. You could spend an entire day here enjoying one or more of the following: horseback riding, hiking, all-terrain vehicles, snorkel tours, Jet Skis, target shooting, canoeing, volleyball, helicopter rides, tennis, a petting zoo, garden tour, badminton, kayak rides, and a ride around the ranch that includes a narrated ranch and movie set tour. Kualoa Ranch was the setting for several major Hollywood films, including *Windtalkers, Jurassic Park, Mighty Joe Young,* and *Godzilla.* In addition to its scenic mountainside headquarters and broad coastal valley, it includes an ancient fishpond, plant nursery, and aquaculture ponds. Our favorite activity here? Relaxing at Secret Island, a remote beach where you can nap in a hammock, play volleyball, go snorkeling, play table tennis, and more.

Touring Tips Numerous tour packages are available, most including a buffet lunch and transportation to and from your hotel. You could also go directly to the ranch and sign up for whatever activities interest you.

Mission Houses Museum — *Zone 2 Greater Honolulu*

Location 553 South King Street

Phone (808) 531-0481

Website www.lava.net/~mhm

Hours Tuesday–Saturday, 9 a.m.–4 p.m.

Admission $10 for adults; $8 for seniors and military personnel; $6 for students ages 6 and over

When to Go Anytime

How Much Time to Allow 1 hour

Author's Rating ★★★; A good bet for history buffs, but boring for kids.

Overall Appeal by Age Group

Pre-school ★	Teens ★★	Over 30 ★★★
Grade school ★½	Young Adults ★★★	Seniors ★★★

Description and Comments This is where the first American Protestant missionaries established their headquarters in 1820. Built between 1821 and 1841, these structures—the oldest surviving Western-style buildings in all of Hawaii—house such original artifacts as furniture, books, quilts, and other household items belonging to missionary families. Visit the white Frame House, which served as home to several of Hawaii's most prominent missionaries; the Chamberlain House, which was used as a storehouse and separate home; and the Coral House, where the first-ever printing in the Pacific was done. (The first printed sheet was produced on January 7, 1922; Chief Keeaumoku had the honor of pulling the lever of a creaky wooden press. Through this printing press the missionaries brought literacy to the Hawaiian nation.) The missionaries also introduced the art of New England quilting to Hawaiian women, and this museum has a sizable collection of some early Hawaiian quilts.

Touring Tips Guided tours are scheduled at 9:30, 10:30, and 11:30 a.m. and 1, 2, and 3 p.m.

Other Things to Do Nearby The museum sits next to historic Kawaiahao Church and is near the Hawaii State Library, Iolani Palace, the State Capitol, the Kamehameha Statue, and State Archives.

National Memorial Cemetery of the Pacific — *Zone 2 Greater Honolulu*

Location 2177 Puowaina Drive

Phone (808) 532-3720

Hours Daily: March 2–September 29, 8 a.m.–6:30 p.m.; September 30–March 1, 8 a.m.–5:30 p.m.; Memorial Day, 7 a.m.–7 p.m.

Admission Free

When to Go Anytime

How Much Time to Allow 1 hour

Author's Rating ★★★; A poignant experience for all.

Overall Appeal by Age Group

Pre-school ½	Teens ★	Over 30 ★★★½
Grade school ★	Young Adults ★★½	Seniors ★★★★

Description and Comments Also known as Punchbowl (the 112-acre site sits inside Punchbowl Crater), this national cemetery is the final resting place for more than 40,000 war veterans (and their family members) who served the United States in World War II, the Korean War, and the Vietnam War. It is a solemn sight, with rows of small, flat, white headstones stretching far across the crater floor. Among those buried here is famed war correspondent Ernest Taylor "Ernie" Pyle. (While serving as a correspondent with the 77th Infantry Division, Pyle was killed on April 18, 1945, by Japanese gunfire on the small Pacific islet of Ie Shima.) Panoramic views of Waikiki, Honolulu, and Pearl Harbor add to the experience here. Each Easter morning, the cemetery is visited by thousands of Hawaii residents and visitors for the annual Easter Sunrise Service.

Pacific Aerospace Museum — *Zone 2 Greater Honolulu*

Location Central lobby, main terminal, Honolulu International Airport

Phone (808) 839-0777

Hours Daily, 9 a.m.–6 p.m.

Admission Free

When to Go Simply put, this is a good place to kill some time while waiting for your return flight home.

How Much Time to Allow 40 minutes

Author's Rating ★★½; Fun for kids and adults alike.

Overall Appeal by Age Group

Pre-school ★★	Teens ★★★½	Over 30 ★★★
Grade school ★★★½	Young Adults ★★★½	Seniors ★★★

Description and Comments A 27-minute multimedia presentation, *The Great Skyquest Theater,* highlights this $3.8 million, 6,500-square-foot mini-museum, which opened in December 1991. The presentation—staged in three adjoining theaters—traces the history of aviation in Hawaii and the Pacific region and includes an account of the infamous Japanese attack on Pearl Harbor. Hands-on exhibits include a computerized globe that displays flight distances and lengths, a "learn to fly" lesson, a model of the moon, and (our favorite) a full-scale NASA space shuttle flight deck.

Polynesian Cultural Center — *Zone 4 The North Shore*

Location 55-370 Kamehameha Highway

Phone (800) 367-7060 or (877) 722-1411

Website www.polynesia.com

Hours Monday–Saturday, 12:30–9 p.m.; villages close at 6 p.m.

Admission General admission is $40 for adults and $24 for children ages 3–11 and includes admission to 7 Polynesian villages, canoe rides, the Pageant of Long Canoes, and a tram tour. Special deluxe packages featuring an IMAX film, a buffet, and the evening show *Horizons* are as follows: Ambassador Package, $105 for adults and $71 for children; Luau Package, $75 for adults and $51 for children; and Buffet Package, $55 for adults and $37 for children. Evening show with no dinner option is offered for $40 for adults and $24 for children.

When to Go Anytime. If you enjoy watching Samoan fire-knife dancers, however, be sure to come during the World Fire-Knife Dance Championships, which are held each year in April or May.

How Much Time to Allow All day, including 2½ hours' drive time to and from Waikiki

Author's Rating ★★★★½; Most popular paid visitor attraction in Hawaii.

Overall Appeal by Age Group

Pre-school ★★★	Teens ★★★★½	Over 30 ★★★★½
Grade school ★★★★	Young Adults ★★★★½	Seniors ★★★★½

Description and Comments Set on 42 acres in the Mormon university town of Laie, home of Brigham Young University–Hawaii, the Polynesian Cultural Center delivers a cultural experience that includes re-created villages representing the cultures of Samoa, Fiji, Tahiti, Tonga, New Zealand, Marquesas, and Hawaii.

Friendly native Pacific Islanders, dressed in traditional attire, eagerly share their arts, crafts, songs, and dances. Most of them are students at the neighboring BYU-H campus. They work part time at PCC in exchange for tuition, room, board, and books. Hands-on demonstrations include coconut husking, wood carving, lau hala weaving, poi pounding, and tapa making. Waterways and lush gardens are the settings for canoe rides, a tram tour, and a colorful pageant of canoes. The seven-story-high IMAX theater adds to the experience with a film tracing the history of Polynesia.

A variety of buffet/show packages is available, culminating in an impressive evening show featuring a cast of more than 150 dancers and musicians. Alcohol is not part of the program at this Mormon institution.

Queen Emma Summer Palace — *Zone 2 Greater Honolulu*

Location 2913 Pali Highway

Phone (808) 595-3167

Hours Daily, 9 a.m.–4 p.m.

Admission $6 for adults; $4 for seniors; $1 for children under age 15

When to Go Anytime

How Much Time to Allow 1 hour

Author's Rating ★★★; Worth a visit for Hawaiian history students.

Overall Appeal by Age Group

Pre-school ½	Teens ★★½	Over 30 ★★★½
Grade school ★★	Young Adults ★★★½	Seniors ★★★½

Description and Comments Maintained and operated by the nonprofit Daughters of Hawaii, this charming white-frame house served as a summer retreat for Queen Emma, consort to Alexander Liholiho (King Kamehameha IV). Many of the queen's possessions are on display here, including an opulent gold necklace and various wedding and baby gifts presented to Emma by England's Queen Victoria. This was among the first Hawaiian properties to be listed on the National Register of Historic Places.

Other Things to Do Nearby Behind the palace, off Puiwa Road, is Nuuanu Valley Park, a serene hideaway favored for its shady trees.

Royal Mausoleum — *Zone 2 Greater Honolulu*

Location 2261 Nuuanu Avenue

Phone (808) 587-0300

Hours Monday–Friday, 8 a.m.–4:30 p.m.

Admission Free

When to Go Anytime

How Much Time to Allow 45 minutes

Author's Rating ★★½; Not your typical visitor attraction.

Overall Appeal by Age Group

Pre-school ½	Teens ★★	Over 30 ★★
Grade school ★½	Young Adults ★★	Seniors ★★★

Description and Comments Considered the most sacred burial ground in the entire state, this three-acre site is the resting place for six of the eight Hawaiian monarchs: Kings Kamehameha II, III, IV, and V; King Kalakaua; and Queen Liliuokalani. (The bones of Kamehameha I were hidden at a secret location on the Kona Coast of the island of Hawaii; William Lunalilo, or Kamehameha VI, per his wishes, was buried in a private tomb on the grounds of Kawaiahao Church.) This current site was prepared in 1865 by Kamehameha V to replace the original royal burial tomb on the grounds of Iolani Palace.

Touring Tips Call ahead to arrange for guided tours.

Sea Life Park — *Zone 3 Windward Oahu*

Location 41-202 Kalanianaole Highway

Phone (808) 259-7933

Hours Daily, 9:30 a.m.–5 p.m.

Admission $25 for adults; $12.50 for children ages 4–12; free for children under age 4

When to Go Anytime

How Much Time to Allow 3–4 hours

Author's Rating ★★★½; Even if you have similar attractions back home, this is a family fun spot.

Overall Appeal by Age Group

Pre-school ★★★★	Teens ★★★★	Over 30 ★★★★
Grade school ★★★★★	Young Adults ★★★★	Seniors ★★★★

Description and Comments The first feature you encounter on entering the park is the 300,000-gallon Hawaiian Reef Tank, filled with more than 2,000 species of reef fish, rays, hammerhead sharks, and other colorful marine life. From there, head to the Rocky Shores exhibit, which provides above- and below-water views of marine life in a tidal zone, and then the Sea Turtle Lagoon, where you'll get an up-close look at Hawaii's protected green sea turtles. Children especially will want to drop by the Discovery Pool, where they can hold tiny sea critters, like sea cucumbers and spiny sea stars.

Other don't-miss exhibits include the Sea Lion Pool (you can purchase fish to feed the sea lions), Sea Bird Sanctuary, and Penguin Habitat (home to a successful breeding colony of Humboldt penguins). At Whaler's Cove, you can view the park's dolphins, whales, and Kekaimalu, the world's only known "wholphin" (half false killer whale, half dolphin). The park offers three live shows: The Hawaii Ocean Theater, a 400-seat amphitheater, features performances by bottlenose dolphins, sea lions, and penguins. Whaler's Cove is the site of an entertaining show built around the amazing leaps and flips of the bottlenose dolphins. And the Kolohe Kai Sea Lion Show, in Makapuu Meadow, spotlights a group of delightful sea lions and their trainers.

Also on the premises are two eateries: the Sea Lion Café and Rabbit Island Bar and Grill. Two gift shops—the Sea Life Park General Store and Little Treasures—offer a wide assortment of T-shirts, souvenirs, and park-related merchandise.

The special program Dolphin Adventures is offered three times daily. Dolphin Adventures lets you learn how the park's trainers use positive reinforcement to train the dolphins. Better yet, you'll have an opportunity to get in the water and interact with specially trained dolphins. The cost is $99 per person, and participants must be at least 13 years of age.

Splash University, meanwhile, also gives you an insider's look at how these friendly mammals are trained. You'll learn a few signals that dolphins respond to and participate in training sessions during shallow-water interaction. The cost is $79 for adults and $67 for children ages 4–12 (children under age 12 must be accompanied by an adult). Splash University is held four times daily.

The Swim with the Sting Rays program offers participants an opportunity to swim with rays and learn their eating habits. The cost is $49 per person.

"Tuition" costs include general admission into Sea Life Park. Each program lasts approximately one hour. Be sure to bring swimwear and a towel. Call (808) 259-2500 for more information or to make a reservation.

Touring Tips "The Hawaiian Reef Show" begins at 9:50 a.m.; "Hawaii Ocean Theater" at 10 a.m.; "Kolohe Kai Sea Lion Show" at 11 a.m.; and "Whaler's Cove" at 11:15 a.m. The show rotation continues throughout the day, with the final set starting at 2:45 p.m.

Other Things to Do Nearby Sandy Beach and Makapuu Beach are just a few minutes away by car.

Senator Fong's Plantation and Gardens — *Zone 3 Windward Oahu*

Location 47-285 Pulama Road

Phone (808) 239-6775

Website www.fonggarden.com

Hours Daily, 9 a.m.–4 p.m.

Admission $10 for adults; $8 for seniors; $6 for children ages 5–12

When to Go Anytime

How Much Time to Allow 90 minutes

Author's Rating ★★★; A Windward Oahu outing featuring family-style aloha spirit.

Overall Appeal by Age Group

Pre-school ★★	Teens ★★★	Over 30 ★★★★
Grade school ★★½	Young Adults ★★★	Seniors ★★★★

Description and Comments Hiram Fong was the first Asian-American to serve in the U.S. Senate, retiring in 1977. Today, Fong and his family run this 725-acre private estate, with tropical flower gardens, more than 100 different fruits and nuts, and scenic views of Windward Oahu. Hands-on activities here include lei-making lessons using flowers picked from nearby gardens. A 50-minute tram tour takes visitors through valleys and tropical forests. A snack bar, fruit stand, and gift shop are on site.

Touring Tips Narrated tram tours are scheduled daily at 10:30 and 11:30 a.m. and 1, 2, and 3 p.m. Reservations are not needed.

Tropic Lightning Museum — *Zone 6 Central Oahu*

Location Schofield Barracks

Phone (808) 655-0438

Hours Tuesday–Saturday, 10 a.m.–4 p.m.

Admission Free

When to Go Anytime

How Much Time to Allow 30 minutes

Author's Rating ★★½; Strictly for military buffs.

Overall Appeal by Age Group

Pre-school ★	Teens ★★	Over 30 ★★
Grade school ★	Young Adults ★★	Seniors ★★★★

Description and Comments This cozy museum documents the history of Schofield Barracks and the famed "Tropic Lightning" 25th Infantry Division, which fought in World War II, the Korean War, and the Vietnam War.

U.S. Army Museum — *Zone 1 Waikiki*

Location Battery Randolph, Fort DeRussy, at the intersection of Kalia and Saratoga Roads, next to the Hale Koa Hotel; validated parking available in Fort DeRussy's Saratoga parking lot

Phone (808) 438-2821

Hours Tuesday–Sunday, 10 a.m.–4:30 p.m.

Admission Donations accepted

When to Go Anytime

How Much Time to Allow 1 hour

Author's Rating ★★★½; A wealth of war memorabilia, and you can't beat the price.

Overall Appeal by Age Group

Pre-school ★	Teens ★★★	Over 30 ★★★½
Grade school ★★★	Young Adults ★★★½	Seniors ★★★

Description and Comments Built in 1909, the Battery Randolph served as an imposing military fortress, ready to defend Waikiki from attacking battleships. (It was a part of the military's "Ring of Steel" that encircled Oahu.) However, when it outlived its usefulness, officials faced a dilemma: The structure was nearly impossible to tear down. Its walls were 22 feet thick (solid concrete) and built to withstand a direct hit from a 2,000-ton artillery shell. Any attempt to bring it down with explosives would undoubtedly cause damage in the surrounding areas of Waikiki. In 1976, the battery was transformed into the 13,500-square-foot U.S. Army Museum, recalling the history of the American army in the Pacific.

Included here are more than 2,000 artifacts and 1,900 photographs tracing the U.S. military's presence in Hawaii. The artifacts range from small (medals and tags) to huge (a Japanese battle tank). One popular exhibit pays tribute to the 100th/442nd Regimental Combat Team, a unit made up of local and mainland Japanese-American men who overcame prejudice to enlist in the U.S. Army during World War II. They became the most highly decorated unit in the war, living up to their battle cry of "Go for broke." A gift shop is available on the premises.

USS Arizona *Memorial* — *Zone 6 Central Oahu*

Location 1 Arizona Memorial Place

Phone (808) 422-0561 or (808) 422-2771

Website www.arizonamemorial.org

Hours Daily, 7:30 a.m.–5 p.m. Program runs 8 a.m.–3 p.m., weather permitting (shuttle boats to the memorial leave every 15 minutes between 8 a.m. and 3 p.m.)

Admission Free

When to Go Anytime

How Much Time to Allow Between 2 and 4 hours. Due to the popularity of this attraction, you are likely to wait in line for an hour or more. The program itself lasts about 75 minutes.

Author's Rating ★★★★; A solemn, moving experience.

Overall Appeal by Age Group

Pre-school ★½	Teens ★★★½	Over 30 ★★★★½
Grade school ★★★	Young Adults ★★★½	Seniors ★★★★★

Description and Comments The museum exhibits numerous historic photos and touching memorabilia from December 7, 1941, the day Japanese warplanes bombed Pearl Harbor. Visitors see a 23-minute film depicting the attack as well as events that led to it. Then you are transported to the memorial via shuttle boat. The memorial is a white structure that sits over the sunken *Arizona,* where 1,102 men went down with the ship and remain entombed. A marble wall pays tribute to the 1,177 sailors and marines who perished during the surprise attack. The memorial, designed by a Honolulu architect, was made possible after a benefit concert staged in Honolulu in 1961 by an ex-G.I. by the name of Elvis Presley.

Touring Tips Tickets are issued on a first-come, first-served basis. Each guest must pick up his or her own ticket in person at the ticket office.

Other Things to Do Nearby The USS Battleship *Missouri* and USS *Bowfin* Submarine and Park are both in the immediate vicinity.

USS Battleship Missouri *Memorial* — *Zone 6 Central Oahu*

Location Ford Island, Pier Fox Trot 5

Phone (808) 423-2263 or (877) MIGHTY-MO

Website www.ussmissouri.com

Hours Daily, 9 a.m.–5 p.m.

Admission General admission: $16 for adults; $8 for children ages 4–12

When to Go Anytime

How Much Time to Allow 90 minutes–2 hours

Author's Rating ★★★★; Forms an appropriate bookend to the USS *Arizona* Memorial.

Overall Appeal by Age Group

Pre-school ★½	Teens ★★★½	Over 30 ★★★★½
Grade school ★★★	Young Adults ★★★½	Seniors ★★★½

Description and Comments One of America's most storied battleships now calls Pearl Harbor home as an interactive museum and memorial. The 45,000-ton "Mighty Mo" is the last of four Iowa-class battleships built during World War II. It was on the deck of the *Missouri* that Japan officially surrendered to the Allied Forces, marking the end of World War II in the Pacific theater. The *Missouri* earned three battle stars for missions in Iwo Jima, Okinawa, and Japan during that war, then five more while serving in the Korean War. The *Missouri* also served during the Persian Gulf War. In 1986, it became the first battleship to circumnavigate the world.

Buses transport visitors to Ford Island, where the ship is anchored. Touring Mighty Mo, which is nearly three football fields long, you'll be able to view documents and photographs and hear a portion of a speech made by Gen. Douglas MacArthur.

Touring Tips A Chief's Guided Tour is available; it includes head-of-the-line privileges and a tour led by a crew member: $20 for adults; $16 for military personnel; $13 for children ages 4–12; $11 for children of military personnel. All tickets must be purchased before 4 p.m.

Other Things to Do Nearby The USS *Arizona* Memorial and USS *Bowfin* Submarine Museum and Park.

USS Bowfin *Submarine Museum and Park* — *Zone 6 Central Oahu*

Location 11 Arizona Memorial Drive

Phone (808) 423-1341

Website www.bowfin.org

Hours Daily, 8 a.m.–5 p.m.

Admission Entry to both museum and submarine: $8 for adults; $6 for seniors and military personnel; $3 for children ages 4–12. Entry to museum only: $4 for adults; $2 for children ages 4–12

When to Go Anytime

How Much Time to Allow 1 hour–90 minutes

Author's Rating ★★★½; Excellent for military and history buffs.

Overall Appeal by Age Group

Pre-school ★½	Teens ★★★½	Over 30 ★★★★
Grade school ★★★	Young Adults ★★★½	Seniors ★★★★½

Description and Comments Nicknamed the "Pearl Harbor Avenger," the *Bowfin* is credited with 44 enemy ship sinkings on nine patrols. It is one of only 15 World War II U.S. submarines still in existence. Visitors can check out the interior of the vessel and examine defused torpedoes. The park houses a museum filled with submarine history, featuring outdoor exhibits and a mini-theater.

Other Things to Do Nearby The USS *Arizona* Memorial and USS Battleship *Missouri* Memorial.

Waikiki Aquarium — *Zone 1 Waikiki*

Location 2777 Kalakaua Avenue

Phone (808) 923-9741

Website www.mic.hawaii.edu/aquarium

Hours Daily, 9 a.m.–5 p.m.

Admission $7 for adults; $5 for seniors, military personnel, and college students; $3.50 for children ages 13–17 and people with disabilities; free for children age 12 and under

When to Go Anytime

How Much Time to Allow 1 hour

Author's Rating ★★★½; Excellent small aquarium by the sea.

Overall Appeal by Age Group

Pre-school ★★★	Teens ★★★★	Over 30 ★★★½
Grade school ★★★½	Young Adults ★★★½	Seniors ★★★½

Description and Comments The Waikiki Aquarium's history is no mere fish story. Built in 1904, it is the third-oldest public aquarium in the United States and has distinguished itself as a living classroom for anyone interested in Hawaii's ocean life. The aquarium is one of the first facilities in the world to successfully breed mahimahi (also known as dolphin fish) and the first in the United States to breed the chambered nautilus. Although not very large, the facility houses more than 2,000 ocean creatures representing some 350 different species. Here you can learn about endangered species, like the Hawaiian monk seal, and threatened species, like the Hawaiian green sea turtle. A gallery of aquariums display colorful reef fish, coral, a giant clam, jellyfish, and mahimahi. It's a great companion experience for your snorkeling adventures. In addition to the live exhibits, several educational classes focusing on Hawaii's marine environment are available. Call for an updated schedule and class fees.

Other Things to Do Nearby The Honolulu Zoo is within easy walking distance.

Maui

Alexander and Baldwin Sugar Museum — *Zone 7 Central Maui*

Location 3957 Hansen Road

Phone (808) 871-8058

Website www.sugarmuseum.com

Hours Monday–Saturday, 9:30 a.m.–4:30 p.m.

Admission $5 for adults; $2 for children ages 6–17

When to Go Anytime

How Much Time to Allow 45 minutes

Author's Rating ★★★; A look at Maui's sugar plantation history.

Overall Appeal by Age Group

Pre-school ★½	Teens ★★½	Over 30 ★★★½
Grade school ★★	Young Adults ★★★	Seniors ★★★½

Description and Comments Formerly the residence of a factory superintendent, this museum houses a number of artifacts, photographs, and a working scale model of sugar-processing machinery.

Bailey House Museum — *Zone 7 Central Maui*

Location 2375-A Main Street

Phone (808) 244-3326

Website www.mauimuseum.org

Hours Monday–Saturday, 10 a.m.–4 p.m.

Admission $5 for adults; $4 for seniors; $1 for children ages 7–12

When to Go Anytime

How Much Time to Allow 1 hour

Author's Rating ★★★; Worth a stop for history buffs.

Overall Appeal by Age Group

Pre-school ★½	Teens ★★½	Over 30 ★★★½
Grade school ★★	Young Adults ★★★	Seniors ★★★½

Description and Comments The Bailey mission home, built in 1833 of lava rock and native woods, sits on land given to the missionaries by Hawaiian chiefs. Hawaiians attended reading and writing classes here, using Hawaiian language books printed on Maui. Today the Bailey House displays Hawaiian artifacts, including tapa, weaving, featherwork, and tools made out of stones, shells, and bones. A gallery of paintings from the late 1800s portrays the beauty of the Valley Isle, and the outside gardens reveal rare native plants, a koa wood canoe, and a surfboard once used by legendary surfer/swimmer Duke Kahanamoku. A gift shop offers crafts, apparel, Hawaiian music, and books.

The Bailey House Museum is one of the few places that you can see a Maui oo, an extinct bird last seen on Molokai in 1904. The black bird with bright yellow wing feathers lies in a glass case with its little feet crossed as if it had just dropped out of the sky. It became extinct 100 years ago. The Kauai oo *(Moho braccatus)* was last seen in the Alakai Swamp in 1986. The oo trophy is so rare that curators of the Bernice Pauahi Bishop Museum of Natural Science in Honolulu keep a solitary taxidermy specimen in a dark safe. If you happen to be in London, you may see a cape once worn by Hawaiian kings made of 20,000 bright yellow oo thigh feathers at the Pitt-Rivers Museum at the University of Oxford. Writer Simon Winchester called the oo cape "certainly one of the most remarkably lovely things in any museum in England."

Other Things to Do Nearby The Hawaii Nature Center and Kepaniwai Park are a short drive away.

Baldwin Home Museum — *Zone 9 West Maui*

Location 120 Dickenson Street

Phone (808) 661-3262

Hours Daily, 10 a.m.–4 p.m.

Admission $5 for families; $3 for adults; $2 for seniors

When to Go Anytime

How Much Time to Allow 1 hour

Author's Rating ★★★; A peek into Hawaii's missionary era.

Overall Appeal by Age Group

Pre-school ★½	Teens ★★★	Over 30 ★★★½
Grade school ★★	Young Adults ★★★	Seniors ★★★½

Description and Comments This two-story structure was the home of Reverend Dwight Baldwin, a Protestant medical missionary from 1838 to 1871. Today the home and its grounds, lovingly restored by the Lahaina Restoration Foundation, give visitors a glimpse of what life was like for nineteenth-century missionary families in Lahaina. On display are various household items and furniture, photographs, and other historic artifacts. Ask for a free self-guided tour map of Lahaina's other restored treasures.

Other Things to Do Nearby Located at Dickenson and Front Streets, the Baldwin Home is one of several historic sights in Lahaina. The *Brig Carthaginian* and Wo Hing Temple are within easy walking distance.

Brig Carthaginian — *Zone 9 West Maui*

Location Lahaina Harbor

Phone (808) 661-3262

Hours Daily, 10 a.m.–4 p.m.

Admission $5 for families (any size); $3 for adults; $2 for seniors

When to Go Anytime

How Much Time to Allow 75 minutes

Author's Rating ★★★; A cool way to learn about the whaling era of the mid-1800s.

Overall Appeal by Age Group

Pre-school ★★	Teens ★★★	Over 30 ★★★½
Grade school ★★½	Young Adults ★★★½	Seniors ★★★½

Description and Comments This 93-foot ship, a replica of a nineteenth-century brig, is a maritime museum featuring whale exhibits, audiovisual displays, and an original whale boat. The square-rigged ship is typical of the vessels that brought the first commerce to the Hawaiian islands. A video about humpback whales is shown.

Other Things to Do Nearby The Wo Hing Temple and Baldwin Home Museum are a short walk away.

Haleakala National Park — *Zone 10 Upcountry Maui*

Location The park extends from the 10,023 foot summit of Haleakala down the southeast flank of the mountain to the Kipahulu coastline near Hana. The summit area is accessible from Kahului via Roads 37, 377, and 378. The park's Kipahulu area, at the east end of the island between Hana and Kaupo, can be reached via Highway 36. Driving time is about 3–4 hours each way.

Phone (808) 572-9306

Website www.haleakala.national-park.com

Hours Park Ranger Headquarters is open daily, 9 a.m.–4 p.m.; the Visitor Center is open daily, sunrise–3 p.m. (Overnight camping is permissible. The Hosmer Grove Campground in the summit area, located just inside the park's entrance, can be used without a permit; all other camping areas require permits.)

Admission $10/vehicle, good for 7 days

When to Go Anytime. Haleakala is renowned as a setting for dramatic sunrises and sunsets, although most people come for sunrise. Be sure to arrive at least 30 minutes before either event.

How Much Time to Allow Half a day, depending on whether you plan to spend time hiking or taking part in one of the park's programs

Author's Rating ★★★★; One of the great natural wonders of the world.

Overall Appeal by Age Group

Pre-school ★★	Teens ★★★½	Over 30 ★★★★
Grade school ★★★	Young Adults ★★★★	Seniors ★★★★

Description and Comments Haleakala ("House of the Sun"), a dormant volcano that last spilled lava a bit more than 200 years ago, was designated as a national park in 1961. The park consists of nearly 29,000 acres, most of it wilderness. In the summit area, see the Park Ranger Headquarters and Haleakala Visitor Center, which houses a variety of cultural and natural history exhibits. Rangers are on duty and can be a tremendous help in making the most out of your visit. In the Kipahulu area, see the Kipahulu Ranger Station/Visitor Center. Each facility has a selection of books, maps, postcards, and other souvenirs for sale.

Touring Tips Check the park's bulletin board for a schedule of daily programs and guided hikes. Obey all posted warning signs. It can be cold at the summit, so be prepared. Due to the high elevation and reduced oxygen at the park, anyone with heart or respiratory conditions is advised to check with his doctor before visiting.

Hana Cultural Center — *Zone 10 Upcountry Maui*

Location 4974 Uakea Road

Phone (808) 248-8622

Website www.planet-hawaii.com/hana

Hours Daily, 10 a.m.–4 p.m.

Admission Donations accepted

When to Go Anytime

How Much Time to Allow 1 hour

Author's Rating ★★★; A reward after the long journey to Hana.

Overall Appeal by Age Group

Pre-school ★★	Teens ★★½	Over 30 ★★★
Grade school ★★½	Young Adults ★★★	Seniors ★★★

Description and Comments This cultural center is home to a quaint museum that features more than 500 artifacts, 600 books, 5,000 historic photographs of the Hana district, and, oddly enough, 680 Hawaiian bottles. Opened in 1983, the nonprofit museum houses Hawaiian quilts, poi boards, stones, kapa, ancient tools, fish hooks, gourd bowls, stone lamps, and a century-old fishing net. Also featured are tributes to some of Hana's most notable personalities. The cultural center also includes a series of old Hawaiian hale (houses), the historic Hana courthouse, and a jailhouse.

Hawaii Experience Theater — *Zone 9 West Maui*

Location 824 Front Street

Phone (808) 661-8314

Hours Daily, 10 a.m.–10 p.m. Tickets go on sale at 9:30 a.m.

Admission $6.95 for adults; $3.95 for children ages 4–12 (younger children free). If you purchase $25 worth of merchandise at the gift shop, you receive a free ticket to the show.

When to Go Anytime

How Much Time to Allow 50 minutes

Author's Rating ★★★½; A diversion in the heart of Lahaina.

Overall Appeal by Age Group

Pre-school ★★★	Teens ★★★½	Over 30 ★★★½
Grade school ★★★½	Young Adults ★★★½	Seniors ★★★½

Description and Comments A planetarium-like theater with a 60-foot-tall domed screen, this attraction features a spectacular 40-minute film, *Hawaii: Islands of the Gods,* shown every hour.

Other Things to Do Nearby Historical attractions, including the Wo Hing Temple and Baldwin Home Museum, are within easy walking distance.

Hawaii Nature Center — *Zone 7 Central Maui*

Location 875 Iao Valley Road

Phone (808) 244-6500

Website www.hawaiiweb.com/maui/html/sites/hawaii_nature_center.html

Hours Daily, 10 a.m.–4 p.m.

Admission $6 for adults; $4 for children ages 4–12

When to Go Anytime

How Much Time to Allow 1 hour

Author's Rating ★★★★; Good hands-on learning experience.

Overall Appeal by Age Group

Pre-school ★★★	Teens ★★★★	Over 30 ★★★★
Grade school ★★★★	Young Adults ★★★★	Seniors ★★★★

Description and Comments The Nature Center's Interactive Science Arcade features more than 30 interactive exhibits celebrating Maui's natural environment. The main exhibit hall features an amazing 10-foot-high, 30-foot-long, three-dimensional replication of four streams that feed into the Iao Stream. Aquariums, rain forest explorations, arcade games, telescopes, and live insect and animal exhibits are among the other highlights. The gift shop features an extensive selection of naturethemed merchandise. All proceeds go to environmental education programs for Maui elementary-school children.

Touring Tips Guided nature walks are offered daily. Call for reservations (required).

Other Things to Do Nearby Visit Kepaniwai Cultural Park and the Bailey House Museum.

Hui Noeau Visual Arts Center — *Zone 10 Upcountry Maui*

Location 2841 Baldwin Avenue

Phone (808) 572-6560

Website www.huinoeau.com

Hours Monday–Friday, 8 a.m.–4 p.m. Gallery hours are Saturday, 10 a.m.–4 p.m.

Admission Donations accepted

When to Go Anytime

How Much Time to Allow 1 hour

Author's Rating ★★★; A haven for art lovers.

Overall Appeal by Age Group

Pre-school ★★	Teens ★★★	Over 30 ★★★½
Grade school ★★½	Young Adults ★★★	Seniors ★★★½

Description and Comments Occupying a beautiful nine-acre estate in Makawao, this nonprofit art center features works by both local and international artists. The estate itself is a historic landmark (built in 1917 for Harry and Ethel Baldwin) dotted with pine and camphor trees and adorned with an immaculate formal garden and reflecting pool. The arts center features classes and workshops for aspiring artisans, and exhibits are open to the public on Saturdays. The gift shop offers a selection of original artworks, note cards, books, and other gift items.

Kepaniwai Cultural Park — *Zone 7 Central Maui*

Location Iao Valley Road

Phone (808) 243-7389

Hours Daily, 7 a.m.–7 p.m.

Admission Free

When to Go Anytime

How Much Time to Allow 1 hour

Author's Rating ★★★; A pleasant stop if you're in the area.

Overall Appeal by Age Group

Pre-school ★★	Teens ★★★	Over 30 ★★★½
Grade school ★★½	Young Adults ★★★	Seniors ★★★½

Description and Comments Picturesque gardens and architectural pavilions representing Hawaii's different ethnic groups.

Other Things to Do Nearby The Hawaii Nature Center and Bailey House Museum.

Kula Botanical Garden — *Zone 10 Upcountry Maui*

Location RR 4, Box 288

Phone (808) 878-1715

Hours Daily, 9 a.m.–4 p.m.

Admission $5 for adults; $1 for children ages 6–12

When to Go Anytime

How Much Time to Allow 90 minutes

Author's Rating ★★★; A botanist's dream come true.

Overall Appeal by Age Group

Pre-school ★★	Teens ★★½	Over 30 ★★★
Grade school ★★½	Young Adults ★★½	Seniors ★★★½

Description and Comments Kula, blessed with a mild, cool climate and fertile soil, is the home of this five-acre wonderland originally owned by Princess Kekaulike. Opened in 1969, the garden today features more than 1,700 tropical plants, including exotic flora such as proteas, heliconias, orchids, anthurium, and gingers.

Lahaina-Kaanapali and Pacific Railroad — *Zone 9 West Maui*

Location 975 Limahana Place, Suite 203

Phone (808) 661-0089 or (808) 661-0080

Hours 12 rides scheduled daily, beginning at 9:45 a.m.

Admission $15.95 for adults; $9.95 for children ages 3–12 (round-trip)

When to Go Anytime

How Much Time to Allow 90 minutes

Author's Rating ★★★; A short train ride offering views of the West Maui coastline.

Overall Appeal by Age Group

Pre-school ★★½	Teens ★★	Over 30 ★★
Grade school ★★★	Young Adults ★★	Seniors ★★½

Description and Comments The "Sugar Cane Train," with its 1890s locomotive and distinctive whistle, was used by the Pioneer Mill to transport sugar crops until the early 1950s. Today, the train shuttles visitors between Lahaina and the resort area of Kaanapali. The six-mile route through a cane field lasts about 40 minutes each way. A friendly conductor shares the history of Maui's sugar industry.

Maui Ocean Center — *Zone 8 South Maui*

Location Maalaea Harbor Village, 192 Maalaea Road

Phone (808) 270-7000

Website www.mauioceancenter.com

Hours Daily, 9 a.m.–5 p.m.

Admission $19 for adults; $13 for children ages 3–12; seniors and military personnel receive discount

When to Go Anytime

How Much Time to Allow 2 hours

Author's Rating ★★★★; A must for understanding island marine life.

Overall Appeal by Age Group

Pre-school ★★★★½	Teens ★★★★★	Over 30 ★★★★★
Grade school ★★★★★	Young Adults ★★★★★	Seniors ★★★★½

Description and Comments The star attraction is the 600,000-gallon ocean aquarium tank with a walk-through acrylic tunnel so that you can get a good view of the inhabitants, including a six-foot tiger shark and other sharks, spotted eagle rays, mahimahi, triggerfish, sea turtles, eels, and a dazzling array of colorful reef fish. Other exhibits include a supervised touch pool for kids, allowing them to hold sea critters; interactive displays about the humpback whale; and smaller aquariums affording a close look at eels, shrimp, coral, and other sea life. The Reef Café and Seascape Café and Bar provide food and drinks, and the large gift shop carries logo and ocean-themed goods.

Other Things to Do Nearby The center overlooks busy Maalaea Harbor, where tour cruise boats come and go. Try combining a trip to the aquarium with a snorkeling tour to look at the sea creatures in the wild.

Maui Tropical Plantation and Country Store — *Zone 7 Central Maui*

Location 1670 Honoapiilani Highway

Phone (808) 244-7643

Hours Daily, 9 a.m.–5 p.m.; tour hours, 9 a.m.–5 p.m.

Admission Free; tram tours cost $9.50 for adults and $3.50 for children ages 5–12

When to Go Anytime

How Much Time to Allow 75 minutes

Author's Rating ★★★; When you want to know more about tropical crops, this is the place. Pick up fresh fruits at the country store.

Overall Appeal by Age Group

Pre-school ★★	Teens ★★★	Over 30 ★★★★
Grade school ★★½	Young Adults ★★★½	Seniors ★★★★

Description and Comments From the Visitor Center, head out to the plantation's 50-acre garden, which is filled with tropical plants, including pineapple, sugarcane, papaya, guava, star fruit, anthuriums, and protea. A restaurant and plant nursery are also available.

Touring Tips Narrated tram tours of the garden are available. The rates are $8.50 for adults (plus tax) and $3.50 for children ages 5–12. The tour lasts about 40 minutes.

Tedeschi Winery — *Zone 8 South Maui*

Location Ulupalakua Ranch, about 10 miles past the junction of Highways 377 and 37 in Kula

Phone (808) 878-6058

Website www.mauiwine.com

Hours Daily, 9 a.m.–5 p.m.; guided tours are held from 10:30 a.m. to 1:30 p.m.

Admission Free

When to Go Anytime

How Much Time to Allow 1 hour

Author's Rating ★★★; Worth a taste for wine lovers.

Overall Appeal by Age Group

Pre-school ★½	Teens ★★½	Over 30 ★★★
Grade school ★★	Young Adults ★★★	Seniors ★★★

Description and Comments Tedeschi Vineyards is known for its island-style wine, including Maui Blanc pineapple wine. Wines are available for tasting and purchase at the tasting room in the King's Cottage, once used as a retreat by King Kalakaua. Hawaii-made specialty goods, books, and gifts are also on sale.

Touring Tips The tour explains how the wines are processed and bottled. But it's not necessary to take a tour to enjoy sampling the wines and walking through the shady lawns and gardens.

Whalers Village Museum — *Zone 9 West Maui*

Location Whalers Village (3rd floor), 2435 Kaanapali Parkway

Phone (808) 661-5992

Website www.whalersvillage.com/museum

Hours Daily, 9:30 a.m.–10 p.m.

Admission Free

When to Go Anytime

How Much Time to Allow 1 hour

Author's Rating ★★½; Displays and historic artifacts about whaling will entertain the family if they get restless shopping.

Overall Appeal by Age Group

Pre-school ★★	Teens ★★½	Over 30 ★★½
Grade school ★★½	Young Adults ★★½	Seniors ★★½

Description and Comments This museum traces the history of Lahaina's colorful whaling era, roughly from 1825 to 1860. Among more than 100 items on exhibit are a six-foot model of a whaling ship, harpoons, maps, logbooks, and an extensive collection of scrimshaw.

Wo Hing Temple Museum — *Zone 9 West Maui*

Location 858 Front Street

Phone (808) 661-3262

Website www.lahainarestoration.org/temple

Hours Daily, 10 a.m.–4 p.m.

Admission Donations accepted

When to Go Anytime

How Much Time to Allow 30 minutes

Author's Rating ★★½; Good for historians; young kids will be bored.

Overall Appeal by Age Group

Pre-school ★	Teens ★★	Over 30 ★★½
Grade school ★★	Young Adults ★★½	Seniors ★★★

Description and Comments A Buddhist shrine is the centerpiece of this restored Chinese temple, which provides a revealing look at how early Chinese settlers lived in Lahaina. Old photographs and artifacts are also on exhibit. A cookhouse (built separately from the main building to reduce the risk of a house fire) sits just to the right of the building. Two Hawaii films shot in 1898 and 1906 by Thomas Edison are among the highlights. The temple is affiliated with Chee Kung Tong, a Chinese fraternal society with branches throughout the world.

Other Things to Do Nearby The Baldwin Home Museum and *Brig Carthaginian* are nearby.

The Big Island of Hawaii

After Dark in The Park — *Zone 12 Hilo and Volcano*

Location Hawaii Volcanoes National Park (See separate listing page 233.)

Phone (808) 985-6000

Website www.nps.gov/havo

Hours Tuesday, 7 p.m.

Admission Free

When to Go Tuesday

How Much Time to Allow 2 hours

Author's Rating ★★★★★; It's the next best thing to seeing Pele's lava eruptions.

Overall Appeal by Age Group

Pre-school ★	Teens ★★★	Over 30 ★★★★★
Grade school ★★	Young Adults ★★★★	Seniors ★★★★★

Description and Comments After Dark in The Park attracts locals and visitors curious about the natural and supernatural facets of Hawaii's culture.

The once-a-week program features Hawaiian musicians, storytellers, artists, scientists, historians, and local authors who offer insights on everything from lava flows and Madame Pele to hula. Hawaiian elders and other Pacific Islanders perform chants, songs, and dance. The variety of topics is as big as the park: Pacific humpback whales, limu (seaweed), hurricanes and tsunamis, fishing (ancient and modern), the alien species found in submarine volcanoes, shipwrecks, coral reefs, Pacific migrations, the gooney birds of Midway Island, tiger sharks, marine archaeology, endangered Hawaiian monk seals, and the revival of arts like celestial navigation and ocean sailing brought about by the Hokulea outrigger canoe voyages. The free program is offered at 7 p.m. every Tuesday at Kilauea Visitor Center, Hawaii Volcanoes National Park.

Touring Tips After a day in the park, go to After Dark in The Park, then head down Chain of Craters Road to watch the lava flow. Bring a windbreaker, water, and a flashlight.

Other Things to Do Nearby America's most exciting national park (the only one with a live volcano) is right outside your door.

Ahuena Heiau — *Zone 11 Kona*

Location Next to Kamakahonu Beach, fronting the King Kamehameha's Kona Beach Hotel

Phone (808) 329-2911

Hours Always open

Admission Free

When to Go Anytime

How Much Time to Allow Up to 1 hour

Author's Rating ★★½; One of Hawaii's most treasured heiau.

Overall Appeal by Age Group

Pre-school ★	Teens ★★	Over 30 ★★★
Grade school ★★	Young Adults ★★½	Seniors ★★★

Description and Comments Rebuilt by King Kamehameha I, this historic *heiau*—a temple of peace dedicated to Lono, the god of fertility—is part of a free walking tour offered at the King Kamehameha's Kona Beach Hotel. The heiau was used by ancient Hawaiians to pray for bountiful harvests, healthy children, and good weather. The tallest structure is the *anuu* (oracle tower), where the *kahuna* (priest) received messages from the gods. Kamehameha spent the last seven years of his life in this area. Many Hawaiians still believe the heiau is a site of great spiritual significance, so access to the temple's platform is strictly forbidden. The grounds surrounding the platform are open to the public.

Touring Tips Guided tours held Monday–Friday at 1:30 p.m. For self-guided tours, stop by the hotel's guest services desk to pick up a free brochure detailing the history of the heiau.

Other Things to Do Nearby Hulihee Palace is just minutes away by car.

Akatsuka Orchid Gardens — *Zone 12 Hilo and Volcano*

Location Off Highway 11, just north of Volcano Village (on the way to Hawaii Volcanoes National Park)

Phone (888) 967-6669

Website www.akatsukaorchid.com

Hours Daily, 8:30 a.m.–5 p.m.

Admission Free (self-guided tours)

When to Go Anytime

How Much Time to Allow 45 minutes

Author's Rating ★★★; The variety of orchids is astounding.

Overall Appeal by Age Group

Pre-school ★	Teens ★★½	Over 30 ★★★
Grade school ★★½	Young Adults ★★★	Seniors ★★★½

Description and Comments This six-acre garden is recognized as a world leader in the hybridization of orchids, nurturing more than 400,000 plants. Many of the latest varieties were developed by noted horticulturist Mori Akatsuka. A gift shop offers orchids that can be shipped home.

Other Things to Do Nearby Hawaii Volcanoes National Park is minutes away by car.

Amy B. H. Greenwell Ethnobotanical Garden — *Zone 11 Kona*

Location 82-6188 Mamalahoa Highway, off Highway 11 in Captain Cook

Phone (808) 323-3318

Website www.bishopmuseum.org/greenwell

Hours Monday–Friday, 8:30 a.m.–5 p.m.

Admission A $5 donation is requested.

When to Go Anytime

How Much Time to Allow 1 hour

Author's Rating ★★★; A first-class garden with lots of photo ops.

Overall Appeal by Age Group

Pre-school ★★	Teens ★★½	Over 30 ★★★
Grade school ★★	Young Adults ★★★	Seniors ★★★★

Description and Comments Owned by the Bishop Museum, this 12-acre ethnobotanical garden features more than 250 varieties of plants, including ten native varieties that are on the endangered species list. These plants were used by ancient Hawaiians for food, medicine, and other daily necessities. Some of the crops on display include banana, breadfruit, sugarcane, and taro.

Touring Tips A guided tour is offered at 10 a.m. on the second Saturday of every month. Helpful information for self-guided tours is provided.

Astronaut Ellison S. Onizuka Space Center *Zone 11 Kona*

Location Keahole-Kona International Airport

Phone (808) 329-3441

Website www.planet-hawaii.com/astronautonizuka

Hours Daily, 8:30 a.m.–4:30 p.m.

Admission $3 for adults; $1 for children under age 12

When to Go While waiting for your flight out of Kona (arrive a halfhour early at the airport)

How Much Time to Allow 30 minutes

Author's Rating ★★★½; A hands-on attraction with equal parts fun and education.

Overall Appeal by Age Group

Pre-school ★★	Teens ★★★½	Over 30 ★★★
Grade school ★★★★	Young Adults ★★★	Seniors ★★★

Description and Comments This space museum features ten interactive exhibits and more than a dozen audiovisual displays, including an authentic *Apollo 13* space suit and a Space Theater showing NASA videos. You can launch a miniature space shuttle, log in to the space shuttle's computer program to learn about the system's components, and even attempt a "rendezvous" with an object in outer space. Proceeds from the gift shop help maintain the center, which is named in honor of Hawaii's first astronaut, Ellison S. Onizuka. Born and raised in the Kona area, Onizuka was among the shuttle crew members who perished in the *Challenger* explosion as it launched into space on January 28, 1986.

Hawaii Tropical Botanical Garden *Zone 12 Hilo and Volcano*

Location 2717 Old Marmalahoa Highway Onemea, RR 143A, 7 miles north of Hilo. Watch for a sign that says SCENIC ROUTE 4 MILES LONG, turn right, then drive to the garden's headquarters and registration area.

Phone (808) 964-5233

Website www.htbg.com

Hours Daily, 8:30 a.m.–4 p.m.

Admission $15 for adults; $5 for children ages 6–16

When to Go Anytime

How Much Time to Allow 1 hour–90 minutes

Author's Rating ★★★½; One of the most beautiful spots in the state.

Overall Appeal by Age Group

Pre-school ★★	Teens ★★½	Over 30 ★★★½
Grade school ★★½	Young Adults ★★★	Seniors ★★★★

Description and Comments This 45-acre nature preserve, opened to the public in 1984, offers a unique tropical rain forest experience. Visitors are provided with trail maps for self-guided tours. At the entrance, you're greeted by helpful volunteers who will answer any questions and even supply you with mosquito repellent or an umbrella in the event of rain. A 500-foot-long boardwalk leads you through a steep ravine filled with banana, bamboo, ferns, and other tropical plants. From there, other trails bring you to waterfalls, a lily pond, streams, an aviary, and more than 2,000 plant species, including palms, ferns, orchids, bromeliads, heliconia, ginger, and fruit trees collected from around the world. Upon your return, drop by the gift shop to browse through local arts and crafts, books, and other items. Proceeds go toward the preservation of the garden.

Hawaii Volcanoes National Park — *Zone 12 Hilo and Volcano*

Location About 30 miles from Hilo, traveling down Highway 11 (follow the road signs and turn left into the park entrance)

Phone (808) 985-6000

Website www.hawaii.volcanoes.national-park.com or www.nps.gov/havo

Hours The park itself is open 24 hours a day year-round; the Visitor Center is open daily, 7:45 a.m.–5 p.m.

Admission $10/vehicle. Admission is good for 7 days.

When to Go Anytime; the best time of day to view eruption activity is after sunset

How Much Time to Allow At least half a day

Author's Rating ★★★★★; Hawaii's premier attraction. Don't expect up-close views of fountaining lava, however.

Overall Appeal by Age Group

Pre-school ★	Teens ★★★★	Over 30 ★★★★½
Grade school ★★★½	Young Adults ★★★★½	Seniors ★★★½

Description and Comments The 377-acre Hawaii Volcanoes National Park, established in 1916 by the National Park Service, is certainly one of the world's top wonders. Kilauea Volcano has been spewing lava continuously since 1983. Begin at the Visitor Center, which houses a gallery of volcano exhibits and a 200-seat mini-theater showing a terrific 23-minute film about the history of Hawaii's volcanoes and their significance to the Hawaiian culture. Park rangers are on hand to answer any questions and offer suggested itineraries at the park.

Next door, the Volcano Art Center offers a wide range of works by some of Hawaii's top artists. Drive on into the park to find the Thomas A. Jaggar Museum, which features exhibits spotlighting Hawaii's volcanic history, current seismic activity, land formations, and a profile of Madame Pele, Hawaii's goddess of fire, whose home is Halemaumau Crater and whose handiwork is evident in the eruptions of Kilauea.

From the museum, you can drive to any and all public trails in the park. Be respectful of the surroundings, which native Hawaiians regard as sacred to their culture. (See separate listing for After Dark in the Park, page 230.)

Other Things to Do Nearby The tranquil village of Volcano is a mile from the park.

Hulihee Palace — *Zone 11 Kona*

Location 75-5718 Alii Drive

Phone (808) 329-1877

Website www.huliheepalace.org

Hours Monday–Friday, 9 a.m.–4 p.m.; Saturday and Sunday, 10 a.m.–4 p.m.

Admission $5 for adults; $4 for seniors; $1 for children under age 18

When to Go Anytime

How Much Time to Allow 45 minutes

Author's Rating ★★★; A historic treasure in the heart of Kailua-Kona.

Overall Appeal by Age Group

Pre-school ★★	Teens ★★★	Over 30 ★★★★
Grade school ★★½	Young Adults ★★★½	Seniors ★★★★

Description and Comments Operated by the Daughters of Hawaii, this handsome Victorian structure was built in 1838 out of lava rock, coral, koa, and ohia wood for Governor John Kuakini. It later served as a vacation retreat for Hawaiian royalty. Among the treasures here are kahili (feathered staffs), stone tools, tapa, jewelry, and a collection of javelins that once belonged to Kamehameha I. *Note:* Photography and videotaping are not allowed inside the palace.

Touring Tips Tours are offered throughout the day.

Other Things to Do Nearby Ahuena Heiau and the Kailua Candy Company are among the notable stops located in Kailua-Kona. A ten-minute drive from Kailua-Kona leads you to Holualoa, a town of artists' studios.

Kaloko-Honokohau National Historical Park — *Zone 11 Kona*

Location Situated at the base of Hualalai Volcano, 3 miles north of Kailua-Kona and 3 miles south of the Keahole-Kona International Airport (along Highway 11)

Phone (808) 329-6881

Website www.nps.gov/kaho

Hours Daily, 8 a.m.–3:30 p.m.

Admission Free

When to Go Anytime

How Much Time to Allow 1 hour

Author's Rating ★★★; Worthwhile stop for anyone interested in Hawaiian history.

Overall Appeal by Age Group

Pre-school ★★	Teens ★★½	Over 30 ★★★
Grade school ★★½	Young Adults ★★★	Seniors ★★★½

Description and Comments This 1,300-acre park features more than 200 archaeological sites, including heiau, petroglyphs, fishing shrines, holua (stone slides), and fishponds. Several species of endangered animals and plants live here. Picnicking, fishing, snorkeling, swimming, bird-watching, and hiking are among the activities you can enjoy here. Overnight camping is not permitted.

Kamuela Museum — *Zone 11 Kona*

Location Waimea, at the intersection of Highways 25 and 19

Phone (808) 885-4724

Hours Daily, 8 a.m.–5 p.m.

Admission $5 for adults; $2 for children under age 12

When to Go Anytime

How Much Time to Allow 1 hour

Author's Rating ★★½; Not worth going out of your way to see, but it has several intriguing exhibits.

Overall Appeal by Age Group

Pre-school ★½	Teens ★★½	Over 30 ★★★
Grade school ★★½	Young Adults ★★★	Seniors ★★★

Description and Comments This cozy museum features an eclectic collection of island artifacts. Among the historical prizes are antique American furniture and Chinese porcelain.

Lyman Mission House and Museum — *Zone 12 Hilo and Volcano*

Location Hilo, 276 Haili Street, a few blocks up from Hilo Bay

Phone (808) 935-5021

Website www.lymanmuseum.org

Hours Monday–Saturday, 9:30 a.m.–4:30 p.m.

Admission $7 for adults; $5 for seniors; $3 for children ages 17 and under

When to Go Anytime

How Much Time to Allow 1 hour

Author's Rating ★★★; Good small museum about Hawaii's missionary and plantation life.

Overall Appeal by Age Group

Pre-school ★	Teens ★★½	Over 30 ★★★
Grade school ★★	Young Adults ★★★	Seniors ★★★★

Description and Comments The mission house was built in 1839 for David and Sarah Lyman, the first Christian missionaries to Hilo. This well-preserved New England–style home is the oldest standing wooden frame structure on the island and houses missionary-era furnishings, clothing, photographs, and other artifacts. Guides provide detailed information throughout the 25-minute tour. The adjacent two-story museum, built in 1973, showcases Hawaii's natural and cultural histories. Exhibits here include mineral and shell collections, original documents, historic photographs, and period pieces reflecting the many people who immigrated to the Islands. A gift shop is located on the ground floor.

Other Things to Do Nearby The Pacific Tsunami Museum is a few minutes away on Kamehameha Avenue.

Mauna Loa Macadamia Nut Visitor Center — *Zone 12 Hilo and Volcano*

Location On Highway 11, 5 miles south of Hilo. Turn onto Macadamia Road and drive to the road's end (you'll pass through Mauna Loa's 2,500-acre orchard)

Phone (808) 966-8618 or (888) 628-6556

Website www.maunaloa.com

Hours Daily, 8 a.m.–6 p.m.

Admission Free

When to Go Anytime

How Much Time to Allow 1 hour

Author's Rating ★★★½; Life story of everyone's favorite nut, complete with free samples.

Overall Appeal by Age Group

Pre-school ★★	Teens ★★★½	Over 30 ★★★½
Grade school ★★★½	Young Adults ★★★½	Seniors ★★★½

Description and Comments Head to the Visitor Center first and enjoy a free sampling of Mauna Loa's macadamia nut products, then head outside and watch a brief video presentation about Mauna Loa and the macadamia nut industry. A mini-factory shows how macadamia nut chocolates are made. Adjacent to the Visitor Center is the company's nut-processing plant, where you can watch the proceedings through large viewing windows (helpful signs explain the process). Also on the premises is a pleasant nature walk through tropical foliage and a snack shop serving macadamia nut ice cream, soft drinks, Kona coffee, and other treats.

Other Things to Do Nearby Both Nani Mau Gardens and Panaewa Rainforest Zoo are just minutes away by car.

Nani Mau Gardens — *Zone 12 Hilo and Volcano*

Location 421 Makalika Street (From Hilo, drive about 3 miles south on Highway 11. Look for the Nani Mau Gardens sign and turn left onto Makalika Street)

Phone (808) 959-3500

Website www.nanimau.com

Hours Daily, 8 a.m.–5 p.m.

Admission $10 for adults; $5 for children ages 6–18

When to Go Anytime

How Much Time to Allow 1 hour–90 minutes

Author's Rating ★★; The price is a little steep for our tastes, but Nani Mau certainly lives up to its name, which means "forever beautiful."

Overall Appeal by Age Group

Pre-school ★½	Teens ★★★	Over 30 ★★★½
Grade school ★★	Young Adults ★★★	Seniors ★★★½

Description and Comments This botanical garden, established in 1970, grows more than a hundred varieties of tropical fruit trees and some 2,000 varieties of tropical flowers, including anthuriums, orchids, and bromeliads. A handy map is provided on entry into the garden. Highlights include the Orchid Walkway, Hibiscus Garden,

Bromeliad Garden, Lily Pond, Polynesian Garden, European Garden, Fruit Orchard, and Annual Garden. Everything here is immaculately maintained, with the exception of the Japanese Garden, which is somewhat disappointing. A restaurant and gift shop are also on the premises.

Touring Tips A 35-minute tram tour is available for an additional $6.

Other Things to Do Nearby Attractions in the vicinity of Nani Mau Gardens include the Mauna Loa Macadamia Nut Visitor Center and Panaewa Rainforest Zoo.

Onizuka Center for International Astronomy and Mauna Kea Observatory — *Zone 12 Hilo and Volcano*

Location Take Highway 200 to the Visitor Information Station, at the 9,300-foot elevation level on Mauna Kea

Phone (808) 961-2180

Website www.ifa.hawaii.edu/info/vis

Hours Visitor Information Station: Monday–Thursday, 5:30–10 p.m.; Friday, 9 a.m.–noon, 1–4:30 p.m., and 6–10 p.m.; Saturday and Sunday, 9 a.m.–10 p.m.

Admission Free

When to Go Anytime; nights for stargazing, weekends for summit visits

How Much Time to Allow Half a day, or night

Author's Rating ★★★½; An "out-of-this-world" experience, especially for visitors who are able to ascend to Mauna Kea's summit.

Overall Appeal by Age Group

Pre-school ★	Teens ★★★★½	Over 30 ★★★★½
Grade school ★★	Young Adults ★★★★½	Seniors ★★★½

Description and Comments The Onizuka Center offers several fascinating displays covering the observatory's history, programs, and accomplishments. The Visitor Information Station offers free tours to the 13,796-foot summit of Mauna Kea every Saturday and Sunday from 1 to 5 p.m. (weather permitting). Visitors should arrive promptly by 1 p.m., as participants are required to spend an hour of acclimation time here before ascending to higher elevations (see other warnings listed below in Touring Tips). At 2 p.m., participants return to their four-wheel-drive vehicles (regular cars cannot do this trek; check with your car rental agency about a four-wheel-drive vehicle) and are led to the summit, perhaps the finest spot on Earth for stargazing. The clear, dark skies allow astronomers in observatories from 11 countries to peer into deep space.

Every night, the Visitor Information Station holds a stargazing program from 6 to 10 p.m. The program begins with an astronomy video, followed by a discussion of astronomy and Mauna Kea, then moves outside to observe celestial delights through two large telescopes: star clusters, double stars, white dwarfs, planetary nebulas, star-forming nebulas, supernova remnants, supernovas, planets, galaxies, and all of the constellations visible in Hawaii. Even at 9,300 feet, the Visitor Information Station enjoys clear, dark skies at a higher elevation than most of the other major telescopes on the planet. Bring binoculars and flashlights with red filters. Most important, dress warmly—temperatures up there drop to 40–55° on summer nights and 26–50° on winter nights.

Important note: Be sure that you have a full tank of gas before driving up Mauna Kea. The steep grade, combined with the lower oxygen level, makes engines run inefficiently. Fuel is not available for purchase on Mauna Kea.

Touring Tips Children under age 16, pregnant women, and those with respiratory, heart, and severe obesity conditions are not allowed to travel to the summit. Be aware that the weather conditions at Mauna Kea can be quite severe, including freezing temperatures, snow, and high winds. Also, scuba divers must wait at least 24 hours after their last dive before ascending to the summit. The drive up to the summit requires a four-wheel-drive vehicle; consult your rental car agency before planning a visit to Mauna Kea.

Pacific Tsunami Museum — *Zone 12 Hilo and Volcano*

Location 103 Kamehameha Avenue in downtown Hilo

Phone (808) 935-0926

Website www.tsunami.org

Hours Monday–Saturday, 9 a.m.–4 p.m.

Admission $7 for adults; $2 for children ages 6–17; $6 for seniors

When to Go Anytime

How Much Time to Allow 1 hour

Author's Rating ★★★; Sad but riveting reminder of the power of tidal waves and an important chapter in Hilo's history. Will make you look twice at that calm bay.

Overall Appeal by Age Group

Pre-school ★★	Teens ★★★★	Over 30 ★★★★½
Grade school ★★★	Young Adults ★★★★	Seniors ★★★½

Description and Comments The Pacific Tsunami Museum pays tribute to the hundreds of Hilo residents who perished during the horrific tsunamis that struck the city in 1946 and 1960. It also educates today's residents about what to do when the next tsunami hits. Exhibits include informative video presentations and startling photographs.

Other Things to Do Nearby The Lyman Mission House and Museum is a few blocks away.

Panaewa Rainforest Zoo — *Zone 12 Hilo and Volcano*

Location Mamaki Street, off Highway 11 south of Hilo

Phone (808) 959-7224

Hours Daily, 9 a.m.–4 p.m.

Admission Free

When to Go Anytime

How Much Time to Allow 1 hour

Author's Rating ★★½; The kids will love it.

Overall Appeal by Age Group

Pre-school ★★★	Teens ★★★	Over 30 ★★½
Grade school ★★★½	Young Adults ★★★	Seniors ★★½

Description and Comments This 12-acre zoo in the Panaewa Rainforest Reserve is the only tropical rain forest zoo in the United States. It spotlights the world's rainforest animals, reptiles, and birds, including a Bengal tiger, water buffalo, pygmy hippos, spider monkeys, deer, iguanas, feral goats, tapirs, and vultures—most of which can't be seen in the Islands—as well as some native birds, including the nene goose, Hawaii's state bird. Picnic tables and rain shelters are provided for rest and relaxation.

Touring Tips The tiger feeding is at 3:30 p.m. every day.

Other Things to Do Nearby The Mauna Loa Macadamia Nut Visitor Center and Nani Mau Gardens are minutes away by car.

Parker Ranch Visitor Center and Historic Homes — *Zone 11 Kona*

Location Parker Ranch Shopping Center, 67-1185 Mamalahoa Highway

Phone (808) 885-7655

Hours Monday–Saturday, 9 a.m.–5 p.m.

Admission Visitor center: $5 for adults, $3.75 for children ages 4–11; historic home: $8.50 for adults (children and seniors discount); both attractions: $12 for adults, $9.50 for children

When to Go Anytime

How Much Time to Allow 2 hours

Author's Rating ★★★½; A good look at the Hawaiian paniolo way of life.

Overall Appeal by Age Group

Pre-school ★★½	Teens ★★★½	Over 30 ★★★½
Grade school ★★★½	Young Adults ★★★½	Seniors ★★★½

Description and Comments One of the largest privately owned ranches in the United States, the 225,000-acre Parker Ranch owns the town of Waimea (also known as Kamuela), in the heart of Big Island "paniolo country." The Parker Ranch Visitor Center traces the storied history of the Parker family through a variety of displays, photographs, artifacts, and a 20-minute video. In 1809, a sailor from Massachusetts named John Palmer Parker arrived in the Islands, befriended King Kamehameha I, and married a Hawaiian princess. At the king's behest, Parker began domesticating the wild horses and cattle that roamed free and were harming the fertile slopes of Mauna Kea, and he was given a two-acre land grant in thanks. In the 1850s, Parker began purchasing more land in the area, laying the foundation for Parker Ranch. Today, guided or self-tours reveal Puuopelu, a handsome ranch home with a fine art collection, and a replica of Mana Hale, the Parker family homes compound located about three-fourths of a mile from the Visitor Center. The Parker Ranch Store carries an assortment of paniolo apparel, hats, boots, buckles, music, artwork, greeting cards, and books.

Touring Tips Wagon rides are now available. They last about 45 minutes to an hour and cost $8.50 for adults and $6 for children ages 4–11.

Puuhonua O Honaunau National Historical Park — *Zone 11 Kona*

Location Approximately 22 miles south of Kailua-Kona. From Highway 11, turn onto Highway 160 at the Honaunau Post Office near Mile Marker 103. Follow the road for about 3½ miles to the park's entrance.

Phone (808) 328-2326

Website www.nps.gov/putio

Hours Visitor Center: daily, 8 a.m.–4:30 p.m. Picnic area: Monday–Thursday, 6 a.m.–8 p.m.; Friday–Sunday, 6 a.m.–11 p.m.

Admission $5 for one car, or $3 for adults; free for children under age 16

When to Go Anytime. If you visit during the weekend closest to July 1, you can take part in the park's annual cultural festival, featuring Hawaiian games, hula performances, and arts and crafts demonstrations.

How Much Time to Allow 1–2 hours

Author's Rating ★★½; One of Hawaii's most sacred cultural history attractions.

Overall Appeal by Age Group

Pre-school ★	Teens ★★½	Over 30 ★★★
Grade school ★★	Young Adults ★★½	Seniors ★★★★

Description and Comments In ancient Hawaii, this area, flanked by huge lava rock walls, served as a place of refuge or sanctuary where minor offenders and refugees of war could seek safety and redemption. You'll find self-guided tour brochures and maps at the park's Visitor Center. You can listen to an audio message along the center's mural wall or sit in on an orientation discussion in the amphitheater. Then explore Hale O Keawe Heiau, built in 1650, as well as wooden kii images, canoe sheds, and other ancient artifacts and structures. Stop and observe cultural demonstrators working at their crafts; they are friendly and eager to share their knowledge of Hawaiiana. Hikers can follow a mile-long trail that hugs the Kona coastline and is dotted with several archaeological sites, including heiau.

Touring Tips Orientation talks at the Visitor Center are scheduled at 10, 10:30, and 11 a.m. and 2:30, 3, and 3:30 p.m.

Other Things to Do Nearby Kealakekua Bay, where Captain Cook landed and met his death, is a five-minute drive north.

Puukohola Heiau — *Zone 11 Kona*

Location On the north end of the Kohala Coast near Kawaiahae Harbor. From the intersection of Route 270 and Highway 19, drive a quarter-mile north of Route 270 to the park's access road.

Phone (808) 882-7218

Website www.nps.gov/puhe

Hours Daily, 7:30 a.m.–4 p.m.

Admission $1

When to Go Anytime. In mid-August, the park stages a cultural festival featuring Hawaiian food and games, hula performances, a royal court procession, and arts and crafts demonstrations.

How Much Time to Allow 1 hour

Author's Rating ★★★; Important site for Islands cultural history.

Overall Appeal by Age Group

Pre-school ★	Teens ★★½	Over 30 ★★★
Grade school ★★	Young Adults ★★½	Seniors ★★★★

Description and Comments Two historic heiau—Puukohola and Mailekini—are within a short walk of the Visitor Center. Puukohola, with its huge stone walls facing the sea, looks like the war temple it was. The site was originally constructed in 1550 and rebuilt by Kamehameha I in 1790 when he launched his efforts to unite the Islands into a kingdom. (There is, in fact, a third heiau, Hale O Kapuni, which rests underwater and is not visible.) Hiking and tours of the park (both guided and self-guided) are among the activities available here.

Other Things to Do Nearby Spencer Beach County Park is within walking distance.

Sadie Seymour Botanical Gardens — *Zone 11 Kona*

Location 76-6280 Kuakini Highway

Phone (808) 329-7286

Hours Daily, 9 a.m.–5 p.m.

Admission Donations accepted

When to Go Anytime

How Much Time to Allow 1 hour

Author's Rating ★★★; A beautifully kept Eden for nature lovers.

Overall Appeal by Age Group

Pre-school ★★	Teens ★★½	Over 30 ★★★½
Grade school ★★½	Young Adults ★★★	Seniors ★★★★

Description and Comments Maintained and operated by the Kona Outdoor Circle, this international garden features beautiful landscapes and exotic flora representing areas from throughout the globe, including Hawaii, the Pacific region, Asia, Central America, South America, and Africa. Brochures for self-guided tours are available.

Suisan Fish Market and Auction — *Zone 12 Hilo and Volcano*

Location Hilo, 85 Lihiwai Street, at the corner of Banyan Drive and Lihiwai Street

Phone (808) 935-9349

Hours Monday–Saturday, opens at 7 a.m.

Admission Free

When to Go Anytime

How Much Time to Allow 30 minutes

Author's Rating ★★½; For early risers with an appreciation of "fishy" business.

Overall Appeal by Age Group

Pre-school ★	Teens ★★★	Over 30 ★★★
Grade school ★★★	Young Adults ★★★½	Seniors ★★★

Description and Comments The public is invited each morning to watch brokers representing restaurants and markets from around the state bid on the day's freshest catches, including ahi (tuna), mahimahi, snappers, marlin, swordfish, and squid. Consumers may purchase fresh fish at the market next door.

Other Things to Do Nearby Visit downtown Hilo.

Volcano Winery — *Zone 12 Hilo and Volcano*

Location Off Highway 11, 30 miles south of Hilo. Turn onto Pii Mauna Drive and follow the road (also called Golf Course Road on some maps)

Phone (808) 967-7772

Website www.volcanowinery.com

Hours Daily, 10 a.m.–5:30 p.m.

Admission Free

When to Go Anytime

How Much Time to Allow 1 hour

Author's Rating ★★½; A great stop for sweet-wine lovers on the way to (or from) Hawaii Volcanoes National Park.

Overall Appeal by Age Group

Pre-school ★	Teens ★★	Over 30 ★★★
Grade school ★★	Young Adults ★★½	Seniors ★★★

Description and Comments The southernmost winery in the United States, this 18-acre vineyard, at the 4,000-foot elevation mark, produces 100% tropical honey and tropical fruit blend (half-grape, half-fruit) wines. Visit the tasting room and sample unique flavors including Macadamia Nut Honey Wine, Lehua Blossom Honey Wine, Guava Chablis, Passion Chablis, and Volcano Blush.

Other Things to Do Nearby Winery borders Hawaii Volcanoes National Park.

Wakefield Botanical Gardens — *Zone 11 Kona*

Location City of Refuge Road

Phone (808) 328-9930

Hours Monday–Friday, 11 a.m.–3:30 p.m.; Saturday and Sunday, 8 a.m.–4 p.m.

Admission Free

When to Go Anytime

How Much Time to Allow 1 hour

Author's Rating ★★½; For botany lovers.

Overall Appeal by Age Group

Pre-school ★★	Teens ★★½	Over 30 ★★★
Grade school ★★½	Young Adults ★★★	Seniors ★★★½

Description and Comments More than a thousand varieties of plants coexist in this small (five-acre) botanical garden and macadamia nut orchard.

Kauai

Grove Farm Homestead — *Zone 13 Kauai*

Location Just off Nawiliwili Road outside Lihue

Phone (808) 245-3202

Hours Monday, Wednesday, and Thursday, guided tours at 10 am. and 1 p.m.; reservations required

Admission Donations of $5 for adults and $2 for children ages 12 and under are requested

When to Go Anytime

How Much Time to Allow 90 minutes

Author's Rating ★★½; A good visit if you're interested in the island's plantation history.

Overall Appeal by Age Group

Pre-school ★½	Teens ★★½	Over 30 ★★★
Grade school ★★	Young Adults ★★★	Seniors ★★★½

Description and Comments This peaceful 80-acre homestead, owned by a prominent plantation family, provides a revealing glimpse of plantation life during the nineteenth century. The complex encompasses a museum, washhouse, teahouse, and other plantation buildings.

Other Things to Do Nearby Kauai Museum is a short drive away on Rice Street in Lihue.

Guava Kai Plantation — *Zone 13 Kauai*

Location At the end of Kuawa Road, off Highway 53 in Kilauea

Phone (808) 828-6121

Hours Daily, 9 a.m.–5 p.m.

Admission Free

When to Go Anytime

How Much Time to Allow 45 minutes

Author's Rating ★★½; A pleasant stop near Kauai's scenic north shore.

Overall Appeal by Age Group

Pre-school ★½	Teens ★★½	Over 30 ★★★
Grade school ★★½	Young Adults ★★★	Seniors ★★★

Description and Comments Visit the plantation's Visitor Center and enjoy free samples of guava juice. Here you can learn how the fruit is grown and processed. Take a stroll through the plantation's gardens.

Other Things to Do Nearby The Kilauea Point National Wildlife Refuge is just a few minutes away by car.

Kauai Museum — *Zone 13 Kauai*

Location 4428 Rice Street

Phone (808) 245-6864

Hours Monday–Saturday 9 a.m.–4 p.m.

Admission $5 for adults; $4 for seniors; $3 for children ages 13–17; $1 for children ages 6–12

When to Go Anytime

How Much Time to Allow 75 minutes

Author's Rating ★★★½; History museum with a slightly different take on the past.

Overall Appeal by Age Group

Pre-school ★★	Teens ★★★	Over 30 ★★★½
Grade school ★★★	Young Adults ★★★	Seniors ★★★★

Description and Comments This compact little museum in a coralblock building in downtown Lihue says as much as most schoolchildren or people on vacation can absorb about Hawaii's mysterious history at one time. Some of its exhibits of treasured artifacts and written legends are presented along a curving ramp like a timeline. It dates the earliest migrations of Polynesian voyagers from about A.D. 200, a few centuries earlier than the commonly accepted theory. Kauai, always the independent kingdom, is said to have been the home of ancient Tahitian alii who settled along the Wailua River and left behind many signs of their residence—including temples, birthing stones, and house sites. Kauai was never conquered by Kamehameha I like the other islands, but joined the kingdom voluntarily. Later, the Hawaiian sugar industry was born in Koloa. This particular history of the Garden Isle, within the overall history of Hawaii, comes to life through the extensive collection of displays and artifacts.

Kilauea Point National Wildlife Refuge — *Zone 13 Kauai*

Location Turn off Highway 56 near Mile Marker 23, then take Kolo Road down to Kilauea Road.

Phone (808) 828-1413

Hours Daily, 10 a.m.–4 p.m.

Admission $2 for adults; free for children age 16 and under

When to Go Anytime

How Much Time to Allow 75 minutes

Author's Rating ★★½; The views from Kilauea Point are breathtaking.

Overall Appeal by Age Group

Pre-school ★★	Teens ★★★½	Over 30 ★★★★
Grade school ★★★	Young Adults ★★★½	Seniors ★★★★

Description and Comments A variety of wildlife can be viewed from Kilauea Point, including more than a dozen species of seabirds, spinner dolphins, Hawaiian green sea turtles, Hawaiian monk seals, and, during the winter months, humpback whales. A 52-foot-high lighthouse, built in 1913, once boasted the largest lens of its kind in the world. It was deactivated in 1976 and is now listed on the National Register of Historic Places.

Other Things to Do Nearby The Guava Kai Plantation is minutes away by car.

Kilohana Plantation — *Zone 13 Kauai*

Location Puhi, 3-2087 Kaumualii Highway

Phone (808) 245-5608; carriage information (808) 246-9529

Hours Monday–Saturday, 9:30 a.m.–9:30 p.m; Sunday, 9:30 a.m.–5 p.m. A 20-minute carriage ride is available (no reservations required), and a 1-hour horse-drawn wagon tour of the cane fields is offered 11 a.m. and 2 p.m., Monday–Thursday.

Admission Free. The carriage ride costs $10 for adults and $5 for children under age 12. The wagon tour costs $24 for adults and $12 for children.

When to Go Anytime

How Much Time to Allow 1–2 hours

Author's Rating ★★★; Shoppers will like the boutiques and galleries; kids will enjoy the carriage ride.

Overall Appeal by Age Group

Pre-school ★★½	Teens ★★★	Over 30 ★★★★
Grade school ★★★	Young Adults ★★★½	Seniors ★★★★

Description and Comments This 35-acre estate, owned by the kamaaina Wilcox sugar plantation family, was built in 1935 and today features a wealth of agricultural displays, antiques, and other treasures from Kauai's plantation era. Shops, galleries, and a restaurant are available.

Kokee Natural History Museum — *Zone 13 Kauai*

Location Kokee State Park

Phone (808) 335-9975

Website www.aloha.net/~kokee

Hours Daily, 10 a.m.–4 p.m.

Admission $5 donation requested

When to Go Anytime

How Much Time to Allow 1 hour

Author's Rating ★★★; A surprisingly good museum worth a visit if you're in the area.

Overall Appeal by Age Group

Pre-school ★½	Teens ★★½	Over 30 ★★★½
Grade school ★★½	Young Adults ★★★	Seniors ★★★★

Description and Comments This is an intimate museum focusing on the island's ecology, geology, and climatology. Featured are stone artifacts, shells, samples of native Hawaiian woods, and an informative display about weather systems in the Pacific region (including information on Hurricane Iniki, which devastated Kauai in September 1992). The museum's gift shop has an impressive selection of Hawaiian books, maps, and hiking guides.

Limahuli Garden — *Zone 13 Kauai*

Location In Haena, near Haena State Park, North Shore

Phone (808) 826-1053

Website www.ntbg.org

Hours Tuesday–Friday and Sunday, 9 a.m.–4 p.m.

Admission Guided tours are $15 for adults (reservations required); self-guided tours are $10 (no reservations needed); children under age 12 are admitted free

When to Go Anytime

How Much Time to Allow 2 hours

Author's Rating ★★★★; Photographers, gardeners, and those who just want to walk in the rain forest will find few more appealing places than this.

Overall Appeal by Age Group

Pre-school ★	Teens ★★	Over 30 ★★★
Grade school ★½	Young Adults ★★½	Seniors ★★★

Description and Comments This award-winning 17-acre garden and 990-acre forest preserve—it was named America's Natural Botanical Garden of the Year in 1997 by the American Horticultural Society—features terraced taro patches, gardens, and a lush rain forest walk. Three distinct ecological zones are found within the garden.

Moir Gardens — *Zone 13 Kauai*

Location Kiahuna Plantation, 2253 Poipu Road

Phone (808) 742-6411

Website www.plantationgardens.net

Hours Daily, 24 hours

Admission Free

When to Go Anytime

How Much Time to Allow 1 hour

Author's Rating ★★★; A living symbol of why Kauai is the Garden Isle.

Overall Appeal by Age Group

Pre-school ★★	Teens ★★½	Over 30 ★★★½
Grade school ★★½	Young Adults ★★★	Seniors ★★★½

Description and Comments Nearly 4,000 varieties of plant life are featured in this garden, which surrounds the former home of Koloa Plantation Company's last plantation manager. Lagoons, lily ponds, trees, and flowers provide photo opportunities. A highlight here is one of the finest cactus gardens in the world.

Touring Tips Free guided tours are held Thursday at 10 a.m.

Other Things to Do Nearby Lawai and Allerton Gardens are a short drive away in Lawai.

National Tropical Botanical Garden Lawai and Allerton Gardens — *Zone 13 Kauai*

Location Near the end of Lawai Road in Lawai

Phone (808) 332-7361, tour information; (808) 742-2623, reservations

Website www.ntbg.org

Hours The Visitor Center is open daily, 8:30 a.m.–5 p.m.

Admission For guided tours: $25 for adults; $15 for children ages 13–18; $10 for children ages 6–12 (not recommended for toddlers). Reservations required.

When to Go Anytime

How Much Time to Allow About 2½ hours for guided tours

Author's Rating ★★½; The experience here is so serene, it borders on therapeutic.

Overall Appeal by Age Group

Pre-school ★	Teens ★★★	Over 30 ★★★
Grade school ★½	Young Adults ★★½	Seniors ★★★

Description and Comments The National Tropical Botanical Garden in Lawai is a 186-acre Eden that boasts one of the world's largest collections of rare and endangered tropical flora, including palms, heliconia, orchids, and other plants that have been collected from tropical regions throughout the world. Neighboring Allerton Garden, meanwhile, features a large collection of flora and beautiful waterfalls, gazebos, and a bamboo jungle. A gift shop offers a charming collection of Islands gift items.

Touring Tips Lawai Garden has guided tours every Monday at 9 a.m. and 1 p.m. Allerton Garden offers guided tours Tuesday–Saturday at 9 and 10 a.m. and 1 and 2 p.m. Reservations are required.

Waioli Mission House Museum — *Zone 13 Kauai*

Location Grove Farm Homestead

Phone (808) 245-3202

Hours Tuesday, Thursday, and Saturday, 9 a.m.–3 p.m. Guided tours are available

Admission Donations of $5 for adults and $2 for children age 12 and under are requested

When to Go Anytime

How Much Time to Allow 1 hour

Author's Rating ★★½; Recommended for anyone interested in Hawaii's missionary era.

Overall Appeal by Age Group

Pre-school ★½	Teens ★★½	Over 30 ★★★
Grade school ★★	Young Adults ★★½	Seniors ★★★½

Description and Comments Built in 1837, this structure was the home of missionaries Lucy and Abner Wilcox. The New England–style Waioli Mission Hall and Waioli Huiia Church are located on adjoining grounds. What brings it to life are docents in period dress who act the part.

Molokai

Molokai Museum and Cultural Center — *Zone 14 Molokai*

Location On Kalae Highway, just west of Kaunakakai

Phone (808) 567-6436

Hours Monday–Saturday, 10 a.m.–2 p.m.

Admission $2.50 for adults; $1 for students ages 5–18

When to Go Anytime

How Much Time to Allow 1 hour

Author's Rating ★★½; Not terribly exciting, but filled with history.

Overall Appeal by Age Group

Pre-school ★★½	Teens ★★½	Over 30 ★★★
Grade school ★★	Young Adults ★★★	Seniors ★★★½

Description and Comments The museum is a converted sugar mill established in 1878 by Rudolph Wilhelm Meyer, an engineer and surveyor who arrived on Molokai in 1851 and married a Hawaiian princess. Now listed on the National Register of Historic Places, the mill houses original machinery and other artifacts from the island's sugar plantation days. Guided tours and Hawaiian cultural programs are offered.

Molokai Ranch — *Zone 14 Molokai*

Location 100 Maunaloa Highway

Phone (808) 552-2791

Website www.molokai-ranch.com

Hours Monday–Saturday, 7:30 a.m.–4:30 p.m.

Admission Prices for activities range from $35–$50 for target archery and $45–$65 for outrigger canoe paddling to $80–$105 for a paniolo roundup (rodeo); half- and full-day children's activities range from $30–$75

When to Go Anytime

How Much Time to Allow Half a day

Author's Rating ★★★★★; Molokai's biggest attraction has something for the entire family.

Overall Appeal by Age Group

Pre-school ★★½	Teens ★★★★½	Over 30 ★★★★
Grade school ★★★★	Young Adults ★★★★½	Seniors ★★★½

Description and Comments Encompassing more than 53,000 acres (a third of the island), Molokai Ranch is the place to find many great outdoor activities. At the ranch's Outfitters Center, you can sign up for a horseback ride or learn basic cowboy skills—you can even compete in the Malihini Rodeo. Fancy camping is one of the ranch's newer offerings, at a seaside cluster of well-appointed solar tent cabins by remote Kaupoa Beach, with a full schedule of activities, meals, and transportation included. The activities include mountain biking, snorkeling, hiking, kayaking, outrigger canoe paddling, archery, a ropes challenge course, and winter whale watching.

Part Eight

Great Outdoors

Outdoor Hawaii is what the Islands are all about. The weather seldom intrudes, the scenery lures you, no snakes or toxic plants block your path, and you have abundant choices, from lolling on hundreds of beaches to climbing Diamond Head Crater, from plunging in waterfall pools to learning to surf. Golf is so popular that we devoted a lengthy section to various courses (see page 299). Activities and guided tours can be arranged by a concierge or hotel activity desk or you can arrange many on your own.

Hawaii by Sea: Get Wet

The Beach Experience

A swimming pool may look inviting, but head for the beach first. The Hawaiian Islands boast some of the world's finest beaches on 180 collective miles of sandy shoreline—243 beaches, all open to the public. Sands come not only in traditional gold but also in black, green, or red. Some beaches have natural splendor (such as Hanalei or Lanikai) or resort action (like Waikiki or Kaanapali), but we're confident you will find beaches in Hawaii that meet your every need: strolling, water sports, or just lying around.

Hawaii's beaches often top the "Best Beach in America" list compiled by geologist Stephen Leatherman ("Dr. Beach") of Florida International University, who rates beaches on environmental quality, aesthetics, water safety, and amenities (visit www.topbeaches.com to learn more).

Beaches may not be exactly the same from visit to visit. Beaches that are big in winter can be small in summer; the reverse is also true. Kilauea Volcano is still building beaches on the southeast shoreline of the Big Island, which is the youngest and least eroded in the chain and consequently has the fewest beaches. Kauai, oldest of the major islands, is ringed with scenic strands of sand of all shapes and sizes. Storms rage in every decade or so to remodel island sands, and human-caused coastal erosion is as much a problem in the Aloha State as it is anywhere else. Some beaches vanish overnight under high tides, like Kahaluu Beach, known as Disappearing Sands Beach, on the Kona coast.

Lucky beachcombers can find treasures like shells and glass fishing floats on certain beaches, including those on north and east shores of Kauai and Oahu. We have also found shells on Kihei beaches. People-watchers are endlessly entertained at crowded beaches, such as Waikiki. Seekers of solitude can leave resort beaches and easily find remote strands, where the only footprints are their own. But the resorts are located on certain beaches because the sands are superlative, so plenty of residents take advantage of public accesses to use them, and so can you.

Many resorts have public trails to walk or jog while you're checking out the beach action and perhaps looking for whales, like Wailea and Kaanapali Resorts on Maui or Mauna Lani and Mauna Kea on the Big Island. Hawaiian resorts on all islands have public beach access, parking, rest rooms, and shower facilities in addition to their private guest amenities. Several also maintain publicly accessible historic sites. The public is welcome in hotel restaurants, spas, stores, and bars.

Though the beaches are grand, the water is even better. Even the most devoted sun-seeking beachgoers who don't want to get their hair wet can't resist a refreshing dip in the ocean. The sea water is clear, ideal in temperature, and salty enough to make you quite buoyant. To swim easily in the ocean is a joyous experience and one of the most special aspects of Hawaii.

The same mid-Pacific location that keeps Hawaii waters clean and warm demands great respect for the sea. Like any other natural environment, Hawaii seas are not entirely hazard-free. The biggest dangers are seasonal surf and currents, posted on most park beaches. Heed lifeguards and warning signs and never turn your back on the ocean. Many Hawaii beaches are sheltered by reefs, but those that are not get pounded, usually in winter, by relentless waves that slap the shore with such force that they can knock the unwary off their feet and send them out to sea. Folks on Kauai refer to part of Lumahai Beach as "Tourist Beach" because of the number of newlyweds and others swept away while posing for photos at the shoreline with their backs to big waves.

You can see and hear rising surf; it's an awesome phenomenon, best observed safely from shore. When the surf comes up, village stores may even shut down while local surfers head out to catch some waves. But novices are wise to consider big-wave surfing strictly a spectator sport. Swimming is out of the question. By the same token, most bodysurfers have heard of fabled Sandy Beach on Oahu's south shore, a pinnacle challenge for that sport. But when the water is rampaging, the wicked shore break can break necks too. It's Hawaii's most dangerous beach.

Currents are insidious, because you can't always tell when and where they are. The major Hawaiian Islands are sunken mountains with deep, steep sides and resulting strong currents. Kealaikahiki Channel, off the south coast of Lanai, is famous for a powerful current that leads straight to Tahiti, 1,500 miles away. (That's what "Kealaikahiki" means—"the way to Tahiti.") Should you get carried out by a rip current, don't panic. Figure out which direction is perpendicular to the current and also leads toward shore, and swim across the current toward safety.

Shark attacks are rare in Hawaiian waters, but sharks themselves are not. Don't swim or surf alone at sunset when the predators feed. Most hazardous are invasions of jellyfish—box jellyfish, which appear often at Waikiki and Ala Moana beaches nine or ten days after the full moon, and are nasty enough that lifeguards issue warnings and supply soothing vinegar to treat the stings.

You might also encounter the milder Hawaiian version of Portuguese man-o-war, known as blue bottles, which float in from time to time. Your first clue to their presence might be stepping on a small, blue balloon that pops along the debris line onshore. On the water's surface, this jellyfish appears as an innocent floating bubble, but the unseen trailing blue tendril leaves a burn that stings like a knife blade. Our hint for a quick antidote is the blue-colored aloe vera gel widely sold in Hawaii as a sunburn soother. Be sure to keep a bottle in your beach bag. A dab on a blue-bottle sting will extinguish the fire for most victims. More extreme allergic reactions may require quick, expert medical care.

Swimmers and snorkelers sometimes run into coral heads and find later they got cut or scraped in the process. Coral cuts tend to infect quickly, and the antidote in this case is hydrogen peroxide, the WD-40 of tropical living. Put that in your beach bag too.

Obviously, a foremost beach bag item should be sunscreen. No paleskin wants to return home from the Islands without a golden Hawaiian tan. But go easy—this tropical sun is strong, the ocean air is clear, and burns happen very quickly, particularly on children. Don't go out without sunscreen in Hawaii—it's that simple. Apply it before you go outside; reapply it after swimming, snorkeling, or sweating a lot; and try to avoid midday exposure. You can get a great tan at 9 a.m. or after 3 or 4 in the afternoon, even with SPF 15 sunscreen. If skin cancer doesn't scare you, maybe wrinkles will (take a good look at the skin on senior surfers).

One other precaution about your beach bag. Leave your most valuable belongings in your room or in a safe when you head for the beach. If you carry a good camera or money, don't leave it unattended. You wouldn't tempt fate at home; don't do it in Hawaii, either.

Hawaii's Top Beaches

Our Picks: Hawaii's Best Beaches

Oahu Lanikai Beach
Maui Wailea Resort Beaches
Big Island Kaunaoa Beach (Mauna Kea Beach Resort)
Kauai Hanalei Bay Beach
Molokai Papohaku Beach
Lanai Hulopoe Beach

Oahu

Ala Moana Beach Park — *Zone 2 Greater Honolulu*

Location 1201 Ala Moana Boulevard, directly across from Ala Moana Center

Activities Swimming, surfing, bodyboarding, scuba diving, fishing

Special Appeal Safe swimming, good for kids, nearness to Waikiki and Ala Moana Center, park facilities, shade

Comments This shoreline oasis, stretching for more than a mile between Waikiki and Honolulu, is one of America's best urban beach parks and the most popular with local families. The beach is a narrow half-mile stretch of white sand with a deep swimming channel. Thanks to light surf, it's considered one of the most swimmable beaches in Hawaii and one of the best for children.

Lifeguards are on duty daily. Magic Island, a 30-acre man-made extension at the eastern end of the park, is a popular spot for picnicking and jogging. Facilities include softball fields, tennis courts, a lawn bowling area, food concessions, showers, rest rooms, the McCoy Pavilion, and more than 100 acres of picnic areas. Parking is limited, on the road between the park and beach and in a lot near Magic Island.

Kailua Beach Park — *Zone 3 Windward Oahu*

Location 450 Kawailoa Road, Kailua

Activities Swimming, surfing, windsurfing, bodyboarding, bodysurfing, canoeing, kayaking, beachcombing, sailing, boating

Special Appeal Good walking, gentle waves, scenery, occasional brisk trades, shade, dunes, picnic areas

Comments "Best Beach in America" winner. The crescent-shaped, golden-sand beach is more than two miles long. The waters are ideal for swimming, surfing, and sailing. This is one of Hawaii's best-known windsurfing and kayaking areas. Inexperienced surfers, bodyboarders, and bodysurfers will find waves they can handle. Facilities include rest rooms, showers, a snack stand, equipment rentals, and picnic areas. Lifeguards are on duty daily.

Lanikai Beach — *Zone 3 Windward Oahu*

Location Fronting Mokulua Drive, Lanikai

Activities Swimming, kayaking, canoe paddling, snorkeling, windsurfing, surfing, sailing, fishing

Special Appeal Beauty, some shade, safe for small kids and swimmers, uncrowded on weekdays

Comments One of Oahu's best family beaches. This scenic, mile-long stretch of golden beach with a vivid aqua and green lagoon bordered by photogenic islets is Hawaii's best for swimming. Waves are docile, thanks to the sheltering reef, and thus offer safe swimming for children, the handicapped, and the elderly. It's a favorite spot for paddlers and for kayakers who head out to the Mokulua, two islets about three-fourths of a mile offshore. Both are state seabird sanctuaries, but the larger, more accessible Moku Nui is a popular target for boaters and swimmers. Human access is restricted to its beaches. The Mokulua, particularly at sunrise, frame a breathtaking scene often used in ads and TV commercials, so it may look familiar to you. This neighborhood beach lacks public facilities or lifeguards. The beach is widest at the middle and northern ends. The southern end has been experiencing severe erosion. Public access is marked with signs on Mokulua Drive.

(For a terrific view of the Windward Coast and passing whales in winter, hike up Ka Iwa Ridge behind the community. As you drive into the one-way Lanikai loop, take the first right on Kaelepulu, park near the cul de sac, and go uphill next to the fence. This is not for people afraid of narrow-ridge heights, but it's an easy climb to the concrete World War II bunkers and back.)

Sandy Beach — *Zone 2 Greater Honolulu*

Location 8800 Kalanianaole Highway, Hawaii Kai, south shore

Activities Bodyboarding, bodysurfing, skimboarding, fishing

Special Appeal Daredevil bodysurfing

Comments Great local atmosphere. The 1,000-foot-long beach at the base of Koko Crater is known for its challenging shore break and feats of daring performed by local experts in wave riding. Some of Oahu's best bodysurfers, skimboarders, and bodyboarders strut their stuff here, and it's worth a visit to see them in action. Because the beach is subject to treacherous surf throughout the year, you should swim only when the waves are flat. Lifeguards are on duty daily. Rest rooms, showers, and picnic areas are available.

Sunset Beach — *Zone 4 The North Shore*

Location 59-100 Kamehameha Highway, Sunset Beach

Activities Surfing, bodysurfing, bodyboarding, summer swimming

Special Appeal Big-wave surfing, scenic beauty

Comments Some of the biggest winter waves in the world pound ashore along the coast from here to Haleiwa. This is the fabled North Shore, nirvana for surfers. This mile-long beach and its neighbors draw expert surfers from all parts of the world. In summer, the golden sands stretch to a strand of more than 200 feet in width, popular with swimmers and bodysurfers. But the beach narrows in winter, when waves rise ten feet or more and the pounding surf sometimes forces evacuations. The annual Triple Crown of Surfing professional events are held here. Lifeguards are on duty daily. Portable rest rooms are available.

Neighboring North Shore beaches include Ehukai Beach, home of the world-renowned Banzai Pipeline, a curling wave that skilled surfers ride through, and Waimea Bay Beach, whose most famous wave is the 30-foot signature monster wave that introduced the television show *Hawaii 5-0,* still in reruns.

Waikiki Beach — *Zone 1 Waikiki*

Location Fronting Waikiki resort area

Activities Swimming, surfing, bodyboarding, snorkeling, outrigger canoe riding, sailing, kayaking, fishing

Special Appeal Beachgoers of all ages, from the old-timers who play chess and cards in the sidewalk pavilions to the bikinied multitudes bronzing in the sand and the surfers offshore

Comments The world's most famous beach is a two-mile stretch of golden sand, from Hilton Hawaiian Village on one end to the cluster of high-rises at the base of Diamond Head at the other. Great for strolling the new beachside walkway, swimming, sunbathing, water sports, and people-watching. The average water temperature ranges 77° to 82°, depending on the season. Beachgoers are most concentrated in front of four neighboring hotels—Sheraton Waikiki, Royal Hawaiian, Outrigger Waikiki Beach, and Sheraton Moana Surfrider—and least crowded in the Kapiolani Park beach areas, such as Queen's Surf Beach (by the aquarium) and Sans Souci Beach (by the New Otani Kaimana Beach Hotel).

Waikiki Beach is an amalgam of several beaches (in order from Ewa to Diamond Head): Duke Kahanamoku Beach, Fort DeRussy Beach, Gray's Beach, Kuhio Beach, Queen's Surf Beach, and Sans Souci Beach. Sans Souci is our favorite—it's low-key and safe for swimming. Public facilities and services throughout Waikiki include rest rooms, showers, equipment rentals, snacks, and surfing lessons. You can sign up for outrigger canoe and catamaran rides from the beach. Lifeguards are on duty daily. Free parking is limited to the streets of Kapiolani Park.

Maui

Kaanapali Beach — *Zone 9 West Maui*

Location Honoapiilani Highway, fronting Kaanapali Beach Resort

Activities Swimming, bodysurfing, bodyboarding, snorkeling, scuba diving, windsurfing, kayaking, sailing, fishing

Special Appeal Places to hang for teens and young people, coastal walkway, boats that cruise from beach landings

Comments This is a popular resort beach. Swimming conditions are good when the surf is flat; this is subject, however, to strong currents and surf. The base of Black Rock, a volcanic cinder cone jutting up at the center of the four-mile beach, is a great spot for snorkeling and diving. A lifeguard is on duty at the Lahaina end. Beach concessions and outdoor showers are available at various points along the walkway that links Kaanapali's neighboring hotels and condos.

Kapalua Beach — *Zone 9 West Maui*

Location Lower Honoapiilani Highway, Kapalua Resort

Activities Swimming, snorkeling, scuba diving, sailing, kayaking

Special Appeal Quiet atmosphere, good swimming, safe for kids, great scenery

Comments This secluded strand in front of Kapalua Bay Hotel is one of Maui's best-looking and best swimming beaches. Lava promontories protect both sides of the beach from rough water. Public facilities are available, but no lifeguards are on duty. The sunset is often spectacular, spotlighting Molokai across the channel.

Makena State Park — *Zone 8 South Maui*

Location Makena Alanui, Makena

Activities Swimming, surfing, snorkeling, bodysurfing, bodyboarding, fishing

Special Appeal Scenic beauty, undeveloped nature, walking (Big Beach)

Comments Makena State Park at Maui's southern end has two scenic golden-sand beaches: Big Beach and Little Beach. Big Beach, 3,300 feet long, is Maui's longest beach and a favorite spot for experienced bodyboarders and bodysurfers. Little Beach, meanwhile, is a small cove with gentler ocean conditions, a good prospect for novice wave riders. No lifeguards are on duty, nor are there public rest rooms or showers. Secluded Little Beach is one of Hawaii's most popular "unofficial" nude beaches, even though public nudity is prohibited by law.

Wailea Resort Beaches — *Zone 8 South Maui*

Location On Wailea Alanui, Wailea

Activities Swimming, bodysurfing, bodyboarding, snorkeling, scuba diving, windsurfing, kayaking, sailing, fishing

Special Appeal Scenic beauty, resort surroundings, public access facilities

Comments Wailea Resort has five golden-sand beaches: Polo, Wailea, Ulua, Mokapu, and Keawakapu. Wailea Beach, shared by the Four Seasons Maui, Grand Wailea, and the public, is an appealing golden crescent about 1,000 feet long and a "Best Beach in America" winner. The waters are clear, with gentle waves to ride and a singular view dotted with neighboring islands. Snorkel along the rocky promontory that defines one side of the beach, where green sea turtles frequent the waters.

Ulua is the centermost beach, 1,000 feet long and 200 feet wide, between the Renaissance Wailea and Outrigger Wailea Beach. Locals regard the offshore reef here as one of Maui's best snorkeling spots. A deeper reef, excellent for scuba diving, is about 100 yards out from shore.

Wailea Resort's 1.5-mile coastal trail links public accessways to all the beaches and private hotel and condo properties. The southern end of the trail, between the Four Seasons and Kea Lani, features a showcase Hawaiian native plant garden and historic house.

Public facilities include rest rooms and showers. Beach concessions offer surfboard rentals and instruction. No lifeguards are on duty.

Big Island of Hawaii

Anaehoomalu Beach — *Zone 11 Kona*

Location Queen Kaahumanu Highway, Waikoloa Beach Resort, south shore of Anaehoomalu Bay, by historic fishponds and Outrigger Waikoloa Beach Hotel

Activities Swimming, surfing, snorkeling, scuba diving, windsurfing, kayaking

Special Appeal Scenic setting, historic features

Comments This beach is a picture-perfect finger of golden sand with palms for shade, on a bay where ancient kings played. Suitable for a wide range of ocean activities, this beach is favored for windsurfing. Novices can frolic in the calmer waters near shore, which they may share with sea turtles. Expert riders enjoy the more challenging wave conditions farther offshore. Public rest rooms and showers are available. No lifeguards are on duty.

Green Sand Beach — *Zone 11 Kona*

Location Mamalahoa Highway near Naalehu at the southern tip of the island; turn off on South Point Road to Ka Lae (South Cape). The paved road ends at Kaulana Boat Ramp. This beach is about 2.5 miles east via a dirt road. You can park at the ramp and hike in or use a four-wheel-drive vehicle.

Activities Beachcombing, fishing

Special Appeal Green sand

Comments An off-the-beaten-path beach for active adventurers, but perhaps a bit rugged for little kids. The sand is green, fragments of olivene rock. High surf throughout the year can pose danger. No lifeguards are on duty. Beachcombers can hunt for gemstone-sized lumps of pale green olivine, a volcanic phenomenon.

This is the most famous green-sand beach, but if your kids are pining to see green sand, try searching the shore from the public beach park at Kaupulehu between Kona Village Resort and Four Seasons Hualalei. We have found green mixed with white coral and black lava sands there.

Hapuna Beach State Recreation Area — *Zone 11 Kona*

Location Queen Kaahumanu Highway, Kohala Coast; look for a highway sign for the entrance to the park

Activities Swimming, surfing, bodyboarding, bodysurfing, snorkeling, camping

Special Appeal Biggest Big Island strand, the only one with camp cabins

Comments Hapuna Beach is a gold-sand jewel stretching more than half a mile and more than 200 feet across. It is very popular with bodyboarders and bodysurfers and can get crowded on weekends and holidays. Public rest rooms, showers, camping shelters, and picnic pavilions are available. Lifeguards are on duty daily and can inform you of current ocean conditions, which are often rough during the winter. Walk up the coastal path in front of the Westin Hapuna Beach Prince a short distance and you'll discover a hidden snorkeling cove teeming with fish.

Kaunaoa Beach — *Zone 11 Kona*

Location Queen Kaahumanu Highway, fronting the Westin Mauna Kea Beach Hotel within Mauna Kea Resort, Kohala Coast

Activities Swimming, surfing, bodyboarding, bodysurfing, snorkeling

Special Appeal Great protected swimming, friendly waves, scenic setting

Comments There's no finer way to begin your day than with a morning swim on this beach, the Big Island's best. The water is clear, calm enough to swim across from one side of the 2,500-foot strand to the other, and sends waves that roll you lazily to shore. The neighboring hotel is one of the oldest and most venerated, and this beach is one good reason why. The water is inviting to ocean enthusiasts of all types, from snorkelers to bodysurfers. No lifeguards are on duty, but hotel beach attendants know current ocean conditions. Public facilities are available. If you stay after dark, stroll along the coastal walk to a floodlit platform to watch the manta rays that come to shore to feed on smaller creatures drawn to the light.

Pololu Beach — *Zone 11 Kona*

Location Highway 270, North Kohala; park at the end of the road and take the 15-minute hike down an ancient switchback trail from the Pololu Lookout

Activities Beachcombing, surfing, bodyboarding, fishing

Special Appeal Scenic beauty, hiking, beachcombing

Comments A scenic black-sand beach with plenty of photo ops. No lifeguards or public facilities are provided. Because this remote beach is exposed to treacherous surf throughout the year, do not swim here unless the ocean is flat. This is a favored site for beachcombers, who scour the shoreline for treasures blown in by storms or high surf.

Kauai

Hanalei Bay — *Zone 13 Kauai*

Location Weke Road, Hanalei Pavilion Beach Park, behind the village of Hanalei on Kauai's north shore

Activities Swimming, surfing, bodyboarding, bodysurfing, snorkeling, windsurfing, sailing, fishing, canoeing

Special Appeal Spectacular scenic setting, seasonally gentle bodysurfing waves, walking, winter surfing

Comments Hanalei Bay is a dream come true. The golden sands extend about two miles around the scenic bay. On one side, the clear waters stretch out toward Japan; on the other is a bowl of lush, green mountains ribboned with waterfalls and capped with jagged volcanic peaks. The bay shore is bordered by private homes with public access via walkways and a trio of beach parks—Black Pot Beach Park, Waioli Beach Park, and Hanalei Pavilion Beach Park in the center. Rest rooms and showers are available at each. In summer, visiting yachts moor in the calm waters. In winter, the boats head for safer shelter because the surf can exceed ten feet, making Hanalei popular with the best surfers. Lifeguards are stationed at Black Pot Beach Park by the pier at the mouth of Hanalei River.

Kalapaki Beach — *Zone 13 Kauai*

Location Fronting Kauai Marriott Resort on Nawiliwili Bay in Lihue

Activities Swimming, surfing, bodyboarding, bodysurfing, snorkeling, windsurfing, sailing, fishing

Special Appeal Walking, safe swimming for kids, passing ships, restaurants and bars close by

Comments One of Kauai's busiest beaches, this strand is protected by cliffs and a seawall. The inlet between the cliffs leads to Nawiliwili's natural harbor and the Huleia River and Menehune Fish Pond behind it. While picnicking or playing on the beach, you may see large ships cruise by on their way into the harbor. Kalapaki is a safe playground for young children and a training ground for novice surfers. Showers and rest rooms are provided for the public courtesy of the Kauai Marriott. Picnic facilities are available at Nawiliwili Park, adjacent to Kalapaki. No lifeguards are on duty.

Kee Beach — *Zone 13 Kauai*

Location End of Kuhio Highway, Haena State Park, North Shore; park along the road or in the small lot

Activities Swimming, snorkeling, fishing

Special Appeal Movie-set beauty *(Thornbirds),* views of Na Pali Coast, near-shore snorkeling

Comments The reef surrounding Kee Beach breaks the waves, except for the giants of winter, and provides excellent snorkeling conditions. The shallow, protected lagoon is home to several species of rainbow-colored fish and offers safe swimming. No lifeguards are on duty, but public rest rooms, outdoor showers, and some parking are provided. This area is the staging point for hikers bound for the Kalalau Trail, 12 miles along the precipitous Na Pali wilderness coast to Kalalau State Park beach, a true hiking commitment. Less devoted hikers will enjoy the scenic first two miles of the (often muddy) trail to Hanakapiai Valley, where a stream littered with boulders runs from a scenic inland waterfall to the sea. The surf is rough there, so save the swim for your return to Kee Beach.

Lumahai Beach — *Zone 13 Kauai*

Location Kuhio Highway, at the foot of Lumahai Valley, North Shore; on the Hanalei end, park along the highway, then follow the trail down to the beach; on the far end, park in a grove of ironwood trees

Activities Surfing, bodyboarding, bodysurfing, snorkeling, windsurfing, sailing, fishing

Special Appeal Scenic splendor, walking

Comments Some 4,000 feet long, this beautiful strip of shoreline was made famous in the movie *South Pacific.* It remains one of the most photographed beaches in the state. This beach is great for appreciating wild beauty from shore, but with no protective reef, swimming or even wading can be very risky. No lifeguards are on duty.

Poipu Beach Park — *Zone 13 Kauai*

Location Hoowili Road, just off of Poipu Beach Road, Poipu Beach Resort, South Shore

Activities Swimming, bodysurfing, bodyboarding

Special Appeal Kids' tidepool, resort beach

Comments More than 1,000 feet long, Poipu Beach is a popular playground shared by public parks and accessways and private hotels, restaurants, and condo resorts. Portions are sheltered enough for safe swimming by young children. Rest rooms, showers, and picnic tables are available; lifeguards are on duty daily. Wave riders should avoid the area past Brennecke's, a rocky and hazardous point.

Polihale State Park (Barking Sands) — *Zone 13 Kauai*

Location Kaumualii Highway, Kekaha, end of the road on the west shore

Activities Surfing, bodyboarding, windsurfing, summer swimming, camping

Special Appeal Wide expanses of wild beauty at the foot of Na Pali

Comments Polihale, 17 miles long and 300 feet wide, is Hawaii's biggest beach. The "Barking Sands" are dunes that squeak and bark under your feet when walked on, special effects thanks to the composition of the coral sands. Hawaiians named such sites *ke*

one kani (musical sands). In summer, the reef protects a plunge known as Queen's Pond. Facilities include rest rooms, showers, parking, and a pavilion. No lifeguards are on duty.

Secret Beach *Zone 13 Kauai*

Location Kuhio Highway, near Kalihiwai Road, Kilauea, between Kilauea Point and Kalihiwai Bay; public access via a dirt road

Activities Swimming, surfing, bodyboarding, bodysurfing, snorkeling, windsurfing, sailing, fishing

Special Appeal The island's best-known nude beach

Comments This 3,000-foot-long golden beach is "secret" because it's not visible from any roads, not just because it is a favorite nude beach. From land, it can be seen only from the Kilauea Point National Wildlife Refuge. A haven for hippies in the early 1970s, Secret Beach is now a popular summer swimming spot. Winter surf, however, poses danger for swimmers. There are no public facilities or lifeguards here. *A reminder:* Nude sunbathing is technically against the law in Hawaii, but certain beaches are so remote that no one seems to mind.

Shipwreck Beach *Zone 13 Kauai*

Location Fronting the Hyatt Regency Kauai in Poipu Beach Resort, South Shore

Activities Surfing, bodyboarding, bodysurfing, windsurfing, fishing

Special Appeal Coastal trail, dunes walk

Comments Shipwreck Beach got its name from an unidentified wooden boat that lay crashed onshore for years until Hurricane Iwa washed it away in 1982. Low-lying rocks keep this golden-sand beach from being good for swimming, but bodysurfers and bodyboarders love it, especially in summer. The beach's most interesting sunbathers are often endangered Hawaiian monk seals or green sea turtles, who surf the waves between the Hyatt and nearby Embassy Vacation Resort. Public rest rooms and showers are available. A coastal walkway about a mile long along the cliffs leads to sand dunes that once served as a Hawaiian burial site. No lifeguards are on duty, but ocean conditions are posted.

Tunnels Beach *Zone 13 Kauai*

Location Kuhio Highway, about a half-mile beyond Haena Beach Park, North Shore

Activities Surfing, bodyboarding, snorkeling, scuba diving, windsurfing, beachcombing, fishing

Special Appeal Scenic splendor, seasonal shells, shade, near-shore reef tunnels

Comments Tunnels is a grainy, gold-sand beach with good summer snorkeling around reefs and coral heads close to shore. Its name refers to the reef "tunnels" that are found in the lagoon inside of Makua Reef, a popular scuba-diving spot. When the surf's up, Tunnels is one of Kauai's best surfing spots for expert wave riders. Rest rooms and showers are available at the public beach park. No lifeguards are on duty.

Molokai

Papohaku Beach *Zone 14 Molokai*

Location Kaluakoi Road, just beyond Kaluakoi Resort

Activities Surfing, bodyboarding, bodysurfing, snorkeling

Special Appeal Broad strand, wild beauty, shady picnics, great sunset views of Oahu

Comments Two miles long and 400 feet wide, Papohaku Beach is the biggest beach on Molokai and one of the only sandy Molokai beaches that is easily accessible for families. This isn't a swimming beach, but board riders favor it. It has a wilderness atmosphere but with good paved road access and public beach park facilities: rest rooms, showers, parking, and camping sites sheltered in the shoreline keawe forest. Dangerous swimming conditions exist because the beach is fully exposed to the force of the sea and surf. High surf conditions can occur any time of year. No lifeguards are on duty.

Sandy Beach — *Zone 14 Molokai*

Location Kamehameha V Highway, 7 miles past the Wave Crest Resort, Kaunakakai, at Mile Marker 21, East End

Activities Swimming, bodysurfing, snorkeling, diving

Special Appeal Good swimming, views of Maui

Comments It's not easy to find a swimming beach on Molokai, which has rough open seas, sheer cliffs, and muddy fishponds. This small, reefsheltered pocket beach is a rare exception. Soft, golden sands and gentle waters make it great for kids. Don't stub your toes on the rocky bottom while admiring the West Maui Mountains across the channel. Rest rooms are available, but no lifeguards are on duty. Good swimming conditions also prevail at nearby Waialua Beach, just before Mile Marker 19.

Lanai

Hulopoe Beach Park — *Zone 15 Lanai*

Location Route 440, Manele Road near Manele Bay Hotel, 8 miles from Lanai City

Activities Swimming, surfing, bodyboarding, bodysurfing, snorkeling, fishing, picnicking, camping

Special Appeal Kids' tidepool, shade, scenic features

Comments This is the only beach park on Lanai, a former pineapple plantation transformed into a luxury resort enclave. But it's a fine one, another Hawaii strand recognized as a "Best Beach in America." It features a large tidepool carved into a lava cliff with all-season swimming for children. Palms offer shade along the golden beach, which is 1,500 feet long and 200 feet wide. Swimming is subject to wave action, but it's usually calm enough inshore. Snorkeling is rewarding along the sheltering lava headland, a place to explore on shore too. Public rest rooms, showers, picnic areas, and campsites are provided by the private owner. Camping at the three sites, limited to six people each, costs $5 per person per night for up to a week and requires a $5 permit from Lanai Company. Write Attn: Camping Permits, P.O. Box 310, Lanai City, HI 96763, or call (808) 565-8206. Facilities include rest rooms, showers, picnic tables, grills, and drinking water.

Kayaking: Different Strokes

Since the first voyagers landed in Hawaii from the South Pacific, paddling the seas has been a way of life. Outrigger canoe paddling is a fiercely competitive local sport. You'll often see paddlers practicing offshore. Today's Hawaiian kayaks are made of fiberglass and come in a variety of shapes and sizes.

The biggest kayak contest, the annual World Championship Kayak Race, takes off from Kepuhi Beach on Molokai each May with solo paddlers who run across the dunes and beach carrying their kayaks, jump in when they hit water, and paddle to Oahu 32 miles away.

For expert ocean kayakers, we recommend a summertime trip along Kauai's picturesque Na Pali Coast, when the sea is calm. In summer, the eastern Molokai shore from Halawa to Kalaupapa also offers wilderness kayaking and beach camping. (Read *Paddle Your Own Canoe,* by solo kayaker Audrey Sutherland.)

Novices can rent a kayak in Kailua and head out for the Mokulua islets off Oahu's Lanikai Beach. On Kauai, paddle down the peaceful Huleia, Wailua, and Hanalei Rivers. Maui kayakers may find themselves whale watching closer than most in winter, when the humpbacks loll around quiet inshore waters. On the Big Island, tranquil Hilo Bay is perfect for kayaking. Try riding gentle waves to shore for a thrill, or maybe a splash, in Kauai's Hanalei Bay, Oahu's Mamala Bay, or Maui's Wailea Bay.

Rentals for single-person kayaks are \$30–\$35 for a full day; for tandem kayaks, about \$42–\$50 per day. A short lesson is usually included in the price, and all kayaking equipment can be transported to the beach for you. Any of the following outfitters can rent equipment and teach you how to use it. Kayak Kauai Outbound in Hanalei and Outfitters Kauai in Poipu Beach have rental equipment and guides for Na Pali Coast outings. The listed firms offer paddles on the Huleia, Wailua, and Hanalei Rivers.

KAYAK RENTALS

Oahu		
Go Banana Kayaks	Kapahulu	(808) 737-9514
Kailua Sailboards and Kayaks	Kailua	(808) 262-2555
Twogood Kayaks	Kailua	(808) 262-5656
Maui		
Maui Ocean Activities	Kaanapali Beach	(808) 667-2001
South Pacific Kayaks	Kihei	(808) 875-4848
Tradewind Kayaks	Kihei	(808) 879-2247
Big Island		
A. Banyan Bicyle, Kayak and Scuba Adventure	Hilo	(808) 933-1228
Hawaii Pack and Paddle	Captain Cook	(808) 328-8911
Ocean Safari's Kayak Tours and Rentals	Kailua-Kona	(808) 326-4699

KAYAK RENTALS *(continued)*

Kauai		
Kayak Kauai Outbound	Hanalei	(800) 826-9844
Kayak Wailua	Kapaa	(808 822-3388
Outfitters Kauai	Poipu Beach	(808) 742-9667

Scuba: Dive, Dive, Dive

A growing segment of diving enthusiasts have discovered Hawaii's particular underwater treasures—lava caverns, reefs full of fish, humpbacks, and other sea life.

Most dive excursions require participants to be certified by a scuba training organization, such as the Professional Association of Diving Instructors (PADI), National Association of Underwater Instructors (NAUI), National Association of Scuba Diving Schools (NASDS), or World Association of Scuba Instructors (WASI). Specialized dives—including explorations of wrecks and caves and night diving—require more advanced training.

Most divers arrive certified, but certification courses are offered at dive shops throughout the islands. Rates range from $75 for a beachside lesson to $300 or more for full open-water instruction and certification (an additional $10–$20 for a scuba certification card). Equipment is provided.

Would-be divers can see how it feels by way of introductory dives, usually conducted in a pool. Participants receive basic instruction, get fitted for scuba gear, and dive with the instructors. The entire experience lasts two to four hours, with rates ranging from $100 to $150.

Dive tour rates range from $75 to $250, depending on the size of the boat, equipment, and number of dives included on the trip. Booking deposits are usually required, refundable if you cancel in advance. Expect to spend at least half a day for a guided scuba adventure. The actual time you spend in the water will vary—the deeper the water you're in, the faster you use your air supply—but usually it's between 90 minutes to 2 hours. The diver-to-guide ratio has a legal maximum of six to one.

A few tips:

- In choosing a dive operator, ask about their experience in the business, safety expertise, type of boat, type of dive destination, and so on to make sure they meet your expectations and needs.
- Be careful where you put your hands and feet underwater. Some marine life—such as eels, jellyfish, and scorpionfish—can bite or sting. Do not touch any animal you

don't recognize. Try to avoid touching or crushing coral, leaving a permanent dent in the underwater environment.

- Never dive alone.
- If you're attempting underwater photography for the first time, shoot from within four feet. For best results, use an underwater camera with a 15mm or 20mm lens.

A fun alternative in the sea is snuba tours, where snorkelers can go underwater tethered by a breathing tube to an air-supply float on the surface. Snuba of Oahu (call (808) 396-6163) offers shallow-water diving for people age eight and older on three bays; Snuba Big Island (call (808) 326-7446) guides snuba dives in Kailua-Kona. Wet-Wonderful (call (888) 945-DIVE) offers snuba on Kauai.

Hawaii has more than 250 diving sites, with depths ranging from 20 to 150 feet. The most popular and one of the best is Molokini, a crescent-shaped sunken cinder cone about three miles off the coast of South Maui, near Kahoolawe. Molokini, a Marine Life Conservation District, has high visibility and thriving ocean life, including reef fish, sea turtles, and manta rays. But it gets swamped with snorkelers and tour boats as the day goes on. One solution is to book one of the boats that leave early directly from the nearest Maui beach, at Makena or Wailea, rather than those that depart from Maalaea Harbor.

A favorite South Maui site is La Perouse Pinnacle, in the middle of picturesque La Perouse Bay beyond Makena. The pinnacle rises 60 feet from the sea floor to about 10 feet below the ocean's surface and is exceptional for snorkeling as well as shallow dives. Look for brilliant damselfish, triggerfish, puffers, and wrasses.

Divers of all skill levels probe Five Caves in Makena. Lava ridges and small pinnacles provide food and shelter for angler fish, sea turtles, eels, and white-tipped sharks. The waters here are around 30–40 feet deep and can be accessed from shore as well as boat.

Lanai's deep, clear waters (there is little runoff on this dry island) draw divers from around the world. At Cathedrals, off the south shore, a stained-glass effect occurs when sunlight pours through the holes in twin underwater caves. This dive is for experienced divers only.

If diving with giant wintering whales is your dream, sign up with Capt. Ed Robinson on Maui, who knows how to find them. Nautilus Dive Center in Hilo offers divers a chance to see the underwater lava flow from Kilauea Volcano. Kona Aggressor II offers weeklong luxury diving excursions aboard a yacht (call (800) 344-KONA). Lucky Boy Charters in Kilauea, Kauai (call (808) 828-1601), offers trips to dive and fish off the private island of Niihau and uninhabited islet of Nihoa.

Here are some dive company recommendations.

SCUBA DIVING OUTFITTERS

Oahu		
Aaron's Dive Shops	Kailua	(808) 262-2333
Aloha Dive Shop	Hawaii Kai	(808) 395-5922
Clark's Diving Tours	Honolulu	(808) 923-5595
Maui		
Ed Robinson's Diving Adventures	Maui	(808) 879-3584
Lahaina Divers	Maui	(808) 667-7496
Maui Dive Shop	five offices	(800) 542-3483
Mike Severns Diving	Kihei	(808) 879-6596
The Big Island of Hawaii		
Jack's Diving Locker	Kailua-Kona	(808) 329-7585
Kohala Divers	Kawaiahae	(808) 882-7444
Nautilus Dive Center	Hilo	(808) 935-6939
Kauai		
Dive Kauai Scuba Center	Kapaa	(808) 822-0452
Fathom Five Divers	Poipu Beach	(808) 742-6991
Seasport Divers	Poipu Beach	(808) 742-9303

Snorkeling: Exploring the Undersea World

Although not as "deep" an experience as scuba diving, snorkeling is an underwater adventure anyone can do. Just wade in backward in your flippers, look through your face mask, and breathe through your J-tube.

Some practical snorkeling tips:

- Know how to swim. Although some snorkeling spots are shallow, being able to swim is the best way to ensure your own safety in the water.
- Novices should practice in shallow water.
- Always snorkel with a buddy or in groups.
- Don't stray too far from shore or the boat.
- Check your snorkel gear carefully before entering the water. Popular wisdom requires you to spit on your mask and rub it around the lens before dunking it in saltwater and then putting it on. Make sure it fits, airtight, to your face.

The most famous snorkeling spot is Oahu's Hanauma Bay, the best place for novice snorkelers. Huge schools of friendly reef fish populate this picturesque bay, which often seems overpopulated by snorkelers. Here are some excellent snorkeling beaches.

Hanauma Bay Nature Preserve — *Zone 1 Waikiki*

Location 7455 Kalanianaole Highway, at Koko Head Regional Park, Hawaii Kai, South Shore. Head east on the H-1 Freeway, which turns into Kalanianaole Highway, and go up the hill just beyond Hawaii Kai.

Phone (808) 396-4229

Activities Snorkeling, scuba diving

Comments Just wade in and look down: You are surrounded by glamorous tropical fish that teem in this too-tame bay. By day Hawaii's most popular dive spot teems with people peeking at tropical fish; on Saturday night there are more fish than folks. Now open for night divers from 6 to 10 p.m. Saturday nights only, Hanauma Bay attracts the brave and curious who probe shadows in search of nocturnal creatures like hawksbill turtles, polka-dotted moray eels, and big-eyed (the better to see you) yellowfin goatfish. Bring your own dive light or rent one.

This U-shaped bay aquarium in a broken crater, a third of a mile point to point, has near-shore reefs ideal for novice snorkelers and more challenging reefs further out. Lifeguards are on duty daily. Facilities include rest rooms, showers, picnic areas, a snack bar, and snorkel rentals. Ask at the beach desk about free educational tours of the bay. The parking fee is $1 per vehicle, and admission is $3 for all nonresidents over the age of 12. Hanauma Bay is open six days a week (closed on Tuesday) from 6 a.m. to 7 p.m. Smoking is prohibited. Feeding reef fish—once a favorite pastime—is now kapu. Go early, before 8 a.m. if possible, as incoming vehicles are turned away when the parking lot is full.

Ahihi-Kinau Preserve — *Zone 8 South Maui*

Location On remote south shore of Maui, beyond Makena, at end of a dirt road

Activities Snorkeling

Comments Black, barren lava reefs reach into aquamarine pools full of tropical fish. The best snorkeling on Maui is in this scenic 2,000-acre nature preserve on the rugged south coast, where Haleakala last spilled red-hot lava into the sea in 1790. It's difficult to reach but easy to enjoy. No facilities.

Kealakekua Bay — *Zone 11 Kona*

Location On Kona coast of the Big Island, south of Kailua-Kona and downhill from Captain Cook

Activities Snorkeling, scuba

Comments An octopus's garden is shared by free-swimming moray eels, parrotfish, and, once in a while, a pod of spinner dolphins in this deep blue, mile-wide bay that's the Big Island's best snorkeling spot. Coral heads, lava tubes, and underwater caves provide an excellent habitat for Hawaii's tropical fish, and the warm, clear water is a natural attraction for snorkelers. Snack bar, bathroom, and showers are available.

Kee Beach — *Zone 13 Kauai*

Location End of Kuhio Highway, Haena State Park, North Shore; park along the road or in small lot

Activities Swimming, snorkeling, fishing

Comments Here you can float like a leaf on a pond, sucking air through a snorkel and watching little yellow fish dart here and there in crystal-clear water. You can float face up, staring at green-velvet cathedral cliffs, under a blue sky with long-tailed tropical birds riding tradewinds. Palms rustle, a wave breaks. If this isn't perfection, what is? Bathrooms, showers, and parking are available.

Kaupoa Beach — *Zone 14 Molokai*

Location West End, on Molokai Ranch property (limited to ranch guests, unless you can navigate a boat there)

Activities Summer snorkeling, swimming, beachcombing, sunbathing

Comments Head for Kaupoa Beach by ranch bus or on horseback, swap boots for flippers, and take a plunge in the warm saltwater, soothing after a morning in the saddle on Molokai Ranch. Horses graze under coco palms. You snorkel with triggerfish. The trail boss grills rib-eye steak. Way, way out west on Molokai, this is what surf and turf is all about. Facilities include beachside bar and dining pavilion, showers, and bathroom.

Five Needles — *Zone 15 Lanai*

Location Off remote south shore of Lanai

Activities Snorkeling, swimming

Comments Spiky sea stacks dominate an almost secret snorkel spot on Lanai's rugged, seldom-seen south side. Go there only by kayak, sailboat, or launch, mostly by tours departing from Maui. Take *Navatek II* or *Trilogy* from Maui's Maalea Harbor for this unforgettable outing (see information on guided tours below). Clarity of water and abundant sea life make this snorkel site excellent. No facilities.

Guided Tours

Guided snorkeling adventures are available on every island, priced from $35. In addition, many shops rent snorkeling equipment, including fins, masks, snorkels, and gear bags. Most snorkel and dive shops accept major credit cards. Guided snorkel tours take about half a day. Instruction for beginners is available. Snorkel outings are weather dependent.

Snorkel Bob's, one of the most popular outfits, has locations on Oahu (call (808) 735-7944); Maui (call (808) 879-7449, (808) 669-9603, or (808) 661-4421); the Big Island (call (808) 329-0770); and Kauai, (call (808) 823-9433 or (808) 742-2206). Here are our favorite guided snorkel tours.

Oahu

Avoid the hassle—go to Hanauma Bay with B. T. Snorkel on a three-hour van and snorkel tour that includes all gear and transportation from Waikiki hotels to the bay and back for under $15. It's the best deal. Call (808) 396-8144.

Maui

Navatek II, an 82-foot, 149-passenger SWATH vessel (it's a smooth cruiser), sails from Maalaea Harbor to Lanai's remote south shore on the

"Voyage of Discovery," the best family snorkel adventure because of its high-tech boat. It's stable to calm queasy stomachs, easy to get on and off in deep water, and the crew grills hamburgers to order for lunch. *Navatek II* and several other snorkel sail cruises are operated by Royal Hawaiian Cruises. Call (800) 852-4183.

Trilogy, a 64-foot cutter-rigged sailing catamaran operated by brothers Jim and Rand Coon and their families, takes blue-water sailors on six-hour snorkel excursions to Lanai, Molokini, or Kaanapali. Trilogy Excursions is the veteran operator for Maui-to-Lanai sails with a well deserved reputation for delivering a superior experience. Call (888) MAUI-800, or visit www.sailtrilogy.com.

The Big Island of Hawaii

Fair Wind II, a 60-foot catamaran run by Puhi and Mendy Dant since 1971, delivers 100 snorkelers to Kealakekua Bay every morning for a four-and-a-half-hour snorkel dive. The big, safe boat is a solid favorite of families. Call (800) 677-9461, or visit www.fair-wind.com.

Kauai

Hold on for a wet ride to Kauai's remote beaches, sea caves, and waterfalls with a picnic and snorkeling stop. Captain Zodiac (a.k.a. Clancy Greff) pioneered rides on 15-passenger, 20-foot fortified rubber rafts down Na Pali Coast in the 1970s and is still going strong. Call (800) 422-7824.

Molokai

Walter Naki of Molokai Action Adventures takes four snorkelers on four- or six-hour dives in seldom-explored territory aboard his 21-foot Boston whaler. Call (808) 558-8184.

Surfing: Catch a Wave

Hawaii's own kings perfected surfing, and no place does it better. Hawaii offers the most consistent surf, biggest waves, and deepest tubes. The best big-wave surfers test their skills here in the winter when Oahu's North Shore turns into the world's surfing capital and the setting for annual professional competitions. No one knows exactly when surfing originated, but many historians believe Polynesians were already well versed in the sport when they migrated to the Hawaiian Islands nearly 2,000 years ago. Big Island petroglyphs depict board-riding figures. Ancient Hawaiians called surfing *hee nalu* (wave sliding). Only the high chiefs enjoyed access to the best surf spots. King Kamehameha I was said to be an avid surfer.

Today, waves are shared according to skill. Beginning surfers can get quick lessons from Waikiki beach boys or sign up for more formal training with an expert instructor, such as Hans Hedemann, a veteran pro and former surfing champion. **Hans Hedemann Surf School** (call (808) 924-7778) offers lessons on the beach at Waikiki. Equipment is provided.

Lessons for one or two students or groups up to five per instructor are conducted in areas where the waves are small and the beach relatively crowd-free. Students learn the basics on the beach, including ocean safety and how to paddle a surfboard, how to get up and stand on the board, proper foot placement, and where to shift body weight. Next they get in the water to do it again, and then catch a real wave and ride it. Once you get the hang of it, you'll learn other basic maneuvers, such as turning your board to move in a certain direction.

Surfers come in all shapes, sizes, and ages. You should know how to swim and expect to do a lot of paddling and kicking in the water. Most schools have a minimum age of five to seven years for surfing lessons. "If you think you can do it, you probably can," said one instructor. Hedemann said almost everyone is "up and riding" on their first lesson. Then you may be hooked for life, because the feeling of being one with the sea, flying in on a cresting wave, is a thrill like no other.

Other recommended surfing schools include **Hawaiian Watersports** (call (808) 255-4352; www.hawaiianwatersports.com) on Oahu, and **Buzzy Kerbox Surf School** (call (808) 573-5728; kerbox@aol.com) and the **Nancy Emerson School of Surfing** (call (808) 244-7873) on Maui. Surfing instruction is available year-round.

Group rates are generally about \$60 for one-hour lessons to \$225–\$250 for all-day lessons. Private lessons are about \$85–\$125 for one-hour lessons and \$425–\$450 for all-day lessons. Multiday and weeklong rates are also available. Book at least a day in advance, although most surf schools will try to accommodate last-minute students.

For experienced surfers able to deal with surfing etiquette and crowds, Oahu is the place to be, with the widest choice of quality surf spots in the state. Surf conditions are good somewhere on the island nearly year-round, and plenty of surf breaks are just right for less-than-expert surfers. Weather forecasters routinely report surf conditions on radio and television. Maui has some great surf spots near Lahaina and just past Paia. Kauai has excellent surf spots at Hanalei, Princeville, and elsewhere on its north shore and at Poipu and south shore locales. Big Island has a few good surfing areas, like Anaehoomalu at Waikoloa Resort, although many are inaccessible by car. A helpful book on the best surf spots is the *Surfer's Guide to Hawaii* by Greg Ambrose (published by Bess Press), which includes tips, descriptions, and maps.

Keep in mind the following safety and etiquette tips before heading out to ride Hawaiian waves.

- Check with lifeguards first. They can point out the hazardous rip currents, jagged reefs, and tricky waves to avoid. Obey posted warnings.
- Never surf alone, and make sure someone on shore knows where you are.
- Be considerate of other surfers. Don't drop in on someone else's wave.

- Don't surf after dark.
- Use leg ropes to control your board, for your safety and the safety of fellow surfers.
- If you get in trouble, don't panic. Signal for help by raising one arm vertically.

Windsurfing: Ride the Wind

A whole different sport seeks to challenge the wind as well as the waves—the combination of sailing and surfing known as windsurfing or board sailing. A day of brisk tradewinds prompts a hatch-out of butterfly-like sails as windsurfers zip here and there across the water, enjoying the pure sensation of natural speed. In Hawaii, where water sports are a way of life, many ocean devotees surf when the waves are right, windsurf when the winds are right, and kayak when it's calm. Expert windsurfers will want to try their hands or just watch the pros at **Kanaha Beach** and **Hookipa Beach** on Maui's North Shore, known as "the Aspen of windsurfing," where the world's top wave riders gather to take advantage of strong winds and optimum waves. **Diamond Head Beach Park** near Waikiki is favored for wave-jumping, quite a spectacle to watch. Windsurfers fly up the face of a wave and soar, sometimes doing somersaults and other feats before returning to water.

To learn to windsurf on Oahu, cross the Koolau to **Kailua** and **Lanikai Beaches** on Windward Oahu for scenic rides and gentle seas, although periodic blustery tradewinds will sideline the beginners and bring out the experts. Robbie Naisch was one of the early stars of windsurfing, and **Naish Windsurfing Hawaii** in Kailua (call (808) 261-6067; www.naishsails.com) is the oldest windsurf shop in the state. There you can buy or rent gear and accessories and sign up for lessons at all skill levels. Private lessons are $55; lessons for two are $75, including equipment rental. Naish also pioneered the new spin-off sport of kitesurfing—windsurfing with the extra speedy lift of a hang-gliding kite attached, popular on Kailua Bay.

Ocean Sports Waikoloa provides windsurfing services at **Anaehoomalu Bay** at Waikoloa Beach Resort on the Big Island (call (888) SAIL-234; www.hawaiioceansports.com). On Kauai, **Anini Beach** on the North Shore near Princeville is a good place to learn the sport. Sailboard rentals are $25–$40 for a full day. **Alan Cadiz's HST** (call (808) 871-5423; www.hstwindsurfing.com) on Maui offers two-and-a-half-hour lessons for $69.

Charter Sportfishing: Reely Big Ones

If you've ever dreamed of hooking a 1,000-pound "grander" Pacific blue marlin, go to the Kona Coast, the best place to land the fish of a lifetime.

The giants, lesser marlin, and desirable food fish roam the seas off all islands, but the best chance of hooking a trophy fish is off Kona, considered the big-game fishing capital of the world. Kona has an optimal fishing environment, thanks to the seas that plunge to great depths right outside the mouth of Honokohau Harbor and to the hulking volcanoes that tend to block onshore winds and high seas. A charter boat may chase a fish on a line for many miles and hours (or days), but it rarely has to go farther than five or six miles out to sea to hook one.

About 100 charter boats operate out of Honokohau Harbor. Contact one of the charter boat associations to choose yours. They handle plenty of boats and customers and can connect you with people who want to share a charter, put you on a tag-and-release boat, or connect you with a crew that will give you a share of your edible catch. Most captains have commercial fishing licenses and keep the food fish caught on their boat to sell, sharing proceeds with the crew. Marlin over 50 pounds are not considered good to eat, particularly after they have been dragged all over the sea. **Kona Charter Skippers Association** (see contact info on following page) also offers fishing trip packages and group bookings.

We suggest browsing the Internet, asking other fishermen, and checking activity guides to familiarize yourself with your fishing options. Experience and frequency of trips, plus electronic gear, help your captain know where the fish are biting. Most charters offer half-, three-quarter-, and full-day fishing adventures that last four, six, and eight hours. Departures are usually 7 a.m., with half-day charters returning by noon and full-day charters returning by 4 p.m. Prices vary according to the size and amenities of the boat, among other factors.

To maximize your chances of landing a big-game fish, book a full-day charter. It can take an hour or more to catch live bait—usually an *aku,* a skipjack tuna of up to 20 pounds—and when you add the time required to handle lines and tackle for both small bait and big game, you won't have much time left for fishing on a half-day excursion. Half-day charters often use lures as a result, and big marlin seem to prefer live bait.

Walk-up bookings are available, but it's better to make your reservations in advance so that you can get the type of boat you want and, if you choose, share a charter with someone. A deposit is usually required (up to half the charter cost) and is refundable up to 48 hours prior to the fishing date. Most charters accept major credit cards and personal checks.

Most boats are licensed to hold six passengers, plus the captain and two deckhands, but four passengers is a more comfortable crowd. The crew provides instruction and equipment. You don't need a fishing license for offshore fishing. Bring your own food and drinks (liquor is allowed) for the ice chest, and sun and seasickness protection. Shorts, swimsuits, and T-shirts are appropriate wear, plus a sweatshirt or light jacket as needed.

Charter boats range in size from 25 to 58 feet, with the average being 33 to 35 feet. If you're new to sportfishing (most Kona fishermen are, other than participants in the frequent jackpot money tournaments) you may want to splurge on a midsized or larger boat so that you enjoy the experience of luxuriating on the water, even if the fish aren't biting that day. But remember—the size of the boat doesn't guarantee the catch. The fish don't care how much you spend or how big your boat is.

Three types of marlin roam Hawaiian waters: black, blue, and striped. Though the chances are good that a marlin will strike your bait, the odds of actually landing one of the tenacious fighters are about one in three. With luck, you might catch one of the "granders"—a trophy marlin of 1,000 pounds or more. You can see what one looks like on the wall of the King Kamehameha Beach Hotel in Kailua-Kona.

You won't need the strength of an Olympian to land a giant marlin. If you're using up to 130-pound test line, the drag is about 40 or 50 pounds, meaning the most you have to worry about pulling in is between 40 and 50 pounds. If you can pull 20 pounds around for a while, you can reel in a marlin. What you may need is staying power. Some big-game fish fight for hours before exhausting themselves. Other fish in the sea you might want to meet are ahi (yellowfin tuna) and other tuna species, ono (wahoo), mahimahi (dolphin fish), and other billfish and spearfish. Some Kona boats go after snappers, onaga, opakapaka, and other bottom fish using a rigorous Asian fishing method called jigging. The *Sea Strike* is one (call (800) 264-4595, or visit www.kona-fishing.com).

Mahimahi, ono, and marlin are present throughout the year, except for striped marlin, which is a winter fish. Spearfish are also more abundant in the winter months, and ahi are more numerous in summer. Or you might want to try some inland bass fishing on Kauai's South Shore freshwater reservoirs. **JJ's Big Bass Tours** (call (808) 332-9219) and **Cast & Catch Freshwater Bass Guides** (call (808) 332-9707) will take you there.

HAWAII OCEAN SPORTFISHING CHARTERS

Operator	Phone	
Statewide		
Sportfish Hawaii	(877) 388-1376	www.sportfishhawaii.com
Big Island, Kona		
Capt. Bob's Kona Coast Sportsfishing Charters	(808) 895-7000	www.konacharters.com
Charter Skippers Association	(800) 7-MARLIN	www.konabiggamefishing.com
Kona Activities Center	(808) 325-0769; (808) 329-3171	

HAWAII OCEAN SPORTFISHING CHARTERS *(continued)*

Operator	Phone	
Oahu		
Inter-island Sportsfishing	(877) 806-FISH	www.maggiejoe.com
Maui		
Fish Maui	(808) 879-3789	www.fishmaui.com
Kauai		
Anini Fishing Charters	(808) 828-1285	www.kauaifishing.com
Kai Bear Sportfishing	(808) 652-4556	www.kaibear.com
Lahela Ocean Adventures	(808) 635-4020; (866) 226-8340	www.sport-fishing-kauai.com
Sport Fishing Kauai	(808) 742-7013	www.fishing-kauai-hawaii.com
Molokai		
Alyce C Sportfishing	(808) 558-8377	www.worldwidefishing.com

Whale Watching

Two-thirds of the Pacific humpback whale population migrates to warm Hawaiian waters each winter to breed, bear, and nurse their young. Few sights match the spectacle of a whale leaping out of the sea.

Whales cruise so close to shore, you can often see them from coastal roads and hotel lanai. For a closer look, take a whale-watching cruise if you are in Hawaii between mid-December and mid-April. Whale-watching excursions are offered throughout Hawaii, but are concentrated off the south and west coasts of Maui, the heart of the whale migration.

Luck plays a big role in seeing actions by large creatures on the move, but some tours offer substantial expertise and special equipment, such as state-of-the-art hydrophones that let you hear whale songs, and support marine conservation nonprofits like Pacific Whale Foundation and Whales Alive.

Experience makes a big difference between whale watching and whale "glimpsing," as federal law requires boats to stay at least 100 yards away from the whales. Some cruises guarantee sightings by giving you a rain check if you don't actually see a whale.

Whale-watching boats come in all sizes, from rubber rafts that bounce through the surf to large, motorized catamarans and sleek sailing sloops, and offer a wide range of comforts, such as shaded decks, beverages, and marine heads.

Daily humpback whale–watching cruises cost $20–$60 for adults and $12–$30 for children age 11 and under. Book your tour several days in advance during holiday periods. Most tours last two to three hours and provide snacks and juice. Some tours offer hotel transportation. Wear swimsuits or casual attire, and bring binoculars and cameras.

Tip: To see whales best from shore, get to an elevated viewing post that gives you a better perspective. Look for whale spouts, geysers of sea spray that shine in the sun and seem to disappear into thin air. Look for large black bodies poking their noses above water as they "spy-hop," possibly to get a better look at you.

If you're in the resort area of Wailea, Maui, check the telescope in front of the Outrigger Wailea Beach. The first person to report a whale sighting to the café each day gets a free breakfast.

Though humpbacks visit the Islands only in winter, Hawaii has five other whale species that can be viewed throughout the year—sperm whales, pilot whales, melon-headed whales, false killer whales, and beaked whales. Big Island boat captain Dan McSweeney, based in Kailua-Kona, is one of the few operators who offers year-round whale-watching adventures spotlighting these lesser-known marine mammals, with tours out of Honokohau Harbor three times a week.

Informative websites on humpback whales include www.pacificwhale.org and www.ilovewhales.com. The following is a list of some whale-watching tours.

WHALE-WATCHING CRUISE OPERATORS

Operator	Phone	Website
Maui		
Maui Princess	(808) 661-8397; (800) 275-6969	www.mauiprincess.com
Pacific Whale Foundation	(808) 249-8811; (800) 942-5311	www.pacificwhale.org
Whale Mist Charters	(808) 667-2833	
Big Island of Hawaii		
Dan McSweeney's Year-Round Whale Watch	(808) 322-0028	www.ilovewhales.com
Hawaii Sailing Co. (luxury yacht)	(808) 776-1505	
Oahu		
Honolulu Sailing Co.	(808) 239-3900; (800) 829-0114	www.honsail.com
Royal Hawaiian Cruises	(808) 848-6360	www.atlantisadventures.com
Kauai		
Capt. Andy's Sailing Adventures	(800) 535-0830	www.sailing-hawaii.com
Capt. Zodiac Raft Expeditions	(808) 329-3199	www.captainzodiac.com

Shark Watching

You've seen it on TV: A big shark, jaws wide, lunges at the human diver in the submerged steel cage. Now, you can experience a real-life close encounter with a shark in Hawaii. A 26-foot launch takes you three to four miles off Oahu's North Shore to the deep blue sea where big tiger sharks roam crystal-clear waters looking for lunch. You get locked in a "shark proof" cage and lowered into the 200-foot depths while scores of 15-foot sharks come in close to see if you are something to eat. You can stay in the cage until you scream, or conquer your fear of sharks. Either way, you leave with great awe and respect. Thrill-seekers from England, Ireland, Canada, New Zealand, Australia, and Japan and nearly every state have survived the encounter. Odds are you will too. The two-hour adventure departs at 7 a.m. from Haleiwa Small Boat Harbor on Oahu's North Shore. Bring swimsuit, T-shirt, sunscreen, snorkel and mask, and your underwater camera. Cost is $120 a person. Contact North Shore Shark Adventure at Haleiwa Small Boat Harbor (call (808) 228-5900; www.hawaiisharkadventures.com).

While sharks abound in Hawaiian water, they are seldom seen. Most attacks tend to occur offshore of Olowalu Beach in the West Maui resort area. On that reef-fringed coast, the Islands' first permanent shark warnings now stand, posted after a rash of shark attacks, several fatal, on snorkelers, divers, and surfers. Eight signs are now posted along a one-mile stretch of Olowalu Beach. Hawaii averages three or four shark attacks annually.

Hawaii by Land

Hiking: Take to the Trails

Hiking is the most popular off-beach outdoor activity in Hawaii. Conditions are generally fine for meeting the natural environment face to face, and the natural environment is extraordinary. There's something Garden of Eden–like about walking on a forest trail edged with leaves bigger than your head and seeing tropical fruit like mountain apple, guava, wild mango, and avocado, surrounded by jungle greenery and waterfall streams—especially when it's within minutes of downtown Honolulu and Waikiki. Waterfall trails lead to waterfall pools, ideal spots to cool off after a tropical trek. There's a certain historic continuity to hiking on trails that were carved by ancient trekkers and smoothed by generations' footsteps long before other means of land travel were available in the Islands. The experience is truly rewarding, with few dangers.

About those dangers: Rain forest means slippery, muddy trails and mosquitoes (take bug repellent). Waterfall valleys are steep and narrow and can flash-flood quickly after cloud-burst deluges upstream, with frightening and sometimes fatal results. Dry hikes on lumpy lava and steep, crumbly dirt trails require paying close attention to your footing and drinking lots of water. No matter what the locals do, don't hike in rubber slippers (beach thongs). Use supportive footwear suitable for Hawaiian red-dirt treks, muddy forest jaunts, or rough lava trails. Don't let the views keep you from watching where you put your feet. It is *Blue Lagoon* and *Castaway* rolled into one, but stand still while you admire the scenery. Stick to the trails. Rain-forested mountains swallow up injured or missing hikers from sight almost instantly. If possible, carry a charged cell phone on remote ventures.

Inviting though the streams may be, don't drink the water or swim with open cuts and risk getting leptospirosis, a wild pig–related bacterial fever. You can get that within minutes of downtown Honolulu too (at Kapena Falls, a swimming hole wildly popular with kids despite the danger of disease).

Easy-to-reach hiking spots on Oahu include **Manoa Falls,** a highly traveled trail directly behind Waikiki in upper Manoa Valley. The hike is about 1.5 miles round-trip through a rain forest, with a waterfall. Park near the trailhead off Upper Manoa Road.

The arid, south-shore area around Makapuu Head includes a series of trails with fantastic views of Windward Oahu and the sea. **Mount Tantalus,** on the Honolulu side of Manoa Valley, has several well-marked trails off Round Top Drive, flourishing with guava, bamboo, lilikoi (passion fruit), and other tropical vegetation. In upper Makiki, the **Hawaii Nature Center** operates exhibits and guides hikes aimed at helping children discover the outdoors.

For a moderately strenuous Oahu hike, tackle all or part of **Koolaupoko Trail,** a recent, well-maintained option. Park at the hairpin curve on the Windward side of the Pali Highway and walk back behind Mt. Olomana through the mountain rain forest, past waterfalls, down to Waimanolo, eight miles. If the round-trip is too much, do it one way and get someone to meet you at the other end. Or hike partway and turn around.

Clubs such as Hawaiian Trail and Mountain and student groups from Chaminade University and other local colleges also post helpful information and maps for Oahu and Neighbor Islands hiking. **Kapalua Nature Center** is Kapalua Resort's ecotourism arm. The resort offers guided hiking tours in its 17,000 acres of Upcountry watershed and pineapple plantation lands. Once a year by lottery, a dozen hikers are dropped off by helicopter with a guide at the top of Puu Kukui to walk on a boardwalk through high-country bogs to see rare and endangered species of plants and birds.

Experienced hikers on Kauai can retrace the footsteps of early Hawaiians along the **Kalalau Trail** that traverses the stunning Na Pali Coast. An easy hike goes from the Kilauea Point National Wildlife Refuge on the North Shore, where knowledgeable guides recount area history and information on a variety of seabirds that nest in the refuge and other wildlife. If you are not a hiker but want to walk through the lush Kauai countryside, go to Limahuli Gardens, a small branch of the National Tropical Botanical Gardens, near the north end of Kuhio Highway. It features native Hawaiian plants and trees along a one-mile hilly loop path through a small scenic valley.

Guided hiking tours can be booked throughout Hawaii, to bring the countryside to life as only personal experience can. This is the best way for visitors to see private and inaccessible country; discover shy, indigenous creatures; and understand the context of what they see.

The newest guided hike on Windward Oahu is a **Kualoa Ranch** trek over a ridge connecting two wild valleys that goes down to the shoreline at Molii Fishpond (phone (808) 237-7321; www.kualoa.com). Our suggestions for hiking guides include **Oahu Nature Tours** (phone (808) 924-2473; www.oahunaturetours.com) and, on the Big Island, experts Rob Pacheco and staff of **Hawaii Forest and Trail** (phone (808) 331-8505; www.hawaii-forest.com) and Hugh Montgomery and staff of **Hawaiian Walkways** (phone (808) 775-0372; www.hawaiianwalkways.com).

Island bookstores and the Internet offer a wealth of information about island hikes. For free trail maps, call the Department of Forestry and Wildlife at (808) 587-0166. Several books are available for those hoping to discover more of Hawaii on foot.

National and State Parks

Hawaii's two national parks and 52 state parks encompass more than 50,000 acres on Oahu, Maui, the Big Island, Kauai, and Molokai. In addition, a number of federal and state historic parks and monuments designate cultural sites worthy of your attention.

Hawaii Volcanoes National Park, home to the world's most active volcano, is one of the nation's oldest and best national parks and a must-see for Big Island visitors. If you're traveling with children, you owe it to yourselves to discover this park together, particularly if Pele, the fire goddess who lives in Halemaumau Crater, is producing any spectacular eruptions during your trip. (Call for eruption updates, (808) 985-6000, or check the website at http://hvo.wr.usgs.gov.) Your best chance of seeing red lava flows is after sunset at the end of Chain of Craters Road. Park rangers are posted there 2–8 p.m. daily. (See below for details.)

Also on the Big Island, **Puuhonua O Honaunau,** the Place of Refuge on the South Kona Coast, is a national historic park on the site of an ancient waterfront sanctuary. A temple has been reconstructed there, within the remaining lava-rock walls built centuries ago. The place has an air of peace you can't miss even on a quick walk-through. It's worth the time to watch local people demonstrate ancient skills and games and help you understand something about old Hawaiian life. There's an annual summer cultural festival in late June or early July.

On the north end of the Kona/Kohala coast, **Puukohola National Historic Site** is an archaeological monument by the sea, the preserved temple from which King Kamehameha I set out to conquer the other islands and unite them into a kingdom in the 1700s. There is an annual cultural pageant here in August.

On Maui, **Haleakala National Park's** 10,023-foot summit is a great place for watching the sun rise, hiking in the vast caldera, and marveling at the claw-footed native Hawaiian nene geese. These endangered state birds of Hawaii evolved special feet for life on cinders. You can also see silversword plants, which are found nowhere else.

Four state parks are especially noteworthy: **Kakaako Waterfront Park** along the downtown Honolulu shoreline, on Oahu; **Iao Valley State Park** on Maui; and **Kokee State Park** and **Waimea Canyon State Park** on Kauai. Each provides scenic settings, exceptional views, and activities for young and old. Information on these parks is included below.

For more information on Hawaii's state parks, write to the Division of State Parks, 1151 Punchbowl Street, Room 310, Honolulu, HI 96813, or call (808) 587-0300.

Overall Safety Tips and Park Regulations

- Guard against tropical sunburn.
- Do not drink from streams and ponds or expose an open cut or abrasion to the water. Harmful bacteria may pose a serious health risk.
- Never leave your valuables unattended in a car at a scenic lookout.
- Drinking or possession of alcoholic beverages is prohibited in parks.
- Build fires only in fireplaces and grills. Portable stoves and other warming devices may be used in designated picnicking and camping areas.
- Do not disturb any plants or geological, historical, and archaeological features.
- Skating and skateboards are prohibited where posted.

National Parks

Hawaii Volcanoes National Park — *Zone 12 Hilo and Volcano*

Location Highway 11, about 30 miles from Hilo; follow the road signs and turn left into the park entrance

Phone (808) 985-6000

Website www.nps.gov/havo

Hours Daily, 7:45 a.m.–5 p.m. Once you are admitted, the park is open all day, every day.

Admission $10 per vehicle, good for a week; $5 per person for people hiking or biking in; $20 for a year-long pass; $10 for a seniors' lifetime pass

When to Go Anytime. The best time to see red lava is after sunset.

How Much Time to Allow At least half a day, including early evening if the lava is flowing

Comments The 377-acre Hawaii Volcanoes National Park was established in 1916, but the mighty spectacle of Kilauea in action has drawn visitors since the 1800s. Then, hardy adventurers were housed in a grass shack on the rim of Halemaumau Crater, fire goddess Pele's legendary home. Now Volcano House lodge stands on the rim, an interesting spot for sunset cocktails.

Kilauea Volcano has been erupting in its current phase since 1983. It runs on its own schedule, sometimes fuming quietly, rarely fountaining, more usually spilling fire and liquid rock down its slopes, creating new real estate and black-sand beaches. Live volcanic action is not guaranteed during your visit, but the park features are well worth the trip even when the volcano is quiet. A variety of natural "attractions" compete for attention; we suggest that you take in as many as you can, but don't miss the Thomas A. Jaggar Museum, an excellent interpretive center where seismographs and easy-to-understand exhibits help illustrate the scientific theories of volcanic works, and Hawaiian artist Herb Kane's murals illustrate the Hawaiian theory, the legend of Pele.

Just outside the museum is one of several overlooks along the trail to view Halemaumau Crater—2.5 miles wide and more than 400 feet deep—within Kilauea Caldera. Halemaumau means "House of Ferns," named for greenery that once grew there between eruptions. Now it looks like a cinder pit. That must be the way Pele likes it, and many islanders still believe she lives there, causing eruptions when she is displeased. Her fiery temper is said to be appeased by gifts of gin, a modern embroidery on the legend. Pele is also said to direct her wrath, in the form of really bad luck, on anyone who steals her rocks. The post office and Volcano House are deluged with tons of rocks each year sent back by hapless miscreants. If you want our advice, leave the lava alone.

MADAME PELE'S ROCK GARDEN

If you take Madame Pele's lava rocks home, even by mistake, something awful could happen to you. That's the threat of Pele's Curse, which akamai Hawaii folks know is a myth fabricated by a Big Island tour guide in the 1950s. Yet, each year thousands of hot rocks come back to Hawaii from around the world, returned by folks with hard luck tales of woe—personal calamities, accidents, injuries, and death. In case you've been snorkeling, Madame Pele is the goddess of fire and volcanoes in ancient Hawaiian mythology. She is revered as one of the most powerful Hawaiian deities. Traditional Hawaiian culture maintains that rocks are conductors of many forms of *mana* (spiritual energy) found in nature. For decades, rangers at Hawaii Volcanoes National Park and other recipients of rock returns tossed the rocks with little or no ceremony back on the black lava beds. Now, the rocks are welcomed home by a Hawaiian kahuna at Ka Ahu Paepae o Hoaka Hoomalu, a special rock garden at the Marriott Outrigger Waikola Beach Hotel on the Big Island's Kohala Coast.

The new garden sits at the center of a sacred crescent of five volcanic summits: Haleakala, Mauna Kea, Mauna Loa, Kohala, and Hualalai. Everyone who returns a rock receives a personal letter from the resort's Hawaiian cultural affairs office informing them that their rock is now safe in "a sheltered resting place where a sense of care will prevail." Anyone may attend the ceremony, held at high noon on the first Wednesday of each month, in the garden area south of the Queen Kaahumanu wing.

Start your park tour at the Visitor Center, which houses volcano exhibits and a 200-seat mini-theater showing a terrific 23-minute film about the history of Hawaii's volcanoes and their significance to the Hawaiian culture. Park rangers can answer questions, suggest itineraries, and conduct an introductory hike from the center. Next door, the Volcano Art Center offers a good selection of works by some of Hawaii's top artists, including Herb Kane, Peggy Chun, Rocky Jensen, and Dietrich Varez.

Guide map in hand, drive into the park, where you'll soon find the Jaggar Museum and other features. A word of caution: Sulfuric fumes from the craters and steamy fumaroles may be hard on pregnant women, small children, and people with breathing problems. If this includes you, roll the windows up and head for less fumy features. Otherwise, drive across the caldera floor and stop to look into the yawning fire pit, a ten-minute walk from the parking area. This is the world's only drive-in volcano, predictable enough to observe up close.

The park includes 150 miles of trails of varying difficulty. For an easy walk, Devastation Trail is a good choice that illustrates some of the havoc caused by volcanic action. It is a mile round-trip, paved and wheelchair accessible, through an area that was devastated by the hot fallout from lava fountains from a 1959 Kilauea Iki eruption. Look for golden strands in the *pahoehoe* lava called Pele's hair, as well as "lava tree" molds formed when hot lava surrounded a tree trunk and burned the tree but left the round form of rock cooling on the outside.

Chain of Craters Road will take you down to the sea, about half an hour's drive through a moonscape of smooth, ropy *pahoehoe* lava (one of two kinds of lava—the other is *aa,* the rough clumps seen on the Kona Coast). The road once traversed the region, but now it dead-ends in more lava. It has been revised many times by recent flows and could be changed again at any time. Watch the coastline for a telltale plume of white smoke—that's where the lava meets the sea.

For a moderate to challenging hike, try the four-mile loop of Kilauea Iki Trail, which descends 400 feet through rain forest; crosses the Kilauea Iki crater floor, which might still feel warm under your feet; and returns via the crater rim. Look for birds, insects, steam vents, and cinder cones. Allow two or three hours and bring water. Be prepared for wet weather and steep, rocky terrain. The trail begins at the Lava Tube parking area.

Stop at Thurston Lava Tube on the way out. The 20-minute walk through lush tree ferns leads into a large, cave-like (and lighted) tube formed by a long-ago lava river.

To get a closer view of the current interaction of lava and ocean, drive to the opposite side of the lava flow, near Kalapana, and take advantage of an access added in 2001. Kilauea's active flow left the park boundaries to ooze over county jurisdiction areas where former flows buried subdivisions, beaches, graveyards, and the road. Hawaii County officials rebuilt the end of Highway 130 so that viewers can park and walk a short coastal trail to a viewing area, rather than the former, challenging six-mile hike from the other side of the older flow that trespassed on buried property. Reach the new access by turning off the Hilo-Volcano road, Highway 11, at Keaau and taking Highway 130 through Pahoa.

At the end of the road, park and follow signs to the nearest designated lookout, currently a bluff over the place where molten magma of some 2,000° drips or rolls into the ocean in a billow of steam, sizzling and spitting and writhing like an agonized creature as fire battles water and eventually loses. The sight is mesmerizing and unforgettable. You are walking on the newest land on Earth. You are watching creation happen.

But stay on the bluff, away from the fragile beach shelf that could crack off and fall in any time. County rescue squads are churlish about saving witless tourists and might charge you for the privilege. Overnight camping is available at the park via free permit (see "Camping in the Wilds," page 284).

Overall, be respectful of the park surroundings, which Hawaiians regard as sacred to their culture, and the buried neighborhoods, still people's homes.

After Dark in The Park, an award-winning interpretative program, features Hawaiian musicians, storytellers, artists, scientists, historians, and local authors who share knowledge of Hawaii's rich natural and supernatural culture. The free program is offered at 7 p.m. every Tuesday at Kilauea Visitor Center, Hawaii Volcanoes National Park. (See page 230 for details.)

Haleakala National Park — *Zone 10 Upcountry Maui*

Location The park extends from the top of Haleakala ("House of the Sun") down the southeast flank of the mountain to the sea at Kipahulu near Hana, including scenic waterfall pools at Oheo Gulch. The summit area is accessible via Roads 37, 377, and 378 up the mountain through Kula, a 3-hour round-trip drive from the Kahului area below. Add more time to get to and from resort areas. Kipahulu, at the east end of the island between Hana and Kaupo, can be reached via Hana Highway. Driving time is 3 to 4 hours each way between Kahului and Kipahulu.

Phone (808) 572-9306

Website www.nps.gov/hale

Hours Park Ranger headquarters open daily, 7:30 a.m.–4 p.m. The Visitor Center is open daily, sunrise–3 p.m.

Admission $10 per vehicle, good for a week; $5 per person not in vehicles

When to Go Anytime. Haleakala is renowned for dramatic sunsets and sunrises, a mystic experience that draws people from slumber in the middle of the night to be there on time. Be sure to arrive at least 30 minutes early. It's also well worth the 3-hour round-trip drive (from Kahului) at other times of day—including after dark, when it is a fabulous place for stargazing.

How Much Time to Allow Up to half a day, depending on whether you take part in park programs. Rangers offer guided hikes on all Haleakala's trails, at the cindery summit, in the cloud forest, or down below in the lush tropical forests of Kipahulu. This is a good option. Take your pick of environments.

Comments Haleakala, a dormant volcano, became a separate national park in 1961. The park consists of 29,000 acres, most of it wilderness. At the summit, the park headquarters and Visitor Center house cultural and natural-history exhibits.

In the Kipahulu area, trails begin at the Ranger Station/Visitor Center. The Kuloa Point Trail is an easy half-mile loop toward the ocean that affords a look at the pools and waterfalls, as well as the sea and the Big Island, but go early or late if you want to avoid crowds. Enjoy a picnic on the grass next to the remnants of an ancient fishing shrine and house site.

Check the park bulletin board for a schedule of daily programs and guided hikes. Obey posted warnings. Because the weather at the summit is unpredictable—temperatures range from 40° to 65° but with windchill factored in, can dip below freezing—wear lightweight, layered clothing and comfortable, sturdy shoes. No restaurants or gas stations are available in the park. People with heart or breathing programs should use caution because of the high elevation and thin air.

Limited drive-in and wilderness overnight camping is permitted in the crater and below at Kipahulu. The Hosmer Grove Campground in the summit area is located just inside the park entrance (see "Camping" section for details on Haleakala camping).

Oahu State Parks

Diamond Head State Monument — *Zone 1 Waikiki*

Location Diamond Head Road, between Makapuu and 18th Avenues

Comments Woke up jet-lagged? Go climb Diamond Head! Early in the day when it's cool, you can make the moderate climb to the summit in about 45 minutes to enjoy panoramic views of Waikiki, Honolulu, mountains, and ocean. Ask your hotel concierge for a trail map. You can sign up for a guided walk sponsored by the Clean Air Team of Hawaii (call (808) 948-3299) on Saturday mornings at 9 a.m.

Heeia State Park — *Zone 3 Windward Oahu*

Location 46-465 Kamehameha Highway at Kealohi Point, Heeia

Comments Beautiful views of Kaneohe Bay, Mokolii (better known as Chinaman's Hat), and the majestic Koolau Mountains. Adjacent to the ancient Heeia fishpond.

Kaena Point State Park — *Zone 5 Leeward Oahu*

Location The end of the road, Farrington Highway, Makua

Comments A 778-acre park located at the northwest end of Oahu. Picnicking and shore-fishing are popular. You can view Kaneana, a large sea cave that is the legendary home of a shark-man. Bring drinking water.

Kakaako Waterfront Park — *Zone 2 Greater Honolulu*

Location End of Ahui or Ohe Streets off Ala Moana Boulevard, Honolulu

Comments A little-known 35-acre waterfront park located in downtown Honolulu, favored by residents who come here during lunch and pau hana (after work). A waterfront promenade, amphitheater, and picnic areas highlight this scenic park.

Maui State Parks

Iao Valley State Park — *Zone 7 Central Maui*

Location End of Iao Valley Road (Highway 32) in Iao Valley, behind Wailuku

Comments The centerpiece is Iao Needle, a pinnacle that rises 1,200 feet from the forested valley floor. Be prepared to share it with tour buses that stop for photo ops. Take a look at the multicultural architectural heritage village below. Think about how this placid area was the scene of one of the bloodiest ancient battles. In 1790, King Kamehameha fought to gain control of Maui, and in the aftermath, so many bodies blocked Iao stream that they named the site Kepuniwai (damming of the waters).

Waianapanapa State Park — *Zone 10 Upcountry Maui*

Location End of Waianapanapa Road, off Hana Highway, Hana

Comments This remote, ocean-view campground features rustic cabins sleeping four to six at $55 per night and free tent camping for up to five days in a grassy open field surrounded by trees. Seek reservations as far in advance as possible, as this is a prized spot. Permits can be obtained at any state parks office. Write to the Maui office at Division of State Parks, P.O. Box 1049, Wailuku, Maui, HI 96793, or call (808) 984-8109.

Rest rooms, outdoor showers, picnic tables, grills, and drinking water are available for tent campers. Each cabin has kitchen, living room, bedroom, and bathroom with bedding, linens, and utensils provided. Amenities include good hiking trails, native forest, cave, heiau, a black-sand beach sprinkled with tiny blue shells, and fishing. Ocean conditions seldom are safe for swimming.

Big Island State Parks

Akaka Falls State Park — *Zone 12 Hilo and Volcano*

Location End of Akaka Falls Road (Highway 220), Hilo

Comments Free and open year-round. Get off the highway and see some inland wonders now and then, like this sizable waterfall and its jungle valley. It's a short walk through the tropical vegetation to scenic points overlooking the falls; picnic facilities are available.

Lapakahi State Historical Park — *Zone 11 Kona*

Location Akoni Pule Highway, North Kohala

Comments This archaeological dig of an ancient Hawaiian fishing village is worth a stop while en route through Kohala District. You can roam through on a self-guided tour and imagine what life was like back then. Interpretive helpers will answer questions. (Call (808) 889-5566.)

Kohala Historical Sites State Monument — *Zone 11 Kona*

Location On a coastal dirt road to the left off Akoni Pule Highway, Hawi

Comments If you're going to pick one ancient temple site, visit Mookini Heiau, believed to be the oldest and largest sacrificial temple, with huge stone walls and a spooky atmosphere. Nearby is the reputed birth site of Kamehameha I, Hawaii's greatest king. (Call (808) 974-6200.)

Wailuku River State Park — *Zone 12 Hilo and Volcano*

Location Off Waianuenue Avenue, Hilo

Comments Free and open year-round, this 16-acre park is the home of Rainbow Falls, named for the brilliant color bands that form through a misty waterfall. Boiling Pots, a series of pools that appear to "boil" after frequent rains, is nearby. The cave beneath the waterfall is said to be the home of Hina, mother of the demigod Maui.

Kauai State Parks

Kokee State Park — *Zone 13 Kauai*

Location High up Kokee Road, 15 miles from Kekaha. This park and Waimea Canyon State Park adjoin.

Comments Far from any beach, Kokee is a special place for its upcountry atmosphere and native plants and birds. Picnicking, camping, and hiking are the best ways to enjoy this 4,345-acre park, the site of a lookout with an arresting view of Kalalau Valley. Camp cabins are available with woodstoves to ward off the upcountry chill. Trails of varying difficulty lead off through the woods; pick one that suits your time frame. Even the easy walks take you into native forest. The forest includes California redwoods among the ohia and koa trees. The Alakai Swamp is a boggy treasure for birders intent on seeing or hearing rare native species. The 11-mile Nualolo-Awaawapuhi Loop, with dramatic vistas of the Na Pali Coast, is one of Hawaii's best hikes. In summer, a very short trout season draws local anglers. (Call (808) 245-6001 for weather info.)

The adjoining 1,866-acre park overlooks spectacular Waimea Canyon, which you can explore on horseback or on foot. It's often likened to the Grand Canyon for its colorful striated geologic layers and steep walls.

Tent camping is free at Kokee with a five-night limit, but it requires a permit. Permits can be obtained at any state parks office. For more information, write to the Kauai office at Division of State Parks, 3060 Eiwa Street, Lihue, HI 96766, or call (808) 241-3444. Rest rooms, showers, picnic tables, sinks, and drinking water are provided.

Kokee Lodge has a dozen cabins that sleep up to six people each. The older cabins have a large dormitory-style room, bathroom, and kitchen; newer cabins offer two bedrooms, living room, kitchen, and bathroom. Rates are $45 per night for the two-bedroom cabins, $35 per night for the dorm-style ones. For cabin reservations, write to Kokee Lodge at P.O. Box 819, Waimea, HI 96796, or call (808) 335-6061.

Other accommodations are available at Kokee State Park. For information, call Camp Sloggett (phone (808) 335-6060), Kokee Methodist Camp (phone (808) 335-3492), or Hongwanji Camp (phone (808) 332-9563). Rates are $40–$96 per night.

A restaurant at the lodge offers Continental breakfast and lunch daily. The Kokee Museum, located adjacent to the lodge, spotlights Kauai's natural history (see Part Seven, "Hawaii's Attractions").

Neighboring Waimea Canyon State Park is located at the bottom of Waimea Canyon, along the Waimea River and Koaie and Waialae streams. Access is via the Kukui Trail, located 7.5 miles north on Waimea Canyon Road.

Free tent camping is available for up to four nights at five campsites on the canyon floor, with a permit. Write the Division of Forestry and Wildlife, 3060 Eiwa Street, Room 306, Lihue, HI 96766, or call (808) 274-3444.

The best is Lonomea Camp, located six miles from Kukui trailhead. Lonomea has pit toilets, a picnic table, and roofed shelters. Wiliwili Camp, at the base of the trail, also has those facilities. Hipalau Camp has no toilets but offers a roofed shelter, picnic table, and two refreshing pools fed by waterfalls. Bring your own drinking water.

Wailua River State Park — *Zone 13 Kauai*

Location Along banks of Wailua River off Kuhio Highway, Wailua

Comments Historic 1,092-acre site within a river valley. Picnicking, boating, and fishing are available, along with paid boat tours to the much-ballyhooed Fern Grotto. Our advice is to skip the touristy grotto ride and, instead, search out the heiau, ancient refuge, and birth stones that are among the historic landmarks in this valley, once reserved for ancient chiefs.

Molokai State Parks

Palaau State Park — *Zone 14 Molokai*

Location End of Kalae Highway, Palaau

Comments This 230-acre park overlooks historic Kalaupapa, the place where people stricken with Hansen's disease (leprosy) were once banished. It's open 24 hours a day, and picnicking and camping are available. A short trail leads to aptly named Phallic Rock, a monolith reputed to enhance fertility among women who sleep beside it overnight. Donations accepted.

Camping in the Wilds

Hawaii has more than 120 campsites and campgrounds on six main islands, with sites ranging from beaches and open mountain terrain to lush green valleys and rain forests. Nearly all are within the jurisdiction of a county, state, or federal agency and require camping permits. Book as far ahead as possible, and be prepared to take part in a lottery-style competition to get permits, because residents like camping too. It's an affordable way to vacation in the Islands.

Bring a tent with a rain flap or tarp for overnight showers, a ground pad, and lightweight sleeping bags to sleep on (more than in, unless you're headed for cool higher altitudes). You'll need bug repellent and your own drinking water, or you'll need to bring what's necessary to purify any water to drink by boiling it or adding some sort of purifier.

Hawaii has no animals to encounter in the wilds, except occasional feral pigs and goats. You can scare them away by shouting or making sudden movements. Otherwise, leave them alone and they'll extend the same courtesy. No island plants are poisonous to the touch (except, for some people, mango, which is a relative of poison ivy), but some are poisonous if eaten. Hawaii does have some creepy bugs of tropical proportions, capable of nasty stings—not the big German brown cockroaches that terrorize visitors but giant centipedes, five inches or longer, scorpions in rocky areas, and black widow or brown recluse spiders under damp wood. Shake out your shoes and bed gear before using them, and wear shoes or use a flashlight to watch your step even in soft grass at night.

If you want to camp without lugging all the gear from home, rent equipment from suppliers such as those listed below, most of which also rent kayaks, mountain bikes, and other outdoor equipment.

CAMPING EQUIPMENT RENTALS

Oahu

Bike Shop
1149 South King Street
Honolulu, HI 96814
Phone: (808) 596-0588

Omar the Tent Man
94-158 Leoole, Warehouse A
Waipahu, HI 96797
Phone: (808) 677-8785,
(888) 242-8556

Kauai

Kayak Kauai
P.O. Box 508
Hanalei, HI 96714

Big Island

Safari Activities Rent-It
75-5785 Kuakini Highway
Kailua-Kona, HI 96740
Phone: (808) 334-0464,
(800) 406-4555

CAMPING EQUIPMENT RENTALS *(continued)*

Maui	Molokai
West Maui Sports & Fishing Supplies 1287 Front Street Lahaina, HI 96761 Phone: (808) 661-6252, (888) 498-7726	Molokai Off-Road Tours & Taxi P.O. Box 747 Kaunakakai, HI 96748 Phone: (808) 553-3369, (808) 552-2218

Where to Camp

Here are suggested campsites, in addition to the state parks covered previously. A good resource to learn more is *Camping Hawaii* by resident camping expert Richard McMahon. Camping information is available on the Hawaii Visitors and Convention Bureau website (www.gohawaii.com).

Oahu

Bellows Beach Park — *Zone 3 Windward Oahu*

Location 41-043 Kalanianaole Highway; located at Bellows Air Force Station, about 2.5 miles northwest of Waimanalo. On Kalanianaole Highway, turn right at the sign marking BAFS and follow the road to the park.

Type of Camping Weekend tent camping only, Friday noon to Monday 8 a.m.

Permits Applications accepted no earlier than two Fridays before the requested camping dates. You must apply in person at any satellite city hall on Oahu or at the Dept. of Parks and Recreation, 650 South Street, Honolulu. Call (808) 523-4525.

Cost Free

Comments Fifty campsites share an ironwood forest by the beach. Picnic tables, rest rooms, drinkable water, and outdoor showers are available. Gentle bodysurfing waves make Bellows a favorite. Swimming and beachcombing are popular year-round.

Camp Mokuleia — *Zone 4 The North Shore*

Location Farrington Highway (Highway 930), about 4 miles west of Waialua (toward the ocean)

Type of Camping Cabins, lodge, and tent sites

Permits Write to Camp Mokuleia at 68-729 Farrington Highway, Waialua, HI 96791, call (808) 637-6241, or e-mail info@campmokuleia.com.

Time Limit None

Cost Tent camping: $8 per person per night; cabins: $160 (14 beds) or $200 (22 beds) per night; lodge: $65 (rooms with shared bath), $65–$75 (with private bath), $100 (suites). Optional meal service ranges from $5 to $7 per meal.

Comments The best of four campsites on Mokuleia Beach. Used primarily by groups. The area is peaceful, a sample of the rugged beauty of the North Shore. Swimming and snorkeling are good in summer, but the surf gets rough in winter. The tent area is sparse on facilities, but all campers may use the facilities at the main camp section.

Kualoa Beach Park — *Zone 3 Windward Oahu*

Location Kamehameha Highway, country end of Kaneohe Bay. From Honolulu, head west on the H-1 to the Likelike Highway exit. Drive through the tunnel, turn on Kahekili Highway, and drive about 9 miles to the park entry on the right.

Type of Camping Tents only

Permits Applications accepted no earlier than two Fridays before the requested camping dates. Group campers must apply for a permit in person at the City Dept. of Parks and Recreation, 650 South Street, Honolulu. Call (808) 523-4525; others can also apply at any satellite city hall on Oahu.

Time Limit 5 nights, from Friday at 8 a.m. to Wednesday at 8 a.m.

Cost Free

Comments Facilities include rest rooms, showers, picnic tables, sinks, a volleyball court, drinking water, and a public phone. Amenities include scenic views, tranquil atmosphere, the beach, and a commanding photo op: Mokolii islet just offshore. Gates to the park close at 8 p.m. and reopen at 7 a.m. Vehicles cannot leave or enter the campgrounds during the night.

Maui

Haleakala National Park

Get groceries and gas before you get to the park, at Kula or lower communities. Three camping alternatives are available in the park, listed below.

Hosmer Grove — *Zone 10 Upcountry Maui*

Location 6,800-foot level, just off Haleakala Crater Road; watch for the sign indicating Hosmer Grove, which is almost 10 miles from the Crater Road turnoff

Type of Camping Tent and vehicle camping. Vehicles must stay in the parking lot.

Permits None. The campground is limited to 25 people, with no more than 12 in a single group.

Time Limit 3 nights

Cost Free

Comments The campsite, a grassy clearing surrounded by trees, has a covered pavilion with two picnic tables and two grills, rest rooms, and drinkable water. Hiking is the activity of choice. A half-mile loop nature trail begins at one end of the parking lot. Pick up hiking trail information at the park headquarters. Bring extra blankets—it can get cold at night.

Wilderness Cabins and Tent Campground — *Zone 10 Upcountry Maui*

Location Inside Haleakala Crater, on the Halemauu Trail

Type of Camping Tent and cabin camping

Permits Tent permits are issued at the park headquarters on a first-come, first-served basis on the day of use. The campground is limited to 25 people, with no more than 12 in a single group. Reservations for Holua, Paliku, and Kapalaoa wilderness cabins must be made 3 months in advance. Be sure to include alternate dates. Write to Haleakala National Park, P.O. Box 369, Makawao, HI 96768, or call (808) 572-9306.

Time Limit 2 consecutive nights

Cost Free for tent campers. The 3 cabins are $40 (accommodate 1–6 people) and $80 (7–12 people) per night.

Comments Awe-inspiring views of Haleakala Crater, big enough to contain Manhattan with room to spare, are among the highlights here at the near-7,000-foot elevation. You are likely to meet the endangered nene goose, Hawaii's state bird. Facilities for tent camping are sparse, and the campground is rocky. Cabins contain bunks with mattresses (but no linens), table, chairs, cooking utensils, and a wood-burning stove with firewood.

Kipahulu Campground — *Zone 10 Upcountry Maui*

Location Hana Highway, about 10 miles past Hana

Type of Camping Tent and vehicle camping

Permits None. Space is limited to 100 people, on first-come, first-served basis. On busy holiday weekends, arrive early to get your space.

Time Limit 2 consecutive nights

Cost Free

Comments Camping in this extraordinary spot, a grassy area overlooking the sea and the Oheo Gulch pools and waterfalls, is so memorable that even noncampers ought to get a tent and give it a try. Facilities include rest rooms, picnic tables, and grills, plus the showers and pools provided by nature. Bring drinking water. No food or gas is available. Swimming and jungle hiking are right at hand.

Exploring the infamous curvy road to Hana and its real-Hawaii villages, swimmable waterfall pools, and botanical gardens can be one of Maui's finer nonresort experiences, when you combine the long drive with an overnight stay in the Hana area. Lodging is limited in Hana, and camping at Kipahulu or Waianapanapa (see section on state parks above) is a great alternative.

The Big Island of Hawaii

Hawaii Volcanoes National Park

Two drive-in campgrounds (Namakani Paio and Kulanaokuaiki) are located within the national park. These facilities are free, once you pay the entry fee to the park, and are available on a first-come basis, with no reservations, permits, or check-in required. Stays are limited to 7 days in a month, not to exceed 30 days per year. Get groceries and gas before you arrive. Volcano village has two small groceries (look for locally made Lilikoi curd for a tropical treat), and Hilo and Keaau have supermarkets.

Namakani Paio Campground — *Zone 12 Hilo and Volcano*

Location Hawaii Volcanoes National Park, 5 miles west of park entrance on Route 11

Type of Camping Tent, vehicle, and rustic cabin camping

Permits None. For cabin reservations, write Volcano House, P.O. Box 53, Volcano, HI 96718, or call (808) 967-7321. Reservations should be made as far in advance as possible for summer and holiday periods. Cabins are $40 per night for up to 4 people; $8 for additional people

Comments Located at a 4,000-foot elevation, this scenic campground is surrounded by towering eucalyptus and native ohia trees. Tents are pitched on an open grassy field or under trees. Facilities include a large pavilion with two grills and a fireplace (pack your own firewood; it's not available in these woods), picnic tables, barbecue pits, rest rooms, sinks, and potable water. Tent campers can rent showers from Volcano House, which operates ten cabins near the campground. Each cabin has a pair of single bunks and a double bed, picnic table, and outdoor barbecue grill. Toilets, sinks, and showers are provided in a separate building for cabin renters. Expect cool, damp weather. Bring warm clothing, as it tends to get chilly at night—as low as the 30s at this elevation.

Kulanaokuaiki Campground *Zone 12 Hilo and Volcano*

Location Hawaii Volcanoes National Park, about 5 miles down Hilina Pali Road

Type of Camping Tent and vehicle camping

Comments Located at 2,700-foot elevation. No drinking water is available at this new campground. It has three campsites, two of them wheelchair-accessible. Facilities include barbecue grills, a vault-type toilet, and picnic tables.

Kilauea State Recreation Area *Zone 12 Hilo and Volcano*

Location Kalanikoa Road, Volcano, a half mile from Haaii Volcanoes National Park

Type of Camping Cabin camping

Permits None. It's always in high demand. Seek reservations from any state parks office; or write to the Big Island office at Division of State Parks, P.O. Box 936, Hilo, HI 96720. Call (808) 974-6200.

Cost $45 per night for 1–4 people, $5 for each additional person up to 6.

Time Limit 5 nights

Comments Count yourself lucky if you're able to stay at this two-bedroom cabin, which is comfortably nestled within a shady grove of trees and ferns, with full kitchen, living/dining room, and a bathroom. Blankets and linens are provided.

Kalopa State Recreation Area *Zone 12 Hilo and Volcano*

Location Highway 19, Hamakua coast, 7 miles from Honokaa

Type of Camping Tent and cabin camping

Permits Obtain at state parks offices in the Islands. Write to the Big Island office at Division of State Parks, P.O. Box 936, Hilo, HI 96720, or call (808) 974-6200.

Time Limit 5 nights

Cost Free for tent campers. Cabins are $55 per night for 1–4 people, $5 per additional person.

Comments Located in a deep forest of ohia trees, this well-maintained park houses a campground, picnic area, and two cabins. Facilities in a concrete-block building include rest rooms, showers, sinks, and drinking water. The nearby picnic area features a covered pavilion with several tables. The cabins each contain a pair of bunk rooms, toilets, showers, and sinks. Cabin users share a dining hall with a fireplace and kitchen.

Mauna Loa Summit Cabins *Zone 12 Hilo and Volcano*

Location Eastern rim of Mauna Loa summit crater. Take Highway 11 to Mauna Loa Road; drive up the narrow road until it ends at a trailhead and parking lot. Hike the trail 7.5 miles to Red Hill Cabin. Mauna Loa Cabin is located 11.6 miles farther up the trail.

Type of Camping High-altitude tent and cabin camping

Permits Permits are first-come, first-served at Hawaii Volcanoes National Park Visitor Center. Limited to 8 people per night per group. For more information, write to the Hawaii Volcanoes National Park, Volcano, HI 96718, or call (808) 985-6000.

Time Limit 3 nights

Cost Free

Comments Used by die-hard hikers able to make the thin-air trek. Located at the 13,250-foot level, Mauna Loa Cabin is near the edge of Mokuaweoweo, Mauna Loa's breathtaking caldera. It offers 12 bunk beds and spare mattresses (so additional people can sleep on the floor). An enclosed pit toilet is behind the cabin. Bring your own stove and drinking water (the water here needs to be treated before use). Tent camping is allowed, but try to get the cabin if at all possible; temperatures can dip below freezing at night. Bring warm clothes. At this elevation, even snow is possible any time. Altitude sickness can pose another problem for lowlanders.

Spencer Beach Park — *Zone 11 Kona*

Location Highway 19, Kohala Coast, south of Kawaihae

Type of Camping Tent and vehicle camping

Permits Book your reservations early, particularly during the summer. Write to the Dept. of Parks and Recreation, County of Hawaii, 25 Aupuni Street, Hilo, HI 96720, or call (808) 961-8311.

Time Limit 1 week during the summer, 2 weeks during the rest of the year

Cost $5 per day for adults; $2 per day for children ages 13–17; $1 per day for children age 12 and younger

Comments Spencer Beach Park offers some of the best camping on the Big Island, with plenty of picnic tables and a large pavilion, rest rooms, sinks, washrooms, changing areas, and showers. The water is drinkable. Swimming and snorkeling are popular here. The campground is located next to Puukohala Heiau National Historical Site.

Kauai

Kalalau Valley, Na Pali Coast State Park — *Zone 13 Kauai*

Location End of Kalalau Trail, about 11 miles from Kee Beach. Experienced hikers walk in, but this precipitous trail, which has been subjected to 1,000 years of erosion since the ancient Hawaiians first used it, is not for novices. A whitewater tour raft will shuttle campers in the summer months. The cost is $60 each way. Call (808) 826-9371.

Type of Camping Tents only

Permits Camping in Kalalau is restricted to 60 people per day, so try to obtain a permit as far in advance as possible. For more information, write to the Division of State Parks, 3060 Eiwa Street, Lihue, HI 96766, or call (808) 241-3444.

Time Limit 5 nights

Cost $10 per person per night

Comments Kalalau has become too popular to feel alone in the jungle, but it still has appeal as a singular tropical fantasy come to life with its magnificent golden-sand beach, waterfalls, and steep cliffs. The camping area stretches a half-mile behind the beach. The only facilities are toilets and water from nearby Hoolea Falls. Pack your own drinking water. Safe swimming in summer only. Most of your fellow travelers in this isolated wilderness are likely to have shed their clothes, since the tradition is to go au naturel.

Molokai

Papohaku Beach Park — *Zone 14 Molokai*

Location Just off Kaluakoi Road, western shore. Head west on Highway 460 to the turnoff to the Kaluakoi Resort; continue past the hotel along Kaluakoi Road

Type of Camping Tent and vehicle camping

Permits Available at the Pauole Center Multipurpose Building in Kaunakakai. For advanced reservations and more information, write to the Maui County Parks Dept., P.O. Box 526, Kaunakakai, HI 96748, or call (808) 553-3204.

Time Limit 3 nights

Cost $3 per person per night

Comments This site is both easily accessible and fairly isolated. Facilities include rest rooms, showers, picnic tables, grills, and drinking water. One drawback is that the beach is unsuitable for swimming.

Bicycling: Pedal Power

Exploring Hawaiian Islands by bike puts you in touch with your surroundings at your own speed. Most of the islands have mountains in the middle, which add a challenging element.

A few biking tours are available. **Backroads,** the well-known bike vacation agency in Berkeley, California (call (800) 462-2848 or visit www.backroads.com), has inn-to-inn trips on the Big Island and multi-sport adventures on Maui and Lanai. **Bicycle Adventures** in Olympia, Washington (call (800) 443-6060 or visit www.bicycleadventures.com) has six- and eight-day Big Island trips in winter combining biking and B&B stays.

Bike path systems are still being developed in the place that needs them most: busy, trafficky Oahu. Kailua on the Windward side recently added bike lanes through beach park areas and up the Pali Highway. The City and County of Honolulu are developing a master plan for a bikeway system throughout the city. In the meantime, TheBus has free bike carriers on front; bikers can take the bus between biking points.

Ala Moana Beach Park in Honolulu and **Kapiolani Park** in Waikiki offer scenic, comfortable biking in late afternoon and around sunset. For fitness-minded cyclists, a grueling ride is the winding road up to the 2,013-foot summit of Mount Tantalus.

The roads on Neighbor Islands are more often traffic-free. The Big Island's wide-open spaces, decent roads, and challenging landscape have plenty of bike appeal. Maui has bike-friendly lanes, some with stunning views of neighboring Molokai, Lanai, and Kahoolawe. One candidate is the one-lane road around Maui's northwest end between Kahului and Kapalua. The scenery and the winding road slow everyone down. Stop and get a refreshing shaved ice at Kahakuloa. Or drive up to Kula, on the 3,000-foot shoulder of Haleakala, and cruise along the hilly country road to Ulupalakua and back, through flower farms, jacaranda trees, botanical gardens, and pastures.

One popular cycle adventure is cruising down the steep and scenic slopes of Hawaii's volcanoes—best known on Maui, where several tour companies will outfit you with special bikes and gear, then take you to the top of 10,023-foot Haleakala, and guide you safely down the mountain, 38 miles to the seashore past pasturelands, farms, and forests. Some companies also provide hotel transportation and a snack; others offer unguided tours, letting you set your own pace. Be forewarned—some deceptive grades and curves coming down the mountain have launched even experienced bikers over the side. If you elect to go on your own, take the curves more slowly than you normally would. Dress in layers; the top third of the ride is virtually alpine, while the bottom is tropical. Downhill tours are also available on Oahu, the Big Island, and Kauai.

Hawaii is a terrific place for mountain biking, offering a wide range of terrain, scenic sites, and tracks.

For off-road bike adventures, go to **Molokai Ranch** on Molokai, where you can stay in a plushy tent cabin, eat communally in camp pavilions, and do your pedaling thing on the 52,000-acre ranch's superb single-track. Mountain biking is one of several activities included in the price of your stay. Here and elsewhere, the rugged trails provide optimal riding conditions, from dusty coastlines to lush forests.

The favorite Maui venue for mountain bikers is **Polipoli State Park,** where you'll find more than ten miles of single-track that wind through thick forests of eucalyptus and redwood trees. On Oahu, other good trails are found in **Mililani** in central Oahu, at **Maunawili** in Windward Oahu, in **Pupukea** on the North Shore, and at **Kaena Point** in Leeward Oahu.

The Big Island offers a wide range of mountain-biking experiences. Experts in the high-altitude sport can ride through a forest at **Mauna Loa,** on the crater rim, cruise the green pastures in **North Kohala,** and more. A mountain-biking trail map is available free of charge at most Big Island bike shops, or call the Big Island Visitors Bureau at (808) 961-5797.

Kauai has five single-tracks and nine dirt roads open to mountain bikes. Coastal treks here count numerous scenic stops and spectacular views among the rewards of biking at **Kokee State Park** and **Waimea Canyon.**

Plenty of dirt roads on Lanai call to mountain bikers, as well as the challenging climb to the summit of **Lanaihale,** the island's highest point at 3,370 feet.

Keep in mind these biking safety tips:

- Wear a helmet, comfortable shoes, and close-fitting clothing.
- If possible, carry a first-aid kit and cell phone in case of emergency.
- Familiarize yourself with your rental bike and the tropic heat and humidity before riding off.

- Ride with a partner or a group.
- Bring drinking water, sunscreen, and sunglasses.
- If traveling in a group, keep at least five lengths between riders.
- Don't use headphones or get distracted by views while riding.
- Novice mountain bikers should avoid narrow, single-track trails, which sometimes skirt the edge of dangerous cliffs. Instead, ride on the dirt roads. Be careful on the Big Island, where rough and craggy lava rocks pose a shredding danger to tires and skin.

Hawaii Bicyling League (call (808) 735-5756) issues a newsletter for local biking enthusiasts. A good resource is John Alford's *Mountain Biking the Hawaiian Islands.* The book features maps and photos as well as detailed descriptions of Hawaii's best biking trails. You can order through www.bikehawaii.com.

Daily rentals run $25–$40 for a mountain bike and $20 for a road bike.

BIKE RENTAL SHOPS

Oahu

Barnfield's Raging Isle Surf and Cycle (808) 637-7707

Big Mountain Rentals (808) 926-1644

Maui

Extreme Sports Maui (808) 871-7954 (877) 376-6284

Haleakala Bike Co. (808) 575-9575 (888) 922-2453

Island Biker (808) 877-7744

South Maui Bicycles (808) 874-0068

West Maui Bicycles (808) 661-9005

The Big Island

C&S Outfitters (808) 885-5005

Da Kine Bike Shop (808) 934-9861

Hilo Bike Hub (808) 961-4452

HP Bike Works (808) 326-2453

Mauna Kea Mountain Bikes (808) 883-0130; (888) 682-8687

Kauai

Kauai Cycle & Tour (808) 821-2115

Outfitters Kauai (808) 742-9667

Molokai

Molokai Bicycle (808) 553-3931

Horseback Riding: Back in the Saddle

You may not think of Hawaii as part of the Wild West, but there's no more western state. Horses were brought to the islands more than a century ago, and a grateful populace, who had either walked or sailed everywhere, eagerly took to riding. Horseback riding is a great way to get off the roads and into the countryside of the vast ranches that invite visitors onto their lands for tropical trail rides. In the Islands, the wide-open spaces lead between volcanoes, along beaches and sea cliffs, and into jungled valleys with waterfalls. The horses are well trained and know their trails, leaving you free to enjoy the views.

Riding adventures are available on all islands, with colorful and personable guides to share local lore. Rates are reasonable, ranging from $55 per person for a one-hour ride to $85–$100 for a two-hour trek. Call for age and weight restrictions if you're concerned: The minimum age for riders is usually eight years old, and the maximum weight ranges to 275 pounds. Book your reservation at least a day in advance, or a week ahead if you have a group. Most rides are limited to 10 to 12 people. You can secure your reservation with a credit card, and most operators also accept traveler's checks or cash. Plan to call on the morning of your ride (or leave a phone number where you can be reached) to check on weather conditions. All riders must sign liability waivers.

A short orientation on horsemanship and safety precautions for island conditions precedes the tour. Previous riding experience is not a requirement; first-time riders are common. Operators will ask your experience level and match you to an appropriate horse. The group will go at the pace of the least experienced rider. Certain ranches offer intermediate- and advanced-level rides. Most island stables use thoroughbreds and quarter horses.

Rides include stops for a picnic lunch or barbecue, a sampling of local fruit, or a cooling swim. Full-cover shoes are mandatory, long pants are suggested, and sun protection is recommended.

HORSEBACK RIDING ADVENTURES

Oahu		
Correa Trails	Waimanolo	(808) 259-9005
Happy Trails Hawaii	North Shore	(808) 638-7433 www.happytrailshawaii.com
Kualoa Ranch & Activity Club	Windward Coast	(808) 237-7321 www.kualoa.com
Maui		
Makena Stables	South Maui	(808) 879-0244
Mendes Ranch and Trail Rides	Northwest Maui	(808) 871-5222 (808) 249-0446
Thompson Ranch	Kula	(808) 878-1910
The Big Island		
Paniolo Riding Adventures	Honokaa	(808) 889-5354
Waipio on Horseback	Waipio Valley	(808) 775-7291
Kauai		
CJM Country Stables	Poipu Beach	(808) 742-6096 www.cjmstables.com
Esprit de Corps Riding Academy	Kapaa	(808) 822-4688 www.kauaihorses.com
Princeville Ranch Stables	North Shore	(808) 826-6777

HORSEBACK RIDING ADVENTURES *(continued)*	
Molokai	
Molokai Ranch Outfitters Center	(808) 552-2791 www.molokairanch.com
Lanai	
Lodge at Koele Stables	(808) 565-7300 www.lanai-resorts.com

Hawaii by Sky

Hang-Gliding: Free as a Bird

Imagine soaring high above Hawaii's wilderness, mountain ridges, rain forests, azure bays, and jagged sea coasts. Hang-gliding is growing in popularity in the Islands, and you can sign up for an instruction course followed by a memorable tandem flight with your instructor, using a traditional glider or a motor-powered glider. **Hang-Gliding Maui** (call (808) 572-6557) offers several adventures using a motorized glider ($95 for a half-hour and $165 for a full hour).

Skydiving: A Leap of Faith

Whether you're searching for the ultimate in aerial views or simply seeking thrills, skydiving may be your choice. **Skydive Hawaii** provides skydiving experiences for novices and experts alike at Dillingham Air Field in Mokuleia on Oahu. The half-day experience includes training and instruction, 15 minutes of flight time to a cruising altitude of 13,000 feet, the jump (in tandem with a professional sky diver), a 5,000-foot free fall, and 6 or 7 minutes of gliding down to Earth via parachute. The cost, $250 per person, includes transportation to and from Waikiki ($180 if you drive yourself). Call (808) 637-9700.

Biplane Riding: Get Loopy

If the romance of the biplane appeals, you can choose flight-seeing—or with a strong enough stomach, a heart-thumping aerobatic adventure, which includes a dizzying repertoire of loops, spins, rolls, and hammerheads. **Stearman Biplane Rides** (call (808) 637-4461) at Dillingham Air Field on North Shore Oahu offers single-passenger rides aboard a restored 1941-vintage, open-cockpit Stearman N2S biplane. A 20-minute North Shore flight is $125; a 40-minute tour over historic Pearl Harbor is $175. Add $35 for an extra ten minutes of aerobatic action.

Also at Dillingham Air Field (call (808) 677-3404), **Tsunami Aviation** features the state-of-the-art aerobatic sport biplane PITTS S2B, billed as the "Formula One racer of airplanes." **Glider Rides** offers an exciting 20-minute ($85) flight with all kinds of topsy-turvy maneuvers—it'll literally turn the island upside-down for you.

Spas: For Your Health

Hawaiians have an ancient word that describes the modern concept of spa treatments for good health: *hooponopono,* or making things right. Hawaii is a healthy place by its very nature and cultural tradition.

Spas devoted to rejuvenation and pampering care are now open on all islands, at moderately priced resorts as well as the luxury spreads, where they are a required amenity. You can find Hawaiian practitioners of ancient healing arts using Hawaiian medicinal plants, massage, and relaxation techniques. Look for spas that use Hawaiian medicinal plants and seaweeds, ocean water, peaceful surroundings, and methods like lomilomi, a vigorous rubbing technique, and hot lava-rock massage to promote good health. All spas offer European, Asian, New Age, and other modern therapeutic techniques.

Spa treatments have become a guy thing, luring men beyond the workout room to the relaxing massages, facials, pedicures, and manicures that women have long enjoyed. Spa treatments are not cheap, but it is easy to treat yourself to some first-class therapeutic pampering on all islands. Several spa programs take advantage of the Hawaiian outdoors—you'll find private outdoor massage cabanas near the sea and open-air facilities within spa buildings. You don't have to be a resort guest for a spa timeout, but be prepared to pay higher fees. Set aside a little money to take home some spa lotions and potions. Most hotels also offer fitness facilities so you can keep up your workout regimens or start new ones.

Here are some top spa choices.

Oahu

Hilton Hawaiian Village — *Zone 1 Waikiki*

Phone (808) 951-6546 (Holistica Hawaii); (808) 949-4321

Hours Daily, 6 a.m.–9 p.m. (fitness); 9 a.m.–9 p.m. (spa)

Comments Hilton's new spa opened in fall 2001 in two floors of the new Kalia Tower at the state's largest hotel with some very interesting innovations. It is a traditional spa and salon operated by Mandara Spa, which runs luxury spas in Asia and the Caribbean as well as aboard cruise ships and on Maui at the Outrigger Wailea Beach.

The spa is also integrated with a high-tech, medically based wellness center focused on comprehensive health evaluations—the Holistica Hawaii Health Center—offering diagnostic evaluation by a physician and electron beam tomography screening tests to detect heart problems and other disease (the tests are fast, easy, and noninvasive, using a $2 million ERT scanner). The program, with multilingual staff, also offers personal trainers and nutrition, fitness, and lifestyle workshops. The tests can be used to scan bone density, brain tissue, internal organs, and the colon—a "virtual colonography" alternative to a colonoscopy. Programs range from a half-day executive workup to a seven-day evaluation. Spa treatments are coordinated with the medical program.

After the program is completed, patrons get a full health summary on their own CD-ROM with all lab and imaging assessments and, later, follow up with their personal doctors. Patrons can volunteer to be part of weight control, anti-aging, and immune enhancement research. For additional details about the wellness center and case histories, visit www.holistica.com.

Mandara Spa incorporates Balinese treatments in the mix of Hawaiian, European, and Asian techniques. It created some new treatments based on Hawaiian ingredients, notably the chocolate macadamia nut scrub and the vanilla-pikake (jasmine) facial. Hawaiian ingredients have been used in a variety of other treatments—ground Kona coffee, fresh coconut, sea salt, limu kala seaweed, ti leaves, and traditional protective plants. Or you could opt for the Kalia tropical pikake-papaya bath. Facilities include 25 private "wet and dry" and massage treatment rooms and some spa suites for couples, friends, and families to share treatments; infinity pool, whirlpool, and sundeck; all the usual showers, lockers, salon services, sauna, and steam rooms, as well as a café with spa cuisine and a boutique. Guests can also schedule massages in their rooms between 9 a.m. and midnight.

Spa treatments can be reserved with a credit card; the fee will be forfeited in case of cancellations with less than two hours' notice before the appointment. Children can have spa services but must be accompanied by a parent or guardian for treatments unless they are age 16 or older.

Massages start at $98; packages, $145 for one guest and $290 for two in a suite. The two-and-a-half-hour indulgence called "Exploration in Chocolate" is $450 for two sharing a suite.

Service charges of 15% and state taxes are added to the bill; additional tips are at your discretion.

Ihilani Resort and Spa — *Zone 5 Leeward Oahu*

Phone (808) 679-0079

Website www.ihilani.com

Hours Daily, 7 a.m.–7 p.m.

Comments The 35,000-square-foot Ihilani Spa offers some 70 services and treatments, many based on distinctive Hawaiian products and ingredients, including piped-in sea water from the adjoining shore. The spa menu includes a wide range of hydrotherapies, fitness, and relaxation programs, massage treatments, aromatherapies, skin care treatments, and salon services.

Men's and women's lounges are equipped with steam room, sauna, Needle Shower Pavilion, Roman pool, relaxation area, and other amenities. Use fee for hotel guests—$20 during 7–11 a.m. and 2–7 p.m.—is waived if you purchase a spa treatment. The fee for others is $25, plus any treatment fees. The facility also has weight and cardiovascular workout rooms, with classes led by trained staff. Proper athletic footwear is required.

Appointments are scheduled in advance, and patrons who are not hotel guests need a credit card to hold a reservation. Cancel or reschedule any appointment for a treatment at least four hours in advance to avoid being charged half of the treatment fee. No-shows will be charged the full fee. You can request a male or female therapist and alert the spa to any allergies or medical conditions.

Individual treatments range from $25 for a brow or chin wax to $110 for an age-protection facial. Half- and full-day treatment programs are available, ranging from $190 to $390. A 17% service charge is added for each treatment.

The Ihilani is one of two places in the United States to offer thalassotherapy, an underwater full-body massage using 180 pulsating jet streams of warm sea water.

Fresh sea water is pumped directly into the spa for each treatment. The massage lasts 25 minutes and costs $60. Contact the spa for a complete list of services or visit www.ihilani.com.

Maui

Grand Wailea Resort Hotel and Spa — *Zone 8 South Maui*

Phone (808) 875-1234

Website www.grandwailea.com

Hours Treatments, 10 a.m.–7 p.m.; fitness/workout rooms, 6 a.m.–8 p.m.; beauty salon, 8 a.m.–7 p.m.

Comments The Grand Wailea's Spa Grande is Hawaii's largest at 50,000 square feet, a favorite with the spa-going world. In 1998, readers of *Condé Nast Traveler* voted the Grand Wailea as the top spa resort.

The Spa Grande has an "East meets West" philosophy, mixing traditional Hawaiian healing techniques with European, American, Indian, and Asian spa therapies. Everything's here: massage treatments, aromatherapy, body treatments, facials, hair care, manicures, pedicures, waxings, yoga, meditation instruction, racquetball, basketball, and more. Prices range from $20 for a nail polish change up to $270 for a one-hour "massage-in-stereo" (two therapists working on you simultaneously). Most soothing is the spa's Termé Wailea Hydrotherapy Circuit, a refreshing hour-long treatment. You begin with a quick shower, enjoy some quality time in a Roman bath, and visit the steam room and sauna before being escorted for a personalized loofah scrub, a cleansing treatment that exfoliates surface skin cells and produces healthier-looking skin. The treatment continues with your choice of specialty baths—Moor mud, limu/seaweed, aromatherapy, tropical enzyme, and mineral salt—followed by a Swiss jet shower. Sound invigorating? The cost is $50 for hotel guests and $75 for non–hotel guests.

Non–hotel guests pay a $30 surcharge added to the first spa treatment (salon and wellness services not included). The surcharge is waived if you book two or more spa treatments on the same day. You must be at least 16 years old to use the spa; minors may receive treatments if accompanied by a parent or guardian. Non–hotel guests need a major credit card to reserve an appointment. A 50% charge is assessed for no-shows and cancellations less than two hours prior to your appointment. All spa and salon services are subject to an additional 15% service charge plus tax.

Use of the cardiovascular and weight-training gyms and all fitness classes are complimentary for guests of the hotel. Nonguests are charged $15 a day.

The Big Island of Hawaii

Four Seasons Resort Hualalai — *Zone 11 Kona*

Phone (808) 325-8000 or (808) 325-8200

Website www.fourseasons.com

Hours Daily, 6 a.m.–8 p.m.

Comments The Hualalai Sports Club and Spa is available only to resident members and guests of the Four Seasons Resort Hualalai. Here you'll find the full range of facilities, not in smelly closed-up quarters but in the open air as much as possible: 17 indoor/outdoor body treatment rooms, outdoor saunas and steam rooms, private outdoor garden showers, an open-air equipment gym and aerobics gym, a 25-meter outdoor Olympic-style lap pool, half-court basketball arena, Cybex strength machines, free-weight equipment, treadmills, stationary bikes, tennis courts, and a volleyball court. Lockers and showers are provided, and robes, slippers, shorts, and T-shirts are available on request.

The sports club offers a variety of fitness classes, including high- and low-impact aerobics and aqua aerobics. Spa therapies include several types of massages ($110 for 50 minutes, $140–$160 for 80 minutes), hydrotherapy and body treatments ($65–$125 for 50 minutes), and various combination packages. Fitness die-hards with money to burn can sign up for the multiday Fitness Fantastic package ($700–$1,200), which includes a fitness assessment, three personal training sessions, three 50-minute massages (you'll need them), a hike, and two golf or tennis lessons. For those who prefer to be pampered, the Hualalai Masque package ($400+) includes your choice of the seaweed or Dead Sea mud masque treatment, plus a Vichy shower massage and a 50-minute Swedish or lomilomi massage.

Provide at least four hours' notice if you need to cancel or reschedule your appointment to avoid being charged in full (24 hours' notice is required from December 15 to January 3). Children under the age of 14 are not allowed into the spa. When making an appointment for a spa treatment, you'll be asked to arrive 20 minutes ahead of time to shower and enjoy the sauna, steam bath, whirlpool, and a cold dip.

Kauai

Hyatt Regency Kauai Resort & Spa — *Zone 13 Kauai*

Phone (808) 742-1234

Webite www.spa.hyatt.com

Hours Daily, 6 a.m.–8 p.m.

Comments The hotel's ANARA Spa was considered state of the art when it opened in 1991, and it has kept up with the times enough to remain one of Hawaii's best spa facilities. Here you'll find no fewer than ten massage rooms that overlook private gardens, a 25-meter heated lap pool in the center of the courtyard, a Turkish steam room, a Finnish sauna, and open-air "shower gardens" carved from lava rock. Combine all this with Kauai's built-in therapeutic value and you have the makings of a very refreshing and invigorating experience.

Admission into the spa is $5 for hotel guests and $25 for non–hotel guests and includes use of the fitness center. Appointments for treatments should be booked at least a day in advance (especially for treatment packages). Non–hotel guests must reserve their bookings with a major credit card. Cancellation notice must be given at least four hours in advance; otherwise, you'll be charged in full. No one under the age of 16 is allowed in the spa at any time.

Here's a sampling of ANARA Spa services and prices: A half-hour massage is $65, an hour-long massage is $110; one-hour body treatments are $110, herbal wraps are $50; manicures are $40 and pedicures are $65. Treatment packages range from $155 (1½ hours) to $375 (6 hours). Locker rooms are available.

Call the hotel for a full menu of services.

HEALTH CLUBS AND FITNESS CENTERS

In addition to health spas, there are health clubs and fitness centers in the Islands, if your hotel doesn't offer one. Daily rates are $12–$20, and weekly rates begin at $40.

Oahu

Spa Fitness Center, (808) 949-0026

24-Hour Fitness,
(808) 923-9090 in Waikiki
(808) 486-2424 in Honolulu

Maui

Gold's Gym, (808) 874-2844 in Kihei
(808) 242-6851 in Wailuku
(808) 667-7474 in Lahaina

24-Hour Fitness, (808) 877-7474

HEALTH CLUBS AND FITNESS CENTERS *(continued)*	
The Big Island	**Kauai**
The Club in Kona, (808) 326-2582	Kauai Athletic Club, (808) 245-5381
Gold's Gym, (808) 334-1977	Kauai Gym, (808) 823-8210

Golf: Tee Time

If you look at the Hawaiian Islands as a chain of golf courses in the middle of the Pacific Ocean, you'll begin to see the challenges they pose. Ninety courses on six islands, with exotic names like Hapuna, Ko Olina, Koolau, and Mauna Lani, are set like jewels by the sea, in black lava beds, on turquoise lagoons, near volcanoes, beside lush rain forests, and deep in jungle valleys. Nowhere else on Earth can you tee off to whale spouts, putt under rainbows, or play around a live volcano. But be forewarned: Many of these courses feature hellish natural hazards—razor-sharp lava, gusty tradewinds, distracting views, an occasional wild pig, and, always, the tropical heat.

You can play at night on Kauai's Poipu Bay Golf Course, which features "Golf Glow," a unique after-dark activity for groups on a nine-hole putting course or a three-hole regular course. The holes are illuminated with glow sticks, and players are provided with glow balls.

There is one major handicap—that big blue ocean between you and the Islands poses a time and distance problem. It's impossible to play all of Hawaii's great courses unless you move here and take up golf full time (which some duffers do).

Ever since a Scotsman opened Oahu's first golf course in 1898, the game spread across the Islands like red-hot lava. Seven 18-hole golf courses blanket the Big Island's Kona/Kohala Coast alone. Golf is now an important attraction in Hawaii and serious business. Golf employs more people here than do sugar and pineapple—2,870 people in all, including 240 golf pros. Last year, visitors and residents played more than 4.8 million rounds of golf.

Best and Most Challenging Courses in Hawaii

Koolau Golf Course, Oahu

"The toughest golf course in America," according to *Men's Journal,* was originally built as a private club for Tokyo high-rollers. But Koolau Golf Course on the Windward side opened to the public after the global recession pinched Japan. The 7,310-yard, par 72 course with a slope rating of 155 was designed by Dick Nugent. It offers "demoralizing" hazards like ravines, monster bunkers, a jungle of foliage, and a lone mango tree that blocks the tiny landing approach to the 18th hole, a 474-yard par 4.

Ko Olina Golf Club, Oahu

The par 72, 18-hole Ted Robinson Ko Olina Golf Club course beckons at Ko Olina Resort on Oahu's western shore. This wide-open course abounds with lakes, ponds, brooks, and waterfalls. The par 5 fifth hole is rated most difficult. It plays 528 yards to a small narrow neck green guarded by a pond full of black swans.

Gold Course at Wailea Resort, Maui

Three championship courses distinguish Wailea Resort in South Maui: the newer Gold and Emerald courses, as well as the par 72, 18-hole Blue course, considered the Grand Lady of Wailea. *Golf for Women* magazine recently named the Wailea Golf Club one of the three most women-friendly golf facilities in the country. The Gold course at Wailea gilds the lily on this island already noted for great courses. This Robert Trent Jones Jr. course is a rugged, natural-style 7,070-yard, par 72 layout that plays over the foothills of 10,023-foot Mt. Haleakala.

Kapalua Resort, Maui

Surrounded by a pineapple plantation on Maui's northwest coast, Kapalua Resort's 1,500 tidy acres include three of the world's most beautiful and challenging 18-hole courses—the Village, Bay, and Plantation courses.

The par 3 fifth hole on the Bay course gives everyone butterflies; it's a 205-yard-long shot across Oneloa Bay from the back tees. With the nearly constant wind at your back, you may dodge the surf but hit the bunkers that shield the green's front, back, and right sides.

The Challenge at Manele and the Experience at Koele, Lanai

Lanai may have more deer than people, but it boasts two stunning resort golf courses—the Experience at Koele and the Challenge at Manele. The Jack Nicklaus–designed Challenge is a target-style course carved from lava cliffs by the sea. The water hazard on the par 3, signature 12th hole at Manele is a wave-lashed coast of jagged lava. This course on the south coast of Lanai will test your patience and increase your impolite vocabulary. Or face the Experience's signature hole, which plays into a ravine from a knoll 250 feet above the fairway of this upland course. The layout begins high on the slopes of 3,366-foot Mt. Lanaihale, complete with Norfolk pine forest and a gallery of deer, pheasant, and wild turkey. Designed by Greg Norman and Ted Robinson, this course features the only bentgrass greens in Hawaii.

Hapuna Prince Course, The Big Island

Native grasslands and wild flowers cover old lava flows that rumple the layout of this environmentally aware 18-hole golf course above the Kohala

Coast. Designed by Arnold Palmer and Ed Seay, Hapuna is a 6,875-yard, par 72 course that makes extensive use of the rugged terrain (it stretches from the shore to 700 feet above sea level). One of *Golf* magazine's top ten new golf courses in the United States when it opened, Hapuna was cited for environmental sensitivity and called "the course of the future."

Hualalai Golf Course, Kaupulehu, The Big Island

Jack Nicklaus was among the first to tee off on Hualalai, his par 72, 18-hole PGA championship course carved out of black lava on the Kona Coast. He made it look so easy. You can play this course only if you are a guest at the new Four Seasons Resort Hualalai or a resident of Hawaii's newest, most exclusive golf retreat.

Mauna Lani, The Big Island

If the Smithsonian Institution ever seeks a golf course for its collection, Mauna Lani is a likely candidate. Set in black lava beside the blue Pacific, this course is, thanks to man and nature, a work of art. Carved from nineteenth-century lava flows, the two 18-hole Francis H. Ii Brown North and South courses feature two striking ocean holes that challenge pros and amateurs who try to beat the records of Arnold Palmer, Lee Trevino, and Raymond Floyd. The signature sixth hole, a 199-yard par 3, is a seascape portrait of lush greens, azure sea, charcoal lava, and gold sand all under a vivid blue sky.

Princeville Resort, Kauai

When designer Robert Trent Jones Jr. first saw the plateau on Kauai's North Shore that would become Princeville's golf links, he said he became "truly nervous." It's a reaction most golfers have today when they tee off at Princeville. With its awesome setting above scenic Hanalei Bay and challenging holes (the 205-yard, par 3 seventh tee addresses a wide-mouthed gorge), the Prince course is rated by some as the most difficult in Hawaii. The famed 27-hole Makai course, one of the top 100 courses in the United States, features three separate nines: the Ocean, the Woods, and the Lake; the Ocean/Lake combo is the most popular.

Golf, Your Way

Hawaii's famous courses are high on the life-lists of most players who plan their vacations around golf. It's a passion fanned by sunny scenes in televised winter tournaments from resorts like Kapalua, where the water feature might be a humpback in the background, or fabled Mauna Kea and Mauna Lani on the Big Island, with their implausible green-on-lava oases under the volcanoes. When you've got that dream, nothing else will satisfy it. However, golf in Hawaii isn't necessarily an expensive indulgence. Hawaii residents who can't afford world-class resort greens fees are equally hooked on the game, and they play golf year-round as often as possible. The Islands' resort, municipal, public, military, semiprivate, and private courses, running the gamut of designers, challenges, layouts, and expense, share a measure of distracting natural beauty.

Devoted golfers will no doubt have a course in mind when they choose where to stay. If you just want to play some golf in Hawaii and not base your vacation around it, be your own concierge and make your own arrangements, so that you can choose the time and place you want to play and the fees you want to pay. Hotels will recommend their neighboring courses to keep their guests close to home. That may be exactly what you had in mind, because fees are lower and tee times often more readily available to resort guests. Plenty of them offer package rates for room, car, and golf with other extras thrown in. If you want to roam, your options include some enticing public and municipal courses—the perennially top-ranked Wailua municipal course on Kauai, for instance—where great golf experiences may cost half the fees of resort courses. Think how top-this options, like the Volcano course at 4,000 feet on the edge of Kilauea, or the historic jewel of a plantation course at Ironwood Hills on Molokai, will play later at your local clubhouse.

Here are some helpful resources:

- The Aloha Section PGA annual directory of Hawaii's golf courses. Call (808) 593-2230 to receive the free guide.
- *Maui Golf Review,* a free monthly golf guide with reliable and well-researched information, at www.mauigolfreview.net or call (808) 874-8300.
- *Discover Hawaii's Best Golf,* an 86-page book by golf writer George Fuller. Issued in 1999 by Island Heritage Publishing, this volume provides vivid descriptions and photos of the state's top courses.

Tee times are usually easy to reserve; the busiest times are weekends and winter tourist season. Oahu has the biggest crowd of golfers and the most competition for bookings. Your hopes may be dashed at that course right across the canal from Waikiki: Ala Wai Golf Course is the busiest in the nation. Koolau Golf Club, on the other side of the mountains, is considered the most difficult course in the nation, according to *Men's Journal.*

Most courses allow you to request a tee time at least a few days in advance. If you're looking for a last-minute tee time, try **Stand-By Golf,** which gives visitors a discount. The company makes a small margin on each booking, you get discounted rates, and the course managers are happy to fill in empty time slots. Call (808) 922-2665.

Shorts are acceptable attire on Hawaiian courses. Collared shirts are often required and a good idea anyway to avoid sunburn on the back of your neck. Soft-spiked shoes are the latest trend.

GREENS FEES	
Based on one 18-hole round, with or without cart:	
Resort Courses $110–$200	**Semiprivate Courses** $25–$135
Private Courses $50–$100	**Public Courses** $14–$135
Municipal Courses $42–$54	**Military Courses** $9–$40

Top Picks among Golf Courses in Hawaii

Oahu

Ala Wai Golf Course — *Zone 1 Waikiki*

Established 1931

Location 404 Kapahulu Avenue, Honolulu, HI 96815 (mauka of the Ala Wai Canal; the entrance is on the right off Kapahulu Avenue)

Phone (808) 733-7387

Status Municipal, 18 holes, par 70

Tees *Men's:* 5,861 yards. *Ladies'* 5,095 yards.

Fees $42 daily. Cart: $14. Accepts tee times a week in advance. Accepts VISA, MC

Facilities Driving range lit for night play, pro shop, and restaurant. Club rentals available

Comments Busiest municipal course in the United States, averaging more than 500 rounds of golf per day. Hawaii's oldest municipal course and local favorite underwent a face-lift in the late 1980s. This is a flat course with some hilly mounds around the greens. The Ala Wai Canal comes into play on three holes. Collared shirts required, no cut-offs.

Coral Creek Golf Course — *Zone 5 Leeward Oahu*

Established 1999

Location 91-1111 Geiger Road, Ewa Beach, HI 96706 (Head west on H-1 to Ewa Beach. Take Fort Weaver Road and turn left on Geiger Road.)

Phone (808) 441-4653

Status Public, 18 holes, par 72

Tees *Championship* (coral tees): 6,870 yards, (gold tees): 6,480 yards. *Men's* (blue tees): 6,025 yards. *Ladies'* (red tees): 5,412 yards.

Fees $125. Includes cart. Special $75 twilight rate available after noon. Club rentals: $30. Accepts tee times after the 15th of each month, for the following month. Accepts VISA, MC, AmEx, JCB, and DC

Facilities Driving range, putting green, practice area, pro shop, clubhouse, restaurant, beverage carts, and locker room with showers

Comments Oahu's newest course. Water comes into play on 13 holes, and 6 are lined with coral reefs and interconnected by a coral creek. The signature Hole 18 is a short, 381-yard par 4 that demands a precise downhill approach to an island green.

Hawaii Kai Golf Course — *Zone 2 Honolulu*

Established 1973

Location 8902 Kalanianaole Highway, Honolulu, HI 96825 (From Waikiki, drive east on Kalanianaole Highway past Hawaii Kai commerce. The course is on the left side shortly after Sandy Beach Park.)

Phone (808) 395-2358

Website www.hawaiikaigolf.com

Status Public, 18 holes, par 72 (Championship); 18 holes, par 54 (Executive)

Tees *Championship:* 6,614 yards. *Men's:* 6,222 yards (Championship), 2,116 yards (Executive). *Ladies':* 5,591 yards (Championship), 1,896 yards (Executive).

Fees Championship course: $90 weekdays, $100 weekends. Includes cart. Executive course: $37 weekdays, $42 weekends for 18 holes. $32.75 weekdays, $37.75 weekends for 9 holes. Accepts tee times a week in advance. Accepts VISA, MC, D

Facilities Driving range, putting green, pro shop, and restaurant. Club rentals available

Comments Championship course at the base of Koko Head Crater includes two hidden lakes and large greens. Breezy tradewinds raise the difficulty level a notch. The Executive course, a long par 3 course designed by Robert Trent Jones Sr., is ideal for beginners. Collared shirts required.

Hawaii Prince Golf Club — *Zone 5 Leeward Oahu*

Established 1992

Location 91-1200 Fort Weaver Road, Ewa Beach, HI 96706 (Head westbound on H-1, take Exit 5A, and make a left after the sixth traffic light into the club's parking lot.)

Phone (808) 944-4567

Website www.princehawaii.com

Status Resort, 27 holes, par 36

Tees *Championship* (blue tees): A and B courses: 5,759 yards; B and C courses: 6,801 yards; C and A courses: 6,746 yards. *Men's* (orange tees): A and B courses: 6,237 yards; B and C courses: 6,175 yards; C and A courses: 6,274 yards. *Ladies'* (white tees): A and B courses: 5,275 yards; B and C courses: 5,205 yards; C and A courses: 5,300 yards.

Fees $135. $90 for Prince Hotel guests. Special $50 twilight rate ($40 for hotel guests) after 2 p.m. on weekdays, 2:30 p.m. on weekends. Includes cart. Club rentals: $35. Accepts tee times 14 days in advance. Accepts VISA, MC, AmEx

Facilities Driving range, putting greens, pro shop, locker rooms with showers, tennis courts, clubhouse, and restaurant

Comments Three 9-hole courses are played in three 18-hole combinations, providing tremendous replay value. A total of 90 sand bunkers and 10 lakes adorns the 270-acre courses, which were designed by Arnold Palmer and Ed Seay. This course is built on land formerly used for growing sugarcane. It's suitable for novice and above-average players.

Hickam Golf Course — *Zone 6 Central Oahu*

Established 1966

Location 900 Hangar Avenue, Hickam AFB, HI 96853 (Take the H-1 westbound and follow the signs to Hickam Air Force Base. The sentry will provide directions to the course.)

Phone (808) 449-6490

Status Military, 18 holes, par 72

Tees *Championship:* 6,868 yards. *Men's:* 6,412 yards. *Ladies':* 5,675 yards.

Fees Civilian with military sponsor: $40.50 with cart, $32 without cart. Relative or guest of military: $27.50 with cart, $20 without cart. All rates are half-price after 3:30 p.m. Accepts tee times 3 days in advance. Accepts VISA, MC

Facilities Driving range, putting green, chipping area, practice bunker, pro shop, clubhouse, restaurant, and locker rooms with showers

Comments This is one of the better military courses in the state and one of the busiest in the nation. Lit for night play and surrounded by water. The signature Hole 2 demands a solid tee shot onto a fairway that juts out over water. Collared shirts required; no denim.

Kapolei Golf Course — *Zone 5 Leeward Oahu*

Established 1996

Location 91-701 Farrington Highway, Kapolei, HI 96707 (Head west on H-1, take the Makaha exit, turn left on Makakilo. At the first light, turn left on Farrington Highway. The course is about a mile ahead on the right.)

Phone (808) 674-2227

Status Public, 18 holes, par 72

Tees *Gold:* 7,001 yards. *Championship:* 6,586 yards. *Men's:* 6,136 yards. *Ladies':* 5,490 yards.

Fees $70 weekdays, $90 weekends and holidays. Includes cart. Special $35 twilight rate available on weekdays after 1:30 p.m. (Monday–Wednesday) and 2:30 p.m. (Thursday–Friday). Club rentals: $30. Accepts tee times 7 days in advance. Accepts VISA, MC, AmEx, D

Facilities Driving range, putting green, chipping area, practice bunker, pro shop, and restaurant

Comments Built as a centerpiece for Oahu's ambitious "Second City" development plan. This is a well-contoured, immaculately manicured course, the site of the LPGA's Hawaiian Ladies Open. Water hazards often come into play. The course was designed by noted golf architect Ted Robinson. Collared shirts required.

Ko Olina Golf Club — *Zone 5 Leeward Oahu*

Established 1990

Location 92-220 Aliinui Drive, Ewa Beach, HI 96707 (Head west on H-1; take the Ko Olina exit. The exit loops around to the course.)

Phone (808) 676-5300

Website www.koolinagolf.com

Status Resort, 18 holes, par 72

Tees *Championship:* 6,867 yards. *Men's:* 6,450 yards. *Ladies':* 5,392 yards.

Fees $150. $100 for Ihilani Resort guests. Includes cart. Special twilight rate ($75 for 18 holes, $45 for 9 holes) after 2:30 p.m. Club rentals: $30–$40. Accepts tee times a week in advance. Accepts VISA, MC, AmEx, D

Facilities Driving range, practice area, pro shop, restaurant, and a locker room with showers, steam rooms, and Jacuzzi

Comments Brisk winds make for challenging play. This course is considered to be one of Ted Robinson's best designs. Water hazards pop up throughout the course, including waterfalls, lakes, and ponds. Greens are split-level and multitiered. The course's signature 18th hole—featuring a waterfall to the right of the tee area, spilling into a lake surrounding the green—is a tough finishing hole. Collared shirts required.

Koolau Golf Club — *Zone 3 Windward Oahu*

Established 1992

Location 45-550 Kionaole Road, Kaneohe, HI 96744 (Take Pali Highway toward Kailua, turn left on Kamehameha Highway and then make a left on Kionaole Road. The entrance to the course is on the left.)

Phone (808) 247-7088

Website www.koolaugolfclub.com

Status Public, 18 holes, par 72

Tees *Tournament* (black tees): 7,310 yards. *Championship* (gold tees): 6,797 yards. *Men's* (blue tees): 6,406 yards. *Ladies'* (white tees): 5,102 yards.

Fees $125 daily. Special $75 twilight rate available after 1 p.m. Fees include cart. Club rentals: $35. Accepts tee times up to 30 days in advance. Accepts VISA, MC, and AmEx

Facilities Driving range, putting green, chipping range, snack bar, and pro shop

Comments This is considered the most difficult course in the United States, even though water comes into play on only one hole. The first hole is a 593-yard par 5. The 18th requires a tee shot over a wide ravine with a precipitous sand trap running the length of the fairway on the right. Exceptionally scenic course, in very high demand. Collared shirts required.

The Links at Kuilima — *Zone 4 The North Shore*

Established 1992

Location 57-049 Kuilima Drive, Kahuku, HI 96731 (Head west on H-1, exit onto H-2 Freeway, and stay to the right. Take the Wahiawa exit and stay right to Kamehameha Highway; the course is about a half-hour away.)

Phone (808) 293-8574

Status Resort, 18 holes, par 72

Tees *Men's:* 7,200 yards. *Ladies':* 4,851 yards.

Fees $125. $75 for guests of the Turtle Bay Hilton at Kuilima or Hilton Hawaiian Village in Waikiki. Includes cart. Special $65 ($45 for Hilton guests) twilight rate on weekdays. Club rentals: $30. Accepts tee times 14 days in advance. Accepts VISA, MC, AmEx, D

Facilities Driving range, putting greens, pro shop, and snack bar

Comments Designed by golf legends Arnold Palmer and Ed Seay. This is a tough course because of strong tradewinds and plentiful sand traps. Though the course is near the ocean, only one hole (the 17th) provides close views of the surf. Several holes skirt a marine wildlife sanctuary. The back nine are the most scenic. *Golf* magazine ranked the course as one of the top ten new courses in the United States; *Golf Digest* ranked it fourth among the new resort courses when it opened. No tank tops or cutoffs.

Luana Hills Country Club — *Zone 3 Windward Oahu*

Established 1994

Location 770 Auloa Road, Kailua, HI 96734 (Pali Highway, toward Kailua. After the third stoplight, turn right onto Auloa and then take an immediate left on the winding road to the course.)

Phone (808) 262-2139

Website www.luanahills.com

Status Semiprivate, 18 holes, par 72

Tees *Championship* (black tees): 6,595 yards. *Championship* (blue tees): 6,164 yards. *Men's* (white tees): 5,522 yards. *Ladies'* (yellow tees): 4,654 yards.

Fees Every day, $109 plus tax. Accepts VISA, MC

Facilities Driving range, putting greens, pro shop, locker rooms with showers and Jacuzzi, restaurant, and cocktail lounge

Comments This course is a growing favorite among residents and visitors, so scenic that the city is talking about making it a park. The front nine is carved into the side of Mount Olomana, and the back nine take you through a tropical rain forest. The par 3 11th hole is a scenic masterpiece dominated by a picturesque pond.

Makaha Resort Golf Club — *Zone 5 Leeward Oahu*

Established 1969

Location 84-626 Makaha Valley Road, Waianae, HI 96792 (Head west on Farrington Highway, turn right at Makaha Valley Road, and turn left at the fork.)

Phone (808) 695-9544

Website www.makaharesortgolfclub.com

Status Resort, 18 holes, par 72

Tees *Championship:* 7,077 yards. *Men's:* 6,414 yards. *Ladies':* 5,856 yards.

Fees $125. $115 for guests of Waikiki hotels. Includes cart. Special $85 twilight rate after noon. Club rentals: $20. Accepts tee times 14 days in advance. Accepts VISA, MC, AmEx, D

Facilities Driving range, putting green, chipping area, clubhouse, and restaurant

Comments Formerly the Sheraton Makaha Golf Club. A favorite challenging course offering spectacular views, especially at sunset. Course overlooks the ocean; the back nine play into Makaha Valley. Winds blow down the valley toward the ocean. The par 4 18th hole is one of the most challenging holes on the island, with two bunkers to the left of the fairway, water on the right, and another water hazard fronting the green. Collared shirts required; no denim. Bring a light jacket to be prepared for frequent light rain in the valley.

Pearl Country Club — *Zone 6 Central Oahu*

Established 1967

Location 98-535 Kaonohi Street, Aiea, HI 96701 (West on H-1, take Pearlridge exit, and make a right. Turn right on Kaonohi Street. The entrance is on the right.)

Phone (808) 487-3802

Website www.pearlcc.com

Status Public, 18 holes, par 72

Tees *Championship:* 6,787 yards. *Men's:* 6,232 yards. *Ladies':* 5,536 yards.

Fees $65 weekdays, $70 weekends. Includes cart. Twilight rates: $48 2–3 p.m. and $30 after 3 p.m. 9-hole twilight rate: $20. Club rentals: $30. Accepts tee times 60 days in advance. Accepts VISA, MC, AmEx

Facilities Driving range (lit for night play), pro shop, and locker room with showers

Comments Older, hilly course that remains popular, especially among residents. Difficult lies provide a good challenge. Overlooks Pearl Harbor and the USS *Arizona* Memorial. No tank tops or cut-offs.

Maui

The Dunes at Maui Lani — *Zone 8 South Maui*

Established 1999

Location 1333 Mauilani Parkway, Kahului, HI 96732 (From the Kahului Airport, head toward Lahaina on Dairy Road until you hit Kuihelani Highway 380. The course is 1.5 miles off to the right. The entrance is marked by green flags.)

Phone (808) 873-0422

Website www.dunesatmauilani.com

Status Public, 18 holes, par 72

Tees *Championship:* 6,840 yards. Blue: 6,413 yards. White: 5,833 yards. Red: 4,768 yards.

Fees $98, includes cart; twilight fees, $60 after 2 p.m. Club rentals, $30. Accepts tee times up to 3 months in advance; check cancellation policy. Accepts VISA, MC, AmEx

Facilities Driving range, 15-acre practice facility, putting greens, clubhouse, pro shop, and restaurant

Comments Maui's newest and most surprising course is an Irish linksland–style course incorporating natural sand dunes not on the coast, where Maui has none, but inland, where the sea left them a million or so years ago in a valley. Architect Robin Nelson took advantage of ancient dunes up to 80 feet high to provide drama on several holes. His layout requires thought when playing. There is a peek of the sea now and then, but it's mostly rolling terrain with a forest of thorny kiawe trees. Instead, the killer views are of towering Haleakala. The short par 3 third hole is a classic dune hole fashioned after the sixth at Lahinch in Ireland. The course anchors a residential planned development.

Elleair Maui Golf Course — *Zone 8 South Maui*

Established 1987

Location 1345 Piilani Highway, Kihei, HI 96753 (mauka, or uphill, side of Highway 31 in Kihei)

Phone (808) 874-0777

Website www.elleairmauiresorts.com

Status Public, 18 holes, par 71

Tees *Championship:* 6,801 yards. *Men's:* 6,404 yards. *Ladies':* 6,003 yards.

Fees $59; twilight special after 1 p.m., $45. Carts included. Club rentals: $30. Accepts tee times 30 days in advance

Facilities Driving range, night lit, pro shop, and restaurant

Comments Morning and late afternoon tradewinds usually hit the course, and many holes bring the winds into play. Views of the sea are afforded from most of the greens on this public course. The ninth hole is a long par 4 with a pond on the right side.

Kaanapali Golf Courses — *Zone 9 West Maui*

Established 1962 (North), 1997 (South)

Location 2290 Kaanapali Parkway, Kaanapali Resort, Lahaina, HI 96761 (Take Highway 30 past Lahaina to Kaanapali Beach Resort. Turn left at the first entrance of the golf course.)

Phone (808) 661-3691

Website www.kaanapali-golf.com

Status Resort, 18 holes, par 71 (for both courses)

Tees *Men's:* North: 6,994 yards; South: 6,555 yards. *Ladies':* North: 5,417 yards; South: 5,485 yards.

Fees $130; less for resort guests. Includes cart. Special $80 twilight rate (South course only) noon–2:30 p.m. Twilight rate (both courses) after 2:30 p.m.: $65. Repeat rounds: $42. Club rentals: $30 ($20 twilight rate). Accepts tee times 2 days in advance. Accepts VISA, MC, AmEx

Facilities Driving range, putting green, pro shop, restaurant, and locker room with showers

Comments Two excellent 18-hole courses. The 18th on the North course is one of Hawaii's toughest finishing holes, with water hazards lined up on the right side and the kidney shaped green bordered by two treacherous bunkers on the left. The shorter South course, with more forgiving greens and wider fairways, is the likely preference for less experienced golfers. The North hosts the annual Kaanapali Classic, a Senior PGA Tour event.

Kapalua Golf Club — *Zone 9 West Maui*

Established 1975 (Bay), 1980 (Village), 1991 (Plantation)

Location 300 Kapalua Drive, Kapalua, HI 96761 (Take Highway 30 past Lahaina and Kaanapali to Kapalua Resort; turn left at Kapalua Drive.)

Phone Bay course: (808) 669-8804; Plantation course: (808) 669-0507; Village course: (808) 669-7715

Status Resort. Bay course: 54 holes, par 72; Village course: 18 holes, par 71; Plantation course: 18 holes, par 73

Tees *Men's:* Bay: 6,600 yards; Village: 6,282 yards; Plantation: 7,263 yards. *Ladies':* Bay: 5,124 yards; Village: 4,876 yards; Plantation: 5,627 yards.

Fees $180, $125 for resort guests. Includes cart. Twilight special: All rates are half off after 2 p.m. Club rentals: $35–$45. Accepts tee times 4 days in advance. Accepts VISA, MC, AmEx, D

Facilities Driving range, putting green, pro shop, clubhouse, and restaurants

Comments These three courses are among Maui's best, providing gorgeous views at every turn. The Village course features elevated tee shots on many holes, and the 367-yard, par 4 Hole 6 is one of the most scenic in Hawaii, with stately pines lined up toward the ocean. The Bay course's Hole 5 is one of the world's most dramatic signature holes, requiring a tee shot over Oneloa Bay. The links-style Plantation course, highly regarded by many pros, is the home of the PGA Tour's Mercedes Championships. No tank tops or cut-offs.

Makena Resort Golf Club — *Zone 8 South Maui*

Established 1983 (split into two separate courses in 1994)

Location 5415 Makena Alanui, Makena, HI 96753 (From Kahului Airport, take Dairy Road to Piilani Highway, turn right at the end, then left at the stop sign on Wailua Alanui and go south past Wailea. The entrance is on the left.)

Phone (808) 879-3344

Website www.makenagolf.com

Status Resort, 18 holes, par 72 (for both courses)

Tees *Championship:* North: 6,500 yards; South: 6,600 yards. *Men's:* North: 6,100 yards; South: 6,200 yards. *Ladies':* North: 5,300 yards; South: 5,500 yards.

Fees $175. Includes cart. Special $100 twilight rate available from 1 p.m. Club rentals: $45. Accepts tee times 3 days in advance. Accepts VISA, MC, AmEx

Facilities Practice range, putting green, pro shop, and locker room with showers

Comments Located by the Maui Prince Hotel. Both courses are among the state's best, with views of the ocean, Haleakala, and Molokai, Lanai, and Kahoolawe. This course was designed by noted golf architect Robert Trent Jones Jr. Severe slopes and fast greens make for very challenging play. The lack of strong winds at Makena is a big plus. The South Course's 15th and 16th holes are among Hawaii's most picturesque oceanfront holes. The North course is generally considered the more difficult of the two courses.

Sandalwood Golf Course — *Zone 8 South Maui*

Established 1991

Location 2500 Honoapiilani Highway, Wailuku, HI 96793 (Turn uphill off Highway 30, just south of Wailuku.)

Phone (808) 242-4653

Website www.sandalwoodgolf.com

Status Resort, 18 holes, par 72

Tees *Championship:* 6,433 yards. *Men's:* 5,918 yards. *Ladies':* 5,162 yards.

Fees $80, carts included. Golf Program participants, $70. Club rentals, $35

Facilities Driving range, pro shop, banquet facility, locker rooms, clubhouse, putting and chipping greens, and restaurant

Comments Robin Nelson and Rodney Wright designed this layout among sandalwood trees at Waikapu, nestled into the side of the West Maui Mountains overlooking Maui's isthmus of green cane fields. Sloping fairways and hefty tradewinds can make for a challenging day, along with a lot of elevated greens and par 4s that are long, straight, and into the wind.

Waiehu Golf Course — *Zone 7 Central Maui*

Established 9-hole course opened in 1933; back 9 added in 1966

Location P.O. Box 507, Wailuku, HI 96793 (From Highway 340, make a right just past Waihee Park. The entrance is on the right.)

Phone (808) 244-5934

Status Municipal, 18 holes, par 72 (par 73 for women)

Tees *Men's:* 6,330 yards. *Ladies':* 5,555 yards.

Fees $26 weekdays, $30 weekends and holidays. Cart: $8 per person. Club rentals: $15. Accepts tee times 2 days in advance. Accepts VISA, MC

Facilities Driving range, putting green, pro shop, clubhouse, and restaurant

Comments Maui's only municipal course. The front nine are relatively flat, whereas the back nine are hilly in spots. This course features one lake and more than 40 sand bunkers. Three holes front the ocean. The signature, par 5 Hole 7 plays along the beach.

Wailea Golf Club — *Zone 8 South Maui*

Established 1972 (Blue), 1993 (Gold), 1995 (Emerald)

Location 100 Wailea Golf Club Drive, Wailea, HI 96753 (From Kahului Airport, take Dairy Road to Piilani Highway, drive to southern end of the road and turn right. At the stop sign, turn left on Wailea Alanui.)

Phone Gold and Emerald courses: (808) 875-7450; Blue course: (808) 875-5155

Status Resort, 18 holes, par 72 (all 3 courses)

Tees *Championship:* Gold: 7,078 yards; Emerald: 6,825 yards; Blue: 6,758 yards. *Men's:* Gold: 6,653 yards; Emerald: 6,407 yards; Blue: 6,152 yards. *Ladies':* Gold: 5,442 yards; Emerald: 5,268 yards; Blue: 5,291 yards.

Fees Gold and Emerald: $160, $135 for Wailea Resort guests. Blue: $145, $120 for resort guests. Includes cart. Club rentals: $50. Accepts tee times 5 days in advance. Accepts VISA, MC, AmEx, D

Facilities Driving range, putting greens, pro shop, and restaurant

Comments All three courses have breathtaking ocean and mountain views. The Blue course, with wide, open fairways, is the easiest, but it does have 74 bunkers and 4 water hazards. The Gold course, featuring ancient lava rock walls, ranked as one of *Golf* magazine's ten best new courses in 1993. The Emerald course offers stunning views of Haleakala and the Pacific and is considered a friendlier course for high-handicap players. Its signature hole is the 18th, a 553-yard par 5 challenge with a downhill slope. Collared shirts required.

The Big Island of Hawaii

Hapuna Golf Course — *Zone 11 Kona*

Established 1992

Location 62-100 Kaunaoa Drive, Kohala Coast, HI 96743 (From Kona, drive north along Highway 19 past Waikoloa until you see the roads leading to the Hapuna Beach Prince Hotel on the left. Drive a bit farther; the golf course is on the right.)

Phone (808) 882-1035

Status Resort, 18 holes, par 72

Tees *Tournament:* 6,875 yards. *Championship:* 6,534 yards. *Men's:* 6,029 yards. *Ladies':* 5,067 yards.

Fees $145. $110 for resort guests. Includes cart. Special twilight rate available after 3 p.m. Club rentals: $40. Accepts tee times 2 days in advance. Accepts VISA, MC, AmEx

Facilities Driving range, putting green, pro shop, clubhouse, and restaurant

Comments This is a sister course to Mauna Kea Golf Course. The demanding links-style course is set amid arid lava flows, natural vegetation, and spectacular scenery. Water hazards come into play on four holes. The front nine play into the winds that blow down from Mauna Kea. The 545-yard, par 5 Hole 3 is regarded as one of the best par 5s in the state, with wide expanses, an imposing ravine, a lake, and a series of bunkers. This is another Arnold Palmer–Ed Seay collaboration. Golfers share the course with several endangered bird species, including the nene goose, Hawaii's state bird. Unquestionably, this is one of the Big Island's best. Collared shirts required; no denim.

Hilo Municipal Golf Course — *Zone 12 Hilo and Volcano*

Established 1951

Location 340 Haihai Street, Hilo, HI 96720 (From Hilo, head south on Highway 11, past the Prince Kuhio Plaza. Turn right on Puainako Street, left on Kilauea Avenue, then right on Haihai Street.)

Phone (808) 959-7711

Status Municipal, 18 holes, par 71

Tees *Championship:* 6,325 yards. *Men's:* 6,006 yards. *Ladies':* 5,034 yards.

Fees $20 weekdays, $25 weekends. Cart: $14.50 for 18 holes, $8 for 9 holes. Club rentals: $10. Accepts tee times 7 days in advance

Facilities Driving range, pro shop, and restaurant

Comments The Big Island's municipal course features flat, tree-lined fairways with no sand traps but plenty of water hazards in the form of streams and lakes. This is a good course for average players. Light rains are frequent in Hilo, so pack an umbrella.

Hualalai Golf Club — *Zone 11 Kona*

Established 1996

Location 100 Kaupulehu Drive, Kaupulehu, HI 96740 (Take Mamalahoa Highway. Hualalai Resort and the golf course are just 5 minutes north of the airport.)

Phone (808) 325-8480

Status Private, 18 holes, par 72

Tees *Championship:* 7,117 yards. *Men's:* 6,632 yards. *Ladies':* 5,374 yards.

Fees $160, cart included. Only Hualalai homeowners or guests staying at the Four Seasons Resort Hualalai may play. Club rentals: $50. Accepts tee times up to 90 days in advance. Accepts VISA, MC, AmEx, DC

Facilities Driving range, putting greens, practice area, clubhouse, snack bar, and restaurant

Comments Designed by Jack Nicklaus, this beautiful course is the home of the PGA Senior Tour's Tournament of Champions. The 172-yard, par 3 Hole 17 is the signature hole, with an expansive green that demands precise pin placement. The golf club is the first in Hawaii to be designated an official PGA Tour facility.

Kona Country Club — *Zone 11 Kona*

Established 1985 (Kona), 1991 (Alii)

Location 78-7000 Alii Drive, Kailua-Kona, HI 96740 (From the Kona Airport, drive south on Highway 11, then turn right down Alii Drive. The course is located near the end of the road.)

Phone (808) 322-2595

Website www.konagolf.com

Status Resort, 27 holes, par 72 (for both courses)

Tees *Championship:* Ocean course: 6,579 yards; Mountain course: 6,671 yards. *Men's:* Ocean course: 6,155 yards; Mountain course: 5,828 yards. *Ladies':* Ocean course: 5,499 yards; Mountain course: 4,906 yards.

Fees $130 Ocean, $110 Mountain. Includes cart. Special twilight rate available after 12:30 p.m. Club rentals: $40. Accepts tee times 3 days in advance. Accepts VISA, MC, AmEx

Facilities Driving range, putting green, pro shop, restaurant, and lounge

Comments The Ocean course is a friendly course for golfers in need of a confidence boost, with wide fairways and easy greens. Much of the course hugs the Pacific, with particularly gorgeous vistas from Holes 11–13. The Mountain course, however, has more hazards and tricky hillside lies. The signature 7th hole is a downhill par 4 (438 yards) that plays straight into the wind and requires a tee shot over a water hazard.

Mauna Kea Golf Course — *Zone 11 Kona*

Established 1964

Location 62-100 Mauna Kea Beach Drive, Kohala Coast, HI 96743 (From Kona, drive north on Highway 19 to the Mauna Kea Resort entrance on the left.)

Phone (808) 882-5400

Website www.maunakearesort.com

Status Resort, 18 holes, par 72

Tees *Tournament:* 7,114 yards. *Championship:* 6,737 yards. *Men's:* 6,365 yards. *Ladies':* 5,277 yards.

Fees $195. $130 for resort guests. Includes cart. Special $145 ($110 for resort guests) twilight rate available after 3 p.m. Club rentals: $40. Accepts tee times 2 days in advance. Accepts VISA, MC, AmEx

Facilities Driving range, putting green, pro shop, and restaurant

Comments The first course to be designed using a lava-strewn landscape, this Robert Trent Jones Sr. course is a perennial favorite, although it is quite demanding. The signature hole, the 210-yard, par 3 Hole 3, requires a tee shot over 180 yards of ocean to reach the green. Jones himself rated this hole one of his all-time favorites. The course remains one of Hawaii's top layouts. Collared shirts required.

Mauna Lani Resort — *Zone 11 Kona*

Established 1981 (North), 1991 (split into 2 courses, adding South)

Location 68-1310 Mauna Lani Drive, Kohala Coast, HI 96743 (From Kona, drive north on Highway 19 and turn left at Mauna Lani Drive. The golf course is on the left.)

Phone (808) 885-6655

Website www.maunalani.com

Status Resort, 18 holes, par 72 (for both courses)

Tees *Championship:* North: 6,913 yards; South: 6,938 yards. *Men's:* North: 6,601 yards (blue tees), 6,086 yards; South: 6,436 yards (blue tees), 5,940 yards. *Ladies':* North: 5,383 yards; South: 5,028 yards.

Fees $185. $95 for resort guests. Includes cart. Special $75 twilight rate available from 2 p.m. Club rentals: $35. Accepts tee times 5 days in advance. Accepts VISA, MC, AmEx, D

Facilities Driving range, putting green, pro shop, clubhouse, and restaurant

Comments Both courses have spectacular visual appeal and play. The North course, blessed with rolling terrain and thickets of kiawe trees, is the longer course and requires more strategy off the tee. The 140-yard, par 3 Hole 17 is its signature hole, where your tee shot carries from an elevated tee to (hopefully) a green framed by black lava. The South's signature hole, the 196-yard, par 3 Hole 15, requires a bold tee shot over crashing surf. During the winter, the 15th may feature another distraction: humpback whales, often spotted in the deep waters. Collared shirts required.

Sea Mountain Golf Course — *Zone 12 Hilo and Volcano*

Established 1974

Location P.O. Box 190, Pahala, HI 96777 (Drive south from Hilo on Highway 11 to Mile Marker 56. The course is on the left.)

Phone (808) 928-6222

Status Resort, 18 holes, par 72

Tees *Championship:* 6,492 yards. *Men's:* 6,106 yards. *Ladies':* 5,663 yards.

Fees $42 weekdays, $45 weekends. Guests of Sea Mountain Golf Course Colony Condominiums receive $10 discount. Includes cart. Club rentals: $25. Accepts tee times 3 days in advance. Accepts VISA, MC

Facilities Driving range, putting green, pro shop, and restaurant

Comments The front nine here line a picturesque beach, and the back nine are set against a mountain. Beautiful views from everywhere on the course.

Volcano Golf and Country Club *Zone 12 Hilo and Volcano*

Established 1922 (as 9-hole course); expanded and redesigned in 1967

Location Hawaii Volcanoes National Park, HI 96718 (From Hilo, drive past the Hawaii Volcanoes National Park, and look for Mile Marker 30. Turn right on Golf Course Road.)

Phone (808) 967-8228

Website www.volcanogolfshop.com

Status Public, 18 holes, par 72

Tees *Championship:* 6,503 yards. *Men's:* 6,180 yards. *Ladies':* 5,514 yards.

Fees $62.50. Includes shared cart. Club rentals: $18. Senior discounts available. Accepts tee times 6 months in advance. Accepts VISA, MC, AmEx

Facilities Driving range, putting green, pro shop, restaurant, and lounge

Comments Located beside Hawaii Volcanoes National Park, this course neighbors an active volcano. But the lava flow is a considerable distance away and won't pose a threat. A mostly flat course except for some rolling hills. A pond and three ditches come into play on four holes. Nearly all the tees and some of the greens are elevated. No tank tops or cut-offs.

Waikoloa Beach Golf Club *Zone 11 Kona*

Established 1981

Location 1020 Keana Place, Waikoloa, HI 96743 (From the airport, drive north on Highway 19. Turn left into Waikoloa Beach Resort.)

Phone (808) 885-6060

Website www.waikoloagolf.com

Status Resort, 18 holes, par 70

Tees *Championship:* 6,566 yards. *Men's:* 5,958 yards. *Ladies':* 5,094 yards.

Fees $95. Accepts tee times 4 days in advance. Accepts VISA, MC, AmEx, D

Facilities Driving range, putting green, pro shop, and restaurant

Comments A challenging course with narrow fairways framed by rugged black lava. An ancient petroglyph field borders the sixth, seventh, and eighth holes, adding a unique sense of place. The 479-yard, par 4 Hole 12, meanwhile, leads to the ocean surf. It features a dogleg fairway and green bordered on the right by the Pacific. Collared shirts required.

Waikoloa Kings' Course *Zone 11 Kona*

Established 1990

Location 600 Waikoloa Beach Drive, Waikoloa, HI 96738 (From the airport, drive north on Highway 19. Turn left into Waikoloa Beach Resort, then make a right on Keana Place after the third stop sign.)

Phone (808) 886-7888

Status Resort, 18 holes, par 72

Tees *Championship:* 7,094 yards. *Men's:* 6,594 yards. *Ladies':* 6,010 yards.

Fees $95. Accepts tee times 5 days in advance. Accepts VISA, MC, AmEx, D

Facilities Driving range, putting green, practice sand trap, and pro shop

Comments Designed by Tom Weiskopf and Jay Morrish, this links-style course was voted among *Golf Digest's* "Best New Resort Courses in America" when it opened. A challenging layout characterized by many sand bunkers and lava rock formations with treacherous greens. The signature hole, the 293-yard, par 4 Hole 5, features a long bunker stretching along the left side of the fairway, with two large boulders posing another threat for players trying to reach the green. The course is very playable for resort golfers when played from the regular tees. Collared shirts required.

Waikoloa Village Golf Club — *Zone 11 Kona*

Established 1972

Location 68-1792 Melia Street, Waikoloa, HI 96738 (From the Kona Airport, drive north along Highway 19. Turn right onto Waikoloa Road and look for the golf course on the left.)

Phone (808) 883-9621

Website www.waikoloa.org

Status Resort, 18 holes, par 72

Tees *Championship:* 6,687 yards. *Men's:* 6,142 yards. *Ladies':* 5,558 yards.

Fees $80. Includes cart. Special $55 twilight rate available after 1 p.m. Club rentals: $30. Accepts tee times 3 days in advance. Accepts VISA, MC, AmEx, D

Facilities Driving range, putting green, pro shop, and restaurant

Comments Oldest of the Waikoloa courses, this scenic layout takes you from ancient lava beds to raging surf. Layout features rolling terrain, dogleg fairways, and two lakes that come into play on three holes. No tank tops or cut-offs.

Waimea Country Club — *Zone 11 Kona*

Established 1994

Location P.O. Box 2155, Kamuela, HI 96743 (east of Kamuela, a.k.a. Waimea, on Mamalahoa Highway)

Phone (808) 885-8053

Website www.waimeagolf.com

Status Semiprivate, 18 holes, par 72

Tees *Championship:* 6,661 yards. *Men's:* 6,210 yards. *Ladies':* 5,673 yards.

Fees $65. Includes cart. Special $50 twilight rate available from 12:30 p.m. Club rentals: $35. Senior discounts available. Accepts tee times 2 days in advance. Accepts VISA, MC, AmEx

Facilities Driving range, putting green, and snack shop

Comments Built on open pasturelands, but features enough tall ironwood trees to keep you honest. There are 28 sand bunkers, and water hazards come into play on five holes. Features large, unrelenting greens. All in all, this is a good course for players of all skill levels. No dress code, but bring a jacket or sweater, as weather conditions here are often cool and misty.

Kauai

Kauai Lagoons Resort *Zone 13 Kauai*

Established 1989

Location 3351 Hoolaulea Way, Lihue, HI 96766 (From Lihue Airport, turn left on Ahukini Road, left again on Highway 51, and left again at the stoplight on Kalapaki Beach. The golf course is on the right.)

Phone (808) 241-6000

Website www.kauailagoonsgolf.com

Status Resort, 18 holes, par 72 (for both courses)

Tees *Championship:* Kiele course: 7,070 yards; Mokihana course: 6,960 yards. *Men's:* Kiele: 6,674 yards (blue tees), 6,164 yards; Mokihana: 6,578 yards (blue tees), 6,136 yards. *Ladies':* Kiele: 5,417 yards; Mokihana: 5,607 yards.

Fees $170 for Kiele, $120 for Mokihana. Includes cart. Club rentals: $35. Accepts tee times 30 days in advance. Accepts VISA, MC, AmEx

Facilities Driving range, putting and chipping greens, pro shop, locker rooms with showers, snack bar, and restaurant

Comments Both courses here were designed by Jack Nicklaus. The Kiele course is the more difficult of the two, with many tee shots needing to carry over ravines. The Kiele course is one of Hawaii's best and offers perhaps the best greens. *Golf Digest* ranked the course as one of the 75 best upscale courses in America. The Mokihana course is more favorable to players with higher handicaps. Collared shirts required; no cut-offs.

Kiahuna Golf Club *Zone 13 Kauai*

Established 1983

Location 2545 Kiahuna Plantation Drive, Koloa, HI 96756 (In Poipu, drive down Poipu Road and turn left on Kiahuna Plantation Drive. The entrance is on the left.)

Phone (808) 742-9595

Website www.kiahunagolf.com

Status Resort, 18 holes, par 70

Tees *Championship:* 6,353 yards. *Men's:* 5,631 yards. *Ladies':* 4,871 yards.

Fees $75 before 11 a.m., $65 from 11 a.m. to 2:30 p.m. Special $45 twilight rate available after 2:30 p.m. on weekdays only. Includes cart. Club rentals: $40. Guests staying at selected hotels receive discounts. Accepts tee times 30 days in advance. Accepts VISA, MC, AmEx, D

Facilities Driving range, putting green, pro shop, and snack bar

Comments A challenging layout built around historic Hawaiian sites. The course features narrow fairways, water hazards, and plenty of tradewinds. Designed by Robert Trent Jones Jr. Collared shirts required.

Poipu Bay Resort Golf Course *Zone 13 Kauai*

Established 1991

Location 2250 Ainako Street, Koloa, HI 96756 (In Poipu, follow Poipu Road to Ainako Street and make a right. The course is just past the Hyatt Regency Kauai.)

Phone (808) 742-9489

Status Resort, 18 holes, par 72

Tees *Championship:* 6,959 yards. *Men's:* 6,499 yards (blue tees), 6,023 yards. *Ladies':* 5,241 yards.

Fees $120–$170 before noon, $95–$115 after noon. Includes cart. Special twilight rate available after 3 p.m. Guests staying at selected hotels are eligible for discounts. Club rentals: $40. Accepts tee times 7 days in advance. Accepts VISA, MC, AmEx

Facilities Driving range, putting and chipping greens, practice sand bunkers, pro shop, locker room with showers, clubhouse, and restaurant

Comments Water hazards come into play on 11 holes at this immaculate course; more than 80 bunkers add to the challenge. The 501-yard, par 4 Hole 16 is lined by a lake on one side of the fairway and the ultimate water hazard—the ocean—on the other. The 201-yard, par 3 Hole 17 is another spectacular setting, boasting awesome coastal views from the tee. This is the site of the PGA Grand Slam of Golf, a two-day event featuring the winners of golf's four major championships. Collared shirts required.

Princeville Resort Golf Courses — *Zone 13 Kauai*

Established 1973 (Makai), 1990 (Prince)

Location Makai course: 4080 Leiopapa Road, Princeville, HI 96722 (From Kuhio Highway, turn right into the Princeville Resort. The golf course is 1 mile away, on the left.) Prince course: 5-3900 Kuhio Highway, Princeville, HI 96722 (From Kuhio Highway, drive past the Princeville Airport. The golf course is on the right.)

Phone Makai course: (808) 826-3580; Prince course: (808) 826-5000

Website www.princeville.com

Status Resort. Makai: 27 holes, par 36; Prince: 18 holes, par 72

Tees *Championship:* Makai: 3,430 yards (Ocean), 3,456 yards (Lakes), 3,445 yards (Woods); Prince: 7,309 yards. *Men's:* Makai: 3,157 yards (Ocean), 3,149 yards (Lakes), 3,204 yards (Woods); Prince: 6,960 yards (blue tees), 6,521 yards, 6,005 yards (gold tees). *Ladies':* Makai: 2,802 yards (Ocean), 2,714 yards (Lakes), 2,809 yards (Woods); Prince: 5,338 yards.

Fees Makai: $125. Guests staying at Princeville pay $105–$110. Prince: $175. $130–$150 for resort guests. Includes cart. Club rentals: $35. Accepts tee times 14 days in advance. Accepts VISA, MC, AmEx

Facilities Makai: Driving range, putting and chipping greens, pro shop, and snack bar; Prince: All of the above plus more putting greens, a full-service spa, and a restaurant

Comments The Makai course is actually three separate 9-hole courses that combine to form three different 18-hole layouts. The Ocean course's signature hole, appropriately, requires a tee shot over a stretch of ocean. Lakes come into play on three holes on the Lakes course and one hole on the Woods course. The Scottish links–style Prince course provides a challenge with its rolling hills and multitude of ravines. Views? You can see the ocean from every tee. *Golf Digest* has rated the Prince course as Hawaii's best. Collared shirts required.

Wailua Golf Course — *Zone 13 Kauai*

Established 1920 (as 6-hole course); expanded and redesigned in 1962

Location 3-5350 Kuhio Highway, Lihue, HI 96746 (From Lihue on Kuhio Highway, drive north to Kapaa. The golf course is on the right.)

Phone (808) 246-2793 or (808) 241-6666

Status Municipal, 18 holes, par 72

Tees *Championship:* 6,981 yards. *Men's:* 6,585 yards. *Ladies':* 5,974 yards.

Fees $25 weekdays, $35 weekends and holidays. 50% discount rates available after 2 p.m. Cart: $14. Club rentals: $15 with $50 deposit. Accepts tee times 7 days in advance. Accepts only traveler's checks or cash

Facilities Driving range, putting green, pro shops, and shower rooms

Comments One of the best municipal courses in the United States. This is a challenging course with elevated tees. It has served as the site of past Men's Public Links Amateur Championships. No tank tops or cut-offs.

Molokai

Note: At press time, Kaluakoi Golf Course at Kaluakoi Resort was closed pending ownership changes. But golfers vacationing on Molokai could be agreeably surprised to discover the following course.

Ironwood Hills Golf Course — *Zone 14 Molokai*

Established 1928

Location Kalae Highway, Kualapuu, HI 96757 (just before the Molokai Mule Ride barn, 15 minutes from the airport)

Phone (808) 567-6000

Status Public, 18 holes; 9 holes, par 34

Tees *Championship:* 3,088 yards. *Middle:* 2,816 yards. *Forward:* 2,409 yards.

Fees $14 for 18 holes; $10 for 9. Rental clubs and carts, $7 each for 9 holes. Tee times reservations advised. Accepts VISA, MC

Facilities Driving range, pro shop, and food service. Metal spikes allowed

Comments Historic upcountry course designed for Del Monte Plantation executives. One of the oldest courses in Hawaii, it has been preserved as a literal link to the past. Its rustic hilly layout, set in the Molokai highlands, is a challenging test with brisk tradewinds in the afternoons and fairways of tightly woven Kukuya grass framed by tall stands of island pine, eucalyptus, and the ironwoods for which it is named. Golfers must drive through narrow shoots of trees, and battle long uphill holes into the wind. After teeing off on the sixth hole, those in the know take only the clubs they need to finish and a driver for the seventh, leaving the rest under a tree for the steep climb to the seventh. Views of this and neighboring islands are breathtaking.

Lanai

The Challenge at Manele — *Zone 15 Lanai*

Established 1993

Location P.O. Box 310, Lanai City, HI 96763 (transportation via Lanai Resorts shuttle)

Phone (808) 565-2222

Website www.manelebayhotel.com

Status Resort, 18 holes, par 72

Tees *Championship:* 7,039 yards. *Men's:* 6,684 yards. *Ladies':* 5,024 yards.

Fees $205. $185 for guests staying at the Lodge at Koele, Manele Bay Hotel, or Hotel Lanai. Club rentals: $50 for full round. Accepts tee times 30 days in advance. Accepts VISA, MC, AmEx

Facilities Driving range, putting and chipping greens, locker rooms, pro shop, and restaurant

Comments Designed by Jack Nicklaus. This is a links-style course that offers great ocean views from every hole. Fairways are open; greens are small and fast. Built on the side of a hill, the course features several changes of elevation and requires several blind tee and approach shots. Winds often come into play. Bring extra balls for Hole 12, a 202-yard par 3 that includes a tee shot across 200 yards of Pacific Ocean. The tee area on a cliff 150 feet above the crashing surf is the picturesque spot where Bill and Melissa Gates were married in 1994. Archaeological sites are among the features. Collared shirts required; no denim.

The Experience at Koele — *Zone 15 Lanai*

Established 1991

Location P.O. Box 310, Lanai City, HI 96763 (transportation via Lanai Resorts shuttle)

Phone (808) 565-4653

Website www.manelebayhotel.com

Status Resort, 18 holes, par 72

Tees *Championship:* 7,014 yards. *Men's:* 6,217 yards. *Ladies':* 5,425 yards.

Fees $205. $185 for guests of the Lodge at Koele, Manele Bay Hotel, or Hotel Lanai. Club rentals: $50. Accepts tee times 30 days in advance. Accepts VISA, MC, AmEx

Facilities Driving range, putting and chipping greens, executive putting course, clubhouse, and snack bar

Comments A magnificent course designed by golf greats Greg Norman and Ted Robinson. The front nine were carved from the side of a mountain, and the back nine are more open and flat. Water features are prominent, with seven lakes, streams, and waterfalls. The par 4, 444-yard Hole 8 is the signature, featuring a 250-foot drop from tee to fairway, with a lake bordering one side and thick shrubs and trees lining the other. Even Jack Nicklaus needed seven attempts to get the ball in play here. Hole 17 is surrounded by a lake. Collared shirts required; no denim.

Spectator Sports

Even without a major professional sports franchise, the islands of Oahu, Maui, Hawaii, and Kauai host major sporting events throughout the year. If you're looking to augment your beach time, here's a game plan.

Football

Hawaii's claim to pro football fame is the game the players all want to play: the **NFL Pro Bowl,** the all-star game that celebrates the end of the season, a week after the Super Bowl, usually in late January. It is held at the 50,000-seat Aloha Stadium on Oahu. It's usually sold out weeks in advance, so inquire early for tickets, (808) 486-9300; for credit card orders, call (808) 484-1122. The players and families are in town for pregame festivities and practice for the week preceding the game.

College football all-stars, meanwhile, head for Maui each January for the annual **Hula Bowl.** After being held on Oahu for years, this contest has found new life on the Valley Isle, with the 20,000-seat War Memorial Stadium in Wailuku filled to capacity with rabid fans and, not coincidentally, talent scouts from every NFL team. Call (808) 545-7171 for tickets.

Golf

A handful of major winter professional golf events brings Hawaii's gorgeous links into the snowbound homes of golf fans via television. In early January, the **Mercedes Championships** at Kapalua, Maui, features top players competing for more than $2.5 million in prize money. Call (808) 669-2440.

Formerly the Hawaiian Open, the new **Sony Open** on Oahu draws the PGA's best to the Waialae Country Club in Kahala. This January tournament kicks off the official PGA Tour season, with another $2.5 million purse. Call (808) 523-7888.

Also in January is the **MasterCard Championship,** which gathers winners from the previous year's Senior PGA Tour to the Hualalai Golf Club on the Big Island. This tournament, featuring more than $1 million in prize money, kicks off the Senior PGA Tour. Call (808) 325-8480.

In February, the Kapolei Golf Course on Oahu hosts the annual **Sunrise Hawaiian Ladies Open,** a 54-hole medal play competition featuring top women's golfers from the United States and Japan. Call (808) 674-2227.

One of the final stops on the Senior PGA Tour is the **EMC Kaanapali Classic** on Maui. Held in October, this event annually draws some of the game's greatest legends and old-time favorites. Call (808) 661-3691.

November brings the **MasterCard PGA Grand Slam** to the Poipu Bay Course on Kauai. This 36-hole, two-day event features the winners of golf's four major PGA championships (Master's, British Open, U.S. Open, and PGA Championship). Call (808) 742-1234.

Ocean Sports

A surf meet provides a different kind of experience for sports fans. It's a good chance to see Hawaii's most prized individual sport at its finest while hanging out at the beach. Admission is always free.

Competitors take to the water in four-man heats, each lasting 20–30 minutes. The surfers ride as many waves as they can. A panel of five judges uses a point system to name the winners. Criteria include the size of the waves, length of the rides, board control, and creative maneuvers.

The most prestigious surfing competition is the **Triple Crown** of surfing, held in November and December. The best professional wave riders from around the world gather on Oahu's North Shore for the **Ocean Pacific Pro** at Alii Beach Park in Haleiwa, **World Cup of Surfing** at Sunset Beach, and **Pipeline Masters** at the famous Banzai Pipeline at

Ehukai Beach Park. The events occur on the four days of best surf conditions during a period of about two weeks. Recently, a special longboard competition was launched at Alii Beach Park. Call (808) 638-7700 or visit www.triplecrownofsurfing.com.

Summer brings the **Outrigger Hotels Oceanfest,** a colorful ocean sports festival headlined by the **Hawaiian International Ocean Challenge,** which features the world's top lifeguards in a variety of ocean-related competitions on Oahu. Other Oceanfest events include kayak, paddleboarding, and canoe races, as well as the **Wahine Windsurfing Classic.** Call (808) 521-4322.

You won't be able to follow all the action of the annual **Bankoh Na Wahine O Ke Kai** and the **Bankoh Mokokai Hoe,** two 41-mile outrigger canoe races from Mokokai to Waikiki. (The women's wahine race is held in late September, while the men's race takes place in early October.) But you can watch the colorful finale as the six-member canoe teams paddle to a finish on the beach. Both events draw international outrigger canoe teams from Australia, Canada, and Tahiti, as well as Hawaii and other states.

Track

Few events are as physically demanding as the zenith of all triathlons, the **Ironman Triathlon World Championship** held each October on the Big Island, where the world's top triathletes plunge into a 2.4-mile ocean swim followed by a 112-mile bike race and a 26.2-mile marathon. Unless it's the annual **Ultraman,** which ups the ante to a 6.2-mile swim, 251.4-mile bike ride, and 52.3-mile run. Fair warning: The weekend of the Ironman is often Kailua-Kona's busiest of the year, and certain visitor necessities, like car rentals, may be hard to come by. Call (808) 329-0063.

College Basketball

College basketball fanciers focus on Honolulu each year around Christmastime for the annual **Outrigger Hotels Rainbow Classic Basketball Tournament,** arguably the nation's best eight-team holiday tournament. A tradition launched in the mid-1960s, the Rainbow Classic has a reputation for spotlighting future first-round NBA draft picks. Certainly enough scouts attend the tourney to find them. College teams compete with equal fervor in the annual women's **Asahi Rainbow Wahine Classic** staged in late November, also in Honolulu. Watch for college all-stars in the annual **Aloha Basketball Classic** tournament in Honolulu in mid-April, and you may be previewing more pro standouts of the future.

Part Nine

Dining in Hawaii

Experiencing Hawaii's Multicultural Cuisine

The New Hawaii Regional Cuisine

Hawaii has cuisine by the bucketful. Good, no-nonsense food dating to the earliest Polynesian voyagers. Bright, colorful food representing the rainbow of cultures that came together on the sugar and pineapple plantations. Hearty favorites of backyard barbecues and plate-lunch stands. Until relatively recently, these flavors—soy, miso, ginger, Filipino fish sauces, the hot peppers of Chinese Szechuan cooking—simply weren't represented within the staid continental-cuisine establishment that represented upscale dining.

All of this changed in the late 1980s, when a few young chefs dared to be different, experimenting with fresh fish from Hawaiian waters, seasonings from Asia, and the best in local produce. Their styles differed—classic French, Mediterranean, Asian—but they all had solid culinary training and had paid their dues in hotel and restaurant kitchens throughout the country.

By 1991, 12 of them organized formally and gave what they were doing a name: Hawaii Regional Cuisine. It meant cooking fresh from the market—no more frozen fish or canned vegetables—and taking it all to an international level of sophistication. Island farms grew along with the restaurant industry, providing baby greens, exotic mushrooms, vine-ripened tomatoes, pencil-thin asparagus. HRC chefs still use foie gras, truffles, dayboat scallops, caviar—all of the finer imported things—but make them work in combination with hearts of palm from the Big Island, corn from Kahuku, sweet potatoes from Molokai.

The Ultimate Buffet

The island food scene offers a smorgasbord of possibilities, born of a plantation heritage that brought together immigrants from throughout the Pacific beginning in the 1800s. Already in place, of course, were the staples of the native Hawaiian diet: taro, breadfruit, coconuts, bananas, yams, and sweet potatoes, to mention just a few. Chinese, Japanese, Filipino, Portuguese, and other laborers adapted their traditional dishes to ingredients available locally. In community kitchens and plantation homes, they borrowed from each other, creating the makings of a cuisine found nowhere else in the world. Later immigrants—from Puerto Rico and Southeast Asia, especially—have also contributed to Hawaii's stewpot, so that lemongrass and kaffir lime, gandule rice and pigeon peas all have become part of the eating scene.

Perhaps the best place to sample this ethnic variety is at an okazuya, or Japanese delicatessen. Although Japanese in origin, Hawaii's okazuya are as likely to offer Filipino adobo, Puerto Rican gandule, Chinese chow mein, or a fusion dish such as Korean kim chee fried rice. The best part is you won't have to guess about unfamiliar foods. Everything's laid out under glass; you just point and pick. Find these family-run take-out places all over town (for example Mitsuba, (808) 841-3864; Fukuya, (808) 946-2073; or Gulick, (808) 847-1461). These places close early, though, and parking can be tight. Consider it part of the adventure.

Quick Eats

The island version of fast food is the plate-lunch diner, modeled after the old-fashioned drive-in. These establishments reach far beyond burgers and fries, however, to offer specialties such as katsu (fried pork or chicken cutlet), teriyaki (soy-marinated grilled pork, beef, or chicken), and big, warm plates of island-style beef stew. Or order a combination—a mixed plate. Expect a yeoman's quantity of food, accompanied by two scoops of steamed white rice and a big spoonful of macaroni salad. A carbo-loaders dream. Favorite chains include Grace's Inn, L&L Drive-Inn, Loco Moco Drive Inn, and Zippy's.

More strictly defined ethnic restaurants abound at the carryout level as well. Korean chains such as Yummy Bar-B-Q and Kim Chee offer a good introduction to a range of traditional dishes, with illustrated menu boards to make the choosing easy. Casual Japanese noodle houses with their steaming bowls of ramen, udon, and soba abound throughout Waikiki, downtown Honolulu, and every neighborhood. Just take a walk. Small Chinese, Thai, and Vietnamese places offer inexpensive meals (Chinatown is a good place for an introduction).

The ultimate Hawaiian carryout food is Spam musubi. The consummate fusion of American, Japanese, and local tastes, it incorporates a hearty scoop of rice molded into a rectangle, topped with a slice of luncheon meat, wrapped in a sheet of nori, or fried seaweed. Find it in take-out delis, supermarkets, and convenience stores (7-Eleven is the biggest producer). Completely portable, a Spam musubi is the perfect picnic food.

Fish Facts

One of the most frequently voiced questions about Hawaii Regional Cuisine concerns a clear-cut definition, including the identity of signature ingredients and dishes. As the genre evolved, certain fresh fish emerged as ingredients unique to the Islands. In the past, mahimahi had always been the fish identified with Hawaii. Today, mahimahi, a mild white fish, remains a favorite, but a vast array of other types of fish, which once were caught by fishermen only for their home tables, are now found on restaurant menus.

For the uninitiated, choosing a fish dish can be a challenge, as fish are known by any number of names—local, mainland, and scientific—and often are served in a multitude of preparations listed and described on menus. To allay some of the confusion and encourage the use of fish that are not so well known, the Department of Business, Economic Development, and Tourism promotes a statewide Seafood Festival during the month of July and has published a chart naming and describing various fishes. Following is an abbreviated guide that can help you in choosing a fish dish from an Island menu, though it's always best to ask your waiter for specific descriptions, particularly regarding preparations.

Aku, Skipjack tuna Red, translucent flesh turns to firm ivory-colored meat when cooked. The high fat content makes this fish good sliced raw for sashimi.

Bigeye ahi, Bigeye tuna Light red flesh cooks to creamy white. The high fat content makes this fish good sliced raw for sashimi.

Yellowfin ahi, Yellowfin tuna Light red flesh cooks to creamy white. The high fat content makes this fish good sliced raw for sashimi.

Shutome, Broadbill swordfish Firm, well-textured, mild-flavored pinkish meat cooks to white.

Mahimahi, Dolphinfish Firm, light flesh cooks to delicate, sweet white meat.

Ono, Wahoo Delicate pink meat is flaky and sweet when cooked.

Opah, Moonfish Rich, large-grained flesh ranges from pink to orange to bright red throughout the fish.

Moi, Threadfish Islanders like the moist, mild white meat of this fish steamed, though some chefs prepare it crisp-fried with its edible scales.

Monchong, Bigscale, or Sickle pomfret Delicately flavored, smooth, well-textured flesh cooks to moist white meat.

Onaga, Ruby, or Long-tailed snapper The onaga's pale pink flesh, which has a delicate flavor, is considered a good-luck food when served raw. It's also delicious cooked.

Opakapaka, Crimson snapper A favorite fish in Hawaii restaurants, with pink flesh that has a mild flavor whether sautéed, grilled, or baked.

If there is a signature dish for Hawaii Regional Cuisine, it's ahi sashimi, served in any number of restaurants of all ethnic persuasions. Sometimes a block of tuna is quickly seared, then thinly sliced for blackened ahi, or sometimes the buttery red fish is simply chilled, sliced, and laid on a bed of shredded cabbage and served with a hot soy-wasabi dipping sauce.

On the cooked scene, a second widely served fish that could symbolize Hawaii Regional Cuisine is often designated as "local-boy style." One popular restaurant uses ono, a white fish, for the preparation, which is flavored with nori-seaweed-soy vinaigrette and sizzling hot peanut oil. It's the kind of dish that might pop up at a backyard barbecue or a home luau, along with mounds of white rice.

Luau Lore: To Go or Not to Go?

If you have never been to a luau, it's one of those things you really should experience. Bear in mind, you don't go to a luau for fine dining; it's most fun to go with friends; and finally, you've got to mentally put yourself in a "hang-loose mode"—wear your wildest print outfit, tuck a flower behind your ear, and be prepared to go barefoot during dinner.

Visitors can experience leisurely and romantic luaus in a garden or on the beach in front of their hotels, or at elaborate, rollicking affairs on a secluded shoreline presented by professional outfits such as Paradise Cove or Germaine's on Oahu. Some commercial luaus include pageantry, with participants dressed like early Hawaiian royalty; all of them include a Polynesian show. Before dinner, guests might have a chance to wade barefoot into the sun-warmed ocean to help pull in the *hukilau* net filled with flopping fish.

In old Hawaii, the most popular way of preparing food was to *kalua* the meat—chicken, dog, or fish—in an underground oven, and the heart and soul of any luau is still the preparation and unearthing of the *imu.* Though dog is no longer part of the menu, current luau food is reasonably authentic, except for such items as teriyaki steak, barbecued chicken, and macaroni and potato salads, added to suit all tastes along the buffet line. You'll still find pig roasted to moist tenderness in the *imu,* then shredded; poi, pounded into a paste-like consistency from the cooked taro corm; sweet potatoes; marinated lomi salmon, small pieces of fish with chopped tomatoes and onions; and sometimes opihi, a Hawaiian shellfish plucked from wave-washed rocky shorelines and eaten raw as a special delicacy. Chicken or squid luau serves a vegetable dish made of the tender leaves of the taro plant cooked in coconut milk. Many Island feasts ladle out chicken long rice, a tasty dish of chicken cooked with slithery translucent noodles made of rice flour and garnished with green onions, and frequently you'll find laulau, little green bundles of taro leaf, which taste like spinach and contain pork and fish. Luau menus are light on vegetables, but usually fresh pineapple, bananas, and other fruits are found on every table. Relishes—Hawaiian salt, inamona made of ground kukui nuts, stalks of green onions, and individual bowls of poi—are also placed on every table. Dessert consists of a white cake with layers of haupia, a pudding of sweetened coconut milk thickened with cornstarch, all crowned with a fluffy white frosting and shredded coconut. Additional haupia cut into finger-sized rectangles always tops off a luau.

The entertainment at one of these feasts is like a mini-tour of Polynesia. Hawaii's contribution includes the haunting chants that perpetuate the legends of the past, as well as the graceful hula. And yes, someone in your party is likely to get dragged onto the stage, so take a camera and capture that Kodak moment, or maybe snap Mom digging into the poi bowl with two fingers, the traditional way to enjoy it.

Our final word about poi comes from an expert. Chef Sam Choy, a "local boy" if ever there was one, says, "You must have poi with your luau whether you like it or not. It just isn't a luau without it."

Island Dining Scenes

Oahu, with the largest population and the highest visitor count (about five million annually), and as the center of commerce and transportation, naturally has more restaurants than any other island. Fine dining is concentrated in the Waikiki area; however, many former hotel chefs have opened restaurants of their own on the edges of Waikiki or in shopping centers near residential areas. Hotel restaurants tend to be more expensive, but often they enjoy special ocean-side settings and big-name chefs. The cost doesn't keep local residents away; we dine in high-profile restaurants for special celebrations, for business lunches, and with visiting guests.

On the Neighbor Islands, you'll find the best hotel restaurants on Maui at Wailea, Kaanapali, Makena, and Kapalua Resorts; on the Big Island along the Kohala Coast; on Kauai at Poipu and Princeville; and on Lanai in the two major hotels, the Lodge at Koele and Manele Bay Hotel.

Office workers in downtown Honolulu frequent nearby restaurants—perhaps an ethnic gem in Chinatown, an upbeat contemporary getaway in the Aloha Tower Marketplace, or a favorite hangout on Restaurant Row. A multitude of ethnic restaurants with reasonably priced menus can also be found on the Diamond Head edge of Waikiki along Kapahulu Avenue and a few miles away in Kaimuki.

In the tourist meccas of Lahaina on Maui and Kailua-Kona on the Big Island, many restaurants are of the casual open-air kind. Interestingly, the little upcountry residential town of Waimea on the Big Island has a growing reputation for good food prepared by good chefs in reputable restaurants—Merriman's, Edelweiss, Parker Ranch Grill, Koa House, and Daniel Thiebaut, to mention just a few.

Trends

When Hawaii Regional Cuisine became a recognized movement, chefs sometimes went overboard concocting dishes with a combination of flavors that confused the palate. As with any new movement trying to gain a foothold, sanity eventually returned. Dishes in today's upscale restaurants are still beautiful to behold, but the trend now is toward flavors that are balanced in courses that complement each other.

Most chefs are aiming toward simplicity and freshness, with the true flavor of meat, fish, and poultry enhanced by fresh herbs. Though the vogue continues to lean toward healthier preparations, with lighter sauces made of fruit coulis or puréed vegetables, meat is on the rebound. People do, however, like variety, and fish and seafood continue to be popular, as evidenced by a proliferation of new seafood bars and buffets.

Wine continues to increase in popularity as an important accompaniment. The best restaurants allow experimentation by making available many wines by the glass, so you can match each course to the wine best suited. More and more restaurants are listing suggested wines on the menu that have been matched to the entrées by in-house sommeliers or by Hawaii's only master sommelier, Chuck Furuya.

Microbreweries have finally come into their own in a number of Island restaurants. Some are mainland imports; a few, such as Waimea Brew Pub on Kauai and Kona Brewing Company on the Big Island, are local endeavors. In all, you'll find beers made and named for their Island-grown ingredients and flavors, and you'll generally find that the brewpubs offer contemporary food attractively served at reasonable prices.

The Melting Pot Is Sizzling

Food festivals held throughout the Islands celebrate Hawaii's bounty in terms of both fresh produce and celebrated chefs. On Oahu, the summer Taste of Honolulu brings chefs to the scenic grounds of city hall. The Taste at Kapolei does the same in the fall on the west side of the island at Ko Olina harbor. Maui hosts the Ulupalakua Thing (an agricultural fair), the Kapalua Food & Wine Festival, and Taste of Lahaina. The capital of food events, however, would have to be the Big Island's Kona-Kohala Coast, which features the Kona Coffee Festival, the Big Island Festival, and a continuing round of upscale dining celebrations at the various resorts.

The Restaurants

Our Favorite Island Restaurants: Explaining the Ratings

We have developed detailed profiles for the best restaurants and for those that offer some special reason to visit, be it decor, ethnic appeal, or bargain prices. Each profile features an easily scanned heading that allows you to quickly check out the restaurant name, cuisine, overall rating, cost, quality rating, and value rating.

Cuisine In a locale where Hawaii Regional Cuisine has been seeking to define itself only since 1992, categorizing cuisine becomes a challenging endeavor. Hawaii Regional Cuisine, itself, is an olio of ethnic foods, so we've ended up with dishes that incorporate Asian flavors, Hawaiian flavors, Cajun flavors, Pacific Rim flavors, Mediterranean flavors, and more. Many chefs prefer not to be categorized at all, as they are afraid this will limit others' perception of their creativity. In most cases, we let restaurant owners or chefs name their own categories. In many cases, fusion cuisines are called simply "contemporary cuisine." Even restaurants that once served classic French cuisine now prepare sauces with a lighter hand and are innovative about using Island-grown ingredients, one of the prerequisites of Hawaii Regional Cuisine. You can get an idea of the type of food served from the heading, then glean a better understanding by reading the detailed descriptions of specialty items and other recommendations.

Overall Rating The overall rating encompasses the entire dining experience, including style, service, and ambience, in addition to the taste, presentation, and quality of the food. Five stars is the highest rating possible and connotes the best of everything. Four-star restaurants are exceptional, three-star restaurants are well above average, and two-star restaurants are good. One star indicates an average restaurant that demonstrates an unusual capability in some area of specialization—for example, an otherwise unmemorable place that has great saimin (noodle soup).

Cost To the right of the cuisine is an expense description that provides a comparative sense of how much a complete meal will cost. A complete meal for our purposes consists of an entrée with a vegetable or side dish and a choice of soup or salad. Appetizers, desserts, drinks, and tips are excluded. Categories and related prices are listed below:

Inexpensive	$14 and less per person
Moderate	$15–$30
Expensive	More than $30 per person

Quality Rating To the right of the cost appear stars that rate food quality on a scale of ★–★★★★★, where ★★★★★ is the best rating attainable.

It is based expressly on the taste, freshness of ingredients, preparation, presentation, and creativity of the food served. There is no consideration of price. If you want the best food available, and cost is not an issue, you need look no further than the quality ratings.

Value Rating If, on the other hand, you are looking for both quality and value, then you should check the value rating. Remember, the perception of value can vary from state to state and country to country. Hawaii is a tourist destination, so restaurant prices in the state probably compare favorably with prices in New York, San Francisco, and other major tourist destinations, but not so favorably with smaller, residential towns. Because it is a common perception that hotel restaurants are universally overpriced (where else would you pay $4–$6 for a glass of orange juice?), we have indicated restaurants of this sort with a ★★ rating rather than a discouraging ★. The ★★ is meant to convey that yes, the restaurant charges perhaps more than you would pay for a similar entrée somewhere else, but because the setting, service, and preparation are exceptional, it's still worth the splurge. We wouldn't want to rate the restaurant a ★, causing a reader to automatically forgo a special dining experience. The value ratings are defined as follows:

★★★★★	Exceptional value; a real bargain
★★★★	Good value
★★★	Fair value; you get exactly what you pay for
★★	Somewhat overpriced
★	Significantly overpriced

Locating the Restaurant On the far right is a designation for geographic zone. This zone description will give you a general idea of where the restaurant described is located. We've divided the six major islands into the following 15 geographic zones.

Zone 1	Waikiki
Zone 2	Greater Honolulu
Zone 3	Windward Oahu
Zone 4	The North Shore
Zone 5	Leeward Oahu
Zone 6	Central Oahu
Zone 7	Central Maui
Zone 8	South Maui
Zone 9	West Maui
Zone 10	Upcountry Maui
Zone 11	Kona
Zone 12	Hilo and Volcano
Zone 13	Kauai
Zone 14	Molokai
Zone 15	Lanai

Payment We've listed the type of payment accepted at each restaurant using the following codes:

AMEX	American Express
CB	Carte Blanche
D	Discover
DC	Diners Club
JCB	Japan Credit Bank
MC	MasterCard
VISA	VISA

Who's Included Restaurants open and close frequently in Hawaii, so most of those we've included have a proven track record. However, some of the newest upscale restaurants owned and operated by chefs who have become local celebrities have been included to keep the guide as complete and up-to-date as possible. Local chains, such as Sam Choy's and Roy's, are included, as are a few franchises that have a distinctly Hawaiian look in food and decor. Also, the list is highly selective. Our leaving out a particular place does not necessarily indicate that the restaurant is not good, only that it was not ranked among the best in its genre. Detailed profiles of individual restaurants follow in alphabetical order at the end of this chapter. In the section titled "More Recommendations," we've named reputable restaurants that you might want to try for a specific reason—for pizzas, bagels, plate lunches—that don't otherwise merit a full description. These are listed according to their island location, but you might notice that every "best" category may not have a listing on each island. This is not an oversight; an omitted island simply may not have a good restaurant that fits the category.

THE BEST HAWAIIAN RESTAURANTS

Island Cuisine and Name	Overall Rating	Price	Quality Rating	Value Rating	Zone
OAHU					
American					
Diamond Head Grill	★★★	Mod/Exp	★★★½	★★	1
Chinese					
Double Eight Chinese Restaurant	★★★★	Inexp	★★★★½	★★★★★	2
The Golden Dragon	★★★★	Mod	★★★★½	★★★	1
Contemporary					
Hoku's	★★★★	Mod/Exp	★★★★½	★★★	2
3660 On the Rise	★★★★	Mod	★★★★½	★★★	2
The Surf Room	★★★½	Mod/Exp	★★★½	★★★	1
Dukes Canoe Club Restaurant	★★★	Inexp/Mod	★★★½	★★★★	1
Continental/Pacific Rim					
Hau Tree Lanai	★★★	Mod	★★★½	★★★	1
Euro-Asian					
L'Uraku	★★★★★	Mod	★★★★★	★★★★	2
Indigo	★★★★	Inexp/Mod	★★★★½	★★★★	2
Bali-By-The-Sea	★★★½	Mod/Exp	★★★½	★★	1

THE BEST HAWAIIAN RESTAURANTS *(continued)*					
Island Cuisine and Name	**Overall Rating**	**Price**	**Quality Rating**	**Value Rating**	**Zone**
OAHU *(continued)*					
French					
La Mer	★★★★★	Exp	★★★★★	★★★	1
Michel's at the Colony Surf	★★★★½	Exp	★★★★½	★★	1
Hawaii Regional					
Alan Wong's Restaurant	★★★★★	Mod	★★★★★	★★★★	1
Prince Court Restaurant	★★★★	Mod	★★★★½	★★★	1
Sam Choy's Diamond Head	★★★★	Mod	★★★★	★★★	1
The Pineapple Room	★★★½	Mod/Exp	★★★★	★★★	2
Don Ho's Island Grill	★★★	Inexp	★★★½	★★★½	2
Sam Choy's Breakfast, Lunch, and Crab	★★★	Mod	★★★½	★★★	2
Hawaiian Fusion					
Roy's Restaurant	★★★★★	Mod	★★★★★	★★★	2
Hawaiian Traditional					
Helena's Hawaiian Foods	★★★★	Inexp	★★★★½	★★★★★	2
Italian					
Assaggio Ristorante Italiano	★★★½	Inexp/Mod	★★★★½	★★★★★	6
Sarentino's Top of the "I"	★★★½	Mod/Exp	★★★★	★★★	1
Japanese					
Sansei Seafood Restaurant and Sushi Bar	★★★★	Mod/Exp	★★★★½	★★★★	2, 9
Mediterranean					
Padovani's Restaurant & Wine Bar	★★★★½	Mod/Exp	★★★★★	★★★	1
Cascada	★★★½	Mod	★★★★★	★★★	1
Palomino Eorp Bistro	★★★	Inexp/Mod	★★★½	★★★★	2
Pacific Rim					
Chef Mavro Restaurant	★★★★½	Exp	★★★★★	★★★	1
Seafood					
Orchids	★★★★½	Mod/Exp	★★★★½	★★★	1
John Domini's	★★★½	Mod/Exp	★★★★	★★	1
Steak and Seafood					
Hy's Steak House	★★★	Mod/Exp	★★★★	★★★	1
Buzz's Original Steak House	★★	Inexp/Mod	★★★½	★★★	3

THE BEST HAWAIIAN RESTAURANTS *(continued)*

Island Cuisine and Name	Overall Rating	Price	Quality Rating	Value Rating	Zone
OAHU *(continued)*					
Thai					
Keo's in Waikiki	★★★★	Inexp/Mod	★★★★½	★★★★	1
Singha Thai Cuisine	★★★★	Inexp/Mod	★★★★½	★★★★	1
MAUI					
American					
David Paul's Lahaina Grill	★★★★	Mod/Exp	★★★★½	★★★	9
Contemporary					
Gerard's	★★★★	Mod/Exp	★★★★	★★★★	9
Plantation House Restaurant	★★½	Inexp/Mod	★★★★	★★★	9
Continental					
The Bay Club Restaurant	★★★	Mod/Exp	★★★½	★★★	9
French					
Chez Paul's	★★★★	Mod/Exp	★★★★	★★★	7
Hawaii Regional					
Pacific'O	★★★★½	Mod	★★★★½	★★★	9
Seasons	★★★★½	Mod/Exp	★★★★½	★★★	8
Haliimaile General Store	★★★★	Mod/Exp	★★★★½	★★★	10
Bamboo Bistro	★★★★	Mod	★★★★	★★★	7
Anuenue Room	★★★½	Mod/Exp	★★★★	★★★	9
Hula Grill	★★★	Inexp/Mod	★★★★	★★★★	9
Hawaiian Fusion					
Roy's Kahana Bar & Grill	★★★½	Mod	★★★★	★★★★	9
Roy's Nicolina	★★★½	Mod	★★★½	★★★	9
Mediterranean					
Longhi's	★★★½	Mod	★★★★	★★★★	9
Seafood					
Maalaea Waterfront Restaurant	★★★½	Mod	★★★★½	★★★	7
Mama's Fish House	★★★½	Mod/Exp	★★★★½	★★★	9
Steak and Seafood					
Kimo's	★★½	Inexp/Mod	★★★	★★★★	9

THE BEST HAWAIIAN RESTAURANTS *(continued)*

Island Cuisine and Name	Overall Rating	Price	Quality Rating	Value Rating	Zone
MAUI *(continued)*					
Vietnamese					
A Saigon Café	★★★	Inexp	★★★★	★★★★★	7
THE BIG ISLAND					
American					
Kona Ranch House	★★½	Inexp/Mod	★★★	★★★★	11
Contemporary					
Café Pesto	★★★½	Inexp	★★★★	★★★★	11, 12
The Grill and Lounge at The Orchid	★★★½	Exp	★★★★	★★★	11
Continental					
Edelweiss	★★★½	Mod	★★★★	★★★★	11
Kilauea Lodge	★★★½	Mod	★★★★	★★★	12
French/Asian					
Daniel Thiebaut Restaurant	★★★½	Mod	★★★★	★★★★	11
Hawaii Regional					
Batik Restaurant	★★★★½	Exp	★★★★½	★★★	11
CanoeHouse	★★★★½	Mod/Exp	★★★★½	★★★	11
Coast Grille	★★★★½	Mod/Exp	★★★★½	★★★	11
Merriman's	★★★★½	Mod/Exp	★★★★½	★★★	11
Sam Choy's Restaurant	★★★	Mod	★★★★	★★★★	11
Hawaii Regional/Southwestern					
Oodles of Noodles	★★★½	Inexp/Mod	★★★★½	★★★★★	11
Hawaiian Fusion					
Roy's at the Kings Shops	★★★★½	Mod	★★★★½	★★★★	11
Pahu ia at Four Seasons	★★★★½	Exp	★★★★½	★★★	11
Italian					
Donatoni's	★★★★½	Mod/Exp	★★★★½	★★★	11
Pacific Rim					
Huggo's	★★½	Mod	★★★½	★★★	11
Steak and Seafood					
Harrington's	★★	Mod	★★★½	★★★★	12

THE BEST HAWAIIAN RESTAURANTS *(continued)*

Island Cuisine and Name	Overall Rating	Price	Quality Rating	Value Rating	Zone
THE BIG ISLAND *(continued)*					
Thai					
Royal Siam Thai	★★★½	Inexp	★★★★	★★★★★	12
KAUAI					
American					
Shells, at the Sheraton Kauai Hotel	★★★½	Mod/Exp	★★★★	★★★	13
Contemporary					
Postcards	★★★½	Mod	★★★★	★★★★	13
Brennecke's Beach Broiler	★★★	Mod	★★★½	★★★★	13
Continental					
Café Hanalei and Terrace	★★★★	Exp	★★★★½	★★★	13
Hawaiian Fusion					
Roy's Poipu Bar & Grill	★★★★	Mod	★★★★½	★★★	13
Island Eclectic					
Hamura Saimin	★	Inexp	★★★½	★★★★★	13
Italian					
Plantation Gardens	★★★½	Mod	★★★★	★★★	13
Casa di Amici	★★½	Mod	★★★★	★★★	13
Pacific Rim					
A Pacific Café	★★★★½	Mod	★★★★½	★★★	13
The Beach House	★★★	Mod	★★★★	★★★	13
Tidepools	★★★	Mod/Exp	★★★½	★★★	13
Seafood					
Duke's Canoe Club	★★★	Inexp/Mod	★★★★	★★★★	13
Steak and Seafood					
Keoki's Paradise	★★★½	Mod	★★★★	★★★★	13
Thai/Chinese					
Mema Thai Chinese Cuisine	★★	Inexp/Mod	★★★★	★★★★★	13
MOLOKAI					
Hawaii Regional					
Maunaloa Room	★★★★	Mod/Exp	★★★★½	★★★	14

THE BEST HAWAIIAN RESTAURANTS *(continued)*

Island Cuisine and Name	Overall Rating	Price	Quality Rating	Value Rating	Zone
THE BIG ISLAND *(continued)*					
Island					
The Village Grill	★★	Mod	★★★½	★★★	14
Hotel Molokai Restaurant	★★	Inexp	★★★	★★★★★	14
Pizza and Sandwiches					
Molokai Pizza Café	★★	Inexp	★★★½	★★★★	14
LANAI					
American					
Henry Clay's Rotisserie	★★★	Mod	★★★½	★★★★	15
Contemporary					
The Formal Dining Room, The Lodge at Koele	★★★★½	Exp	★★★	★★★	15
Hawaii Regional/Mediterranean					
Ihilani	★★★★½	Exp	★★★★½	★★★	15
Island Eclectic					
Blue Ginger Café	★	Inexp	★★★	★★★★★	15

THE BEST HAWAIIAN RESTAURANTS BY ZONE

OAHU: Zones 1–6

Alan Wong's Restaurant
Assaggio Ristorante Italiano
Bali-By-The-Sea
Buzz's Original Steak House
Cascada
Chef Mavro Restaurant
Diamond Head Grill
Don Ho's Island Grill
Double Eight Chinese Restaurant
Duke's Canoe Club Restaurant
The Golden Dragon
Hau Tree Lanai
Helena's Hawaiian Foods
Hoku's
Hy's Steak House
Indigo
John Domini's
Keo's in Waikiki
La Mer
L'Uraku
Michel's at the Colony Surf
Orchids
Padovani's Restaurant & Wine Bar
Palomino Euro Bistro
The Pineapple Room
Prince Court Restaurant
Roy's Restaurant
Sam Choy's Breakfast, Lunch, and Crab
Sam Choy's Diamond Head

THE BEST HAWAIIAN RESTAURANTS BY ZONE *(continued)*

OAHU: Zones 1–6 *(continued)*

Sansei Seafood Restaurant and Sushi Bar
Sarento's Top of the "I"
Singha Thai Cuisine
The Surf Room
3660 On the Rise

MAUI: Zones 7–10

Anuenue Room
Bamboo Bistro
The Bay Club Restaurant
Chez Paul's
David Paul's Lahaina Grill
Gerard's
Haliimaile General Store
Hula Grill
Kimo's
Longhi's
Maalaea Waterfront Restaurant
Mama's Fish House
Pacific'O
Plantation House Restaurant
Roy's Kahana Bar & Grill
Roy's Nicolina
A Saigon Café
Sansei Seafood Restaurant and Sushi Bar
Seasons

THE BIG ISLAND: Zones 11–12

Batik Restaurant
Café Pesto
CanoeHouse
Coast Grille
Daniel Thiebaut Restaurant
Donatoni's
Edelweiss
The Grill and Lounge at The Orchid
Harrington's
Huggo's
Kilauea Lodge
Kona Ranch House
Merriman's
Oodles of Noodles
Pahu ia at Four Seasons
Royal Siam Thai
Roy's at the Kings Shops
Sam Choy's Restaurant

KAUAI: Zone 13

The Beach House
Brennecke's Beach Broiler
Café Hanalei and Terrace
Casa Di Amici
Duke's Canoe Club
Hamura Saimin
Keoki's Paradise
Mema Thai Chinese Cuisine
A Pacific Café
Plantation Gardens
Postcards
Roy's Poipu Bar & Grill
Shells, at the Sheraton Kauai Hotel
Tidepools

MOLOKAI: Zone 14

Hotel Molokai Restaurant
Maunaloa Room
Molokai Pizza Café
The Village Grill

THE BEST HAWAIIAN RESTAURANTS BY ZONE (*continued*)

LANAI: Zone 15

Blue Ginger Café
The Formal Dining Room, The Lodge at Koele
Henry Clay's Rotisserie
Ihilani

More Recommendations

Best Bagels

Oahu

This Is It Bakery and Deli 443 Cooke Street, Honolulu (808) 597-1017

Best Bakeries

Oahu

Mary Catherine's Bakery 2820 South King Street, Honolulu (808) 946-4333

Maui

Komoda Store & Bakery 3674 Baldwin Avenue, Makawao (808) 572-7261. For cream puffs and macadamia nut cookies.

Kauai

Kilauea Bakery and Pau Hana Pizza Kong Lung Center, Kilauea (808) 828-2020

Molokai

Kanemitsu Bakery 79 Ala Malama Street, Kaunakakai (808) 553-5855. For Molokai bread and lavosh.

Best Breakfasts

The Big Island

Pahu Ia Four Seasons Hualalai, 100 Kaupulehu Drive, Kaupulehu-Kona (808) 325-8000

Kauai

Eggbert's 4-484 Kuhio Highway, Coconut Marketplace, Kapaa (808) 822-3787

Best Brewpubs

Oahu

Brew Moon 1200 Ala Moana Boulevard, Honolulu (808) 589-1818

Maui

Maui Brews 900 Front Street, Lahaina (808) 667-7794

The Big Island

Kona Brewing Company and Brew Pub 75-5629 Kuakini Highway, Kailua-Kona (808) 329-2739

Kauai

Whaler's Brewpub 3132 Ninini Point Street, Lihue (808) 245-2000

Best Deli Food

Oahu

This Is It Bakery and Deli 443 Cooke Street, Honolulu (808) 597-1017

Maui

Pauwela Café 375 West Kuiaha Road, Haiku (808) 575-9242

The Big Island

A Piece of the Apple 75-5799 Alii Drive, Suite 2A, Kailua-Kona (808) 329-4668

Lanai

Pele's Other Garden 811 Hausten Street, Lanai City (808) 565-9628

Best Down-Home Local Atmosphere

Oahu

La Mariana Restaurant and Bar 50 Sand Island Access Road, Honolulu (808) 848-2800

The Big Island

Bamboo Restaurant Akoni Pule Highway, Hawi (808) 889-5555

Kauai

Green Garden Highway 50, Hanapepe (808) 335-5422

Best Fresh Fish

Maui

Mama's Fish House 799 Poho Place, Kuau (808) 579-8488

The Big Island

Seaside Restaurant 1790 Kalanianaole Avenue, Hilo (808) 935-8825

Best Golf Course Restaurants

Oahu

Bird of Paradise Hawaii Prince Golf Course, Ewa Beach (808) 689-2270

Maui

Sea Watch 100 Wailea Golf Club Drive, Wailea (808) 875-8080

The Big Island

The Club Grill Hualalai Resort, 100 Kaupulehu Drive, Kaupulehu-Kona (808) 325-8525

Kauai

Princeville Restaurant and Bar Prince Clubhouse, 5-3900 Kuhio Highway, Princeville (808) 826-5050

Lanai

The Challenge at Manele Bay Clubhouse Manele, Lanai (808) 565-2230

Best Hamburgers

Oahu

Kua Aina Sandwich 66-214 Kamehameha Highway, Haleiwa (808) 637-6067; 1116 Auahi Street, Honolulu (808) 591-9133

Maui

Cheeseburger in Paradise 811 Front Street, Lahaina (808) 661-4855

Kauai

Bubba's Hawaii 4-1421 Kuhio Highway, Kapaa (808) 823-0069; Hanalei (808) 826-7839; Maui (808) 891-2600

Best Hawaiian Food

Oahu: Local-Style

Ono Hawaiian Foods 726 Kapahulu Avenue, Kapahulu (808) 737-2275

Oahu: Upscale

Parc Café Waikiki Parc Hotel, 2233 Helumoa Road, Waikiki (808) 931-6643. Wednesday and Friday lunch buffet.

Best Hawaiian Food *(continued)*

Maui

Pukalani Country Club Restaurant 360 Pukalani, Pukalani (808) 572-1325

The Big Island

Kuhio Grille 111 East Puainako, Prince Kuhio Plaza, Suite A106, Hilo (808) 959-2336

Kauai

Aloha Diner 971F Kuhio Highway, Waipouli (808) 822-3851

Best Ice Cream (Locally Made)

Call listed numbers for other outlets.

Oahu

Bubbie's Homemade Ice Cream and Desserts Kahala Mall Shopping Center, Kahala (808) 739-2822; 1010 University Avenue, Honolulu (808) 949-8984

The Big Island

Tropical Dreams Ice Cream Kress Building, Kamehameha Highway, Hilo (808) 935-9109; Kohala Coffee Mill, Akoni Puli Highway, Hawi (808) 889-5577

Kauai

Lappert's Ice Cream 1-3555 Kaumualii Highway (808) 335-6121

Best Italian Cuisine

Oahu

Donato's Restaurant Manoa Marketplace, Waikiki (808) 988-2000

The Big Island

Donatoni's Hilton Waikoloa Village, 425 Waikoloa Beach Drive, Waikoloa (808) 886-1234

Kauai

La Cascata Princeville Hotel, Princeville Resort (808) 826-9644

Best Japanese Teahouses

Oahu

Natsunoya Tea House 1935 Makanani Drive, Honolulu (808) 595-4488. Minimum of ten diners.

Kauai

Hanamaulu Restaurant, Tea House and Sushi Bar 1-4291 Kuhio Highway, Hanamaulu (808) 245-2511

Best Luau

Oahu

Paradise Cove 92-1089 Aliinui Drive, Kapolei (808) 842-5911

Maui

Old Lahaina Luau 1251 Front Street, Lahaina (808) 667-1998

The Big Island

Kona Village Resort Queen Kaahumanu Highway, Kaupulehu-Kona (808) 325-5555

Kauai

Paina o Hanalei Princeville Hotel, Princeville Resort (808) 826-9644

Best Mexican Cuisine

Oahu

Rosie's Cantina Haleiwa Shopping Plaza, Haleiwa (808) 637-3538

Maui

Pollis 1202 Makawao Avenue, Makawao (808) 572-7808

Kauai

La Bamba 4261 Rice Street, Lihue (808) 245-5972

Best Pizza

Oahu

Pizza Bob's Haleiwa Haleiwa Shopping Plaza, Haleiwa (808) 637-5095

Maui

Pizza Paradiso Express Whaler's Village, 2435 Kaanapali Parkway, Kaanapali (808) 667-0333

The Big Island

Bianelli's Gourmet Pizza and Pasta 75-240 Nani Kailua Drive, Kailua-Kona (808) 326-4800

Kauai

Brick Oven Pizza State Highway 50, Kaumualii Highway, Kalaheo (808) 332-8561

Best Pizza *(continued)*

Molokai

Molokai Pizza Café Kaunakakai Place on Wharf Road, Kaunakakai (808) 553-5655

Best Places to Hang Out

Oahu

The Pier Bar Aloha Tower Market Place, 1 Aloha Tower Drive, Honolulu (808) 536-2100

Maui

Hula Grill's Beach Bar Whaler's Village, 2435 Kaanapali Parkway, Kaanapali (808) 667-6636

The Big Island

Kona Inn Restaurant 75-5744 Alii Drive, Kailua-Kona (808) 329-4455. Go at sunset.

Best Plate Lunches

Oahu

Kakaako Kitchen 1200 Ala Moana Boulevard, Honolulu (808) 594-3663

Maui

Sam Sato's in Wailuku Millyard 1750 Wili Pa Loop, Wailuku (808) 244-7124

The Big Island

Island Grinds Hilo Bay Front on the beach near Suisan Fish auction, Hilo (808) 895-0625. Lunch wagon.

Kauai

Mixed Plate Ching Young Village, 5-5190 Kuhio Highway, 3E4, Hanalei (808) 826-7888

Best Romantic Restaurants

In all cases, ask for a table with an ocean view.

Oahu

Michel's 2895 Kalakaua Avenue, Waikiki (808) 923-6552

The Big Island

Pahu Ia Restaurant at Four Seasons Hualalai 100 Kaupulehu Drive, Kaupulehu-Kona (808) 325-8000

Kauai

Tidepools Hyatt Regency Kauai, 1571 Poipu Road, Poipu (808) 742-1234

Best Seafood Buffets

Oahu

Orchids at Halekulani 2199 Kalia Road, Waikiki (808) 923 2311

Maui

The Terrace at the Ritz-Carlton 1 Ritz-Carlton Drive, Kapalua (808) 669-6200

Kauai

Café Hanalei and Terrace Princeville Resort, Princeville (808) 826-2760. Friday night only.

Best Shave Ice

Oahu

Matsumoto Shave Ice 66-087 Kamehameha Highway, Haleiwa (808) 637-4827

Maui

Tobi's Ice Cream and Shave Ice 1913 South Kihei Road, Kihei (808) 891-2440

The Big Island

Oodles of Noodles 75-1027 Henry, Suite 102, Kailua-Kona (808) 329-9222

Best Steak Houses

Oahu

Ruth's Chris Steak House Restaurant Row, Honolulu (808) 599-3860

Maui

Outback Steak House 4405 Honoapiilani Highway, Honoapiilani (808) 665-1822

Best Steak Houses *(continued)*

The Big Island

Big Island Steak House Kings Shops, Waikoloa Beach Drive, Waikoloa (808) 886-8805

Kauai

Kalaheo Steak House 4444 Papalina Road, Kalaheo (808) 332-9780

Best Sunday Brunch

Oahu

Orchids Halekulani, 2199 Kalia Road, Waikiki (808) 923-2311

Maui

Grand Wailea Hotel 3850 Wailea Alanui Drive, Wailea (808) 875-1234

The Big Island

The Terrace Manua Kea Beach Hotel, 62-100 Mauna Kea Beach Drive, Kohala Coast (808) 882-7222

Kauai

Café Hanalei and Terrace Princeville Resort, Princeville (808) 826-2760

Best Sushi Bars

Oahu

Kacho Waikiki Parc Hotel, 2233 Helumoa Road, Waikiki (808) 924-3535

East Maui

Hakone Maui Prince Hotel, 5400 Makena Alanui Road, Makena (808) 874-1111

West Maui

Sansei Restaurant and Sushi Bar Kapalua Shops, 115 Bay Drive, Unit 115, Kapalua (808) 669-6286

The Big Island

Imari at Hilton Waikoloa Village 425 Waikoloa Beach Drive, Kohala Coast (808) 886-1234

Best Thai Cuisine

Oahu

Singha Thai 1910 Ala Moana Boulevard, Honolulu (808) 941-2898

The Big Island

Royal Siam Thai 70 Malama Street, Hilo (808) 961-6100

Bangkok Houses 75-5626 Kuakini Highway, Building 5, Kailua-Kona (808) 329-7764

Kauai

Mema Thai Chinese Cuisine Wailua Shopping Plaza, 4-361 Kuhio Highway, Kapaa (808) 823-0899

Best Theme Restaurants

Oahu

All Star Café King Kalakaua Plaza, 2080 Kalakaua Avenue, Waikiki (808) 955-8326

Maui

Bubba Gump Shrimp Company 889 Front Street, Lahaina (808) 661-3111

The Big Island

Hard Rock Café 75-5815 Alii Drive, Kailua-Kona (808) 326-7655

Best Vegetarian

Oahu

Down to Earth Deli 2525 South King Street, Honolulu (808) 947-7678

Maui

The Vegan 115 Baldwin Avenue, Paia (808) 579-9144

The Big Island

Sibu Café 75-5695 Alii Drive, Kailua-Kona (808) 329-1112. Also serves Asian food.

Kauai

Hanapepe Café & Espresso 3830 Hanapepe Road, Hanapepe (808) 335-5011

Best Vegetarian *(continued)*

Molokai

Outpost Natural Foods 70 Makaena Street, Kaunakakai (808) 553-3377

Best Vietnamese Cuisine

Oahu

A Little Bit of Saigon 1160 Maunakea, Honolulu (808) 528-3663

Maui

A Saigon Café 1792 Main Street, Wailuku (808) 243-9560

Best Views

Oahu

John Domini's 43 Ahui Street, Honolulu (808) 523-0955

Maui

The Bay Club Kapalua Bay Hotel, 1 Bay Drive, Kapalua (808) 669-5656

The Big Island

Pavilion Mauna Kea Beach Hotel, 62-100 Mauna Kea Beach Drive, Kohala Coast (808) 822-7222

Kauai

Café Hanalei and Terrace Princeville Resort, Princeville (808) 826-2760

Lanai

Manele Bay Clubhouse Manele Bay Resort, Manele (808) 565-2230

Restaurant Profiles

Oahu

Alan Wong's Restaurant ★★★★★

HAWAII REGIONAL | MODERATE | QUALITY ★★★★★ | VALUE ★★★★ | ZONE I

1857 South King Street, 3rd floor, Waikiki/Honolulu; (808) 949-2526; www.alanwongs.com

Reservations Highly recommended **When to go** Anytime, but less crowded 5–6:30 p.m. **Entrée range** $15–$30 **Payment** VISA, MC, AMEX, DC, JCB **Service rating** ★★★★★ **Parking** Valet or limited onstreet parking **Bar** Full service **Wine selection** Extensive, mostly domestic, good selection by the glass **Dress** Dressy resort attire **Disabled access** Good, via elevator **Customers** Islanders and visitors

Dinner Every day, 5–10 p.m.

Setting & atmosphere Situated a short cab ride out of Waikiki, Alan Wong's is hard to spot if you're unfamiliar with South King Street, but the third-floor restaurant is worth the search. Local artwork decorates the walls, and sparkly lights hang overhead. An exhibition kitchen on one side of the comfortable restaurant showcases the action indoors, while outdoors, lanai diners look across part of the city to the Koolau Mountains.

House specialties "Da Bag," an appetizer in a billowy foil pillow, is pierced at the table to yield aromatic kalua pig, steamed clams, spinach, and shiitake mushrooms. Pacific flavors continue throughout the meal in desserts such as "The Coconut," an eye-catching ball of Hawaiian Vintage Chocolate filled with haupia sorbet nestled in tropical fruits and lilikoi sauce.

Other recommendations The chef's sense of humor and his seemingly effortless ability to fuse Asian, Hawaiian, and Continental flavors are evident in such menu favorites as poke pines (ahi tartare fried in a crispy, spiky shell), duck nacho (Chinese-style duck on tapioca-scallion chips), and sautéed shrimp and clams (with a spicy lemongrass/black-bean sauce served with pasta). Even mashed potatoes take on new meaning when served as roasted garlic smashed potatoes to accompany shellfish.

Summary & comments Alan Wong is among Hawaii's most creative and accomplished chefs, known for his artistry and the hands-on care he continues to provide in his kitchen despite his many new projects. In recent years other prominent hotel chefs have opened freestanding restaurants, but Wong's King Street location has withstood the competition and remains the favorite special-occasion destination. The ultimate way to sample his style is the always-evolving five-course tasting menu ($65; $90 with wines).

Assaggio Ristorante Italiano ★★★½

ITALIAN | INEXPENSIVE/MODERATE | QUALITY ★★★★½ | VALUE ★★★★★ | ZONE 6

Mililani Town Center, 95-1249 Meheula Parkway, Mililani; (808) 623-4693

Reservations Suggested **When to go** Anytime **Entrée range** Lunch $9–$14, dinner $10–$19 **Payment** All major credit cards **Service rating** ★★★ **Parking** Free, in shopping-center lot **Bar** Full service **Wine selection** Average, but featuring a nice selection of Italian wines, 7 by the glass **Dress** Casual **Disabled access** Good **Customers** Mostly locals

Lunch Every day, 11:30 a.m.–2:30 p.m.

Dinner Sunday–Thursday, 5–9:30 p.m.; Friday and Saturday, 5–10 p.m.

Setting & atmosphere A family-friendly atmosphere, but dressy enough to make this a special-occasion spot for the suburbs. Assaggio has a clean, contemporary, open feel—upscale, but not intimidating. The name means "to taste." The restaurant is a distance from town, but consider it for a lunch stop on a trip to see the waves on the North Shore. It's a short hop off the H-2 freeway.

House specialties This is fairly simple Italian food, but the menu is large, with choices for everyone, from the spaghetti-and-meatballs kid to the adult with a taste for veal scaloppine with eggplant and mushrooms. Chicken Assaggio is crunchy and flavorful, smothered in garlic, peppers, and mushrooms in wine sauce. The spicy house arrabiata sauce is another no-fail favorite, served with ziti or fresh fish. Sicilian chicken is a hearty comfort meal made with potatoes, peppers, mushrooms, and wine sauce.

Other recommendations The Caesar salad for two is excellent; it is tossed and served at the table. Also popular are the ravioli dishes, osso buco, and the many treatments of veal scaloppine (saltimbocca, alla piccata, alla sorrentino, and alla rollatini).

Summary & comments Chef/owner Thomas Ky came to this country as a refugee from Vietnam, escaping his homeland alone and destitute as a 14-year-old. He learned English and worked in Chinese restaurants, sometimes several at a time. But once he found work at an Italian restaurant, he identified his calling and within 18 months had saved enough money to go into his first restaurant partnership. Ky does not cultivate celebrity, but he is as successful as any of Hawaii's restaurateurs if not more so. There are three other Assaggios (Ala Moana Center, Hawaii Kai, and Kailua). The Ala Moana location may be most convenient for visitors, but the Mililani restaurant is the most consistent in quality, as Ky personally spends most of his time in this kitchen.

Bali-By-The-Sea ★★★½

EURO-ASIAN | MODERATE/EXPENSIVE | QUALITY ★★★★ | VALUE ★★★ | ZONE 1

Hilton Hawaiian Village Hotel, 2005 Kalia Road, Waikiki; (808) 941-BALI, restaurant (808) 949-4321; www.hawaiianvillage.hilton.com

Reservations Highly recommended **When to go** Sunsets are most pleasant **Entrée range** $25.50–$30.95 **Payment** All major credit cards **Service rating** ★★★★★ **Parking** Valet or hotel lot **Bar** Full service **Wine selection** Exceptional; the wine selection has been named "The Best" in 1999 in the local Hale Aina Awards—half a dozen wines are available by the glass **Dress** Resort attire, collared shirts and slacks for gentlemen **Disabled access** Good **Customers** Hotel guests and Islanders for special occasions

Dinner Monday–Saturday, 6–10 p.m.

Setting & atmosphere White linens, candlelight, and fine china and crystal impart an elegance to this romantic, though large, open-air restaurant that overlooks ocean and lagoon vistas. Diamond Head looms beyond the window tables.

House specialties The regular menu hints of Chef Jean-Luc Voegeles's French background. Escargot in phyllo with warm ratatouille and roasted garlic beurre blanc followed by succulent rack of lamb crusted with macadamia nuts and herbs are two of Voegeles's classic presentations. Complete dinners climax with a showy presentation of truffles in a miniature chocolate replica of Diamond Head swirling with dry ice.

Other recommendations From half a dozen appetizers you might choose char siu and shiitake pot-stickers with port wine balsamic glaze or shrimp and scallop Provençales. Seafood lovers often go for Island bouillabaisse as a main course.

Summary & comments It's not only the open-air dining with soft breezes and lapping waves carrying in from the ocean that make this prize-winning restaurant a favorite of those ready to pop the question, but also the knowledge that they'll receive impeccable service as well as good food to win a sweetheart's heart and hand.

Buzz's Original Steak House ★★

STEAK AND SEAFOOD | INEXPENSIVE/MODERATE | QUALITY ★★★½ | VALUE ★★★
ZONE 3

413 Kawailoa Road, Kailua; (808) 261-4661

Reservations Highly recommended **When to go** Anytime **Entrée range** $11–$30 **Payment** No credit cards **Service rating** ★★★ **Parking** Free in adjacent lot **Bar** Full service **Wine selection** Adequate, many by the glass **Dress** Casual **Disabled access** Good **Customers** Islanders, tourists brought in by Islanders

Lunch Every day, 11 a.m.–3 p.m.

Dinner Every day, 5–10 p.m.

Setting & atmosphere Across the street from Kailua Beach and bordered on one side by Kaelepulu Stream, Buzz's has the appeal of an old-fashioned beach house. The wait-help wears Polynesian prints and T-shirts to serve customers at wooden-topped tables and booths indoors and on an outdoor deck. Inside, the bar is a local gathering spot for beachgoers and the young people of this family-oriented small windward town a little less than 15 miles from Waikiki.

House specialties Salad lovers invariably remember Buzz's bar because avocado is generally among the offerings of tossed greens, sprouts, olives, bacon bits, sesame seeds, and the like. This is a good place to choose fresh fish; thick, juicy steaks; prime rib; and rack of lamb accompanied by a baked potato. If you want good, straightforward food without all the fancy coulis, aïoli, and other sauces of today's trendy cuisine, Buzz's is the place.

Other recommendations Share an artichoke surprise, a whole artichoke with a butter, herb, and garlic dipping sauce for an appetizer, before sampling fresh fish prepared Chinese-style. You'll catch whiffs of peanut oil, soy sauce, garlic, ginger, and cilantro when this dish is served.

Summary & comments If you sit at the last table on the open-air deck, you'll notice a little plaque commemorating the fact that President and Mrs. Clinton dined at that table during a stopover in the Islands. Lunch at Buzz's is a pleasant way to take a break from a day spent windsurfing or sunning at the nearby beach.

Cascada ★★★½

MEDITERRANEAN WITH ISLAND FLAIR | MODERATE | QUALITY ★★★★ | VALUE ★★★
ZONE I

Royal Garden Hotel, 440 Olohana Street, Waikiki; (808) 945-0270; www.royalgardens.com

Reservations Recommended **When to go** Anytime **Entrée range** $18–$26 **Payment** All major credit cards **Service rating** ★★★★½ **Parking** Complimentary valet or limited on-street **Bar** Full service **Wine selection** Adequate, 10 wines by the glass **Dress** Casual resort attire **Disabled access** Good **Customers** Tourists and Islanders for special occasions

Breakfast Every day, 6:30–9:30 a.m.

Lunch Every day, 11 a.m.–2 p.m.

Dinner Every day, 6–10 p.m.

Setting & atmosphere You'll feel as if you made your own special discovery when you wander up a Waikiki side street to this boutique hotel. The restaurant sports a handpainted trompe l'oeil ceiling that depicts trellises, birds, and flowers. Tables are set inside and out on a marble terrace beside a soothing waterfall that feeds into a swimming pool.

House specialties Whatever you do, don't miss sampling the gnocchi with ricotta cheese and spinach, a delicious accompaniment to Mongolian lamb chops or pan-seared pork tenderloin.

Other recommendations Salmon tartare, Thai spring rolls, and crab cakes with chipotle sour cream and avocado tomatillo sauces are tried-and-true favorites among the appetizers. Opt for entrées like seafood risotto or fresh Island fish for a lighter meal.

Summary & comments *Gourmet* magazine named Cascada one of America's Top Tables. Dining here is like finding a peaceful Mediterranean oasis in the middle of frantic Waikiki. Cascada works equally well for a serious business meeting or a quiet tête-à-tête.

Chef Mavro Restaurant ★★★★½

PACIFIC RIM | EXPENSIVE | QUALITY ★★★★★ | VALUE ★★★ | ZONE I

1969 South King Street, Waikiki/Honolulu; (808) 944-4714; www.chefmavro.com

Reservations Highly recommended **When to go** Anytime **Entrée range** $27–$38; prix fixe menus: $48–$72 without wines, $66–$96 with wines **Payment** VISA, MC, AMEX, DC, JCB **Service rating** ★★★★★ **Parking** Valet only **Bar** Full service **Wine selection** Good **Dress** Dressy resort attire **Disabled access** Good **Customers** Islanders

Dinner Tuesday–Sunday, 6–9:30 p.m.

Setting & atmosphere Gleaming pink marble at the entry foretells the simple elegance of the interior. A graceful arch divides the upper and lower portions of the dining area, with banquette seating beside two walls of etched glass windows. The intimate 68-seat restaurant is lit with pinpoint lights with tiny shades suspended like stars from the ceiling and decorated with sprays of orchids for a peaceful, refined atmosphere.

House specialties Chef/owner George Mavrothalassitis changes his menu every two months, but one dish remains constant. His salt-crusted onaga is elegantly presented at the table, the fish-shaped pastry carefully lifted to reveal a fillet of succulent and steaming longtail snapper. The chef has been preparing the dish the same way for ten years; he says he is a bit tired of making it, but his customers won't let him remove it from the menu. The essence of Chef Mavro is the pairing of food and wine, and the best way to appreciate his cuisine is through his tasting menus. He offers a choice of three- to six-course dinners, each dish paired with wine, for $67 to $120. Every few weeks, the chef presents his new dishes to the staff and a few guest tasters; they try the dishes with a variety of wines and vote on the best pairings. Majority rules and sets the menu for the next two months.

Other recommendations Coriander-crisped beef entrecôte was a featured dish in *Wine Spectator* magazine, paired with an Italian Chianti. It is served with artichoke barigoule, slow-roasted tomatoes, angel-hair pasta, and an anchovy–Pinot Noir sauce. A true comfort dish that plays on favorite island flavors is the island chicken and oxtail pot au feu, with its deeply flavored star anise consommé, vegetables, and Yukon gold potatoes, served with wasabi-flavored rice. The restaurant has recently entered a partnership with the new Hawaiian Vanilla Co., so the pastry chef's new creations with that flavoring, such as Hawaiian Vanilla tapioca, are worth a visit.

Summary & comments Chef George Mavrothalassitis opened Chef Mavro in 1988 with the goal of creating an intimate restaurant in the finest French tradition. He built his reputation for contemporary French cuisine as executive chef at the Halekulani when it was first awarded five diamonds by AAA. In 2003, he was named Best Chef of the Pacific Northwest/Hawaii by the James Beard foundation, only the third Hawaii chef to receive the honor.

Diamond Head Grill ★★★

CONTEMPORARY AMERICAN | MODERATE/EXPENSIVE | QUALITY ★★★½ | VALUE ★★
ZONE 1

W Hotel, 2885 Kalakaua Avenue, Waikiki; (808) 922-3734; www.whotels.com

Reservations Highly recommended, but not required **When to go** Anytime **Entrée range** $22–$42 **Payment** VISA, MC, AMEX, DC, D, JCB **Service rating** ★★★★½ **Parking** Valet or on-street meters **Bar** Full service **Wine selection** Extensive, nearly 2 dozen wines by the glass, including champagne **Dress** Resort attire, no beach wear **Disabled access** Good, via elevator **Customers** Islanders and tourists

Dinner Every day, 5:30–10 p.m.; a lighter bistro menu is available Thursday–Saturday, 10–11:30 p.m.

Setting & atmosphere The second-floor location of this restaurant, opened in 1998, is a winner, thanks to Los Angeles architect Steve Jones, who incidentally designed Wolfgang Puck's outlets. It's atmosphere is light and airy, with tables nicely spaced, and the view of Diamond Head outside a huge picture window seems bigger than life. Jan Kasprzycki's vivid mural beside the entry staircase adds a sophisticated touch. The main dining area seats 150, with a serpentine martini and appetizer bar on one side; a separate banquet room holds 125. And a glass-enclosed "Chefs Table" is perfect for ten guests.

House specialties A delicately flavored white snapper called opakapaka—a longtime island favorite—is crusted with porcini mushrooms, then sautéed and served on a bed of red bliss potato salad and Dungeness crab ragout. For non–fish lovers, two full-flavored specialties are the guava- and mustard-crusted rack of lamb (with goat cheese and roasted garlic gratin) and braised short ribs (with soybean puree and plum wine demi-glace). Chocolate lava cake with coffee ice cream is another memory-maker.

Other recommendations It's hard to pass up appetizers like kalua pork lumpia with mango guacamole and spicy mustard sauce and a lighter grilled portobello mushroom with grilled asparagus, Gorgonzola, and polenta. Selections from the stone oven include rotisserie pork panini with smoky mozzarella, sun-dried tomato aïoli, and arugula on a rustic flat bread.

Entertainment & amenities Live music offered Wednesdays and Thursdays, plus late-night entertainment in a club atmosphere on Fridays and Saturdays.

Summary & comments This restaurant opened under the helm of the charismatic celebrity chef from Maui, David Paul Johnson. Johnson was replaced less than two years later with David Reardon, a well-respected hotel chef, but Reardon left soon afterward, leaving the kitchen in the hands of one of the sous-chefs, Todd Constantino. The restaurant is still seeking its center amid all this change.

Don Ho's Island Grill ★★★

HAWAII REGIONAL COMFORT FOOD | INEXPENSIVE | QUALITY ★★★½ | VALUE ★★★½
ZONE 2

Aloha Tower Marketplace, 1 Aloha Tower Drive, Honolulu; (808) 528-0807; www.donho.com

Reservations Recommended **When to go** Sunset for best views of a working harbor **Entrée range** $5.95–$16.95 **Payment** VISA, MC, AMEX, DC, JCB **Service rating** ★★★★ **Parking** Valet or in adjacent pay lot **Bar** Full service, good selection of tropical drinks **Wine selection** Adequate **Dress** Casual **Disabled access** Good if using valet **Customers** Islanders and tourists

Lunch & dinner Every day, 10 a.m.–9 p.m.

Setting & atmosphere This restaurant is a Polynesian nostalgia trip right back to the Hawaii depicted by Hollywood in the 1940s and 1950s. Walls are covered with surfboards, paddles, rattan, and Don Ho memorabilia and pictures. The salad bar is nestled in an outrigger canoe. The restaurant opens to views of busy Honolulu Harbor on one side, and a thatched-roof bar just outside the confines of the restaurant also overlooks the harbor. Pillars decorated like palm trees and a bamboo-lined bar with stools covered in colorful Polynesian prints are all part of the yesteryear atmosphere.

House specialties Most fun for sharing is the surfboard pizza with a variety of toppings presented at the table on a miniature surfboard resting on two big pineapple cans. You can get a cheeseburger anytime, but the chop chop salad with rotisserie roast pork and crispy Oriental vegetables is only one of many more interesting choices.

Other recommendations Stir-fry dishes—teriyaki beef with broccoli, Phoenix and Dragon with shrimp and chicken, Chinatown noodles, etc.—come in big portions, but the fresh Island fish is better. It comes macadamia-nut-and-pesto crusted, or luau-roasted with Hawaiian salt, or local-style with ginger, shoyu, sesame oil, and chives.

Entertainment & amenities Seven days a week musicians grace the stage during afternoon happy hour, while bigger-name entertainers often appear on weekends and for special events.

Summary & comments People say they haven't seen anything like this place in 30 years, since Don Ho's heyday. The atmosphere receives bigger raves than the food, however. Ho tends to show up several nights a week, generally after 10 p.m.

Double Eight Chinese Restaurant ★★★★

CHINESE | INEXPENSIVE | QUALITY ★★★★½ | VALUE ★★★★★ | ZONE 2

1113 Maunakea Street, Chinatown; (808) 526-3887

Reservations None taken **When to go** Anytime **Entrée range** Lunch or dinner, $8–$9 **Payment** VISA, MC **Service rating** ★★★ **Parking** Metered parking on street or in public lots nearby **Bar** None **Wine selection** None **Dress** Casual **Disabled access** One step up from sidewalk **Customers** Locals, some tourists

Lunch Every day, 10:30 a.m.–3 p.m.

Dinner Every day, 4:30–10 p.m.

Setting & atmosphere Double Eight is a small, bare-bones noodle house, presenting honest Chinese food in Hong Kong style. It's clean and comfortable, right in the middle of Honolulu's bustling Chinatown. Plan a few hours of shopping and browsing in this area, with Double Eight as the perfect spot to rest and replenish.

House specialties The hot pot casseroles are savory, satisfying bowls of warm comfort. Try chicken with mushrooms, pig's feet with bean curd, a seafood mix, or tofu and vegetables. The flavors mix wonderfully. One hot pot and some noodles would feed two to three. The cake noodles, thin and crispy, are especially good. They're on the menu with chicken, but pay an extra six bits and you can have them with any of the toppings, such as sour cabbage and pork or beef and broccoli.

Other recommendations Double Eight does well by many traditional specialties, particularly ginger chicken (poached and served cold), spicy salt-and-pepper shrimp (quick-fried with heads attached), Kung Pao chicken, and eggplant with garlic sauce.

Summary & comments Double Eight is one of those true "finds" for a traveler—an affordable place with character and great food. Best of all, it's a place that locals have come to for years, and these are people with a lot of access to Chinese food. They're good judges.

Dukes Canoe Club Restaurant ★★★

CONTEMPORARY | INEXPENSIVE/MODERATE | QUALITY ★★★½ | VALUE ★★★★
ZONE 1

Outrigger Waikiki Hotel, 2335 Kalakaua Avenue, Waikiki; (808) 922-2268; www.outrigger.com

Reservations Accepted **When to go** Anytime **Entrée range** $7.95–$23.95 **Payment** VISA, MC, AMEX, D, DC **Service rating** ★★★ **Parking** Valet or hotel lot **Bar** Full service **Wine selection** Good **Dress** Daytime, off-the-beach casual; at night, it's still casual **Disabled access** Good if using valet **Customers** Islanders, beach boys, tourists

Breakfast Every day, 7–11 a.m.

Lunch Every day, 11 a.m.–5 p.m.

Dinner Every day, 5–10 p.m.—a simpler menu is served in the Barefoot Bar 5 p.m.–midnight

Setting & atmosphere *Pau hana* (after work) surfers, paddlers, and tourists hang out at the big wooden bar watching the sunset over Waikiki Beach in this casual, oceanfront eatery. Historic photos, surfboards, and saltwater aquariums bring back memories of the days when Duke Kahanamoku was an Olympic swimmer and surfer extraordinaire.

House specialties At dinner try a huge slab of prime rib or awesome fresh fish—ahi, mahimahi, ono, or opakapaka—available in five preparations: baked, firecracker, Parmesan- and herb-crusted, hibachi-style teriyaki, or simply grilled. At lunch this is a convenient spot for anything from a burger to huli huli chicken to Thai-style seafood coconut curry.

Other recommendations Breakfast and lunch buffets and a salad bar at dinner boast value "grinds," or if you prefer table service you might order burgers, fries, pasta, and salads.

Entertainment & amenities From 4 to 6 p.m. thoroughly modern musicians play island sounds. On Friday, Saturday, and Sunday, dance bands keep the lower lanai jumping.

Summary & comments Dukes is one of the most popular places to hang out after a day on Waikiki Beach for both Islanders and tourists, partly because it opens right onto the sand, but also because local surfers are rightly proud of the great Hawaiian swimmer this restaurant commemorates.

The Golden Dragon ★★★★

CHINESE | MODERATE | QUALITY ★★★★½ | VALUE ★★★ | ZONE 1

Hilton Hawaiian Village Hotel, 2005 Kalia Road, Waikiki; (808) 946-5336; www.hawaiianvillage.hilton.com

Reservations Highly recommended **When to go** Anytime except Monday **Entrée range** $9–$30 **Payment** All major credit cards **Service rating** ★★★★½ **Parking** Valet or validated self-park in hotel's garage **Bar** Full service **Wine selection** Good **Dress** Resort attire **Disabled access** Good if using valet **Customers** Hotel guests, Waikiki tourists, Islanders

Dinner Tuesday–Sunday, 6–9:30 p.m.

Setting & atmosphere Ask to sit on one of the open-air lanai that extend out from the restaurant, for the most romantic views over the Hilton Hawaiian Village lagoon and the little coconut-clad island that rests in its center. The dining room itself has the imperial grandeur of a modern Oriental palace. Golden dragon statues greet you at the entrance, and one wall is lined with lacquer screens decorated with Oriental figures. Tempting aromas float from a circular, glass-enclosed "smoke room" that displays plump juicy roasted ducks. At the back of the restaurant, a private room secluded by a glass partition etched in a lily design is available for groups.

House specialties A few signature items on the Cantonese menu are a legacy to Chef Dai Hoy Chang, who opened this first Chinese restaurant in Hawaii. Imperial beggar's chicken has to be ordered 24 hours in advance; then, when the waiter presents the dish, he shares the legend with you. A beggar who stole a chicken had only lotus leaves to wrap it in. He improvised a pan by covering the leaves with mud from the lily pond and cooking the whole thing in a campfire. At the Golden Dragon, beggar's chicken arrives at the table in its clay encasement, and the diner is given a beribboned "good luck hammer" to crack it, after which the waiter peels away the clay and the lotus leaves and carves the juicy chicken.

You can see the Peking duck, another traditional dish, hanging in the glass house in the restaurant's center before you eat it. It's carved at the table and served with plum sauce rolled in Mandarin pancakes by your waiter, an easy, non-messy way to eat a dish that could otherwise have you licking your fingers all through the meal.

Other recommendations Islanders traditionally love the succulent chunks of cold ginger chicken and a tangy lemon chicken dish, but personally, we would opt for the shelled lobster meat with a delicate curry sauce and haupia (coconut pudding). Two chef's signature dinners for $32 and $39 per person feature enough food that you can tuck leftovers in your hotel mini-fridge for dinner the next night.

Summary & comments Don't say no when the tea lady offers to tell your fortune (at no extra cost), though you must reveal your birth year so she can determine which animal sign you are in the Chinese zodiac. You'll be amazed at how often the fortune fits your personality. *Gourmet* magazine named the Golden Dragon one of America's Top Tables in 1997 and 1998.

Hau Tree Lanai ★★★

CONTINENTAL/PACIFIC RIM | MODERATE | QUALITY ★★★½ | VALUE ★★★ | ZONE 1

New Otani Kaimana Beach Hotel, 2863 Kalakaua Avenue, Waikiki; (808) 921-7066; www.kaimana.com

Reservations Recommended, especially for dinner **When to go** Anytime; at dinner sunset is preferred **Entrée range** Breakfast $9.50–$12.95, lunch

$7.95–$14.95, dinner $17.50–$35 **Payment** VISA, MC, AMEX, DC, D, JCB **Service rating** ★★★★ **Parking** Valet or on-street meters **Bar** Full service **Wine selection** Good, some selections by the glass **Dress** Casual for breakfast and lunch, resort attire at dinner **Disabled access** Good, with ramp to the beach-level terrace **Customers** Waikiki visitors, hotel guests, Islanders

Breakfast Monday–Saturday, 7–11 a.m.; Sunday, 7–11:30 a.m.

Lunch Monday–Saturday, 11:30 a.m.–2 p.m.; Sunday, noon–2 p.m.

Dinner Every day, 5:30–9 p.m.

Setting & atmosphere A favorite, unpretentious place for Islanders to take out-of-town guests, the Hau Tree Lanai's linen-draped tables are snuggled under a spreading hau tree on the beach at the Diamond Head end of Waikiki. If you want a beach-edge table, go early, about 5:30 p.m., and be sure to make reservations noting your request.

House specialties Hau Tree Lanai's signature dish is fresh opakapaka (snapper) Oriental style, steamed and garnished with hot peanut oil, soy sauce, cilantro, and green onions. Other favorites among the main courses include filet mignon teamed with the day's fresh catch, seafood penne pasta, shrimp scampi, or, on the wilder side, Thai pesto black tiger prawns and scallops with garlic chili-pepper fried rice. Complete dinners can be made of any entrée item for $6 extra, which adds soup or salad, dessert, and coffee or tea.

Other recommendations The manager recommends filet Madagascar, sautéed and served with a creamy green peppercorn sauce, potatoes, and vegetables. Appetizers encompass and combine international flavors ranging from Cajun blackened ahi sashimi, to chicken and vegetable lumpia, to hoisin duck quesadilla.

Summary & comments Dawdle over dessert at sundown and eventually you'll see someone you know heading home from paddling or surfing. The Hau Tree Lanai is often named Oahu's best outdoor dining location in local competitions.

Helena's Hawaiian Foods ★★★★

TRADITIONAL HAWAIIAN | INEXPENSIVE | QUALITY ★★★★½ | VALUE ★★★★★
ZONE 2

1240 North School Street, Honolulu; (808) 845-8044

Reservations None taken **When to go** Anytime **Entrée range** Lunch or dinner, $6–$12 **Payment** No credit cards accepted **Service rating** ★★★ **Parking** A few spots in a small attached lot **Bar** None **Wine selection** None **Dress** Casual **Disabled access** Restaurant would be easily negotiated by wheelchairs, but there are two shallow steps up from the parking lot **Customers** Locals

Lundh & dinner Tuesday–Friday, 11:30 a.m.–7:30 p.m.

Setting & atmosphere Helena's is a clean, down-to-earth, no-frills eatery. with the door painted red for good luck. On the walls you will find lithographs by Jean Charlot, gifts from the late artist that were personally framed and delivered. Also on the wall: owner Helen Chock's James Beard Foundation Award. In 2000, the restaurant was named a Regional Classic, a special designation for locally owned, neighborhood eateries that best reflect the character of their communities.

House specialties The menu is small and entirely devoted to traditional Hawaiian foods. It has remained unchanged for more than 50 years. The pipi kaula short ribs are exceptional—chewy on the outside and pull-apart moist on the inside. The flavoring is one-of-a-kind, drawn from Helena's grill, where they hang to dry slightly before cooking. Butterfish collars, made from the sweet, delicate meat just behind the fish's gills, are served fried or stewed (fried is better, crunchy and flavorful). Salt beef with watercress, soft cubes of brisket in a mellow broth, is perfect comfort food.

Other recommendations Lomi salmon, squid luau, and kalua pig, all luau specialties, are done well at Helena's. Refreshing squares of haupia, or coconut gelatin, are the perfect ending to the meal. You can order à la carte and assemble your own mixed plate. Most items are in the $3 range. Or you can choose one of four preset menus, priced at $6–$12. Whatever you have, don't forget a bowl of poi.

Summary and comments Owner Helen Chock ran Helena's almost single-handedly in one location beginning in 1946, winning the hearts of an extremely devoted clientele. In 2001, after collecting her James Beard Award, she lost her lease and moved to this location, which has all the clean brightness of a new site. Her grandson is now the principal owner, but Chock is in the kitchen daily, a tiny but unmistakable presence.

Hoku's ★★★★

CONTEMPORARY INTERNATIONAL | MODERATE/EXPENSIVE | QUALITY ★★★★½
VALUE ★★★ | ZONE 2

Kahala Mandarin Hotel, 500 Kahala Avenue, Honolulu; (808) 739-8777 or (808) 739-8888; www.mandarin-oriental.com

Reservations Highly recommended **When to go** Anytime **Entrée range** Lunch $14.95–$29.95, dinner $26.50–$32.50, vegetarian entrée at $21.95 **Payment** All major credit cards **Service rating** ★★★★★ **Parking** Valet or validated in hotel garage **Bar** Full service **Wine selection** Extensive, including half a dozen ports **Dress** Resort attire **Disabled access** Good **Customers** Hotel guests, repeat local diners

Lunch Monday–Friday, 11:30 a.m.–2:30 p.m.

Dinner Monday–Sunday, 5:30–10 p.m.

Setting & atmosphere Hoku's is a stylish restaurant where every table has a panoramic vista of the Pacific, thanks to a multilevel layout. An open kitchen at one end of the dining room showcases a kiawe wood grill, woks, a tandoori oven, and a wood-burning pizza oven. A sushi bar offers additional tidbits.

House specialties Hoku's satisfies international appetites in a single appetizer: Indian naan bread with an island-style ahi poke dip. Other dishes do justice to the flavors of the world—tandoori chicken salad, herb-crusted onaga (longtail snapper), and wok-fried prawns in garlic, ginger, and chiles. Among the more spectacular dishes is the seafood tower—a chilled mountain of prawns, crab claws, mussels, sashimi, octopus, and lobster, served with six dipping sauces. For the ultimate appetizer (serves four), order it with champagne.

Other recommendations The chef's tasting menu, which changes frequently, tops out at $65 for five courses, but it allows you to sample a bit of the best of everything. A similar business lunch special includes a salad, the chef's special entrée of the day, and tiramisu for dessert. The remodeled veranda offers a tasty and generous curry bar during lunch on weekdays, with a sampling of Indian, Japanese, and Thai curries, all the condiments, and three types of rice. Afternoon tea, featuring an exotic selection of loose-leaf teas, beautifully poured, and accented with pastries and mini-sandwiches, is an elegant treat.

Entertainment & amenities The restaurant is adjacent to a veranda where live music is featured nightly.

Summary & comments Chef Wayne Hirabayashi has come into his own at Hoku's, having taken over from the formidable Oliver Altherr. Under Altherr the restaurant was named top restaurant in *Honolulu Magazine's* Hale Aina Awards, interrupting a streak of wins by the formidable Alan Wong's. They were big shoes to fill, but Hirabayashi, an extremely hardworking and accomplished chef, has definitely made his mark.

Hy's Steak House ★★★

STEAK AND SEAFOOD | MODERATE/EXPENSIVE | QUALITY ★★★★ | VALUE ★★★
ZONE 1

Waikiki Park Heights Condominium, 2440 Kuhio Avenue; (808) 922-5555; www.hyshawaii.com

Reservations Recommended **When to go** Anytime **Entrée range** $19.95–$47.95, market price may be slightly higher **Payment** All major credit cards **Service rating** ★★★★½ **Parking** Valet in garage **Bar** Full service **Wine selection** Hy's has a wine list that never ends! **Dress** From dressy attire to resort casual **Disabled access** No ramp for stairs, but staff will help; wheelchair lift available **Customers** Islanders and tourists

Dinner Sunday–Thursday, 6–10 p.m.; Friday and Saturday, 6–11 p.m.

Setting & atmosphere Meat lovers revel in the traditional formal candlelit ambience found beyond the massive carved doors to this elegant, Old World club–like room. Rich, warm wooden wall paneling with heavy carved filigree accenting ceiling moldings, gleaming brass chandeliers, and a huge beveled mirror reflect tables dressed in pretty pink cloths.

House specialties Start with a grand, garlicky Caesar salad and proceed to your favorite steaks: The Only, a tender New York Strip broiled over kiawe and served with the restaurant's secret sauce; or T-bone, prime rib, or filet of beef Wellington topped with foie gras (in season) and mushroom druxelles, baked in a light pastry and served with Cabernet truffle sauce. Châteaubriand is also a popular choice not always found in other restaurants. Hy's signature dessert is bananas Foster, a French-Creole version of fresh bananas, orange juice, liqueurs, butter, brown sugar, cinnamon, and rum, flambéed table-side and served over ice cream.

Other recommendations Seafood combos, lamb, scallops, and scampi can also be ordered with twice-baked potatoes (whipped with sour cream and butter) or with pan-fired O'Brien potatoes, steak fries, steamed rice, or rice pilaf, all accompanied by Hy's famous cheese bread.

Entertainment & amenities Audy Kimura, winner of eight Na Hoku Hanohano Awards, strums the guitar and sings Wednesday through Saturday evenings.

Summary & comments Even though it's in the heart of Waikiki, Hy's has a loyal *kamaaina* (longtime resident) following.

Indigo ★★★★

EURO-ASIAN | INEXPENSIVE/MODERATE | QUALITY ★★★★½ | VALUE ★★★★ | ZONE 2

1121 Nuuanu Avenue, Honolulu; (808) 521-2900; www.indigo-hawaii.com

Reservations Recommended **When to go** Anytime **Entrée range** $8.25–$16.95, vegetarian $7.25 **Payment** VISA, MC, D, DC, JCB **Service rating** ★★★★ **Parking** Valet, street, or nearby Gateway Plaza lot **Bar** Full service **Wine selection** Good, many by the glass **Dress** Casual **Disabled access** Good if using valet **Customers** Islanders and their out-of-town guests, businesspeople at lunch, pre– and post–Hawaii Theatre attendees

Lunch Tuesday–Friday, 11:30 a.m.–2 p.m.

Dinner Tuesday–Saturday, 6–9 p.m.

Setting & atmosphere Great care has been taken to create a tropical Eurasian retreat in the heart of old Honolulu by chef/owner Glenn Chu. The indoor part of the restaurant is set in a historic building erected in 1903. With a high ceiling, suspended fans circling lazily overhead, antique carved panels from Indonesia, and big paintings of Chinese goddesses by local artist Pegge Hopper, you get the feeling you've traveled back in time to some exotic foreign locale for lunch. The back of the building opens onto Chinatown Gateway Park. Diners on the lanai are surrounded by lush greenery, with paper lanterns hung overhead and Balinese umbrellas placed here and there. A bar at the edge of the lanai is roofed with ironwood shingles brought from Indonesia.

House specialties Appetizers here give diners a chance to taste a variety of textures and flavors, from little steamed, filled dumplings, to spring rolls, to deep-fried wonton and shrimp lumpia served with chipotle aïoli and tangerine sauce. Miso salmon, breast of chicken with peanut sauce, and steamed fish with a soy-oyster-sesame dressing are flavorful entrées.

Other recommendations Regulars won't let Chef Chu take the crab-tomato-and-garlic soup off the menu. The pizzettas—duck or chicken—are also good for a light meal, especially if you want to try the signature dessert: Madame Pele's chocolate volcano, a cone-shaped mound of mousse spouting raspberry coulis and crème anglaise, arrives at the table amid a cloud of dry-ice smoke announced by a resonating gong.

Summary & comments Located across the park from the historic Hawaii Theatre, Indigo is a perfect spot for a preperformance dinner. Romantics might like to mention any special occasions when making a reservation, as one table is screened by greenery and set near a bubbling waterfall. Chu has bottled a line of his special sauces, such as raspberry-hoisin sauce, which can be purchased at the restaurant.

John Domini's ★★★½

SEAFOOD | MODERATE/EXPENSIVE | QUALITY ★★★★ | VALUE ★★ | ZONE 1

43 Ahui Street, Honolulu; (808) 523-0955; www.johndominis.com

Reservations Recommended **When to go** Sunset brings out gorgeous colors over Diamond Head, even though you don't see the setting sun itself **Entrée range** $19.95–$68.95 **Payment** VISA, MC, AMEX, DC, JCB **Service rating** ★★★½ **Parking** Valet **Bar** Full service **Wine selection** Good, 8 wines by the glass **Dress** Resort attire **Disabled access** Good **Customers** Tourists and Islanders for special occasions

Brunch Sunday seafood buffet, 9 a.m.–1 p.m.

Dinner Sunday–Thursday, 6–9:30 p.m.; Friday and Saturday, 5:30–9:30 p.m.

Setting & atmosphere On the lower level of this split-level restaurant, a saltwater fishpond is filled with Island fish, stingrays, and lobsters, so you get an effect of water all around, from the ocean outside to the pool inside. A moss-rock wall, koa furnishings, orchids throughout the restaurant, and green pothos vines hanging from the ceiling create the effect of a cool tropical oasis. Near the entry a large, comfortable lounge and 20-seat bar is a fine place to drop by with friends for an appetizer and a glass of wine.

House specialties Island fish served in half a dozen different preparations are John Domini's area of expertise. Everyone loves the opakapaka (snapper) en papillote (in a parchment bag), served with freshly made pasta and sautéed vegetables du jour. Mild, moist moi steamed with lemon, shoyu, and ginger delights local diners, though tiger prawns, sautéed scampi-style or stir-fried with black-bean sauce, are also high on the list of favorites. Abalone with white wine and capers, though costly, is another delicacy seldom seen on standard menus. The restaurant is known for live lobster—Hawaiian spinies or live Maine lobster—fresh from the tank.

Other recommendations You can order good things to precede dinner, like stuffed mushrooms with crab and hollandaise, or, for an Island flair, ahi poke (made with raw fish). Then, if you haven't gotten your fill of good things, John Domini's Bailey's mud pie in an Oreo cookie crust filled with ice cream and dressed in Bailey's liqueur sauce is a perfect way to end a meal.

Entertainment & amenities A four-piece band, including a vocalist, renders contemporary pop music on Friday and Saturday nights.

Summary & comments John Domini's is a five-time Ilima winner for fine dining, an award offered annually by *Honolulu Advertiser* and Diamond Head Theater. We hear that service tends to be inconsistent.

Keo's in Waikiki ★★★★

THAI/ISLAND | INEXPENSIVE/MODERATE | QUALITY ★★★★½ | VALUE ★★★★
ZONE 1

Ambassador Hotel, 2028 Kuhio Avenue, Waikiki; (808) 951-9355; www.ambassadorhotelofwaikiki.com

Reservations Recommended, but not required **When to go** Anytime **Entrée range** $8.95–$16.95 **Payment** All major credit cards **Service rating** ★★★★½ **Parking** Valet **Bar** Full service **Wine selection** Adequate **Dress** Resort attire **Disabled access** Good **Customers** Tourists and Islanders

Breakfast Every day, 7–11 a.m.

Lunch Every day, 11 a.m.–2 p.m.

Dinner Every day, 5–10:30 p.m.

Setting & atmosphere Creative chef/owner Keo Sananikone designed and decorated this newest of his five Keo's restaurants with teak furnishings, Thai carvings, and Hawaiian artwork. In the heart of Waikiki, the restaurant still has the ambience of a quiet refuge, with indoor and outdoor seating at linen-draped tables surrounded by blooming orchids.

House specialties Locally grown filet of catfish, deep-fried with a tapioca crust, and evil jungle prince (a delicious concoction of shrimp, chicken, or beef in a spicy coconut milk sauce) are favorites.

Other recommendations You can feel free to try any dishes that sound good, as the chef adapts his Thai recipes to suit Western tastes using coconut milk with no preservatives, prime meat, seafood, poultry, and fresh herbs and produce grown on his own four-acre farm.

Summary & comments At the grand opening celebration in January 1999, celebrities, whose pictures line the walls, showed up, just as they used to at the old Keo's on Kapahulu Avenue, now closed. It's fun to try family-style dining here, with each person choosing a different dish and sharing. Keo's has received numerous awards from local and national publications.

La Mer ★★★★★

NEOCLASSICAL (CONTEMPORARY) | EXPENSIVE | QUALITY ★★★★★ | VALUE ★★★
ZONE 1

Halekulani Hotel, 2199 Kalia Road, Waikiki; (808) 923-2311; www.halekulani.com

Reservations Highly recommended **When to go** Sunset for most romantic atmosphere **Entrée range** $36–$43 **Payment** VISA, MC, AMEX, DC, JCB **Service rating** ★★★★★ **Parking** Valet **Bar** Full service **Wine selection** Extensive **Dress** Dressy attire **Disabled access** Good, via elevator **Customers** Hotel guests, Islanders for special occasions

Dinner Every day, 6–10 p.m.

Setting & atmosphere Serene, understated elegance focuses your attention on spectacular views of Diamond Head and glowing sunsets over the ocean, interrupted only by the gracious service of haute cuisine prepared by the French chef. Soft sand colors, reflecting mirrors, waiters in white dinner jackets, and the best of all beachfront views at this second-level fine restaurant can keep you dallying over dinner for more than three hours, despite the fact that the service is the best in the Islands. There's a big bar situated near the restaurant's entry, but it doesn't seem to attract much of a bar crowd.

House specialties La Mer's signature fish tartare, a combination of raw hamachi, ahi, and salmon, is served with three caviars and three coulis. Two complete dinners of four and six courses are also offered nightly for $85–$105. La Mer's soufflé with lilikoi sauce has gained regional fame for dessert.

Other recommendations Avoid the most expensive appetizers, such as foie gras of duck for $34, or Beluga caviar for $105, unless, of course, price is no object. Sample medallions of fresh Scottish salmon with golden gnocchi and caviar sauce, or veal chop sautéed with chanterelles.

A sip of Port with a selection of French cheeses and walnut bread can be a perfect finish to the meal, though the symphony of La Mer desserts—a selection that includes poached pear with sabayon cream, almond biscuit Napoleon with hazelnut and coffee cream, or candied chestnut nougat in a chocolate tower—is perfect for more than one sweet tooth.

Entertainment & amenities Music drifts up from atrium below during dinner hour.

Summary & comments This is one of the few restaurants where jackets are suggested but long-sleeve dress shirts are required for men, and on breezy winter nights when the windows are open, women might also want to bring a light wrap. At press time, La Mer was Hawaii's only AAA Five Diamond Award restaurant.

L'Uraku ★★★★★

EURO-JAPANESE | MODERATE | QUALITY ★★★★★ | VALUE ★★★★ | ZONE 2

1341 Kapiolani Boulevard, Honolulu; (808) 955-0552; www.luraku.com

Reservations Recommended **When to go** Anytime; for value you might try a weekender lunch menu, 4 courses including appetizer, salad entrée, and dessert, for $15–$18 **Entrée range** Lunch $8.95–$17.50, dinner $15.75–$27.50, vegetarian $17.50 **Payment** VISA, MC, AMEX, DC, JCB **Service rating** ★★★★★ **Parking** Complimentary self-parking in garage **Bar** Full service **Wine selection** Good, 20 wines by the glass **Dress** Dressy casual **Disabled access** Good, via elevator from parking building **Customers** Islanders and a few tourists

Lunch Every day, 11 a.m.–2 p.m.

Dinner Every day, 5:30–10 p.m.

Setting & atmosphere L'Uraku has a festive, contemporary setting that comes alive in vibrant colors and multicolored napkins on snowy white linen-covered tables. Kiyoshi, an artist whose pictures are displayed on the walls, hand-painted table vases, menu covers, and cheerful umbrellas that hang suspended from the ceiling. A big marble-topped black bar near the entrance to the dining room is a good place to relax if you forgot to make reservations.

House specialties In the finest dining experiences, each dish should offer up a little surprise in the way the flavors merge. L'Uraku offers many specialties in this vein—veal cheeks, slow-cooked and flavored with soy sauce, so tender they melt like butter; papio filet, pan-seared with a fragrant caper-butter sauce; lobster tomalley, marinated in its own juices, soy sauce, and mirin, then quickly fried with the shell on. The restaurant's approach to miso-yaki butterfish, a Japanese classic, is among the best you'll find in Hawaii.

Other recommendations Assemble your own tasting menu by combining appetizers with downsized portions that the chef calls "Just a Taste," all in the $5–$9 range. Foie gras and pepper-seared ahi is touched with a raspberry reduction, yielding a perfect combination of savory and sweet. Sizzling moi carpaccio is flavored with the house-secret ponzu sauce (Japanese soy-citrus) and explodes with flavor. Try also the seared sea scallop served on a ragout made of bacon and salted mustard cabbage with a creamy kabayaki beurre blanc. That same mustard cabbage shows up in the house classic crab cake. L'Uraku regulars would emphasize the baked oyster—plump, succulent, and topped with crab meat and avocado.

Summary & comments L'Uraku bills its style as Euro-Japanese, and that is no gimmicky pretension. The food here personifies the Japanese respect for clean, balanced flavors and artistry of presentation, fused with all the sophistication and depth of a fine French menu. In the last few years, Chef Hiroshi Fukui has taken his place among the three or four best chefs in the Islands. The dishes here surprise the palate with their complex levels of flavor, yet the chef always respects the freshness of his key ingredients and never covers them up with fussiness, loud spices, or brash sauces. The food here, unlike much traditional Japanese cooking, is extremely wine-friendly, and the staff is well trained in offering suggestions for excellent pairings. For something different, though, L'Uraku carries several premium sakes. Ask for a suggestion.

The Euro-Japanese cuisine of Hiroshi Fukui, one of Honolulu's rising stars, is a treat (his twice-a-year contemporary kaiseki dinners are an experience) and a real deal on weekends, when a four-course lunch (miso butterfish, pan-seared scallops, lamb chops, steak) is only $15. It's Honolulu's best weekend special.

Michel's at the Colony Surf ★★★★½

FRENCH/CONTINENTAL | EXPENSIVE | QUALITY ★★★★½ | VALUE ★★ | ZONE I

Colony Surf Condominium, 2895 Kalakaua Avenue, Waikiki; (808) 923-6552

Reservations Highly recommended **When to go** Sunset **Entrée range** $26–$68.95 **Payment** VISA, MC, AMEX, DC, JCB **Service rating** ★★★★★ **Parking** Valet **Bar** Full service **Wine selection** Extensive, a dozen wines by the glass **Dress** Dressy **Disabled access** Good **Customers** Tourists, hotel guests, Islanders for special occasions

Dinner Every day, 5:30–9 p.m.

Setting & atmosphere For the romantically inclined, a seat at the ocean's edge, with flickering lights from torches casting shadows on surfers headed home in the setting sun, plus the lights of hotels twinkling all along Waikiki's crescent of white sand, is a languid mood setter. This is a fine restaurant and table-side service from carts is still the norm.

House specialties Michel's food has traditional roots, but it's beautifully presented in updated versions, so you may want to sip a perfectly-iced cocktail while you peruse the menu. Then choose the chef's Hudson Valley foie gras, sautéed and served with a sweet-and-sour poha berry sauce, or steak tartare. Michel's is probably the only restaurant left in Hawaii that prepares steak tartare table-side, where the waiters mix in crushed capers and onions, Tabasco, ground pepper, and Worcestershire sauce with flair and serve the dish on toast points. Take your time: There's lobster bisque or Caesar salad to come, unless you go straight to an entrée of beef Wellington.

Other recommendations Escargots are a good garlicky introduction to Châteaubriand or a lighter crab capellini, sautéed scallops, or opakapaka with oyster mushrooms. Don't miss ordering a flambéed dessert to experience the waiters' artistry one last time. Crêpes suzettes, crème brûlée, or strawberries Romanoff (with vanilla cream Grand Marnier and kirsch sauce) are heavenly finales.

Summary & comments Plan on an extended dining experience; you may even want to finish dinner with a snifter of Hennessy X.O. Michel's is that kind of place—dreamy, traditional, and lethargy-inducing. And the sunset can't be beat—on a good evening you may even see the infamous green flash as the sun sets on the ocean's horizon.

Orchids ★★★★½

SEAFOOD/INTERNATIONAL | MODERATE/EXPENSIVE | QUALITY ★★★★½ | VALUE ★★★
ZONE 1

Halekulani Hotel, 2199 Kalia Road, Waikiki; (808) 923-2311; www.halekulani.com

Reservations Highly recommended **When to go** Anytime, but sunset is best, particularly if you sit outside **Entrée range** $27–$38 **Payment** VISA, MC, AMEX, DC, JCB **Service rating** ★★★★ **Parking** Valet **Bar** Full service **Wine selection** Extensive **Dress** Resort attire **Disabled access** Good **Customers** Tourists and Islanders

Breakfast Every day, 7:30–11 a.m.

Brunch Sunday, 9:30 a.m.–2:30 p.m.

Lunch Every day, 11:30 a.m.–2 p.m.

Dinner Every day, 6–10 p.m.

Setting & atmosphere This lovely, light, and airy room is decorated with orchids and has a peaceful feeling even when crowded. Ask to sit outdoors, where the view of Diamond Head seems bigger than life, and Waikiki Beach is just beyond the green lawn.

House specialties A well-stocked seafood bar set smack in the middle of the room is only one highlight of Orchids. As a full dinner, it's priced at entrée rates, but as an appetizer course with an entrée it's priced at a remarkable bargain (if you can eat that much), particularly considering that the buffet carries lobster thermidor (rich lobster meat prepared with a brandy cream sauce), as well as opakapaka with cucumber slices and wasabi mashed potatoes, garnished with fresh ginger and a citrus-mirin-sake sauce. Oysters on the shell, shrimp, ahi poke, smoked ono, seafood salads, and house-cured gravlax are just part of this bountiful buffet.

Other recommendations Baked Australian prawns stuffed with king crab and served with freshly made fettuccini, or aromatic five-spice chicken roasted in the tandoori oven, are a few of the interesting treats on a menu that ranges from imaginative to traditional—rack of lamb, filet, and lobster, for example. Lemon curd tart or Halekulani's own tropical sorbets in pineapple, guava, lilikoi, and lychee flavors are light, refreshing desserts.

Entertainment & amenities Sunday and Monday, 8:30–10:15 p.m., a pianist plays classical music in the restaurant's atrium; during the rest of the week, it's light jazz and contemporary tunes for diners' listening pleasure.

Summary & comments A perfect evening might begin with a cocktail outside at sunset at House without a Key next door, then dinner on the covered patio at Orchids.

Padovani's Restaurant & Wine Bar ★★★★½

MEDITERRANEAN/ISLAND FLAIR | MODERATE/EXPENSIVE | QUALITY ★★★★★
VALUE ★★★ | ZONE 1

Doubletree Alana Hotel, 1956 Ala Moana Boulevard, Honolulu; (808) 946-3456; www.padovanirestaurants.com

Reservations Recommended **When to go** Anytime **Entrée range** Breakfast \$9–\$22, lunch \$14–\$19 (prix fixe, \$28), dinner \$20–\$34, multicourse degustation menus \$48–\$75 **Payment** VISA, MC, AMEX, DC, JCB **Service rating** ★★★★★ **Parking** Valet **Bar** Full service **Wine** selection Excellent; several wines by the glass in the restaurant, 24 in the Wine Bar. **Dress** Resort attire **Disabled access** Good **Customers** Hotel guests, tourists, Islanders

Breakfast Every day, 6–10 a.m.

Lunch Every day, 11:30 a.m.–2 p.m.

Dinner Every day, 6–10 p.m.

Setting & atmosphere Attention has been paid to every detail to create an elegant, gracious setting that reflects Island-inspired touches used in fine estate homes in Hawaii. A *maile* lei painted on the wooden floor at the entry leads to the carpeted interior past a polished cherry-wood wine cruvinet. It dispenses several wines by the glass. Nothing but the best—Riedel crystal, Frette linens, Bernardaud china, and Christofle flatware—complements the Old World cart service. Rich golds, jade greens, and cherry-wood furnishings under a low ceiling add a warm, intimate touch. Light fixtures that are held by geometric chevrons have the look of 1930s Ossipoff-designed homes and were actually taken from a Hawaii *kamaaina* home.

House specialties Philippe Padovani's Mediterranean-inspired dishes rely on herbs and natural seasonings to bring out the peak flavors of ingredients. The menu is divided into "Earth's Bounty" and "Flavors from the Sea," with a full range of appetizers and entrées on each side. The chef's best dishes burst with unique flavors and freshness. Begin the meal, for example, with Hawaiian sweet corn fresh clam chowder or vichyssoise of kiawe-smoked salmon and crab, elegant soups that will amaze you by how creamy and light they can be at the same time. Follow up with bouillabaisse of free-range chicken, crispy confit of duck leg, and pan-fried duck liver or the chef's favorite fish, John Dory, grilled.

The chef and his partner/brother, Pierre, are masters at desserts—more than a dozen are listed on the menu, from a luscious panna cotta of lemongrass and Hawaiian fruits to a crème brûlée with the unexpected pleasure of fresh ginger in the flavoring. The best way to experience them is to order the $15 Symphony of Desserts, with its many mini-portions. The Padovanis are also famed for their fresh sorbets and ice creams.

Other recommendations The upstairs Wine Bar offers a less expensive, more casual alternative to the Padovani experience. A generous menu of smaller plates is offered here. Half-portions of dishes such as grilled shrimp fettuccini are available, along with sandwiches, salads, an appetizer cart, carved roast of the day, and a selection of French cheeses.

Padovani has crafted a line of truffles made with Hawaiian Vintage Chocolate and filled with nougat, amaretto, ginger, fruits, and liqueurs. They are available at his shop in the Royal Hawaiian Shopping Center as well as in gift boxes at the restaurant.

Summary & comments Chef/owner Philippe Padovani has a distinguished culinary background in Hawaii as one of the founding chefs of the Hawaii Regional Cuisine movement. On his arrival from France, he first served as executive chef of La Mer at the Halekulani Hotel; then he went to the Ritz-Carlton, Mauna Lani, where he launched the Big Island Bounty food festival; and finally he was executive chef at Manele Bay Hotel on Lanai. Padovani's Bistro & Wine Bar is a family venture with his wife, Pierrette, managing restaurant service, and his brother, Pierre, serving as pastry chef.

Palomino Euro Bistro ★★★

MEDITERRANEAN | INEXPENSIVE/MODERATE | QUALITY ★★★½ | VALUE ★★★★
ZONE 2

Harbor Court, 66 Queen Street, Honolulu; (808) 528-2400; www.palamino.com

Reservations Recommended **When to go** Anytime **Entrée range** Lunch $5.95–$18.95, dinner $6.94–$22.95 **Payment** VISA, MC, AMEX, DC, D **Service rating** ★★★½ **Parking** Valet or self-park in Harbor Court garage **Bar** The full-service bar has one of the largest selections of scotch in town, plus a good selection of champagnes, a dozen beers on tap, and grappa (Italian brandy) **Wine selection** Good, many by the glass **Dress** Casual **Disabled access** Via an elevator and ramps in the restaurant **Customers** Downtown office workers during lunch, Islanders and some tourists at dinner

Lunch Monday–Friday, 11:15 a.m.–2:30 p.m.; lunch is served until 3:30 p.m. in the lounge

Dinner Sunday–Thursday, 5–10 p.m.; Friday and Saturday, 5–11 p.m.

Setting & atmosphere Palomino seems very cosmopolitan in a glamorous way, with its extraordinary views of Honolulu Harbor through soaring windows and an interior that shines with rose marble–topped tables and counters, highlighted with African woods and Art Deco hand-blown glass ceiling fixtures.

House specialties Palomino's food is rustic Mediterranean-style in approach, well-seasoned with fresh herbs and spices and smoke-infused flavors. A 60-foot exhibition kitchen turns out spit-roasted tenderloins, and cracker-thin crusted pizzas come from a wood-burning oven.

Other recommendations Palomino is surprisingly affordable—maybe that's why Islanders can't stay away. The most expensive dinner entrée is whole-roasted Island snapper with Israeli couscous and Moroccan spices for less than $30. Pasta dishes are among the most reasonable, starting at less than $10 and topping out under $20, with spit-roasted seafood ravioli made with prawns, scallops, salmon, and Dungeness crab mascarpone and rosemary-lemon beurre blanc.

Summary & comments A curved marble bar that seats 70 is a fun place to meet friends, but be sure to use the valet parking; otherwise you'll get dizzy circling to the top of the parking building past floors of reserved stalls.

The Pineapple Room ★★★½

HAWAII REGIONAL | MODERATE/EXPENSIVE | QUALITY ★★★★ | VALUE ★★★
ZONE 2

Third floor of Liberty House, Ala Moana Center, Honolulu; (808) 945-8881

Reservations Recommended **When to go** Anytime **Entrée range** Lunch $13.50–$16.75, dinner $20–$29 **Payment** All major credit cards **Service rating** ★★★ **Parking** Free in the shopping center lot **Bar** Full service **Wine selection** Extensive **Dress** Casual **Disabled access** Good **Customers** Locals, business crowd, tourists

Lunch Every day, 11 a.m.–3 p.m.

Tea Monday–Saturday, 3–5 p.m.

Dinner Monday–Saturday, 4–9 p.m.

Setting & atmosphere The Pineapple Room is located in a department store, but in design and menu it challenges any definition of a shopping-center operation. It has its own entrance but is also accessible through the store, so if you have to wait for a table, you can always distract yourself with some shopping. The decor is warm and elegant, but with contemporary lines that don't intimidate. A large exhibition kitchen fills one corner of the room; consider taking a seat at the counter there if the restaurant is busy.

House specialties Chef de Cuisine Steven Ariel trained at the side of the acclaimed Alan Wong and is accomplished both in the Hawaii Regional Cuisine tradition and in meeting Wong's strict standards. His creativity is displayed in large and small ways—for example, grilled salmon served on a bed of tea-flavored risotto that is rich, unique, and ultimately satisfying; or an Asian slaw that is a fresh, tangy mix of crunchy textures. Wood-fired pizzas are another specialty, topped with lobster, portobello mushrooms, or kalua pig. Pineapple Room crab cakes are generous and flavorful.

Whatever you eat here, leave room for dessert. Pastry chef Mark Okumura's chocolate crunch bars, granitas, tapiocas, and other specialties are all necessary evils.

Other recommendations Specials are extensive and change daily; they're always worth a look. The Pineapple Room also offers afternoon tea for $15, including plates of small bites, both savory and sweet. After-work drink specials and finger foods are served at the bar. On many Thursday nights, the restaurant offers five-course menus with wines. Sommelier Mark Shishido is considered among the best in the state for matching foods with wines, so these dinners are sure to offer some eye-opening pairings.

Summary & comments The Pineapple Room is the second of Alan Wong's Hawaii restaurants, but it is different in menu and philosophy from his original King Street site. It is more casual and more accessible, with a bit lower price tag. The restaurant is a good spot to take a break while shopping, but it is also a destination in itself, drawing special-occasion diners attracted by the food, not the shopping.

Prince Court Restaurant ★★★★

HAWAII REGIONAL | MODERATE | QUALITY ★★★★½ | VALUE ★★★ | ZONE I

Hawaii Prince Hotel, 100 Holomoana Street; (808) 944-4494; www.princehawaii.com

Reservations Highly recommended; required for Chef's Studio **When to go** Anytime, though sunset provides the loveliest view **Entrée range** $19–$28 **Payment** VISA, MC, AMEX, DC **Service rating** ★★★★ **Parking** Valet or self-parking in hotel garage ($1 with validation) **Bar** Full service

Wine selection Extensive, many domestic and imported Bordeaux and Burgundies, 20 wines by the glass **Dress** Resort attire **Disabled access** Good, via elevator **Customers** Islanders, hotel guests, tourists

Breakfast Every day, 6–10:30 a.m.

Brunch Sunday, 11:15 a.m.–1 p.m.

Lunch Every day, 11:30 a.m.–2 p.m.

Dinner Monday–Thursday, 6–9:30 p.m.; Friday–Sunday, 5:30–9:30 p.m.

Setting & atmosphere Views of boats bobbing lazily at the Ala Wai Yacht Harbor and sometimes a rainbow over nearby Magic Island through floor-to-ceiling windows give this spacious restaurant nearly as much appeal for lunch or Sunday brunch as for an evening repast. Tropical flowers on the tables add a Hawaiian touch.

House specialties The most popular item on the menu is a seafood extravaganza that includes Kona lobster, Island shrimp, and sea scallops with coconut saffron sauce, but the lemongrass crab-crusted opakapaka (red snapper) on seasoned crab with a Thai curry sauce comes in a close second. All dishes are artistically presented, but the best time to schedule dinner might be on Tuesday or Wednesday, for a Chef's Studio dinner, which includes a "flight" of wines (three matched to four courses). Three courses are prepared in front of guests in the restaurant, and then guests get a mini-tour of the kitchen while the chef completes the dessert course.

Other recommendations Monday, Tuesday, and Wednesday evenings, an appetizer shellfish bar featuring poke, sashimi, smoked fish, oysters, California hand rolls, and more, followed by a demi-entrée of the diner's choice, is a great way to sample a variety of Hawaii's seafood specialties. Friday and Saturday nights, an abundant seafood buffet is a highlight.

The menu at Prince Court changes monthly, but a dessert standby is chocolate soufflé with vanilla ice cream and crème anglaise.

Summary & comments Prince Court offers spectacular buffets. Make it easy on yourself and use valet parking, as it's a tiresome drive up many levels to find an empty space in the parking garage.

Roy's Restaurant ★★★★★

HAWAIIAN FUSION | MODERATE | QUALITY ★★★★★ | VALUE ★★★ | ZONE 2

Hawaii Kai Corporate Plaza, 6600 Kalanianaole Highway; (808) 396-7697; www.roysrestaurant.com

Reservations Highly recommended **When to go** Anytime, though sunsets over Maunalua Bay are especially mood-inducing **Entrée range** $16–$33 **Payment** All major credit cards **Service rating** ★★★★½ **Parking** Free in adjacent lot **Bar** Full service **Wine selection** Extensive, 10 wines by the glass **Dress** Casual **Disabled access** Good, via elevator **Customers** Islanders and tourists

Dinner Monday–Friday, 5:30–9:30 p.m.; Saturday, 5–10 p.m.; Sunday, 5–9:30 p.m.

Setting & atmosphere The lounge downstairs is fine in the evening for drinks and pupus, but upstairs is where the dining action is. The best tables, arranged around an exhibition kitchen, are those that are farthest from it and closest to the floor-to-ceiling windows, which look out over Maunalua Bay. This high-ceilinged restaurant is generally a full and vibrant (translate: noisy) place, a sign, says Chef Roy Yamaguchi, that people are having a good time. Soft pink walls decorated with artwork by Island artists, white tablecloths, and fresh flowers on the table complete the picture.

House specialties An extensive menu of special items, up to 20, which change every night, is where Roy's Restaurant shines. In addition, eight to ten different fresh fish in a myriad of preparations are available nightly. Tops on the list is steamed fish of the day drizzled with sizzling hot peanut oil and served with rice and Chinese vegetables. Crispy Thai chicken stuffed with Chinese noodles and an exotic mushroom-fungus served with chutney and macadamia nut curry sauce is a poultry favorite.

Other recommendations Some dainty eaters like to confine themselves to the appetizers, perhaps a cassoulet of escargot or teriyaki-glazed duck breast in Chinese black bean sauce, so they'll have room for dessert of hot chocolate soufflé or a cobbler made of fresh, seasonal fruit.

Entertainment & amenities Various musical entertainers perform in the downstairs lounge on weekends.

Summary & comments This is the original of Chef Roy Yamaguchi's 30-plus restaurants. The number literally grows by the month as Yamaguchi, in partnership with Outback Steakhouse, continues to open outlets across the country. The restaurant never feels like a chain operation, however. Yamaguchi has an unerring sense of flavor and has trained his staff well in maintaining his exceptional standards when he is away tending to his empire.

Sam Choy's Breakfast, Lunch, and Crab and Sam Choy's Diamond Head ★★★

HAWAII REGIONAL | MODERATE | QUALITY ★★★½ | VALUE ★★★ | ZONES 1 AND 2

580 North Nimitz Highway, Honolulu; (808) 545-7979; www.samchoy.com
449 Kapahulu Avenue, 2nd level, Waikiki; (808) 732-8645

Reservations Recommended for dinner **When to go** Anytime **Entrée range** Lunch $6.50 and up, dinner $26.95 **Payment** VISA, MC, AMEX **Service rating** ★★★½ **Parking** Valet or nearby lot **Bar** Full service. A brewmaster at Choy's Big Aloha Brewery within the spacious BLC turns out 8 varieties of beer. His latest is Hibiscus White, infused with Island ingredients like Kau orange peel, hibiscus, and coriander. **Wine selection** Good **Dress** Casual **Disabled access** Good **Customers** Islanders, businesspeople at lunch, large family groups and others at dinner

Brunch *Sam Choy's Diamond Head:* Sunday, 9 a.m.–noon

Breakfast *Breakfast, Lunch, and Crab:* Monday–Friday, 6:30–11:30 a.m.; Saturday and Sunday, 6:30–11 a.m.

Lunch *Breakfast, Lunch, and Crab:* Every day, 10:30 a.m.–4 p.m.

Dinner *Breakfast, Lunch, and Crab:* Every day, 5–10 p.m.; *Sam Choy's Diamond Head:* Monday–Thursday, 5:30–9:30 p.m.; Friday–Sunday, 5–9 p.m.

Setting & atmosphere Breakfast, Lunch, and Crab has a lively atmosphere, with an exhibition kitchen, showcases full of fresh seafood, and table seating in more than one room for true old salts and junior sailors. It's a big restaurant with fun touches, like a fishing sampan with tables in it, and a fountain or two in the middle of the dining room so you can rinse your hands conveniently after ripping into cracked crab legs.

Sam Choy's Diamond Head restaurant is less casual, with views of Diamond Head through an open window and an exhibition kitchen with counter seating, as well as linen-draped tables. It is no less popular, however.

House specialties At Diamond Head entrées such as local-style osso buco with Chinese noodles and shiitake mushrooms, seafood laulau (choice items wrapped in ti leaves and steamed), or the "Choy-sized" salad of the day served in a tortilla shell with local greens shock diners with their sheer sizes. At BLC, the focus is on seafood, with crab and lobster served steamed Chinese-style with black beans, roasted with garlic, or as part of a huge clambake.

Other recommendations To truly experience Sam Choy's food, you must try the poke (pronounced po-kay), a traditional Hawaiian appetizer of cubes of raw fish served with onions, soy sauce, seaweed, and various seasonings and oils. The closest Western approximation would be ceviche, but that's really not accurate. Choy is a serious aficionado of poke and offers it in many preparations with international flair. He even offers it fried for those who just can't do raw fish.

Summary & comments Chef/owner Sam Choy has become an industry in himself, with television shows, cookbook projects, and nationwide guest chef stints filling his calendar. He consults daily with his chefs, but the day-to-day running of his restaurants has passed to Elmer Guzman (Diamond Head) and Aurelio Garcia (BLC). Guzman has a special interest in island reef fish—the unglamorous but flavorful specimens that seldom find a place on upscale menus. The adventurous fish lover would do well to check out his daily specials.

Sansei Seafood Restaurant and Sushi Bar ★★★★

CONTEMPORARY JAPANESE/PACIFIC RIM | MODERATE/EXPENSIVE | QUALITY ★★★★½ VALUE ★★★★ | ZONE 2

Restaurant Row, 500 Ala Moana Boulevard, Honolulu; (808) 536-6286

Reservations Recommended for dinner **When to go** Anytime **Entrée range** Lunch $4–$8, dinner $16–$24 **Payment** All major credit cards **Service rating** ★★★½ **Parking** Validated for Restaurant Row lot **Bar** Full service **Wine selection** Extensive list of wines by the glass and premium sakes **Dress** Casual **Disabled access** Good **Customers** Locals, business crowd, late-night club crowd, some tourists

Lunch Monday–Friday, 11 a.m.–2 p.m.

Dinner Every day, 5–10 p.m.; half-price specials after 10 p.m.

Late-night Every day, 10 p.m.–1 a.m.

Setting & atmosphere Owner D. K. Kodama likes his restaurants compact, active, and noisy. When this location debuted, it was more open, with seating spread out; Kodama felt the place seemed lonely at times, so he remodeled to collect the action around an open sushi bar on one side and a crowded bar on the other. Two private dining rooms are available. The decor is heavy on wood and blends Japanese with casual island sensibilities.

House specialties Concentrate on the appetizers and sushi rolls here. They're designed for sharing and play into the Sansei philosophy that dining should be fun. Entrées can be an overwhelming mix of competing flavors and are not the restaurant's strong point. Try instead the ahi tataki, with its strips of seared tuna in a tangy ponzu (soy-citrus) sauce and tossed with a refreshing mix of sprouts. Calamari salad is a favorite, its sweet, spicy sauce a perfect pairing for a cold beer. Mango salad crab roll, the tempura shrimp roll, and 69 roll (a California roll with strips of eel wrapped around the outside) all take the staid, Japanese sushi tradition and stand it on its head. If you deserve a treat, order the foie gras nigiri sushi, the best dish in the house, but an indulgence at $16.95 for two pieces.

Other recommendations Menu prices are half-off from 5:30 to 6 p.m. nightly. Drink specials and half-price sushi are offered after 10 p.m. Sansei is a great place to experiment with sushi and wine. Kodama and his staff have given a great deal of thought to ways of pairing the flavors in their contemporary sushi creations with fine wines from France, California, and Germany. Sansei offers a number of premium sake choices as well, for a more traditional sushi pairing.

Summary & comments Kodama is one of Hawaii's most charismatic and ambitious chefs. His original Maui restaurant perfected his formula of bold, colorful dishes that invite sharing and smiles. On Oahu, his secret weapon is his mother, Sandy, who works the dining room, offering extremely personal, friendly service. The staff and even the customers call her "Mom."

Sarento's Top of the "I" ★★★½

ITALIAN | MODERATE/EXPENSIVE | QUALITY ★★★★ | VALUE ★★★ | ZONE I

Ilikai Hotel, 1777 Ala Moana Boulevard, Waikiki; (808) 955-5559; www.ilikaihotel.com

Reservations Recommended **When to go** Sunset is most romantic if sitting at window tables **Entrée range** $15.95–$42.95 **Payment** VISA, MC, AMEX, DC, D, JCB **Service rating** ★★★★½ **Parking** Discounted with validation in hotel garage **Bar** Full service **Wine selection** Extensive **Dress** Resort attire **Disabled access** Adequate, via elevator **Customers** Tourists and Islanders

Dinner Every day, 5:30–9:30 p.m.

Setting & atmosphere The ride in the glass-sided elevator to Sarento's, perched high atop the Ilikai Hotel, sets a fantasy mood for this top-notch Italian restaurant. Waiters in dark jackets help adjust your lighting, individually controlled at booths that enjoy panoramic views of the Ala Wai Yacht Harbor, Waikiki's bright lights, and the beach or Diamond Head. The decor in this restaurant is as beautifully Italian (with graceful archways and a green-and-white tiled exhibition pizza and dessert kitchen) as the food. Frescoes on the walls of two cozy private dining rooms and in the main restaurant show scenes typical of the Mediterranean area—a mother cooking, grapes being crushed, gardens. One scene of a large family at the dining table depicts one of the restaurants, three owners, Aaron Placuorakis, his wife, two children, grandfather Sarento, grandmother, uncles, and aunts.

House specialties The risotto here has got to be among the best in Honolulu, and at a moment's notice, the chef can stir together any of dozens of variations. Homemade pastas, pizza from a wood-burning oven, osso buco, filet wrapped with pancetta and topped with fontina cheese, and crisp Jerusalem artichoke chips are superb choices.

Other recommendations Lobster ravioli with mushroom cream sauce is a soul-satisfying entrée. Top dinner off with cool tiramisu made of ladyfingers, espresso, mascarpone cheese, and liqueurs. *Hint:* One way to keep the dinner cost down here is to go between 5:30 and 6:30 p.m. for an early evening special that includes soup or salad, a choice of several entrées, and dessert. Pizzas are also a value if chosen as an entrée, ranging from $12.95 to $16.95.

Summary & comments By request, guests can take a gander at the restaurant's wine cellar and view a bottle of $9,500 Chateau Cheval Blanc stored with some 3,000 other wines.

Singha Thai Cuisine ★★★★

THAI | INEXPENSIVE/MODERATE | QUALITY ★★★★½ | VALUE ★★★★ | ZONE 1

Canterbury Place, 1910 Ala Moana Boulevard, Waikiki; (808) 941-2898

Reservations Highly recommended for dinner, accepted for lunch **When to go** Anytime **Entrée range** $11.95–$31.95 **Payment** VISA, MC, AMEX, DC, JCB **Service rating** ★★★★½ **Parking** Free with validation in Canterbury Place lot **Bar** Full service **Wine selection** Extensive **Dress** Casual **Disabled access** Good **Customers** Tourists

Dinner Every day, 4–11 p.m.

Setting & atmosphere After dark Singha's exotic magic emerges, though it's not so evident during the lunch hour. During dinner, lights twinkle on the restaurant's mirrors and golden Buddha, and a fountain tinkles in the open-air patio dotted with orchids. Outdoor patio seating at umbrella tables is right next to the street but set at a lower level and surrounded by a wall so it feels like a private garden.

House specialties Blackened ahi summer rolls with a soy-ginger-sesame dipping sauce and shredded green mango, and boneless breast of duck with Panang curry sauce, successfully combine Hawaii regional and Thai cuisine. Seafood lovers go for the grilled jumbo black tiger prawns with Thai peanut sauce, or lobster tail with Singha's signature Thai chili, ginger, and light black-bean sauce.

Other recommendations If you have qualms about choosing a balanced number of dishes from the à la carte menu, sampling menus for two, three, four, or five people are composed of an appetizer sampler plus an ample variety of entrées and rice, plus dessert, for just under $30 per person.

Entertainment & amenities Thai dancers in extravagant headdresses and colorful silk costumes perform on a tiny stage, while rose petals float through the air.

Summary & comments Named Honolulu's best Thai restaurant by Gayot's *The Best of Hawaii Guide, Zagat Survey, Honolulu Advertiser's* Ilima Awards, and *Honolulu Magazine's* Hale Aina Awards. Chef/owner Chai Chaowasaree's food is a work of art (melons might be carved into flower shapes, for example) that balances fresh Island ingredients and flavors with Thai spices, fresh herbs, and reduced sauces.

The Surf Room ★★★½

CONTEMPORARY | MODERATE/EXPENSIVE | QUALITY ★★★½ | VALUE ★★★ | ZONE 1

Royal Hawaiian Hotel, 2259 Kalakaua Avenue; (808) 923-7311; www.royal-hawaiian.com

Reservations Highly recommended **When to go** Sunset **Entrée range** Breakfast $10–$21, lunch $10–$20, dinner $25–$40 **Payment** VISA,

MC, AMEX, DC, D, JCB **Service rating** ★★★★ **Parking** Valet or validated self-parking in hotel garage **Bar** Full service **Wine selection** Good **Dress** Resort attire **Disabled access** Good **Customers** Hotel guests, other tourists, and Islanders for special occasions

Breakfast Every day, 6:30–11:30 a.m.

Lunch Every day, 11:30 a.m.–2:30 p.m.

Dinner Every day, 6–10 p.m.

Setting & atmosphere Near the entry to The Surf Room at the Mai Tai Bar, a hula dancer performs old favorites, such as "Lovely Hula Hands" or "The Hawaiian Wedding Song," to live Hawaiian music, while rustling palm trees and lapping ocean waves furnish a dreamy backdrop. The best seating is right beside the sands of Waikiki Beach, where you can watch couples stroll by in the moonlight.

House specialties Though Cajun-spiced crab pot-stickers might not sound Hawaiian, the plump little Chinese dumplings with a mustard cream sauce are a great way to dive into this menu, which claims to focus on the flavors of Hawaii. Pan-fried Pacific salmon in a balsamic vinegar glaze with shiitake-garlic mashed potatoes, or togarashi-peppered ahi with Maui onion, Kau orange relish, and lime-soy vinaigrette are two Island favorites.

Other recommendations A three-course dinner selection dubbed the Art of Food and Wine includes two glasses of wine for $39.95. Friday seafood buffets and Sunday brunches draw repeat visitors. If you've got a big appetite, the breakfast buffet is lovely to dawdle over.

Summary & comments The open-air atmosphere beside Waikiki Beach makes The Surf Room special, so for its fullest impact, request a table as close as possible to the sand. After dining, wander through the elegant old hotel and take a moment to enjoy what is left of the big trees and green lawns at the front entrance. This is the Waikiki from a more gracious era.

3660 On The Rise ★★★★

CONTEMPORARY | MODERATE | QUALITY ★★★★½ | VALUE ★★★ | ZONE 2

3660 Waialae Avenue, Kaimuki; (808) 737-1177; www.3660.com

Reservations Highly recommended **When to go** Anytime **Entrée range** $19–$25 **Payment** VISA, AMEX, MC, DC, D, JCB **Service rating** ★★★★½ **Parking** Free in garage **Bar** Full service **Wine selection** Well-rounded; primarily California wines; many great matches for Chef Siu's Euro-Asian-Island flavors **Dress** Resort attire **Disabled access** Good **Customers** Islanders and their visiting guests

Dinner Sunday, Tuesday–Thursday, 5:30–9 p.m.; Friday and Saturday, 5:30–10 p.m.; closed Monday

Setting & atmosphere Jade green marble floors, a black marble bar, frosted glass panels, and light wood accents are a cool background for this busy restaurant, where repeat clientele are likely to table-hop, saying hello to friends. Indoor tables seat 88, while a street-side lanai surrounded by plants holds another 25.

House specialties Appetizers of ahi katsu, duck confit ravioli, potato-crusted crab cake; entrées of flaky tempura catfish with ponzu sauce, Chinese steamed opakapaka (red snapper), or Angus New York steak alaea. Dessert lovers rave about the pastry chef's bread puddings.

Other recommendations Desserts are so good that it makes sense to order a sampler of three appetizers to share. Dine lightly on seared scallops with ahi taro cake and allow yourself to go crazy on desserts of warm chocolate soufflé cake with mocha sauce and ice cream or mile-high Waialae pie, which combines vanilla and coffee ice cream, macadamia brittle, and caramel and chocolate sauces for a sweet treat. For lunch, hale ice tea is a cooling limeade/tea blend, while French-press coffeepots make rich coffee to go with your favorite after-dinner cognacs.

Summary & comments Chef Russell Siu's chic restaurant has won countless awards and always places near the top overall in the Hale Aina Awards, but for the last two years the restaurant has won first place for its desserts. 3660 has the feel of a favorite neighborhood restaurant because it's outside Waikiki and is not a showy place, but the service and food make it worth the cab fare from your hotel.

Maui

Anuenue Room ★★★½

HAWAII REGIONAL | MODERATE/EXPENSIVE | QUALITY ★★★★ | VALUE ★★★ | ZONE 9

Ritz-Carlton Hotel, 1 Ritz-Carlton Drive, Kapalua; (808) 669-1665; www.ritzcarlton.com

Reservations Highly recommended **When to go** Anytime except Sunday and Monday **Entrée range** $27–$42 **Payment** VISA, MC, AMEX, DC, D, JCB **Service rating** ★★★★★ **Parking** Valet or free self-parking in hotel lot **Bar** Full service **Wine selection** Extensive, 20 wines by the glass **Dress** Dressy resort attire **Disabled access** Good **Customers** Resort guests and Islanders on special occasions

Dinner Tuesday–Saturday, 6–9 p.m.

Lounge Every day, 5:30–11 p.m.

Setting & atmosphere This elegant room is dressed in rich koa wood, brocade draperies, and chandeliers, giving it an Old World, club-like atmosphere. The walls are decorated with landscapes of the Kapalua area by local artists, and impressive formal arrangements of flowers highlight the entry and the dining areas. A separate dining room with wall sconces carved in the shape of pineapples holds private parties of a dozen.

House specialties Start with the seared duck foie gras, a duck confit highlighted with pineapple and vintage port. For an entrée, barbecued rack of lamb with a *paniolo* (cowboy) glaze of poha berry and Zinfandel has a reputation as the best lamb on Maui, though lighter appetites might prefer orange-shoyu caramelized salmon served with gingered jasmine rice and Kau lime.

Other recommendations For big splurges, grilled Keahole lobsters are fresh from aquaculture tanks on the Big Island, or you can sample the succulent warm lobster in a hearts-of-palm salad dressed with fresh mango and black truffle vinaigrette. To complete what's sure to be a truly special evening, plan ahead and order the rich and light-as-air Grand Marnier or chocolate soufflé when you order your entrée, so it will be ready when you are.

Entertainment & amenities The Anuenue Lounge, next to the dining room, features live entertainment Tuesday–Saturday, 8–11 p.m.

Summary & comments To make a night of it, you might plan on coffee and cognac in the lounge after dinner. People do get out on the dance floor to cut the light fantastic. *Anuenue,* by the way, is the Hawaiian word for "rainbow"; the restaurant is so designated because rainbows are sometimes visible over the ocean from the Anuenue Room's windows.

Bamboo Bistro ★★★★

HAWAII REGIONAL | MODERATE | QUALITY ★★★★ | VALUE ★★★ | ZONE 7

300 Maalaea Road, Suite 300, Wailuku; (808) 243-7374

Reservations Recommended **When to go** Anytime **Entrée range** Lunch $6–$13, dinner $20–$30 **Payment** All major credit cards **Service rating** ★★★ **Parking** Complimentary valet **Bar** Full service **Wine selection** Good, 18 wines by the glass **Dress** Resort attire **Disabled access** Good **Customers** Locals, tourists

Lunch Tuesday–Sunday, 11:30 a.m.–3 p.m.

Dinner Tuesday–Sunday, 5:30–9 p.m.

Setting & atmosphere High, open ceilings and a sweeping view of Maalaea harbor and Maui's south shoreline give the Bamboo Bistro a comfortable, airy feel. You might see green sea turtles or even whales if you're there in the right season. Floors are covered in locally grown eucalyptus, walls in blond bamboo, the bar in black bamboo. The decor is Polynesian, but not the tacky type.

House specialties Take your food in small portions here. The chef advocates the Spanish style of tapas dining—although he calls it "tropas," for a tropical touch. Everything on the menu is available in sampling portions, family-style on platters for sharing, or as full-sized entrées. The fresh catch of the day may be ordered four tempting ways—simply grilled, herb-grilled, sesame-crusted, or steamed in banana leaf. Sauces are seamlessly paired with each presentation, from a spicy passion fruit to accompany the sesame-crusted fish to soy-mustard butter for the herb-grilled. Accompaniments include sweet potato Palau, with its surprising mix of coarsely mashed purple Okinawan sweet potato, banana, and taro. Meat dishes include succulent and tender spare ribs braised in black vinegar and star anise, and New York steak with a Szechuan-style salt-and-pepper rub.

Other recommendations Don't miss the salad specialties. A bed of baby greens is tossed with sweet strawberries in a Maui onion vinaigrette, then topped with goat cheese baked in phyllo dough. "Pure gastronomic bliss," one reviewer called it. Maui asparagus is served with hearts of palm in a coconut vinaigrette. The house Caesar salad is lightly dressed and includes slabs of ahi sashimi.

Summary & comments Chef Peter Merriman was the initial driving force behind the Hawaii Regional Cuisine movement, and his dedication to fresh local produce is legendary. When he opened his first restaurant on the Big Island, Merriman would climb coconut trees, dive for fresh shellfish, and make with farmers deals they couldn"t refuse so they'd grow top-quality tomatoes for him. A devotion to freshness is what drives the Bamboo Bistro.

The Bay Club Restaurant ★★★

CONTINENTAL | MODERATE/EXPENSIVE | QUALITY ★★★½ | VALUE ★★★ | ZONE 9

Kapalua Bay Hotel, 1 Bay Drive, Kapalua; (808) 669-5656; www.kapaluabayhotel.com

Reservations Highly recommended **When to go** Sunset **Entrée range** Lunch $9.75–$14, dinner $25–$38 (vegetarian $21) **Payment** VISA, MC, AMEX, DC, JCB **Service rating** ★★★★ **Parking** In adjacent lot **Bar** Full service **Wine selection** Good **Dress** Resort attire **Disabled access** Good **Customers** Islanders and tourists

Lunch Every day, 11:30 a.m.–2 p.m.

Dinner Every day, 6–9 p.m.

Setting & atmosphere Considered one of the loveliest oceanfront settings on Maui. Tables on the open-air deck fill up quickly, so it's best to make reservations and go early for the full romantic effect of sunset. Inside, the restaurant resembles a gracious *kamaaina* beach home, with a fireplace near the entry, a piano surrounded by comfortable linen-draped tables, and low lighting.

House specialties From the moment you sit down to dinner, you can munch on crispy lavosh lavished with salmon mousse. At lunch, the

Monte Cristo sandwich filled with ham, turkey, and Swiss cheese and sautéed in an egg batter is one of the most reasonable items on the menu. Caesar salad prepared table-side precedes main courses such as scallops and prawns with white truffle risotto and a veal demi-glace, or a half roasted duck with butternut squash, or a more traditional filet mignon with chanterelles and foie gras sauce.

Other recommendations Hawaiian fish are caught fresh daily and can be ordered Mediterranean style (with tomato concasse, lemon, capers, parsley, garlic, and anchovies, in white wine butter sauce) or Oriental style (with shiitake mushrooms, scallions, cilantro, and soy and sesame oil sauce).

Summary & comments Shuttles run from Kapalua Bay and the Ritz-Carlton Kapalua, so resort guests do not need a rental car. However, for those staying at Kapalua Bay Hotel, a palm-shaded path along the ocean's edge is pleasant for a pre- or post-dinner stroll. Diners may charge checks to their rooms in either hotel.

Chez Paul's

FRENCH | MODERATE/EXPENSIVE | QUALITY ★★★★ | VALUE ★★★ | ZONE 7

Highway 30 (4 miles south of Lahaina), Olowalu Village; (808) 661-3843

Reservations Highly recommended **When to go** Anytime **Entrée range** \$22–\$36 **Payment** VISA, MC, AMEX, D **Service rating** ★★★★ **Parking** Free in adjacent lot **Bar** Full service **Wine selection** Good; wine cellar in restaurant **Dress** Resort attire **Disabled access** Good **Customers** Islanders, a few tourists

Dinner Every day, seatings at 6 p.m. and 8:30 p.m.

Setting & atmosphere You might smell the garlic wafting in through your open car window if you drive past this little blink-and-you'll-miss-it roadside restaurant at Olowalu. Classical French Provençal cuisine is served at 14 linen-covered, candlelit tables. Two mirror-lined walls make the place look bigger, and banquette seating upholstered in green splashed with pink roses adds an Old World touch. A private dining room seats 22.

House specialties Repeat customers often order poisson des iles (fresh fish) with beurre-blanc sauce, or medallions of veal simmered in chardonnay, lemon, and orange jus, while the dessert to die for is profiteroles, puff pastry with ice cream in a warm chocolate sauce.

Other recommendations Regulars regard as "très bien" an appetizer of escargots de Bourgogne presented in their shells in garlic butter. We favored the opakapaka Provençal (snapper with fennel and artichokes). Another recommended entrée is the Tahitian, duck à l'orange presented with a variety of tangy fruits.

Summary & comments It's a nice surprise to learn that here, unlike on many contemporary French menus, soup or salad and vegetables are included with entrée items. Chez Paul's is owned by Belgium-born Lucien Charbounier, who joined with Chef Patric Callares in 1999 to update the menu. Chez Paul's was named Maui's best French restaurant by the readers of *Maui News* in 1998 and has been recommended in *Travel/Holiday* magazine.

David Paul's Lahaina Grill ★★★★

CONTEMPORARY AMERICAN | MODERATE/EXPENSIVE | QUALITY ★★★★½
VALUE ★★★ | ZONE 9

127 Lahainaluna Road, Lahaina; (808) 667-5117; www.lahainagrill.com

Reservations Highly recommended **When to go** Early or late to avoid the 7 p.m. crowd **Entrée range** $24–$37 **Payment** VISA, MC, AMEX, DC **Service rating** ★★★★★ **Parking** On street or in adjacent lot **Bar** Full service **Wine selection** Extensive, many by the glass **Dress** Resort wear **Disabled access** Good, separate wheelchair access **Customers** Islanders and tourists

Dinner Every day, 6–10 p.m.

Setting & atmosphere This lively bistro, composed of two dining rooms plus the Chef's Table (which provides an exceptional, personalized dining experience for up to eight guests), is located next door to the old restored Lahaina Inn. The restaurant has a Victorian ceiling of pressed-tin panels embossed with an abstract design. Soft peach, blue, and sand tones in the decor are set off by simple black chairs at candlelit tables set with white linens, Mikasa china, and fresh flowers. In addition, the full menu is available for those seated at the bar.

House specialties David Paul's signature dish of tequila shrimp with firecracker rice competes with the kalua duck with reduced plum wine sauce, seasonal vegetables, and Lundberg rice for first place on the dinner menu. Kona coffee–roasted rack of lamb boasts a full-flavored Kona coffee Cabernet demi-glace served with garlic mashed potatoes.

Other recommendations The vegetarian eggplant Napoleon and the Maui onion-crusted seared ahi (tuna) with vanilla bean rice and an apple cider soy-butter vinaigrette are light enough to reserve room for dessert—a luscious triple berry pie of raspberries, blueberries, and black currants topped with crème fraîche, or the Hawaiian Vintage Chocolate decadence, a flourless torte served with chantilly cream and raspberry port sauce. "Flights" of wine are offered nightly. Generally these consist of a tasting of three wines, either whites or reds.

Entertainment & amenities Thursday through Saturday evenings, a jazz pianist plays and sings.

Summary & comments If you'd like a quiet little table in the corner for a romantic dinner, ask for Table #28, #29, or #34. These tables for two are tucked into an out-of-the-way corner of the restaurant, where you can check out the action in the dining room, but the action can't check you out! A few of David Paul's most recent awards include *Honolulu Magazine's* Hale Aina Award, received six years in a row for Best Maui Restaurant, as well as the 1998 Legendary Service Award, as voted by the readers of *Maui News.*

Gerard's ★★★★

CONTEMPORARY ISLAND/FRENCH | MODERATE/EXPENSIVE | QUALITY ★★★★
VALUE ★★★★ | ZONE 9

Plantation Inn, 174 Lahainaluna Road, Lahaina; (808) 661-8939; www.gerardsmaui.com

Reservations Recommended **When to go** Anytime **Entrée range** $26.50–$32.50 **Payment** All major credit cards **Service rating** ★★★★★ **Parking** In nearby lot **Bar** Full service **Wine selection** Excellent, 10 wines by the glass **Dress** Casual resort attire **Disabled access** Good for garden-level dining, adequate via a back entry for in-house dining **Customers** Tourists and Islanders for special occasions

Dinner Every day, 6–8:30 p.m.

Setting & atmosphere Seated in this plantation-style inn, diners in Gerard's might feel as if they are eating in someone's gracious old-fashioned home dining room. Walls are papered in a pink-and-beige floral design, windows are stained glass, and tables are lit with candle lamps. You can also sit outside on a porch screened with plantings.

House specialties Starting with the appetizers, people rave about the calamari sautéed with lime and ginger and the shiitake and oyster mushrooms in puff pastry. Though the menu changes annually, chef/owner Gerard Reversade's confit of duck and his roasted Hawaiian snapper, served with vegetables and potato puree or rice pilaf, are a constant.

Other recommendations Islanders go for ahi tartare with taro chips; mainlanders love the fresh Kona lobster and avocado salad. Rack of lamb with mint crust is filling, but most people find room to share spoons over crème brûlée or flourless chocolate cake.

Summary & comments Reversade opened this special restaurant in 1982, and over the years his traditional French cuisine has been adapted to Island tastes, so sauces are lighter and hints of Island flavors and ingredients show up. He has been featured on PBS's *Country Cooking* and the Discovery Channel's *Great Chefs of America.* The wine list repeatedly receives *Wine Spectators'* award of excellence.

Haliimaile General Store ★★★★

HAWAII REGIONAL | MODERATE/EXPENSIVE | QUALITY ★★★★½ | VALUE ★★★
ZONE 8

900 Haliimaile Road, Haliimaile; (808) 572-2666; www.haliimailegeneralstore.com

Reservations Highly recommended for dinner **When to go** Anytime Monday–Friday **Entrée range** $17–$32 **Payment** VISA, MC, DC, D, JCB **Service rating** ★★★★½ **Parking** In adjacent lot **Bar** Full service **Wine selection** Good, many by the glass **Dress** Casual **Disabled access** Adequate, via ramp **Customers** Islanders and tourists

Lunch Monday–Friday, 11 a.m.–2:30 p.m.

Dinner Monday–Friday, 5:30–9:30 p.m.

Setting & atmosphere Chef/owner Bev Gannon's Hawaii Regional Cuisine is famous throughout the Islands, but you'll still feel as if you've made a discovery when you search out the restaurant, located in a restored 1920s plantation store in the middle of nowhere, surrounded by sugarcane and pineapple fields. The only drawback is that the noise level inside can be irritating if you like peace while dining.

House specialties The crab boboli is legendary for lunch, while for dinner it's a good idea to check the fish preparations, as they vary every night. As an appetizer, sashimi Napoleon, a crispy wonton layered with smoked salmon, ahi tartare, and sashimi and served with a spicy wasabi vinaigrette, is always in demand. Rack of lamb Hunan-style keeps Islanders coming back for more.

Other recommendations Paniolo ribs done with a secret lime barbecue sauce and coconut seafood curry also have local enthusiasts. As pastry chef, Gannon's daughter Theresa whips up chocolate macadamia nut caramel pies, lilikoi cheese torte (a sweet tart), gingerbread with caramelized pears, a variety of crème brûlées, and piña colada cheesecake.

Summary & comments Chef Bev Gannon was one of the founding members of the Hawaii Regional Cuisine movement and has been featured many times in national publications such as *Bon Appétit.* Locally the restaurant has won the Best Maui Restaurant title and is a favorite stomping ground for Upcountry residents. *Hint:* It's a treat to see the store after dark during the Christmas season, when it's dressed in full holiday regalia.

Hula Grill ★★★

HAWAII REGIONAL | INEXPENSIVE/MODERATE | QUALITY ★★★★ | VALUE ★★★★
ZONE 9

Whalers Village, 2435 Kaanapali Parkway, Kaanapali; (808) 667-6636; www.hulagrill.com

Reservations Recommended for dinner **When to go** Anytime, but it's best to sit on the open lanai at sunset **Entrée range** Lunch $6.95–$10.95, dinner $14.95–$24 **Payment** VISA, MC, AMEX, D, DC **Service rating** ★★★★ **Parking** Validated, in shopping center garage **Bar** Full service **Wine selection** Good, 10 wines by the glass **Dress** Casual **Disabled access** Good **Customers** Tourists and Islanders

Lunch Every day, 11 a.m.–10:30 p.m. (pizzas, salads, sandwiches served through the dinner hour in the casual Barefoot Bar area)

Dinner Every day, 5–9:30 p.m.

Setting & atmosphere Hula Grill is set in a re-created Hawaiian plantation home, with the main dining room an open-air lanai at the ocean's edge. During the day you'll see beachgoers sunning and walking along Kaanapali's golden sands; at night flickering torches light the path along the beach. Near the entry, koa walls and shelves in a library area are decorated with Hawaiian collectibles, while an exhibition kitchen allows you to watch the chefs if there's a wait for a table. Smokers can relax in a stepped-down waterfall room or a designated section of the Barefoot Bar.

House specialties Even the appetizers are special at Hula Grill. As a starter you can order Asian-style dim sum, such as scallop and lobster pot-stickers served in bamboo baskets, or Hawaiian-style *pupus*, like wok-charred ahi seared on the outside, sashimi-style on the inside, and served with a dipping sauce of wasabi and shoyu.

Hula Grill's signature entrée is macadamia nut roasted fresh Island opakapaka, garnished with a sauce made of Hana rum and mango and served with bamboo rice. Some diners swear by the Hawaiian seafood gumbo, a linguini dish with fresh shrimp, fish, clams, and scallops that can be ordered from mild to spicy hot.

Other recommendations At lunch this is a great place to pop by for a casual bite to eat, maybe a warm focaccia chicken sandwich with Monterey Jack cheese, roasted poblano pepper, avocado, and tomato–chili pepper aïoli. Pizzas topped with Puna goat cheese, fresh spinach, tomato, and mushrooms come crispy hot from the kiawe wood–fired oven. You might want to share Hula Grill's famous dessert—a homemade ice-cream sandwich, made with two chocolate macadamia-nut brownies, vanilla ice cream, and raspberry puree and whipped cream.

Entertainment & amenities It's easy to slip off the beach for a Lava Flow, a piña colada–like drink made with fresh coconut, pineapple juice, and rum and topped with a strawberry "eruption," during happy hour, when a guitarist and vocalist entertain from 3 to 5 p.m. Hawaiian musicians return during dinner hours from 6:30 to 9 p.m., and hula dancers sway at table-side around 7 p.m. every night.

Summary & comments Chef Peter Merriman is the same Big Island chef who was instrumental in officially founding the Hawaii Regional Cuisine movement. Merriman's other restaurant on Maui offers a completely different dining experience than Hula Grill, though both are true to fresh Island ingredients. Hula Grill has won the Restaurant of Distinction Award and been named as the Maui restaurant with the best ambience for three years in a row by the readers of *Maui News.*

Kimo's ★★½

STEAK AND SEAFOOD | INEXPENSIVE/MODERATE | QUALITY ★★★ | VALUE ★★★★ ZONE 9

845 Front Street, Lahaina; (808) 661-4811; www.kimosmaui.com

Reservations Recommended for dinner **When to go** Anytime; to sit outside in the upstairs dining room, go early—it's first-come, first-seated **Entrée range** Lunch $6.95–$10.95, dinner $6.95–$23.95 **Payment** VISA, MC, AMEX, DC, D, JCB **Service rating** ★★★½ **Parking** Limited on-street or use Lahaina Center lot and walk a couple of blocks **Bar** Full service **Wine selection** Good, 8 wines by the glass **Dress** Casual **Disabled access** Access to the main dining room upstairs is inadequate for wheelchairs, but seating is available downstairs in a secondary dining area near the bar **Customers** Tourists, some Islanders

Lunch Every day, 11 a.m.–3 p.m.

Pupus Every day, 3–5 p.m.

Dinner Every day, 5–10:30 p.m.

Bar Every day, open until 1:30 a.m.

Setting & atmosphere This two-level restaurant is a casual place where it's easy to drop by for lunch or a cocktail downstairs at sunset, then find your way upstairs for dinner. Kimo's takes full advantage of its ocean's-edge setting, with an open lanai perched one story above the rocks and lapping waves. Signal flags promote the sailing motif, and tropical foliage adds an Island touch. At night, flaming torches cast flickering shadows on the spreading limbs of a rustling monkeypod tree. You can order from the full menu or a lighter menu at the bar, which seats 22 downstairs.

House specialties Kimo's fresh fish might be ono, ahi, onaga, au, mahi, opah, opakapaka, or lehi, depending on what comes in on any given day. Of four preparations, Kimo's Style, baked in garlic, lemon, and sweet basil glaze, has widespread approval.

Other recommendations Meat eaters swear by the prime rib, but fence-sitters are likely to choose the top sirloin and Tahitian shrimp (touched up with a bit of garlic and cheese) combination. Try a lighter, healthier lunch, such as the veggie sandwich that boasts Maui onions, fresh tomatoes, sprouts, cheese, and avocado, and then you can afford to top it off with the dessert that sailors swim to shore for—the original hula pie, a wedge of vanilla macadamia-nut ice cream nestled in an Oreo cookie crust.

Entertainment & amenities Kimo's is the place to be Friday and Saturday nights from 10 p.m. to midnight, when live rock-and-roll music livens the night. Monday–Friday, 7–8 p.m., there's live Hawaiian music.

Summary & comments Interestingly, local people voted Kimo's, in the heart of touristy Lahaina, Maui's best restaurant in the *Honolulu Advertiser's* Ilima Awards. The restaurant has neither a "big-name" chef nor a nationwide reputation, but Kimo's entrées come with Caesar salad, carrot muffins, sour cream rolls, and steamed herb rice, so you don't go broke ordering à la carte. Generous portions and fairly priced food of a consistent quality probably had a lot to do with the vote too. It's one of the nicest Lahaina bars to sit in and have a drink at sunset.

Longhi's ★★★½

MEDITERRANEAN/ITALIAN | MODERATE | QUALITY ★★★★ | VALUE ★★★★ | ZONE 9

888 Front Street, Lahaina; (808) 667-2288; www.longhi-maui.com

Reservations Recommended for dinner **When to go** Anytime **Entrée range** Breakfast $2.50–$12.50, lunch $8–$16, dinner $17–$27, except for lobster at $55 **Payment** AMEX, VISA, MC, DC, D, JCB **Service rating** ★★★ **Parking** Free valet at dinner, free self-parking in adjacent lot **Bar** Full service **Wine selection** Extensive, many Italian wines and 3 house wines, 20 by the glass **Dress** Casual **Disabled access** Good for downstairs dining **Customers** Tourists and Islanders

Breakfast Every day, 7:30–11:30 a.m.

Lunch Every day, 11:45 a.m.–4:45 p.m.

Dinner Every day, 5–10 p.m.

Setting & atmosphere This sleek, cosmopolitan, open-air restaurant has a fun and casual ambience. Big black-and-white tiles cover the floor downstairs, interrupted only by a wide staircase that leads upstairs to additional koa-topped tables open to the tradewinds.

House specialties Here, nobody wants to stop at just one appetizer, even if it's as good as the grilled portobello mushrooms with goat-cheese pesto. Follow it with shrimp Longhi, a classic first, served on opening night more than 20 years ago. Plump white shrimp are sautéed in butter, lemon juice, and white wine, then fresh Maui basil and tomatoes are simmered before it's all served on garlic toast. Fresh white fish, often onaga, prepared with white wine and garnished with grapes, is another longtime specialty.

Other recommendations The in-house bakery prepares oven-fresh cinnamon buns, macadamia-nut rolls, coffee cakes, quiches, and cheesy jalapeño and pizza bread. Pastas, freshly made on the premises, and salads, all composed of fresh vegetables, are available both at lunch and dinner. Desserts are presented on a tray and served to you even as you point your finger at macadamia-nut pie, cheesecake, or strawberry mousse cake, though you may want to order a special chocolate or Grand Marnier soufflé in advance.

Entertainment & amenities Longhi's is the place to be on Friday nights from 9:30 p.m. to closing, when various live bands play music to swing to on the upstairs dance floor.

Summary & comments Created in 1976 by "a man who loves to eat," Bob Longhi, the restaurant has remained a family affair, with son Peter the general manager and daughter Carol O'Leary an executive chef. It's a winning combination, as the restaurant won best overall restaurant in the *Maui News* readers poll in 1998 and has repeatedly received *Wine Spectator's* Best Award of Excellence since 1988. Longhi's has an all-verbal menu, which can prove irritating or exciting, depending on your mood. On the plus side, it gets diners to interact with the waiter, new menu items can be introduced easily, and you can get a true description of the food that you order. On the other hand, it can be difficult to remember all the choices (especially if you've had a libation or two), and it's easy to lose track of what you're spending.

Maalaea Waterfront Restaurant ★★★½

SEAFOOD/CONTINENTAL | MODERATE | QUALITY ★★★★½ | VALUE ★★★ | ZONE 7

50 Haouli Street, Maalaea; (808) 244-9028; www.waterfrontrestaurant.com

Reservations Highly recommended **When to go** Sunset for outside **Entrée range** $17.95–$54 **Payment** VISA, MC, AMEX, DC, D, JCB **Service rating** ★★★½ **Parking** Free in upper level of adjacent condominium garage **Bar** Full service **Wine selection** Extensive, 30 by the glass **Dress** Resort attire **Disabled access** Adequate, via elevator **Customers** Islanders and tourists

Dinner Every day, 8:30 p.m.–closing

Setting & atmosphere Remodeled in 1998, this elegant oceanfront restaurant has pretty textured pale green walls, white tablecloths decorated with candles and tropical flowers, and scenic Island paintings on the walls. Outdoor dining on the deck is lovely on a balmy night, but bring a sweater if the tradewinds are up.

House specialties Depending on what the fishermen bring in, seven or eight different kinds of Island fish are served daily in your choice of nine preparation styles. This means there are always 50 or more choices to make while you nibble on homemade bread slathered with the house's special beer-cheese spread or watch the table-side preparation of your Caesar salad.

Other recommendations Besides the rack of lamb, Maalaea Waterfront specializes in game meats, so you might find venison, red deer, pheasant, or ostrich, on a rotating basis. For dessert, the white chocolate blueberry cheesecake will satisfy every cheesecake aficionado.

Summary & comments Maalaea Waterfront Restaurant is a family endeavor, opened in 1990 by the Smiths: Bob, the chef; Gary, the manager; and Rick, the detail man. Their success is evidenced by the fact that the restaurant has repeatedly been named by the readership of *Maui News* as the restaurant with the best seafood and best service. Local voters repeatedly mention the warmth of the proprietors and the intimate ambience of the room.

Mama's Fish House ★★★½

SEAFOOD | MODERATE/EXPENSIVE | QUALITY ★★★★½ | VALUE ★★★ | ZONE 9

799 Poho Place, Kuau; (808) 579-8488; www.mamasfishhouse.com

Reservations Highly recommended **When to go** Anytime, but sunset is most romantic **Entrée range** Lunch $14–$28, dinner $27–$36 **Payment** VISA, MC, AMEX, DC, D, JCB **Service rating** ★★★★ **Parking** Valet or adjacent lot **Bar** Full service **Wine selection** Excellent, half a dozen by the glass **Dress** Casual resort wear **Disabled access** Good, but it's some distance from the lot **Customers** Tourists and Islanders

Lunch Every day, 11 a.m.–3 p.m.

Pupus Every day, 2:30–3 p.m.

Dinner Every day, 5–9:30 p.m.; closed Christmas Day

Setting & atmosphere You'll find Mama's reminiscent of a rambling, open-air beach house, at the end of a gecko-patterned walkway beside the ocean, with cool green lawns and shady coconut palms out front. A wooden bar and wooden paneling inside are made of tropical almond, monkeypod, and mango wood. It's a perfect place to while away an afternoon over a Mai Tai Roa Ae—the same kind of fresh fruit and rum concoction originated by Trader Vic's years ago—or to sample other retro drinks: Singapore Slings of Raffles hotel fame, Zombies, and Scorpions.

House specialties Fishermen get written credit for catching the fresh fish on this menu, so the fish is always top-notch, whether you have ono, ahi, uku, or opah. Preparations include sautéed with garlic butter, white wine, and capers; grilled with Thai red curry; fried with Maui onion, chili pepper, and avocado; or served with honey-roasted macadamia-nut-lemon sauce. A signature dish, Pua me hua Hana, features sautéed fish with fresh coconut milk and lime juice served surrounded by fresh tropical fruit and accompanied by Molokai sweet potatoes.

Other recommendations To sample Island-style cooking, try a laulau, a bundle of mahimahi baked in ti leaves and served with tender, moist kalua pig. Another imaginative entrée with local flair is crispy kalua duck with mango-mui glaze served with baby bok choy and wild rice. Traditionalists can always get Black Angus New York steak or veal shank roasted with Asian spices served with portobello mushrooms, wasabi mashed potatoes, and Kula vegetables.

Summary & comments In 1999, the Fish House added rattan tables and chairs and decorated an open-air area near the entrance to look like old Hawaii—they dubbed it "Grandma's Living Room." The room has become a popular spot for locals, who come to hang out, listen to the strains of vintage music, and nibble on *pupus* rather than order a full-blown meal from a menu that most Islanders consider "higher end." In contrast to the windsurfers who show up from nearby Hookipa Beach, there are occasional celebs—Jason Alexander, for one—who have discovered the charms of Mama's Fish House and Grandma's Living Room. For five consecutive years, Mama's has won a five-diamond award from *Hospitality Sciences.* Locally, *Maui News* readers have named it as serving the best seafood, and it has been named a restaurant of distinction in *Honolulu Magazine*'s Hale Aina Awards.

Pacific'O ★★★★½

HAWAII REGIONAL | MODERATE | QUALITY ★★★★½ | VALUE ★★★ | ZONE 9

505 Front Street, Lahaina; (808) 667-4341; www.pacificomaui.com

Reservations Recommended **When to go** Sunset for best ocean views **Entrée range** Lunch $8.50–$14.50, dinner $19–$25 **Payment** VISA, MC, AMEX, DC, JCB **Service rating** ★★★★ **Parking** Free in lot across the street **Bar** Full service **Wine selection** Excellent **Dress** Casual **Disabled access** Adequate, but it's a long way from the parking lot **Customers** Tourists and Islanders

Lunch Every day, 11 a.m.–4 p.m.

Dinner Every day, 5:30–9 p.m.

Setting & atmosphere This is a pleasant spot for indoor or outdoor dining at tables shaded by umbrellas and set right at the edge of the ocean. Inside, ceiling fans suspended above the checked marble floor lazily stir the air. A long bar is bordered by tables beside windows wide open to the ocean breezes and to views of three islands.

House specialties You'll see why Chef James McDonald has won Taste of Lahaina competitions ever since 1993 when you try his appetizer of prawns and basil wontons served with a spicy sweet-and-sour sauce and Hawaiian salsa. Another Taste of Lahaina winner is Asian gravlax, slices of house-cured salmon on a warm sweet-potato applejack with wasabi chive sour cream, radish sprouts, and caviar.

Other recommendations Artistic presentations include fresh fish, prepared seared in sesame with Kula lettuce and wasabi, or tandoori-flavored with Indonesian spices and caramelized Maui pineapple, or crispy deep-fried in a seaweed wrapper, or steamed in shiitake-sake bouillon in an old-fashioned Chinese bamboo steamer. A melt-in-your-mouth dessert of pineapple lumpia and macadamia-nut ice cream is a beautiful blend of texture and taste.

Entertainment & amenities Thursday–Saturday nights, 9 p.m.–midnight, the indoor/outdoor restaurant at ocean's edge attracts jazz aficionados with live jazz performances.

Summary & comments The same chef/owner, James McDonald, also owns Io, a black-and-white metallic modern restaurant next door.

Plantation House Restaurant ★★½

CONTEMPORARY | INEXPENSIVE/MODERATE | QUALITY ★★★★ | VALUE ★★★ | ZONE 9

Kapalua Resort, Plantation Course Clubhouse, 2000 Plantation Club Drive, Kapalua; (808) 669-6299; www.theplantationhouse.com

Reservations Recommended for dinner **When to go** Anytime **Entrée range** Lunch $6.50–$13, dinner $21–$25 **Payment** VISA, AMEX, MC, DC **Service rating** ★★★ **Parking** In adjacent lot **Bar** Full service **Wine selection** Extensive **Dress** Casual **Disabled access** Good, drop off at front door **Customers** Golfers, tourists, and Islanders

Breakfast & lunch Every day, 8 a.m.–3 p.m.; light menu 3–5 p.m.

Dinner Every day, 5:30–9 p.m.

Setting & atmosphere Cool mountain breezes and views of velvety-green fairways and distant blue ocean are a calming backdrop seen through paned windows that open to catch the breeze. Natural light woods, comfortable rattan chairs, and lazy overhead fans add to the relaxing atmosphere. A double-sided fireplace creates a warm glow in the evening, and by the bar, a big mural of workers in the pineapple fields depicts Kapalua's plantation past.

House specialties Plantation House is known for Australian double-cut lamb chops with rosemary-bordelaise sauce and for fresh Island fish—try the Taste of the Rich Forest preparation, done with a mushroom crust on a bed of tot soi (Chinese spinach) with garlic mashed potatoes. Fresh fish specials inspired by the Mediterranean are seasonal and changed monthly.

Other recommendations A wide variety of appealing choices exists: smoked salmon Benedict dotted with capers for breakfast; chicken Caesar salad, burgers, or pasta at lunch; and desserts that range from old-fashioned Molokai sweet bread pudding to flashy bananas Foster, or da kine brownie with vanilla ice cream, chocolate sauce, whipped cream, and macadamia nuts.

Summary & comments Chef Alex Stanislaw is coaxing this restaurant away from typical golf-course food to provide a more elevated dining experience in the Pacific Rim style. Specials incorporate the flavors of Italy and southern France, showcasing fresh local produce. The aim now is more fish and salads, less meat and starch. Plantation House is a work in progress, but it is a good alternative to the pricier restaurants of the Kapalua Resort hotels. Guests of both hotels may charge meals to their rooms and ride a free shuttle to the restaurant.

Roy's Kahana Bar & Grill and Roy's Nicolina ★★★½

HAWAIIAN FUSION | MODERATE | QUALITY ★★★★ | VALUE ★★★★ | ZONE 9

Kahana Gateway Shopping Center, 4405 Honoapiilani Highway, Kahana; (808) 669-6999; www.roysrestaurant.com

Reservations Highly recommended **When to go** Anytime **Entrée range** $13–$26 **Payment** VISA, MC, AMEX, DC, D, JCB **Service rating** ★★★★½ **Parking** Free in shopping center lot **Bar** Full service **Wine selection** Excellent, 10–15 by the glass **Dress** Casual **Disabled access** Good, via elevator to upstairs restaurants **Customers** Tourists and Islanders

Dinner *Nicolina:* Every day, 5:30–9:30 p.m.; *Roy's Kahana Bar & Grill:* Every day, 5:30–10 p.m.

Setting & atmosphere Even owner Roy Yamaguchi admits there's not a lot of difference between these two restaurants that sit side by side on an upstairs level of a West Maui shopping center. Originally, he opened them with differing concepts in mind, but found that people liked his original ideas, so both restaurants are guided by the same corporate chef, and both offer 20 to 25 specials nightly. Roy's Kahana has a long bar near the entry and a centrally located open kitchen, so the high noise level seems to make it more suited to a lively, younger crowd, while Nicolina has a quieter appeal. Nicolina's kitchen is enclosed, but diners can enjoy lanai seating. Both have wooden-topped tables and local artwork that changes every six weeks; the art is available for sale.

House specialties Since items change so rapidly, you never know what you'll find, but everything is made with the freshest local ingredients and has Euro-Asian and international flavorings. Appetizers like Szechuan baby-back ribs or Roy's shrimp and pork spring rolls with hot sweet mustard and black bean sauce set a spicy scene for perhaps a lighter entrée. Lemongrass-crusted shutome (swordfish) reflects a touch of Thailand, with sticky rice and basil peanut sauce. Hibachi-style salmon and blackened ahi entrées are signature items in both restaurants.

Other recommendations The left side of the menu is made up of Roy's signature dishes, prepared the same throughout the chain, down to the garnishes. The right side reflects the in-house chef's daily inspirations, which lean more toward Hawaiian than Asian flavors. For a standard dish worth a taste, try the dim sum "canoe" for two, a sampling of the traditional Chinese treats done up with more Hawaiian ingredients.

Summary & comments Roy Yamaguchi has won so many awards that it's difficult to credit them to his specific restaurants. *Gourmet* magazines Top Tables, *Honolulu* magazine's top 20, *Maui News*'s best overall Maui restaurant, the James Beard Foundation, and many others applaud this imaginative and energetic chef, whose name was attached to more than 20 Roy's restaurants (with plans for more) throughout the country in 2002.

A Saigon Café ★★★

VIETNAMESE | INEXPENSIVE | QUALITY ★★★★ | VALUE ★★★★★ | ZONE 7

1792 Main Street, Wailuku; (808) 243-9560

Reservations Recommended, especially for dinner **When to go** Anytime **Entrée range** $6.75–$17.95 **Payment** VISA, MC, AMEX, DC, D, JCB **Service rating** ★★★★ **Parking** In adjacent lot **Bar** Full service **Wine selection** Limited **Dress** Casual **Disabled access** Good **Customers** Islanders and a few tourists

Lunch & dinner Every day, 10 a.m.–8:30 p.m.

Setting & atmosphere Sit at the low wooden bar with roll-around chairs, or choose a Formica-topped table or booth for lunch and dinner in this basic, white-walled restaurant minimally decorated with Vietnamese carved and lacquered art. A gold statue of Buddha greets guests at the door, ceiling fans whir overhead, and the TV might be on at the bar. It's a low-key place that can be difficult to find because there is no sign.

House specialties It's almost de rigueur to start with cha gio (fried spring rolls)—little deep-fried bundles of ground pork, long rice, carrot, and onion wrapped in rice paper; the waiter will show you how to roll them in romaine lettuce with mint leaves and vermicelli noodles, then dip them in sweet-sour garlic sauce before enjoying them. Among any number of in-demand Vietnamese entrées, garden party shrimp dipped in a light batter, deep-fried, and served with sautéed ginger and green onions on bean sprouts and lettuce (with rice on the side) is one of the most delicious.

Other recommendations With 92 items on the menu, it's hard to make a choice, let alone describe the best. Green papaya salad is a much-loved starter. For lunch, any of the noodle soups—with seafood and chicken, calamari and shrimp, or wonton, and others—provide a big bowl of steaming goodness. There are several rice-in-a-clay-pot variations done with chicken, catfish, shrimp, or pork.

Summary & comments Everybody loves A Saigon Café, and regulars love the proprietor, Jennifer Nguyen, as well. Nguyen opened the restaurant in January 1996, but the identifying sign is still stored in a box somewhere. The sprightly, hardworking proprietor says, "We've been so busy, we've never gotten around to putting it up!"

Sansei Seafood Restaurant and Sushi Bar ★★★★

JAPANESE/PACIFIC RIM | MODERATE/EXPENSIVE | QUALITY ★★★★½ | VALUE ★★★★
ZONE 9

The Shops at Kapalua, 115 Bay Drive, Kapalua; (808) 669-6286; www.sanseihawaiian.com

Reservations Highly recommended **When to go** Anytime **Entrée range** $12.95–$37.95 **Payment** VISA, MC, AMEX, D, JCB **Service rating** ★★★★ **Parking** In shopping-village lot **Bar** Full service **Wine selection** Extensive **Dress** Resort attire **Disabled access** Adequate **Customers** Islanders and tourists

Dinner Every day, 5:30–10 p.m.; karaoke Thursday–Friday from 10 p.m.

Late-night Tuesday–Saturday, 10 p.m.–2 a.m.

Setting & atmosphere Booths and tables fill up fast in the intimate 120-seat restaurant, which includes a sushi bar and cocktail lounge area, so reservations are wise. Restaurant decor blends a bit of Japan with a Maui plantation look. The glass panel of the entry door is etched with a pineapple, and a window beyond the bar showcases a garden of tropical plants. There are samurai pictures on the walls, and the sushi bar, with its scalloped awning, could have come straight from Tokyo.

House specialties The idea here is to try a lot of dishes and share. With sushi this is a no-brainer, and Sansei offers up delicious tidbits from crab and mango salad hand roll to spider rolls with soft-shell crab to bagel rolls with smoked salmon, Maui onion, and cream cheese. The familystyle concept applies to the entrées as well. Pass around the house special Peking duck breast with shiitake potato risotto. Other favorites: Asian rock shrimp cake and nori ravioli of shrimp and lobster.

Other recommendations Pay attention when the waiter describes nightly specials like asparagus tempura and fresh fish preparations, or try shrimp tempura deep-fried in a light-as-air batter, or a healthy preparation of grilled fresh mahimahi on Kula greens. Granny Smith baked apple tart is a pure American finish to any meal.

Entertainment & amenities Sansei's karaoke after 10 p.m. on Thursday and Friday draws a happy crowd.

Summary & comments Even big-name Maui chefs gather at this casual restaurant set unobtrusively in the Kapalua Shops center. Chef/owner D. K. Kodama says his menu reflects the way he likes to eat, with playful flavors and bits of this and that. In 1999, Sansei was named Best Maui Restaurant by *Honolulu Magazine*'s Hale Aina Awards, and in 1998 *Maui News* readers called it the best sushi bar on Maui.

Seasons ★★★★½

HAWAII REGIONAL | MODERATE/EXPENSIVE | QUALITY ★★★★½ | VALUE ★★★
ZONE 8

Four Seasons Resort, 3900 Wailea Alanui, Wailea; (808) 874-8000; www.fourseasons.com

Reservations Highly recommended **When to go** Sunset is spectacular from the panoramic seating on the lower level **Entrée range** $36–$42; multi-course tasting menus, $78–$145 **Payment** AMEX, VISA, MC, DC, D, JCB **Service rating** ★★★★★ **Parking** Complimentary valet or self-parking in covered hotel lot **Bar** Full service **Wine selection** Extensive; tops on the list is a 1994 Silver Oak Alexander Valley for $160; a dozen wines by the glass **Dress** Resort attire, jackets optional **Disabled access** Good, via elevator **Customers** Hotel guests and Islanders for special occasions

Dinner Tuesday–Saturday, 6–9:30 p.m.

Setting & atmosphere Seasons enjoys a spectacular setting, with sweeping ocean vistas the entire length of Wailea's coastline offering glimpses of the island of Kahoolawe through the tops of swaying coconut palms. Superbly executed service complements the understated decor of crisp white linen tablecloths, oversized hurricane lamps, and unassuming French china. Natural materials accent the decor with caramel-colored marble side tables, slate tile floors on the lower lanai, and heavy rattan and leather chairs throughout.

House specialties One of Hawaii's most popular fish, onaga, is seared crispy on top with julienned endives and pureed snow peas, or you might want to try an updated version of an old favorite, roasted rack of lamb in a Cabernet sauce paired with Camembert potato soufflé and confit tomato.

Other recommendations Salad of charbroiled Keahole (Big Island) lobster and Molokai sweet-potato puree; for dessert, the Hawaiian Vintage Chocolate Surprise is made of chocolate over Tahitian vanilla ice cream.

Entertainment & amenities A Hawaiian trio serenades diners with traditional sounds of Hawaii from 7 to 10 p.m. nightly, and a dance floor beckons romantics. In the adjacent lobby lounge, a guitarist strums contemporary tunes from 8:30 to 11 p.m.

Summary & comments This is the only restaurant on Maui with a master sommelier. Repeat diners say Seasons is what a hotel restaurant should be. It has a gracious elegance that makes an Absolut martini straight up with a twist, stirred not shaken, just right as a pre-dinner cocktail. Free shuttles operate between all Wailea hotels, so if a post-dinner snifter of Remy Martin XO also seems just right, you need not worry about driving your car.

The Big Island

Batik Restaurant ★★★★½

HAWAII REGIONAL | EXPENSIVE | QUALITY ★★★★½ | VALUE ★★★ | ZONE 11

Mauna Kea Beach Hotel, 62-100 Mauna Kea Beach Drive, Kohala Coast; (808) 882-7222; www.maunakeabeachhotel.com

Reservations Highly recommended **When to go** Anytime **Entrée range** $29–$48, vegetarian $24, prix fixe menus $65–$85 **Payment** VISA, MC, AMEX, DC, JCB **Service rating** ★★★★★ **Parking** Valet or hotel parking lot **Bar** Full service **Wine selection** Extensive **Dress** Evening resort wear **Disabled access** Adequate, via elevator **Customers** Tourists and Islanders celebrating special occasions

Dinner Monday, Wednesday–Friday, and Sunday, 6:30–9 p.m.; closed Tuesday and Saturday for house luau and clambake/seafood buffet

Setting & atmosphere This is Mauna Kea Beach Hotel's premier restaurant, and care has been taken to do everything right. Batik panels decorating one wall are authentic, there are candles and tropical flowers on the tables, and a bronze charger rests under fine china plates for a look of burnished elegance. Patio tables overlooking Kaunaoa Bay were added in 1999 for those who prefer outdoor dining.

House specialties Thai-style curries are the house specialty and the most often ordered entrée on the menu, though some people prefer to choose traditional items like beef Wellington, crispy salmon with saffron pepper jus, or lobster tail with saffron risotto. Meals are accompanied by tandoori oven–baked naan bread. Starters, such as langostinos sautéed in garlic and served with angel-hair pasta with lobster sauce, or scallop ravioli with ginger-lime sauce, are as satisfying as the entrées.

Other recommendations The number-one choice from the decadent dessert menu is a Grand Marnier soufflé, but the warm Valrhona chocolate cake comes a close second.

Entertainment & amenities A classical solo guitarist strums tunes every evening. After dinner in the Batik Lounge, a jazz duo performs from 9 to 11 p.m. nightly.

Summary & comments This place was once on the stuffy side, but today jackets are only recommended, and the food and decor have been finely honed to provide a high-quality dining experience.

Café Pesto ★★★½

CONTEMPORARY | INEXPENSIVE | QUALITY ★★★★ | VALUE ★★★★ | ZONES 11, 12

Wharf Road and Mahukona Highway, Kawaihae Center, Kawaihae; (808) 882-1071; 308 Kamehameha Avenue, Hilo; (808) 969-6640; www.cafepesto.com

Reservations Accepted **When to go** Anytime **Entrée range** $13–$28 **Payment** All major credit cards **Service rating** ★★★ **Parking** Adjacent parking lot **Bar** Full service **Wine selection** Limited, some by glass **Dress** Casual **Disabled access** Good **Customers** Islanders and tourists

Lunch Every day, 11 a.m.–4:30 p.m.

Dinner Sunday–Thursday, 4:30–9 p.m.; Friday and Saturday, 4:30–10 p.m.

Setting & atmosphere Café Pesto in Hilo and at Kawaihae Harbor both have a bright, cheerful outlook, with black-and-white flooring and big windows reflecting a contemporary Art Deco theme. Kawaihae has a more intimate feeling, with a low ceiling, while the Hilo restaurant is in the historic S. Hata Building, which retained the high ceiling of turn-of-the-twentieth-century architecture when it was restored.

House specialties Café Pesto is known for its use of fresh Island ingredients and simple healthy preparations. A wood-burning pizza oven fired on kiawe or ohia produces ten different pizzas, including one where you compile as many ingredients as you like. The Marguerite cheese pizza is most popular, but the Oriental al pesto pizza is a top vegetarian choice, with eggplant, sundried tomatoes, and roasted garlic.

Other recommendations Pastas are great; risottos are creamy and good, particularly the seafood risotto made with Keahole lobster, prawns, scallops, and grilled local fish. A beef tenderloin of Kamuela Pride beef comes with lobster tempura and garlic prawns served with mozzarella mashed potatoes. The macadamia-crusted apple pie and the chocolate ganache torte are desserts to diet for.

Summary & comments Café Pesto won the local Hale Aina Award for Best Big Island Restaurant in 1999. Diners pen comments such as "Move the restaurant to where we live," or "You cook better than my wife, but don't tell her." Both restaurants have a smoke-free policy.

CanoeHouse ★★★★½

HAWAII REGIONAL | MODERATE/EXPENSIVE | QUALITY ★★★★½ | VALUE ★★★
ZONE 11

Mauna Lani Bay Hotel & Bungalows, 68-1400 Mauna Lani Drive, Kohala Coast; (808) 885-6622; www.maunalani.com

Reservations Highly recommended **When to go** Sunset **Entrée range** $23–$50 **Payment** All major credit cards **Service rating** ★★★★ **Parking** Valet or hotel lot **Bar** Full service **Wine selection** Good **Dress** Resort attire **Disabled access** Adequate, but it's some distance from the parking **Customers** Resort and hotel guests and Islanders

Dinner Sunday–Thursday, 6–9 p.m.; buffet on Friday and Saturday

Setting & atmosphere A torchlit path with a little bridge over a koi-filled stream and the ocean waves lapping on the beach a few steps away set the scene for a romantic evening. Inside, a huge koa canoe is the focal point. You can choose semi-privacy by sitting in a raised booth, choose to be in the middle of things at a table, or join the conviviality at a central bar.

House specialties Imaginative entrées include stir-fried soba noodles with miso-sake marinated mahimahi, and grilled lemon-pepper scallops with wild-mushroom mashed potatoes.

Other recommendations It's tempting to order two appetizers, perhaps kalua pork spring rolls or baby-back ribs grilled with guava hoisin sauce, instead of an entrée, just so you can try the intriguing preparations. If you still have room for a decadent dessert, try the CanoeHouse Chocolate Pillar, a rich torte with vanilla sauce and fresh berries.

Summary & comments The food is innovative, the setting lovely, and wines suggested for each entrée are available by the glass. It almost makes paying the hefty bill worth it.

Coast Grille ★★★★½

CONTEMPORARY/HAWAII REGIONAL | MODERATE/EXPENSIVE | QUALITY ★★★★½ VALUE ★★★ | ZONE 11

Hapuna Beach Prince Hotel, 62-100 Kaunaoa Drive, Kohala Coast; (808) 880-1111; www.hapunabeachprincehotel.com

Reservations Recommended **When to go** Sunset under the stars if you sit outside overlooking the ocean **Entrée range** $20–$50 **Payment** VISA, MC, AMEX, DC, JCB **Service rating** ★★★★ **Parking** Valet or hotel lot **Bar** Full service **Wine selection** Extensive **Dress** Resort wear **Disabled access** Adequate, via elevator and curving ramp walkway **Customers** Hotel and resort guests and Islanders for special occasions

Dinner Every day, 6–9:30 p.m.

Setting & atmosphere This is a big, spacious restaurant where you can sit at interior tables (which is a waste of an exhilarating view), out on the deck, or at banquettes that face the ocean when the breeze is a little too nippy for comfort. Tables inside the multilevel, circular building seem dwarfed under a high ceiling but give you a nice feeling of privacy from neighboring diners. Natural woods and soft lighting tone down the empty effect.

House specialties The oyster bar is a rare find in Island restaurants, while Kona lobster, raised just down the coast, comes in a steamer basket with shrimp, Manila clams, and Waipio taro ravioli. The hotel is the home of the Sam Choy Poke Contest, a blessing for seafood lovers, as many types of poke, generally made of raw fish, seaweed, and spices, are available.

Other recommendations For non–seafood lovers, there's peppercorn-crusted lamb rack with star anise sauce, or grilled smoked veal chop. The dessert sampler eases the pain of making a decision, but you might want to order the warm chocolate pudding with fresh nutmeg ice cream in advance so this creamy rich treat will be ready when you are.

Summary & comments Sit outside at sunset on summer and fall evenings to fully appreciate the view of turquoise ocean and white sand.

Daniel Thiebaut Restaurant ★★★½

FRENCH ASIAN | MODERATE | QUALITY ★★★★ | VALUE ★★★★ | ZONE 11

65-1259 Kawaihae Road, Kamuela; (808) 887-2200; www.danielthiebaut..com

Reservations Suggested **When to go** Anytime **Entrée range** Lunch $8.50–$15, dinner $20–$26.50 **Payment** All major credit cards **Service rating** ★★★★ **Parking** Free, on site **Bar** Full service **Wine selection** Extensive, with 35 selections by the glass **Dress** Casual **Disabled access** Good **Customers** Locals, tourists

Lunch Monday–Friday, 11:30 a.m.–1:30 p.m.

Dinner Every day, 5:30–9:30 p.m.

Setting & atmosphere Daniel Thiebaut is set in the former Chock In Store and Family Home, which has been part of this ranching community since the turn of the twentieth century. The character of the cheerful yellow structure has been preserved, with five dining rooms that reflect the room's original uses: a dress shop, for instance, plus the general store and the family's dining parlor. Warm wood floors and period furnishings reflect the plantation times. Vintage Hawaiiana is a large part of the decor.

House specialties Local produce is at its freshest in this cool, mountain farming community, and Thiebaut's takes advantage of the bounty. French techniques are applied in combination with Asian flavors. The chef's signature Hunan-style rack of lamb comes with an eggplant compote and goat cheese made in nearby Mauna Kea. Salmon is served with ravioli filled with spicy wasabi and topped with kaffir lime sauce. A corn cake flavored with a lemongrass-coconut-lobster sauce is also a house favorite.

Other recommendations Lunch is quite affordable here, and it's an eclectic mix of dishes—from two eggs any style (with roasted tomato) to a mixed grill of lamb chop, beef tenderloin, and chicken sausage. Several vegetarian entrées are on the menu, including avocado spring roll with smoked tomato coulis, pad thai noodles with tofu and wild mushrooms, and macadamia-crusted tofu with cilantro-tahini sauce.

Summary & comments Chef Daniel Thiebaut came to the Kohala Coast from his native France by way of such diverse assignments as the Manila Hotel, Gleneagles Hotel in Scotland, and Switzerland's Winter Resort. As you would expect from a chef with that résumé, he came to Hawaii as a hotel resort chef, but he has chosen a more intimate expression for his own restaurant, opened in 1998. Daniel Thiebaut was recognized in *Condé Nast* in 2001 as one of the 100 hottest new restaurants in the world.

Donatoni's ★★★★½

ITALIAN | MODERATE/EXPENSIVE | QUALITY ★★★★½ | VALUE ★★★ | ZONE 11

Hilton Waikoloa Village, 425 Waikoloa Beach Drive, Waikoloa; (808) 886-1234; www.hilton.com

Reservations Highly recommended **When to go** Anytime **Entrée range** $19.25–$45 **Payment** All major credit cards **Service rating** ★★★★½ **Parking** Valet or complimentary hotel parking lot **Bar** Full ser-vice **Wine selection** Extensive wine and champagne list **Dress** Resort attire **Disabled access** Adequate, at some distance from the parking lot **Customers** Hotel and resort guests, some Islanders

Dinner Every day, 6–10 p.m.

Setting & atmosphere This is an intimate, romantic restaurant reminiscent of old Italy, and it seems even more dreamy if you have the chance to sit outdoors next to a saltwater canal where boats drift by in the moonlight—almost like being in Venice.

House specialties With a name like Sascia Marchesi, is it any wonder the Milanese-born chef is an expert in preparing the northern Italian cuisine served at Donatoni's? Among his best dishes are Torre Di Granseola e Vitello (king crab and veal scaloppini with lemon sauce) and a daily fresh catch of fish served with risotto and fresh asparagus.

Other recommendations Delectable pastas may be ordered as appetizers or entrées. Traditional tiramisu and exquisite crème brûlée take top dessert honors at this restaurant.

Entertainment & amenities A violinist strolls from table to table in the evenings.

Summary & comments More than one publication has lauded Donatoni's for its Italian food and romantic atmosphere. Oddly, the romantic ambience is nearly as heady inside (with opulent chandeliers and pretty upholstered booths and chairs) as it is outside beside the waterway.

Edelweiss ★★★½

CONTINENTAL | MODERATE | QUALITY ★★★★ | VALUE ★★★★ | ZONE 11

Highway 19, Waimea; (808) 885-6800

Reservations Recommended **When to go** Anytime for dinner except Sunday and Monday; go early on weekends to avoid waiting **Entrée range** $18.50–$24.50 **Payment** VISA, MC, AMEX **Service rating** ★★★★ **Parking** In adjacent lot **Bar** Full service **Wine selection** Average **Dress** Casual **Disabled access** Good **Customers** Islanders and some tourists

Lunch Tuesday–Saturday, 11:30 a.m.–1:30 p.m.

Dinner Tuesday–Saturday, 5–8:30 p.m.

Setting & atmosphere You feel as if you're back in Bavaria in this charming chalet-restaurant with rustic redwood furnishings, traditional blue-and-white curtains, and rich aromas of robust food wafting from the kitchen over the room's 15 tables.

House specialties You'll always find a delicious rack of lamb on the menu. Complete dinners include everything but dessert, for which you can choose the three-layer raspberry, vanilla, and chocolate Edelweiss torte, or rice pudding.

Other recommendations More than a dozen specials might be served nightly—Texas wild boar, venison ragout, Black Forest chicken, veal chalet Emily—so you never get tired of the menu.

Summary & comments Edelweiss has been a Big Island favorite for years, steadily withstanding competition from new, trendy restaurants that have come and, in many cases, gone from the Big Island dining scene. A word of warning: Sometimes the chef gets a little heavy on the salt.

The Grill and Lounge at The Orchid ★★★½

CONTEMPORARY | EXPENSIVE | QUALITY ★★★★ | VALUE ★★★ | ZONE 11

The Orchid Hotel, 1 North Kaniku Drive, Kohala Coast; (808) 885-2000; www.orchid-maunalani.com

Reservations Highly recommended **When to go** Anytime **Entrée range** $28–$50 **Payment** All major credit cards **Service rating** ★★★★½ **Parking** Valet or free self-parking in hotel lot **Bar** Full service **Wine selection** Extensive **Dress** Dressy resort attire **Disabled access** Good, via elevator **Customers** Hotel and resort guests, Islanders for special occasions

Dinner Every day, 6:30–9:30 p.m.

Setting & atmosphere Comfortable club-like atmosphere, with richly polished koa wood bar and wall paneling, enhances relaxed dining. Tables are covered in beige Frette linens and softly lit with candle lamps. Chairs are upholstered in rich tapestry, while the walls are hung with scenes by local artists.

House specialties The Grill and Lounge is especially good for the grilled meat items on the menu. Rack of lamb is crusted with pesto accompanied by apple-smoked bacon, sweet potato, and wild mushrooms, and garnished with tropical fruit chutney. Veal chops are similarly crusted with Parmesan and served with a sweet corn risotto and Waimea tomato fondue. To start, Maui onion soup topped with imported Gruyère and Reggiano cheeses, or warm baby-spinach salad garnished with fresh buffalo mozzarella, sets the taste buds tingling.

Other recommendations The oven-roasted breast of organic chicken (mainlanders might call it "free-range") oozes melted Puna goat cheese and is served with baby bok choy and roasted garlic potatoes. Dessert lovers have to ask which selections of soufflés are available nightly, though for a lighter conclusion, you might opt for the apple Florentine served in a crust of crisp macadamia-nut butter snaps.

Entertainment & amenities Classical guitarist Charles Brotman, whose instrumental CDs can be found in Island music outlets, strums contemporary tunes most evenings. Couples often linger a while to take advantage of the restaurant's dance floor.

Summary & comments The Grill and Lounge has been recognized by Gayot's *The Best of Hawaii* for fine dining.

Harrington's ★★

STEAK AND SEAFOOD | MODERATE | QUALITY ★★★½ | VALUE ★★★★ | ZONE 12

135 Kalanianaole Street, Hilo; (808) 961-4966

Reservations Recommended **When to go** Dinner any day but Wednesday **Entrée range** $14.75–$27.95 **Payment** VISA, MC **Service rating** ★★★★ **Parking** In adjacent lot **Bar** Full service **Wine selection** Adequate, about 30 wines **Dress** Casual dress, no tank tops, no swimwear for women **Disabled access** Good **Customers** Tourists and Islanders

Lunch Monday–Friday, 11 a.m.–2 p.m.

Dinner Monday–Saturday, 5–9:30 p.m.; Sunday, 5–9 p.m.

Setting & atmosphere Harrington's is in an old brown freestanding building on the edge of the Ice Pond in Hilo; it's best viewed in kinder lighting after dark. Inside, hanging plants and other greenery, blue tablecloths, and tropical flowers on the tables create an intimate atmosphere.

House specialties Among reliable choices like prime rib, New York steak, and teriyaki steak offerings, the Slavic steak is a tasty chilled mainland sirloin sliced thin and topped with a savory garlic butter sauce.

Other recommendations Dinners, including seafood selections—fresh fish, lobster, prawns, calamari, scallops—come with a choice of starch and salad. If you're a vegetarian in a world of steak eaters, opt for the eggplant parmigiana. Waiters tempt you by presenting desserts on a tray. If you can't say no, try the house cheesecake with strawberries or lilikoi.

Entertainment & amenities On Thursday, Friday, and Saturday nights a musician livens up the lounge with contemporary Hawaiian music.

Summary & comments The menu in this old standby may have been updated by new ownership several years ago, but basically if you liked steak and seafood restaurants 20 years ago, you'll find this pleasant restaurant comforting in a world of nouvelle cuisine.

Huggo's ★★½

PACIFIC RIM/MEDITERRANEAN | MODERATE | QUALITY ★★★½ | VALUE ★★★ ZONE 11

75-5828 Kahakai Road, Kailua-Kona; (808) 329-1493; www.huggos.com

Reservations Recommended **When to go** Sunset for most romantic lighting **Entrée range** $16.95–$37 **Payment** VISA, MC, D, DC, JCB **Service rating** ★★★ **Parking** Adjacent lot **Bar** Full service **Wine selection** Adequate, a dozen by the glass **Dress** Casual **Disabled access** Good **Customers** Islanders and tourists

Lunch Every day, 11:30 a.m.–2:30 p.m.

Dinner Every day, 5:30–10 p.m.

Setting & atmosphere With tables in an open-air restaurant set just above water's edge, Huggo's proved such a popular place for sunset watchers that the owners opened an adjacent waterfront lounge with a similar view next door called Huggo's on the Rocks. The new bar, which serves lunch and *pupus* at dinner, is also a popular hangout for longtime Huggo's loyalists. The established restaurant is decorated with marine memorabilia, big anchors, lamps that must have come from some ocean-going vessel at one time, rope lines, and natural wood. One open-to-the-elements deck has half a dozen tables shaded by big umbrellas.

House specialties The fresh local seafood is the reason Huggo's has earned a dedicated following. Try sesame-crusted mahimahi or coconut-kiwi ono, both delicately flavored white fish adeptly seasoned.

Other recommendations A number of vegetarian choices and a juicy cut of certified Angus prime rib gives non–seafood lovers a chance to enjoy Huggo's casual atmosphere and fine food.

Entertainment & amenities Performers render live contemporary music nightly at the adjacent bar.

Summary & comments Ask for a table by the window to fully appreciate Huggo's oceanfront appeal.

Kilauea Lodge ★★★½

CONTINENTAL | MODERATE | QUALITY ★★★★ | VALUE ★★★ | ZONE 12

19-4055 Old Volcano Road, Volcano Village; (808) 967-7366; www.kilauealodge.com

Reservations Highly recommended **When to go** Anytime; post-nighttime lava viewing is always fun **Entrée range** $15.50–$33 **Payment** VISA, MC **Service rating** ★★★½ **Parking** Adjacent lot **Bar** Full service **Wine selection** Good, some wines by the glass **Dress** Casual. Bring a sweater; Volcano nights can be cool **Disabled access** Adequate, via lift **Customers** Islanders and tourists

Dinner Every day, 5:30–9 p.m.

Setting & atmosphere This mountain lodge, surrounded by tree ferns in the cool, secluded Volcano area, dates from 1938, when the property was a scouting retreat. The dining room has a stone fireplace, vaulted cedar ceiling, hardwood floors, local artwork, and a rustic, remote appeal.

House specialties The cool climate is great for duck l'orange with red cabbage and potatoes du jour or a rich seafood Mauna Kea, pasta made with bay shrimp, prawns, fresh ahi, scallops, mushrooms, capers, and basil-wine sauce. Lighter appetites go for the fresh Island fish. The Lodge's signature dessert is Portuguese sweet bread pudding garnished with a variety of fruit sauces.

Other recommendations This is a cozy place to sip a full-bodied red wine and nibble away on an appetizer, such as Brie cheese deep-fried in coconut batter and served with brandied apples and bread.

Summary & comments Kilauea Lodge has long been considered *the* place to eat in Volcano, and people from Hilo often drive the half hour from town to enjoy the "getting-away-from-it-all" feeling the Lodge provides.

Kona Ranch House ★★½

AMERICAN | INEXPENSIVE/MODERATE | QUALITY ★★★ | VALUE ★★★★ | ZONE 11

75-5653 Ololi Street, Kailua-Kona; (808) 329-7061

Reservations Recommended **When to go** Anytime **Entrée range** Breakfast $4.75–$11, lunch $5.95–$12, dinner $10.95–$37.95 **Payment** VISA, MC, AMEX, DC, D, JCB **Service rating** ★★★ **Parking** In adjacent lot **Bar** Full service **Wine selection** Limited, all by glass **Dress** Casual **Disabled access** Good **Customers** Islanders and tourists

Breakfast Every day, 6:30 a.m.–2 p.m.

Lunch Every day, 10 a.m.–4 p.m.

Dinner Every day, 4–9 p.m.

Setting & atmosphere This family-style restaurant is divided into two sections. The Paniolo Room has booths handy for a quick lunch; the Plantation Lanai is nicer for dinner or Sunday brunch, with white wicker chairs, flowers, and candles in the evening.

House specialties Known for good breakfasts of omelets, eggs Benedict, and pancakes, this place is especially busy on Sunday mornings. At dinner, big barbecue platters are the draw, but the menu is so varied you'll find Tex-Mex and vegetarian items as well.

Other recommendations You can choose fresh local fish—ahi, mahimahi, and ono—prepared broiled, Cajun, sautéed, and fried. Meals come with salad, vegetables, and starch.

Summary & comments Ample food, reasonable prices, and pleasant surroundings—this family restaurant has been an Island favorite since 1981.

Merriman's ★★★★½

HAWAII REGIONAL | MODERATE/EXPENSIVE | QUALITY ★★★★½ | VALUE ★★★
ZONE 11

Opelo Plaza II, Highway 19 and Opelo Road, Waimea; (808) 885-6822; www.merrimanshawaii.com

Reservations Highly recommended **When to go** Anytime for dinner **Entrée range** $12.95–$25.95 **Payment** VISA, MC, AMEX, JCB **Service rating** ★★★★★ **Parking** In adjacent lot **Bar** Full service **Wine selection** Extensive **Dress** Casual **Disabled access** Good **Customers** Tourists and Islanders

Lunch Monday–Friday, 11:30 a.m.–1:30 p.m.

Dinner Every day, 5:30–9 p.m.

Setting & atmosphere Set in the heart of Big Island cowboy country, Merriman's is a classy, understated restaurant with an exhibition kitchen. Artwork by local artists is ever-changing and available for purchase. Light colors and potted palms add to the contemporary ranch country feel.

House specialties Chef/owner Peter Merriman serves fresh, locally raised meat and produce, available in dishes that reflect the cooking styles of Hawaii's various cultures. The restaurant's signature dish is original wokcharred ahi, seared, sashimi-rare on the inside, available as an appetizer or an entrée. New York steaks are from nearby Parker Ranch, but the lamb is raised at Kahua Ranch and prepared differently each day. You might find herb-roasted leg of lamb served with mango port wine jus, or a rack of lamb. Lokelani Farms grows special tomatoes just for Merriman's; organic spinach, grown at Honopua Farms, is tossed with hot balsamic vinegar and garnished with pipi kaula (spicy dried beef) and crumbled bacon.

Other recommendations Fresh Island fish is served sautéed with shellfish and vegetable nabemono, herb-grilled on mango chutney, or sesame-crusted with spicy lilikoi sauce and tomato papaya relish. Vegetarians will appreciate pan-fried Asian cake noodle served with a medley of vegetables: broccoli, snow peas, cauliflower, and carrots, with a spicy blackbean sauce. Dessert lovers say the coconut crème brûlée is the best they've had, though some prefer the lilikoi passion-fruit mousse.

Summary & comments This is probably the Big Island's favorite restaurant. The chef/owner's reputation for the best food on the island is so widely known that visitors (including celebrities like Robert Redford and Kevin Costner) drive from miles away to Merriman's for special occasions. *Hint:* Take a sweater, as the restaurant can get cool in the chilly Waimea night.

Oodles of Noodles ★★★½

HAWAII REGIONAL/SOUTHWESTERN FUSION | INEXPENSIVE/MODERATE
QUALITY ★★★★½ | VALUE ★★★★★ | ZONE 11

75-1027 Henry Street, Suite 102, Kailua-Kona; (808)-329-9222

Reservations Not necessary **When to go** Anytime **Entrée range** Lunch or dinner $8–$17 **Payment** All major credit cards **Service rating** ★★★★ **Parking** Free in the adjoining shopping-center lot **Bar** Full service **Wine selection** Good, 17 wines by the glass **Dress** Casual **Disabled access** Good **Customers** Locals, tourists

Lunch and dinner Every day, 11 a.m.–9 p.m.

Setting & atmosphere Chic and contemporary, Oodles of Noodles shows off clean lines in its slate floors, warm wood furnishings, and brightly painted walls. Original art by Dietrich Varez, Shelly Maudsley White, and Debra Thompson provide even more personality.

House specialties Noodles obviously rule here, and it's a cross-cultural menu, pasta being an international language. You'll find Japanese udon, Italian linguine, Chinese chow mein, Thai rice noodles, all in seemingly endless presentations. Go simple with a steaming bowl of Vietnamese pho or a local favorite, saimin, made especially savory with duck broth and lup cheong (Chinese sausage). Or sample one of the Signature Noodles, such as wok-spiced ahi in a casserole with orecchiette pasta, or Southwestern-style fettuccini with grilled chicken and ancho-chipotle chili cream.

Other recommendations The restaurant also offers an extensive selection of salads and vegetarian entrées that, again, tour the world. Visit Asia through sweet-sour Thai salads topped with grilled fish or chicken and crispy noodles. You can go Mediterranean with linguine in a traditional presentation with kalamata olives, tomatoes, and roasted garlic.

Summary & comments Chef Amy Ferguson Ota is the former executive chef at the Ritz-Carlton Mauna Lani, among the first women to attain that level with a U.S. luxury hotel group, but she gave that up to run this intimate, freestanding restaurant. Ota began her career in Texas and was influential in the development of a regional cuisine in the Southwest, then in Hawaii became a founding member of the Hawaii Regional Cuisine chefs. Her specialty is blending the two styles with a solid foundation in classic French cooking. In 1995 she was nominated for a James Beard Award for the Pacific Northwest region, which includes Hawaii.

Pahu ia at Four Seasons ★★★★½

HAWAIIAN FUSION | EXPENSIVE | QUALITY ★★★★½ | VALUE ★★★ | ZONE 11

Four Seasons Resort Hualalai, 100 Kaupulehu Drive, Kaupulehu-Kona; (808) 325-8000; www.fourseasons.com

Reservations Recommended **When to go** Sunset is most romantic **Entrée range** $25–$43; 4-course chef's tasting menu plus dessert, $65; with wine pairings, add $20 **Payment** VISA, MC, AMEX, D, JCB **Service rating** ★★★★★ **Parking** Complimentary valet or hotel lot **Bar** Full service **Wine selection** Extensive **Dress** Resort wear **Disabled access** Adequate, via paved pathways **Customers** Hotel and resort guests and Islanders celebrating special occasions

Breakfast Every day, 6–11:30 a.m.

Dinner Every day, 5:30–10 p.m.

Setting & atmosphere Outdoor deck seating features candlelit tables, with spotlights illuminating the rhythmic surf, and is romantic even for hand-holding at breakfast. Cross a wooden bridge suspended across a natural fishpond to reach the polished mahogany-and-teak interior, where a four-foot rectangular aquarium that stands nine feet tall holds colorful reef fish. Candles in black sand in hurricane lamps light individual tables. Check out three original hand-colored woodcuts by Charles Bartlett (circa 1921–1922)—"Duke Kahanamoku," "Surfing at Waikiki," and "Hawaiian Fisherman"—displayed on restaurant walls.

House specialties There's a mind-boggling daily breakfast buffet that's even more extensive on Sundays for brunch. At dinner, an Ahi, Ahi, Ahi appetizer features the popular tuna in a trio of preparations: sashimi, seared, and poke. Steamed opakapaka Oriental style with shiitake mushrooms, Chinese parsley, and ginger-shoyu is both good and good for you.

Other recommendations As with most top-notch hotel restaurants, you'll find a plethora of fresh Island fish on the menu, which may save enough on calories that you'll feel no guilt at plunging into the kope pukolu (coffee trio), a tower of classic tiramisu and cappuccino crème brûlée on a cinnamon sugar puff pastry, and homemade espresso ice cream wrapped in a coconut wave cookie. On the other hand, Vintage Chocolate soufflé, a melt-in-your-mouth warm delight, is also a spectacular finish to a meal.

Entertainment & amenities Island entertainers torch dance nightly from 6:30 to 9:30 p.m.

Summary & comments This is the closest to the beach you could possibly sit without spreading a towel in the sand for a picnic, but the price may reduce you to opting for a real picnic next time.

Royal Siam Thai ★★★½

THAI | INEXPENSIVE | QUALITY ★★★★ | VALUE ★★★★★ | ZONE 12

70 Mamo Street, Hilo; (808) 961-6100

Reservations Accepted **When to go** Any time except Sunday **Entrée range** $7.95–$12.95, vegetarian dishes start at $4.95 **Payment** VISA, MC,

AMEX, DC, D **Service rating** ★★★ **Parking** On street **Bar** Full service **Wine selection** Very limited **Dress** Casual **Disabled access** Adequate **Customers** Islanders and some tourists

Lunch Monday–Saturday, 11 a.m.–2 p.m.

Dinner Every day, 5–8:30 p.m.

Setting & atmosphere This small restaurant seats about 50 at booths that line the walls and central tables covered with pink-and-white striped tablecloths. Pictures of the Thai king and queen, Buddha, and Thai dancers hang on the walls. Sprays of orchids and potted trees add a colorful touch.

House specialties Diners always love the deep-fried spring rolls made with either vegetables only or pork and vegetables and served in the traditional way, with mint and lettuce leaves to roll them in and a sweet-sour sauce for dipping. The most popular entrée on the menu is Buddrama, chicken prepared with spinach and peanut sauce, though curries, which can be ordered mild, medium, or hot, are also favored. Choose yellow or green curry with chicken, beef, or shrimp, or a healthy vegetarian curry with basil, green peas, and eggplant.

Other recommendations The chef's favorites are Thai garlic shrimp and cashew chicken with orders of sticky rice. Thai jasmine rice and brown rice are other starchy choices.

Entertainment & amenities The sound system plays subdued Thai music to set the mood.

Summary & comments Quality- and value-wise, though it's certainly not fancy, this is sometimes called the best food in Hilo. In 1999 the restaurant expanded, adding a second room that can seat about 25 people. It can be booked for private parties, though it's normally used for dinner seating.

Roy's at the Kings Shops ★★★★½

HAWAIIAN FUSION | MODERATE | QUALITY ★★★★½ | VALUE ★★★★ | ZONE 11

Kings Shops, 250 Waikoloa Beach Drive, Waikoloa; (808) 886-4321; www.roysrestaurant.com

Reservations Highly recommended **When to go** Early to avoid crowds **Entrée range** $14–$27 **Payment** All major credit cards **Service rating** ★★★★ **Parking** Shopping-center lot **Bar** Full bar **Wine selection** Very good, some by the glass **Dress** Casual, no tank tops for men, no swimwear **Disabled access** Good **Customers** Islanders and tourists

Lunch Every day, 11:30 a.m.–2 p.m.

Dinner Every day, 5:30–9:30 p.m.

Setting & atmosphere This Roy's, with green carpets, a green marble bar, an exhibition kitchen, and window tables that overlook a golf course lake, is the nicest yet of Roy Yamaguchi's popular restaurants in Hawaii.

House specialties Sample grilled Szechuan-style baby-back ribs or Thai noodle peanut chicken salad at dinner, or choose among entrées like imu-roasted pork laulau, pizza, or sweet sake-glazed shrimp. Blackened Island ahi, served in spicy hot soy-mustard-butter sauce, is a Roy's standby. More than half a dozen fish and their preparations change nightly, as do appetizers, pizzas, pastas, salads, and soups.

Other recommendations Salads and sandwiches at lunch are complete meals, such as the teriyaki Big Island beef sandwich or fresh Island fish of the day with ponzu sprout salad, as are the pastas, like penne pasta with Neopolitan sauce and chicken, shrimp, or beef.

Summary & comments It's no problem matching a wine to any of the Euro-Asian flavors, given the extensive wine list. Youngsters are welcome; Roy's offers a children's menu and crayons. According to the chef's mood and the ingredients available, more than 30 menu items may change nightly, so go often; you'll never get bored with the food.

Sam Choy's Restaurant ★★★

HAWAII REGIONAL | MODERATE | QUALITY ★★★★ | VALUE ★★★★ | ZONE 11

Kaloko Light Industrial Park, 73-5576 Kauhola Street, Bay 1, Kailua-Kona; (808) 326-1545; www.samchoys.com

Reservations Highly recommended for dinner **When to go** Anytime **Entrée range** $16.95–$24.95, daily specials can top out at $31.95 **Payment** VISA, MC, D **Service rating** ★★★★ **Parking** In adjacent lot **Bar** None **Wine selection** Bring your own **Dress** Casual **Disabled access** Good **Customers** Islanders and tourists

Breakfast & lunch Every day, 6 a.m.–2 p.m.

Dinner Tuesday–Saturday, 5–9 p.m.

Setting & atmosphere During the day, Sam Choy's is a casual, local-style restaurant frequented not only by workers from the surrounding area but also by visitors looking for real local food. In the evening, the room undergoes a transformation with white cloths and colored napkins added to the tables, but you can still watch the cooks zip around the open kitchen.

House specialties Islanders love the seafood laulau, an assortment of fresh fish, vegetables, and spinach steamed in a luau leaf. Equally famous is Sam's seafood trio, three types of local fresh fish, one served seared, one ogo-crusted in crispy tempura, and one macadamia-nut crusted. All meals come with soup or salad and a choice of rice or potato.

Other recommendations Duck, lamb chops, macadamia nut–crusted pork loin, and teriyaki steak round out a dinner menu that's sure to round out an average person's body. Big hearty breakfasts of stew omelets or fried poke (barely seared seafood and seaweed) are filling, and omelets come with rice, home fries, or hash browns, and toast and jelly. At lunch, specials change daily, but a big steaming bowl of saimin (Island-style noodle soup) is always on the menu.

Summary & comments Sam Choy is Hawaii's most famous, and his restaurants are known almost as much for their *big* portions as for the high-quality food with a real local touch and robust flavors. Expect to take home enough food for the next day's lunch.

Kauai

The Beach House ★★★

PACIFIC RIM | MODERATE | QUALITY ★★★★ | VALUE ★★★ | ZONE 13

5022 Lawai Road, Poipu; (808) 742-1424; www.the-beach-house.com

Reservations Highly recommended **When to go** Sunset **Entrée range** $18.95–$32.50 **Payment** VISA, MC, AMEX, DC, JCB **Service rating** ★★★★ **Parking** Valet or street **Bar** Full service **Wine selection** Extensive **Dress** Resort wear **Disabled access** Good; valet parking is free for disabled **Customers** Tourists and Islanders

Dinner *May 2–October 1:* Every day, 6–9:30 p.m.; *October 2–May 1:* Every day, 5:30–9:30 p.m.

Setting & atmosphere Artwork by local artists can be purchased right off the walls, if you have time to tear your eyes away from floor-to-ceiling windows that showcase Poipu's best ocean view. It's most romantic at sunset, when surfers and frolicking whales might still be spotted.

House specialties A kiawe wood–burning grill adds a flavorful touch to kal-bi-style lamb rack or Jawaiian pork tenderloin with jerk spices.

Other recommendations The on-property chef, under the guiding wing of Kauai's well-known chef Linda Yamada, prepares such delicacies as wok-charred mahimahi in a ginger-sesame crust and lime-ginger sauce, or seared sea scallops with a polenta herb crust and papaya-avocado guacamole. Save calories on a stack of portobello mushrooms with spring vegetables, then splurge on Toasted Hawaiian, a white-chocolate cake layered with haupia (coconut pudding), white-chocolate mousse, macadamia nuts, and caramel sauce.

Summary & comments Make reservations early and request a seat by the window for the full effect of this beach area's stunning views. In 1998, The Beach House won honors as the top restaurant on Kauai in the local Hale Aina Awards.

Brennecke's Beach Broiler ★★★

CONTEMPORARY | MODERATE | QUALITY ★★★½ | VALUE ★★★★ | ZONE 13

2100 Hoone Road, Poipu Beach; (808) 742-7588; www.brenneckes.com

Reservations Recommended **When to go** Sunset **Entrée range** $9–$35 **Payment** All major credit cards **Service rating** ★★★ **Parking** In 2 adjacent lots **Bar** Full service **Wine selection** Limited **Dress** Casual **Disabled access** Poor, but staff will carry wheelchairs up the stairs **Customers** Tourists and Islanders

Lunch Every day, 11 a.m.–4 p.m.

Dinner Every day, 4–10 p.m.

Setting & atmosphere Climb the stairs to this restaurant situated across from Poipu Beach Park in a freestanding blue building. Then sit by an open window so you can see surfers, palms, blue ocean, and golden sands just beyond the petunia-filled window boxes.

House specialties After a trip to the salad bar, specialties called *makai* (from the ocean) and *mauka* (from the land) arrive sizzling from the kiawe charcoal broiler. Fresh Island fish, Hawaiian spiny lobster, or Brennecke's signature scampi with choice of barbecue, teriyaki, or garlic sauce will satisfy most diners.

Other recommendations Sea breezes through the open windows and a varied menu of Kauai *pupus,* including fresh sashimi caught by local fishermen, New York steak and mushrooms, and nachos with peppers, make this a great spot for a glass of wine or one of Brenneckes world-famous mai tais.

Entertainment & amenities The restaurant sound system usually carries either 1960s or Hawaiian tunes.

Summary & comments Brennecke's is handy if you've had enough sun and sand but still want a peaceful beachside ambience while you eat a big burger for lunch. The open-air view makes this place an old favorite. For quick and casual snacks, Brennecke's Deli downstairs serves cool shave ice and sandwiches with your choice of fillings.

Café Hanalei and Terrace ★★★★

CONTINENTAL (WITH ISLAND INGREDIENTS) | EXPENSIVE | QUALITY ★★★★½ VALUE ★★★ | ZONE 13

Princeville Hotel, Princeville; (808) 826-2760; www.princeville.com

Reservations Recommended **When to go** Anytime, though sunsets are best **Entrée range** $26.95–$31.95, (vegetarian dish $21.95); 3-course dinner $43.95 **Payment** All major credit cards **Service rating** ★★★★★ **Parking** Valet or hotel lot **Bar** Full service **Wine selection** Good **Dress** Resort wear **Disabled access** Good, via elevator **Customers** Resort and hotel guests, Islanders for special events

Breakfast Every day, 6:30–11 a.m. (includes buffet)

Lunch Every day, 11 a.m.–2:30 p.m.

Dinner Every day, 5:30–9:30 p.m.

Setting & atmosphere Café Hanalei and Terrace enjoys the most stunning view of any restaurant on Kauai; it overlooks Hanalei Bay and Makana Peak (the jutting spire of land that gained fame as Bali Hai in the movie *South Pacific*). A placid reflecting pool is on one side of the covered terrace seating, and when rain sprinkles over the bay, it becomes an artist's extravagant scene; sometimes a vivid rainbow arches across the misty sun-streaked sky. Inside, the restaurant is surrounded by towering windows and the ceiling is two floors above the lobby level.

House specialties The restaurant's Sunday brunch buffet is both a gourmand's and a glutton's dream come true, with made-to-order omelets, seafood, salads, and a dessert spread that requires at least two trips. Breakfast buffets the rest of the week are well stocked with Island fruit. At dinner the most popular entrée is steamed Hawaiian snapper, a sweet, white fish prepared with fresh ginger, cilantro, and shiitake mushrooms. Such a low-calorie meal calls for a decadent dessert—Kona coffee crème brûlée or chocolate macadamia-nut pie.

Other recommendations Sushi addicts are lucky if they come by on Saturday, Sunday, Tuesday, or Wednesday: On those nights, sushi chefs handcraft these little balls of rice and seafood to order in the restaurant.

Entertainment & amenities The lilting music of a pianist and a vocalist filters down from an upstairs lobby bar to diners who eat inside.

Summary & comments The view is what people remember, but the food and service also make dining a pleasure.

Casa di Amici ★★½

ITALIAN/CONTEMPORARY | MODERATE | QUALITY ★★★★ | VALUE ★★★ | ZONE 13

2301 Nalo Road, Poipu; (808) 742-1555

Reservations Requested **When to go** Thursday–Saturday if you like piano music **Entrée range** $13–$27 **Payment** VISA, AMEX **Service rating** ★★★★ **Parking** In adjacent lot **Bar** Full service **Wine selection** Excellent **Dress** Casual **Disabled access** Good **Customers** Islanders and tourists

Lunch Tuesday–Friday, 11:30 a.m.–2:30 p.m.

Dinner Every day, 6–9 p.m.

Setting & atmosphere Windows open to the balmy air around this comfortable Poipu restaurant. Casa di Amici means "house of friends," and with rattan furnishings under ceiling fans inside and sweeping views to the ocean on the deck outside, it feels like the *kamaaina* home the building once was. A small open-air bar is near the entry, where a big fish tank is filled with colorful reef fish for your diversion.

House specialties The Italian menu is translated into English, so you can figure out what you're getting when you mix and match your favorite pasta with perhaps a salsa arrabiatta—spicy tomato with sautéed pancetta and chilis. The most popular item on the menu is a porcini-crusted chicken breast in a sun-dried cherry, port wine, and mushroom sauce.

If you like bold flavors, try Japanese mahogany-glazed salmon served on frijole chorittos and black beans, or salmon steak painted with heavy soy sauce, sprinkled with furukake, baked and garnished with jalapeño-tequila aïoli, and served on a corn husk.

Other recommendations Picatta (as in veal picatta) and marsala sauces are particularly flavorful and rich. The chef loves Mexican/Southwestern food, so he's proud of his chili verde risotto. He has fun with risotto, creating classic four-cheese risotto, Indian curried lamb, kalua (usually pork), and other variations. Besides the bananas Foster, a dessert with a tropical appeal is Sugarloaf—upside-down cake topped with lilikoi cream.

Summary & comments Some entrées are available in light portions, but once you taste the house scampi with a good red wine, you may want more. Because of the variety of ethnic flavors in his preparations, the French-trained chef/owner describes his restaurant as "the most un-Italian Italian restaurant you'll ever be in." It has been given high marks by *Zagat,* the *Los Angeles Times, Gourmet,* and the *Chicago Tribune.*

Duke's Canoe Club ★★★

SEAFOOD | INEXPENSIVE/MODERATE | QUALITY ★★★★ | VALUE ★★★★ | ZONE 13

Kauai Marriott Resort and Beach Club, Kalapaki Beach, Lihue; (808) 246-9599; www.marriotthotels.com/lihhi

Reservations Recommended **When to go** Anytime; for cocktails at the Barefoot Bar, show up 4–6 p.m. for reasonable prices and live entertainment **Entrée range** $10.99–$24.99, market price for lobster **Payment** VISA, MC, AMEX, D **Service rating** ★★★½ **Parking** In adjacent lot **Bar** Full service **Wine selection** Adequate **Dress** Casual **Disabled access** Adequate **Customers** Tourists and Islanders

Lunch Every day, 11:30 a.m.–11:30 p.m. downstairs

Dinner Every day, 5–10 p.m.

Setting & atmosphere At this Polynesian-style restaurant with open-air views onto Kalapaki Beach, diners can sit downstairs at the Barefoot Bar for lunch, snacks, afternoon cocktails, and people-watching, or amble upstairs for dinner. A stream and waterfall, edged by lush plantings, create an outdoor garden effect even in the building's cool, shady interior.

House specialties Fresh fish is the name of the game after a trip to Duke's "all-you-care-to-eat" salad bar. Entrées come with salad, herbed rice, muffins, and sourdough bread. Best of the five preparations for fish is "Duke's Style," baked in garlic, lemon, and sweet basil glaze, although if you want to spice things up a bit, you might go for the "Firecracker Fresh Fish" preparation with tomato-chili-cumin aïoli, served with black bean, Maui onion, and avocado relish.

Other recommendations Macadamia-nut-and-crab wontons are such delicious little deep-fried pockets of Dungeness crab, cream cheese, and macadamia nuts served with a mustard plum sauce, you might be tempted to limit dinner to these appetizers and a trip to the salad bar.

Entertainment & amenities A strolling trio of guitar and ukulele players presents Hawaiian-style dinner music in the restaurant upstairs. Downstairs on Thursday and "Tropical Friday" afternoons, a band entertains, and tropical drinks are a special happy hour price.

Summary & comments This is a casual place to grab a hamburger as you come off Kalapaki Beach for lunch or enjoy a mai tai at sunset, and then climb the stairs for a pleasant dinner. Service isn't always as attentive as it should be. *Keiki* (children's) dinner items make this a reasonably "nice" place to take kids, a welcome change from fast-food dinners.

Hamura Saimin ★

ISLAND ECLECTIC | INEXPENSIVE | QUALITY ★★★½ | VALUE ★★★★★ | ZONE 13

2956 Kress Street, Lihue; (808) 245-3271

Reservations Not accepted **When to go** This little café is always busy, especially on rainy days, but right after opening there might be a lull **Entrée range** $5–$15 **Payment** Cash or traveler's checks **Service rating** ★★ **Parking** Limited in lot and on street **Bar** None, diners can bring libations **Wine selection** None **Dress** Casual **Disabled access** Accessible, but there is no ramp over an entry step **Customers** Islanders and adventuresome tourists

Lunch & dinner Monday–Saturday, 10 a.m.–midnight; Sunday, 10 a.m.–9 p.m.

Setting & atmosphere This is down-home Hawaii on a dusty side street in Lihue. The restaurant is in a single-board, plantation-style building, with louvered windows that let in a breath of air on a muggy summer day. Counter space fills the center of the restaurant, there are a few tables, and you'll note good-luck porcelain cat statues and other Island touches.

House specialties Everybody ends up at Hamura at one time or another for a big steaming bowl of saimin that's especially good on a wet, windy Kauai winter day. The saimin special bowl has a little bit of everything:

noodles garnished with vegetables, wonton, fish cake, chopped boiled egg, sliced pork, green onion, and sliced luncheon meat.

Other recommendations Soup is the ticket at Hamura, but carnivores will love the grilled chicken skewers and beef sticks. Manapua, big bread-like buns with a savory filling, are also favored, while lilikoi chiffon pie is a don't-miss dessert.

Summary & comments Hamura Saimin has been a Lihue standby for so long it's an institution. Go for a steaming bowl of soup, but don't expect to be blown away by fancy food or service; just enjoy the fun of having a unique local experience.

Keoki's Paradise ★★★½

STEAK AND SEAFOOD | MODERATE | QUALITY ★★★★ | VALUE ★★★★ | ZONE 13

Poipu Shopping Village, Poipu; (808) 742-7535; www.keokisparadise.com

Reservations Recommended **When to go** Anytime **Entrée range** \$8.94–\$23.95, or market price **Payment** VISA, MC, AMEX **Service rating** ★★★ **Parking** In adjacent lot **Bar** Full service **Wine selection** Good **Dress** Casual **Disabled access** Good **Customers** Tourists and Islanders

Lunch Every day, 11 a.m.–1:30 p.m.

Dinner Every day, 5:30–10 p.m.

Setting & atmosphere From outside in the generally crowded parking lot of this centrally located resort shopping center, you wouldn't expect to find a pleasant, cool boathouse-style restaurant set on a peaceful lagoon with tropical foliage and a thatched-roof bar. It takes you back to the Hawaii depicted on movie screens in the 1950s.

House specialties Fresh seafood, from starters of sashimi or chowder to a fresh-catch entrée served in your choice of five preparations and sauces, is most popular. Types of fish served depend on what is delivered that day and could range from ahi (tuna) to ulua (pompano) to opah (Hawaiian moonfish). For dessert, the hula pie with an Oreo cookie crust filled with ice cream is made for sharing.

Other recommendations For a taste of local flavor, order Koloa pork ribs glazed with plum sauce or Balinese chicken marinated in lemongrass and served with a lemon shoyu sauce, or try both in a combination plate. A variety of steaks is served with garlic mashed potatoes.

Summary & comments You can get just about any down-to-earth food you're in the mood for. You feel as if you are getting your money's worth, as healthy-sized entrées all include Keoki's Caesar-style salad, fresh-baked bread, and herbed rice, all served in a pleasant Polynesian setting.

Mema Thai Chinese Cuisine ★★

THAI/CHINESE | INEXPENSIVE/MODERATE | QUALITY ★★★★ | VALUE ★★★★★
ZONE 13

Wailua Shopping Center, 4-361 Kuhio Highway, Kapaa; (808) 823-0899

Reservations Accepted **When to go** Anytime **Entrée range** $7.95–$16.95 **Payment** VISA, MC, AMEX, D, DC **Service rating** ★★★ **Parking** In adjacent lot **Bar** Full bar **Wine selection** Limited **Dress** Casual **Disabled access** Good **Customers** Islanders and tourists

Lunch Monday–Friday, 11 a.m.–2:30 p.m.

Dinner Every day, 5–9:30 p.m.

Setting & atmosphere Set in a strip mall, Mema Thai Chinese is surprisingly attractive, with pretty pink linen tablecloths and lovely Oriental rosewood chairs. Orchid sprays add to the gracious atmosphere.

House specialties Curries come in colors of the rainbow—red, green, and yellow—made with your choice of vegetables, chicken, pork, beef, shrimp, fish, or other seafood. A local dish named evil jungle prince, a savory blending of coconut milk, basil, and red chili, can also be ordered with seafood (including calamari), poultry, or meat.

Other recommendations There's plenty to satisfy vegetarians here; many dishes can be ordered with tofu instead of meat, such as rice noodles with cabbage, mushrooms, and carrots, or stir-fried broccoli with oyster sauce.

Summary & comments *Thai Scene* magazine once named Mema "one of the ten best Thai restaurants outside Thailand." You may want to sit toward the back of the semi-divided room, away from the bar and the entrance to the kitchen, for the most peaceful dining experience.

A Pacific Café ★★★★½

PACIFIC RIM | MODERATE | QUALITY ★★★★½ | VALUE ★★★ | ZONE 13

Kauai Village Shopping Center, 4-831 Kuhio Highway, Suite 220, Kapaa; (808) 822-0013

Reservations Highly recommended **When to go** Anytime, but it's less crowded 5:30–6:30 p.m. **Entrée range** $22–$26 **Payment** VISA, MC, AMEX, D, DC **Service rating** ★★★★★ **Parking** Shopping center lot **Bar** Full service **Wine selection** Extensive, several by the glass **Dress** Casual **Disabled access** Good **Customers** Islanders and tourists

Dinner Every day, 5:30–10 p.m.

Setting & atmosphere The pretty-in-pastel restaurant has light-colored wooden tables, a few colorful tropical floral arrangements, and paintings from nearby Wyland Art Galleries decorating the walls.

House specialties The wok-charred mahimahi served with julienned vegetables and lime-ginger sauce is an award winner that never fails to please. Another popular standby on what is otherwise a most inventive menu is the certified Black Angus New York steak.

Two desserts have a loyal following: Crème brûlée is pure ambrosia enveloped in a crispy pastry crust. Or you can order a hot Vintage Chocolate tart, which takes 15 minutes to bake. Order the tart while you're still eating, or relax over coffee while you wait its preparation.

Other recommendations Almost too pretty to eat, the tiger eye sushi is sliced into thin, melt-in-the-mouth slices that resemble tiger eyes, because the ahi (tuna) that it's made of encases green asparagus and tobiko roe. The ahi is dipped in tempura, then flash-fried, so the inside slices remain sushi rare.

Summary & comments For years this classy Kapaa community restaurant has been *the* place to go for beautifully presented dishes with complex flavors made with homegrown ingredients. Chef/owner Jean Marie Josselin works with an Island farmer who grows herbs, lettuces, fruit, and vegetables to meet the restaurant's specific requirements.

Plantation Gardens ★★★½

ITALIAN | MODERATE | QUALITY ★★★★ | VALUE ★★★ | ZONE 13

Kiahuna Plantation, 2253 Poipu Road, Poipu; (808) 742-2216; www.outrigger.com

Reservations Recommended **When to go** Anytime after 5:30 p.m. for dinner; for cocktails and pizza, drop by 4–5:30 p.m. **Entrée range** $13.95–$27.95 **Payment** VISA, MC, AMEX, DC **Service rating** ★★★★ **Parking** In adjacent lots **Bar** Full service **Wine selection** Excellent **Dress** Kauai casual **Disabled access** Good **Customers** Tourists and Islanders

Dinner Every day, 5:30–10 p.m.

Setting & atmosphere Gardens with torchlit paths, rock work, a rich wood interior, and veranda dining offer a lovely setting for Italian food served in a historic Polynesian home, which once belonged to an early sugar baron.

House specialties Many items on the menu change monthly, but Plantation Gardens is known for its fresh fish and house-made pastas. The signature pasta dish, pappardelle fantasia, is a wide saffron pasta sautéed in white wine, herbs, and spices and tossed with fresh garden vegetables and shrimp. Fish of the day varies depending on what the fishermen bring to the door. If you hang out around the display kitchen, you can watch your pizza with portobello mushrooms, pancetta, and fontina cheese emerge sizzling from the wood-burning oven. A kiawe broiler gives steaks and fish that special smoky flavor.

Other recommendations Currently on the menu, manzo brasato is slow-roasted pot roast served with mascarpone mashed potatoes (whipped with sweet Italian cream cheese), served with gravy and fresh veggies of day, which might be bok choy and Koloa asparagus when in season.

The restaurant is famous for a classic tiramisu, but the banana lilikoi cream cheesecake with cream cheese frosting is equally decadent.

Entertainment & amenities If you're lucky, you may hit a weekend summer night when a rising Kauai group might drop by to play.

Summary & comments Fresh herbs are plucked from the garden out back, and Island fish might have been picked or caught only hours before reaching your table.

Postcards ★★★½

CONTEMPORARY | MODERATE | QUALITY ★★★★ | VALUE ★★★★ | ZONE 13

5-5075 A Kuhio Highway, Hanalei; (808) 826-1191

Reservations Highly recommended **When to go** Anytime for dinner **Entrée range** $14–$22, fish are market price **Payment** VISA, MC, AMEX **Service rating** ★★ **Parking** In adjacent lot **Bar** None **Wine selection** BYOB **Dress** Casual **Disabled access** Adequate **Customers** Islanders and tourists

Brunch Sunday, 8 a.m.–noon

Breakfast Every day, 8–11 a.m.

Dinner Every day, 5–9 p.m.

Setting & atmosphere Set in a small restored single-board plantation-style house with a front porch, the restaurant has the charm of an earlier era.

House specialties Gourmet vegetarian cuisine and savory seafood dishes draw repeat visitors. Start with an organic salad, or Thai summer rolls with spicy peanut sauce, then plunge into fresh fish or shrimp tacos or sample the taj triangles, crusty phyllo pastry filled with potatoes, peas, carrots, and Indian spices served with tropical chutney. Youngsters love the fresh fruit smoothies and cheese quesadillas.

Other recommendations If you're tired of hotel food, this is possibly Hanalei's next-best bet for breakfast. Sunrise Scramble features sautéed tofu with onions, garlic, and herbs mixed into the eggs. Other highlights include a full espresso bar, Irish red-roasted potatoes, homemade muffins, fresh orange juice, and Hanalei hotcakes.

Summary & comments Guests sign the guest book with notes like "We ate here three nights in a row" and "The best seafood in the Islands."

Roy's Poipu Bar & Grill ★★★★

HAWAIIAN FUSION | MODERATE | QUALITY ★★★★½ | VALUE ★★★ | ZONE 13

Poipu Shopping Village, 2360 Kiahuna Plantation Drive, Poipu Beach; (808) 742-5000; www.roysrestaurant.com

Reservations Highly recommended **When to go** Early for a quieter dinner, later for a livelier crowd **Entrée range** $17–$32 **Payment** VISA, MC, AMEX, DC, D **Service rating** ★★★★ **Parking** In shopping-center lot **Bar** Full bar **Wine selection** Excellent, many wines by the glass **Dress** Casual **Disabled access** Good **Customers** Tourists and Islanders

Dinner Every day, 5:30–9 p.m.

Setting & atmosphere Chef/owner Roy Yamaguchi's sleek shopping-center restaurant is a mecca for fans of what he dubs Euro-Asian Pacific cuisine—Asian seasonings mixed with French techniques. The restaurant has an airy feeling, with windows that let in the night air. The exhibition kitchen is enclosed by glass, so the noise level is kept down. A newer expansion and lounge area across a public walkway brings shoppers seemingly through the middle of the restaurant.

House specialties Hibachi-style salmon and oven-roasted pot roast have emerged from a long list of specials as steady favorites. Seafood lovers might choose fresh seared opakapaka (snapper) with orange shrimp butter and Chinese black-bean sauce. Dark-chocolate soufflé and volcanic puffed pastry filled with caramelized apple are dessert winners.

Other recommendations It's fun to go for dim sum and appetizers followed by a pizza from the wood-fired oven, so you have a chance to sample a number of the culinary creations available. Or, couples might share appetizers like lemongrass shrimp sticks with Thai chili cocktail sauce, pot-stickers with spicy peanut satay sauce, or escargot cassoulet with caramelized onions and creamy polenta.

Summary & comments Diners return again and again to this popular restaurant in Poipu, so Roy's chefs make sure they will never get bored with the menu by offering 25 or more specials nightly.

Shells, at the Sheraton Kauai Hotel ★★★½

AMERICAN | MODERATE/EXPENSIVE | QUALITY ★★★★ | VALUE ★★★ | ZONE 13

Sheraton Kauai Hotel, 2440 Hoonani Road, Poipu Beach; (808) 742-1661; www.sheraton-kauai.com

Reservations Recommended **When to go** 6–7 p.m. for sunset ocean view **Entrée range** $15.50–$36 **Payment** VISA, MC, AMEX, DC, D, JCB **Service rating** ★★★★ **Parking** Valet or hotel lot **Bar** Full service **Wine selection** Good **Dress** Resort wear **Disabled access** Good **Customers** Tourists

Breakfast Every day, 6:30–11 a.m.

Dinner Every day, 5:30–9:30 p.m.

Setting & atmosphere Floor-to-ceiling windows let the tradewinds and the sound of the waves drift off the ocean to diners on the lanai and inside this high-ceilinged restaurant. The airy, tropical room has rattan furnishings set under elaborate shell chandeliers that remained intact through Hurricane Iniki, which destroyed the hotel in 1992.

House specialties Baby rack of lamb prepared with herb and hoisin sauce is *ono* (delicious), though you might prefer the fresh fish and prawns served with spicy pineapple, baked sweet potato, Kauai slaw, and steamed rice, for a touch of Island flavor.

Other recommendations Appetizer crab cakes are a perennial favorite, but the restaurant is really known for a dessert called Mount Waialeale, a mountain of chocolate-mousse cake piled with sorbet and Island fruit.

Summary & comments This big, pretty hotel dining room is located adjacent to The Point, a great spot for pre-dinner cocktails indoors or out-doors, where the ocean view is even more encompassing. Note that children ages 12 and under eat free (maximum two children per table).

Tidepools ★★★

PACIFIC RIM | MODERATE/EXPENSIVE | QUALITY ★★★½ | VALUE ★★★ | ZONE 13

Hyatt Regency Kauai, 1571 Poipu Road, Poipu Beach; (808) 742-6260

Reservations Highly recommended **When to go** Anytime **Entrée range** $22–$40 **Payment** VISA, MC, AMEX **Service rating** ★★★★ **Parking** Valet or hotel lot **Bar** Full service **Wine selection** Adequate **Dress** Resort attire **Disabled access** Make pre-arrangements; it's quite a distance from the parking lot via an elevator and a service tunnel **Customers** Tourists, hotel guests, a few Islanders for special events

Dinner Every day, 6–10 p.m.

Setting & atmosphere Romantic tropical atmosphere makes this restaurant special for honeymooners and longtime lovers. Torchlit paths lead to the restaurant, which floats on a fish-filled lagoon; some thatched dining huts hold single candlelit tables for total privacy under Kauai's starry skies.

House specialties Tidepools serves interesting grilled entrées seasoned with Hawaiian alaea sea salt, such as chicken breast filled with Puna goat cheese and a lemongrass butter sauce, or pork chops topped with Asian pear marmalade, but fish and seafood are truly most appropriate for this watery restaurant. Macadamia nut–crusted Island fish with Kahlua, lime-ginger butter sauce, and jasmine fried rice is the signature dish. A selection from ten kinds of Island fish is offered nightly, and the server can describe each fish in detail. You can order four different preparations: sautéed with lilikoi butter, grilled with papaya and mango relish, steamed with sweet chili and lime sauce, or blackened with Hana Bay rum pineapple sauce.

Other recommendations Combination plates are the most expensive, but by ordering from a menu of ten combination items you can sample meat *and* seafood. Don't miss banana chocolate silk, a heavenly combination of bittersweet chocolate silk with bananas and cream, crème anglaise, and caramelized macadamia nuts.

Summary & comments You don't need to be afraid to take the kids to eat at Tidepools. The restaurant actually offers a children's menu, with most items from $5 to $11—pasta, hamburger, chicken nuggets—and they will be enchanted by the surrounding lagoons.

Molokai

Hotel Molokai Restaurant ★★

ISLAND ECLECTIC | INEXPENSIVE | QUALITY ★★★ | VALUE ★★★★★ | ZONE 14

Box 1020, Kamehameha Highway, Kaunakakai; (808) 553-5347; www.hotelmolokai.com

Reservations Accepted **When to go** Anytime **Entrée range** $10–$19 **Payment** VISA, MC **Service rating** ★★★ **Parking** Free in hotel lot **Bar** Full service **Wine selection** Adequate **Dress** Casual **Disabled access** Good **Customers** Tourists and Islanders are split about 50-50

Lunch Every day, 11:30 a.m.–2 p.m.

Dinner Every day, 6–9 p.m.

Setting & atmosphere Being right on the beach in this open-air restaurant enhances the feeling of old Polynesia imparted by decorative tiki carved pillars and outrigger canoes pulled up on the nearby shore. You can sit under the roof at candlelit tables, or at plastic tables arranged on the adjacent pool deck.

House specialties Cockeyed Molokai coconut shrimp, dipped in batter, rolled in coconut, and deep-fried may not be good *for* you, but it's good. Soups and specialties change daily, so one night the theme might be Oriental, with Chinese food, another it might be country-and-western, featuring barbecued back ribs and chicken, while Friday and Saturday, prime rib is the featured dinner.

Other recommendations This is truly a menu with something for everyone. There's Chinese chicken salad or taco salad, and mahimahi comes with your choice of caper sauce, papaya-pineapple relish, or pepper sauce. If you've been hanging loose at the bar, down a big bowl of manauele (taro) boy chili or Molokai stew before heading out into the night.

Entertainment & amenities Island-style musicians make this one of the few places to hang out after dark on Molokai on Friday and Saturday nights.

Summary & comments For a hotel restaurant, prices are surprisingly reasonable, and the management's goal is to keep them low in hopes of building a clientele of loyal Molokai residents.

Maunaloa Room ★★★★

HAWAII REGIONAL | MODERATE/EXPENSIVE | QUALITY ★★★★½ | VALUE ★★★
ZONE 14

The Lodge at Molokai Ranch, #8, Maunaloa; (808) 660-2725; www.molokairanch.com

Reservations Recommended **When to go** Anytime **Entrée range** $19–$39 **Payment** AMEX, MC, VISA **Service rating** ★★★★ **Parking** Free in hotel lot **Bar** Full service **Wine selection** Good **Dress** Resort wear **Disabled access** Excellent **Customers** Tourists, Islanders for a very special occasion

Breakfast Monday–Saturday, 7–10 a.m.

Brunch Sunday, 11 a.m.–1 p.m.

Lunch Every day, 10 a.m.–4 p.m.

Dinner Every day, 6–9 p.m.; Wednesday, prime rib buffet

Setting & atmosphere Inside, the decor follows a ranch theme with wooden tables, chairs with pineapple print seats, and chandeliers with electric candles in a wagon wheel shape. Views from an open-air deck stretch three miles to the ocean. Deck chairs are metal with woven lau hala seats and backs that sport the Molokai Ranch logo, the profile of a cow.

House specialties The chef describes his menu as Molokai Regional because he buys as many ingredients locally as possible and blends flavors originating with the various ethnic groups that populate Molokai. He also mixes his own spices and grows many of his herbs just outside the Lodge. This is one of the few menus that feature Molokai opihi (a crunchy limpet that is an island delicacy) as an appetizer or pan-seared venison as an entrée. Corn and crab bisque, followed by macadamia nut–crusted catch of the day on spinach surrounded by lobster-coconut curry sauce and garnished with pineapple-ginger relish are two of the menu's stars.

Other recommendations Big, tender, crispy coconut shrimp come with an orange-ginger sauce for a tasty appetizer. A truly Island-style entrée is panko-crusted ahi (tuna) wrapped around a fern shoot, packaged in nori (seaweed), and seared crisp on the outside and rare on the inside. Cut into slices, it's served with rice and a fern shoot salad. A carving station at Sunday brunch might feature prime rib, lamb, or other succulent meats. Brunch will run you $22.95, or $27.95 with champagne.

Summary & comments Bar none, the Maunaloa Room serves the finest haute cuisine on the island. It's also the priciest restaurant on Molokai, but dining here is a splurge you should enjoy at least once during an island visit. After dinner, it's a pleasure to relax in the Great Room with its enormous stone fireplace and listen to acoustic Hawaiian music strummed and sung by a ranch *paniolo* (cowboy). Often, a hula dancer joins him—either a pretty Molokai *wahine* (lady) or, when the bar next door is slow, the bartender might render a dance or two.

Molokai Pizza Café ★★

PIZZA AND SANDWICHES | INEXPENSIVE | QUALITY ★★★½ | VALUE ★★★★ ZONE 14

15 Kaunakakai Place, on Wharf Road, Kaunakakai; (808) 553-3288

Reservations Not accepted **When to go** Anytime **Entrée range** $4.50–$12.99 **Payment** Cash only **Service rating** ★★ **Parking** Adjacent lot **Bar** None **Wine selection** None **Dress** Casual **Disabled access** Good **Customers** Locals and tourists

Breakfast Available all day

Lunch & dinner Monday–Thursday, Sunday, 11 a.m.–10 p.m.; Friday and Saturday, 11 a.m.–11 p.m.

Setting & atmosphere This is a clean, air-conditioned café with booths and tables in a spacious room. It's a family kind of place, often decorated with artwork and thank-you cards by schoolkids. Some of the Formica-topped tables are set in a smaller, quieter area at the front of the restaurant away from kids, and there is also outside lanai dining, where guests are welcome to bring their own wine or beer to enjoy with dinner.

House specialties Fresh fish is served at market price whenever available. Wednesday nights a Mexican menu featuring burritos, fajitas, tacos, and nachos is added for variety, and Sunday nights prime rib is the big draw.

Other recommendations You can order pizza by the piece, or a Molokini pizza for a single person, or get a big one to go or to eat in. Chicken dinners come with rice or french fries and hot veggies. Sandwiches, pasta, salads, and frozen yogurt are also on the menu.

Entertainment & amenities Strolling musicians are hired for big private parties and sometimes for special holidays.

Summary & comments Eventually everyone stops by the Pizza Café. Kids hang out here after school, and tourists stop by for a slice of pizza, as it's one of the few places that serve until 10 p.m. nightly.

The Village Grill ★★

ISLAND ECLECTIC | MODERATE | QUALITY ★★★½ | VALUE ★★★ | ZONE 14

Maunaloa Highway, Maunaloa Town; (808) 552-0012

Reservations Recommended **When to go** Anytime; 5–6 p.m. for the early-bird special; it gets busier later **Entrée range** $17–$24.50 **Payment** VISA, MC, AMEX, DC **Service rating** ★★★ **Parking** Adjacent lot **Bar** Full service **Wine selection** Adequate, with several wines in a reasonable price range **Dress** Casual **Disabled access** Good **Customers** More tourists than Islanders, but a good mix

Dinner Every day, 6–9 p.m.

Setting & atmosphere Remodeled in 1998 by Molokai Ranch, the former Jojo's Café still sports a historic bar that once graced Oahu's Pearl City Tavern, but it now has a bronze countertop with a lariat design. The restaurant has a western feeling, with light fixtures sporting western-designed shades, and saddles and cowboy pictures on the wall, but most people prefer to sit outside on the screened deck to enjoy the stars above this quiet little town.

House specialties Good, filling entrées like prime rib, New York steak, and pizza are flavored with locally grown herbs. There's always a fresh catch of the day that can be ordered sautéed, broiled, or Cajun style, plus lobster and king crab. Try a "sky high pie" for dessert, a mound of vanilla, macadamia, and coffee-flavored ice cream in a graham cracker crust with custard, strawberry, and chocolate sauces.

Other recommendations Wok-seared Asian stir-fry, with veggies, shrimp, and scallops, and baby-back ribs impart a Molokai flavor. A local favorite for dessert is lilikoi-coconut cream pie, a coconut–passion fruit cream pie on a macadamia cookie crust made with a layer of haupia (coconut pudding), glazed with passion fruit, and topped with whipped cream and toasted coconut flakes.

Summary & comments Much of the fun here comes from cooking your own entrée on a stone grill brought to your table. Dinner in this small-town restaurant makes you feel as if you're rubbing elbows with the local folks, even though tourists are likely to be sitting at the next table.

Lanai

Blue Ginger Café ★

ISLAND ECLECTIC | INEXPENSIVE | QUALITY ★★★ | VALUE ★★★★★ | ZONE 15

409 Seventh Avenue, Lanai City; (808) 565-6363

Reservations Accepted, but requested only for large parties **When to go** Anytime **Entrée range** \$5.50–\$13.95 **Payment** VISA, MC **Service rating** ★★★ **Parking** Street **Bar** Full service **Wine selection** Limited **Dress** Casual **Disabled access** Good **Customers** Islanders, *kamaaina* travelers

Breakfast Every day, 6–11 a.m.

Lunch & dinner Every day, 11 a.m.–9 p.m.

Setting & atmosphere Set in a little single-board plantation building in Lanai City's main square. Diners order and pick up food at the counter and eat at tables draped with plastic cloths in this old, somewhat grubby-looking restaurant. An inexpensive alternative to Lanai's costly hotel dining rooms.

House specialties Try the tasty vegetarian breakfast omelet that comes with rice, or order fresh-baked apple turnovers or cinnamon rolls to carry back to your hotel, as this is Lanai's only bakery outside the hotel bake shops. For lunch, the bacon-cheddar cheeseburgers are better than Big Macs, but you might want to try the local soup called saimin, a generous steaming bowl of noodle soup garnished with sliced fish cake, green onions, and shredded egg. At dinner, sautéed mahimahi with capers, onions, and mushrooms is the signature dish. Top it off with an ice-cream dessert. Blue Ginger serves Dave's ice cream, made in the Islands with local ingredients.

Other recommendations Banana or blueberry pancakes accompanied by cappuccino for breakfast. For dinner, if an Island-style plate with a choice of teriyaki beef, katsu chicken, hamburger steak with gravy, plus rice and macaroni salad sounds like too much cholesterol for one meal, there's also New York steak with a baked potato or shrimp scampi.

Summary & comments This has been a Lanai hangout owned by the same family for years. Blue Ginger and the little deli called Pele's Other Garden, located across the park, are the best independent restaurants around the square in central Lanai City.

The Formal Dining Room, The Lodge at Koele ★★★★½

CONTEMPORARY | EXPENSIVE | QUALITY ★★★★½ | VALUE ★★★ | ZONE 15

Lodge at Koele, Keomuku Drive, Lanai City; (808) 565-7300; www.lanai-resorts.com

Reservations Highly recommended **When to go** Anytime, but sunset is generally more peaceful; the restaurant can get crowded by 7 p.m. **Entrée range** $34–$42 **Payment** VISA, MC, AMEX, DC, JCB **Service rating** ★★★★★ **Parking** Valet, hotel lot **Bar** Full service **Wine selection** Excellent **Dress** Jacket required **Disabled access** Adequate **Customers** Hotel guests, other tourists, and visiting Neighbor Islanders

Dinner Every day, 6–9:30 p.m.

Setting & atmosphere Relaxed elegance sums up the ambience of this refined restaurant overlooking the fountain, a man-made lake, and the croquet lawn of Koele Lodge. With fine silver and sparkling crystal, twinkling lights in the chandelier, and a fire in the dining room's own fireplace, this is a peaceful place for a romantic dinner.

House specialties The chef makes flavorful soups with Lanai-grown herbs and produce and creates dishes that fit the cool lodge atmosphere: onaga with garlic butter, corn, and spinach; roasted Lanai venison loin rolled in pancetta; and foie gras served with a balsamic reduction.

Other recommendations Rack of lamb with English mint cake. A lighter option is seared Hawaiian ahi with foie gras, cauliflower/parsnip puree, and veal reduction.

Entertainment & amenities Dinner music, often traditional Hawaiian melodies, piano, or classical musical scores, drifts in from the adjoining lobby. You can extend what is sure to be an expensive evening by relaxing in the Lodge's lobby after dinner with a snifter of brandy in front of a crackling fire in either of two massive fireplaces.

Summary & comments This could be the perfect place to pop the question, as lovers enjoy an intimate feeling of isolation in this quiet dining room. Tables are far enough apart to whisper sweet nothings, and the food is delicious. No wonder The Formal Dining Room keeps winning awards.

Henry Clay's Rotisserie ★★★

AMERICAN COUNTRY | MODERATE | QUALITY ★★★½ | VALUE ★★★★ | ZONE 15

Hotel Lanai, 828 Lanai Avenue, Lanai City; (808) 565-7211; www.hotellanai.com

Reservations Highly recommended **When to go** Anytime **Entrée range** $12–$28 **Payment** VISA, MC; guests of all 3 island hotels have signing privileges to their rooms **Service rating** ★★★ **Parking** Hotel lot; many people ride a shuttle from Lanai's other 2 hotels **Bar** Full service **Wine selection** Good, especially California wines, many of which are available by the glass **Dress** Casual **Disabled access** Adequate **Customers** Tourists and Islanders

Dinner Every day, 5:30–9 p.m.

Setting & atmosphere Two fireplaces create a warm glow on knotty pine walls, oak floors, and a granite-topped bar. Rich floral tapestries in mauve, green, and gold, Island scenes by Lanai artists, and outdoor lanai seating add to the old Hawaii country charm. Diners can watch the chefs and rotisserie action through a display window into the kitchen.

House specialties The chef/owner, Henry Clay Richardson, has ties to the South, so his ragin' Cajun shrimp is only one example of some of the Louisiana-style menu items. The restaurant is recognized for rotisserie chicken and wild game, including venison, quail, rabbit, and duckling, as well as fresh-caught Hawaiian fish. Salads—Caesar or Hawaiian greens with Roma tomatoes, feta cheese, and Maui onions—are à la carte, but meals come with fresh vegetables, rice or potatoes, and French bread.

Other recommendations For a bit more of the southern flavor, try seafood jalapeño pasta or eggplant Creole. Everything is made from scratch, so you can't miss by sampling the pâté, clam chowder, or pecan pie.

Summary & comments Lanai visitors often say this is the best dinner value on the island, considering the cost in comparison with the major hotel restaurants.

Ihilani ★★★★½

HAWAII REGIONAL/MEDITERRANEAN | EXPENSIVE | QUALITY ★★★★½ | VALUE ★★★ ZONE 15

Manele Bay Hotel, 1 Manele Road, Lanai City; (808) 565-7700; www.lanai-resorts.com

Reservations Highly recommended **When to go** Anytime **Entrée range** $32–$40; vegetarian menu, $28–$32 **Payment** VISA, MC, AMEX, DC, JCB **Service rating** ★★★★★ **Parking** Valet **Bar** Full service **Wine selection** Extensive **Dress** Jacket required **Disabled access** Good **Customers** Tourists and visiting Neighbor Islanders

Dinner Every day, 6–9:30 p.m.

Setting & atmosphere Fine china, silver, and lace-bedecked tables under hand-blown Italian crystal chandeliers are a lovely backdrop for dining in this formal dining room, which boasts a soothing view of pool and ocean from tables on an upper and lower bank.

House specialties The chef presents picture-perfect food in entrées such as roasted pheasant breast with foie gras and Madeira truffle sauce, pan-fried veal loin, or sautéed opakapaka (snapper) served with ragout of white beans, pancetta, and fresh thyme. Many of the more than a dozen desserts include sweets and truffles made of Hawaiian Vintage Chocolate. Diners can order an extensive selection of gourmet cheeses from the à la carte menu.

Other recommendations A nightly degustation menu of six or seven courses can be ordered paired with wines for $95 or sans wines for $65 per person. Prices may change according to what is featured. You might begin with oysters, then sample Maine lobster with shiitake mushrooms, proceed to pan-fried ahi, and savor a main course of roasted muscovy duck breast in red wine port sauce with Molokai sweet-potato puree and sautéed endive. Next, a selection of cheeses and walnut bread is served, plus a dessert selection followed by Hawaiian Vintage Chocolates and mignardises.

Entertainment & amenities Classical background music is set at a pleasant listening level.

Summary & comments This is the kind of dining experience that is more than just grabbing a bite to eat. Expect to take several leisurely hours to do all the courses justice.

Part Ten

Shopping

In Hawaii, when the sun gets too hot, the sunburned go shopping. And what a bazaar they'll find—everything from funky T-shirts to worldly imports and a growing selection of made-in-Hawaii clothing, art, sports gear, and jewelry.

Because the Islands have attracted an increasingly international crowd—particularly free-spending young Japanese for whom Hawaii has become a cheap ticket to European designer boutiques—shopping prospects have soared from dismal to extraordinary in recent years.

Smart-shopping Americans found they could bargain for the best selection this side of Hong Kong in Asian pearls, jewelry, antiques, and other imports. The trickle-down effect also lured American discount stores, that in turn brought everyday prices down in other Islands stores. When sugar plantations shut down, the company-owned stores, where so many workers shopped exclusively, soon followed. That left a lot of young people with better jobs and bigger dreams and more money to spend than their immigrant field-worker parents ever had. Obviously, retail makes up a large share of the Hawaiian economy.

The Aloha State is known for high costs, understandable because most of the goods—and every piece of glass, nail, and board in the buildings that contain them—are imported. But the low sales tax of 4%, charged at 4.176%, makes purchases more palatable, and some items just can't be found anywhere else. Besides, there's no going home empty-handed after an enviable trip to Hawaii, so bring an extra suitcase and get ready to shop! Here are suggestions to maximize the experience.

Buy Hawaiian

Local arts and crafts are flourishing. Finding them is often as much fun as giving them for gifts. Local wares sold by their makers dominate the frequent arts and crafts fairs held throughout the Islands. Particularly fine are the **Pacific Handcrafters Guild** fairs held periodically on Oahu. Hawaiian product stores have sprung up everywhere (see some listed below). Occasionally you'll find local things among the cheap imports in tourist-zone kiosks and souvenir stores. You can find local books, music, aloha wear, and other goods at favorable prices in the national chain stores, such as **Costco, Longs, Sears,** and **Borders,** and in the local chain **ABC** stores.

Hawaii's indigenous products range from inexpensive to very dear. They include foods—macadamia nuts, coffees, teas, wines, tropical jams, syrups, honeys, candies, and real Maui potato chips; soaps and cosmetics with tropical ingredients and fragrances; fiber arts made of coconut leaf, lauhala, or pandanus and other natural materials; aloha print fabrics made into shirts, baby clothes, totes, dresses, glasses cases, and even golf bags; Hawaiian books and music; warm-weather designer clothing; hand-painted clothing; windsurfing and surfboards and equipment; furniture and boxes handmade from tropical woods; one-of-a-kind Hawaiian appliquéd quilts, sewn only with permission of the family that created the design; and gold heirloom jewelry, Niihau shell jewelry, and all kinds of artwork.

One solution to the nice-but-not-too-nice gift dilemma is packaging. Buy some affordable soaps or foods and bed them in an aloha fabric or natural fiber inside a lidded lauhala box, tie it with fiber ribbon, and decorate it with a shell. Gifts are sold prepackaged this way too.

Hawaiian heirloom gold jewelry, monogrammed Victorian-style pieces in an arcane style created for nineteenth-century royals, is the precious gift of choice for special occasions in the Islands. Insider tip: Most women in Hawaii wear at least one solid oval gold bracelet ornately patterned and bearing their name in Hawaiian in black enameled script. Mothers may wear their daughters' bracelets until the girls are older. Many bracelets never come off. Many women wear them by the armload in Hawaii, where it is safe enough and the local style. Admiring them is an effective way to start a conversation and get some hints on designs.

Heirloom jewelry has branched out to include medallions, pendants, watchbands, link bracelets, rings, and earrings for men as well as women. It is sold at jewelry shops throughout the Islands and at jewelry counters in other stores, including the Japanese chain **Daiei.** In Waikiki, you can visit the factory and showroom at **Royal Hawaiian Shopping Center** to watch jewelry being made and buy some, if you wish.

Jewelry prices vary by gold weight and creative design. A bracelet might cost anywhere from $250 for a simple pattern on a thin band to $1,200 or more for a complex design on a larger band. This is a subjective purchase based on design, but do shop around enough to satisfy yourself that the price is fair for what you want. Shop for a bracelet early in your trip, to allow time for sizing and name engraving. The case samples are inscribed "Kuuipo" or "my sweetheart."

Niihau shells are exquisite and extraordinarily expensive if you view them as just another shell necklace. After all, a strand of dyed "coral" costs $10, and a strand of the least expensive Niihau shells costs more than $100 and fancy museum-quality ones can run up to thousands of dollars. Consider that each nearly microscopic Niihau shell is picked off the beach on the private ranch island of Niihau by one of its few inhabitants and then sorted, pierced, and strung into a traditional design. Visitors to Kauai, Niihau's neighbor island, are most likely to learn to appreciate the beauty of these treasures and to see a variety displayed in shops and museums. You may even find some shells on a West Kauai beach.

Specialty Shopping

It's hard to avoid places to shop, beginning with lobby stores in hotels, where stylish, good-quality resort clothing and swimsuits can often be found. In Waikiki, you can run the full gamut by strolling through shops at a luxury hotel like **Halekulani** or **Royal Hawaiian Hotel** and then walking to the varied boutiques of **Royal Hawaiian Shopping Center** and on across the street to **Liberty House** and the colorful jumble of kiosks surrounding the **International Market Place.** Walk out the back to Kuhio Avenue, jump on TheBus and get off at **Ala Moana Center,** which reinvented itself to cater to high-end shoppers on its new upper floors with a Nieman's and plentiful designer boutiques, in addition to its usual wild assortment of department stores, island stores, and restaurants.

On up Ala Moana Boulevard, **Ward Centre** and **Ward Warehouse** are smaller boutique collections of island-style clothes, gifts, and restaurants. On up the street on the left, find **Aloha Tower Marketplace,** a harborfront complex of shops, food, and entertainment with the added amusement of container ships bringing more goods to the active harbor. Shoppers can prowl while mates down a freshly brewed beer at Gordon Biersch and watch the ships go by. If you're looking for national-brand outlet shops, drive out to **Waikele Centre,** west of the airport on H-1, and find familiar names.

We know you can find all the malls and local branches of national chain stores you know and love, so we won't waste your time except to say: Expect slightly higher prices on some items, even at Wal-Mart. **Hilo Hattie's** matching aloha wear and Hawaiian goods are everywhere, and they will find you if you don't find them. But that's not all there is. Here are our recommendations for some places to find local arts and crafts and Hawaiian goods. Hours of operation are subject to change.

Oahu

Alii Antiques of Kailua

Location 21 Malunui Avenue, Kailua; Zone 3, Windward Oahu

Phone (808) 261-1705

Hours Monday–Saturday, 10:30 a.m.–4:30 p.m.

Description Alii has a separate building filled with Hawaiian kitsch and all kinds of treasures, including jewelry. Great place to prowl the island past.

Crazy Shirts

Location International Market Place, Waikiki (more than 20 locations throughout the state); Zone 1, Waikiki

Phone (808) 922-4791

Hours Every day, 8 a.m.–11:30 p.m.

Description Hawaii's homegrown T-shirt shop, featuring hundreds of colorful, local-themed designs, is ubiquitous, but the International Market Place location is the biggest of the line.

Harry's Music Store

Location 3457 Waialae Avenue, Honolulu; Zone 2, Greater Honolulu

Phone (808) 735-2866

Hours Monday–Friday, 9:30 a.m.–5:30 p.m.; Saturday, 9 a.m.–5 p.m.

Description Old Hawaiian records, sheet music, and ukuleles are among the vintage items offered at this small but famous stop for Hawaiian music aficionados.

Hawaiian Ukulele Company

Location Aloha Tower Marketplace, Honolulu; Zone 2, Greater Honolulu

Phone (808) 536-3228

Hours Monday–Saturday, 9 a.m.–9 p.m.; Sunday, 9 a.m.–6 p.m.

Description Specializes in hand-crafted Hawaiian ukulele and other instruments, plus accessories, songbooks, and instruction booklets.

Irene's Hawaiian Gifts

Location Ala Moana Center, Honolulu; Zone 2, Greater Honolulu

Phone (808) 946-6818

Hours Monday–Saturday, 9:30 a.m.–9 p.m.; Sunday, 10 a.m.–7 p.m.

Description Hawaiian gifts and souvenirs, including koa boxes, porcelain dolls, soaps, perfumes, note cards, dish towels, and Hawaiian quilt kits.

Island Treasures

Location 629 Kailua Road, Kailua; Zone 3, Windward Oahu

Phone (808) 261-8131

Hours Monday–Saturday, 10 a.m.–6 p.m.; Sunday, 10 a.m.–4 p.m.

Description Artworks and Hawaiian-style crafts, gifts with flair created locally.

Islands' Best

Location Ala Moana Center, Honolulu; Zone 2, Greater Honolulu

Phone (808) 949-5345

Hours Monday–Saturday, 9:30 a.m.–9 p.m.; Sunday, 10 a.m.–7 p.m.

Description Wide range of Hawaiian gifts and souvenirs, including soaps, crafts, stationery, and arts.

Montsuki

Location 1148 Koko Head Avenue, Honolulu; Zone 2, Greater Honolulu

Phone (808) 734-3457

Hours Monday–Saturday, 9:30 a.m.–4 p.m.

Description Stylish apparel fashioned from vintage silk kimonos.

Native Books & Beautiful Things

Location Ward Warehouse and 222 Merchant Street, Downtown, Honolulu; Zone 2, Greater Honolulu

Phone Ward (808) 596-8885; downtown (808) 599-5511

Hours Ward: Monday–Saturday, 10 a.m.–9 p.m.; Sunday, 10 a.m.–5 p.m. Downtown: Monday–Friday, 8 a.m.–5 p.m.; Saturday, 10 a.m.–3 p.m.

Description Fine collection of Hawaiian books, crafts, artworks, apparel, and gifts.

Nohea Gallery

Location Ward Warehouse, Honolulu; Zone 2, Greater Honolulu (also at Sheraton Moana Surfrider in Waikiki and Kahala Mandarin Oriental in Kahala)

Phone (808) 596-0074

Website www.noheagallery.com

Hours Monday–Saturday, 10 a.m.–9 p.m.; Sunday, 10 a.m.–5 p.m.

Description One of the best galleries for island arts and fine crafts in all media.

Maui

Hasegawa General Store

Location 5165 Hana Highway, Hana; Zone 10, Upcountry Maui and Beyond

Phone (808) 248-8231

Hours Monday–Saturday, 7 a.m.–7 p.m.; Sunday, 8 a.m.–6 p.m.

Description An old-fashioned general merchandise store, so beloved that a song was written about it. Founded in 1910, this family-run store sells the necessities and some frills for residents and visitors to faraway Hana.

Hawaiiana Arts & Crafts

Location Wharf Cinema Center, Lahaina; Zone 9, West Maui

Phone (808) 661-9077

Hours Every day, 10 a.m.–8 p.m.

Description Handmade arts and crafts by some of Maui's best artisans, including raku pottery, woodcrafts, and woven baskets.

Honolua Store

Location Office Road, Kapalua Resort; Zone 9, West Maui

Phone (808) 669-6128

Hours Every day, 6 a.m.–8 p.m.

Description Historic plantation grocery store features books, gifts, and clothing, along with groceries and beverages.

The Big Island of Hawaii

Alapaki's

Location Keauhou Shopping Center, Kailua-Kona; Zone 11, Kona

Phone (808) 322-2007

Hours Monday–Saturday, 9 a.m.–6 p.m.; Sunday, 10 a.m.–5 p.m.

Description A lava rock archway welcomes you into a shop full of made-in-Hawaii ceramics, koa, woven lauhala goods, ukuleles and other instruments, pillows, wall hangings, stationery, and more.

Big Island Candies

Location 585 Hinano Street, Hilo; Zone 12, Hilo and Volcano

Phone (808) 935-8890

Website www.bigislandcandies.com

Hours Every day, 8:30 a.m.–5 p.m.

Description Locally made chocolates and candies. Large windows let you watch confections being made in the adjoining factory.

Cook's Discoveries

Location Waimea Center, Waimea (on Highway 19); Zone 11, Kona

Phone (808) 885-3633

Hours Monday–Saturday, 9 a.m.–6 p.m.; Sunday, 10 a.m.–5 p.m.

Description Somewhat pricey Hawaiian goods include aloha wear, books, art, music, language tapes, hats, stationery, Kona coffee, confections, and other gifts. This is one of the best shops to browse for Big Island arts.

Harbor Gallery

Location Kawaihae Shopping Center, Kawaihae; Zone 11, Kona

Phone (808) 882-1510

Hours Every day, 11:30 a.m.–8:30 p.m.

Description Diverse collection of island art, including koa wood, sculptures, paintings, ceramics, and jewelry.

Hula Heaven

Location Kona Inn Shopping Village, Kailua-Kona; Zone 11, Kona

Phone (808) 329-7885

Hours Every day, 9 a.m.–9 p.m.

Description Vintage collectibles—old aloha shirts in mint condition, antique hula dolls, original menu art.

Sig Zane Designs

Location 122 Kamehameha Avenue, Hilo; Zone 12, Hilo and Volcano

Phone (808) 935-7077

Hours Monday–Friday, 9 a.m.–5:30 p.m.; Saturday, 9 a.m.–3 p.m.

Description Zane's striking Hawaiian prints in fabric, dresses, shirts, and pareos.

Kauai

Kong Lung Co.

Location Keneke Road, Kilauea; Zone 13, Kauai

Phone (808) 828-1822

Hours Monday–Saturday, 9 a.m.–9 p.m.; Sunday, 10 a.m.–9 p.m.

Description Set in a historic stone building, this is one of Kauai's most famous shops. Collectibles, housewares, jewelry, apparel, and fine gifts make it a worthwhile stop on your way to the North Shore.

Ola's

Location Hanalei Trader Building, Hanalei; Zone 13, Kauai

Phone (808) 826-6937

Hours Every day, 10 a.m.–9:30 p.m.

Description Jewelry, glassware, woodcrafts, soaps and other handcrafted goods are for sale at this fun-to-browse shop.

Yellowfish Trading Company

Location New Hanalei School Center, Hanalei; Zone 13, Kauai

Phone (808) 826-1227

Hours Every day, 10 a.m.–9 p.m.

Description Antiques and knickknacks, vintage aloha shirts, photographs and posters, Hawaiian furniture, and kitchenware.

Molokai

Big Wind Kite Factory

Location 120 Maunaloa Highway, Maunaloa; Zone 14, Molokai

Phone (808) 552-2364

Hours Monday–Saturday, 8:30 a.m.–5 p.m.; Sunday, 10 a.m.–2 p.m.

Description Kites of all shapes, sizes, and designs, some made on site; imported gifts. The friendly owner provides free kite-flying lessons (at an adjacent open field) with "no strings attached."

Lanai

Akamai Trading

Location 408 Eighth Street, Lanai City; Zone 15, Lanai

Phone (808) 565-6587

Hours Monday–Saturday, 9 a.m.–6 p.m.; Sunday, 9 a.m.–5 p.m.

Description General store with an interesting selection of island necessities, souvenirs, gifts, and locally made jams and jellies.

Gifts with Aloha

Location Seventh Street, Lanai City; Zone 15, Lanai

Phone (808) 565-6589

Hours Monday–Saturday, 9:30 a.m.–5:30 p.m.

Description Made-in-Hawaii gifts, including resort wear, koa wood products, scented candles, books, and hand-quilted pillow covers.

Shopping Centers

Oahu

Ala Moana Center

Location Ala Moana Boulevard, next to Waikiki; Zone 2, Greater Honolulu

Phone (808) 955-9517

Website www.alamoanacenter.com

Hours Monday–Saturday, 9:30 a.m.–9 p.m.; Sunday, 10 a.m.–7 p.m.

Number of Stores and Restaurants More than 200

Description Department stores, upscale European and American boutiques, jewelry, gifts, outdoor gifts and gear, drugstore, supermarket, shoes, cartoon art, candy, software, sandals and slippers, swim and beachwear, toys, sports gear, Tahitian and Hawaiian fabrics. This is one of the largest shopping centers in the United States and is certainly one of the most pleasant with its open-air tropical gardens and ponds. Free entertainment daily on the stage in the middle of the Center, usually music and/or dance.

Aloha Tower Marketplace

Location 1 Aloha Tower Drive, foot of Bishop St. downtown; Zone 2, Greater Honolulu

Phone (808) 528-5700

Website www.alohatower.com

Hours Monday–Saturday, 9 a.m.–9 p.m.; Sunday, 9 a.m.–6 p.m.

Number of Stores and Restaurants About 75

Description Hawaiian woodcrafts, furniture, gifts, swimwear, coffee, candies, cartoon art, tropical apparel, cigar shop, shoes, magnets, and perfumes; plus changing goods, imports, and clothing in numerous kiosks. Stores are arrayed at the foot of historic ten-story Aloha Tower, where you can take the elevator to the top, enjoy panoramic views, and imagine the scene when this was the tallest building in town.

International Market Place

Location 2330 Kalakaua Avenue, Waikiki; Zone 1, Waikiki

Phone (808) 971-2080

Website www.internationalmarketplacewaikiki.com

Hours Every day, 10 a.m.–10:30 p.m.

Number of Stores and Restaurants About 150

Description Outdoor maze of kiosks features jewelry, T-shirts, pareo, handbags, touristy souvenirs, and imported knickknacks. Bargain like crazy to improve the prices—everybody here wants to sell.

Pearlridge Shopping Center

Location 231 Pearlridge Center, Honolulu; Zone 6, Central Oahu

Phone (808) 488-0981

Hours Monday–Saturday, 10 a.m.–9 p.m.; Sunday, 10 a.m.–6 p.m.

Number of Stores and Restaurants More than 170

Description Department stores, electronics, outdoor goods, toys, books, drugstores, apparel, candy, lingerie, men's wear, videos, stationers, shoes, glasses, and movies. The most interesting thing about this suburban center is the monorail linking two complexes, which was built so that development would not imperil the prized Sumida watercress farm below. (Better yet, skip the shopping and get some of the superlative watercress, sold in huge bunches at island markets and eaten stems and all.)

Royal Hawaiian Shopping Center

Location 2201 Kalakaua Avenue, Waikiki; Zone 1, Waikiki

Phone (808) 922-0588

Hours Every day, 9 a.m.–11 p.m.

Number of Stores and Restaurants About 160

Description Upscale designer boutiques, biker logos, jewelry factory, sports apparel, collectibles, and island wear. Frequent free entertainment, usually Hawaiian music and dance, by the waterfall at the central Kalakaua entrance.

Ward Centre/Ward Warehouse

Location 1050–1240 Ala Moana Boulevard, Honolulu; Zone 2, Greater Honolulu

Phone (808) 591-8411 or (808) 593-2376

Website www.victoriaward.com

Hours Monday–Saturday, 10 a.m.–9 p.m.; Sunday, 10 a.m.–5 p.m.

Number of Stores and Restaurants 100 (restaurants mostly at Ward Centre; mostly shops at Warehouse)

Description Books and music, gifts, gadgets, stationery, island ceramics, University of Hawaii gear, chocolates, tropical wear, tropical home furnishings, art galleries, bath shop, shoes, crafts, holiday ornaments, sandals and shoes, apparel, toys, and perfumes. Free band concerts, shows, and exhibits throughout the year.

Maui

505 Front Street

Location Front Street, Lahaina; Zone 9, West Maui

Phone (808) 667-2514

Website www.lahainarestaurants.com

Hours Monday–Saturday, 10 a.m.–9 p.m.; Sunday, 10 a.m.–6 p.m.

Number of Stores and Restaurants More than 25

Description Oceanfront boutique mall at the quiet southern end of Lahaina. Unusual shops include Hawaiian products, spa goods, clothing, souvenirs, gifts. Live jazz outdoors at Pacific'O restaurant on Thursday, Friday, and Saturday nights.

Lahaina Center

Location 900 Front Street, Lahaina; Zone 9, West Maui

Phone (808) 667-9216

Website www.lahainacenter.com

Hours Generally, Monday–Saturday, 9 a.m.–10 p.m., Sunday; 9 a.m.–6 p.m.

Number of Stores and Restaurants 30

Description Aloha wear, gifts, sundries, apparel, T-shirts, swimwear, jewelry, children's shop, microbrewery. Free hula shows Wednesday and Friday, 2 and 6 p.m.

Queen Kaahumanu Center

Location 275 Kaahumanu Avenue, Kahului; Zone 7, Central Maui

Phone (808) 877-3369

Website www.kaahumanu.net

Hours Monday–Friday, 9:30 a.m.–9 p.m.; Saturday, 9:30 a.m.–7 p.m.; Sunday, 10 a.m.–5 p.m.

Number of Stores and Restaurants About 75

Description Department stores, books, gifts, toys, cards, jewelry, cartoon logos, dime store, coffee, shoes, apparel, photo processing, movies, and community events.

The Shops at Wailea

Location Wailea Resort, 3750 Wailea Alanui Drive, Wailea; Zone 8, South Maui

Phone (808) 891-6770

Website www.shopsatwailea.com

Hours Every day, 9:30 a.m.–9 p.m.

Number of Stores and Restaurants More than 25

Description Resort wear, upscale designer boutiques, gifts, galleries, woodcrafts and furniture, toys, camera shops, sundries, ice cream, and swim and beachwear. Frequent events and food festivals.

Whalers Village

Location Kaanapali Beach Resort, 2435 Kaanapali Parkway, Lahaina; Zone 9, West Maui

Phone (808) 661-4567

Website www.whalersvillage.com

Hours Every day, 9:30 a.m.–10 p.m.

Number of Stores and Restaurants 60

Description Upscale boutiques, jewelry, scrimshaw, Hawaiian koa furniture, gifts, art galleries, island apparel, and general goods. Free hula performances 7 p.m. nightly except Tuesday and Thursday.

The Big Island of Hawaii

Keauhou Shopping Center

Location 78-6831 Alii Drive, Keauhou; Zone 11, Kona

Phone (808) 332-3000

Hours Monday–Saturday, 9 a.m.–6 p.m.; Sunday, 10 a.m.–5 p.m.

Number of Stores and Restaurants 40

Description Supermarket, drugstore, dime store, hardware, coffee, art gallery, and movies. Craft demonstrations and talk story sessions are held Fridays, 10 a.m.–2 p.m.

Kings' Shops

Location Waikoloa Beach Resort, Kohala Coast; Zone 11, Kona

Phone (808) 886-8811

Hours Every day, 9:30 a.m.–9:30 p.m.

Number of Stores and Restaurants About 40

Description Souvenirs, jewelry, art gallery, T-shirts, gifts, and sunglasses. Free entertainment Tuesday and Thursday evenings.

Prince Kuhio Plaza

Location 111 Puainako Street (off Highway 11, near Hilo airport), Hilo; Zone 12, Hilo and Volcano

Phone (808) 959-3555

Hours Monday–Friday, 9:30 a.m.–9 p.m.; Saturday, 9:30 a.m.–7 p.m.; Sunday, 10 a.m.–6 p.m.

Number of Stores and Restaurants Over 75

Description Department stores, books, videos, drugstore, gifts, apparel, swimwear, and movies.

Kauai

Coconut Marketplace

Location 484 Kuhio Highway, Wailua; Zone 13, Kauai

Phone (808) 822-3641

Hours Monday–Saturday, 9 a.m.–9 p.m.; Sunday, 10 a.m.–6 p.m.

Number of Stores and Restaurants Over 70

Description Gifts, music, jewelry, clothing, Hawaiian products, swimwear, movies. Free entertainment (including hula) daily at 5 p.m.

Kukui Grove Center

Location 3-2600 Kaumualii Highway, Lihue; Zone 13, Kauai

Phone (808) 245-7784

Hours Monday–Thursday and Saturday, 9:30 a.m.–5:30 p.m.; Friday, 9:30 a.m.–9 p.m.; Sunday, 10 a.m.–5 p.m.

Number of Stores and Restaurants Over 50

Description Department store, Kauai products, jeans, shoes, and swim- and beachwear.

Poipu Shopping Village

Location Poipu Beach Resort, 2360 Kiahuna Plantation Drive, Poipu; Zone 13, Kauai

Phone (808) 742-2831

Hours Monday–Saturday, 10 a.m.–9 p.m.; Sunday, 10 a.m.–6 p.m.

Number of Stores and Restaurants About 20

Description T-shirts, art galleries, swimwear, gifts, sandals, sunglasses, cosmetics, and clothing. Free Polynesian shows Tuesdays and Thursdays at 5 p.m.

Swap Meets and Flea Markets

Bargain hunters on Oahu should check out the major swap meet, the **Aloha Stadium Swap Meet** held in the parking lot surrounding Aloha Stadium on Wednesday, Saturday, and Sunday (and some holidays) from 6 a.m. to 3 p.m. You'll find an astounding variety of new and used merchandise, treasures and trash, eel-skin leathers, imports, baskets, fresh produce, plants, and even fresh fish. Feel free to bargain; it's part of the fun. Admission is 50 cents a head for people over age 12. The sun can be relentless, so go early and dress casually for shopping with the local folks. Call (808) 486-6704 for more information.

Part Eleven

Entertainment and Nightlife

Hawaii Nightlife

In Hawaii you can experience Hawaiian music, song, and dance. Or you can see the kind of things that you have back home. But you must at least once go to a luau (**Paradise Cove** or **Germaine's** on Oahu, **Old Lahaina Luau** on Maui, **Kona Village Resort** luau on the Big Island are top choices for commercial luau), see the *Don Ho Show* in Waikiki, and, above all, experience *Ulalena* in Lahaina on Maui. Many other shows are entertaining, and some are hokey, but if you want a good evening out, by all means see the top shows mentioned here. A luau is the traditional cultural event. Don Ho is, well, Don Ho. *Ulalena,* most exciting of all, is simply excellent entertainment, a new but authentic version of the Hawaii story, told in a *Cirque du Soleil*–type production.

Hawaiian music is alive and well, not just at Don Ho's but **Duke's Canoe Club** in Waikiki or **Chai's Island Bistro** and **Henry Kapono's** new club at Aloha Tower Marketplace. You can see Jerry Santos and Olomana at the **Paradise Lounge at Hilton Hawaiian Village.** After a long dry period, popular contemporary Hawaiian musicians are back playing in Waikiki.

The Islands are full of gifted musicians and singers, such as Kealii Reichel, Hookena, Willie K., Amy Hanaialii Gilliom, Makaha Sons of Niihau, the Peter Moon Band, Robbie Kahakalau, and Na Leo Pumehana, to name a few. They appear on all islands, so check the local papers' entertainment sections.

Oahu is Hawaii's nightlife center with nightclubs, cocktail lounges, local bars, karaoke clubs, adult entertainment clubs, and hostess bars. The nightclub scene revolves around the **Ocean Club, Rumours,** and **Wave Waikiki.**

If you're staying on an outer island, bring a good book. Folks may well draw their shades early. Only a few spots, like Kihei and Lahaina on Maui, stay open after dark with clubs drawing crowds that linger past midnight.

Otherwise, nightlife may be limited to hotel lounge acts (some of which are quite good). You came to the Islands to relax, remember?

Performing Arts

Sooner or later, everyone plays Honolulu. The beach city attracts worldly entertainers who regularly perform at Neal Blaisdell Center, Waikiki Shell, and elsewhere. If your timing's good, you may see the Bolshoi Ballet, the Beach Boys, or even the Rolling Stones (who played Aloha Stadium) and for a lot less than on the mainland. Jazz singer Diana Krall and Sir Elton John appeared one night in adjoining concert halls.

MAJOR CONCERT AND PERFORMING ARTS VENUES

Check *Honolulu Weekly* or the local dailies for appearances and dates. Here are some contact numbers and general locations for many of the concert venues in Hawaii.

Oahu		
Aloha Stadium	Zone 6	(808) 486-9300
Hawaii Theatre Center	Zone 2	(808) 528-0506
Neal Blaisdell Center Arena	Zone 2	(808) 591-2211
Neal Blaisdell Concert Hall	Zone 2	(808) 591-2211
Waikiki Shell	Zone 1	(808) 527-5400
Maui		
Maui Arts and Cultural Center	Zone 7	(808) 242-7469

Dinner Shows

Waikiki isn't Las Vegas, nor does it want to be, so don't expect extravaganzas. Your choices are limited to a few entertaining dinner shows—something of an oxymoron. People who enjoy good food don't usually go to dinner shows. Food is often mediocre, tickets are expensive ($129 for a magic show), seating is clumsy, and, with few exceptions, the shows are forgettable. But here are seven shows worth a look because they can only be seen in the Islands, dinner entrées are of sufficient variety to satisfy even picky eaters, and, in most cases, the price of admission won't cause sticker shock.

Oahu

Blue Hawaii: The Show

Location Waikiki Beachcomber Hotel, Waikiki

Phone (808) 923-1245

Show Times Nightly, Tuesday; dinner seating 5 p.m., cocktail seating 5:45 p.m., show time 6:15 p.m.

Length 75 minutes

Cost Dinner show: adult $56.64, children ages 3–13 $28.32; Cocktail show: adult $27.84, children ages 3–13 $13.92; Deluxe dinner: adult $75.84.

Creation—A Polynesian Odyssey

Location 120 Kaiulani Avenue, Ainahau Showroom, Sheraton Princess Kaiulani Hotel, Waikiki

Phone (808) 931-4660

Show Times Shows Tuesday, Thursday–Sunday. Dinner seating at 5:15 p.m.; cocktail seating at 6 p.m.

Length 90 minutes

Cost $105 per adult ($72 per child age 7–12) for the premium dinner; $62 per adult ($34.50 per child) for the buffet dinner, first show; and $32 per adult ($21 per child) for the cocktail show.

Discounts Discount coupons available inside "Best of Oahu" booklets. Hotel guests receive a two-for-one coupon.

Type of Seating Long tables facing the stage. First come, first served.

Menu All-you-can-eat buffet. Prime rib, shoyu chicken, chow mein noodles with vegetables and char siu, beef curry stew, mahimahi, fresh salad, fruits, cakes, and ice cream. The premium dinner is a sit-down meal of lobster tail, tenderloin steak, salad, rice or potato, dessert, and two drinks.

Vegetarian Alternative Salads at buffet.

Beverages Mai tai, draft beer, soft drinks, juice, coffee.

Description and Comments High-tech stage show follows Polynesian voyagers with vivid sound and light effects. Good choice for young families.

Don Ho Show

Location 2300 Kalakaua Avenue, Hoku Hale Showroom, Waikiki Beachcomber Hotel, Waikiki

Phone (808) 923-3981

Website www.donho.com

Show Time Sunday–Thursday, 7 p.m.

Length 90 minutes

Cost $52 per adult ($26 per child age 6–20) for the dinner show; $32 per adult ($16 per child) for the cocktail show; for the show only (no dinner), adults are $20, children are $10.

Discounts None.

Type of Seating Table seating.

Menu A sit-down dinner of chicken, prime rib, mashed potatoes, salad, and dessert.

Vegetarian Alternative Varies nightly.

Beverages Tropical drinks, wine, beer, soft drinks, juice, tea, coffee.

Description and Comments Over age 70 now, Don Ho is still the king of Waikiki, attracting full-house audiences five nights a week. He also attracts bright young talent in Hawaii and offers them a chance to shine in his show.

Magic of Polynesia

Location 2300 Kalakaua Avenue, Waikiki Beachcomber Hotel, Waikiki

Phone (808) 971-4321

Show Times 2 shows nightly, 6:30 and 8:45 p.m. Dinner seating at 5 p.m.; cocktail seating at 6 and 8 p.m.

Length 75 minutes

Cost $137 per adult ($97 per child age 4–11) for deluxe dinner; $69 per adult ($49 per child) for the standard dinner; $42 per adult ($32 per child) for the cocktail show.

Discounts Entertainment Book coupons offer 20% off for the cocktail show.

Type of Seating Table seating. Smaller tables seat 10; larger tables in rows seat 40. First come, first served. A seat toward the back gives better overall view.

Menu Sit-down dinner of roast beef, chicken, rice, steamed vegetables, cake.

Vegetarian Alternative Steamed noodles with vegetables. Request in advance.

Beverages Tropical drinks, wine, beer, soft drinks, juice, coffee.

Description and Comments John Hirokawa, a local boy taught by David Copperfield, delivers superb illusionist skills with Polynesian themes in family-oriented magic show.

Society of Seven

Location 2335 Kalakaua Avenue, Main Outrigger Showroom, Outrigger Waikiki Hotel, Waikiki

Phone (808) 922-6408

Website www.angelfire.com/hi/societyofseven

Show Times 2 shows Tuesday–Sunday, 7 p.m. and 8 p.m.

Length 80 minutes

Cost Cocktail show: adults $36.48, children ages 5–20 $21.12; Alii buffet: adults $52.60, children ages 5–20 $42.24.

Discounts None.

Type of Seating Cabaret-style table seating.

Menu Buffet includes meats, fish, chicken, rice, salad bar, and dessert. Sit-down dinner includes choice of prime rib, chicken, or fish and starch, vegetables, and dessert.

Vegetarian Alternative Pasta or salad.

Beverages Tropical drinks, beer, wine, mixed drinks, soft drinks, juice, coffee.

Description and Comments Hawaii's longest running show (30 years and counting), for one reason: It's good fun. Comedy, Broadway tunes, musical skits, impressions, oldies, contemporary hits, and audience participation make for a fun evening.

Maui

Ulalena

Location Maui Myth and Magic Theater, 878 Front Street, Lahaina

Phone Toll-free (877) 688-4800, (808) 661-9913

Website www.ulalena.com

Show Times Tuesday, 6 p.m. and 8:30 p.m.; Wednesday–Saturday, 6 p.m.

Length 90 minutes

Cost $48 adults, $38 children, $28 under age 10.

Discounts None.

Type of Seating $10 million, state-of-the-art theater with stadium seating; features live Hawaiian chant and music with 8-channel surround sound.

Food Snack bar in lobby.

Beverages Beer, wine, soft drinks, juice, coffee.

Description and Comments Best original, creative show in Hawaii. A *Cirque du Soleil* production by the Montreal troupe blends island myth and fact in culturally keen theatrical performance. If you go to Maui, you must see Ulalena.

Warren & Annabelle's

Location 900 Front Street, Lahaina

Phone (808) 667-6244

Show Times 2 shows, Monday–Saturday, 5 p.m. and 7:30 p.m.

Length 120 minutes

Cost $40. Guests must be age 21 or older. Special *pupu* (hors d'oeuvres) packages are available: $70.20 includes show, appetizer platter, 2 drinks; and $77.95 includes show, appetizer platter, dessert, 2 drinks, and coffee. Prices include tax and tip.

Discounts Coupons offering a 20% discount available in hotel lobbies.

Type of Seating Table seating for *pupus* and cocktails. Intimate 78-seat theater (stadium seating). First come, first served.

Menu Unless you order *pupu*, everything is à la carte. *Pupu* menu includes spicy crab cakes, coconut-battered shrimp, chicken satay, and crab-stuffed mushrooms. Desserts include chocolate truffle cake, crème brûlée, and New York–style cheesecake.

Vegetarian Alternative Request in advance.

Beverages Tropical drinks, specialty drinks, beer, wine, soft drinks, juice, coffee.

Description and Comments "Close-up" magician Warren Gibson performs sleight-of-hand tricks in the cozy theater with Annabelle, a piano-playing ghost who takes requests.

Before- and After-Dinner Lounges

Major resort hotels on all the islands offer good Hawaiian music, jazz, and a place to dance or relax with an after-dinner drink and enjoy the evening. Here are some of the best.

Oahu

Duke Canoe Club, Outrigger Waikiki (808) 922-2268 Open-air beach club full of young couples full of beer and mai tais boogeying to Hawaiian music.

House without a Key, Halekulani (808) 923-2311 Sophisticated, elegant open-air setting ideal for sunset cocktails.

Lewers Lounge, Halekulani (808) 923-2311 When you want the most romantic hideaway, come and hear late-night jazz in the finest hotel.

Mai Tai Bar, Royal Hawaiian Hotel (808) 923-7311 Beach bar nonpareil. Here you can sip a cool one in your swimsuit and watch babes and hunks go by.

Paradise Lounge, Hilton Hawaiian Village (808) 949-4321 The living-room setting is a cozy venue for Olomana, one of Hawaii's best-loved Hawaiian-music groups.

Maui

Anuenue Lounge, Ritz-Carlton, Kapalua (808) 669-6200 Dark koa-wood lounge for sophisticated couples who want dancing after dark to grand piano tunes.

Hula Moons, Outrigger Wailea Beach Resort (808) 879-1922 Nostalgic bar filled with old photos and vintage art with live Hawaiian music on weekends.

Tsunami, Grand Wailea Resort (808) 875-1234 High-tech disco with dressy couples dancing to DJed Top 40 tunes. Loud, noisy, and fun.

Big Island of Hawaii

Billfish Bar, King Kamehameha's Kona Beach Hotel (808) 329-3111 Big fish on the wall, big fish tales at the bar, and big drinks too. Hawaiian music, weekends only.

Honu Bar, Mauna Lani Bay Hotel and Bungalows (808) 885-6622 A favorite Kohala Coast nightspot, this chic wine bar full of couples offers jazz, dancing, and late-night dinners.

Shipwreck Bar, Kona Village Resort (808) 325-5555 Lift a mai tai toast to Johnno Jackson, who hit the reef in 1959 aboard his 42-foot schooner (the hull forms the bar) and founded Kona Village. No music, just ocean breezes and strong drinks.

Kauai

Duke's Canoe Club, Kauai Marriott Resort and Beach Club (808) 245-5050 Beachside shrine to Duke Kahanamoku, Hawaiian music on weekends.

Stevenson's Library Hyatt Regency Kauai Resort and Spa (808) 742-1234 Koa wood–lined old boy's club (ladies welcome) lined with books, vintage art. Jazz in the evening.

Dance Clubs and Nightspots

Anyone who wants to whoop it up in the tropic night should make plans to do all their boogeying on Oahu, although Maui shows some signs of a burgeoning nightlife. You can find late-night amusement on Lahaina's Front Street on Maui, but don't expect a scene elsewhere. The legal drinking age is 21. Clubs come and go; schedules and formats change often. Check with your hotel concierge for up-to-the-minute details.

NIGHTCLUBS BY ZONE

Zone 1: Waikiki	
The Cellar	No-frills bar and dance venue
Esprit Lounge	Live music nightclub and hotel lounge
Fusion Waikiki	Alternative club
Hard Rock Café	Internationally known music-themed restaurant
Nashville Waikiki	Authentic Waikiki watering hole
Scruples Beach Club	Waikiki beach bar that's not on a beach
Wave Waikiki	Alternative nightclub and rare alternative live music venue
Zone 2: Greater Honolulu	
Brew Moon	Hip island dining spot; beer brewed on site
Don Ho's Grill	Nostalgic, casual, pier-side hangout
Kapono's	Local Hawaiian music on Honolulu waterfront
Ocean Club	Chic downtown nightclub and discotheque
Rumours	Oldies disco and nightclub

NIGHTCLUBS BY ZONE *(continued)*	
Zone 8: South Maui	
Hapa's Brew Haus	Locals-meet-tourists Neighbor Island hangout
Zone 9: West Maui	
Maui Brews	10,000-square-foot eatery and club in Lahaina

Oahu

Brew Moon

HIP ISLAND DINING SPOT FEATURING ECLECTIC DECOR AND BEER BREWED ON SITE

Who Goes There 20–45 crowd; office workers, college kids, and professionals

1200 Ala Moana Boulevard, Honolulu (at Ward Centre); (808) 593-0088; www.brewmoon.com **Zone 2** *Greater Honolulu*

Cover $5–$10 (varies) **Minimum** None **Mixed drinks** $4–$7 **Wine** $4.50 and up **Beer** $3.25–$6.25 **Dress** Anything from aloha shirts to casual business attire **Specials** "Zero Gravity Hour" offers $3–$5 beers, $4–$6 wine, and half-price appetizers, including their addictive Beer Crackers, tasty Fire-Roasted Ribs, and hefty Heavy Metal Nacho platter; 4–7 p.m. daily **Food available** Jambalaya, chicken curry, herb-crusted sirloin, burgers, shakes, and daily fish specials

Hours Monday–Wednesday, 11 a.m.–1 p.m.; Thursday–Saturday, 11 a.m.–2 a.m.; Sunday, 2 p.m.–midnight

What goes on One of Honolulu's newest venues where customers can people-watch, mingle, and listen to music ranging from Top 40 hits to reggae beats to blues to jazz. Occasionally, live contemporary Hawaiian and jazz are performed Wednesday (9 p.m.–midnight) or Sunday (5–8 p.m.) nights.

Setting & atmosphere Brewpub with a view of Waikiki and Honolulu. Dining room features Art Deco furniture and eclectic menu. Check on their beers online at www.brewmoon.com.

If you go Try going at "Zero Gravity Hour" to catch half-priced Lunar Sampler—five four-ounce servings of Brew Moon beer—or other award-winning beers.

The Cellar

NO-FRILLS BAR AND DANCE VENUE

Who Goes There 18–30; 20-somethings, people-watchers, visitors, and curfew breakers

Waikiki Imperial Hotel, 205 Lewers Street, Waikiki; (808) 923-9952 **Zone 1** *Waikiki*

Cover $5 **Minimum** None **Mixed drinks** $3.75 and up **Wine** $5 **Beer** $3.50 **Dress** Casual **Specials** $1.50 drink specials are offered throughout the night **Food available** None

Hours Wednesday, Friday, and Saturday, 8 p.m.–4 a.m.; Tuesday, Thursday, and Sunday, 9 p.m.–4 a.m.; closed Mondays

What goes on A variety of entertainment and dance themes, including Top 40 hits, hip hop, R&B music, and a male dance revue every Wednesday, Friday, and Saturday, 8–10 p.m. Dancing nightly.

Setting & atmosphere Dark and smoke-filled, always packed with two bars. Nightly drink specials and a come-as-you-are attitude.

If you go Call ahead to find out what the evening's theme is. If the all-male revue isn't for you, check out Ladies' Night on Wednesdays.

Don Ho's Grill

NOSTALGIC, CASUAL PIER-SIDE HANGOUT

Who Goes There 21–55; visiting families, beach boys, and music lovers

1 Aloha Tower Drive (Aloha Tower Marketplace), Honolulu; (808) 528-0807; www.donho.com **Zone 2** *Greater Honolulu*

Cover Varies **Minimum** None **Mixed drinks** $4.75–$6.50 **Wine** $5 and up **Beer** $3 and up **Dress** Board shorts, sandals, khakis, and the obligatory aloha shirt **Specials** Happy hour daily, 4:30–6:30 p.m.; half-priced appetizers and $2 draft beers **Food available** Seared ahi, calamari, pizzas, sandwiches, and salads

Hours Monday–Wednesday, Sunday, 11 a.m.–11 p.m.; Thursday–Saturday, 11 a.m.– 2 a.m.

What goes on Live Hawaiian entertainment daily. Sunday–Wednesday, 6–8:30 p.m.; Thursday–Saturday, 9 p.m.–closing.

Setting & atmosphere Open-air Polynesian-style retro shrine to the man who made "Tiny Bubbles" an anthem. Rattan chairs and bamboo furniture fill this harbor-front restaurant decorated with photographs and memorabilia from Ho's heyday. Sometimes he even appears here.

If you go Explore the waterfront and go up Aloha Tower to the observation deck.

Esprit Lounge

LIVE MUSIC NIGHTCLUB AND HOTEL LOUNGE

Who Goes There 18–45; locals, hotel guests, professionals, and live music fans

Sheraton Waikiki Hotel, 2255 Kalakaua Avenue, Waikiki; (808) 922-4422; www.starwood.com **Zone 1** *Waikiki*

Cover None **Minimum** 2 drinks **Mixed drinks** $5.25–$6.50 **Wine** $5 and up **Beer** $3.50–$4.25 **Dress** Casual **Specials** None **Food available** Pizzas, sandwiches, hot wings, and nachos

Hours Sunday–Thursday, 8:30 p.m.–12:30 a.m.; Friday and Saturday, 8:30 p.m.–1 a.m.

What goes on This is a popular and stylish nightspot where the entertainment ranges from energetic live shows with local bands to dancing (R&B, Top 40). Entertainment is featured 8:30 p.m.–12:30 a.m. Tuesday–Thursday and 8:30 p.m.–1:30 a.m. Friday and Saturday.

Setting & atmosphere A dark, candle-lit room connected to the hotel's beach bar/lounge. On the left, cocktail tables and shimmering lights hang over a small dance floor next to the main stage. On the right, a relaxed, open-air beach bar lounge area.

If you go Go early for live music acts.

Fusion Waikiki

AN ALTERNATIVE CLUB

Who Goes There 21–28; night owls, retro geeks, and cool-kid wannabes

2260 Kuhio Avenue, 2nd floor, Waikiki; (808) 924-2422 **Zone 1** *Waikiki*

Cover $5 Friday and Saturday, free the rest of the week **Minimum** None **Mixed drinks** $4.25 and up **Wine** $5 and up **Beer** $3 and up **Dress** Come with what you have on, as long as it isn't ragged, tattered, or torn **Specials** DJs and drink specials nightly; karaoke on Mondays; well-drink specials on Thursdays; Kids Club on 1st and 3rd Sundays (on the lower level) drops the minimum age for entry to 18 **Food available** None

Hours Monday–Thursday, 9 p.m.–4 a.m.; Friday and Saturday, 8 p.m.–4 a.m.; Sunday, 10 p.m.–4 a.m.

What goes on Dancing nightly. Occasional live entertainment and club circuit parties. Friday and Saturday nights are reserved for the club's weekly male revue show.

Setting & atmosphere Up a narrow staircase, a small, dark alternative club full of couples. Energy, spunk, and character—from patrons who don't care where you come from, what you do, or where you have to be.

If you go Be prepared to stay late, because the serious action starts after midnight.

Hard Rock Café

INTERNATIONALLY KNOWN MUSIC-THEMED RESTAURANT

Who Goes There 18–50; tourists, music lovers, T-shirt collectors

1837 Kapiolani Boulevard, Waikiki; (808) 955-7383 **Zone 1** *Waikiki*

Cover Tuesday only for Battle of the Bands **Minimum** None **Mixed drinks** $4 and up **Wine** $4.50 and up **Beer** $3.50–$4 **Dress** Casual **Specials** None **Food available** Hard Rock Café's pig sandwiches, pot roast, grilled fajitas, burgers, barbecue chicken

Hours *Dining:* every day, 11:30 a.m.–11 p.m.; *bar:* Saturday–Thursday, 11:30 a.m.–12:30 a.m.; Friday, 11:30 a.m.–1:30 a.m.

What goes on Live entertainment Friday and Saturday, 10 p.m.–1 a.m.

Setting & atmosphere Same place, different artifacts. Honolulu has Eddie Van Halen's guitar, a bust of Mick Jagger, and an outfit worn by No Doubt's Gwen Stefani.

If you go Long wait—sometimes up to an hour—to eat. Get a table outside to avoid conversation-killing decibel levels in main room.

Kapono's

LOCAL HAWAIIAN MUSIC ON HONOLULU WATERFRONT

Who Goes There Locals, tourists, and Hawaiian music lovers (age 21 and over)

1 Aloha Tower Drive (Aloha Tower Marketplace), Honolulu; (808) 536-2161
Zone 2 *Greater Honolulu*

Cover Call Entertainment Hotline for schedule and cover, (808) 537-9611 **Minimum** None **Mixed drinks** $4.25–$5.50 **Wine** $5 and up **Beer** $3 and up **Dress** Aloha attire, shorts, sandals, casual wear **Specials** Happy hour 4–8 p.m. $2 draft beer, 25% off drinks, wine **Food available** Open for lunch, *pupus*, and dinner featuring Chef Russell Siu's local cuisine

Hours Every day, 11 a.m.–2 a.m.

What goes on Hawaiian music every night. Singer and guitar player Henry Kapono, one of Hawaii's top performers, appears and hosts Willie K., Kapena, John Cruz, and Fiji.

Setting & atmosphere Indoor/outdoor bistro and club on Honolulu waterfront.

If you go Go early on weekends to see big-name Hawaiian entertainers.

Nashville Waikiki

AUTHENTIC WAIKIKI WATERING HOLE

Who Goes There 21–30; college cowpokes, country bumpkins, and the occasional curious visitor

2330 Kuhio Avenue, Waikiki; (808) 926-7911 **Zone 1** *Waikiki*

Cover None **Minimum** None **Mixed drinks** $4–$6.50 **Wine** $4 **Beer** $3 and up **Dress** From blue jeans to shorts, from boots to sandals; shirts and footwear are required; 10-gallon hats are optional **Specials** Nightly line-dancing lessons offered 7–9 p.m. **Food available** Chips and popcorn

Hours Every day, 4 p.m.–4 a.m.

What goes on Music provided by Hawaii's top country DJs nightly. Pool tournaments Sundays and Tuesdays; dart tournaments Wednesdays.

Setting & atmosphere Two-step in hula-land at Waikiki's only country-and-western bar. This joint has bullhorns, saddles, copper paneling, drink specials, and a posse-sized dance floor.

If you go If line dancing doesn't do it for you, try Vegas Night, on Wednesdays.

Ocean Club

CHIC DOWNTOWN NIGHTCLUB AND DISCO

Who Goes There 23–35 (no one under 23 admitted); urbanites, locals, tourists, and singles

500 Ala Moana Boulevard (Restaurant Row); (808) 526-9888; www.oceanclubonline.com **Zone 2** *Greater Honolulu*

Cover Tuesday–Thursday, $4 after 8 p.m.; Friday, $5 after 8 p.m.; Saturday, $5 after 9 p.m. **Minimum** None **Mixed drinks** $1.75 and up **Wine** $3.75 and up **Beer** $3.50–$3.75 **Dress** Gap and Banana Republic; men must wear collared shirts; hats and athletic wear prohibited **Specials** $2 for most drinks and $2.50 for beer Tuesdays and Paddlers' Night on Thursdays; Thursdays, win cap for wearing aloha shirt, free cover **Food available** Calamari, spring rolls, crab dip, teriyaki steak, chicken wings, and nachos

Hours Tuesday–Thursday, 4:30 p.m.–2 a.m.; Friday, 4:30 p.m.–3 a.m.; Saturday, 6 p.m.–3 a.m.; closed Sundays and Mondays; available for private parties

What goes on Live local musicians perform on a sporadic basis. Dancing Tuesday–Thursday nights to Top 40 hits, R&B, hip hop, and urban beat.

Setting & atmosphere Trendy spot features two bars, a kitchen that pumps out high-end *pupus*, and an open-air lounge. Expect loud music, cheap drinks, and a young crowd.

If you go Sooner or later everyone shows up here, but don't go here to celebrate your 21st birthday. Only those age 23 and over are allowed. Guests 21 and over are welcome on Thursday (Paddlers' night) and for private parties.

Rumours

OLDIES DISCO AND NIGHTCLUB

Who Goes There 18–45; tourists and locals

Ala Moana Hotel, 410 Atkinson Drive, Honolulu; (808) 955-4811
Zone 2 *Greater Honolulu*

Cover $5 Friday and $10 Saturday after 9 p.m.; free before 9 p.m. daily and on Wednesday **Minimum** 2 drinks **Mixed drinks** $3.75 and up **Wine** $3.75 and up **Beer** $4.50 and up **Dress** Anything goes except beach wear, tank tops, and slippers **Specials** Free *pupus* daily 5–9 p.m.; dance to the music of the 1960s and 1970s during Big Chill Night on Fridays **Food available** Nachos, potato wedges, steak strips, veggie platters, pizzas, burgers, wontons, and cheesecake slices

Hours Thursday, 5 p.m.–1 a.m.; Friday, 5 p.m.–4 a.m.; Saturday, 9 p.m.–3 a.m.; Sunday, 5–9 p.m.; closed Tuesday, but available for private parties

What goes on Different theme every night, from ballroom dancing and country music to Top 40 mixes and Latin dancing. Wednesday karaoke.

Setting & atmosphere Waiters/waitresses decked out in formal black-and-white attire. Rust-colored, old-style lounge chairs, two-story club. Huge TV screen flanks dance floor.

If you go Bring your dancing shoes and be prepared to strut your stuff. People will be watching.

Scruples Beach Club

WAIKIKI BEACH BAR THAT'S NOT ON A BEACH

Who Goes There 18–25; tourists, people-watchers, and celebrities

2310 Kuhio Avenue, Waikiki; (808) 923-9530 **Zone 1** *Waikiki*

Cover $5 for those age 21 and over; Friday–Saturday after 10 p.m. $10; $15 for age 18–21 **Minimum** 2 drinks **Mixed drinks** $4.75 and up **Wine** $4.75 and up **Beer** $4.75 and up **Dress** Jeans, skirts, trousers, and shorts; no athletic wear **Food available** None

Hours Every day, 9 p.m.–4 a.m.

What goes on Dancing to Top 40, alternative, and reggae beats.

Setting & atmosphere This club is so tacky it's cool—from the bamboo-paneled walls to plastic palm leaves hanging from the pillars. There isn't anything in the way of food or views—unusual for a beach bar—but what you get is a dance floor open to 4 a.m. and a bikini contest every Thursday night at midnight.

If you go Check out Wall of Fame to see who got here before you—Robert De Niro, Jim Carrey, and Jean-Claude Van Damme, to name a few.

Wave Waikiki

ALTERNATIVE NIGHTCLUB AND RARE ALTERNATIVE LIVE MUSIC VENUE

Who Goes There 18–28; college kids, eccentric folk, jocks, and alterna-lovers

1877 Kalakaua Avenue, Waikiki; (808) 941-0424 **Zone 1** *Waikiki*

Cover $5–$7 **Minimum** 2 drinks **Mixed drinks** $5 **Wine** $4–$5 **Beer** $4–$6.50 **Dress** Slacker garb and Gen-X gear is the norm **Specials** Each week boasts a different drink special; happy hour 9–10 p.m. and 1–4 a.m.; 18 and up on Mondays **Food available** None

Hours Every day, 9 p.m.–4 a.m.

What goes on Live entertainment (various themes, including classic and alternative rock) and DJs nightly 9 p.m.–4 a.m. Live bands are featured Wednesday–Friday, and Thursday is Ladies' Night.

Setting & atmosphere Two-story hot spot hosts live alternative bands. Large, wooden dance floor fronts the Wave's big-screen TV and performance stage.

If you go Take a cab; parking is scarce and pricey. Kick back in air-conditioned, second-floor lounge, with full-service bar and a people-watching perch.

Maui

Hapa's Brew Haus

LOCALS-MEET-TOURISTS NEIGHBOR ISLAND HANGOUT

Who Goes There 21–35; celebrities, locals, and visitors

41 East Lipoa Street, Suite 4A, Kihei; (808) 879-9001 **Zone 8** *South Maui*

Cover Varies **Minimum** None **Mixed drinks** $4–$6 **Wine** $5–$7 **Beer** $4 and up **Dress** Come as you are **Specials** Ladies' Night every Thursday **Food available** Pizzas, burgers, and sandwiches

Hours Every day, 4 p.m.–2 a.m.

What goes on Nightly entertainment featuring a variety of live bands, dancing, bikini contests, and comedy acts.

Setting & atmosphere The hot spot on the Valley Isle.

If you go Go before 8:30 p.m. to enter free.

Adult Entertainment

Since World War II, when prostitution was legal and soldiers and sailors queued up for Hotel Street hookers in Chinatown, Hawaii's nightlife has been X-rated. Not a whole lot has changed since then. Streetwalkers work Waikiki after dark and strippers dance "totally naked" in clubs near the convention center. So-called adult clubs and services are advertised in the sports pages of the *Honolulu Advertiser* and the *Honolulu Star-Bulletin* as well as the Yellow Pages of Honolulu's phone book. Oahu's most popular establishments, like **Rock-za** and **Femme Nu,** are on Kapiolani Boulevard near the Hawaii Convention Center and on Keeaumoku Street, near Ala Moana Center.

Tip: Avoid clubs on Hotel Street in Chinatown, where transsexual hookers work street corners, and drugs (mostly crack) are readily available despite police presence.

Subject Index

Accommodations Index

Note: Page numbers in **bold face** type indicate hotel profiles.

Restaurant Index

Note: Page numbers in **bold face** type indicate restaurant profiles.